Investment Protection in Southeast Asia

Investment Protection in Southeast Asia

A Country-by-Country Guide on Arbitration Laws and Bilateral Investment Treaties

Edited by

Loretta Malintoppi and Charis Tan

BRILL
NIJHOFF

LEIDEN | BOSTON

Cover illustration: Courtesy of National Library Board, Singapore 2016.

Library of Congress Cataloging-in-Publication Data

Names: Malintoppi, Loretta. | Tan, Charis.
Title: Investment protection in Southeast Asia: a country-by-country guide on arbitration laws and bilateral investment treaties / edited by Loretta Malintoppi and Charis Tan.
Description: Leiden ; Boston : Brill Nijhoff, 2017. | Includes bibliographical references and index.
Identifiers: LCCN 2016036873 (print) | LCCN 2016037657 (ebook) | ISBN 9789004335240 (hardback : alk. paper) | ISBN 9789004335257 (E-book)
Subjects: LCSH: Investments, Foreign—Southeast Asia. | International commercial arbitration—Southeast Asia. | Southeast Asia—Commercial treaties.
Classification: LCC KNC747.I57 2017 (print) | LCC KNC747 (ebook) | DDC 346.59/092—dc23
LC record available at https://lccn.loc.gov/2016036873

Typeface for the Latin, Greek, and Cyrillic scripts: "Brill". See and download: brill.com/brill-typeface.

ISBN 978-90-04-33524-0 (hardback)
ISBN 978-90-04-33525-7 (e-book)

This book is printed on acid-free paper and produced in a sustainable manner.

Printed by Printforce, the Netherlands

To Ezra: Yours is the Earth and everything that's in it

Contents

Foreword

This book was conceived as a handy reference guide to investment protection in the region, intended to give a quick answer to the top few questions a potential investor might ask when considering investment in a particular jurisdiction. Thus, while not an exhaustive treatise on all aspects of investment protection, each chapter is intended to cover a few key areas: (a) arbitral legislation and institutions in the country; (b) investment-related domestic laws; (c) an analysis of the bilateral investment treaties ("BITs") entered into by that State; and (d) a summary of cases involving the State or its investors.

Besides providing a broad overview of the arbitration and investment laws in place in each country, the study of publicly available BITs concluded by each State was intended as an attempt to identify (to the extent possible) trends based on the scope of various clauses commonly found in BITs. The observations in this regard highlight the differing standards of protection provided by various treaties, and demonstrate how substantive protections under the treaties may be differentiated in spite of their seeming similarity. However, we excluded from the analysis an in-depth study of investment chapters of free trade agreements ("FTAs") signed by the State, as those chapters have to be read in the context of each FTA. FTAs cover various aspects of trade and investment promotion and protection much more comprehensively, and the clauses of the investment chapter must be interpreted in the light of other provisions of the agreement. Nonetheless, some authors have chosen to make observations on significant FTAs concluded by a State or by ASEAN, though the treatment of FTAs herein is by no means exhaustive. Separately, the chapters mention some multilateral investment-related treaties and organizations to which the relevant State is a party; these were intended merely as a sampling of the State's involvement in such instruments and fora.

Each chapter in this book was conceived as a standalone chapter, and thus some notes are repeated in a number of chapters, wherever they are relevant. To the extent possible, chapters have also been reviewed by local counsel practising in the jurisdiction covered, and their contributions have been acknowledged in the relevant chapters. By its very nature, the information contained in this book is fluid and subject to development. However, the authors have endeavoured to ensure that the information is accurate as of May 2016, and to anticipate developments where this was possible.

While an exhaustive treatment of the subject of investment promotion and protection would be beyond the scope of this work, we hope that this book may provide a useful tool for practitioners and investors considering investments in the region.

Loretta Malintoppi
Charis Tan
Eversheds LLP
Singapore
Singapore, June 2016

Notes on Contributors

Cameron Forsaith

Cameron is a Senior Associate with Eversheds LLP, based in London. He specialises in international dispute resolution with a focus on both international commercial and investment treaty arbitrations. Outside of contentious proceedings he advises on cross-jurisdictional enforcement risk, claims under international investment law and investment structuring to access investment treaty protections, and arbitration and conflict of laws issues. Cameron is qualified as a lawyer in England & Wales and Australia, and holds undergraduate degrees in arts and law from the University of Queensland and a Master of Law from the University of Cambridge.

Steven Gibson

Steven is a Legal Manager at Bouygues Energies & Services UK, part of the international Bouygues Group, and advises on projects and disputes in the construction and engineering, and energy, sectors. Prior to joining Bouygues, he was an Associate at the international law firm Eversheds, working in both Singapore and the UK, advising clients in a number of jurisdictions. This included advising on a substantial concession agreement dispute in the Maldives, and advising an oil and gas operator based in Russia on several large projects, and international arbitrations.

Natasha Harrington

Natasha was a Senior Associate in Eversheds' public international law and international arbitration group in Paris. Natasha specialises in public international law, investor-State arbitration and international commercial arbitration.

Natasha also advises Governments, international organisations, NGOs and private corporations on matters involving international law. Her work includes the application of international law in domestic courts. She has recently advised a State and an international organisation on immunities under international and municipal laws.

Natasha is committed to pro bono work, and has spoken at a seminar and written a number of articles on international humanitarian law for non-profit organisations. Natasha also teaches a seminar in the law and procedure of international courts and tribunals at Sciences Po in Paris.

Before joining Eversheds, Natasha completed a twelve-month pupillage at Essex Court Chambers, a "magic circle" set. She gained experience in commercial law and proceedings before the English Courts.

Natasha obtained a BA with Distinction (first class) in Law with Law Studies in Europe (France) from Merton College, University of Oxford. She completed the Bar Vocational Course at BPP Law School, London, where she was classed Outstanding.

Kate Lan

Kate is a senior associate in Eversheds Singapore and specialises in international commercial and construction arbitration, investment treaty arbitration and public international law. Prior to joining Eversheds, Kate worked in the dispute resolution practice of the largest law firm in South East Asia, where she appeared regularly before the Singapore courts. She has acted for and advised States, State entities, private multinational companies and corporations on a broad spectrum of litigation and arbitration disputes, including SIAC, ICC, ICSID as well as UNCITRAL *ad hoc* arbitrations. She regularly writes articles and recently contributed a chapter to the book, Arbitration in Singapore: A Practical Guide (Sweet & Maxwell, 2014) which was edited by the Honourable The Chief Justice Sundaresh Menon. Kate is qualified as an Advocate and Solicitor of the Supreme Court in Singapore and as a Solicitor of the Senior Courts of England and Wales.

Natalie Limbasan

Natalie was previously from Eversheds Paris, and is currently a Legal Advisor at the *Organisation for Economic Co-operation and Development* (OECD), headquartered in Paris. She specialises in public international law, including the law of treaties, international investment law, international organisations law and issues of personality and recognition under public international law. Prior to joining the OECD, Natalie was a lawyer in private practice, focusing on public international law and international arbitration, both investment and commercial. Natalie is qualified as a lawyer in England & Wales.

Loretta Malintoppi

Loretta is dually-qualified (Paris and Rome Bars) and is registered to practice as a Foreign Lawyer in Singapore since 2012. She specializes in both international commercial and investment arbitration. She acts as counsel, advocate and arbitrator and has represented private companies, States and State entities in proceedings under a variety of arbitration rules, including ICSID, ICC, UNCITRAL, SIAC, LCIA and DIAC.

Loretta also appears as counsel and advocate in State-to-State disputes before the International Court of Justice and in *ad hoc* arbitrations. She was a Member for Italy of the ICC International Court of Arbitration from 2000 to 2009 and was a Vice-President of the ICC Court until 2013.

Loretta has written a number of articles on investment arbitration and State-to-State litigation and has co-authored the second edition of Prof. Schreuer's *The ICSID Convention – A Commentary* published by Cambridge University Press in 2009. She is also a member of the Advisory Board of the Investment Treaty Forum of the British Institute of International and Comparative Law, the Editorial Board of The Law and Practice of International Courts and Tribunals, editor of the series International Litigation in Practice Series, and a member of the editorial advisory board of the Journal of World Investment and Trade. Loretta is regarded by the legal directory Chambers Global as a leading individual in international arbitration.

Vishal Melwani

Vishal is a Principal in the Hong Kong office of Lipman Karas. Vishal's accounting background has added value to clients in a number of arbitrations and commercial litigation cases on which he has acted as a solicitor. In addition to being a Canadian and Hong Kong Certified Public Accountant, Vishal is also an associate member of the Hong Kong Institute of Arbitrators, a distinguished professional mentor of the Chinese University of Hong Kong Faculty of Law, and is on the panel of accredited general mediators of the Hong Kong Mediation Accreditation Association Limited. Vishal was also ranked as a "leading lawyer" in the 2013, 2014 and 2015 editions of the Chambers Asia Pacific Guide.

Charis Tan

Charis practices at Eversheds LLP, Singapore, and specialises in public international law, international investment and commercial arbitration, and the upstream oil and gas industry.

She has been admitted as an Advocate and Solicitor of Singapore, an Attorney and Counselor-at-Law of the State of New York, and a Solicitor of England & Wales.

Charis has advised States and multinational corporations on a wide range of public international law issues, including in high profile State-to-State disputes before the International Court of Justice, and on issues such as land and maritime boundary delimitation, law of the sea, State-to-State bilateral co-operation agreements, national development issues, State responsibility and the law of treaties.

She has also worked on a wide range of investment treaty and commercial arbitrations under the rules of major arbitration institutions, including ICSID, ICC, SIAC and SCC, as well as *ad hoc* proceedings under UNCITRAL Rules. Charis has also been appointed as an arbitrator.

Charis acts for National Oil Companies (NOCs) and International Oil Companies (IOCs) in both contentious and non-contentious matters, including the drafting and review of PSAs, JOAs, farm-in agreements, cooperation agreements, and advising on complex issues of domestic and international unitization, and participation. A unique area of her specialization is where the practice of oil and gas crosses into the public international law sphere, such as where blocks straddle disputed boundaries.

Charis is recommended by Asia Pacific Legal 500 for international arbitration.

Alvin Yap

Alvin is an associate in Eversheds' Singapore office. He practises international arbitration and public international law. He has represented MNCs, State-owned entities and Governments in commercial and investment arbitration under a wide variety of arbitral institution rules, including SIAC, ICC, ICSID and FOSFA Rules. He has experience in advising States, international and national oil companies on national boundary issues and related upstream oil and gas matters, such as cross-border unitization and joint development zones.

Laura Yvonne Zielinski

Laura is an associate with Eversheds in Paris, specializing in public international law and international commercial and investment treaty arbitration. A native of Germany, Laura studied in France, Spain and the US. She obtained her first law degree from Sciences Po Paris and holds an LLM from Columbia Law School. She is New York qualified and is fluent in German, French and English with working knowledge of Spanish.

Introduction

While the growing number of BITs and international investment agreements ("IIAs") have been accompanied by a steady growth of investor-State arbitration, the number of cases involving South East Asian States and investors from this region remains relatively low in comparison with other parts of the world.

According to the ICSID 2016 Caseload Statistics,[1] the number of cases involving States from South and East Asia and the Pacific has remained stable since 2015, at 8% of all ICSID claims. Of the new cases registered by the Centre in 2015, 4% concerned State parties from South and East Asia and the Pacific. While 13% of the arbitrators, conciliators and *ad hoc* Committee members appointed in 2015 came from South and East Asia and the Pacific, this figure pales in comparison with Western Europe's 50%, but is more than double the percentage relating to South America. The only South East Asian nationalities to feature in ICSID's list of arbitrators appointed in 2015 are Singapore (with one appointment) and Malaysia. It is, however, notable that – of the top 20 nationalities of arbitrators, conciliators and *ad hoc* Committee members appointed under the ICSID Convention and the ICSID Additional facility Rules – none are Asian.

That said, a number of considerations point to an increase of investor-State arbitration in region, in spite of the challenges currently faced by this form of dispute resolution.

First, there has been significant reform in the IIAs, including the adoption of new provisions on the powers of States to issue joint interpretations of the relevant treaties, interventions by non-disputing States, and greater transparency in the process of dispute resolution under IIAs.

Second, as investor-State cases have started to be brought by investors from South East Asia, local lawyers, including government lawyers, are acquiring the knowledge and expertise necessary to handle the complex issues of private and public international law arising from these cases. As the learning curve of the legal profession grows, it is to be expected that investment arbitration will become a concrete option for resolution of investor-State disputes.

Third, a number of South East Asian countries have undergone a process of modernization of their legislative system, and have become more open to

1 https://icsid.worldbank.org/apps/ICSIDWEB/resources/Documents/ICSID%20Web%20Stats%202016-1%20(English)%20final.pdf.

 | DOI 10.1163/9789004335257_002

international arbitration through a reform of their laws and the opening of new arbitration centers. Most countries in the region have engaged in investment policy reviews and adopted new model BITs or domestic investment laws. Indonesia's draft model BIT is in the process of being finalized[2] and Thailand adopted a new Model BIT in 2013, which is, however, not in the public domain.[3]

Fourth, there exists significant economic data that may point to an increase in the number of investor-State disputes in the future. Foreign direct investment ("FDI") inflows to the region remain strong. With a growth of 10% in combined inflows to a historical high of $381 billion in 2014, East and South-East Asia together continue to be the largest recipient region in the world.[4] Outbound FDI is also growing;[5] investors from the region are taking greater risks and increasingly investing in countries in Africa, Latin America and Eastern Europe. Long-term investment plans in infrastructure in South East Asia are expected to grow further, and a number of ASEAN Member States have also begun to open transport industries to foreign participation. This could lead to more intraregional FDI. For example, Indonesia has recently allowed foreign investments in service industries such as port management as part of the Government's efforts to enhance Indonesia's status as an important maritime port destination.

Fifth, a review of the system is being carried out at the multilateral level, particularly with the work of UNCTAD and UNCITRAL, bringing together different stakeholders to discuss investment issues, a process which is also affecting South East Asian countries.

Sixth, a future increase in both Asian claimants and respondents in ISDS cases appears to be backed up by the most recent caseload statistics. The years 2014 and 2015 have seen utilisation of investment arbitration by investors from China, Korea and Japan, a factor which may be a sign of a growing legitimacy and attraction of investor-State dispute settlement ("ISDS") in Asia as a whole.

When it comes to the investment trends that can be identified in the region, even though the vast majority of existing investment protection instruments remain bilateral, there appears to be a growing tendency for Southeast Asian States to enter into fewer BITs and increasingly conclude investment chapters of FTAs. In addition, there is an increase of multilateral and regional

2 http://unctad.org/en/PublicationsLibrary/webdiaepcb2016d1_en.pdf.

3 Nottage, Luke R., *op. cit.*

4 http://unctad.org/en/PublicationsLibrary/wir2015_en.pdf.

5 Nottage, Luke R., "The TPP Investment Chapter and Investor-State Arbitration in Asia and Oceania: Assessing Prospects for Ratification" (April 20, 2016). Sydney Law School Research Paper No. 16/28. Available at SSRN: http://ssrn.com/abstract=2767996.

agreements instead of purely bilateral instruments. In this respect, the recent signature of the Trans-Pacific Partnership ("TPP"), as an "FTA of the 21st century" with a wide scope of application coming in line with strongly liberal trends, is significant.

It is also important to underscore that, while ASEAN has always been more of a consultative forum, there increasingly is a willingness for ASEAN Member States to use the group as a platform to enter into multilateral instruments for trade and investment promotion and protection. This reflects the potential of ASEAN to play an enlarged role in this aspect in the region.

Ultimately, only time will tell how things will develop in the region and whether ISDS will overcome its many challenges. However, it seems that after years of disproportionately low levels of ISDS involving parties from South East Asia, and notably a scarcity of claimants from the region, the recent case-load statistics and the other factors highlighted above point to an increased uptake by investors in the region and may signal a change for the future. The aim of this book is to assist various stakeholders, and notably investors and practitioners, in acquiring basic information relating to the framework of international investments in South East Asian States.

Loretta Malintoppi
Charis Tan
Eversheds LLP
Singapore
Singapore, June 2016

CHAPTER 1

Association of Southeast Asian Nations (ASEAN)[1]

I Introduction

ASEAN was established on 8 August 1967 with the signing in Bangkok, Thailand, of the ASEAN Declaration (also known as the "Bangkok Declaration") by Indonesia, Malaysia, the Philippines, Singapore and Thailand. Brunei Darussalam subsequently joined on 7 January 1984, followed by Vietnam on 28 July 1995, Lao PDR and Myanmar on 23 July 1997, and Cambodia on 30 April 1999.[2]

In line with the aims and purposes of ASEAN to accelerate its economic growth and promote active collaboration and mutual assistance on matters of common interest in the economic field,[3] the first investment-related agreement in ASEAN emerged with the signing of the Agreement on Promotion and Protection of Investment in ASEAN ("ASEAN IPPA") by Brunei, Indonesia, Malaysia, the Philippines, Singapore and Thailand in 1987. The ASEAN IPPA focussed on protecting and promoting investments within the ASEAN region and amongst Member States *inter se*.[4] Following the establishment of the ASEAN Economic Community ("AEC"), the ASEAN Investment Area ("AIA") and the ASEAN Free Trade Area ("AFTA"), the investment treaty regime in ASEAN has shifted its focus from investments amongst ASEAN Member States to attracting and facilitating foreign direct investment ("FDI") flows into ASEAN from outside of the region.

The AEC seeks to achieve regional economic integration and envisages a single market and production base for all ten rapidly growing economies in ASEAN with a total population of 622 million and a combined GDP of USD2.6 trillion.[5] The amount of FDI flowing into ASEAN rose for the third consecutive year from USD 117.7 billion in 2013 to USD 136.2 billion in 2014, exceeding

---

1 This chapter has been drafted by Ms Kate Lan of Eversheds LLP, Singapore.

2 See http://www.asean.org/asean/about-asean/. ASEAN has its headquarters in Jakarta.

3 See the ASEAN Declaration, available at: http://www.asean.org/the-asean-declaration-bangkok-declaration-bangkok-8-august-1967/.

4 See Preamble of the ASEAN IPPA, available at: http://www.asean.org/storage/images/2012/Economic/AIA/Agreement/Agreement%20among%20the%20Government%20of%20Brunei%20Darussalam.pdf.

5 See http://www.asean.org/storage/2015/12/AEC-at-a-Glance-2015.pdf.

 | DOI 10.1163/9789004335257_003

FDI inflows to China for the first time since 1993.[6] These figures also meant that ASEAN is now the largest recipient of FDI in the developing world.[7] Investments from ASEAN Member States reached USD 24.4 billion in 2014 from USD 19.4 billion in the previous year.[8] Intra-ASEAN investment accounted for 18% of the total FDI into the region, making ASEAN the second largest investor in its own region.[9] ASEAN is also a major source of FDI for other countries. FDI flows from ASEAN to countries outside the region rose by 19% to USD 80 billion in 2014. The AEC-2015 blueprint paves the way for further growth in FDI flows into ASEAN as investors are expected to take advantage of the opportunities and benefits from the single market and production base of an integrated ASEAN.

The upward trend in FDI flows into ASEAN is underscored by significant developments in the legal framework surrounding the investment regime in ASEAN, which includes the signing in 2009 of the ASEAN Comprehensive Investment Agreement ("ACIA") and five free trade agreements ("FTAs") amongst ASEAN Member States and Japan, the Republic of Korea, China, Australia and New Zealand, as well as India, respectively (the "Dialogue Partners"), in quick succession between 2008 and 2014.

II Investment Regime in ASEAN

The investment regime in ASEAN (which includes the key legal instruments that this chapter discusses in greater detail below) falls under the purview of the AEC. The AEC's main objectives, as set out in the AEC Blueprint 2015, are to explore and foster economic cooperation amongst ASEAN Member States through consultations on economic, financial, trade and investment policies, with the aim of achieving regional economic integration by 2015. In 2015, the AEC released the AEC Blueprint 2025, which acknowledged that the overall vision remained relevant, but that the AEC Blueprint 2025 would build on the AEC Blueprint 2015 on the basis of five characteristics: (i) A Highly Integrated and Cohesive Economy; (ii) A Competitive, Innovative, and Dynamic ASEAN; (iii) Enhanced Connectivity and Sectoral Cooperation;

6 ASEAN Investment Report 2015, Infrastructure Investment and Connectivity, available at: http://www.asean.org/storage/images/2015/November/asean-investment-report/ASEAN%20Investment%20Report%202015.pdf.

7 *Ibid.*

8 *Ibid.*

9 *Ibid.*

(iv) A Resilient, Inclusive, People-Oriented, and People-Centred ASEAN; and (v) A Global ASEAN.[10]

The AIA and AFTA fall within the AEC. The oversight and implementation of the ACIA fall under the AIA while the FTAs come within the ambit of the AFTA.

1 *AIA*

The AIA Council is the Ministerial body under the ASEAN Economic Ministers responsible for overseeing the implementation of the ACIA.[11] It is composed of the Secretary-General of ASEAN and Ministers responsible for investment from the ten Member States.[12] The Coordinating Committee on Investment ("CCI"), which is made up of senior officials responsible for investment and other officials from other government agencies, supports the AIA Council in carrying out its functions.[13] Through the AIA Council and the CCI, ASEAN seeks to implement and encourage Member States to draw on the benefits of the ACIA, while at the same time promote the ACIA to foreign investors.

The AIA Council's immediate objectives include promoting the ACIA and reaching out to businessmen and investors to create awareness of the benefits of the ACIA, enhancing the capacity of ASEAN and the Member States in implementing the ACIA, and developing a regional cooperation work programme aimed at supporting the work of ASEAN on investment liberalisation, protection, promotion and facilitation.[14]

2 *AFTA*

AFTA is a trade bloc established in 1992 pursuant to the signing of the Agreement on Common Effective Preferential Tariff ("CEPT") Scheme for the ASEAN Free Trade Area which was signed in Singapore on 28 January 1992 (the "AFTA Agreement").

The AFTA Agreement was originally signed by Brunei, Indonesia, Malaysia, Philippines, Singapore and Thailand in 1992. Vietnam, Laos, Myanmar and Cambodia subsequently signed the AFTA Agreement upon joining ASEAN.

---

10 See AEC Blueprint 2025, para. 3, available at: http://www.asean.org/storage/images/2015/November/aec-page/AEC-Blueprint-2025-FINAL.pdf.

11 See http://www.asean.org/asean-economic-community/asean-investment-area-aia-council/overview/.

12 *Ibid.*

13 *Ibid.*

14 *Ibid.*

The AFTA Agreement seeks to further economic growth of the ASEAN region through the liberalisation of investment and trade within ASEAN by, *inter alia*, eliminating tariff barriers among ASEAN Member States.[15]

The AFTA Council (comprising one nominee from each ASEAN Member State and the Secretary-General of the ASEAN Secretariat) is responsible for the implementation of the AFTA Agreement. Under the AFTA Agreement,[16] Member States are obliged to explore measures on border and non-border areas of cooperation to supplement and complement the liberalisation of trade, including the removal of barriers to foreign investments.

III ACIA

1 *History and Overview*

In 1987, Brunei, Indonesia, Malaysia, Singapore, Philippines and Thailand signed the ASEAN IPPA. The ASEAN IPPA was the first investment–related agreement that ASEAN Member States concluded. It was primarily focussed on the protection and promotion of investments within the ASEAN region. The ASEAN IPPA was amended by way of a Protocol dated 12 September 1996 (the "Protocol"),[17] which, *inter alia*, added Vietnam as a party to the ASEAN IPPA, emphasized the agreement to establish the AFTA, and updated the ASEAN IPPA to reflect the rapid development in the global investment environment and the commitments which Member States had made under various international and regional investment agreements.

A second agreement, the Framework Agreement on the ASEAN Investment Area ("AIA Agreement"), was signed in 1998 by Lao and Myanmar, in addition to the Parties to the ASEAN IPPA (as amended by the Protocol). The AIA Agreement was designed to further enhance the process of FDI policy liberalisation, promotion, facilitation and harmonisation that was already

---

15 See Agreement on the Common Effective Preferential Tariff Scheme for the ASEAN Free Trade Area, available at: http://www.asean.org/storage/images/2012/Economic/AFTA/Common_Effective_Preferential_Tariff/Agreement%20on%20the%20Common%20Effective%20Preferential%20Tariff%20Scheme%20for%20the%20ASEAN%20Free%20Trade%20Area.pdf.

16 See Article 5(C) of the AFTA Agreement.

17 See the Protocol to Amend the Agreement among the Governments of Brunei Darussalam, the Republic of Indonesia, Malaysia, the Republic of the Philippines, the Republic of Singapore, and the Kingdom of Thailand for the Promotion and Protection of Investments, available at: http://www.asean.org/storage/images/2012/Economic/AIA/Agreement/Protocol%20to%20Amend%20the%20Agreement%20among%20the%20Governments.pdf.

taking place in ASEAN pursuant to the establishment of the AFTA and the implementation of the ASEAN Industrial Co-operation Scheme.[18]

On 26 February 2009, the ACIA was signed by all ten ASEAN Member States in Thailand. The ACIA entered into force on 29 March 2012, replacing the ASEAN IPPA and AIA Agreement, which were terminated upon the entry into force of the ACIA.[19] The ACIA aims to create a free and open investment environment through the consolidation and expansion of existing agreements[20] between ASEAN Member States.[21] The ACIA is key to realising the establishment of the AEC. The cornerstones of the single market and production base envisaged by the AEC are: having non-discriminatory treatment extended to ASEAN and ASEAN-based investors, providing for transparent rules and regulations, and ensuring that investors and their investments enjoy protection. ASEAN seeks to achieve these goals via the implementation of the ACIA.

The "Guiding Principles" in Article 2 of the ACIA set out the clear and overarching objective of the agreement – to create a liberal, facilitative, transparent and competitive investment environment in ASEAN. The ACIA also contains substantive investment protections commonly found in Bilateral Investment Treaties ("BITs"), such as provisions on fair and equitable treatment, full protection and security, most favoured nation treatment, and expropriation, as well as dispute resolution provisions in the event that a dispute arises between an investor and a Member State or between two Member States. Besides the usual provisions found in BITs, the ACIA also contains provisions aimed at enhancing cooperation between ASEAN States in the promotion and facilitation of investment, and ASEAN integration.

2 *Definition of Investment*

The term "investment" is defined broadly in the ACIA[22] as every kind of asset, owned or controlled by an investor, including but not limited to, the following:

- movable and immovable property and other property rights such as mortgages, liens or pledges;

18 See Preamble to the AIA Agreement, available at: http://www.asean.org/storage/images/2012/Economic/AIA/Agreement/Framework%20Agreement%20on%20the%20ASEAN%20Investment%20Area%20(AIA)%201998.pdf.

19 Article 47 of the ACIA. However, note that Article 2(e) specifies as a guiding principle of the ACIA that there shall be no back-tracking of commitments made by Member States under the AIA Agreement and the ASEAN IPPA.

20 See the ASEAN IPPA and the AIA Agreement.

21 See http://www.aseanbriefing.com/news/2013/04/12/introduction-to-the-asean-comprehensive-investment-agreement.html.

22 Article 4(c) of the ACIA.

- shares, stocks, bonds and debentures and any other forms of participation in a juridical person and rights or interests derived therefrom;
- intellectual property rights which are conferred pursuant to the laws and regulations of each Member State;
- claims to money or to any contractual performance related to a business and having financial value;
- rights under contracts, including turnkey, construction, management, production or revenue-sharing contracts; and
- business concessions required to conduct economic activities and having financial value conferred by law or under a contract, including any concessions to search, cultivate, extract or exploit natural resources.

An "investment" also includes amounts yielded by investments, in particular, profits, interest capital gains, dividend, royalties and fees, and it is stated that any alteration of the form in which assets are invested or reinvested shall not affect their classification as investment.[23] However, Article 4[24] also makes clear that an "investment" does not include claims to money that arise solely from commercial contracts for sale of goods or services, or the extension of credit in connection with such commercial contracts.

Additionally, for an asset to be considered as an "investment" which falls to be protected under the ACIA, it must possess the characteristics of an investment, including the commitment of capital, the expectation of gain or profit, or the assumption of risk.[25] It appears from the wording of Article 4,[26] therefore, that, if an asset falls within one of the categories set out in Article 4(c) of the ACIA but lacks the characteristics of an investment, that asset would not be considered an investment regardless of the form it might take.

3 *Definition of Investor*

An "investor" under the ACIA is defined as a natural person of a Member State[27] or a juridical person of a Member State that is making, or has made, an investment in the territory of another Member State.[28]

23 *Ibid.*

24 See footnote 3 of Article 4(c) of the ACIA.

25 See footnote 2 of Article 4(c) of the ACIA.

26 *Ibid.*

27 Refers to the Governments of Brunei, Cambodia, Indonesia, Lao, Malaysia, Myanmar, the Philippines, Singapore, Thailand, and Vietnam; see Preamble of the ACIA.

28 Article 4(d) of the ACIA.

A "natural person" refers to a national, citizen or permanent resident of a Member State.[29] It is stipulated that the nationality, citizenship or right of permanent residence must have been obtained in accordance with the laws, regulations and national policies of the relevant Member State.[30]

A "juridical person" is defined as any legal entity which has been duly constituted or otherwise organised under the applicable law of a Member State, whether for profit or otherwise, and whether privately-owned or government-owned, and includes any enterprise, corporation, trust, partnership, joint venture, sole proprietorship, association, or organisation.[31]

4 *Scope*

The ACIA applies only to investments in existence in the territory of a Member State on and after the date of entry into force of the agreement.[32] An investment will be covered by the ACIA only if it has been made in accordance with the laws, regulations and national policies of the relevant Member State, and where applicable, specifically approved in writing[33] by the competent authority of a Member State.[34] Subrogation rights are recognised, provided that the subrogated or transferred right or claim is not greater than the original right or claim of the investor.[35]

Importantly, the scope of application of the ACIA is limited to certain sectors agreed upon by all Member States, such as manufacturing, agriculture,

29 Article 4(g) of the ACIA. With regard to the treatment of "permanent residents" of a Member State, note the reservations made by Cambodia, Indonesia, Myanmar, Philippines, Thailand, Vietnam and Brunei, as set out at Articles 6 and 7 of the Headnote of the List of Reservations found in the Schedule to the ACIA.

30 *Ibid.*

31 Article 4(e) of the ACIA.

32 Articles 3(2) and 4(a) of the ACIA.

33 Annex 1 of the ACIA sets out the required procedures to be complied with where specific approval in writing is required for covered investments by a Member State's domestic laws, regulations and national policies. These include informing all other Member States through the ASEAN Secretariat of the contact details of its competent authority responsible for granting such approval and informing the applicant in writing the outcome of the application within four months from the date of application. The relevant Member State is also obliged to inform an applicant in writing any additional information required in the case of an incomplete application. In the event that the application is denied, an applicant must also be informed of the reasons and afforded with the opportunity to submit a new application.

34 Article 4(a) of the ACIA.

35 Article 15 of the ACIA.

fishery, forestry, mining and quarrying, or services incidental to manufacturing, agriculture, fishery, forestry, mining and quarrying.[36]

The ACIA specifically excludes application[37] to taxation measures, subsidies or grants provided by a Member State, government procurement, services supplied in the exercise of governmental authority by the relevant body or authority of a Member State, and measures adopted or maintained by a Member State affecting trade in services.[38]

Notwithstanding the above, a Member State may deny the benefits of the ACIA to an investor[39] from another Member State if it is owned or controlled by an investor from a non-Member State or the denying Member State and the investor do not have substantive business operations in the territory of the other Member State.[40] An investor[41] from another Member State may also be prevented from relying on the benefits of the ACIA by a Member State if it is found to be owned or controlled by investors from a non-Member State and the denying Member State does not maintain diplomatic relations with the non-Member State.[42] In addition, a Member State may also deny the benefits of the ACIA to investors of another Member State and to investments of that investor if such investor has made an investment in breach of the domestic laws of the denying Member State by misrepresenting its ownership in those areas of investment which are reserved for investors of the denying Member State.[43]

5 *Substantive Protections*

Fair and Equitable Treatment and Full Protection and Security

Each Member State is obliged to accord to covered investments of investors of another Member State "Fair and Equitable Treatment" ("FET") and "full protection and security".[44] FET requires each Member State not to deny justice

36 Article 3(3) of the ACIA; other sectors may be included if agreed upon by all Member States. Note that Article 3(3) of the ACIA is subject to the Reservations set out in Article 9.

37 Article 4 of the ACIA; see Article 5 which applies notwithstanding Article 4. See also Article 17 on General Exceptions.

38 As provided under the ASEAN Framework Agreement on Services signed in Bangkok, Thailand on 15 December 1995; see Article 4(e) of the ACIA.

39 A "juridical person" as defined in Article 19(3) of the ACIA.

40 Articles 19(1)(a) and (b) of the ACIA.

41 A "juridical person" as defined in Article 19(3) of the ACIA.

42 Article 19(1)(c) of the ACIA.

43 Article 19(2). Note that a Member State has to first notify the Member State of the investor prior to exercising its right to deny the investor the benefits of the ACIA.

44 Article 11(1) of the ACIA.

in any legal or administrative proceedings in accordance with the principle of due process,[45] while full protection and security requires each Member State to take such measures as may be reasonably necessary to ensure the protection and security of the covered investments.[46]

The ACIA also clarifies that a breach of another provision of the ACIA or of a separate international agreement would not in itself equate to a breach of the FET provision found in the ACIA.[47]

Non-Discrimination

The ACIA prohibits arbitrary and discriminatory treatment of covered investments by Member States. This principle of non-discrimination is central to a number of provisions which deal with a Member State's treatment of a covered investment in relation to the transfer,[48] expropriation[49] and compensation[50] relating to the investment.

Free Transfer of Payments

The ACIA provides that each Member State shall allow all transfers relating to a covered investment to be made freely and without delay into and out of its territory.[51] These include transfers of contributions to capital,[52] profits, capital gains, dividends, royalties, license fees, technical assistance, technical and management fees, interest, other current income accruing from any covered investment,[53] proceeds from the total or partial sale or liquidation of any covered investment,[54] payments made under a contract,[55] compensation in cases of strife and expropriation,[56] payments arising out of the settlement of a

45 Article 11(2)(a) of the ACIA.
46 Article 11(2)(b) of the ACIA.
47 *Ibid.*, Articles 11(1)–(3).
48 *Ibid.*, Article 13(h).
49 See Article 14 and Annex 2 of the ACIA.
50 *Ibid.*
51 Article 13(1) of the ACIA.
52 *Ibid.*, Article 13(1)(a).
53 *Ibid.*, Article 13(1)(b).
54 *Ibid.*, Article 13(1)(c).
55 *Ibid.*, Article 13(1)(d).
56 *Ibid.*, Article 13(1)(e).

dispute,[57] earnings and other remuneration of employees working in connection with the covered investment.[58]

Member States are allowed to impose restrictions on capital transactions only in exceptional circumstances specified in the ACIA,[59] *i.e.* where the movement of capital will cause or threaten to cause serious economic or financial disturbance in the Member State, where such measures are taken for the purpose of safeguarding the balance of payments under Article 16, or where such measure is requested by the International Monetary Fund.

A Member State is only allowed to delay or prevent such transfers by reason of its internal laws and regulations,[60] such as those relating to bankruptcy or insolvency,[61] trading or dealing in securities, futures and derivatives,[62] criminal offences or proceeds of crime,[63] taxation,[64] compliance with judgments or orders,[65] social security, public retirement or compulsory savings schemes,[66] severance entitlements of employees,[67] provision of assistance to law enforcement or financial regulatory authorities,[68] and formalities imposed by the central bank or other relevant authorities of a Member State.[69] The application of such local laws and regulations must be exercised by the relevant Member State equitably, in good faith, and in a non-discriminatory manner.[70]

Expropriation

Expropriation, nationalisation and any other measure having an effect equivalent to expropriation or nationalisation of a covered investment by a Member State is generally prohibited unless such a measure taken by the Member State serves a public purpose, is carried out in a non-discriminatory

57 *Ibid.*, Article 13(1)(f).
58 *Ibid.*, Article 13(1)(g).
59 *Ibid.*, Article 13(4).
60 *Ibid.*, Article 13(3).
61 *Ibid.*, Article 13(3)(a).
62 *Ibid.*, Article 13(3)(b).
63 *Ibid.*, Article 13(3)(c).
64 Article 13(3)(f) of the ACIA.
65 *Ibid.*, Article 13(3)(e).
66 *Ibid.*, Article 13(3)(g).
67 *Ibid.*, Article 13(3)(a).
68 *Ibid.*, Article 13(3)(d).
69 *Ibid.*, Article 13(3)(i).
70 *Ibid.*, Article 13(3) of the ACIA.

manner, is carried out on payment of prompt, adequate and effective compensation,[71] and is in accordance with due process of law.[72]

Uncommonly, Annex 2 of the ACIA provides specific guidance on the interpretation of the provision relating to expropriation. Annex 2 elaborates that what amounts to an "expropriation" under the ACIA are situations where an investment is nationalised or otherwise directly expropriated through formal transfer of title or outright seizure, or where an action or series of related actions by a Member State has an effect equivalent to direct expropriation without formal transfer of title or outright seizure.[73] Whether an action or series of actions by a Member State constitutes an "expropriation" is a fact-based inquiry which requires an analysis of the specific facts of the situation in question on a case-by-case basis. In this regard, factors such as the economic impact of the government action, whether the government action breaches the government's prior binding written commitment to the investor,[74] and the character of the government action,[75] have to be taken into account.

Most Favoured Nation and National Treatment

The ACIA requires each Member State to accord to investors as well as investments of another Member State treatment no less favourable than that it accords to investors of any other third Member State.[76] Similarly, any preferential treatment granted by a Member State to investors or investments of any other Member State or a non-Member State under any existing or future agreements or arrangements to which a Member State is a party shall be extended

71 The compensation should: (a) be paid by the relevant Member State without delay; (b) be equivalent to the fair market value of the expropriated investment immediately before or at the time when the expropriation was publicly announced or when the expropriation occurred, whichever is applicable; (c) not reflect any change in value because the intended expropriation had become known earlier; and (d) be fully realisable and freely transferable in accordance with Article 13 of the ACIA between the territories of Member States; see Article 14(2). In the event of a delay in payment, the compensation shall include an appropriate interest in accordance with the laws and regulations of the Member State making the expropriation; see Article 14(3).

72 Article 14 of the ACIA.

73 Annex 2, section 2 of the ACIA.

74 Whether by contract, licence or other legal document; see Annex 2, section 3(b) of the ACIA.

75 This includes the government's objective and whether the action is disproportional to the public purpose exception under Article 14(1) of the ACIA; see Annex 2, section 3(c).

76 Article 6(1) and (2) of the ACIA.

on a "most favoured nation" basis to all Member States.[77] This is commonly known as a "Most Favoured Nation" ("MFN") provision.

The ACIA specifically applies the MFN provision to the admission, establishment, acquisition, expansion, management, conduct, operation and sale or other disposition of investments,[78] but does not extend to investors or investments of other Member States the benefit of any treatment, preference or privilege resulting from any sub-regional arrangements between and among Member States,[79] or any existing agreement notified by Member States to the AIA Council.[80] The MFN provision also does not apply to investor-State dispute settlement procedures that are available in other agreements which Member States are party to[81] and to measures covered by certain obligations arising from the Agreement on Trade-Related Aspects of Intellectual Property Rights in Annex 1C to the WTO Agreement[82] ("TRIPS Agreement").[83]

The ACIA also contains explicit National Treatment provisions[84] which oblige each Member State to accord to investors and investments of any other Member State, treatment no less favourable than that it accords to its own investors with respect to the admission, establishment, acquisition, expansion, management, conduct, operation and sale or other disposition of investments in its territory.

However, it is expressly provided in the ACIA that the National Treatment provisions do not apply to existing measures that are maintained by a Member State at the central, regional and local level of government as set out in the reservation list in the Schedule to the ACIA.[85]

All Member States have submitted a list of reservations setting out measures that do not conform to the obligations under the National Treatment

77 Article 6, footnote 4(b) of the ACIA.

78 *Ibid.*

79 These include but are not limited to Greater Mekong Sub-region ("GMS"), ASEAN Mekong Basin Development Cooperation ("AMBDC"), Indonesia-Malaysia-Thailand Growth Triangle ("IMT-GT"), Indonesia-Malaysia-Singapore Growth Triangle ("IMS-GT"), Brunei-Indonesia-Malaysia-Philippines East ASEAN Growth Area ("BIMP-EAGA").

80 Pursuant to Article 8(3) of the AIA Agreement.

81 Article 6, footnote 4(a) of the ACIA.

82 Note that the "WTO Agreement" refers to the Marrakesh Agreement Establishing the World Trade Organization, done at Marrakesh, Morocco on 15 April 1994, as may be amended.

83 Article 9(5) of the ACIA.

84 *Ibid.*, Article 5.

85 *Ibid.*, Article 9(1).

provisions of the ACIA.[86] The extent of these reservations differs for each Member State,[87] most notably in respect of the sectors[88] in which the reservation is taken and the levels of government maintaining the measure for which such reservations are taken.

Each Member State has also reserved the right to make future reservations on measures that do not conform to the National Treatment provisions in the ACIA in respect of sectors, sub-sectors, industries, products or activities which are unregulated at the time of submission of the reservation lists.[89]

Although the Member States are obliged[90] to reduce or eliminate their respective reservations by 2015 in accordance with the three phases of the Strategic Schedule of the AEC Blueprint,[91] these reservations have yet to be withdrawn at the time of writing. In addition, as is the case for the MFN provision in the ACIA, the National Treatment provisions similarly do not apply to measures covered by certain obligations arising from the TRIPS Agreement.

6 *Compensation of Losses*

Article 12 of the ACIA mandates that each Member State accords to investors of another Member State non-discriminatory treatment with respect to restitution, compensation or other valuable consideration in relation to "covered investments"[92] which suffered losses in a Member State's territory due

---

86 For the detailed list of the reservations made by each of the Member States, see the Schedule to the ACIA.

87 For example, Cambodia stated as part of its reservations that the National Treatment provisions shall not apply to measures relating to land ownership, leasing, transactions or use across all sectors; Indonesia stated as part of its reservations that in foreign investors in all sectors must appoint local distribution agents to sell its products to end users in Indonesia; Lao stated as part of its reservations that foreign investors in all sectors are not allowed to own land but allowed to lease land or to receive grant or concession of land for investment purposes.

88 Refers to either manufacturing, agriculture, fishery, forestry, mining and quarrying, services incidental to these sectors, all or a combination of these sectors (see Article 2(a) of the Headnote to the List of Reservations found in the Schedule of the ACIA).

89 Article 4 of the Headnote to the List of Reservations found in the Schedule of the ACIA.

90 See Article 1 of the Protocol to Amend the ACIA, done at Nay Pyi Taw, Myanmar on 26 August 2014.

91 See the Strategic Schedule for ASEAN Economic Community (available at: http://www.asean.org/storage/images/archive/21161.pdf), which sets out three phases of progressive reduction/elimination of investment restrictions and impediments for the Member States, with the "Final Phase" set for completion in 2015.

92 See Article 4(a) of the ACIA.

to armed conflict, civil strife or state of emergency declared in the relevant Member State.

7 *Investor-State Dispute Settlement*

In the event of a dispute between an investor and a Member State, ACIA parties must first seek a resolution of the dispute by consultation and negotiation through a written request delivered by the investor to the host State.[93] If the dispute is not resolved within 180 days of the receipt by the Member State of the request for consultations, the investor may submit the dispute to arbitration.

The scope of the dispute resolution clause, however, is limited. The investor can only bring a claim against a Member State on the basis that: (i) the Member State has breached an obligation arising under Articles 5 (National Treatment), 6 (MFN Treatment), 8 (Senior Management and Board of Directors), 11 (Treatment of Investment), 12 (Compensation in Cases of Strife), 13 (Transfers) and 14 (Expropriation and Compensation) relating to the management, conduct, operation or sale or other disposition of a covered investment; and (ii) the disputing investor has incurred loss or damage by reason of or arising out of that breach.[94]

An investor has the option of submitting its claim to the courts or administrative tribunals of the Member State,[95] or to arbitration: (i) under the ICSID Convention and the ICSID Rules of Procedure for Arbitration Proceedings;[96] (ii) under the ICSID Additional Facility Rules;[97] (iii) under UNCITRAL Arbitration Rules; (iv) to the Regional Centre for Arbitration at Kuala Lumpur; or (v) to any other regional centre for arbitration in ASEAN. An investor may submit a claim to any other arbitration institution only if the Member State agrees to do so. There is also a "fork in the road" clause whereby an investment

93 Article 31 of the ACIA.

94 *Ibid.*, Article 32.

95 Provided such courts or tribunals have jurisdiction over such claims; see Article 33 (1)(a) of the ACIA.

96 Provided that both the disputing Member State and the non-disputing Member State are parties to the ICSID Convention; see Article 33(1)(b). Note that in the case of the Phillippines, submission of a claim to ICSID and the ICSID Rules of Procedure for Arbitration Proceedings is subject to a written agreement between the disputing parties in the event that an investment dispute arises; see footnote 14 to Aritcle 33(1)(b) of the ACIA.

97 Provided that either the disputing Member State or the non-disputing Member State is a party to the ICSID Convention.

dispute may only be submitted to one forum (to the exclusion of other fora) for determination.[98]

A claim is deemed to be submitted to arbitration when the investor's notice or request for arbitration is received under the applicable arbitration rules.[99] The tribunal shall comprise of three arbitrators unless the parties agree otherwise;[100] with each party appointing one arbitrator[101] and the third (presiding) arbitrator to be agreed by the parties.[102] The ACIA expressly provides that the parties to the dispute are to bear the fees and costs of their respective arbitrators and share equally the costs of the presiding arbitrator and other relevant costs. The tribunal otherwise determines its own procedures.[103]

A unique feature of the investor-State dispute resolution mechanism under the ACIA is that it is mandatory for the tribunal to bifurcate the proceedings where issues relating to jurisdiction or admissibility are raised as preliminary objections; the tribunal has to decide on these preliminary issues first before proceeding to the merits.[104] In other words, unlike most bilateral investment treaty arbitrations where the tribunal usually has discretion as to whether or not bifurcate the proceedings in the event that preliminary objections of jurisdiction or admissibility are raised, the tribunal does not have such discretionary powers in an investor-State arbitration commenced pursuant to the ACIA.

The ACIA also mandates that the place of arbitration be in the territory of a State that is a party to the New York Convention.[105]

The ACIA further provides for rules on, *inter alia*, consolidation of claims,[106] appointment of experts,[107] governing law of the arbitration,[108] issuance and enforcement of awards,[109] and the transparency of arbitral proceedings.[110]

---

98 Article 33(1) of the ACIA.

99 *Ibid.*, Article 33(2).

100 *Ibid.*, Article 35(1).

101 *Ibid.*, Article 35(1)(a).

102 Article 35(1)(b) of the ACIA; the presiding arbitrator shall be a national of a non-Member State which has diplomatic relations with the disputing Member State and non-disputing Member State, and shall not have permanent residence in either the disputing Member State or non-disputing Member State.

103 Article 35(5) of the ACIA.

104 Article 36(1) of the ACIA.

105 *Ibid.*, Article 36(5).

106 *Ibid.*, Article 37.

107 *Ibid.*, Article 38.

108 *Ibid.*, Article 40.

109 *Ibid.*, Article 41.

110 *Ibid.*, Article 39.

It bears noting that unless a disputing party informs the parties and the tribunal that the information that is submitted or to be used in a hearing is confidential, the Member State may make publicly available all awards and decisions produced by the tribunal.[111]

8 *Settlement of State-to-State Disputes*

Disputes between or among Member States concerning the interpretation or application of the ACIA shall be resolved in accordance with the ASEAN Protocol on Enhanced Dispute Settlement Mechanism signed in Vientiane, Lao on 29 November 2004[112] (the "ASEAN Protocol").

The ASEAN Protocol provides for disputes to be resolved between ASEAN Member States, first and as far as possible by amicable settlement through consultation between Member States, failing which the dispute may be escalated to a panel established by the Senior Economic Officials Meeting ("SEOM") at a meeting to be held immediately after the SEOM receives a request for a panel from a complaining Member State.[113]

The panel shall be composed of three panellists unless the parties to the dispute agree to have five panellists.[114] Such panels are comprised of "well-qualified governmental and/or non-governmental individuals, including persons who have served on or presented a case to a panel, served in the [ASEAN] Secretariat, taught or published on international trade law or policy, or served as a senior trade policy official of a Member State".[115]

Panel members are "selected with a view to ensuring the independence of the members, a sufficiently diverse background and a wide spectrum of experience."[116]

When considering nominations to the panel, preference is given to individuals who are nationals of ASEAN Member States. Nationals of Member States whose governments are parties to the dispute are not allowed to serve on a panel concerned with the dispute unless parties to the dispute agree otherwise.[117]

111 *Ibid.*

112 Article 27 of the ACIA.

113 The panel shall be so established by the SEOM unless the SEOM decides by consensus not to establish a panel.

114 Appendix II of the ASEAN Protocol.

115 *Ibid.*, Article 1.1.

116 *Ibid.*, Article 1.2.

117 *Ibid.*, Article 1.3.

The panel may regulate its own procedures.[118] While panel proceedings and deliberations are confidential, a party to a dispute is allowed to disclose statements of its own positions to the public; information submitted by the opposing Member State must however be treated as confidential.[119]

Generally, panel proceedings include written submissions of each party's case and arguments, followed by at least two oral hearings (known as "substantive meetings"), wherein each party presents its own case at a first hearing and formal rebuttals are made in a second hearing.[120]

The panel has to submit its findings and recommendations to the SEOM in the form of a written report within 60 days of its establishment.[121] The panel report shall be adopted by the SEOM within 30 days of its submission by the panel unless a party to the dispute formally notifies the SEOM of its decision to appeal the findings of the panel to the Appellate Body to be established by the ASEAN Economic Ministers ("AEM")[122] or if the SEOM decides by consensus not to adopt the report.[123]

The Appellate Body hears appeals from panel cases and is composed of seven (7) persons, three (3) of whom serve on any one case.[124] The Appellate Body comprises of persons of recognised authority, irrespective of nationality, with demonstrated expertise in law, international trade and the subject matter of the covered agreements generally. Members of the Appellate Body cannot be affiliated with any government and are not allowed to participate in the consideration of any disputes that would create a direct or indirect conflict of interest.[125]

As a general rule, the proceedings[126] of the Appellate Body should conclude within 60 days from the date a party to the dispute formally notifies its decision to appeal the panel report. The Appellate Body will provide the SEOM with

---

118 Article 8 of the ASEAN Protocol.

119 Appendix II of the ASEAN Protocol, Article 2.2 and 2.3.

120 *Ibid.*, Article 2.7.

121 Article 8(2) of the ASEAN Protocol allows an additional 10 days for the panel to submit its findings and recommendations to the SEOM in "exceptional cases".

122 For more details on the constitution, duties and responsibilities of the Appellate Body, see "ASEAN Protocol on Enhanced Dispute Settlement Mechanism Working Procedures for Appellate Review (drawn up pursuant to paragraph 8 of Article 12 of the Protocol)" annexed to the text of the ASEAN Protocol.

123 Article 12(1) of the ASEAN Protocol.

124 *Ibid.*

125 Article 12(3) of the ASEAN Protocol.

126 For working procedures of the Appellate Body and the Appellate Review process, see "ASEAN Protocol on Enhanced Dispute Settlement Mechanism Working Procedures

its report within the 60-day time period, or if more time is required, within 90 days.[127] A party to the dispute may only appeal against a panel report with regard to issues of law covered in the panel report and legal interpretations developed by the panel.[128]

9 *Additional Provisions*

Beyond the usual provisions found in BITs, the ACIA also contains provisions aimed at enhancing cooperation between ASEAN States in the promotion and facilitation of investment, and to enhance ASEAN integration. These overarching objectives are clearly set out in Articles 1[129] and 2[130] of the ACIA at the start of the agreement. In addition to these general provisions, the ACIA contains specific obligations on the part of the Member States which are designed to achieve these objectives.

Appointment of Senior Management and Board of Directors

The ACIA does not permit Member States to compel the investor[131] to appoint persons of any particular nationality to its senior management.[132] However, a Member State may require that a majority of the board of directors of the investor be of a particular nationality or reside in the territory of the Member State, provided that this requirement does not materially impair the ability of the investor to exercise control over its investment.

In other words, while investors are generally given the freedom to appoint any person of their choice for any senior management positions, a Member State may impose a condition on the investor that its board of directors be composed of a majority of its own nationals or residents if such a condition does not materially affect the investor's control over its investment in the Member State.

It is important to note that, with the exception of Lao, each of the Member States have, pursuant to Article 9 of the ACIA, submitted reservations on measures that do not conform to their obligations under Article 8.[133] The extent of

for Appellate Review (drawn up pursuant to paragraph 8 of Article 12 of the Protocol)" annexed to the text of the ASEAN Protocol.

127 Article 12(5) of the ASEAN Protocol.

128 Article 12(6) of the ASEAN Protocol.

129 On Objectives.

130 On Guiding Principles.

131 In this case a "juridical person" as defined under Article 4(e) of the ACIA.

132 Article 8(1) of the ACIA.

133 For the detailed list of the reservations made by each of the Member States, see the Schedule to the ACIA.

these reservations differs across Member States[134] and may apply to all, one, or a combination of sectors.[135]

Special and Differential Treatment for the Newer ASEAN Member States[136]

The ACIA recognises the differing levels of development and sectorial sensitivities across all Member States.[137] In line with this guiding principle, the ACIA accords new ASEAN Member States special and differential treatment through the provision of technical assistance to strengthen their capacity in relation to investment policies and promotion in areas such as human resource development, committing to areas of interests to the newer ASEAN Member States, and, more significantly, "recognising that commitments by each newer ASEAN Member State may be made in accordance with its individual stage of development."[138] This specific allowance which has been afforded to the newer ASEAN Member States may allow an eligible host State to argue that it is entitled to some leeway in the enforcement of some of its investment protection obligations found in the ACIA in light of its stage of development, which would arguably have material impact on the overall effectiveness of the investment protection regime under the ACIA.

---

134 For example, Brunei has stated as part of its reservations that for investment in all sectors, where there are two directors, at least one of the two directors shall be ordinarily resident in Brunei and, where there are more than two directors, at least two of them shall be ordinarily resident in Brunei.

Singapore has stated as part of its reservations that for investment in all sectors only a Singapore citizen, Singapore permanent resident or Singapore Employment Pass holder shall be allowed to register a business without appointing a local manager who has to be a Singapore citizen, Singapore permanent resident or Singapore Employment Pass holder, at least one director of the company shall be resident in Singapore, and all branches of foreign companies registered in Singapore shall have at least two agents resident in Singapore.

Malaysia has stated as part of its reservations that at least two directors of a company incorporated in Malaysia must have their principal or only place of residence in Malaysia.

135 Refers to either manufacturing, agriculture, fishery, forestry, mining and quarrying, services incidental to these sectors, all or a combination of these sectors (see Article 2(a) of the Headnote to the List of Reservations found in the Schedule of the ACIA).

136 Article 23 of the ACIA.

137 *Ibid.*, Article 2.

138 *Ibid.*, Article 23(c).

Transparency[139]

Each Member State is obliged to inform the AIA Council promptly and at least annually of any investment related agreements or arrangements which it has entered into and where preferential treatment was granted, as well as any new law or of any changes to existing laws, regulations or administrative guidelines which significantly affect investments or commitments of a Member State under the ACIA.

Member States must also make publicly available all relevant laws, regulations and administrative guidelines that pertain to or affect investments in its territory, and establish or designate an enquiry point where such information may be obtained when required.

Promotion of Investments[140]

Member States are obliged to cooperate in increasing awareness of ASEAN as an integrated investment area in order to increase foreign investment into ASEAN and intra-ASEAN investments.

This is done through, *inter alia*, encouraging the growth and development of ASEAN small and medium enterprises and multinational enterprises, enhancing industrial complementation and production networks among multinational enterprises in ASEAN, organising investment missions that focus on developing regional clusters and production networks, organising seminars on investment opportunities and on investment laws, regulations and policies, and conducting exchanges on other issues of mutual concern relating to investment promotion.

Facilitation of Investments[141]

Member States have to endeavour to cooperate in the facilitation of investments into and within ASEAN through, *inter alia*, creating the necessary environment for all forms of investments, streamlining and simplifying procedures for investment applications and approvals, promoting dissemination of investment information, establishing one-stop investment centres, strengthening databases on all forms of investments for policy formulation to improve ASEAN's investment environment, undertaking consultation with the business community on investment matters, and providing advisory services to the business community of the other Member States.

---

139 *Ibid.*, Article 21.

140 *Ibid.*, Article 24.

141 Article 25 of the ACIA.

Enhancing ASEAN Integration[142]

By signing on to the ACIA, Member States are deemed to acknowledge and recognise the importance of fostering and enhancing ASEAN economic integration. Member States agree to achieve this purpose by, *inter alia*, harmonising, where possible, investment policies and measures to achieve industrial complementation, build and strengthen capacity of Member States in the formulation and improvement of investment policies to attract investment, share information on investment policies and best practices, and support investment promotion efforts amongst Member States for mutual benefits.

IV ASEAN FTAs

1 *Overview*

ASEAN Member States are currently parties to five FTAs with certain ASEAN Dialogue Partners, namely, Australia and New Zealand, China, India, Japan and South Korea.

The Agreement on Comprehensive Economic Partnership Among Member States of ASEAN and Japan was signed in April 2008 ("ASEAN-Japan FTA"); the Agreement Establishing the ASEAN-Australia-New Zealand Free Trade Area was signed on 27 February 2009 ("ASEAN-Aust-NZ FTA"); the Agreement on Investment Under the Framework Agreement on Comprehensive Economic Cooperation Among the Governments of the Member Countries of ASEAN and South Korea was signed on 2 June 2009 ("ASEAN-Korea FTA"); the Agreement on Investment of the Framework Agreement on Comprehensive Economic Cooperation between ASEAN and China was signed on 15 August 2009 ("ASEAN-China FTA"); and the Agreement on Investment Under the Framework Agreement on Comprehensive Economic Cooperation between ASEAN and India was most recently concluded on 12 November 2014 ("ASEAN-India FTA").

The texts of all five FTAs are publicly available.[143] With the exception of the ASEAN-Japan FTA,[144] which contains an obligation to negotiate an

142 *Ibid.*, Article 26.

143 See http://www.asean.org/asean-economic-community/asean-free-trade-area-afta-council/free-trade-agreements-with-dialogue-partners/.

144 The ASEAN-Japan FTA contains only general provisions which oblige parties to promote economic cooperation, liberalise and facilitate trade and investment (Article 52), and endeavour to create and maintain favourable and transparent conditions in one party for

investment chapter at a later time, but no substantive investment protection obligations,[145] the investment chapters of the FTAs contain substantive provisions commonly found in BITs, as well as provisions aimed at promoting and facilitating investments between ASEAN Member States and the respective Dialogue Partners. The text of several of these provisions broadly mirror those found in the ACIA. One significant difference is the provision on Work Programmes.

2 *Definition of Investment*

The FTAs[146] provide for a relatively broad definition of "investment", similar to that found in the ACIA.[147] Thus "investment" is defined as every kind of asset that an investor owns or controls in the territory of the host State, including shares, stocks, bonds, debentures, loans, movable and immovable property, intellectual property rights, claims to money or contractual performance having financial value, as well as rights under contracts and business concessions.[148]

ASEAN FTAs also provide that investments include returns that are invested, and that the alteration of the form in which assets are invested or reinvested shall not affect their character as investments.[149] The ASEAN-Korea FTA[150] and ASEAN-India FTA[151] contain an additional criterion in their definition of "investment": there must be a commitment of capital; the expectation of gain or profit; or the assumption of risk.

---

investments of investors of the other party in accordance with the laws, regulations and policies of each party (Article 51). Article 51(2) provides that parties shall continue to discuss and negotiate provisions for investment, and that for this purpose, a sub-committee on investment shall be established within one year from the date of entry into force of the agreement. At the time of publication, the ASEAN-Japan FTA has not been amended to incorporate the results of such negotiations pursuant to Article 51(3).

145 See Article 51 of the ASEAN-Japan FTA.

146 In this Part IV, at sections 2–11, unless otherwise stated, the term "FTAs" refers only to the following treaties: the ASEAN-Aust-NZ FTA, the ASEAN-Korean FTA, the ASEAN-China FTA and the ASEAN-India FTA, and excludes the ASEAN-Japan FTA.

147 See Part III, paragraph 2 above.

148 See Chapter 11, Article 2(c) of ASEAN-Aust-NZ FTA; Article 1(j) of ASEAN-Korea FTA; Article 1(d) of ASEAN-China FTA; and Article 2(e) of ASEAN-India FTA.

149 *Ibid.*

150 See Article 1(j).

151 See Article 2(e).

The ASEAN-China FTA specifically states that the "investment" must have been made in accordance with the relevant laws, regulations and policies of the host State.[152] Although this compliance requirement is absent in the respective definitions of "investment" in other FTAs, the latter provide that only investments which have been admitted in accordance with the relevant laws, regulations and policies of the host State will be "covered" by or otherwise entitled to the benefits set out in the respective FTAs.[153] The FTAs[154] recognise that this may require an investment to be specifically approved in writing for protection by the competent authorities, as is the case for investments made in Cambodia, Thailand and Vietnam.

The ASEAN-Aust-NZ FTA[155] and ASEAN-Korea FTA[156] specifically exclude from the term "investment" claims to money that arise solely from commercial contracts for the sale of goods or services by a party in the territory of a State to a party in the territory of another State, and the extension of credit in connection with a commercial transaction (*e.g.* trade financing). Similarly excluded from the definition of "investment" in the ASEAN-Aust-NZ FTA[157] and ASEAN-India FTA[158] are orders and judgments entered in judicial or administrative actions.

3 *Definition of Investor*

The definition of "investor" in the FTAs[159] accords with that found in the ACIA.[160] It includes natural persons who are nationals in a State who is party to the FTA and legal entities duly constituted or incorporated under applicable laws of a party to the relevant FTA. The latter includes profit or non-profit, private or government-owned entities, including corporations, trusts, partnerships, joint ventures, sole proprietorships, associations and cooperatives.

---

152 Article 1(d) of the ASEAN-China FTA.

153 See Chapter 11, Article 2(a) of the ASEAN-Aust-NZ FTA; Article 1(c) of the ASEAN-Korea FTA; and Article 1(1)(b) of the ASEAN-India FTA.

154 See Chapter 11, footnote 1 of the ASEAN-Aust-NZ FTA; Article 3(3) of the ASEAN-China FTA; footnote 1 and Annex 1 of the ASEAN-Korea FTA; and footnote 1 of the ASEAN-India FTA.

155 See Chapter 11, footnote 3 to Article 2.

156 See Article 1(i) and (j).

157 See Chapter 11, footnote 2 to Article 2.

158 See footnote 3 to Article 2.

159 See Chapter 11, Articles 2(d), (e), (f) and (i) of the ASEAN-Aust-NZ FTA; Articles 1(e), (f) and (i) of the ASEAN-China FTA; Articles 1(k), (j) and (o) of the ASEAN-Korea FTA; and Articles 2(f), (g), (h) and (j) of the ASEAN-India FTA.

160 See Part III, paragraph 3 above.

4 *Scope*

The FTAs apply to investments which are made in a State[161] party to the relevant FTA prior to and after the agreement came into force,[162] as well as measures[163] adopted or maintained by a State[164] relating to such investments from the date of entry into force of the relevant FTA, but[165] do not apply to claims made or events which have given rise to claims that occurred prior to the entry into force of the relevant FTA.[166] In addition, the ASEAN-India FTA specifically states that its provisions shall apply to the manufacturing, agriculture, fishery, forestry and mining and quarrying sectors.[167]

Further, as discussed earlier in this Chapter,[168] an investment would be covered by the FTAs only if it has been made in accordance with the laws, regulations and national policies[169] of the relevant State, and where applicable, specifically approved in writing by the competent authority of the relevant State.[170]

---

161 Note that the ASEAN-China FTA only applies to investments of investors of an ASEAN State made in the customs territory of China according as defined by the World Trade Organization ("WTO") at the time of China's accession to the WTO on 11 December 2011; see Article 3(1)(b) of the ASEAN-China FTA.

162 See Chapter 11, Articles 1 and 2(a) of the ASEAN-Aust-NZ FTA; Article 3 of the ASEAN-China FTA; Articles 1(c) and 2 of the ASEAN-Korea FTA; and Article 1 of the ASEAN-India FTA.

163 This includes any measure by a party to the FTA, whether in the form of a law, regulation, rule, procedure, decision, administrative action, or "any other form"; see Chapter 11, Article 2(g) and (h) of the ASEAN-Aust-NZ FTA and Article 2(i) of the ASEAN-India FTA. The ASEAN-China (Article 1(g)) and ASEAN-Korea (Article1(n)) further specify that such measures of "any other form" must be measures that are affecting investors and/or investments.

164 This includes central, regional or local governments and authorities, as well as non-governmental bodies in the exercise of powers delegated by central, regional or local governments and authorities; see Chapter 11, Article 2(g) and (h) of the ASEAN-Aust-NZ FTA; Article 1(g) of the ASEAN-China FTA; Article 1(n) of the ASEAN-China FTA; and Article 2(i) of the ASEAN-India FTA.

165 Excluding the ASEAN-Aust-NZ FTA.

166 See Article 3(2) of the ASEAN-China FTA; Article 2(2)(d) of the ASEAN-Korea FTA; and Article 1(3) of the ASEAN-India FTA.

167 Article 1(5) of the ASEAN-India FTA.

168 See Part IV, paragraph 2 above.

169 Note that Article 1(d) of the ASEAN-China FTA defines "policies" as referring to those affecting investment that are endorsed and announced by the government of a State party and made publicly available in a written form.

170 See Article 1(c) of the ASEAN-Korea FTA. Note that the ASEAN-Aust-NZ FTA (Chapter 11, Article 2(a)), ASEAN-China FTA (Article 3(3)) and ASEAN-India FTA (Article 1(1)

The FTAs, however, generally do not apply to government procurements, subsidies or grants provided by a State party, taxation measures, laws, regulations, policies or procedures governing government procurements, services supplied in the exercise of governmental authority by a relevant body or authority of a State party, and measures adopted or maintained by a State party affecting trade in services[171] or its security interests.[172] Most of the FTAs provide that a State is generally excepted from complying with the provisions of the relevant FTA in respect of:

- measures necessary to protect public morals or to maintain public order;
- measures necessary to protect human, animal or plant life or health;
- measures necessary to secure compliance with laws or regulations which are not inconsistent with the provisions of the relevant FTA (*e.g.* prevention of deceptive and fraudulent practices, protection of privacy and personal data of individuals, and safety);
- measures aimed at ensuring the equitable or effective imposition or collection of direct taxes in respect of investments or investors;
- measures imposed for the protection of national treasures; or
- measures relating to the conservation of exhaustible natural resources.[173]

The FTAs also contain provisions similar to those found in the ACIA relating to circumstances where a State may deny an investor the benefits of the relevant agreement.[174] A host State may deny an investor the benefits of

(b)) provide that in the case of Thailand an investment shall be afforded with protection under the treaty only in cases where the investment by an investor of another State party in the territory of Thailand has been admitted and specifically approved in writing for protection by its competent authorities, in accordance with its domestic laws, regulations and policies. The ASEAN-Aust-NZ FTA (Chapter 11, Article 2(a)) and the ASEAN-India FTA (Article 1(1)(b)) also contain similar requirements for investments to be specifically registered or approved in writing, as the case may be, in the case of Vietnam. The ASEAN-India FTA (Article 1(1)(b)) extends this requirement in respect of Cambodia as well.

171 See Chapter 11, Article 1(2) of the ASEAN-Aust-NZ FTA; Article 3(4) of the ASEAN-China FTA; Article 2(2) of the ASEAN-Korea FTA; and Article 1(2) of the ASEAN-India FTA.

172 See Article 17 of the ASEAN-China FTA; Article 21 of the ASEAN-Korea FTA; and Article 22 and Annexes 1 and 2 of the ASEAN-India FTA.

173 See Article 16 of the ASEAN-China FTA; Article 20 of the ASEAN-Korea FTA; and Article 21 of the ASEAN-India FTA.

174 See Chapter 11, Article 11 of the ASEAN-Aust-NZ FTA; Article 15 of the ASEAN-China FTA; Article 17 of the ASEAN-Korea FTA; and Article 13 of the ASEAN-India FTA.

the FTA if the investor is owned or controlled by an investor from a State which is not a party to the FTA or the host State, and it is established that the investor does not have substantive business operations in the territory of the other State which is a party to the FTA. An investor may also be prevented from relying on the benefits of the FTA by a host State if the investor is found to be owned or controlled by investors from a State which is not a party to the FTA and with which the host State does not maintain diplomatic relations. In addition, an investor may also be denied the benefits of the FTA if such investor has made an investment in breach of the domestic laws of the host State by misrepresenting its ownership in those areas of investment which are reserved for investors of the host State.

Subrogation rights are generally recognised by the FTAs, provided that the subrogated or transferred right or claim is not greater than the original right or claim of the investor.[175]

5 *Substantive Protections*

Fair and Equitable Treatment

The FTAs provide that qualifying investors and/or investments shall be accorded with FET by the host State.[176] Among other aspects, FET requires the host State not to deny the investor justice in any legal or administrative proceedings.[177] States are not required to accord treatment which are in addition to or beyond that which is required under customary international law.[178]

It is also clear that a breach of the FET provision in the FTAs has to be independently established by a claimant – a determination that there has been a breach of another provision of the FTA or of a separate international agreement does not establish that there has been a breach of the FET provision under the relevant FTA.[179]

Full Protection and Security

Qualifying investors and/or investments under the FTAs are accorded full protection and security, which requires States to take such measures as may be reasonably necessary to ensure the protection and security of the qualifying

175 See Chapter 11, Article 10 of the ASEAN-Aust-NZ FTA; Article 12 of the ASEAN-China FTA; Article 14 of the ASEAN-Korea FTA; and Article 10 of the ASEAN-India FTA.

176 See Chapter 11, Article 6 of the ASEAN-Aust-NZ FTA; Article 4 of the ASEAN-China FTA; Article 5 of the ASEAN-Korea FTA; and Article 7 of the ASEAN-India FTA.

177 *Ibid.*

178 *Ibid.*

179 *Ibid.*

investments.[180] However, such measures of "protection and security" do not require treatment in addition to or beyond that which is required under customary international law and do not create additional substantive rights.[181] Similar to FET protection, a determination that there has been a breach of another provision of the FTA or of a separate international agreement does not establish that there has been a breach of the "full protection and security" treatment provision under the relevant FTA.[182]

Non-Discrimination

The FTAs generally prohibit arbitrary and discriminatory treatment of qualifying investors and/or investments by States. This principle of non-discrimination is reflected in a number of provisions in the FTAs, including those that deal with a State's treatment of a qualifying investor and/or investment, such as in relation to the transfer or expropriation of an investment, compensation of an investor, and denial of benefits to the investor.

Free Transfer of Payments

The FTAs[183] contain provisions similar to that found in the ACIA[184] which obliges States to allow all transfers relating to a qualifying investment to be made freely and without delay into and out of its territory. A State is only allowed to delay or prevent such transfers through the equitable, non-discriminatory and good faith application of specified areas of laws and regulations of the State such as those relating to insolvency, securities, crime, taxation and employment.

Expropriation

All of the FTAs[185] expressly prohibit a State from expropriating, nationalising or undertaking any other measures equivalent to expropriation or nationalisation of a qualifying investment unless such a measure was taken by a State for a public purpose, in a non-discriminatory manner, on payment of prompt,

180 See Chapter 11, Article 6 of the ASEAN-Aust-NZ FTA; Article 4 of the ASEAN-China FTA; Article 5 of the ASEAN-Korea FTA; and Article 7 of the ASEAN-India FTA.

181 *Ibid.*

182 *Ibid.*

183 See Chapter 11, Article 8 of the ASEAN-Aust-NZ FTA; Article 10 of the ASEAN-China FTA; Article 10 of the ASEAN-Korea FTA; and Article 11 of the ASEAN-India FTA.

184 See Article 13 of the ACIA; see also above Part III, paragraph 5, sub-paragraph titled "Transfers of Investments".

185 See Chapter 11, Article 9 of the ASEAN-Aust-NZ FTA; Article 8 of the ASEAN-China FTA; Article 12 of the ASEAN-Korea FTA; and Article 8 of the ASEAN-India FTA.

adequate and effective compensation, and in accordance with due process of law.

The FTAs[186] also provide that any measure of expropriation relating to land shall be as defined in the expropriating State's existing domestic laws and regulations and shall be for the purposes of and upon payment of compensation in accordance with the aforesaid laws and regulations.[187]

The ASEAN-China FTA and ASEAN-Korea FTA do not provide any further definitions or explanations on what amounts to or constitutes expropriation or nationalisation under the respective agreements.

The ASEAN-Aust-NZ FTA[188] and ASEAN-India FTA,[189] however, specify that a measure or a series of related measures taken by a State cannot amount to an expropriation unless it interferes with a tangible or intangible property right in a qualifying investment. Both agreements recognise that a qualifying investment may be expropriated either directly[190] or indirectly,[191] and that the determination of whether expropriation has taken place depends on the specific facts of the case or claim.[192] Both these agreements[193] also provide that non-discriminatory actions by a State that are designed and applied to achieve legitimate public welfare objectives, such as the protection of public health, safety and the environment, do not constitute expropriation.

Most Favoured Nation and National Treatment

Only the ASEAN-China FTA and ASEAN-Korea FTA contain MFN provisions.[194] Both agreements, however, exclude from their respective MFN provisions[195] preferential treatment accorded to investors and/or their investments under any existing bilateral, regional and/or international

186 *Ibid.*

187 In respect of the ASEAN-Aust-NZ FTA and ASEAN-Korea FTA, this provision only applies in the case of Singapore and Vietnam.

188 Chapter 11, Annex on Expropriation and Compensation.

189 Article 8(2).

190 Where a qualifying investment is nationalised or otherwise directly expropriated through formal transfer of title or outright seizure.

191 Where a measure or series of related measures by a State has an effect equivalent to direct expropriation without formal transfer of title or outright seizure.

192 See Chapter 11, Annex on Expropriation and Compensation to the ASEAN-Aust-NZ FTA; and Articles 8(2) and (3) of the ASEAN-India FTA.

193 See Chapter 11, Annex on Expropriation and Compensation to the ASEAN-Aust-NZ FTA and Article 8(9) of the ASEAN-India FTA.

194 See Article 5 of the ASEAN-China FTA and Article 4 of the ASEAN-Korea FTA.

195 *Ibid.*

agreements or any forms of economic or regional cooperation with any State which is not a party to the relevant FTA, as well as existing or future preferential treatment accorded to investors and/or investments in any agreement or arrangement between or among ASEAN Member States. Both agreements also exclude the application of their respective MFN provisions *vis-à-vis* future agreements or arrangements to which a State becomes a party. However, in such an event, both agreements[196] oblige a State to accord adequate opportunity to negotiate the benefits granted to another State upon request from that State. These extensive carve-out provisions effectively render the MFN provisions in the ASEAN-China FTA and ASEAN-Korea FTA nugatory as they do not guarantee that the status of ASEAN Member States would be elevated above that of other countries either retrospectively or prospectively.

While all FTAs contain similarly broad provisions on national treatment[197] (*i.e.* qualifying investors and investments are to be accorded with treatment no less favourable than that accorded by a State, in like circumstances, to its own investors and investments), the ASEAN-India FTA goes further to elaborate that such treatment means, at a regional or local level, treatment no less favourable than the most favoured treatment accorded at that regional or local level, in like circumstances, to investors and investments of the State to which it forms a part.[198] The ASEAN-India FTA also clarifies that the determination of whether investments or investors are in "like circumstances" should be made based upon an objective assessment of all circumstances on a case-by-case basis, including, *inter alia*, the sector the investor is in, the location of the investment, the aim of the measure concerned and the regulatory process generally applied in relation to the measure concerned.[199]

The ASEAN-India FTA specifically allows for the exclusion of the application of its "national treatment" provision by allowing a host State to not extend to investors the benefits or privileges arising from customs unions, free trade agreements or similar bilateral, regional or international agreements or arrangements, where the investor's home State is or may become a member, including any arrangements between or among ASEAN Member States.[200]

Extension of financial assistance or measures taken by a State in favour of its investors and investments in pursuit of legitimate public purposes

---

196 *Ibid.* Article 5(1) of the ASEAN-India FTA contains a similar provision.

197 See Chapter 11, Article 4 of the ASEAN-Aust-NZ FTA; Article 4 of the ASEAN-China FTA; and Article 3 of the ASEAN-Korea FTA.

198 See Article 3(2) of the ASEAN-India FTA.

199 Article 3(4).

200 Article 3(3) of the ASEAN-India FTA.

(*e.g.* the protection of health, safety, or the environment) are also excluded from the scope of the "national treatment" provision in the ASEAN-India FTA.[201]

The ASEAN-China FTA,[202] ASEAN-Korea FTA[203] and ASEAN-India FTA[204] permit a State to take measures that do not conform with its obligations under the "national treatment" or MFN provisions (as the case may be), in respect of cross-border capital transactions or transfers, in the event that the State is under the threat of serious balance of payments and external financial difficulties.

6 *Compensation for Losses*

All FTAs contain similar provisions[205] obliging States to grant investors from another State compensation no less favourable than that which they afford to their own investors and investments or to investors of a third State and their investments in the event that such investors suffer losses owing to war or other armed conflict, state of national emergency or civil disturbances in the host State.

7 *Investor-State Dispute Settlement*

The mechanism provided in the FTAs for the settlement of disputes between an investor and a State is largely similar to that in the ACIA.[206] The FTAs[207] provide that in the event of a dispute between an investor and a State, parties are obliged to first attempt to seek an amicable settlement of the dispute through consultations. A claim can only be escalated if the dispute is not resolved within 6 months[208] or 180 days[209] of the receipt of the request for such consultations.

---

201 Article 3(5) of the ASEAN-India FTA.

202 Article 6(1).

203 Article 11(1).

204 Article 12(1).

205 Chapter 11, Article 7 of the ASEAN-Aust-NZ FTA; Article 9 of the ASEAN-China FTA; Article 13 of the ASEAN-Korea FTA; and Article 9 of the ASEAN-India FTA.

206 See Part III, paragraph 8 above.

207 See Chapter 17, Articles 19 and 20 of the ASEAN-Aust-NZ FTA; Article 14 of the ASEAN-China FTA; Article 18 of the ASEAN-Korea FTA; and Article 20 of the ASEAN-India FTA.

208 ASEAN-China FTA and ASEAN-Korea FTA.

209 ASEAN-Aust-NZ FTA and ASEAN-India FTA.

In such an event, the FTAs[210] allow the investor to elect to submit its claim to either the courts or tribunals of the host State,[211] or to arbitration under one of the following: (i) the ICSID Convention and the ICSID Rules of Procedure for Arbitration Proceedings; (ii) the ICSID Additional Facility Rules; (iii) UNCITRAL Arbitration Rules; or (v) any other arbitral rules or to any other arbitral institution if the disputing parties agree. With the exception of the ASEAN-China FTA, the FTAs state that the submission of a claim to a court or tribunal of a State would preclude the investor from submitting the same claim to arbitration. Interestingly, the ASEAN-China FTA[212] allows for a dispute which has been submitted to a competent domestic court to be submitted to arbitration if the investor has withdrawn its case from the domestic court before a final judgment has been rendered in the case. However, this provision in the ASEAN-China FTA does not apply (*i.e.*, the choice of procedure is final) if the dispute has been submitted to the respective competent courts or tribunals of Indonesia, Philippines, Thailand or Vietnam.

In all cases where the investor elects to arbitrate the dispute, the FTAs[213] oblige the investor to provide written notice of its intention to submit its claim to arbitration at least 90 days before the claim is submitted to arbitration. Also noteworthy is the three-year limitation period of such claims which starts running from the time at which the investor became aware or should reasonably have become aware of an alleged breach of an obligation under the relevant FTA which had caused loss or damage to the investor in relation to its investment.[214]

While the ASEAN-Aust-NZ FTA and ASEAN-India FTA contain other specific provisions relating to the arbitral proceedings such as the selection of arbitrators,[215] consolidation of claims,[216] conduct of the arbitration,[217] trans-

---

210 See Chapter 17, Article 21 of the ASEAN-Aust-NZ FTA; Article 14 of the ASEAN-China FTA; Article 18 of the ASEAN-Korea FTA; and Article 20 of the ASEAN-India FTA.

211 The ASEAN-Aust-NZ FTA only allows for a claim to be submitted to the courts or tribunals of a State where the Philippines or Vietnam is the disputing State (Article 21(a)).

212 Article 14(5).

213 See Chapter 17, Article 22 of the ASEAN-Aust-NZ FTA; Article 14(6) of the ASEAN-China FTA; Article 18(7) of the ASEAN-Korea FTA; and Article 20(8) of the ASEAN-India FTA.

214 *Ibid.*

215 Unless the disputing parties agree otherwise, the arbitral tribunal shall comprise three arbitrators, where each of the disputing parties appoints an arbitrator and the third (presiding) arbitrator appointed by agreement of the disputing parties; see Article 23 of the ASEAN-Aust-NZ FTA and Article 20(10) of the ASEAN-India FTA.

216 See Chapter 17, Article 24 of the ASEAN-Aust-NZ FTA.

217 See Chapter 17, Article 25 of the ASEAN-Aust-NZ FTA and Articles 20(12)–(14) of the ASEAN-India FTA. Note that, the ASEAN-Aust-NZ FTA and ASEAN-India FTA (like

parency of the proceedings,[218] governing law,[219] finality and enforcement of awards[220] and costs,[221] the ASEAN-China FTA and ASEAN-Korea FTA are silent on these issues.

8 *State-to-State Dispute Settlement*

The dispute resolution mechanism for disputes between States arising under the respective FTAs are provided for in separate chapters of the relevant FTA[222] or separate agreements between the respective parties,[223] although the procedures involved are similar to a large extent.

They provide that parties should first attempt to resolve the dispute through consultations. Disputing parties are also encouraged to undertake other procedures of good offices, conciliation and mediation with a view to reaching an amicable settlement of the dispute.

A State-to-State dispute may be submitted to an arbitral tribunal for determination if the dispute is not resolved within 60 days from the date of receipt of the request for consultations. Unless parties agree otherwise, the arbitral tribunal shall comprise of three arbitrators. In the case of State-to-State disputes arising under the ASEAN-China FTA, ASEAN-Korea FTA or ASEAN-India FTA, if any party to such dispute fails to appoint an arbitrator within the

---

the ACIA) provide that where issues relating to jurisdiction or admissibility are raised as preliminary objections, the tribunal shall decide the matter before proceeding to the merits.

218 See Chapter 17, Article 26 of the ASEAN-Aust-NZ FTA and Articles 20(17)–(18) of the ASEAN-India FTA.

219 See Chapter 17, Article 27 of the ASEAN-Aust-NZ FTA and Article 20(31) of the ASEAN-India FTA.

220 See Chapter 17, Article 28 of the ASEAN-Aust-NZ FTA and Articles 20(21)–(27) of the ASEAN-India FTA.

221 See Article 20(28)–(3) of the ASEAN-India FTA.

222 In the case of the ASEAN-Aust-NZ FTA, under Chapter 17 of the agreement; in the case of the ASEAN-Japan FTA, under Chapter 9 of the agreement.

223 In the case of the ASEAN-China FTA (see Article 13), under the Agreement on Dispute Settlement Mechanism of the Framework Agreement on Comprehensive Economic Co-operation between ASEAN and China signed in Vientiane, Lao PDR on 29 November 2004 ("China Framework Agreement"); in the case of the ASEAN-Korea FTA (see Article 19), under the Agreement on Dispute Settlement Mechanism Under the Framework Agreement on Comprehensive Economic Cooperation Among the Governments of the Member Countries of ASEAN and Korea signed in Kuala Lumpur, Malaysia on 13 December 2005 ("Korea Framework Agreement"); in the case of the ASEAN-India FTA (see Article 19), under the Agreement on Dispute Settlement Mechanism under the Framework Agreement on Comprehensive Economic Cooperation between ASEAN and India signed in Bangkok, Thailand on 13 August 2009 ("India Framework Agreement").

prescribed time period,[224] then the arbitrator appointed by the other party to the dispute shall act as the sole arbitrator of the tribunal.[225]

The ASEAN-Aust-NZ FTA[226] and ASEAN-Japan FTA[227] provide that a disputing party may request the Director-General of the WTO to make the remaining appointments to the arbitral tribunal in such an event. The dispute resolution agreements also specify nationality, qualifications and other requirements that must be satisfied by prospective arbitrators. Third States who are parties to the relevant FTA and who have substantial interest in a dispute before the arbitral tribunal are also afforded with the opportunity to make written submissions to the tribunal.[228]

The dispute resolution agreements also contain provisions on functions[229] and proceedings[230] of the tribunal, suspension and termination of arbitral proceedings,[231] implementation of the final award, report or rulings of the tribunal,[232] the venue[233] and language[234] of arbitration, as well as

224 See Article 7(2) of the China Framework Agreement; Article 6(2) of the Korea Framework Agreement; and Article 7(2) of the India Framework Agreement.

225 *Ibid.*

226 Article 11.

227 Article 65.

228 See Chapter 17, Article 10 of the ASEAN-Aust-NZ FTA; Article 66 of the ASEAN-Japan FTA; Article 10 of the China Framework Agreement; Article 7 of the Korea Framework Agreement; and Article 8 of the India Framework Agreement.

229 See Chapter 17, Article 12 of the ASEAN-Aust-NZ FTA; Article 67 of the ASEAN-Japan FTA; Article 8 of the China Framework Agreement; Article 9 of the Korea Framework Agreement; and Article 10 of the India Framework Agreement.

230 See Chapter 17, Article 13 of the ASEAN-Aust-NZ FTA; Article 68 of the ASEAN-Japan FTA; Article 9 of the China Framework Agreement; Article 10 of the Korea Framework Agreement; and Article 11 of the India Framework Agreement.

231 See Chapter 17, Article 14 of the ASEAN-Aust-NZ FTA; Article 70 of the ASEAN-Japan FTA; Article 11 of the China Framework Agreement; Article 8 of the Korea Framework Agreement; and Article 9 of the India Framework Agreement.

232 See Chapter 17, Article 15 of the ASEAN-Aust-NZ FTA; Article 71 of the ASEAN-Japan FTA; Article 12 of the China Framework Agreement; Article 14 of the Korea Framework Agreement; and Article 15 of the India Framework Agreement.

233 See Chapter 17, Article 13(9) of the ASEAN-Aust-NZ FTA; Article 68(12) of the ASEAN-Japan FTA; Article 9(2) of the China Framework Agreement; paragraph 15 of the Annex (Rules and Procedures for the Arbitral Panel Proceedings) to the Korea Framework Agreement; and paragraph 11 of the Annex (Rules and Procedures for the Arbitral Panel Proceedings) to the India Framework Agreement.

234 With the exception of the ASEAN-Japan FTA. In the case of the other dispute resolution agreements, see Chapter 17, Article 21 of the ASEAN-Aust-NZ FTA; Article 14 of the China

confidentiality,[235] expenses and costs[236] of the proceedings. A common feature in the dispute resolution agreements is availability of temporary measures of compensation and suspension of concession or benefits in the event that the award, report, recommendations or rulings of the tribunal are not implemented by the relevant State within a reasonable period of time. Such measures may be ordered by the tribunal in the event that disputing parties are unable to reach a mutually satisfactory agreement on compensation through negotiations.[237]

9 *Additional Provisions*

Apart from the usual provisions found in BITs, a number of FTAs also contain provisions on special and differential treatment for the newer ASEAN Member States[238] as well as on transparency,[239] promotion[240] and facilitation[241] of investments aimed at enhancing cooperation between the relevant Dialogue Partner and ASEAN Member States in the area of investment, which are similar to those found in the ACIA.[242]

Framework Agreement; Article 16 of the Korea Framework Agreement; Article 17 of the India Framework Agreement.

235 See Chapter 17, Article 13(10) of the ASEAN-Aust-NZ FTA; Articles 68(8)–(11) of the ASEAN-Japan FTA; Article 9(4) of the China Framework Agreement; paragraph 21 of the Annex (Rules and Procedures for the Arbitral Panel Proceedings) to the Korea Framework Agreement; and paragraph 14 of the Annex (Rules and Procedures for the Arbitral Panel Proceedings) to the India Framework Agreement.

236 See Chapter 17, Article 19 of the ASEAN-Aust-NZ FTA; Articles 73 of the ASEAN-Japan FTA; Article 15 of the China Framework Agreement; Article 17 of the Korea Framework Agreement; and Article 18 of the India Framework Agreement.

237 See Chapter 17, Article 17 of the ASEAN-Aust-NZ FTA; Article 72 of the ASEAN-Japan FTA; Article 11 of the China Framework Agreement; Article 15 of the Korea Framework Agreement; and Article 9 of the India Framework Agreement.

238 See Chapter 11, Article 15 of the ASEAN-Aust-NZ FTA; Article 16 of the ASEAN-Korea FTA; and Article 16 of the ASEAN-India FTA.

239 See Chapter 11, Article 13 of the ASEAN-Aust-NZ FTA; Article 19 of the ASEAN-China FTA; Article 8 of the ASEAN-Korean FTA; and Article 14 of the ASEAN-India FTA.

240 Excluding the ASEAN-Aust-NZ FTA and ASEAN-Korea FTA. In the case of the other FTAs, see Article 20 of the ASEAN-China FTA and Article 17 of the ASEAN-India FTA.

241 Excluding the ASEAN-Aust-NZ FTA and ASEAN-Korea FTA. In the case of the other FTAs, see Article 21 of the ASEAN-China FTA and Article 18 of the ASEAN-India FTA.

242 For detailed analyses on these provisions, see Part III, paragraph 10 above.

It is important to note the impact of the "Work Programme" articles found in most of the ASEAN FTAs[243] *vis-à-vis* the provisions on reservations[244] or non-conforming measures[245] under the relevant FTAs. These articles contain a little-known provision stating that the application of a number of substantive obligations of the State parties (such as those on National Treatment and MFN Treatment)[246] are suspended until the parties' schedules of reservations have entered into force. While the "Work Programme" articles[247] oblige parties to discuss or negotiate the contents of the schedule of reservations or non-conforming measures, as well as the procedures for the modification of such schedule of reservations or non-conforming measures, it is not publicly known at the time of writing whether any of these items have in fact been negotiated or agreed upon. If they have not been agreed upon (and therefore have not entered into force), this would mean that the specified substantive obligations under the respective FTA do not apply.[248] This would mean that qualifying investments made in the relevant host States may not be afforded the full range of substantive treaty protections under the relevant FTA.

Appointment of Senior Management and Board of Directors

The ASEAN-Korea FTA contains a provision relating to the constitution of senior management and boards of directors of a qualifying investor.

Article 7[249] of the ASEAN-Korea FTA mirrors Article 8 of the ACIA in this regard,[250] where investors are free to appoint any person to senior management

243 With the exception of the ASEAN-China FTA. However, refer to the above discussion on the National Treatment and MFN Treatment provisions found in the ASEAN-China FTA.

244 See Chapter 11, Article 12 of the ASEAN-Aust-NZ FTA; Article 9 of the ASEAN-Korea FTA; and Article 4 of the ASEAN-India FTA.

245 See Article 6 of the ASEAN-China FTA.

246 These include obligations relating to National Treatment obligations and Prohibition of Performance Requirements under the ASEAN-Aust-NZ FTA (see Article 12(1)); obligations relating to National Treatment and MFN Treatment under the ASEAN-China FTA (see Article 6(1)); obligations relating to National Treatment, MFN Treatment, Senior Management and Boards of Directors as well as Performance Requirements under the ASEAN-Korea FTA (see Article 9(1)); and obligations relating to National Treatment under the ASEAN-India FTA (see Article 4(1)).

247 See Chapter 11, Article 16 of the ASEAN-Aust-NZ FTA; Article 27 of the ASEAN-Korea FTA; and Article 6 of the ASEAN-India FTA.

248 *Ibid.*

249 Note that the application of Article 7 is subject to Article 27.

250 See above Part III, paragraph 5 on "Appointment of Senior Management and Board of Directors".

positions, but the host State may require the investor to appoint its nationals or residents of the host State to the board of directors if such appointment does not materially affect the investor's control over its investment in the host State. Curiously, the ASEAN-Korea FTA is the only ASEAN FTA which contains such a provision; the rest of the FTAs are silent on the issue.

V International Investment Arbitration Jurisprudence

With regard to the practical application of the investment protection provisions for qualifying investors investing in ASEAN Member States, at the time of writing, there were no investment disputes brought under the ACIA or the FTAs which were in the public domain.

However, there have been two international investment disputes submitted to arbitration under the ASEAN IPPA and the AIA Agreement.

The claimant in *Yaung Chi Oo Trading Pte Ltd., v. Government of the Union of Myanmar*[251] sought to rely on provisions in the ASEAN IGA and AIA Agreement, while *Cemex Asia Holdings Ltd. v. Republic of Indonesia*[252] was brought under the ASEAN IGA.

Each of these cases is considered in detail in the chapters on Myanmar[253] and Indonesia[254] of this book respectively.

VI Outlook: Anticipated Developments

At the time of writing, negotiations on a Regional Comprehensive Economic Partnership Agreement ("RCEP") are underway among ASEAN Member States, Australia, China, India. the Republic of Korea, Japan and New Zealand.

The RCEP is an ASEAN-led process through which ASEAN seeks to strengthen its economic engagements with its Dialogue Partners. It is envisaged that the RCEP will provide a platform for greater economic integration, support equitable economic development and strengthen economic cooperation among the countries involved. When completed, the agreement will be signed by

251 ASEAN I.D. Case No. ARB/01/1.

252 ICSID Case No. ARB/04/3.

253 For a detailed case analysis of *Yaung Chi Oo Trading Pte Ltd., v. Government of the Union of Myanmar*, see the Myanmar chapter.

254 For a detailed analysis of *Cemex Asia Holdings Ltd. v. Republic of Indonesia*, see the Indonesia chapter.

16 countries.[255] The RCEP envisions a transformation of the region into an integrated market of more than three billion people (45% of the world's population), and contribute a third of the world's GDP at about US$17.23 trillion.[256]

The RCEP will cover sectors such as trade in goods, trade in services, investment, economic and technical cooperation, intellectual property, competition, legal and institutional matters.[257] In the area of investment, the RCEP seeks to create a liberal, facilitative and competitive investment environment in the region. RCEP negotiations in this area will cover the four pillars of promotion, protection, facilitation and liberalisation.[258] Apart from the recognised sectors and areas of cooperation, the RCEP will also cover new and emerging issues that are relevant to business realities.[259]

It is not clear at the time of writing whether there will be any changes made to the ACIA or whether the existing FTAs with the Dialogue Partners will be amended or terminated upon the conclusion and entry into force of the RCEP. However, with the establishment of the AEC, together with the AEC-2025 Blueprint, the signing of the RCEP is expected to be a catalyst to the upward trend of FDI flow into ASEAN, and will hopefully further developments in the realm of investment treaty protection and dispute resolution in the region.

---

255 Ten ASEAN Member States and their six Dialogue Partners, Australia, China, India, Japan, Korea and New Zealand.

256 See Singapore Ministry of Trade and Industry, *Factsheet: What You Need To Know About Regional Comprehensive Economic Partnership* (RCEP), dated June 2014, available at: https://www.mti.gov.sg/MTIInsights/SiteAssets/Pages/FACTSHEET-WHAT-YOU-NEED-TO-KNOW-ABOUT/Factsheet%20on%20RCEP%20(June%202014).pdf.

257 *Ibid.*

258 *Ibid.*

259 *Ibid.*

CHAPTER 2

Brunei[1]

I Introduction

Brunei Darussalam ("Brunei") gained independence from Britain on 1 January 1984.[2] It is a national monarchy headed by the Sultan of Brunei.[3] It has two parallel and co-existing court systems – one based on Sharia law and one based on English common law.[4] In 2013, Brunei introduced a penal code that is entirely based on Sharia law, which would apply principally to Muslims although there are certain prescribed offences that may also apply to non-Muslims.

Brunei's economy has traditionally been heavily reliant on the sale of its rich oil and gas resources.[5] In 2014, as part of its long-term national strategy, "Wawasan 2035", Brunei released an Energy White Paper outlining its plans to leverage on its oil wealth to diversify its economy and attract Foreign Direct Investments ("FDI").[6]

FDI into Brunei has been recovering from the effects of the 2008–2009 global financial crisis. Between 2011 and 2012, the FDI flow into Brunei increased from USD 691 million to USD 865 million.[7] In recent years, the source of incoming FDI into Brunei has taken on a more regional focus. While total FDI into Brunei deceased from USD 865 million in 2012 to USD 568 million in 2014,[8] FDI into Brunei from South East Asian countries increased from around USD 93.5 million in 2011 to around USD 132.9 million in 2014.[9]

1 This chapter has been drafted by Mr Alvin Yap of Eversheds LLP, Singapore and reviewed by Mr Bernard Tan Thiam Swee of Abrahams, Davidson & Co of Brunei Darussalam.

2 The Commonwealth, Brunei Darussalam: Constitution and politics: http://thecommonwealth.org/our-member-countries/brunei-darussalam/constitution-politics.

3 *Ibid.*

4 Brunei's Economic Development Board, Prime Minister's Office, Introducing Brunei: http://www.bedb.com.bn/why_intro.html.

5 Brunei's Economic Development Board, Prime Minister's Office, Economic Overview: http://www.bedb.com.bn/why_ecoverview.html.

6 Brunei's Energy White Paper: https://www.usasean.org/sites/default/files/uploads/Energy%20White%20Paper%202014.pdf.

7 UNCTAD World Investment Report 2015, Country Fact Sheet on Brunei: http://unctad.org/sections/dite_dir/docs/wir2015/wir15_fs_bn_en.pdf.

8 *Ibid.*

9 *Ibid.*

 | DOI 10.1163/9789004335257_004

In the World Bank's "Doing Business" 2016 report, Brunei ranks 84th among the 189 economies covered for the ease of doing business (an improvement of 21 places on the 2015 report).[10] Notably, in that same report, Brunei ranks 134th in the degree of protection afforded to minority investors.[11]

II Brunei's National Arbitration and Investment Legislations

1 *Brunei's Arbitration Legislation and Institution*

Brunei's Arbitration Law

Brunei has two legal regimes for arbitration. Domestic arbitrations are governed by the Arbitration Order 2009[12] while international arbitrations are governed by the International Arbitration Order 2009.[13] The latter is based on the UNCITRAL Model Law as amended in 2006.[14] The Arbitration Order 2009 and International Arbitration Order 2009 replaced[15] the 1994 Arbitration Act,[16] which governed both domestic and international arbitrations.[17]

> "International Arbitration" is defined in section 5(2) of the International Arbitration Order 2009. An arbitration is international if:
>
> (a) at least one of the parties to the arbitration agreement, at the time of the conclusion of the agreement, has its place of business in any State other than Brunei;
> (b) the place of arbitration if determined in, or pursuant to, the arbitration agreement, is situated outside the State in which the parties have their places of business;
> (c) the place where a substantial part of the obligations of the commercial relationship is to be performed or the place with which the

10 World Bank Group, *Doing Business Report* 2016: http://www.doingbusiness.org/rankings.

11 *Ibid.*

12 Available at: http://www.agc.gov.bn/AGC%20Site%20Pages/Text%20of%20Orders.aspx.

13 *Ibid.*

14 http://www.uncitral.org/uncitral/en/uncitral_texts/arbitration/1985Model_arbitration_status.html.

15 Section 67 of Arbitration Order 2009.

16 Cap. 173, Laws of Brunei, B.L.R.O. 1/99, available at: http://www.agc.gov.bn/AGC%20Images/LOB/PDF/Chp.173.pdf.

17 Sections 7 and 8 of the 1994 Arbitration Act.

subject-matter of the dispute is most closely connected is situated outside the State in which the parties have their places of business; or

(d) the parties have expressly agreed that the subject-matter of the arbitration agreement relates to more than one country or territory.

Thus, it is likely that on the basis of limb (a) alone, many of the cases involving a foreign investor will be considered international arbitrations, given that a foreign investor will probably have its place of business outside Brunei.

A "domestic arbitration" to which the Arbitration Order 2009 applies is defined as an arbitration that is seated in Brunei which does not fall within any of the limbs of section 5(2) of the International Arbitration Order 2009.[18]

Brunei's Arbitral Institution and Rules

Formed in 2004, the Arbitration Association Brunei Darussalam ("AABD") is the only arbitral institution in Brunei.[19] The AABD maintains a panel of arbitrators from which parties can choose their arbitrators.[20] However, parties are not restricted to choose arbitrators who are on the AABD panel. The AABD can also provide assistance in arranging venues for arbitration hearings.[21]

The President of the AABD serves as the default appointing authority under both the Arbitration Order 2009 and the International Arbitration Order 2009.[22] Thus, in the absence of an agreement for the appointment of arbitrators, or where the agreed procedure fails, an application may be made to the President of the AABD for arbitrator(s) to be appointed.[23]

While there have been no arbitration rules promulgated by the AABD, the ABBD recommends the UNCITRAL Arbitration Rules and practice shows that parties usually choose these Rules.[24]

---

18 Section 3 of the Arbitration Order 2009.

19 International Comparative Legal Guides, Brunei, International Arbitration 2015, para. 15.1 available at: http://www.iclg.co.uk/practice-areas/international-arbitration-/international-arbitration-2015/brunei.

20 *Ibid.*

21 *Ibid.*

22 Section 13(8) of the Arbitration Order 2009 and section 8(2) of the International Arbitration Order 2009.

23 Articles 11(3) and 11(4), UNCITRAL Model Law, First Schedule of International Arbitration Order 2009, sections 13(3), 13(4) and 13(5) of Arbitration Order 2009.

24 International Comparative Legal Guides, Brunei, International Arbitration 2015, para. 6.1, available at: http://www.iclg.co.uk/practice-areas/international-arbitration-/international-arbitration-2015/brunei.

Brunei's Courts and Arbitration

There is no special court in Brunei that hears only arbitration-related cases and applications, although under the Arbitration Order 2009 and the International Arbitration Order 2009 most applications are to be made to the Brunei High Court.

For domestic and international arbitrations, an application to stay court proceedings commenced in breach of an arbitration agreement is made to the court in which proceedings were commenced.[25] Importantly, for international arbitrations, the International Arbitration Order 2009 provides that unless the court (in which the court proceedings were commenced) is satisfied that the arbitration agreement is null and void, inoperative or incapable of being performed, it is mandatory for the court to stay the proceedings.[26] The mandatory imposition of a stay of court proceedings unless the agreement is "null and void, inoperative or incapable of being performed" is narrow and restricted, forming a significant safeguard to limit the extent to which parties who have agreed to arbitration are able to circumvent the arbitral process.

In contrast, under the Arbitration Order 2009, courts retain the discretion not to stay judicial proceedings.[27] Section 6(2) of the Arbitration Order 2009 provides that the court "may" stay proceedings if it is satisfied that: (a) there is insufficient reason for the matter not to be referred in accordance with the arbitration agreement; and (b) the applicant seeking the stay is ready and willing to do everything necessary for the proper conduct of the arbitration.

If a party wishes to challenge the jurisdiction of the arbitral tribunal, the challenge must be raised to the tribunal before the submission of the statement of defence.[28] Under both domestic and international arbitration regimes, the tribunal faced with a challenge to its jurisdiction may rule on its jurisdiction either as a preliminary matter or in an award on the merits.[29] In the event that the arbitral tribunal rules as a preliminary question that it has jurisdiction, any party may apply to the Brunei High Court to decide the matter within thirty

---

25 Section 6(1) read with section 6(5)(b) of International Arbitration Order 2009; section 6(1) read with definition of "court" in section 2(1) of the Arbitration Order 2009.

26 Section 6(2) of International Arbitration Order 2009.

27 Section 6(2) of Arbitration Order 2009.

28 Section 21(4) of Arbitration Order 2009; section 3(1) of the International Arbitration Order 2009 read with Article 16(2), UNCITRAL Model Law, First Schedule of International Arbitration Order 2009.

29 Section 21(8) of Arbitration Order 2009; Article 16(3), UNCITRAL Model Law, First Schedule of International Arbitration Order 2009.

days after receipt of notice of such a ruling.[30] If a party wishes to further appeal against the decision of the Brunei High Court in this matter to the Brunei Court of Appeal, leave of the Brunei High Court is required.[31] In the event that the tribunal rules on its jurisdiction in an award on the merits, a party wishing to challenge this decision may apply to set aside the award before the Brunei High Court. Conversely, where the tribunal rules that it has no jurisdiction, the parties may not apply to the Brunei High Court to challenge this ruling.

Separately, both the Arbitration Order 2009 and International Arbitration Order 2009 provide for arbitrators to have certain powers for the conduct of proceedings and to make interim orders.

Under both statutes, an arbitral tribunal is empowered to make orders or give directions to any party, *inter alia*, to furnish security for costs, for discovery of documents and interrogatories, for the giving of evidence by affidavit, for preservation and interim custody of any evidence.[32] With leave from the Brunei High Court, such orders or directions are enforceable as if they were orders made by the Brunei High Court and judgments may be entered in terms of the orders or directions.[33]

Notably, while section 15(1)(i) of the International Arbitration Order 2009 empowers a tribunal to make an order for an interim injunction, the equivalent provision for domestic arbitrations, section 28(2) of the Arbitration Order 2009, does not appear to vest a tribunal with such a power.

Under section 15(1)(i) of the International Arbitration Order 2009, a tribunal also has the power to make an order for any other "interim measure". An "interim measure" is defined in section 15(8) of the International Arbitration Order 2009 as any temporary measure, whether in the form of an award or in another form, by which, at any time prior to the issue of the award by which the dispute is finally decided, the tribunal orders a party to (a) maintain or restore the *status quo* pending determination of the dispute,[34] (b) take action that would prevent, or refrain from taking action that is likely to cause, current

30 Section 21(9) of Arbitration Order 2009, section 3(1) of the International Arbitration Order 2009 read with Article 16(3), UNCITRAL Model Law, First Schedule of International Arbitration Order 2009.

31 Section 21(10) of Arbitration Order 2009, Section 12(1) of International Arbitration Order 2009.

32 Section 28(2) of Arbitration Order 2009, section 15(1) of International Arbitration Order 2009.

33 Section 28(4) of Arbitration Order 2009, section 15(6) of International Arbitration Order 2009.

34 Section 15(8)(a) of International Arbitration Order 2009.

or imminent harm or prejudice to the arbitral proceedings,[35] (c) provide a means of preserving assets out of which a subsequent award may be satisfied,[36] (d) or preserve evidence that may be relevant and material to the resolution of the dispute.[37] It would thus appear that the categories of "interim measures" that a tribunal may order under the International Arbitration Order 2009 are closed and restricted to those set out in section 15(8)(a) to 15(8)(d) of the International Arbitration Order 2009.

In contrast, under the Arbitration Order 2009, a tribunal is not similarly empowered to make orders or give directions for "any other interim measure". However, the Arbitration Order 2009 empowers the Brunei High Court to make an order for "any other interim measure" for the purpose of and in relation to a domestic arbitration.[38] Thus, in this regard, the ambit of a tribunal's powers is significantly greater in international arbitrations than in domestic arbitrations. Further, the Arbitration Order 2009 notably does not define or set out the categories of "interim measures" which the High Court may order. A credible argument can therefore be made that the High Court can order any interim measure and is not restricted to a closed list of categories of interim measures.

It is also noteworthy that under the International Arbitration Order 2009, it is explicitly provided that a party may, without notice to any other party, make a request to the tribunal for an interim measure together with an application for a preliminary order directing a party not to frustrate the purpose of the interim measure requested.[39] This could be important armoury for an applicant concerned that the respondent party may dissipate its assets to avoid the consequences of a claim. In this regard, section 18 of the International Arbitration Order 2009 sets out a specific regime. For instance, such a preliminary order lasts only for 20 days.[40] The tribunal may then issue an interim measure adopting or modifying the preliminary order after the party against whom the preliminary order is directed has been given notice and had an opportunity to present its case.[41]

With respect to arbitral awards, there is no right of appeal against an arbitration award made under the International Arbitration Order.[42] An aggrieved

35 *Ibid.*, Section 15(8)(b).

36 *Ibid.*, Section 15(8)(c).

37 *Ibid.*, Section 15(8)(d).

38 Section 31(d) of Arbitration Order 2009.

39 Section 17(1) of International Arbitration Order 2009.

40 *Ibid.*, Section 18(4).

41 *Ibid.*

42 Section 31(1) of International Arbitration Order 2009.

party may apply to set the award aside under the limited grounds provided under Article 34(2)(a) of the Model Law,[43] *viz.* (i) a party to the arbitration agreement lacks capacity, or the arbitration agreement was not valid under the law to which the parties have subjected it or, failing any indication thereon, under the law of Brunei; (ii) the party applying to set aside the award was not given proper notice of the appointment of an arbitrator or of the arbitration proceedings or was otherwise unable to present his case; (iii) the award dealt with a dispute not contemplated by or not falling within the terms of the submission to arbitration, or contains decisions on matters beyond the scope of the submission to arbitration; (iv) the composition of the tribunal or the arbitral procedure was not in accordance with the agreement of the parties. Under Article 34(2)(b) of the Model Law, a Brunei court may also set aside the award if the award is in conflict with the public policy of Brunei or if the subject-matter of the dispute in the award is not arbitrable under the laws of Brunei. The Brunei High Court may also set aside the award if the making of the award was induced or affected by fraud or corruption, or if a breach of the rules of natural justice occurred in connection with the making of the award by which the rights of any party have been prejudiced.[44]

Curiously, the International Arbitration Order 2009 does not explicitly state if recourse to set aside an award under Article 34 of the Model Law should be made only to the Brunei High Court or whether it can be made to any other court in Brunei.[45] However, it could be surmised that such recourse may only be made to the Brunei High Court given that Article 6 of the Model Law envisages that the High Court performs the functions referred to in Articles 11(3), 11(4), 13(3), 14, 16(3) and 34(2) of the Model Law.

For domestic arbitration awards, *i.e.* awards made under the Arbitration Order 2009, apart from applying to the High Court to set aside the award on grounds substantially similar to those under the International Arbitration Order 2009,[46] an aggrieved party may also appeal to the Brunei High Court against an award on a question of law.[47] However, parties may, by agreement, exclude the jurisdiction of the Brunei High Court to hear such an appeal.[48] It is also noteworthy that an agreement to dispense with reasons for the award

43 Section 3(1) of International Arbitration Order 2009 gives the Model Law, with the exception of Chapter VIII, the force of law.

44 Section 36 of International Arbitration Order 2009.

45 See Article 6 of the First Schedule of the International Arbitration Order 2009.

46 Section 48(1) of Arbitration Order 2009.

47 *Ibid.*

48 Section 49(2) of Arbitration Order 2009.

shall be treated as an agreement to exclude the jurisdiction of the Brunei High Court to hear an appeal on a question of law.[49] Further, such an appeal may only be brought with the agreement of all parties to the proceedings or with the leave of the High Court.[50]

An award arising from an arbitration seated in Brunei (whether under the purview of the International Arbitration Order 2009 or Arbitration Order 2009) is enforceable, with leave of the High Court, in the same manner as a judgment or order of the High Court to the same effect,[51] and judgment may be entered in the terms of the award.[52]

As regards enforcement of foreign arbitral awards, Brunei has ratified the 1958 New York Convention. A foreign award made in another New York Convention country is therefore enforceable in Brunei.[53] However, the Brunei High Court may refuse enforcement if it is satisfied that the limited grounds set out in section 44(2) of the International Arbitration Order 2009 (which essentially mirror the grounds under Article V of the New York Convention) are proved to its satisfaction, *viz.* (a) a party to the arbitration agreement lacked capacity at the time the arbitration agreement was made; (b) the arbitration agreement was not valid under the law to which parties have subjected it, or, in the absence of any indication in that respect, under the law of the country where the award was made; (c) the party against whom enforcement is sought was not given proper notice of the appointment of the arbitrator or of the arbitration proceedings or was otherwise unable to present his case in the arbitration proceedings; (d) the award dealt with a difference not contemplated by, or not falling within the terms of, the submission to arbitration or contains a decision on a matter beyond the scope of the submission to arbitration; (e) the composition of the arbitral authority or the arbitral procedure was not in accordance with the agreement of the parties or, failing such agreement, was not in accordance with the law of the country where the arbitration took place; or (f) the award has not yet become binding on the parties to the award or has been set aside or suspended by a competent authority of the country in which, or under the law of which, the award was made.

---

49 *Ibid.*

50 Section 49(3) of Arbitration Order 2009.

51 Section 29 of Internatinal Arbitration Order 2009, section 46(1) of Arbitration Order 2009.

52 Section 29 of International Arbitration Order 2009, section 46(2) of Arbitration Order 2009.

53 Section 42(2) of International Arbitration Order 2009.

2 *Brunei's Investment Laws*

The primary legislation on investment in Brunei is the Investment Incentives Order 2001[54] ("IIO"), which offers incentives such as tax relief to investors. The Minister of Industry and Primary Resources administers this legislation.

The IIO introduces a range of categories and activities for investors and businesses to qualify for a range of tax reliefs, investment allowances, loss deductions and exemptions from import duties. There are about 13 categories and business activities which qualify for benefits ranging from Pioneer Enterprises (comprising 24 types of industries or products) to Export Services and investments in New Technology Companies.

For instance, under the IIO as amended via the Investment Incentives (Amendment) Order 2011, the tax relief period of a "Pioneer Service" company is: (a) 8 years or such longer period, not exceeding 11 years, as the Minister may determine, in relation to any qualifying activity other than financial services; and (b) 5 years, which may be extended for a further 5 years as the Minister may determine, in relation to financial services.

Positively, there are few restrictions on foreign ownership of businesses in Brunei. A foreigner cannot operate a sole proprietorship in Brunei.[55] While sole proprietors are not subject to tax in Brunei, they are also personally liable for the obligations undertaken by their businesses.[56] Also, save for certain professions such as legal or medical, foreigners are generally restricted from registering a partnership.

However, it is open for foreigners to register a private company, a public company or a branch of a foreign company in Brunei.[57] A private or public company is required to have at least one director who is ordinarily resident in Brunei if the company has two directors, and at least two directors who are ordinarily resident in Brunei if it has more than two directors.[58]

---

54 Available at: http://www.agc.gov.bn/AGC%20Images/LAWS/Gazette_PDF/2001/EN/s048.pdf. The Investment Incentives Order 2001 was amended via the Investment Incentives (Amendment) Order 2011.

55 Brunei Economic Development Board, Prime Minister's Office, Type of Businesses: http://www.bedb.com.bn/doing_guides_types.html.

56 http://www.bedb.com.bn/doing_guides_business_sole.html.

57 http://www.bedb.com.bn/doing_guides_types.html.

58 Section 138 of Companies Act, as amended by the Companies Act (Amendment) Order 2010.

III Brunei's Bilateral Investment Treaties

1 *Overview*

Brunei signed its first Bilateral Investment Treaty ("BIT") in March 1998 with Germany.[59] Since then, as at the time of writing, it has signed BITs with Bahrain, China, India, Republic of Korea, Oman, South Africa and Ukraine.[60] Of these, as at the time of writing, Brunei's BITs with Bahrain, Germany, India, Republic of Korea and Ukraine have entered into force.

Brunei and India have also entered into a Protocol to the Brunei-India BIT, which contains additional provisions relating to Articles 4 and 5 of the BIT. Similarly, Brunei and Germany entered into a Protocol to the Brunei-Germany BIT, which contains additional provisions relating to Article 3 of this BIT. Brunei and China also entered into a Protocol to the Brunei-China BIT, which contains additional provisions relating to Articles 3 and 6 of the Brunei-China BIT.

2 *Definition of Investment*

Of the 8 BITs that Brunei has signed, the texts of 5 of them are publicly available: those concluded with China, Germany, India, Republic of Korea and Oman. The treaties with China, Oman and South Africa have not yet entered into force. These BITs provide for a relatively broad definition of investment. All of them define "investment" to mean "every kind of asset" and provide non-exhaustive examples of assets that fall within the scope of protection, such as movable and immovable property and any other property rights such as mortgages, liens or pledges; shares, stocks and debentures of a company and any other form of participation in a company; claims to money or any performance under a contract having an economic value; intellectual property rights and business concessions.

Brunei's BITs with Korea, China and India limit qualifying investments to those made in accordance with the laws of the State in which they are made.[61]

All the publicly available BITs also state that any change in the form in which the assets or rights are invested or reinvested shall not affect their character as investments.[62] Such a provision would allow foreign invested enter-

59 http://investmentpolicyhub.unctad.org/IIA/CountryBits/29.

60 http://investmentpolicyhub.unctad.org/IIA/CountryBits/29?type=c.

61 Article 1(1) of the Brunei-Korea BIT, Article 1(b) of the Brunei-India BIT, Article 1(1)(a) of the Brunei-China BIT.

62 Article 1(1)(a) of the Brunei-China BIT, Article 1(1) of the Brunei-Germany BIT, Article 1(b) of the Brunei-India BIT, Article 1(1) of the Brunei-Korea BIT, Article 1(1)(f) of the Brunei-Oman BIT.

prises to change their corporate form, such as from a joint venture company to a wholly foreign owned company, without fear of being excluded from the protection of these BITs by reason of the change alone.

3 *Definition of Investor*

In terms of the general definition of "investor", Bruneian BITs contain different approaches. An "investor" in the Brunei-China BIT means "nationals" and "companies" of a contracting State.[63] The Brunei-Korea BIT defines "investors" as nationals or juridical persons "who invest in the territory of the other Contracting Party".[64] A similar definition is adopted in the Brunei-India BIT, which defines "investors" as any "nationals or companies of a Contracting Party who has made investments in the territory of the other Contracting Party".[65] The Brunei-Germany and Brunei-Oman BITs do not employ the term "investors" but use the terms "nationals" and "companies" in their provisions instead. Under the Brunei-Germany BIT, the protection offered to "nationals" is the same as that offered to "companies". This is also the case for the Brunei-Oman BIT.

Generally, under Brunei's publicly available BITs, "nationals" is defined as natural persons who are accorded the status of nationals of a State pursuant to the laws of that State.[66] This reference to the law of the State in which the person is a national is not unusual and can be found in the Model BITs of several countries, such as Austria,[67] China,[68] Colombia[69] and Italy.[70]

Comparatively, under Brunei's publicly available BITs, the definition of "companies" or "juridical persons" varies. For instance, under the Brunei-India BIT, the definition of an Indian company is restricted to "firms and associations incorporated or constituted or established under the law in force in any part of India".[71] In contrast, the Brunei-Oman and Brunei-Germany BITs give a wider definition to "companies", to mean any kind of judicial entity including partnership, corporation, body corporate, firm, association or other organisation duly incorporated by the law of the State, whether with limited or unlimited

---

63 Article 1(c) of Brunei-India BIT, Article 1(2) of Brunei-China BIT.
64 Article 1(3) of the Brunei-Korea BIT.
65 Article 1(c) of the Brunei-India BIT.
66 Article 1(d) of Brunei-India BIT, Article 1(3)(a) of Brunei-Korea BIT, Article 1(2)(a) of Brunei-China BIT, Article 1(4) of Brunei-Oman BIT, Article 1(4) of Brunei-Germany BIT.
67 Chester Brown (ed.), *Commentaries on Selected Model Investment Treaties*, (Oxford University Press: 2013), p. 22.
68 *Ibid.*, p. 151.
69 *Ibid.*, p. 199.
70 *Ibid.*, p. 327.
71 Article 1(a)(i) of Brunei-India BIT.

liabilities and whether or not the entity is directed to profit.[72] However, under the Brunei-Germany BIT, a qualifying Bruneian company is restricted to one over which Bruneian nationals have a substantial or controlling interest.[73] Under the Brunei-Oman BIT, a company qualifies as an "investor" if nationals of either contracting party have a substantial or controlling interest in the company.[74] This limitation is significant as it means that companies in which nationals of either contracting party are minority shareholders or in some other way lack control over the companies would not qualify for protection under the Brunei-Oman BIT.

Notably, under the Brunei-China BIT, for a company incorporated in either contracting State to qualify for protection under the BIT, it also has to have its "effective seat of management" in that State.[75] This combination of the criteria of incorporation with seat is uncommon. Most BITs use either the place of incorporation *or* the main seat of business as the criterion to qualify for protection.[76] Article I(2) of the ASEAN Agreement for the Promotion and Protection of Investments ("ASEAN Agreement") similarly requires a combination of incorporation and seat for a company to qualify for protection. It provides:

> The term 'company' of a Contracting Party shall mean a corporation, partnership or business association, incorporated or constituted under the laws in force in the territory of any Contracting party wherein the place of effective management is situated.

One case provides an interesting insight on how the test of the "effective seat of management" can be interpreted by investor-State tribunals. In *Yaung Chi Oo v Myanmar*,[77] brought under ASEAN, the Claimant argued that the test of effective management was not fully relevant in Singapore as Singapore applies the test of incorporation to determine corporate nationality.[78] The Tribunal disagreed and held that the ASEAN Agreement requires both local

72 Article 1(5) of Brunei-Germany BIT, Article 1(5) of Brunei-Oman BIT.

73 Article 1(5)(a) of Brunei-Germany BIT.

74 Article 1(5) of Brunei-Oman BIT.

75 Article 1(2)(b) of Brunei-China BIT.

76 Rudolf Dolzer and Christoph Schreuer, *Principles of International Investment Law*, 2nd Ed, (Oxford University Press, 2012), p. 47.

77 *Yaung Chi Oo Trading Pte Ltd v Government of the Union of Myanmar*, ASEAN I.D. Case No. ARB/01/1, 31 March 2003.

78 *Ibid.*, at para. 47.

incorporation and effective management.[79] The Claimant also argued that the test of effective management needs only to be satisfied at the time the investment was made.[80] The Tribunal held that where investment is made over a period of time, effective management of the investing company may be required throughout the period.[81] However, in assessing whether there was effective management during the entire period, a tribunal may take into account the legal requirements of the State of incorporation.[82] The Tribunal also held that there is a presumption that effective management "once established is not readily lost".[83] While these findings made by the Tribunal in *Yaung Chi Oo* are not binding upon another tribunal applying the Brunei-China BIT, they are likely to be helpful in casting light on how the dual test of incorporation and effective management as provided in the Brunei-China BIT is to be applied.

Under the Brunei-China BIT, a company incorporated in a third country would fall under the definition of "companies" under the Brunei-China BIT if nationals or companies of either contracting State have a substantial or controlling interest in that company and the "third country abandons or fails to exercise its right to protect" that company.[84] This requirement that the third country must have abandoned or failed to exercise its right to protect the company is highly unusual. As at the date of writing, it appears that the Brunei-China BIT is the only publicly available BIT that contains such a requirement.

4 *Scope*

All of Brunei's publicly available BITs apply to investments made prior to the entry into force of the relevant treaty.[85] However, the Brunei-Korea BIT specifies that it shall not apply to any dispute concerning investments which was settled before its entry into force.[86] The other publicly available BITs do not state this explicitly.

79 *Ibid.*, at para. 49.
80 *Ibid.*, at para. 47.
81 *Ibid.*, at para. 49.
82 *Ibid.*
83 *Ibid.*, at para. 52.
84 Article 1(2)(b)(ii) of the Brunei-China BIT.
85 Article 11 of Brunei-China BIT, Article 2(3) of the Brunei-Germany BIT, Article 1(1)(f) of Brunei-Oman BIT, Article 11 of Brunei-Korea BIT, Article 2 of the Brunei-India BIT.
86 Article 11 of Brunei-Korea BIT.

Notably, under Article 2(2) of the Brunei-Oman BIT, protection is only accorded where the investment has been approved, if approval is required under the legislation of the contracting State.[87]

5 *Substantive Protections*

Fair and Equitable Treatment

All of Brunei's publicly available BITs contain a "fair and equitable treatment" provision.[88] For instance, Article 2(1) of the Brunei-Germany BIT provides *inter alia* that "[e]ach Contracting Party shall at all times ensure fair and equitable treatment to investments made in its territory by nationals and companies of the other Contracting Party." Article 3(1) of the Brunei-Oman BIT and Article 2(1) of the Brunei-Korea BIT contain largely similar language.

Article 3(2) of the Brunei-India BIT grants protection not only to investments but also to returns. It requires that the "[i]nvestments and returns of investors of each Contracting Party ... be accorded fair, equitable and non-discriminatory treatment". Article 3(1) of the Brunei-China BIT provides, "[i]nvestments and activities associated with investments or investors of either Contracting Party shall be accorded fair and equitable treatment", which offers protection not only to investments but also to "activities associated with investments".

Non-Discrimination

The Brunei-Germany, Brunei-Oman and Brunei-China BITs prohibit arbitrary or discriminatory measures that impair the management, maintenance, use or enjoyment of investments by investors.[89]

The Brunei-India BIT provides that each contracting party shall accord investments and returns of investors of the other contracting party "non-discriminatory treatment".[90]

Article 2(2) of the Brunei-Korea BIT provides: "[n]either Contracting Party shall in any way impair by unreasonable or discriminatory measures the operation, management, use, enjoyment or disposal of investments in its territory by investors of the other Contracting Party".[91] Although it uses the language of

87 Article 2(2) of Brunei-Oman BIT.

88 Article 2(2) of Brunei-Korea BIT, Article 2(1) of Brunei-Germany BIT, Article 3(1) of Brunei-Oman BIT, Article 3(2) of Brunei-India BIT, Article 3(1) of Brunei-China BIT.

89 Article 3(2) of Brunei-China BIT, Article 2(3) of Brunei-Oman BIT, Article 2(2) of Brunei-Germany BIT.

90 Article 3(2) of Brunei-India BIT.

91 Article 2(2) of Brunei-Korea BIT.

"unreasonable" measures rather than "arbitrary" measures, it is arguable that these two terms are interchangeable and do not denote a different standard of protection.[92]

Full Protection and Security

All of Brunei's publicly available BITs accord "full protection and security" to qualifying investments of qualifying investors of the other contracting State.[93] The wording of the relevant articles in the respective BITs is substantially identical. As an example, Article 3(2) of the Brunei-China BIT provides that "[i]nvestments by investors of each Contracting Party shall at all times enjoy full protection and security in the territory of the other Contracting Party." The Brunei-India BIT specifies that investments shall enjoy "full legal protection and security".[94] However, this may not be a material difference as tribunals have interpreted "full protection and security" to include protection against infringement of investors' legal rights.[95]

Expropriation

There are some significant differences among Brunei's publicly available BITs with regard to their provisions on expropriation.

In general, all of Brunei's BITs contain three of the four requirements for a legal expropriation that are usually contained in BITs:[96] (i) the measure must serve a public purpose; (ii) the measure must not be arbitrary or discriminatory; and (iii) the expropriatory measure must be accompanied by compensation.[97] For example, Article 4(1) of the Brunei-China BIT provides:

> Investments of investors of one Contracting Party shall not either directly or indirectly be expropriated or nationalised or subjected to measures having effect equivalent to nationalisation or expropriation (hereinafter together referred to as "expropriation") in the territory of the other Contracting Party except for a public purpose of that Contracting Party

92 Dolzer and Schreuer,*op. cit.*, p. 191.

93 Article 2(3) of Brunei-Oman BIT, Article 2(2) of Brunei-Korea BIT, Article 3(2) of Brunei-India BIT, Article 2(2) of Brunei-Germany BIT, Article 3(2) of Brunei-China BIT.

94 Article 3(2) of Brunei-India BIT.

95 Dolzer and Schreuer, *op. cit.*, p. 163.

96 Andrew Newcombe and Lluís Paradell, *Law and Practice of Investment Treaties: Standards of Treatment* (*Kluwer Law International, 2009*) at paragraph 7.31.

97 Article 4(2) of Brunei-Oman BIT, Article 5(1) of Brunei-Korea BIT, Article 5(1) of Brunei-India BIT, Article 4(2) of Brunei-Germany BIT, Article 4(1) of Brunei-China BIT.

> on a non-discriminatory basis and against appropriate compensation or compensations.

As for the fourth common requirement that the expropriation be "in accordance with due process of law,"[98] it is noteworthy that the Brunei-China, Brunei-Oman and Brunei-Germany BITs do not contain such a requirement. On the other hand, Article 5(1) of the Brunei-India BIT requires that the expropriation be "in accordance with law" and Article 5(1) of the Brunei-Korea BIT provides that the measure has to be taken "in accordance with legal procedures". However, this difference may be more theoretical than real as it has been suggested that the requirement of due process of law is an expression of the requirement of fair and equitable treatment,[99] which all of Brunei's publicly available BITs already provide for.[100]

On the requirement that the measure must serve a public purpose, the Brunei-Oman BIT limits "public purpose" to those that are related to the "internal needs" of the host State.[101] This may have the effect of preventing either contracting party from justifying an expropriation on the basis of foreign policy reasons, although it has been questioned whether such a formulation actually provides any substantive limitation that is not already inherent in the concept of "public purpose."[102] "Public purpose" in the other publicly available BITs are not limited as such.

As mentioned above,[103] the Brunei-India BIT contains a separate Protocol on its Articles 4 and 5. Article 5 sets out provisions relating to expropriation.

The Protocol to the Brunei-India BIT appears to have been signed at the same time as the Brunei-India BIT itself. The intention behind concluding a separate Protocol on Article 5 can be gleaned from paragraph II(a) of the Protocol, which provides: "Article 5 of the [Brunei-India BIT] is intended to reflect customary international law concerning the obligations of the Contracting Parties with respect to expropriation". The provisions of the Protocol to Article 5 therefore appear to have been intended to set out what the Contracting Parties

98 Andrew Newcombe and Lluís Paradell, *Law and Practice of Investment Treaties: Standards of Treatment*, Kluwer Law International, 2009, at para. 7.31.

99 Dolzer and Schreuer, *op. cit.*, p. 100.

100 Article 2(2) of Brunei-Korea BIT, Article 2(1) of Brunei-Germany BIT, Article 3(1) of Brunei-Oman BIT, Article 3(2) of Brunei-India BIT, Article 3(1) of Brunei-China BIT.

101 Article 4(2) of Brunei-Oman BIT.

102 Andrew Newcombe and Lluís Paradell, *op. cit.*, para. 7.32.

103 Section III.1.

determined to be the applicable principles of expropriation under customary international law at the time the Brunei-India BIT was concluded.

Paragraph II(b) of the Protocol to the Brunei-India BIT provides that a "measure of expropriation includes a measure or series of actions that has an effect equivalent to direct expropriation or nationalisation, without a formal transfer of title or outright seizure." Paragraph II(c) of the Protocol provides that the determination of whether a measure or series of measures constitutes a measure of expropriation is on a case-by-case basis, based on factors including: (i) the economic impact of the measure or series of measures; (ii) the extent to which the measure or series of measures interferes with distinct, reasonable, investment-backed expectations; and (iii) the character of the measure or series of measures such as its intent, objectives, purpose and the degree of nexus between the measures and outcome or effects that form the basis of the claim for expropriation. Paragraph II(d) of the Protocol provides that except in rare circumstances, non-discriminatory measures that are designed and applied for legitimate public welfare objectives such as health, safety and the environment, do not constitute measures having an effect equivalent to nationalisation or expropriation. It further provides that these rare circumstances include instances where a measure or series of measures is so severe in the light of its purpose that it cannot be reasonably viewed as having been adopted and applied in good faith.

As regards compensation, expropriation under the Brunei-China BIT requires "appropriate compensation or compensations"[104] while the Brunei-India BIT adopts the language of "fair and equitable compensation."[105] The other publicly available BITs adopt the Hull formula of "prompt, adequate and effective compensation."[106]

All of Brunei's publicly available BITs provide guidance on the valuation of the compensation to be paid when there is expropriation. The Brunei-China BIT provides that the compensation shall be equivalent to the "genuine value of the expropriated investment,"[107] while the other publicly available BITs provide for compensation to amount to, or be computed on the basis of, the "fair market value" of the investment.[108]

---

104 Article 4(1) of Brunei-China BIT.

105 Article 5(1) of Brunei-India BIT.

106 Article 4(2) of Brunei-Oman BIT, Article 4(2) of Brunei-Germany BIT.

107 Article 4(2) of Brunei-China BIT.

108 Article 5(1) of Brunei-India BIT, Article 5(2) of Brunei-Korea BIT, Article 4(3) of Brunei-Germany BIT, Article 4(3) of Brunei-Oman BIT.

In respect of the date of valuation, the Brunei-China BIT states that the value of the investment shall be "immediately before the expropriated action was taken or became publicly known, whichever is the earlier,"[109] and the Brunei-Korea and Brunei-India BITs provide substantially similar valuation dates for the purpose of computing compensation.[110] Under Article 4(3) of the Brunei-Germany BIT, the valuation date of the investment is "immediately prior to the point of time when the actual or threatened expropriation has become publicly known." Under Article 4(3) of the Brunei-Oman BIT, the valuation date of the investment is "immediately prior to the point of time when the decision for expropriation has been taken or became publicly known whichever occurs earlier."

The Brunei-India and Brunei-Germany BITs further provide that where the market value of the expropriated investment cannot be ascertained properly, the compensation shall be determined in accordance with "internationally recognised accounting principles."[111] The Brunei-Oman BIT provides that where the market value of the expropriated investment cannot be ascertained properly, the compensation shall be determined "in accordance with the generally recognised principles of valuation and on equitable principles", taking into account factors such as the capital invested, depreciation, capital already repatriated and the replacement value.[112]

The Brunei-Korea and Brunei-China BITs do not include similar guidance when the "genuine value" or "fair market value" of the expropriated investment cannot be properly ascertained. However, they provide for a right of the investor to prompt review by a judicial or other independent authority of the host State of the investor's case and the valuation of its investments.[113] The Brunei-India BIT also contains a substantially similar provision.[114]

The Brunei-Germany BIT provides that the amount of compensation shall be "subject to review by due process of law"[115] while the Brunei-Oman BIT provides that where the amount of compensation cannot be agreed to between the investor and the host State, the determination of the amount of compensation shall be referred to arbitration.[116]

109 Article 4(2) of Brunei-China BIT.

110 Article 5(2) of Brunei-Korea BIT and Article 5(1) of Brunei-India BIT.

111 Article 5(1) of Brunei-India BIT, Article 4(3) of Brunei-Germany BIT.

112 Article 4(3) of Brunei-Oman BIT.

113 Article 5(3) of Brunei-Korea BIT, Article 4(2) of Brunei-China BIT.

114 Article 5(2) of Brunei-India BIT.

115 Artcile 4(3) of Brunei-Germany BIT.

116 Article 4(5) of Brunei-Oman BIT.

Brunei's publicly available BITs contain different formulations on the issue of compensation to be made to investors who invested in a company incorporated in the host State, in circumstances where the company is then expropriated or nationalised by the host State. The Brunei-Korea BIT provides that the provisions relating to expropriation and compensation shall equally apply to such a situation,[117] while the Brunei-India BIT provides that the provisions relating to expropriation and compensation shall apply only to the extent necessary to ensure fair and equitable compensation.[118] The Brunei-China BIT provides that either the company or the investors be compensated in accordance with the provisions relating to expropriation and compensation, but a Contracting State need not compensate both the company and its investors.[119] The Brunei-Oman BIT provides that a Contracting State shall ensure that "fair and reasonable compensation is received", without specifying whether the company or the investors should be the party receiving the compensation.[120] However, this is unlikely to open the door to double recovery by the company and its shareholders, given the requirement that the compensation be "fair and reasonable".

Umbrella Clauses

The Brunei-Korea, Brunei-China and Brunei-Germany BITs include an obligation on the Contracting Parties to observe any obligation they have undertaken with regard to investments of an investor of the other contracting party.[121] The wording of these provisions are substantially identical. For instance, Article 10(2) of the Brunei-Korea BIT provides:

> Each Contracting Party shall observe any other obligation it has assumed with regard to investments in its territory by investors of the other Contracting Party.

Such a provision is commonly known as an "umbrella clause". This means that State obligations such as those contained in the agreements between investors and the host State can potentially be elevated to treaty obligations.

117 Article 5(4) of Brunei-Korea BIT.
118 Article 5(3) of Brunei-India BIT.
119 Article 4(3) of Brunei-China BIT.
120 Article 4(4) of Brunei-Oman BIT.
121 Article 10(2) of Brunei-Germany BIT, Article 10(2) of Brunei-Korea BIT, Article 10(2) of Brunei-China BIT.

Most Favoured Nation and National Treatment

All of Brunei's publicly available BITs require that the treatment of the investments and investors of the other contracting State be no less favourable than that granted to nationals or companies of third States.[122] For instance, Article 4(2) of the Brunei-India BIT provides:

> In addition, each Contracting Party shall, at all times, accord to investors of the other Contracting Party, including in respect of returns on their investments, treatment which shall not be less favourable than that accorded to investors of any third State.

Such a provision is commonly known as a "Most Favoured Nation" or "MFN" provision and can have the effect of extending to its beneficiaries substantive treaty guarantees such as "fair and equitable treatment" granted to a third State or its nationals. At present, the current state of customary international law remains uncertain on whether a MFN provision may also extend to cover provisions on dispute settlement.[123]

The Brunei-Germany, Brunei-Korea and Brunei-India BITs also contain explicit National Treatment provisions requiring the contracting State to treat qualifying investors and investments at least as favourably as investments of their own investors.[124]

As mentioned above,[125] India and Brunei entered into a Protocol on Articles 4 and 5 of the Brunei-India BIT. Notably, the Protocol on Article 4 of the Brunei-India BIT carves out a reservation to the National Treatment provision for the host State's development considerations, provided that the investments of the investors of the other State are not substantially impaired. It provides that measures undertaken by one contracting party in pursuit of its development objectives to stimulate the creation of industries in its territory and applied only to its investors are not considered to be contrary to obligations of national treatment under Article 4 if they do not "substantially impair established and admitted investments of investors of the other Contracting

---

122 Article 3(1) of Brunei-Korea BIT, Articles 3(1) and 3(2) of Brunei-Germany BIT, Article 3(2) of Brunei-Oman BIT, Article 3(3) of Brunei-China BIT, Articles 4(1) and 4(2) of Brunei-India BIT.

123 Dolzer and Schreuer, *Principles of International Investment Law*, (2nd Ed), Oxford University Press, 2012, p. 211.

124 Article 4(1) of Brunei-India BIT, Articles 3(1) and 3(2) of Brunei-Germany BIT, Articles 3(1) and 3(2) of Brunei-Korea BIT.

125 See Section III 1. Overview.

Party, and are undertaken in accordance with its laws, regulations and policies". Such a reservation allows both States to pursue social policies to develop certain industries.[126] It is not unique and a similar reservation can be found in the Jamaica-Switzerland BIT,[127] Jamaica-Netherlands BIT[128] and Protocol to the Germany-Papua New Guinea BIT.[129]

As regards the Brunei-Germany BIT, Ad Article 3(a) of the Protocol to the Brunei-Germany BIT provides that measures that have been taken for reasons of public security and order, public health or morality shall not be deemed "treatment less favourable" within the meaning of its MFN and National Treatment provisions.

Ad Article 3(b) of the Protocol to the Brunei-Germany BIT provides that "unequal treatment in the case of restrictions on the purchase of raw or auxiliary materials, of energy or fuel or of means of production or operation of any kind, unequal treatment in the case of impeding the marketing of products inside or outside the country, as well as any other measures having similar effects" shall be deemed "treatment less favourable". Such a stipulation is common in German BITs[130] and a substantially similar form can be found in Germany's Model BIT (2009).[131] Interestingly, Article 1(a) of the Protocol to the Brunei-China BIT also contains a substantially similar provision: "any action restricting the purchase of raw or auxiliary materials or of energy or fuel or means of production or operation of any kind, or impeding the marketing of products inside or outside the country and any other measures having similar effect shall be deemed "treatment less favourable" within the meaning of [Articles 3 and 5 of the Brunei-China BIT, which include the MFN and National Treatment provisions]".

All of Brunei's BITs explicitly state that the MFN and National Treatment provisions do not apply to more favourable treatment arising out of customs unions, free trade areas, common markets, and international agreements or domestic legislation relating mainly or wholly to taxation, such as treaties relating to double taxation.[132]

---

126 Andrew Newcombe and Lluís Paradell, *op. cit.*, para. 4.28.

127 Article 3(6) of the Jamaica-Switzerland BIT.

128 Article 3(6) of the Jamaica-Netherlands BIT.

129 Ad Article 3(c) of the Protocol to the Germany-Papua New Guinea BIT.

130 Andrew Newcombe and Lluís Paradell, *op. cit.*, para. 4.20, footnote 178.

131 Chester Brown (ed.), *op. cit.*, p. 308.

132 Articles 3(3) and 3(4) of Brunei-Germany BIT, Article 3(4) of Brunei-China BIT, Article 3(3) of Brunei-Oman BIT, Article 4(3) of Brunei-India BIT, Articles 3(3) and 3(4) of Brunei-Korea BIT.

6 *Repatriation of Capital and Compensation for Losses*

All publicly available BITs signed by Brunei at the time of writing contain provisions allowing for the repatriation or "free transfer" by the investor of capital invested and investment returns, such as the initial and additional capital amounts used to maintain, increase or expand investments, repayment of loans, proceeds accruing from the sale or total or partial liquidation of the investments.[133] It should be noted that at the time of writing, there is no foreign exchange control regulation in force in Brunei and there is also no restriction on repatriation of funds related to investments such as profits, dividends, royalties, loan or repayment and liquidation. The Brunei-Germany BIT provides that the repatriation shall be made within one month from the time the request for the transfer was made.[134] The Brunei-Oman BIT provides that the transfer shall be allowed within one month from the date on which the request for the transfer was made.[135]

The Brunei-China BIT provides that repatriation is subject to the host State's laws and regulations.[136] Notably, the Brunei-Oman BIT requires nationals and companies to perform "their fiscal obligations" before being able to transfer their capital and returns.[137]

Moreover, all of Brunei's publicly available BITs provide that the nationals and companies of one contracting party whose investments suffer losses due to war or other armed conflict, a state of national emergency, revolt or riot shall be accorded treatment no less favourable than the host State's treatment of its own nationals and companies, or nationals or companies of any third country.[138] In other words, the BITs provide MFN and national treatment protection to any losses suffered due to any of the mentioned causes, such as war and armed conflict. Further, these BITs provide that nationals or companies who suffer losses as a result of the requisitioning of their property by forces or authorities, or destruction of their property which was not caused in combat or was not required by the necessity of the situation, shall be accorded restitution or compensation.[139]

---

133 Article 6 of Korea-Burnei BIT, Article 7 of Brunei-India BIT, Article 6 of Brunei-Oman BIT, Article 6 of Brunei-China BIT, Article 6 of Brunei-Germany BIT.

134 Article 6(2) of Brunei-Germany BIT.

135 Article 6(3) of Brunei-Oman BIT.

136 Article 6(1) of Brunei-China BIT.

137 Article 6(1) of Brunei-Oman BIT.

138 Article 5(1) of Brunei-Oman BIT, Article 5(1) of Brunei-China BIT, Article 4(1) of Brunei-Korea BIT, Article 6(1) of Brunei-India BIT, Article 5(1) of Brunei-Germany BIT.

139 Article 5(2) of Brunei-Germany BIT, Article 6(2) of Brunei-India BIT, Article 4(2) of Brunei-Korea BIT, Article 5(2) of Brunei-China BIT, Article 5(2) of Brunei-Oman BIT.

7 *Investor-State Dispute Settlement*

All the publicly available BITs signed by Brunei provide that a dispute arising between a contracting State and an investor shall as far as possible be resolved amicably.[140] The Brunei-India and Brunei-China BITs specify that the dispute shall as far as possible be resolved amicably "through negotiations."[141]

Under the Brunei-Germany BIT, Brunei-Oman BIT and Brunei-Korea BIT, if the dispute cannot be settled within six months, it may then be submitted for arbitration.[142] Under the Brunei-China BIT and Brunei-India BIT, if the dispute cannot be settled within six months, additional steps may have to be taken before the dispute can be submitted to arbitration.

Article 9(2) of the Brunei-China BIT provides that a contracting party may require the exhaustion of a "domestic administrative reconsideration procedure" prior to an investor's submission of the dispute to arbitration. However, the BIT does not give any guidance on what such a procedure may entail, although it has been suggested that it refers to the Chinese courts.[143] If so, this may severely undermine an investor's rights to its remedies for breaches of the Brunei-China BIT, as it may take a long time for a dispute to work its way through the Chinese court system before it can finally be submitted to arbitration.

Article 9(2) of the Brunei-India BIT provides that if a dispute has not been amicably settled within six months, and if both parties agree, the dispute may be submitted: (a) for resolution, in accordance with the law of the host State to its competent judicial, arbitral or administrative bodies; or (b) for international conciliation under the Conciliation Rules of the United Nations Commission on International Trade Law ("UNCITRAL"). If the parties are unable to agree on a dispute settlement procedure provided in Article 9(2) of the Brunei-India BIT, or where a dispute was referred to conciliation but conciliation proceedings were terminated other than by signing of a settlement agreement, a party may then submit the dispute for arbitration.[144]

Where an investor-State dispute is to be submitted for arbitration, all of Brunei's publicly available BITs provide that the dispute shall be submitted

140 Article 9(1) of Brunei-Germany BIT, Article 9(1) of Brunei-India BIT, Article 8(1) of Brunei-Korea BIT, Article 9(1) of Brunei-China BIT, Article 9(1) of Brunei-Oman BIT.

141 Article 9(1) of Brunei-China BIT, Article 9(1) of Brunei-India BIT.

142 Article 8(2) of Brunei-Korea BIT, Article 9(2) of Brunei-Germany BIT and Article 9(2) of Brunei-Oman BIT.

143 John Pappas, *The Future* US-*China* BIT: *Its Likely Look and Effects*, Hong Kong Law Journal, vol. 41, Part 3, 2011, p. 868.

144 Article 9(3) of Brunei-India BIT.

under the Convention on the Settlement of Investment Disputes between States and Nationals of Other States ("ICSID Convention") if both States are contracting parties to the ICSID Convention, unless the parties in dispute agree otherwise.[145] At the time of writing, India is the only counterparty to Brunei's publicly available BITs that has not signed or ratified the ICSID Convention.[146] Consequently, unless the parties in dispute agree otherwise, a dispute brought by investors under the Brunei-China, Brunei-Korea, Brunei-Oman and Brunei-Germany will be submitted under the ICSID Convention.

Until India ratifies the ICSID Convention, Article 9(3)(b) of the Brunei-India BIT provides that if both parties to the dispute agree, the arbitration shall be carried out under the ICSID Additional Facility Rules for the Administration of Conciliation, Arbitration and Fact-Finding Proceedings. Under Article 9(3)(c) of the Brunei-India BIT, if parties do not agree to submit the dispute to the ICSID Additional Facility Rules, the dispute will be submitted to an *ad hoc* tribunal applying the UNCITRAL Arbitration Rules of 1976,[147] subject to certain modifications to the rules stipulated in Article 9(3)(c) of the Brunei-India BIT. These modifications relate to the appointment of arbitrators, the finality of the award and specifying that the tribunal shall state the basis of its decision and give reasons upon the request of either party. Notably, under the Brunei-India BIT, if the necessary appointments of arbitrators are not made within the stipulated periods, either party to the dispute may invite the President of the International Court of Justice to make the necessary appointments,[148] which, while commonly provided for under the State-to-State dispute mechanism under BITs, is not commonly stipulated as part of the appointment procedure for investor-State disputes.

With the exception of the Brunei-India BIT, all of Brunei's publicly available BITs stipulate that during arbitration proceedings or the enforcement of the award, the contracting party involved in the dispute shall not raise the objection that the investor of the other contracting party has "received compensation under an insurance contract in respect of all or part of its loss."[149]

145 Article 9(3)(a) of Brunei-India BIT, Article 9(10) of Brunei-China BIT, Article 8(6) of Brunei-Korea BIT, Article 9(4) of Brunei-Germany BIT, Article 9(4) of Brunei-Oman BIT.

146 https://icsid.worldbank.org/apps/ICSIDWEB/about/Pages/Database-of-Member-States.aspx?tab=FtoJ&rdo=BOTH.

147 See Article 9(3)(c) of Brunei-India BIT.

148 Article 9(3)(c)(ii) of Brunei-India BIT.

149 Article 9(3) of Brunei-Oman BIT, Article 9(3) of Brunei-Germany BIT, Article 9(8) of Brunei-China BIT, Article 8(7) of Brunei-Korea BIT.

8 *State-to-State Dispute Settlement*

All Brunei's BITs stipulate that disputes between the contracting States shall be resolved as far as possible by recourse to diplomatic channels, through consultation and negotiations.[150] The Brunei-Oman BIT further requires that the contracting parties engage in "direct and meaningful diplomatic consultation and negotiations."[151]

All Brunei's BITs further provide that, in the event that diplomatic channels fail to result in a settlement, a dispute shall, upon the request of either contracting party, be submitted for arbitration.[152] The Brunei-India and Brunei-Korea BITs provide that a dispute shall be submitted for arbitration if a dispute cannot be settled within six months.[153] The Brunei-China BIT provides a longer period of nine months,[154] while the Brunei-Germany and Brunei-Oman BITs do not specify a time period for diplomatic settlement to be attempted before a dispute may be submitted for arbitration.

All Brunei's BITs stipulate substantially similar procedures for the appointment of arbitrators: each contracting party shall appoint one arbitrator, and both co-arbitrators shall then agree upon a third arbitrator which is not a national of either contracting party, who shall act as the chairman.[155] The Brunei-Korea, Brunei-China and Brunei-India BITs further require that the third arbitrator be from a State that has diplomatic relations with both contracting parties.[156]

Under all Brunei's BITs, if the stipulated time periods for the appointment of arbitrators are not complied with, either contracting party may invite the President of the International Court of Justice to make the necessary appointments.[157] As is commonly the case, the BITs do not adopt a set of institutional arbitration rules for the arbitration.

---

150 Article 9(1) of Brunei-Korea BIT, Article 10(1) of Brunei-India BIT, Article 8(1) of Brunei-China BIT, Article 8(1) of Brunei-Germany BIT, Article 8(1) of Brunei-Oman BIT.

151 Article 8(1) of Brunei-Oman BIT.

152 Article 8(2) of Brunei-Oman BIT, Article 8(2) of Brunei-Germany BIT, Article 8(2) of Brunei-China BIT, Article 10(2) of Brunei-India BIT, Article 9(2) of Brunei-Korea BIT.

153 Article 10(2) of Brunei-India BIT, Article 9(2) of Brunei-Korea BIT.

154 Article 8(2) of Brunei-China BIT.

155 Article 8(3) of Brunei-Oman BIT, Article 8(3) of Brunei-Germany BIT, Article 8(3) of Brunei-China BIT, Article 10(3) of Brunei-India BIT, Article 9(3) of Brunei-Korea BIT.

156 Article 8(3) of Brunei-China BIT, Article 10(3) of Brunei-India BIT, Article 9(3) of Brunei-Korea BIT.

157 Article 8(4) of Brunei-Germany BIT, Article 8(4) of Brunei-Oman BIT, Article 8(4) of Brunei-China BIT, Article 10(4) of Brunei-India BIT, Article 9(4) of Brunei-Korea BIT.

The Brunei-China BIT provides that the tribunal shall hold meetings in a neutral State to be agreed by both contracting parties[158] and that the tribunal shall reach its award in accordance with the provisions of the Brunei-China BIT and the principles of international law recognised by both Contracting Parties.[159]

9 *Other Provisions*

All Brunei's BITs contain subrogation rights.[160]

The Brunei-China BIT provides that the representatives of the two contracting parties shall hold meetings from time to time for the purpose of *inter alia* reviewing the implementation of the BIT and exchanging legal information and investment opportunities.[161] The Brunei-China BIT also provides that the provisions of the BIT shall remain in force notwithstanding a conflict arising between the contracting parties.[162]

The Brunei-China, Brunei-Germany and Brunei-India BITs also contain provisions relating to the entry of persons into, and sojourn of persons in, the territory of each contracting party, going beyond the usual scope of provisions included in a BIT.

The Brunei-India BIT provides that a contracting party shall, subject to its laws and regulations, permit natural persons of the other contracting party and personnel employed by companies of the other contracting party to enter and remain in its territory for the purpose of engaging in activities connected with investments.[163]

Ad Article 3(d) of the Protocol to the Brunei-Germany BIT provides that the contracting parties shall within the framework of their national legislation give "sympathetic considerations" to applications for the entry into and sojourn of persons of one contracting party in the territory of the other contracting party in connection with an investment. The Brunei-China BIT contains a substantially similar provision to Ad Article 3(d) of the Protocol to the Brunei-Germany BIT.[164]

---

158 Article 8(8) of Brunei-China BIT.

159 Article 8(5) of Brunei-China BIT.

160 Article 7 of Brunei-Korea BIT, Article 8 of Brunei-India BIT, Article 7 of Brunei-Oman BIT, Article 7 of Brunei-Germany BIT, Article 7 of Brunei-China BIT.

161 Article 12 of Brunei-China BIT.

162 Article 13 of Brunei-China BIT.

163 Article 11 of Brunei-India BIT.

164 Article 2(2) of Brunei-China BIT.

10 *Notable Trends*

Brunei has made substantial improvements and introduced reforms making it easier to do business and invest in the country. This has now started to show in a growing FDI inflow in general, however, with a large reliance on the oil and gas sector Brunei FDI remains vulnerable to fluctuating international energy prices.[165]

IV Multilateral Investment Related Treaties and Organizations to which Brunei is a Party

1 *ASEAN – ACIA*

Brunei joined ASEAN on 7 January 1984 as the first non-founding member of ASEAN.[166] ASEAN has entered into several investment-related treaties.[167]

Within ASEAN, the most important treaty relating to investment protection is arguably the ASEAN Comprehensive Investment Agreement ("ACIA") which entered into force on 29 March 2012.[168] Brunei signed the ACIA on 26 February 2009[169] and ratified the ACIA on 9 September 2009.[170] Investors from other States in ASEAN which have also ratified the ACIA can therefore look to the ACIA for investment protection for their investments within Brunei.

The objectives of the ACIA, as stated in Article 1 of the ACIA, are to create a "free and open investment regime in ASEAN" to achieve economic integration, through the principles of, *inter alia*, investment liberalisation, protection, investment promotion and facilitation.

The ACIA contains substantive investment protections commonly found in BITs, such as provisions on MFN treatment,[171] fair and equitable treatment,[172] full protection and security,[173] and rules on expropriation.[174] Article 3(3) of the ACIA states that the ACIA is applicable to several sectors including manufacturing, agriculture, fishery, forestry, mining and quarrying, services incidental

165 ttps://www.wto.org/english/tratop_e/tpr_e/s309_sum_e.pdf.

166 http://www.asean.org/asean/about-asean/overview.

167 See the ASEAN chapter for further details.

168 http://investmentpolicyhub.unctad.org/IIA/CountryOtherIias/29#iiaInnerMenu.

169 *Ibid.*

170 http://agreement.asean.org/agreement/detail/102.html.

171 Article 6 of ACIA.

172 *Ibid.*, Article 11.

173 *Ibid.*, Article 11.

174 *Ibid.*, Article 14.

to these above-mentioned industries and other sectors that may be agreed upon by all member States.

Beyond the usual provisions found in BITs, the ACIA also contains provisions aimed at enhancing cooperation between ASEAN States in the promotion[175] and facilitation of investment,[176] and to enhance ASEAN integration.[177]

Article 32 of the ACIA provides an investor wishing to submit a claim against a Member State with six different choices: (i) the courts or administrative tribunals of the disputing Member State; (ii) under the ICSID Convention and ICSID Rules of Procedure for Arbitration Proceedings if both the disputing Member State and the non-disputing Member State are parties to the ICSID Convention; (iii) under the ICSID Additional Facility Rules if either the disputing Member State or the non-disputing Member State is a party to the ICSID Convention; (iv) under UNCITRAL Arbitration Rules; (v) to the Regional Centre for Arbitration at Kuala Lumpur or any other regional centre for arbitration in ASEAN; or (vi) any other arbitration institution if the disputing parties agree. Resort to any of the above choices will exclude resort to the other options.

2 *APEC*

Brunei has been a Member State of the Asia-Pacific Economic Cooperation ("APEC") since 7 November 1989.[178] Three key APEC investment-related instruments are the Non-Binding Investment Principles ("NBIP"), the Menu of Options, and the Transparency Standards on Investment.

The NBIP sets out 12 investment principles that are broadly similar to the core elements of international investment agreements concluded between APEC Member States, including provisions on transparency, national treatment, fair and equitable treatment, full protection and security, protection from strife, the transfer of funds, and the entry of key personnel. The Menu of Options (or the Options for Investment Liberalization and Business Facilitation to Strengthen the APEC Economies) lists policies for liberalization and business facilitation. The Transparency Standards on investment cover the publication, awareness and availability of investment laws and measures.[179]

175 *Ibid.*, Article 24.

176 *Ibid.*, Article 25.

177 *Ibid.*, Article 26.

178 http://www.apec.org/about-us/about-apec/member-economies.aspx.

179 "Identifying core elements in investment agreements in the APEC region", UNCTAD Series on International Investment Policies for Development, United Nations (New York and Geneva: 2008), available at http://unctad.org/en/Docs/diaeia20083_en.pdf.

3 *OIC – APPGI*

Brunei signed the Agreement on Promotion, Protection and Guarantee of Investments ("APPGI") among Member States of the Organization of the Islamic Conference, now known as Organisation of Islamic Cooperation ("OIC") on 5 June 1981, which came into force on 23 September 1986.[180]

The APPGI seeks to provide and develop a favourable climate for investments. Under the APPGI, contracting parties agree to, *inter alia*, permit the transfer of capital among them and its utilization therein in the fields permitted for investment, guarantee adequate protection and security over any capital invested,[181] provide treatment to investors of any contracting party not less favourable than the treatment accorded to investors belonging to any other State not party to the APPGI.[182]

Under Article 16 of the APPGI, the Host State undertakes to allow the investor the right to resort to its national judicial system to: (i) complain against a measure adopted by its authorities against him; or (ii) to contest the extent of its conformity with the provisions of the regulations and laws in force in its territory; or (iii) to complain against the non-adoption by the Host State of a certain measure which is in the interest of the investor, and which the State should have adopted.

V Multilateral Dispute Settlement Related Treaties

1 *ICSID Convention*

Brunei signed and deposited its ratification of the ICSID Convention on 16 September 2002.[183] The ICSID Convention came into force in Brunei one month later, on 16 October 2002.[184] Brunei did not issue any notification under Articles 25(1), 25(3), 25(4), 54(2), 69 or 70 of the ICSID Convention.[185]

As at the date of writing, there has yet to be a publicly available case brought against Brunei or brought by a Brunei investor under the ICSID Convention.[186]

180 http://investmentpolicyhub.unctad.org/IIA/country/29/treaty/3092.

181 Article 2 of APPGI.

182 *Ibid.*, Article 8(1).

183 https://icsid.worldbank.org/apps/ICSIDWEB/about/Pages/Database-of-Member-States.aspx.

184 *Ibid.*

185 https://icsid.worldbank.org/apps/ICSIDWEB/about/Pages/MembershipStateDetails.aspx?state=ST20.

186 https://icsid.worldbank.org/apps/ICSIDWEB/cases/Pages/AdvancedSearch.aspx.

2 *New York Convention*

Brunei has been a contracting State of the New York Convention since 25 July 1996.[187] As at the date of writing, there has yet to be a publicly available decision of the Bruneian courts interpreting and applying the New York Convention.[188]

Brunei will apply the New York Convention only to recognition and enforcement of awards made in the territory of a contracting State which recognises and will enforce awards made in Brunei.[189]

VI International Investment Arbitration Jurisprudence

As at the date of writing, there has been no known investor-State arbitration against Brunei or any investment treaty arbitration brought by Bruneian nationals. The US Department of State 2015 Investment Climate Statement states that there is no history of expropriation of foreign owned property in Brunei, although there have been cases of domestically owned private property being expropriated for infrastructural development.[190]

It should be noted that under the Brunei Land Acquisition Act, private property may be acquired for a public purpose or for public utility works.[191] The purpose and land or area affected must be made known publicly[192] and compensation is awarded for such acquisition.

VII Outlook: Anticipated Developments

Brunei is a party to the Trans-Pacific Partnership Agreement ("TPP") which was concluded in Atlanta, Georgia, USA on 5 October 2015, after five and a half years of negotiations. The TPP is a comprehensive, high standard regional trade agreement that is widely expected to create new trade and investment opportunities for Brunei in the Asia-Pacific region. The TPP brings together 12 economies from both sides of the Pacific, namely, Australia, Brunei

187 http://www.newyorkconvention.org/contracting-states/list-of-contracting-states.

188 http://www.newyorkconvention.org/court-decisions/decisions-per-country.

189 Section 42(1) of the International Arbitration Order 2009.

190 US Department of State, Brunei Investment Climate Statement 2015 at page 9, available at http://www.state.gov/documents/organization/241706.pdf.

191 Section 3(1) of the Land Acquisition Act.

192 *Ibid.*, Section 5.

Darussalam, Canada, Chile, Japan, Malaysia, Mexico, New Zealand, Peru, Singapore, the United States and Vietnam. Collectively, these countries represent 40% of global GDP, one-third of world trade, and comprise a population of 800 million, making the TPP the largest regional trade agreement at the time of writing.[193] Apart from offering new market access for Bruneian goods and services producers exporting to and investing in TPP markets, the TPP also reinforces the region's commitment to a rules-based trading system by updating international rules that apply to cross-border trade and investment.[194]

Brunei already has existing Free Trade Agreements ("FTAs") through the ASEAN network with 6 of the 11 TPP partners.[195] The TPP represents Brunei's first preferential trade agreement with Canada, Mexico, Peru and the US.[196] While the TPP has been concluded, it will only enter into force when at least six original signatories, accounting for at least 85% of the GDP across the TPP economies, have ratified the agreement. When the TPP comes into force, it will be interesting to see how this agreement will fit into treaty arrangements in Brunei's existing FTAs, BITs, regional investment agreements such as the ASEAN Comprehensive Investment Agreement, as well as the widely anticipated Regional Comprehensive Economic Partnership Agreement ("RCEP") where negotiations are expected to be concluded soon.[197] While the TPP and RCEP might open doors to vast investment opportunities and a jump in FDI inflows to Brunei, these agreements at the same time afford investors in Brunei with greater protection when investing in economies which did not previously have investment agreements with Brunei.[198]

Notably, Brunei, together with Chile, Singapore and New Zealand are parties to the original 2005 Trans-Pacific Strategic Economic Partnership Agreement.

Based on publicly available information, the TPP is slated to boost the competitiveness of participating countries.[199] Its key features include the

---

193 Singapore Ministry of Trade and Industry, *Trans Pacific Partnership Free Trade Agreement* (TPP) *7 Things You Should Know*, available at https://www.mti.gov.sg/MTIInsights/SiteAssets/Pages/TPP/Seven%20things%20you%20should%20know%20about%20the%20TPP%20(Final).pdf.

194 *Ibid.*

195 See: https://aric.adb.org/fta-country and http://www.mofat.gov.bn/Pages/Brunei-Darussalam%27s-Policy-on-Free-Trade----Agreements.aspx.

196 *Ibid.*

197 http://fta.miti.gov.my/index.php/pages/view/60?mid=39.

198 http://www.mofat.gov.bn/Pages/Brunei-Darussalam%27s-Policy-on-Free-Trade----Agreements.aspx.

199 Office of the US Trade Representative, https://ustr.gov/tpp/outlines-of-TPP.

elimination of tariffs and other barriers to goods and services trade and investments and the promotion of investment in innovative products and services, including those related to the digital economy and green technologies.[200] The TPP is also intended to be a living agreement which can be updated from time to time to address trade issues that emerge in the future.[201]

200 *Ibid.*

201 *Ibid.*

CHAPTER 3

Cambodia[1]

I Introduction

Cambodia has a hybrid legal system that is still at a relatively early stage of development following the effects of Khmer Rouge rule and the subsequent civil war. A constitutional monarchy, Cambodia's legal system contains elements derived from French civil law, Vietnamese contract law, and common law.

Foreign Direct Investment ("FDI") inflow to Cambodia is critical to its continued development. Notwithstanding an 8% year-on-year decrease in 2014 to USD 1.7 billion,[2] FDI has nevertheless increased significantly over recent years, rising from USD 928 million in 2009. As at the time of writing, inward FDI stock is some USD 13 billion, or approximately 79% of GDP,[3] with the Republic of Korea, China, and Thailand the largest holders of assets in Cambodia.[4]

Investment protection for foreign investors and their investments is accorded both under domestic law and, to investors from States with which Cambodia has entered into bilateral or multilateral investment treaties, under international investment treaties. Investment protection includes both substantive protections and dispute settlement mechanisms (including investor-State dispute settlement or "ISDS"), the ability to enforce substantive protections being an important safeguard for investors in itself.

The protections conferred under these treaties, and the further development of the rule of law in Cambodia, form an important part of Cambodia's strategy for attracting investment.

1 This chapter has been drafted by Mr Cameron Forsaith, Eversheds LLP, London, and reviewed by Mr So Mosseny of the Extraordinary Chambers in the Courts of Cambodia (ECCC), Phnom Penh, Cambodia. The editors are also grateful to Prof. Mahdev Mohan of the Singapore Management University for his valuable comments.

2 UNCTAD World Investment Report 2015, p. 80, available at: http://unctad.org/en/pages/PublicationWebflyer.aspx?publicationid=1245.

3 UNCTAD World Investment Report 2015, Cambodia Country fact sheet, available at: http://unctad.org/sections/dite_dir/docs/wir2015/wir15_fs_kh_en.pdf.

4 US Department of State, Cambodia Investment Climate Statement 2015, p. 23, available at: http://www.state.gov/e/eb/rls/othr/ics/2015/241508.htm.

 | DOI 10.1163/9789004335257_005

II Cambodia's National Arbitration and Investment Legislation

1 *Cambodia's Arbitration Legislation and National Institution*

Cambodia's Arbitration Law

The law governing arbitration in Cambodia is the Commercial Arbitration Law of the Kingdom of Cambodia (the "Arbitration Law"), adopted in 2006.[5] The Arbitration Law is based on the 1985 UNCITRAL Model Law on International Commercial Arbitration (the "Model Law" or "UNCITRAL Model Law").[6] It continues to remain in effect.[7]

The Arbitration Law sets out the legal framework concerning arbitration and arbitration-related matters (including arbitration agreements, arbitral procedure, arbitral awards and the role of the courts) in Cambodia.

It includes provisions governing:

- the requirements of an arbitration agreement and how the existence of an arbitration agreement impacts upon claims brought before domestic courts (Chapter II);
- the establishment of an independent national arbitration centre (this centre did not exist on adoption of the Arbitration Law – it was ultimately established in 2009 as the National Commercial Arbitration Centre (or "NCAC")) (Chapter III);
- the composition and appointment of arbitral tribunals, including the role of the courts and/or the national arbitration centre in appointing arbitrators (on the request of either party) and determining challenges to arbitrators (on the request of either party, but only after a challenge is heard by the remainder of the tribunal) (Chapter IV);
- the jurisdiction of an arbitral tribunal to determine its own jurisdiction (*kompetenz-kompetenz*) and to order interim measures (Chapter V);
- the conduct of arbitral proceedings, providing for equality and that "each party shall be given a full opportunity to present his case, including representation by any party of his choice",[8] but otherwise

---

5 Available at http://www.cambodiaip.gov.kh/DocResources/372a361b-7a97-44b3-9810-79e5e6ea85f4_c786a043-b88d-4f64-9429-60a330efdc5f-en.pdf, at http://ncac.org.kh/items/LAW-Commercial_Arbitration_(2006)_En.pdf, and at Moser, Appendix 10.1.

6 Haw & Slott in Moser, *Arbitration in Asia*, 2nd ed (2008), CAM-4; Recent Developments In Arbitration Law And Practice: Cambodia in Albert Jan van den Berg (ed), *Yearbook Commercial Arbitration 2006 – Volume XXXI*, pp. 500–501.

7 Note General Editor Cambodia (2015), in Jan Paulsson and Lise Bosman (eds), ICCA *International Handbook on Commercial Arbitration*, Kluwer Law International 1984, Supplement No. 83, March 2015 p. i.

8 Arbitration Law, Article 26.

deferring to the parties' choice and the autonomy of the tribunal (Chapter VI);
- the making of an award, termination of proceedings, and (limited) correction and interpretation of an award (Chapter VII);
- recourse against domestic arbitral awards, which is exclusively by application to set aside (and not by way of appeal or rehearing), to be heard by the Appeal Court, with appeal to the Supreme Court (Chapter VIII, Section II);[9] and
- the recognition and enforcement of foreign and domestic awards (Chapter VIII, Section III).[10]

As noted above, the Arbitration Law applies to all arbitrations in Cambodia, whether domestic or international.

Under the Arbitration Law, an arbitration is international: if the parties to an arbitration agreement have their places of business in different States at the time of the conclusion of that agreement; if any of the following is different from the place of business of the parties: (i) the seat of arbitration; (ii) any place of performance of a substantial part of the parties' obligations; or (iii) the place with which the subject matter of the dispute is most closely connected; or if the parties have expressly agreed that the subject matter of the arbitration agreement relates to more than one country.[11]

There is no express definition of a domestic arbitration, and so if the arbitration is not an international arbitration under the criteria set out above, it will be considered a domestic arbitration.

The principal relevance of this distinction under the Arbitration Law is with regard to the appointment of arbitrators. Under Article 19(5) of the Arbitration Law, the court or NCAC is granted the authority to appoint the arbitrator or arbitrators in certain circumstances. In appointing the arbitrator(s) in all arbitrations, the court or NCAC "shall have due regard to any qualifications required of the arbitrator by the agreement of the parties and to such considerations as are likely to secure the appointment of an independent and impartial arbitrator".[12] However, in an international arbitration, the Arbitration Law provides that the appointing authority must also have regard to the advisability

9 The grounds for the set aside of a domestic award restate those set out in Article V of the New York Convention.

10 The grounds for refusing recognition and enforcement of a foreign award also restate those set out in Article V of the New York Convention.

11 This reflects the position under the UNCITRAL Model Law.

12 Arbitration Law, Article 19(5).

of appointing a sole or third arbitrator of a nationality other than those of the parties.[13]

The Provisions of the Arbitration Law

Comparison with the Model Law

The Arbitration Law is, as noted at the outset, based on the 1985 UNCITRAL Model Law on International Commercial Arbitration.[14] Accordingly, before considering the Arbitration Law's provisions in detail, a helpful starting point for understanding how the provisions of the Arbitration Law differ from the provisions of arbitral legislation in other jurisdictions (and general arbitral practice) is by reference to the differences between the Arbitration Law and the Model Law on which it is based.

The main ways in which the Arbitration Law deviates from the UNCITRAL Model Law are set out below:

- The Arbitration Law governs both domestic and international commercial arbitration,[15] rather than purely international commercial arbitration as under the Model Law.
- Chapter III of the Arbitration Law provides for the establishment of an independent National Arbitration Centre, something which is not provided for under the Model Law. This Centre, which adopted its arbitral rules in 2014 and received its first request for arbitration in 2015, is discussed below.
- Article 36 of the Arbitration Law provides a somewhat more flexible approach to determining the applicable law in the absence of a choice by the parties. As with the Model Law, the Arbitration Law requires that the tribunal first apply any choice made by the parties, but in the absence of such choice enables an arbitral tribunal to "apply the law that it considers appropriate", rather than the Model Law provision that the tribunal "apply the law determined by the conflict of laws rules which it considers applicable" (Article 28(2) of the Model Law).

---

13 *Ibid.*

14 Haw & Slott in Moser, *op. cit.*, pp. 500–501.

15 Arbitration Law, Article 1: "The purpose of this law is to facilitate the impartial and prompt resolution of commercial disputes in accordance with the wishes of the parties, to safeguard the legal rights and interests of the parties, and to promote the sound development of the economy". Arbitration Law, article 2(a): "'Arbitration' means any arbitration whether or not administered by a permanent arbitral institution".

- Article 38 of the Arbitration Law provides that "Upon request by both parties, prior to commencement of formal arbitration proceedings, the arbitral tribunal may confer with the parties for the purpose of exploring whether the possibility exists of a voluntary settlement of the parties' dispute... if the parties determines [*sic*] that it does, the arbitral tribunal shall assist the parties in any manner it deems appropriate...". This invitation to the tribunal, which is not provided for in the Model Law, provides legislative endorsement of a tribunal performing an active role in assisting settlement, albeit only following the request of both parties and only "prior to commencement of the formal arbitral proceedings". The Arbitration Law does not explain the meaning of "formal arbitral proceedings" (which must necessarily be at some point following the appointment of the tribunal), and there is accordingly still room for dispute as to when, precisely, the tribunal can fulfil this mediator-like role.[16]
- Article 39(3) of the Arbitration Law prescribes that an award shall deal with the costs of arbitration – this is of course permitted under the Model Law but is mandated in the Arbitration Law. Further, if the parties have so agreed, or if the arbitral tribunal deems it appropriate, an award may provide for the recovery of legal costs ("reasonable counsel fees"). While there is some provision for the recovery of legal costs in the Cambodian Civil Procedure Code, the principle of cost recovery is relatively undeveloped under Cambodian law and legal procedure, and so if legal cost recovery is desired by parties this should be specified clearly in the parties' agreement.[17]
- Article 41(1)(b) of the Arbitration Law provides that either party may request an "interpretation" or "amplification" of the award from the tribunal – in contrast to the Model Law provision, which does not contain the concept of "amplification", and which only entitles a party to request an interpretation where the parties have so agreed. The concept of "amplification" is not explained, and a disappointed arbitral party might seek to rely on these

16 In many cases, the tribunal will have received a detailed notice of arbitration and response on or shortly following its appointment (depending on the relevant arbitration rules), and some tribunals may consider a mediator-like role in these circumstances as involving a pre-judging of the merits and therefore incompatible with an arbitral tribunal's role. Conversely, other tribunals may see this as no more than managing the proceedings actively.

17 Haw & Slott in Moser, *Arbitration in Asia*, 2nd ed (2008), CAM-11.

differences to justify a relatively more substantial post-award "interpretative" process than is typically associated with arbitration.

- Article 44(3) of the Arbitration Law specifies a time limit of thirty days to apply to the Appeal Court for the setting aside of an award. Any further appeal to the Supreme Court must be made within fifteen days of the decision of the Court of Appeal (Article 43). This is a tighter time-frame than the three-month time limit provided for in the Model Law (Article 34(4)).

Chapter II

Chapter II of the Arbitration Law provides that an arbitration agreement must be in writing, whether as an arbitration clause in a contract or a separate agreement. Chapter II also provides for the effect of an arbitration agreement on the Cambodian courts: the court is (on a party's request) to refer any proceedings the subject of an agreement to arbitration. However, a party may request (and the courts may grant) interim measures of protection, whether before or during an arbitration.

Chapter III

Chapter III of the Arbitration Law provides for the establishment of an independent national arbitration centre, discussed further below under the heading "Cambodian Arbitral Institutions and Rules".

Chapter IV

Chapter IV of the Arbitration Law addresses the composition of an arbitral tribunal. Rather than prescribing a specific procedure, the rules in Chapter IV are in effect a default or fall-back position for use when either: (i) the parties have not agreed upon a specific procedure for the appointment of the tribunal; or (ii) something has gone wrong (or one party alleges something has gone wrong) in the composition of the tribunal, for example, something (allegedly) necessitating the removal of an arbitrator. Chapter IV grants powers in this regard to both the NCAC and the Cambodian courts, and its provisions are discussed in more detail below.

Chapter V

Chapter V of the Arbitration Law confirms the jurisdiction of the arbitral tribunal to rule on its own jurisdiction and (subject to contrary agreement by the parties) to order interim measures. Chapter V adopts the principles of *kompetenz-kompetenz* and the separability of the arbitration agreement. *Kompetenz-kompetenz* is the principle that a tribunal is competent to rule on its own jurisdiction (that is, its competence). Separability is the principle that an arbitration agreement (which is most commonly contained as a clause within a larger underlying contract) is an agreement independent of its underlying contract. These principles do not remove the tribunal or its decisions from the jurisdiction of the courts; and the Cambodian courts' role in deciding these issues is discussed further below under the heading "Autonomy and Independence of Arbitration from Court Proceedings".

Chapter VI

Chapter VI of the Arbitration Law concerns the conduct of arbitral proceedings, setting out a legal framework for those proceedings (including the principles of equality and the right to present one's case) and a default procedure, but deferring to the parties' choice and the autonomy of the tribunal. Chapter VI also confirms that a tribunal (or party with the tribunal's approval) can request the Cambodian courts' assistance in taking evidence.

Chapter VII

Chapter VII of the Arbitration Law concerns the applicable law, the award, and termination of proceedings. It is this chapter (Articles 36–41) that, as discussed above, diverges most significantly from the Model Law provisions. However, Chapter VII requires a tribunal to respect any choice of substantive law made by the parties and to produce a reasoned majority award dealing with the disputed issues (and the arbitration costs).

Chapter VIII

Chapter VIII of the Arbitration concerns the recourse against Cambodian-seated awards, and recognition and enforcement of foreign awards. In both cases, the Arbitration Law closely follows accepted arbitral practice and the requirements of international conventions. However, as described below under the heading "Autonomy and Independence of Arbitration from Court Proceedings", the application of Chapter VIII and the principles it embodies in Cambodia has been uneven to date.

Chapter IX

Interestingly, the final provision of the Arbitration Law provides that "[a]ny provisions in commercial arbitration sector that are contrary to this Law shall be abrogated".[18] Both the target(s) and effect(s) of this provision are somewhat unclear. Similar language in Cambodian legislation generally refers to

18 Arbitration Law, Article 47.

a hierarchy of local laws. While it appears clear that the Arbitration Law is intended to prevail over a contrary provision in, for example, the NCAC Rules, it is not clear how the courts or the Constitutional Council will interpret the Arbitration Law (and international guidance concerning the interpretation of other arbitration legislation in Model Law jurisdictions) while applying Chapter IX, and there are as yet no known government statements or local judicial decisions in this regard.

Cambodian Arbitral Institutions and Rules

As mentioned above, Article 10 of the Arbitration Law expressly envisaged the subsequent establishment of the NCAC.[19] The NCAC was in due course established by Sub-Decree No. 125 dated 12 August 2009 on the Management and Function of the NCAC, and adopted its rules in 2014 (the "NCAC Rules",[20] which were drafted with the assistance of the International Finance Corporation and the Asian Development Bank).

The NCAC Rules are modern and detailed – for example they include express provisions on "arbitration friendly" concepts such as the tribunal's *kompetenz-kompetenz*[21] and the separability of the arbitration clause[22] – there should therefore be no question that parties to an arbitration agreement incorporating the NCAC Rules expressly accept these concepts. As noted above, Chapter V of the Arbitration Law also confirms that these principles apply as a matter of Cambodian arbitration law.

The NCAC's Role under the Arbitration Law and NCAC Rules

In addition to the administrative services typical of any arbitral institution, the NCAC Rules also provide that the NCAC will determine if any objection to "NCAC jurisdiction" made before a tribunal is constituted is "properly submitted to NCAC",[23] and will scrutinise a draft Award produced by a tribunal before

19 The Arbitration Law, adopted in 2006, provided for certain powers and roles to vest in the centre which had not, at that time, been established.

20 Arbitration Rules of the National Commercial Arbitration Center of Kingdom of Cambodia. Available at http://ncac.org.kh/items/Abitration_Rules_(NCAC)_Adopted_Jul_2014_E.pdf, and at Haw & Slott in Moser *op. cit.*, Appendix 10.2.

21 NCAC Rules, Article 19.2.

22 *Ibid.*, Article 19.3.

23 *Ibid.*, Article 19.1. Article 19.1 envisages both objections to the existence or validity of the arbitration agreement, or to the competence of the NCAC to administer an arbitration under that agreement. Any such determination is such determination being without prejudice to a tribunal's power to rule on its own jurisdiction.

it is finalised.[24] Such roles are commonly undertaken by other arbitral institutions (the ICC being perhaps the best known example)[25] under their institutional arbitration rules, but how this role will be interpreted by the NCAC remains untested. For example, while the provisions dealing with the institution's scrutiny of a draft award are similar under both the ICC and NCAC Rules (both Article 35 of the NCAC Rules and Article 33 of the ICC Rules reference the institution's ability to "draw [the tribunal's] attention to points of substance" but "without affecting the [tribunal's] liberty of decision"), it remains to be seen whether the NCAC will interpret its power in the same way.

The Arbitration Law also provides for the NCAC to play a role beyond that of merely administering arbitrations under its Rules. The NCAC also performs a judicial or at least quasi-judicial role under the Arbitration Law in appointing an arbitrator where the party or nominated institution fails to do so (Article 19), determining challenges to an arbitrator (Article 21), and applications to remove an arbitrator on the basis that the arbitration has become "*De Jure* or *De Dacto* unable to perform his functions, or for other reasons fails to act without undue delay" (Article 22). The Arbitration Law provides that arbitral parties can make such applications to either the courts or to the NCAC, "which decision shall be subject to no appeal". Accordingly, the Arbitration Law appears to entitle the challenging party to elect whether to submit its appointment request or challenge to either the courts or NCAC; and where it selects the NCAC, ousts the ability of the courts to consider or reconsider such decision.

Registration of Arbitrators with NCAC

Article 11 of the Arbitration Law provides that an arbitrator, whether a Cambodian national or a foreigner, "shall"[26] register with the NCAC, that the NCAC is obliged to determine whether such an arbitrator is qualified, and that the NCAC will provide a list of such qualified arbitrators on its website. However, Article 11 also provides that "the list is not absolute" and that parties may choose an arbitrator from outside the NCAC's list.

---

24 *Ibid.*, Article 35.

25 See by way of comparison Articles 6(4) and Article 33 of the ICC Rules.

26 The purpose of the use of the mandatory "shall" rather than permissive "may" in Article 11 is unclear; the NCAC's list may well be intended primarily as a form of licensing or regulation for the benefit of Cambodia-resident arbitrators and/or for the protection of Cambodian users of arbitration, rather than a disincentive to the selection of non-list arbitrators.

Cases under the NCAC Rules

The NCAC received its first notice of arbitration in May 2015: a US$150,000 claim by a foreign claimant in relation to the rental of a Phnom Penh factory.[27]

Given the NCAC's recent establishment and the limited use of the NCAC Rules to date, there is presently little guidance as to how the NCAC will exercise its functions under the Arbitration Law, how it will interact with arbitral tribunals and the Cambodian courts, and more generally, the approach that it will take in administering arbitrations.

Despite its central role in the Cambodian arbitral landscape, there is no express requirement in the Arbitration Law that all arbitrations seated in Cambodia must be administered by the NCAC and/or governed by the NCAC Rules, and there seems to be no reason why parties cannot agree to Cambodian-seated arbitrations without reference to the NCAC.[28] Equally, the NCAC Rules expressly envisage that they may be used for arbitrations seated outside of Cambodia.[29]

The consensus among the majority of potential users of the NCAC (and of Cambodian-seated arbitrations more generally) appears to be to adopt a "wait-and-see" approach. Most potential users are (understandably) likely to await the results of the NCAC's first arbitration(s) before agreeing to the application of the NCAC Rules, in preference to foreign-seated arbitrations administered by one of the more established regional or global centres, in their commercial contracts.

Cambodian Courts and Arbitration

Court Powers in Support of Arbitration

There is little guidance as to how the Cambodian Courts will interpret the Arbitration Law provisions in relation to the appointment of an arbitrator (Article 19), a challenge to an arbitrator (Article 21) or an application to terminate the arbitrator's mandate (Article 22). Jurisdiction vests in the Appeal Court and the Supreme Court, with no distinction within the Arbitration Law

27 "Arbitration Body Receives First Complaint", *Cambodia Daily*, 27 May 2015. Available at: https://www.cambodiadaily.com/business/arbitration-body-receives-first-complaint-84450/; Olga Boltenko, "Cambodia's Arbitration Centre sets off on its First Flight", *Kluwer Arbitration Blog*, 10 June 2015. Available at: http://kluwerarbitrationblog.com/blog/2015/06/10-Cambodias-arbitration-centre-sets-off-on-its-first-flight/.

28 Haw & Slott in Moser, *Arbitration in Asia*, 2nd ed (2008), CAM-13.

29 NCAC Rules, Article 2.3.

as to the circumstances in which an application should be made to the Appeal Court rather than the Supreme Court (or vice versa).[30]

As discussed above, the courts share this role (under Articles 19, 21 and 22) with the NCAC, with no express limitation or guidance on when applications should be made to the courts and when they should be addressed to the NCAC. Accordingly, the Arbitration Law appears to entitle a challenging party to elect whether to submit its appointment request or challenge to either the courts or NCAC; and where a party selects the NCAC, the law ousts the ability of the courts to consider or reconsider such a decision. How this sharing of roles and functions will be interpreted by the Cambodian judiciary remains to be seen.

Parties to arbitration may request interim measures of protection from the court: Article 9 of the Arbitration Law replicates the UNCITRAL Model Law and provides: "It is not incompatible with an arbitration agreement for a party to request, before or during arbitral proceedings from a Court an interim measure of protection and for a Court to grant such measure."

Autonomy and Independence of Arbitration from Court Proceedings

The Arbitration Law provides that the Cambodian courts shall (on request) "refer the parties to arbitration", in any case in which "an action is brought in a matter which is the subject of an arbitration agreement", unless the court "finds that the agreement is null and void, inoperative or incapable of being performed".[31] It is unclear whether the Arbitration Law intends that a court stay or terminate the court proceedings when the court refers the parties to arbitration.

A tribunal is empowered to decide upon its own jurisdiction and any objections to that jurisdiction, including any objections regarding the validity of the arbitration agreement.[32]

If a tribunal rules on a jurisdictional objection as a preliminary question, a party may (within 30 days) request that the court decide the issue of jurisdiction,[33] but the tribunal is entitled to continue its proceedings notwithstanding any such request of the courts. Article 24 of the Arbitration Law,

30 See Haw & Slott in Moser, *Arbitration in Asia*, 2nd ed (2008), CAM-11. The Arbitration Law also provides that disputes may be submitted to a Commercial Court, but as at the time of writing, the enabling procedural rules of court have not been passed and this Court has not been established.

31 Arbitration Law, Article 8.

32 *Ibid.*, Article 24.

33 Where such a ruling of the tribunal is the subject of an Award rather than preliminary question, the Award can be challenged on these grounds.

which provides for these issues, replicates the UNCITRAL Model Law exactly, thereby adopting the principles of *kompetenz-kompetenz* and the separability of the arbitration agreement.

In relation to both the setting aside of domestic awards and the recognition and enforcement of foreign awards, an application to set aside or request to refuse recognition or enforcement can only be made on the limited grounds set out in the Arbitration Law (at Article 44, in relation to setting aside applications, and Article 46, on the recognition and enforcement of arbitral awards). Again, these grounds (which are the same in both article 44 and article 46) follow the Article 36 UNCITRAL Model Law and New York Convention grounds closely: lack of capacity of parties; lack of a valid arbitration agreement; lack of notice of appointment of an arbitrator or of the arbitral proceedings or otherwise an inability of a party to present its case; the award dealing with matters outside the submission to arbitration; the composition of arbitral tribunal or arbitral procedure contrary to the agreement of parties or (failing agreement) contrary to the Arbitration Law; the non-arbitrability of the subject-matter of the dispute under Cambodian law; or a violation of Cambodian public policy.

Clauses such as Articles 24, 44 and 46 of the Arbitration Law are considered modern, "arbitration friendly" provisions. However, notwithstanding the content of the Arbitration Law, private commercial arbitration is a relatively new concept in Cambodia. There remains little definitive guidance available as to how the Cambodian courts will apply the relevant laws. This lack of guidance is in part because of the lack of a formal system for the reporting of court cases.

However, there appears to be a general consensus that Cambodian courts will not (or at least, will not necessarily or reliably) stay or terminate court proceedings in favour of arbitration, and may seek to revisit the merits of an arbitral award, notwithstanding the provisions of the Arbitration Law.

It has previously been commented that "the Courts in Cambodia have been reluctant to relinquish their power in regards to commercial disputes. In several recent unpublished court cases, the courts have refused to refer cases to arbitration[34] even when there has been a valid arbitration clause ... In both domestic and international arbitrations the courts are not required to determine the merits of the dispute but it is assumed that the courts of Cambodia would in fact rule on the merits of the dispute even though it is not required ... it should be noted that in Cambodia, even with a carefully drafted arbitration

34 Article 8 of the Arbitration Law provides that the courts "shall" refer such matters to arbitration.

clause, the courts will not refer the case to arbitration and will issue orders and decisions based on the facts of the dispute."[35]

The Cambodian Constitutional Council decision on the constitutionality of the Arbitration Law also suggests the possibility of such interference.[36] That decision found that the Arbitration Law was constitutional, but stated that "Article 5 of the [Arbitration Law] shall be interpreted that the court can intervene upon the request from the parties and that the judicial power shall not be limited".[37]

Similarly, in relation to the enforcement of foreign-seated awards, it appears that prior to 2014 there had been only very limited examples of a party enforcing a foreign arbitral award in Cambodia successfully.[38]

In 2014, the Supreme Court of Cambodia confirmed an earlier decision of the Court of Appeal that recognised and enforced a Korean Commercial Arbitration Board award, in favour of a Korean company, in respect of a real estate development in Phnom Penh.[39] In that case, the relevant enforcement proceedings were commenced in 2012.[40] While evidence of the enforcement of a foreign award does not prove that Cambodia is an arbitration-friendly jurisdiction or that parties can necessarily be confident that their arbitration

35 Haw & Slott in Moser, *Arbitration in Asia*, 2nd ed (2008), CAM-11 and CAM-13. One of the two co-authors of that chapter (Ms Slott) is a member of the NCAC Advisory Council.

36 Constitutional Council Decision No. 075/002/2006, available at: http://www.ccc.gov.kh/english/decision/2006/dec%2075.pdf.

37 Haw & Slott in Moser, Arbitration in Asia, 2nd ed (2008), CAM-12. Article 5 of the Arbitration Law provides: "In matters governed by this Law, no Court shall intervene except where so provided in this Law."

38 See Larkin & Sambo, "Recent Developments in Commercial Arbitration in Cambodia", *Asian Dispute Review* (January 2015) (LexisNexis) (stating no successful enforcement prior to 2014); and Haw & Slott in Moser, Arbitration in Asia, 2nd ed (2008), CAM-12 (referring without further detail to two examples of foreign awards being "upheld" by the Appeal Court since 2001).

39 There is conflicting information as to whether the non-prevailing party (or parties) was Korean or Cambodian – see Larkin & Sambo, "Recent Developments in Commercial Arbitration in Cambodia", *Asian Dispute Review* (January 2015) (LexisNexis), and Olga Boltenko, "Cambodia's Arbitration Centre sets off on its First Flight", *Kluwer Arbitration Blog*, 10 June 2015.

40 "Kookmin bank takes Camko City to court", *Phnom Penh Post*, 20 September 2012, available at http://www.phnompenhpost.com/business/kookmin-bank-takes-camko-city-court. The article is striking (in addition to providing extensive media quotes from "Seng Sivutha, chief judge on the case at the appeals court") in referring to a series of procedural delays – which, it appears, resulted in a 2-year enforcement process.

agreements and arbitral awards will be effective in Cambodia,[41] it does offer hope that the provisions of the Arbitration Law may indeed be interpreted in line with modern arbitral practice.

However, even with a rapid change in approach from the Cambodian courts, the application of the Arbitration Law (including on the stay of court proceedings, the review of jurisdictional rulings, and the recognition and enforcement of awards) is likely to remain inconsistent at best in the coming years.

2 *Cambodia's Investment Laws*

The 1994 Law on Investment and its 2003 amendments (together the "Law on Investment"),[42] and its implementing Sub-Decree (the "Sub-Decree"),[43] provide, *inter alia*, certain substantive guarantees in relation to investments in Cambodia.[44]

Qualifying for Protection

The guarantees and incentives under the Law on Investment are available only to "Qualified Investment Projects".[45]

Establishing a Qualified Investment Project ("QIP") requires an investor to go through an approval process from the Council for the Development of Cambodia ("CDC") for its investment. The CDC is intended as a "one-stop shop" for investment approvals.

Detailed requirements for approval (and the applicable application form which is annexed to the Sub-Decree) are set out in the Sub-Decree. In summary, an applicant must:

---

41 Cf. Larkin & Sambo, *op. cit.*, Asian Dispute Review (January 2015) (LexisNexis), and Olga Boltenko, *op. cit., Kluwer Arbitration Blog*, 10 June 2015.

42 Law on Investment of the Kingdom of Cambodia (August 05, 1994) and Law on the Amendment to the Law on Investment of the Kingdom of Cambodia (Match 24, 2003). Available at: http://www.cambodiainvestment.gov.kh/law-on-investment-august-05-1994-and-law-on-the-amendment-to-the-law-on-investment_030324.html.

43 Sub-Decree on the Implementation of the Law on the Amendment to the Law on Investment of the Kingdom of Cambodia No 111 ANK/BK dated September 27 2005. Available at: http://www.cambodiainvestment.gov.kh/content/uploads/2011/10/Sub-Decree-111-on-Implementation-LOI_050927.pdf.

44 See generally the information available on the CDC website: http://www.cambodiainvestment.gov.kh/investment-scheme/limitation-on-foreign-investment.html.

45 Article 2 of the Law of Investment states that a "Qualified Investment Project" means an investment project which has received a Final Registration Certificate.

- provide the required information pertaining to the investor (including, for example, details of shareholders, directors, etc.);
- provide the required information pertaining to the investment (including, for example, details of the capital to be invested, envisaged use of labour, etc.);
- provide information regarding the envisaged environmental impact of the investment;
- confirm that the investment is not in a sector where investment is prohibited;[46]
- confirm that the investment is not in a sector ineligible for foreign investment incentives;[47] and
- elect the substantive incentive or exemption (discussed below) that will be received by the investor; and
- pay the application fee (7,000,000 riel, currently approximately US$1,750).

If those requirements are met, then save for investment proposals which are related to the national interest or are environmentally sensitive,[48] CDC will issue a Conditional Registration Certificate which lists "all the necessary approvals, authorizations, licenses, permits or registrations which are required for the QIP to be lawfully undertaken" (which will vary by sector and from investment to investment).

The Law on Investment also provides procedural protections designed to give comfort to investors and ensure the efficient operation of the qualification process. For example, Article 7 of the Law on Investment provides that the CDC shall issue either a Conditional Registration Certificate or a Letter of Non-Compliance within three days of receiving an application. If the CDC does not provide one of those two documents within three days (and

46 Section 1 of the Negative List in Schedule 1 of the Sub-Decree: "Production/processing of psychotropic substances and narcotic substances; 2. Production of poisonous chemicals, agriculture pesticide/insecticide and other goods by using chemical substances, prohibited by international regulations or the World Health Organization, that affect the public health and environment; 3. Processing and production of electricity power by using any waste imported from a foreign country; 4. Forestry exploitation business prohibited by Forestry Law".

47 Section 2 of the Negative List in Schedule 1 of the Sub-Decree: These include absolute exclusions from incentives (e.g. professional services, all kinds of commercial activity, tourism) and size or capital limitations (i.e. incentives are available only to projects of sufficient size).

48 Sub-Decree, Article 6.1(d).

so commence the processing of the investor's application), the Conditional Registration Certificate will be considered automatically approved.

It is important to note that where the Law on Investment imposes restrictions on the eligibility of investments in certain sectors, these are limitations on whether an investment can be a QIP (and so receive guarantees and incentives under domestic law), rather than on the possibility of investment altogether. No sector is closed to foreign investment.[49]

Substantive Guarantees & Incentives

The substantive guarantees available to QIPs are set out at Articles 8 to 11 of the Law on Investment:

- A foreign investor shall not be treated in any discriminatory way by reason only of the investor being a foreign investor, except in respect of ownership of land;
- The Government shall not undertake any nationalization policy that would adversely affect private properties of investors in Cambodia;
- The Government shall not fix the price or fee of products or services of a QIP; and
- The Cambodian Government shall permit investors to purchase foreign currencies through the banking system and to remit sums abroad for the following purposes:

  - Payment for imports and repayment of principal and interest on international loans;
  - Payment of royalties and management fees;
  - Remittance of profits; and
  - Repatriation of invested capital.

In addition to these protections, Cambodia also provides registered QIPs with various incentives, which include full or partial exemption from certain duties (particularly import duties) and taxes (for example, profit taxes).[50]

---

49 However, only Cambodian nationals or entities (which must be majority owned by Cambodian nationals or other Cambodian entities) may own land; although foreign investors are entitled to lease and otherwise use land.

50 Although an investor which opts-in to certain incentives (such as the profit tax exemption) may lose other benefits (for example the entitlement to claim depreciation): see Article 14(4) of the Law on Investment, and the application form annexed to the Sub-Decree.

These substantive protections mirror many of the protections available under international investment instruments, particularly the protections from discrimination and, to some extent, the prohibition on unlawful expropriation. However, these are not as extensive as the protections available under international investment treaties.

Further, an investor's ability to enforce these protections may be limited. If a dispute arises in relation to a QIP and it is not resolved within two months of amicable settlement discussions, either party to the dispute may bring the dispute to: (i) conciliation before the CDC ("which shall provide its opinion"); (ii) arbitration "in or outside of Cambodia as agreed by both parties"; or (iii) "trial by the tribunals of the Kingdom of Cambodia".[51] It is open to debate whether this language, without more, would be construed as providing an investor with a right to commence ISDS proceedings without further agreement. Without such a right, however, an investor is only able to submit the dispute to a neutral decision maker if it can rely upon (or make) another separate agreement.

Accordingly, these protections are not a substitute for protection under international investment agreements, and it would be prudent for foreign investors considering investing in Cambodia to ensure that they and their investments are protected under one or more international investment instruments.

III Cambodia's Bilateral Investment Treaties

1 *Overview*

Cambodia signed its first Bilateral Investment Treaty ("BIT") with Malaysia on 17 August 1994. Over the following 21 years it has signed at least 23 BITs,[52] of

51 Article 20, Law on Investment.

52 UNCTAD reports that Cambodia has signed BITs with the following States: Austria, Belarus, China, Croatia, Cuba, Czech Republic, France, Germany, Indonesia, Japan, Republic of Korea, Kuwait, Laos, Malaysia, Netherlands, North Korea, Pakistan, Philippines, Russia, Singapore, Switzerland, Thailand, and Vietnam.

A 2014 publicly available presentation by the Council for the Development of Cambodia (Available at http://www.cdc-crdb.gov.kh/cdc/Donor_Development_Cooperation_Programs/Japan/12th_policy_dialogue_on_oda/downloads/1_2_Cambodia_FDIs_Trend_12_June_2014.pdf) also reports BITs signed with Australia, OPEC, and 'OPIC'; the status of these BITs is unclear.

which at least 11 have entered into force.[53] Out of the 23 BITs, 17 treaties are available from public or subscription access websites.[54]

While a "Cambodia Model BIT" dated March 1998 is publicly available,[55] the extent to which it has been used as a model for Cambodia's BITs is questionable. The provisions of the Cambodian Model BIT are reflected to some extent in a few BITs signed in the years following 1998: this is so with the BITs concluded with Indonesia (1999), the Philippines (2000) and Cuba (2001), although none of these treaties are yet in force.

However, from an analysis of the wording of the relevant treaties, it appears that it was the treaty between Cambodia and Indonesia that served as a *de facto* model for Cambodian negotiators in subsequent treaty negotiations with the Philippines and Cuba. For example, the Cambodia-Indonesia BIT contains a more detailed definition of the "territory" of Cambodia at Article 1(4), a definition which is then repeated in the Philippines and Cuba treaties, and reflected to some extent in the Cambodia-Vietnam BIT (2001, not in force) and Cambodia-Czech Republic BIT (2008, in force since 2009).

In respect of the other BITs entered into by Cambodia, however, the reality is that the BITs concluded with developed States are more likely to reflect the developed State's model BIT.[56]

In that regard, prospective investors may find it useful to note that the Cambodia-Netherlands BIT replicates the provisions of the Netherlands 1997 Model BIT (save for the ISDS provisions in the Cambodia-Netherlands BIT – article 9(1) prescribes a three-month "cooling off" period that does not feature in the Netherlands Model BIT).[57]

---

53 UNCTAD reflects that Cambodia's BITs with the following States have entered into force: China, Croatia, Czech Republic, France, Germany, Japan, Republic of Korea, Netherlands, Singapore, Switzerland, and Thailand (http://investmentpolicyhub.unctad.org/IIA/CountryBits/33#iiaInnerMenu).

54 Of the 23 treaties reported on the UNCTAD International Investment Agreements Navigator website (http://investmentpolicyhub.unctad.org/IIA/CountryIris/33), the treaties with Austria, Belarus, Kuwait, Laos, North Korea, Pakistan, and Russia are unavailable. The Pakistan treaty is however available on a subscription-based website. This section III is based on an analysis of the available treaties only.

55 On the UNCTAD International Investment Agreements Navigator website: http://investmentpolicyhub.unctad.org/IIA/CountryIris/33.

56 By way of example, the Cambodia-Japan BIT is used as the *de facto* Japan Model BIT in Chester Brown's leading text, *Commentaries on Selected Model Investment Treaties* (2013, Oxford University Press).

57 As to the Netherlands Model BIT, see Schrijver & Prislan in Chester Brown (ed.), *Commentaries on Selected Model Investment Treaties*, (2013, Oxford University Press), Ch. 13.

It is also unclear to what extent any of Cambodia's previously negotiated BITs reflect its current negotiating priorities – the only treaties signed since 2008 (with Belarus and Russia, both in 2014) are neither in force nor publicly available.

However, at least in those treaties which are publicly available, Cambodia has not sought to include (or, if it has, has not successfully negotiated) express provisions that carve out broad regulatory spaces for the State in specified areas (or similar provisions which could be seen as "State-friendly"). This is significant given that other States in the region have included such provisions in their treaties. For example, the 2008 Laos-Japan BIT contains general exceptions which permit parties to take, for example, measures "necessary to protect human, animal or plant life or health", or "imposed for the protection of national treasures of artistic, historic or archaeological value".[58] No such provisions appear in Cambodia's network of publicly available BITs.

2 *Definition of Investment*

The publicly available BITs signed by Cambodia generally provide for a broad or classic definition of investment. The majority of these BITs define investment to include any kind of asset; in particular, though not exclusively: movable and immovable property rights and any other rights *in rem*, shares, stocks and debentures of or interests in the property of companies, claims to money or any performance having a financial value, intellectual and industrial property rights and business concessions.[59]

The Cambodia-Pakistan BIT in particular contains a more limited definition and, amongst other things, expressly excludes from the list of qualifying investments construction contracts, time-bound contracts, and contracts to provide a service.[60]

Slightly more than half of Cambodia's publicly available BITs in force (and the Cambodian model BIT) stipulate expressly that the investments shall be made in accordance with the laws and regulations of the State in which they are made. For example, the Cambodia-Indonesia BIT provides that: "The term 'investments' shall mean any kind of asset invested by investors of one Contracting Party in the territory of the other Contracting Party,

58 See Laos-Japan BIT, Article 18; 'Latest Japanese Pacts With Laos and Cambodia Offer Glimpse of Latest Japanese Thinking On Investor Protection', *Investment Arbitration Reporter*, 18 June 2008, available at http://www.iareporter.com/articles/latest-japanese-pacts-with-laos-and-cambodia-offer-glimpse-of-latest-japanese-thinking-on-investor-protection/; and see the chapter on Lao People's Democratic Republic.

59 See generally Article 1 of each of the publicly available treaties in footnote 54 above.

60 Cambodia-Pakistan BIT, Article 1(b) and Article 1(d).

in conformity with the laws and regulations of the latter, including, but not exclusively … movable and immovable property …".[61]

3 *Definition of Investor*

An "investor" (or comparable term)[62] in Cambodia's BITs is generally also defined classically and expansively, to include both nationals (or natural persons) and legal entities of the home State.

Nationals or natural persons are further defined (where at all) as nationals by reference to the law of their home State. Unusually, the Cambodia-Malaysia BIT confers protection on natural persons who are either citizens of the applicable home State, or permanent residents. In contrast, the Cambodia-Cuba BIT requires Cuban investors who are natural persons to have both Cuban citizenship and permanent residence, though no such qualification applies to Cambodian natural persons (who need only have Cambodian nationality under Cambodian law).

Protection for qualifying companies or legal persons is also generally defined with reference to the law of their home State. For example, the Cambodia-Indonesia BIT refers to "legal persons constituted under the law of that Contracting Party".[63]

Under some BITs, the definition of a qualifying investor is somewhat more restrictive. The BITs concluded with Croatia and Pakistan also require that an investor have "real business activities" and that its seat be in its home State. The Germany BIT (in relation to German investors only) also requires that an investor have its seat in Germany; and the Czech Republic BIT requires that a qualifying investor (in addition to being an entity under the home State's law) have its seat in either the Czech Republic or Cambodia.

Conversely, the Netherlands, France and Swiss BITs have a broader definition, extending protection to legal entities controlled, directly or indirectly, by other investors of that host State.

61 See Cambodia-Indonesia BIT, Article 1(1). BITs which do not include this language include those concluded with Germany, Japan, Korea, Malaysia, the Netherlands, Switzerland, and Thailand.

62 For example, the BITs with France, Germany, Singapore and Vietnam refer simply to nationals and companies, and the Netherlands and Philippines BITs use the defined term "nationals" to refer to both natural and legal persons.

63 See Cambodia-Indonesia BIT, Article 1(2).

4 *Scope*

Cambodia's BITs apply to investments made prior to, as well as after, the entry into force of the relevant treaty.[64]

Several Cambodian BITs state expressly that they shall not apply to disputes that have arisen before their entry into force (including the BITs concluded with Croatia, Cuba, the Czech Republic, Indonesia, Japan, Korea, the Netherlands, Pakistan, the Philippines and Vietnam).

5 *Substantive Protections*

Fair and Equitable Treatment

All of Cambodia's publicly available BITs at the time of writing contain a fair and equitable treatment ("FET") standard that is a variation of the classic FET provision.[65]

The Cambodia-Indonesia BIT provides that "[i]nvestments of investors of either Contracting Party shall at all times be accorded fair and equitable treatment and shall enjoy adequate protection and security in the territory of the other Contracting Party"[66] and that "[e]ach Contracting Party shall ensure fair and equitable treatment of the investments of investors of the other Contracting Party and shall not impair, by unreasonable or discriminatory measures, the operation, management, maintenance, use, enjoyment or disposal thereof by those investors".[67]

Some treaties formulate that standard by reference to the laws and regulations of the other Contracting State (such as the treaties entered into with Malaysia and Pakistan).[68] Other treaties reference the (arguably) lesser "in

64 Arguably with the exception of the Cambodia-Thailand BIT, which does not appear to deal with the temporal application of the BIT.

65 China, Article 3(1); Croatia, Article 3(2); Cuba, Articles 2(2) and 3(1); Czech Republic, Article 3(1); France, Article 3; Germany, Article 2(1); Indonesia, Articles 2(2) and 3(1); Japan, Article 4; Korea, Article 3(1); Malaysia, Article 3(1); Netherlands, Article 3(1); Pakistan, Article 3(2); Philippines, Articles 2(2) and 3(1); Singapore, Article 3(2); Switzerland, Article 4(1); Thailand, Article 4(1); Vietnam, Articles 2(2) and 3(1).

66 Article 2(2).

67 Article 3(1). Note that Article 3(1) is replicated in the Cuba, Indonesia, Philippines and Vietnam BITs; and (for the purpose of the FET and non-impairment standards) in the Netherlands BIT.

68 E.g. the Cambodia-Malaysia BIT, Article 3(1): "Investments made by investors of either Contracting Party in the territory of the other Contracting Party shall receive treatment which is fair and equitable in accordance with the laws, regulations and national policies of the -Contracting Parties and not less favorable than that accorded to investments made by investors of any third State."

accordance with international law" standard (including treaties entered into with Croatia and Japan).[69]

The FET provisions of many treaties (including the Netherlands BIT[70] and the Singapore BIT[71]) reflect the Model or *de facto* Model provisions of the other contracting State. As noted above, these are all variations of the classic FET provision. The use of model provisions is significant as it means that, while none of Cambodia's BITs have themselves been considered by an arbitral tribunal (as Cambodia has not been subject to a claim under a BIT, and no BIT claim has yet been brought by a Cambodian investor), there is nonetheless a significant body of arbitral jurisprudence considering the wording of these provisions where they appear in other BITs.

Non-Discrimination

Many of Cambodia's BITs also expressly prohibit arbitrary, unreasonable or discriminatory treatment of qualifying investors and/or investments by Contracting States, in addition to the FET standard.

Such BITs typically contain the Cambodia-Indonesia BIT language, or a close paraphrase thereof: "Each Contracting Party shall ensure fair and equitable treatment of the investments of investors of the other Contracting Party and shall not impair, by unreasonable or discriminatory measures, the operation, management, maintenance, use enjoyment or disposal thereof by those investors."

---

69 E.g. the Cambodia-Croatia BIT, Article 3(2): "Investments or returns of investors of either Contracting Party in the territory of the other Contracting Party shall be accorded fair and equitable treatment in accordance with international law and the provisions of this Agreement".

70 As noted above, the relevant "FET" language in the Cambodia-Netherlands BIT is identical to that contained in the Netherlands Model BIT since 1993: see Schrijver & Prislan in Chester Brown (ed.), *op. cit.*, Ch 13, pp. 560–562; Cambodia-Netherlands BIT, Article 3(1): "Each Contracting Party shall ensure fair and equitable treatment of the investments of nationals of the other Contracting Party and shall not impair, by unreasonable or discriminatory measures, the operation, management, maintenance, use, enjoyment or disposal thereof by those nationals. Each Contracting Party shall accord to such investments full physical security and protection."

71 Ho in Chester Brown (ed.), *op. cit.*, Ch 15, p. 535, discussing Singapore's *de facto* model Investment Guarantee Agreement (Singapore does not have an official Model BIT or Investment Guarantee Agreement, but standard formulations in its BITs and FTA investment chapters suggest a *de facto* Model); Cambodia-Singapore BIT, Article 3(2): "Investments approved under Article 2 shall be accorded fair and equitable treatment and protection in accordance with this Agreement."

Similar or identical language is used in the Croatia,[72] Germany,[73] Korea,[74] Netherlands, Pakistan,[75] Philippines, Swiss, Thailand and Vietnam BITs.

Protection and Security

All of Cambodia's publicly available BITs at the time of writing contain some variation of the protection and security standard.[76] This is expressed in various manners; most commonly as "full protection and security" (as in the Croatia, Czech Republic, Germany, Japan, Korea, Malaysia, Pakistan, and Thailand BITs), but also as "full physical security and protection" (the Netherlands BIT), "adequate protection and security" and "adequate physical security and protection" (BITs concluded with Indonesia, Cuba, Vietnam and the Philippines), or simply "protection" (the China and Singapore BITs).

Expropriation

All of Cambodia's BITs that are publicly available at the time of writing contain a provision prohibiting the expropriation, nationalization and any other measure having an effect equivalent to expropriation or nationalization, unless the measure taken by the host State: (i) serves a public purpose; (ii) is taken under due process of law and/or in accordance with domestic legal procedure; (iii) without discrimination; and (iv) on payment of compensation.[77]

---

72 Article 3(3): "Each Contracting Party shall not in its territory impose mandatory measures on investments by investors of the other Contracting Party concerning purchase of materials, means of production, operation, transport, marketing of its products or similar orders having unreasonable or discriminatory effects."

73 Article 2(2): "Neither Contracting Party shall in any way impair by arbitrary or discriminatory measures the management, maintenance, use or enjoyment of Investments in its territory of nationals or companies of the other Contracting Party."

74 Article 2(3): "Neither Contracting Party shall in any way impair by unreasonable or discriminatory measures the operation, management, maintenance, use, enjoyments or disposal of investments in its territory by investors of the other Contracting Party." (Duplicated in the Thailand BIT).

75 Article 3(1): "...Neither Contracting Party shall impair by arbitrary or discriminatory measures the development, management, maintenance, use, enjoyment, expansion, sale and if it is the case, the liquidation of such investments."

76 China, Article 3(1); Croatia, Article 3(1); Cuba, Articles 2(2) and 3(1); Czech Republic, Article 2(2); France, Article 5; Germany, Article 4(1); Indonesia, Articles 2(2) and 3(1); Japan, Article 4; Korea, Article 2(2); Malaysia, Article 2(2); Netherlands, Article 3(1); Pakistan, Article 3(1); Philippines, Articles 2(2) and 3(1); Singapore, Article 3(2); Switzerland, Article 4(1); Thailand, Article 3(2); Vietnam, Article Articles 2(2) and 3(1).

77 China, Article 4; Croatia, Article 5; Cuba, Article 4; Czech Republic, Article 5; France, Article 5(2); Germany, Article 4(2); Indonesia, Article 4; Japan, Article 12; Korea,

By way of example, the Cambodia-Indonesia BIT provides: "Each Contracting Party shall not take any measures of expropriation, nationalization or otherwise subjected to any other measures, having effect equivalent to nationalization or expropriation (hereinafter referred to as "expropriation") against the investments of an investors of the other Contracting Party except under the following conditions: (a) the measures are taken for a lawful interest and under due process of law; (b) the measures are non-discriminatory; (c) the measures are accompanied by provisions for the payment of prompt, adequate and effective compensation. Such compensation shall amount to the fair market value without delay before the measure of dispossession became public knowledge. Such market value shall be determined in accordance with internationally acknowledged practices and methods or, where such fair market value cannot be determined, it shall be such reasonable amount as may be mutually agreed between the Contracting Parties hereto, and it shall be freely transferable in freely usable currencies from the Contracting Party."

The precise formulations of each treaty vary between States (for example, "prompt, adequate and effective compensation" (the majority of treaties) versus simply "compensation" (as per the BIT concluded with China)), although these differences in expression do not necessarily indicate a different substantive standard.

Further, many of Cambodia's BITs provide an investor with an express right to prompt review of its case by a judicial or other competent authority; these include the Croatia, Czech Republic, Japan, Korea and Pakistan BITs.

The China BIT limits the availability of Investor-State Dispute Settlement ("ISDS") to "a dispute involving the amount of compensation for expropriation". It is debatable whether this merely affords investors a right to resort to arbitration regarding the quantification of compensation or whether the treaty also allows investors to refer disputes regarding whether or not an expropriation has occurred.

Umbrella Clauses

Many Cambodian BITs include an obligation on the Contracting Parties to observe any obligation they have undertaken with regard to investments of an investor of the other Contracting Party, a so-called "umbrella clause".

Article 5; Malaysia, Article 4; Netherlands, Article 6; Pakistan, Article 5; Philippines, Article 4; Singapore, Article 6; Switzerland, Article 6; Thailand, Article 6(1); Vietnam, Article 4.

While the effect of such clauses is contested,[78] it arguably elevates a State's obligations (such as contractual obligations) into obligations protected under the BIT.

Such umbrella clauses are included in the Croatia, Germany, Japan, Korea, Netherlands, Pakistan, Swiss, Singapore and Thailand BITs.[79] The wording of each umbrella clause is relatively similar, save for the umbrella clause contained in the Cambodia-Singapore BIT, which is in unconventional terms and seemingly extends the State's protection not only to its own commitments and those of its agents, but to those of all host State nationals and companies. It states: "...[e]ach Contracting Party shall observe any commitment in accordance with its laws additional to those specified in this Agreement entered into by the Contracting Party, its nationals or companies with nationals or companies of the other Contracting Party as regards their investments."[80]

---

78 See Anthony Sinclair, "The Origins of the Umbrella Clause in the International Law of Investment Protection", (2004) *Arbitration International* 20(4) at 411; Jude Anthony, "Umbrella Clauses Since SGS v. Pakistan and SGS v. Philippines – A Developing Consensus", (2013) *Arbitration International* 29(4) at 607.

79 Croatia, Article 3(1): "Either Contracting Party shall observe any other obligation it may have entered into with regard to specific investments of investors of the other Contracting Party".

Germany, Article 8(2): "Each Contracting Party shall observe any other obligation it has assumed with regard to investments in its territory by nationals or companies of the other Contracting Party."

Japan, Article 4(2): "Each Contracting Party shall observe any obligation it may have entered into with regard to investments of investors of the other Contracting Party."

Korea, Article 10(3): "Either Contracting Party shall observe any other obligation it may have entered into with regard to investments in its territory by investors of the other Contracting Party."

Netherlands, Article 3(4): "Each Contracting Party shall observe any obligation it may have entered into with regard to investments of nationals of the other Contracting Party."

Pakistan, Article 3(1) "... A Contracting Party shall observe any other obligation it may have entered into with regards to investments of investors of the other Contracting Party."

Switzerland, Article 10(2): "Chacune des Parties contractantes se conformera à toutes ses obligations à l'égard des investissements effectués sur son territoire par des investisseurs de l'autre Partie contractante."

Singapore, Article 15(2): "... Each Contracting Party shall observe any commitment in accordance with its laws additional to those specified in this Agreement entered into by the Contracting Party, its nationals or companies with nationals or companies of the other Contracting Party as regards their investments".

80 Article 15, Cambodia-Singapore BIT. This provision, which is reflective of the Singapore Model BIT, was referred to as an "unusually generous formulation of the umbrella

Most Favoured Nation and National Treatment

All of Cambodia's publicly available BITs require that the treatment of the investments of investors from the other Contracting State be no less favourable than that granted to nationals or companies of third states – a so called "Most Favoured Nation" ("MFN") provision.[81]

A majority of Cambodia's BITs also contain a "national treatment" provision, obliging parties to provide treatment not less favourable than that it provides to domestic investors, although the China, Cuba, Indonesia, Malaysia, Philippines and Singapore BITs do not provide such protection.

A good example of such a clause providing for both MFN and national treatment is that contained within the Cambodia-Netherlands treaty: "More particularly, each Contracting Party shall accord to such investments treatment which in any case shall not be less favourable than that accorded either to investments of its own nationals or to investments of nationals of any third State, whichever is more favourable to the national concerned."

The basic form of a clause which does not include national treatment can be found in the Cambodia-Indonesia BIT: "More particularly, each Contracting Party shall accord to such investments treatment which in any case shall not be less favourable than that accorded to investments of investors of any third state."

The vast majority of treaties expressly provide that such MFN clauses do not apply to the benefits of membership of a customs union or free trade area, or to taxation agreements and taxation legislation.[82]

---

clause" – see Ho in Chester Brown (ed), *op. cit.*, page 647. See also the discussion of this provision in the Singapore chapter.

81 China, Article 3(2); Croatia, Article 4; Cuba, Article 3; Czech Republic, Article 3; France, Article 4; Germany, Articles 3 and 4(4); Indonesia, Article 3; Japan, Article 3; Korea, Article 3; Malaysia, Article 3; Netherlands, Article 3; Pakistan, Article 4; Philippines, Article 3; Singapore, Article 4; Switzerland, Articles 4(2) & 4(3); Thailand, Article 4; Vietnam, Article 3.

82 See, e.g., Cambodia-Indonesia BIT, Articles 3(3) and 3(4): "(3) If a Contracting Party has accorded special advantages to investors of any third state by virtue of agreements establishing customs unions, economic unions, monetary unions or similar institutions, or on the basis of interim agreements leading to such unions of institutions, that Contracting Party shall not be obliged to accord such advantages to investors of the other Contracting Party. (4) The provision of this Agreement shall not apply to matters of taxation in the territory of either Contracting Party. Such matters shall be governed by any Avoidance of Double Taxation Treaty between the two Contracting Parties and the domestic laws of each Contracting Party."

Some BITs also contain express carve-outs in relation to specific benefits and sectors; the Cambodia-Japan BIT in particular contains (in its Schedules) carve-outs in relation to a list of existing non-conforming measures and specified sectors and activities.

6 *Repatriation of Capital and Compensation for Losses*

At the time of writing, all publicly available BITs signed by Cambodia contain provisions allowing for the repatriation by the investor of capital invested and investment returns.

Cambodia's BITs also all contain a provision providing for most favoured nation treatment in respect of compensation for losses resulting from war or other armed conflict, revolution, riot or similar events in the territory of the host State.[83] A number of treaties (those concluded with Croatia, Cuba, the Czech Republic, France, Germany, Japan, Korea, Netherlands, Pakistan, the Philippines, Switzerland, Thailand, and Vietnam) also provide for national treatment in respect of such losses.[84] For example, the provisions of the Cambodia-Netherlands BIT state that "Nationals of the one Contracting Party who suffer losses in respect of their investments in the territory of the other Contracting Party owing to war or other armed conflict, revolution, a state of national emergency, revolt, insurrection or riot shall be accorded by the latter Contracting Party treatment, as regards restitution, indemnification, compensation or other settlement, no less favourable than that which that Contracting Party accords to its own nationals or to nationals of any third State, whichever is more favourable to the nationals concerned."

7 *Investor-State Dispute Settlement*

All of the publicly available BITs signed by Cambodia provide for an amicable settlement or "cooling off" period. After the specified period (six months, save for the three-month periods under the Netherlands and Thailand BITs and the 90-day period under the Japan BIT), the dispute may be submitted to formal proceedings.

The majority of BITs provide an investor with a menu of available fora, including one or more of ICSID arbitration, *ad hoc* arbitration under the

83 China, Article 5; Croatia, Article 6(1); Cuba, Article 5; Czech Republic, Article 4(1); France, Article 5(3); Germany, Article 4(3) & 4(4); Indonesia, Article 5; Japan, Article 13; Korea, Article 4(1); Malaysia, Article 3(2); Netherlands, Article 7; Pakistan, Article 6; Philippines, Articles 5; Singapore, Article 7; Switzerland, Article 6(2); Thailand, Article 6(2); Vietnam, Article 5.

84 *Ibid.*

UNCITRAL rules, ICC arbitration, and local court proceedings. However, some treaties provide only one option for arbitration (for example, the Cambodia-Germany BIT provides for ICSID arbitration only, and the Cambodia-Pakistan BIT provides for UNCITRAL arbitration only).

A number of Cambodia's BITs contain "fork in the road clauses",[85] which preclude further dispute resolution proceedings for disputes which have previously been submitted for resolution in another forum. Most commonly, these are intended to foreclose the availability of investor-State arbitration in circumstances where a dispute under the treaty has already been submitted to the local courts. Investors should be particularly mindful of the potential impact of such provisions in considering any potential proceedings to enforce the protections offered under Cambodia's domestic investment law (discussed above) in the local courts, as it is conceivable that such proceedings might operate as an election under the BIT's "fork in the road" clause, or otherwise make a claim before an international forum under the BIT inadmissible.

As noted above, the Cambodia-China BIT limits the right of ISDS to "a dispute involving the amount of compensation for expropriation".[86]

8 *State-to-State Dispute Settlement*

Cambodia's publicly available BITs stipulate that disputes between the Contracting States shall be resolved as far as possible through recourse to diplomatic channels. In the event that diplomatic settlement fails, a dispute shall be submitted to an arbitral tribunal.

Each BIT contains provisions for the appointment of an *ad hoc* tribunal; typically through agreement in the first instance, with a third party (for example the President of the International Court of Justice) making appointments in the absence of agreement.[87]

---

85 For example, the China, Croatia, Czech, Pakistan and Thailand BITs.

86 Cambodia-China BIT, Article 9(3). All disputes (including disputes concerning the amount of compensation for expropriation) may be submitted to the host State courts.

87 For example, Cambodia-Singapore BIT, Article 14(3) and Article 14(4) provide: "(3) Within two months of receipt of the request for arbitration, each Contracting Party shall appoint one arbitrator, and within two months of such appointment of the two arbitrators, the Contracting Parties shall appoint the third arbitrator. (4) If the tribunal shall not have been constituted within four months of receipt of the request for arbitration, either Contracting Party may, in the absence of any other agreement, invite the President of the International Court of Justice to appoint the arbitrator or arbitrators not yet appointed. If the President is a national of either Contracting Party or if he is unable to do so, the Vice-President may be invited to do so. If the Vice-President is a national of either Contracting Party or if he is unable to do so, the Member of the International Court of Justice next

IV Multilateral Investment Related Treaties and Organizations to which Cambodia is a Party

1 *ASEAN – ACIA*

Cambodia is a member of ASEAN, becoming the tenth member on 30 April 1999.[88] ASEAN has the aim and purpose of, *inter alia*, accelerating economic growth, social progress and cultural development in the region, promoting regional peace and stability and promoting active collaboration and mutual assistance on matters of common interest.[89]

Cambodia is a party to the ASEAN Comprehensive Investment Agreement (the "ACIA") which entered into force on 29 March 2012. It aims to create a free and open investment environment through the consolidation and expansion of existing agreements between ASEAN Member States.[90]

The ACIA contains substantive investment protections commonly found in BITs, such as provisions on non-discrimination, MFN treatment, fair and equitable treatment, full protection and security, and expropriation.

Beyond the usual provisions found in BITs, the ACIA also contains provisions aimed at enhancing cooperation between ASEAN States in the promotion[91] and facilitation of investment,[92] and to enhance ASEAN integration.[93]

Where a dispute arises between an investor and a Member State, the ACIA provides for various dispute resolution options, including the submission of a claim under the ICSID Convention, under the UNCITRAL Arbitration Rules, or to the KLRCA or any other regional centre for arbitration in ASEAN.[94] The availability of investor-State dispute settlement distinguishes the ACIA from many other multilateral investment promotion and free trade agreements.

The investment treaties between ASEAN and third States are addressed in greater detail in relevant chapter.

---

in seniority who is not a national of either Contracting Party may be invited to make the necessary appointments, and so on."

88 The other members being Brunei, Indonesia, Laos, Malaysia, Myanmar, Philippines, Singapore, Thailand and Vietnam.

89 ASEAN Overview, available at: http://www.asean.org/asean/about-asean/overview.

90 "Introduction to the ASEAN Comprehensive Investment Agreement", ASEAN *Briefing*, 12 April 2013. Available at: http://www.aseanbriefing.com/news/2013/04/12/introduction-to-the-asean-comprehensive-investment-agreement.html.

91 ACIA, Article 24.

92 *Ibid.*, Article 25.

93 *Ibid.*, Article 26.

94 *Ibid.*, Article 33.

2 *MIGA*

Cambodia is a Member Country of the Multilateral Investment Guarantee Agency (the "MIGA"). MIGA is a part of the World Bank Group and a multilateral investment insurance system against political risks, which offers investment protection for cross-border investments against losses resulting from, *inter alia*, currency transfer restrictions, expropriation and a government's (or, in certain circumstances, a State-owned enterprise's[95]) breach or repudiation of a contract with an investor.

V Multilateral Dispute Settlement Related Treaties

1 *ICSID Convention*

Cambodia is a party to the ICSID Convention (also known as the Washington Convention) of 1966, which established the International Centre for Settlement of Investment Disputes (or ICSID). Cambodia signed the ICSID Convention on 5 November 1993 and deposited its ratification on 20 December 2004. The ICSID Convention entered into force for Cambodia on 19 January 2005.[96] Cambodia has not issued any Article 25(4) notification or other reservation in relation to ICSID jurisdiction.

2 *New York Convention*

Cambodia acceded to the New York Convention on 5 January 1960.[97]

In May 2001, Cambodia passed the Law on the Approval and Implementation of the United Nations Convention on the Recognition and Enforcement of Foreign Arbitral Awards. This Law implements the New York Convention, and specifies the detailed procedures that parties should adhere to when seeking recognition and enforcement of foreign arbitration awards in the Cambodian courts.

Since the passage of that implementing law (and the 2006 Arbitration Law, based on the UNCITRAL Model Law, which now governs the recognition and enforcement of foreign awards), it appears that at least two arbitral awards

95 MIGA Investment Guarantee Guide, July 2015. Available at: http://www.miga.org/documents/IGGenglish.pdf.

96 The list of ICSID member States is available on the ICSID website at: https://icsid.worldbank.org/apps/ICSIDWEB/about/Pages/Database-of-Member-States.aspx.

97 The list of contracting States to the New York Convention is available on the New York Convention website at: http://www.newyorkconvention.org/contracting-states/list-of-contracting-states.

have been "upheld" by the Cambodian Court of Appeal.[98] Further, in 2014, the Supreme Court of Cambodia affirmed a Court of Appeal decision to recognise and enforce a Korean Commercial Arbitration Board against a Cambodian company in favour of a foreign company. The application of the Arbitration Law is, however, likely to remain inconsistent at best in the coming years.[99]

Cambodia did not make any declarations, reservations or other notifications to the New York Convention.[100]

The New York Convention seeks to provide common legislative standards for the recognition of arbitration agreements and court recognition and enforcement of foreign and non-domestic arbitral awards. It obliges parties to ensure that foreign and non-domestic arbitral awards will not be discriminated against but will be recognised and enforced in the same way as domestic awards in each of the signatory States.[101]

The New York Convention does not address investment protection specifically, but rather governs the enforcement of foreign-seated arbitral awards (including those arising out of investments). The Convention, and its application by the Cambodian courts, is therefore critical to ensuring that an arbitral award provides an effective remedy that is enforceable within Cambodia.

In addition to commercial disputes concerning investments, international investment law disputes can be resolved through arbitration under a variety of arbitral rules other than through the ICSID system: most commonly under the UNCITRAL Arbitration Rules, but also often under the Stockholm Chamber of Commerce (SCC) Rules or International Chamber of Commerce (ICC) Rules, whether administered by arbitral institutions such as the Permanent Court of Arbitration or on an *ad hoc* basis. For such awards that will be rendered outside of the enforcement (and annulment) framework of the ICSID Convention, the New York Convention plays a significant role in enforcement.

98 Haw & Slott in Moser, *op. cit.*, CAM-12. However, as discussed in section II above, there is little detail available regarding such enforcement efforts.

99 See the detailed discussion in section II above.

100 Status of the Convention on the Recognition and Enforcement of Foreign Arbitral Awards (New York, 1958): http://www.uncitral.org/uncitral/en/uncitral_texts/arbitration/NYConvention_status.html.

101 See UNCITRAL's comments on the objectives of the New York Convention: "The Convention's principal aim is that foreign and non-domestic arbitral awards will not be discriminated against and it obliges Parties to ensure such awards are recognized and generally capable of enforcement in their jurisdiction in the same way as domestic awards." Available at: http://www.uncitral.org/uncitral/uncitral_texts/arbitration/NYConvention.html.

VI International Investment Arbitration Jurisprudence

Cambodia has been a party to one international investment dispute in the public domain: *Cambodia Power Company v Kingdom of Cambodia and Electricité du Cambodge*.[102]

The claim did not involve claims under any investment treaty, and the Tribunal's jurisdiction was based on the State's consent to arbitrate under various contracts.

As an ICSID claim, however, it may nevertheless provide some guidance as to how Cambodia might be expected to approach any Treaty claim that may be brought against it.

Cambodia Power Company v Kingdom of Cambodia and Electricité du Cambodge (*ICSID* Case No. ARB/09/18)

Tribunal:	Neil Kaplan QC (President, United Kingdom) John Beechey (United Kingdom) Toby Landau (United Kingdom)
Case Initiated:	16 September 2009
Award Rendered:	22 April 2013

Background Facts

The Claimant was a Cambodian company that was wholly owned by Beacon Hill Associates, Inc, a Delaware corporation.

In 1995, the Claimant's owners had successfully won a bid to produce a 60MW electric power plant in Phnom Penh, and to sell that plant's capacity and electricity to Electricité du Cambodge ("EDC"), then a department of the Ministry of Industry, Mines and Energy, for a 20 to 25-year term. In 1996, EDC became a limited liability company owned by the State of Cambodia, and the Claimant's owners formed the Claimant, Cambodia Power Company ("CPC"), a limited liability company under Cambodian law.

Following a series of novations, CPC became party to a power purchase agreement (between the State, EDC and CPC) (the "PPA"), an implementation agreement (between the State and CPC), and a guarantee (between the State and CPC).

102 *Cambodia Power Company v Kingdom of Cambodia and Electricité du Cambodge* ICSID Arbitration ARB/09/18.

CPC contended that from 1998 to 2004, the State of Cambodia and EDC breached their contractual obligations to support the project to build and operate the power plant, and that as a result, CPC was not able to build the power plant.

CPC argued that it ultimately accepted Cambodia's and EDC's repudiation of the project contracts, and that such alleged repudiation caused the Claimant to lose its entire investment and the benefit of its bargain.

The Claimant brought claims totalling some US$300M, under the relevant contract (the PPA, implementation agreement and guarantee) and under customary international law, relying on the three arbitration agreements contained in the PPA, implementation agreement and guarantee. These agreements, as amended and novated, provided for arbitration under the ICSID Rules.

Key Legal Outcomes

- Jurisdiction

The Respondent objected to the Tribunal's jurisdiction over EDC on the basis that EDC was not properly designated to the Centre as an agency of the State within the meaning of Article 25(1) of the Convention.

The Tribunal found that "in order for there to be a '*designation*' of an agency or subdivision of a Contracting State under the Convention, there has to be a written designation which is communicated to the Centre. It may be possible for this to be done other than in a direct communication from the Contracting State to the Centre, such as in a Treaty or Legislation that would inevitably have public notoriety. But in most cases, it would be by direct communication and thus cannot be complied with by the investor itself providing a document to the Centre which contains, or is said to contain, a designation."[103]

Further, that designation, in addition to being a public communication made by the State, "must also represent an unequivocal intention of the State to consider the entity as its agency or subdivision".[104] A mere contractual promise to designate a particular agency in the event that the host State ratified the ICSID Convention (which had not occurred when the relevant contracts were

103 Decision on Jurisdiction, para. 246. The decision is available on the ICSID website at: https://icsid.worldbank.org/ICSID/FrontServlet?requestType=CasesRH&actionVal=showDoc&docId=DC3212_En&caseId=C760.

104 *Ibid.*, para. 259.

signed) did not suffice, and the Claimant was unable to make out any of the criteria necessary for an estoppel to arise under international law.[105]

Accordingly, the matter proceeded against the Kingdom of Cambodia only, on the basis of a contractual agreement to submit to ICSID arbitration.

As a separate issue, the Respondents also objected to the consolidation of claims under three separate contractual agreements into one proceeding. The Tribunal found that the three arbitration agreements (contained in the PPA, implementation agreement and guarantee) were sufficiently compatible, as a matter of contractual interpretation, such that the Respondent was found to have consented to having claims under all three agreements being heard by a single tribunal.[106]

The Respondents also objected that the wording of the relevant arbitration clause did not confer jurisdiction on the Tribunal to consider questions of customary international law. The Tribunal rejected this objection, holding the clauses sufficiently broad and finding that "parties can always consent to exclude customary international law from the scope of their dispute resolution clause. However, one would expect this to be done expressly and unequivocally."[107]

- Merits

The Award rendered on 22 April 2013 remains unpublished, and there is little publicly available information about the merits arguments run by either side.

However, the Kingdom of Cambodia's press release confirmed that the Tribunal held that "the Kingdom of Cambodia did not breach the agreements directly or indirectly through the actions of EDC, and dismissed all of the claims [which would necessarily include the contractual claims and the claims under customary international law] brought against the Kingdom of Cambodia."[108]

The State's press release also indicated that the State was awarded some US$5.6M in legal costs.

105 Both parties accepted these were "(a) a clear and unequivocal statement or conduct; (b) reliance on that statement or conduct by one party; and (c) detriment to the party invoking the estoppel or an advantage to the party who made the statement.": *Ibid.*, para. 261.

106 *Ibid.*, para. 161.

107 *Ibid.*, para. 335.

108 Press Release of the Royal Government of the Kingdom of Cambodia, 26 April 2013. Available at: http://www.pressocm.gov.kh/files/documents/20130426_Press-Release_The-Royal-Government_The-Kingdom_Cambodia_EN.pdf.

VII Outlook: Anticipated Developments

As seen above, Cambodia participated fully in the only claim brought against it under the ICSID Rules to date, in which it appears that it was wholly or at least substantially successful on the merits.

Although no new BITs appear to have come into force since 2009 (the last BIT to come into force was the Cambodia-Czech Republic BIT, on 23 October 2009), Cambodia signed BITs with Belarus and Russia in 2014, and remains publicly committed to negotiating and signing investment treaties. A publicly available June 2014 presentation by the Council for the Development of Cambodia[109] indicates that BITs are under negotiation with Azerbaijan, Egypt, the United Kingdom, Hungary, Iran, Libya, Macedonia, Myanmar, Algeria, Bangladesh, Bulgaria, Malta, Turkey, Russia,[110] Israel, Qatar, Belgium-Luxembourg Economic Union, Ukraine, and the USA.

Further, a 2015 US Department of State report states that Cambodia is planning "[f]uture [BIT] agreements with Algeria, Bangladesh, Belarus, the Belgium-Luxembourg Economic Union, Bulgaria, Myanmar, Egypt, Hungary, Israel, Iran, Libya, Macedonia, Malta, Qatar, Russia, Turkey, the United Kingdom, and Ukraine."[111]

Accordingly, it appears that bilateral investment treaties remain a key part of Cambodia's strategy for attracting FDI.

In relation to arbitration and the rule of law in Cambodia, the NCAC received its first notice of arbitration in May 2015;[112] the proceedings concern the lease of a factory in Phnom Penh between a foreign national and a Cambodian landlord. The Centre's administration of this first proceeding, and how any award is treated in any eventual enforcement action before the courts,

109 Sok Chenda Sophea (Minister Attached to the Prime Minister and Secretary General Council for the Development of Cambodia), "FDIs Trend in Cambodia", Available at: http://www.cdc-crdb.gov.kh/cdc/Donor_Development_Cooperation_Programs/Japan/12th_policy_dialogue_on_oda/downloads/1_2_Cambodia_FDIs_Trend_12_June_2014.pdf.

110 The UNCTAD International Investment Agreements Navigator website indicates this treaty was signed in March 2014. It is not yet in force.

111 US Department of State, Cambodia Investment Climate Statement 2015, page 17. Available at http://www.state.gov/documents/organization/241718.pdf. The UNCTAD International Investment Agreements Navigator website indicates that the Cambodia-Russia treaty was signed in March 2014 and that the Cambodia-Belarus treaty was signed in April 2014. At the time of writing, neither treaty is yet in force.

112 See: https://www.cambodiadaily.com/business/arbitration-body-receives-first-complaint-84450/ and http://kluwerarbitrationblog.com/2015/06/10/cambodias-arbitration-centre-sets-off-on-its-first-flight/.

will substantially influence potential users' perception of the NCAC, and the extent to which commercial parties will agree to arbitrate under the NCAC Rules or refer cases for administration by the NCAC. However, as with any nascent arbitral institution, it is likely to take time for it to be perceived as a "safe" choice for inclusion in arbitration agreements, especially in comparison to its more established competitor institutions within the region.

CHAPTER 4

Indonesia[1]

I Introduction

The Republic of Indonesia declared independence on 17 August 1945[2] and is a unitary democratic republic with a presidential system.[3] The Indonesian legal system is a unique confluence of three legal traditions: Roman-Dutch civil law, customary or "*adat*" law and sharia law.[4]

Indonesia is Southeast Asia's largest economy; displaying growth of 5.02% in 2014[5] and an estimated growth of 4.7% in 2015.[6] Indonesia is a popular destination for foreign direct investment ("FDI"). According to the UNCTAD World Investment Prospects Survey, Indonesia ranks among the top three destinations for FDI in 2014–2016.[7]

In 2014, Indonesia's FDI inflow was USD 22.58 billion.[8] Indonesia Investment Coordinating Board ("BKPM") reported that FDI and domestic direct investment ("DDI") in Indonesia was approximately USD33.38 billion[9] in 2014, marking a 16.2% increase from the previous year.[10]

---

1 This chapter has been drafted by Mr Alvin Yap of Eversheds LLP, Singapore, with assistance from Mr Richard Tyacke, Eversheds LLP, and reviewed by Mr Wisjnu Wardhana of Hakim Dan Rekan, Jakarta, Indonesia.

2 Indonesia Profile – Timeline, BBC, http://www.bbc.co.uk/news/world-asia-pacific-15114517.

3 "Politics and Government", *Portal Nasional Republik Indonesia*, http://www.indonesia.go.id/en/indonesia-glance/politics-and-government.

4 Dewi Savitri Reni, "Update: The Indonesian Legal System and Legal Research", http://www.nyulawglobal.org/globalex/Indonesia1.html#overview.

5 "Indonesia Economic Outlook 2016", Global Business Guide: http://www.gbgindonesia.com/en/main/why_indonesia/2016/indonesia_economic_outlook_2016_economy_not_at_the_mercy_of_global_markets_11430.php.

6 *Ibid.*

7 UNCTAD World Investment Prospects Survey 2014–2016: http://unctad.org/en/PublicationsLibrary/webdiaeia2015d4_en.pdf.

8 Country Fact Sheet: Indonesia, UNCTAD: http://unctad.org/sections/dite_dir/docs/wir2015/wir15_fs_id_en.pdf.

9 Using a conversion rate of 1 Indonesian Rupiah to 0.000072 US Dollar. "Domestic and Foreign Direct Investment Realization in Quarter IV and January – December 2014", *Indonesia Investment Coordinating Board*, 28 January 2015: http://www4.bkpm.go.id/file_uploaded/public/Bahan%20Paparan%20TW%20IV%202014-Eng.pdf.

10 *Ibid.*

 | DOI 10.1163/9789004335257_006

FDI into Indonesia has a strong regional character. In 2014, there were four non-Asian countries in the top ten countries of origin investing into Indonesia.[11] Singapore was the largest contributor by a broad margin, investing around USD5.83 bn, which more than doubled Japanese investment at USD2.7bn.[12]

Indonesia's mining sector was the most popular destination of FDI in 2014, having received approximately USD 4.66 bn of investment, totaling 552 projects. Interestingly, Indonesia's mining sector receives far less attention from domestic investments, ranking 11th on the list of destinations for DDI.[13] Other popular sectors for FDI include the food sector, transportation, warehouse and telecommunication sector and the metal, machinery and electronic industry sector.[14]

II Indonesia's National Arbitration and Investment Legislation

1 *Indonesia's Arbitration Legislation and Institutions*

Indonesian Arbitration Law

Prior to 1999, arbitration proceedings in Indonesia were governed by Articles 615 to 651 of the colonial Dutch Code of Civil Procedure, the *Reglemen op de Burgerlijke Rechtsvordering* (the "RV").[15] This old legal regime for arbitration was criticized for not being comprehensive enough to cover all the arbitration issues. In particular, it was silent on the recognition and enforcement of foreign arbitration awards. Also, some provisions had become outdated and were no longer compatible with modern times. For instance, under this old legal regime, a woman was prohibited from becoming an arbitrator.[16]

On 12 August 1999, the Government of the Republic of Indonesia promulgated Law No. 30 of 1999, on Arbitration and Alternative Dispute Resolution ("Law No. 30 of 1999"), repealing the relevant articles in the RV. However, Law No. 30 of 1999, which is not based on the UNCITRAL Model Law of 1985, should not be seen as a clean break from the old legal regime. In fact, many of the relevant provisions from the RV are reflected in Law No. 30 of 1999.[17] There

11 *Ibid.*

12 *Ibid.*

13 *Ibid.*

14 *Ibid.*

15 Michael J. Moser (ed), *Arbitration in Asia*, 2nd ed (JurisNet, LLC, 2009) at IND-6-7.

16 Hadiputranto, Hadinoto & Partners, *Arbitration in Indonesia, Law No. 30 of 1999 Arbitration and Alternative Dispute Resolutions*, p. 2, available at: http://www.hhp.co.id/files/Uploads/Documents/Type%202/HHP/br_hhp_arbitrationindonesia.pdf.

17 Michael Pryles (ed), *Dispute Resolution in Asia*, (Kluwer Law International, 2006), p. 178.

are, however, a number of features in Law No. 30 of 1999 that set it apart from the old legal regime. In particular, it clarifies the law on the enforcement of foreign arbitral awards and allows parties to apply to an arbitral institution for a binding opinion as to a point of law or the interpretation of a provision in their underlying agreement.[18]

Following the old regime,[19] under Article 5, paragraph 1 of Law No. 30 of 1999, only disputes "in the commercial sector concerning rights which, according to the law and regulations, have the force of law and are fully controlled by the parties in dispute" are arbitrable.[20] Article 5, paragraph 2 of Law No. 30 of 1999 further restricts "disputes that cannot be settled amicably under the regulations and the force of law" from resolution by arbitration.

Previously, Article 616 of the RV enumerated certain disputes that could not be arbitrated, which included any agreement pertaining to gifts and bequests for maintenance, lodging or clothing, divorce, judicial separation or dissolution of martial community property and the legal status of persons.[21] It is likely that disputes that fall under Article 616 of the RV would also be considered to be non-arbitrable under Law No. 30 of 1999.

Article 1, paragraph 3 of Law No. 30 of 1999 defines an arbitration agreement as an agreement "in the form of an arbitration clause set out in a written agreement made by the parties before the dispute occurs, or a separate arbitration agreement made by the parties after the dispute occurs". Thus, an arbitration clause in a third-party agreement that has been incorporated by reference in an underlying agreement between two parties may not be sufficient to constitute a valid arbitration agreement.[22] If so, this would be an important restriction to be noted by persons considering arbitrations seated in Indonesia.

Interestingly, Article 8, paragraph 2 of Law No. 30 of 1999 prescribes the content of a notification of arbitration. A claimant, in its notification of the arbitration, must clearly state: (a) the names and addresses of the parties; (b) reference to the applicable arbitration clause or agreement; (c) the agreement or problem in dispute; (d) the basis for the claim and the amount claimed, if any; (e) the method of resolution desired; and (f) the agreement entered into by the parties concerning the number of arbitrators, or if no such

18 *Ibid.*

19 Michael J. Moser (ed), *op. cit.*, (JurisNet, LLC, 2009) at IND-10-11.

20 Article 5, paragraph 1 of Law No. 30 of 1999, based on an unofficial translation of Law No. 30 of 1999, available at: http://www.hhp.co.id/files/Uploads/Documents/Type%202/HHP/br_hhp_arbitrationindonesia.pdf.

21 Michael J. Moser (ed), *op. cit.*, (JurisNet, LLC, 2009) at IND-10.

22 *Ibid.*, at IND-18.

agreement has been entered into, the claimant may submit a proposal about the odd number of arbitrators desired. Further, Article 8, paragraph 1 of Law No. 30 of 1999 requires the claimant to inform the respondent by registered letter, telegram, telex, fax or email, or by courier that the terms for arbitration between the claimant and the respondent apply.

Article 12 of Law No. 30 of 1999 sets out restrictions of who may be appointed as an arbitrator. Under Article 12, an arbitrator must (a) be competent to perform legal actions; (b) be at least 35 years old; (c) not have a family relationship by blood or marriage to the second degree with one of the disputing parties; (d) not have any financial or other interest in the arbitration award; and (e) have at least 15 years' experience and active expertise in the field. Further, under Article 12, paragraph 2 of Law No. 30 of 1999, judges, prosecutors, courts and other judicial officials may not be appointed as arbitrators. However, it deserves mention there is no restriction in Law No. 30 of 1999 on the nationality of the arbitrator.

If the parties are unable to agree on the choice of arbitrators, or if no terms have been agreed concerning the appointment of arbitrators, the Chairman of the District Court may appoint the arbitrator or the members of the arbitral tribunal.[23] "District Court" is defined in Article 1, paragraph 4 of Law No. 30 of 1999 as the District Court that has jurisdiction over the Respondent's domicile.

With regard to arbitral procedures, Article 28 of Law No. 30 of 1999 provides that the Indonesian language must be used in all arbitration proceedings, although the parties may choose to use another language with the consent of the arbitral tribunal. Parties are free to determine in a written agreement the arbitration procedure to be used, provided that it does not conflict with the provisions of Law No. 30 of 1999.[24] Under Law No. 30 of 1999, all examinations of disputes by the tribunal must be closed to the public.[25] Arbitration proceedings must be conducted in writing[26] but oral proceedings are permissible with the parties' consent, or if deemed necessary by the tribunal.[27] In particular, Article 49, paragraph 1 of Law No. 30 of 1999 provides that, by the instruction of the tribunal or at the request of one of the parties, one or more witnesses or expert witnesses may be called to be heard.

As regards provisional measures, Article 32 paragraph 1, provides that, at the request of one of the parties, the tribunal may make a provisional award

23 Article 13, paragraph 1 of Law No. 30 of 1999.

24 *Ibid.*, Article 31, para. 1.

25 *Ibid.*, Article 27.

26 *Ibid.*, Article 36, para. 1.

27 *Ibid.*, Article 36, para. 2.

or other interlocutory decision on how to organize the examination of the dispute, including awarding a security attachment, ordering the deposit of goods with third parties, or the sale of perishable goods.

Article 57 of Law No. 30 of 1999 provides that the award must be rendered 30 days after the dispute is closed. This is a particularly onerous provision on arbitrators, especially since Law No. 30 of 1999 does not seem to allow a tribunal to extend this time limit even if special circumstances exist. Further, Article 20 of Law No. 30 of 1999 provides that, if an arbitrator or arbitration panel, for no valid reason, fails to render an award within the specified period, the arbitrator(s) may be ordered to pay the parties compensation for the costs and losses caused by the delay.

Indonesia's Arbitral Institutions and Rules

There are several arbitration institutions in Indonesia. The most commonly used is the Badan Arbitrase Nasional Indonesia ("BANI").[28] BANI maintains a panel of local and international arbitrators and utilizes rules of procedures which are available in both Indonesian and English. Currently, BANI has more than 100 listed arbitrators with various professional backgrounds, of which about 30 per cent are foreign nationals.[29] BANI also maintains hearing rooms and provides basic secretarial and other administrative services, including registering BANI awards with the Indonesian courts.[30]

Another arbitration body is the Capital Market Arbitration Board ("BAPMI"), which was set up in 2002 by the Indonesian Capital Supervisory Agency and other Indonesian capital market organizations and associations.[31] Like BANI, BAPMI maintains its own panel of arbitrators.[32] It administers arbitrations relating to capital market disputes.[33] BAPMI also has its own rules, and has additional rules for the conduct of arbitrators.[34]

The National Shariah Arbitration Board was established by the Indonesian Uleme Council in 1993 to resolve disputes arising out of shariah transactions

---

28 Michael J. Moser (ed), *op. cit.*, (JurisNet, LLC, 2009) at IND-11.

29 "Guide to Regional Arbitration – Indonesian National Board of Arbitration (BANI)", Global Arbitration Review online, 2015: http://globalarbitrationreview.com/regional-arbitration/5/category/89/region/19/entry/282/.

30 Michael J. Moser (ed), *op. cit.*, (JurisNet, LLC, 2009) at IND-12.

31 *Ibid.*

32 *Ibid.*

33 *Ibid.*

34 *Ibid.*

or transactions based on Islamic principles.[35] Like BANI and BAPMI, it has its own rules and panels of arbitrators.[36]

Article 34, paragraph 1 of Law No. 30 of 1999 allows a dispute to be conducted through a national or international arbitration institution, with the agreement of the parties. Further, Article 34, paragraph 2 of Law No. 30 of 1999 provides that where a dispute is conducted through an arbitration institution as contemplated in Article 34, paragraph 1, it "should be conducted according to the rules and procedures of the institution chosen, unless otherwise determined by the parties". Therefore, where parties choose a particular arbitral institution to administer their dispute, the rules and procedures of that institution will apply to the arbitration proceedings, provided they do not conflict with Law No. 30 of 1999.[37]

Indonesian Courts and Arbitration

Law No. 30 of 1999 requires the Indonesian Courts to enforce an arbitration agreement. Under Article 3 of Law No. 30 of 1999, the District Court[38] "has no jurisdiction to try disputes between parties bound by an arbitration agreement". Further, Article 11, paragraph 1 provides that the existence of a written arbitration agreement eliminates the rights of the parties to submit the resolution of the dispute or difference of opinion contained in the agreement to the District Court. The Supreme Court has held that the Court must, on its own initiative, dismiss any claim if it does not have jurisdiction.[39] A challenge to the Court's jurisdiction must be brought at the outset of a case, and the Court must rule on it as a preliminary matter before examining the merits.[40]

Article 11, paragraph 2 further provides that the District Court must not interfere in any dispute settlement which has been determined by arbitration, except in particular cases determined in Law No. 30 of 1999, such as in the appointment, removal and replacement of arbitrators, and the enforcement and annulment of awards.

Law No. 30 of 1999 is silent on whether the Indonesian Courts may issue interim measures of protection in aid of arbitration. Given that Article 11, paragraph 2 restricts the Courts' interference in arbitration to the particular cases

35 *Ibid.*

36 *Ibid.*

37 Article 31, para. 1 of Law No. 30 of 1999.

38 As defined in Article 1, para. 4 of Law No. 30 of 1999.

39 Michael J. Moser (ed), *op. cit.*, (JurisNet, LLC, 2009) at IND-21.

40 *Ibid.*

set out in Law No. 30 of 1999, it appears that an applicant seeking interim measures from the Courts in aid of arbitration would be very unlikely to succeed.

As regards interim measures of protection issued by the arbitral tribunal itself, Law No. 30 of 1999 is also silent on whether the Court may enforce such tribunal-ordered interim measures. This may lead to the unfortunate conclusion that interim measures ordered by the tribunal cannot be judicially enforced against uncooperative parties.[41] However, it has been suggested that Article 61, which provides for judicial enforcement of arbitral awards, may extend to interim measures of protection.[42]

Unlike under the old legal regime, a party may not appeal the award to the Courts under Law No. 30 of 1999.[43]

Moreover, in a departure from the UNCITRAL Model Law, Law No. 30 of 1999 does not contain provisions on the setting aside of arbitral awards. Rather, Articles 70 to 72 of Law No. 30 of 1999 provide for three very limited grounds for the annulment of an arbitral award. Under Article 70, an application for annulment may be made only if it is alleged that (a) letters or documents were submitted in the hearing which are admitted to be forged or are declared to be forgeries after the award has been rendered; (b) documents are found after the award has been rendered which are decisive in nature and were deliberately concealed by the opposing party; or (c) the award was made based on fraud committed by one of the parties. If the application is granted, the Chairman of the District Court must determine the consequence of the annulment of the whole or only part of the award.[44]

As regards enforcement of the award, Law No. 30 of 1999 sets out two legal regimes for enforcement, depending on whether the award is an "International arbitration award". Article 1, paragraph 9 of Law No. 30 of 1999 defines an "International arbitration award" as "an award handed down by an arbitration institution or individual arbitrator outside the jurisdiction of the Republic of Indonesia, or an award by an arbitration institution or individual arbitrator, which, under the provisions of Indonesia law, is deemed to be an international arbitration award". An award rendered in an arbitration seated in Indonesia would be a "domestic arbitration award".[45]

---

41 Philip J. McConnaughay, *International Commercial Arbitration in Asia*, (Juris Publishing, Inc., 2002), at 3–17.

42 *Ibid.*

43 Article 60 of Law No. 30 of 1999. See also Philip J. McConnaughay, *International Commercial Arbitration in Asia*, (Juris Publishing, Inc., 2002), at 3–20.

44 Article 72, para. 3 of Law No. 30 of 1999.

45 Michael Pryles (ed), *Dispute Resolution in Asia*, (Kluwer Law International, 2006), at 198.

The First Part of Chapter VI of Law No. 30 of 1999, which contains Articles 59 to 64, sets out the provisions concerning enforcement of a domestic award. Under Article 59, paragraph 1, within 30 days from the date the award is rendered, the original text or an authentic copy of the award must be delivered to the Clerk of District Court and registered there. Otherwise, the award will be rendered unenforceable under Article 59, paragraph 4 of Law No. 30 of 1999.

Article 61 of Law No. 30 of 1999 provides that, if the parties do not implement the award, it may be enforced by an order from the Chairman of the District Court at the request of one of the parties. The Chairman, before issuing such an order, must first examine whether the award fulfils Articles 4 and 5 of Law No. 30 of 1999, which set out the formal requirements for an arbitration agreement and the disputes that are arbitrable.[46] The Chairman must also examine the award to ensure that it does not conflict with public morality and order before issuing the order for its execution.[47] Article 62, paragraph 4 of Law No. 30 of 1999 makes clear that the Chairman of the District Court will not examine the reasons or considerations for the award.

As regards the enforcement of an international arbitration award, this is governed by the Second Part of Chapter VI of Law No. 30 of 1999, which contains Articles 65 to 69. Article 65 makes clear that the Central Jakarta District Court has the authority to handle matters with respect to the recognition and enforcement of international arbitration awards. Article 66 provides that an international arbitration award will only be recognized and enforced in Indonesia if: (a) it is rendered by an arbitrator or an arbitration panel in a country which is bound to Indonesia by a bilateral or multilateral treaty on the recognition and enforcement of international arbitration awards; (b) it is an award within the scope of commercial law under Indonesian law; (c) it does not conflict with public order; (d) it may only be enforced in Indonesia after obtaining a writ of execution from the Chairman of the Central Jakarta District Court; and (e) if the State of the Republic of Indonesia is a party to the dispute in the award, the award may only be enforced after obtaining an *exequatur* from the Supreme Court of Indonesia.

With regard to the requirement under Article 66(a) that the award is rendered by a tribunal in a country which is bound by a bilateral or multilateral treaty on the recognition and enforcement of international arbitration awards, it should be noted that Indonesia has ratified the 1958 New York Convention on the Recognition and Enforcement of Foreign Arbitral Awards.[48] Therefore,

46 Article 62, para. 2 of Law No. 30 of 1999.

47 *Ibid.*

48 Ratified by Presidential Decree No. 34 of 1981.

an award rendered in a dispute of a commercial nature in any other signatory State of the 1958 New York Convention will fall under Article 66(a) of Law No. 30 of 1999. Under Article 67, paragraph 2(c) of Law No. 30 of 1999, the application for enforcement of an international arbitration award must be accompanied by a statement from the diplomatic representative of Indonesia in the country where the international arbitration award was rendered, stating that the claimant's country is bound to Indonesia by a bilateral or multilateral treaty on the recognition and enforcement of international arbitration awards.

No appeal or cassation to the Supreme Court is allowed if a writ of execution is issued by the Chairman of the Central Jakarta District Court under Article 66(d), which recognizes and enforces the international arbitration award.[49] By contrast, if the writ of execution is not issued, which means the award is not recognized and enforceable, an appeal may be made to the Supreme Court.[50]

2 *Indonesia's Investment Laws*

Law No. 25 of 2007 on Capital Investment (the "Investment Law") regulates domestic and foreign investment in Indonesia.[51] It should be noted that under Article 5(2) of the Investment Law, unless otherwise provided by law, foreign capital investment must take the form of a limited liability company under Indonesian law and be domiciled in Indonesia.

One important feature of the Investment Law is found at Article 6(1), which provides that the Indonesian Government shall provide equal treatment to all investors, regardless of their country of origin, who undertake investment activity in Indonesia in accordance with prevailing laws and regulations. Article 6(2) of the Investment Law specifies that Article 6(1) is not applicable to an investor from a country which obtains special rights based on an agreement with Indonesia, such as under a bilateral investment treaty ("BIT"). An investor from a country who has a BIT with Indonesia would have to rely on the BIT for protection, rather than on Article 6(1) of the Investment Law.

Another important feature of the Investment Law is found at Article 7(1), which provides that the Indonesian Government will not undertake any nationalization or "take over the ownership rights of the investor", unless by law. In the event that such nationalization or expropriation occurs, the Government will grant compensation, the amount of which will be specified based on the

49 Article 68 para. 1 of Law No. 30 of 1999.

50 *Ibid.*, Article 68, para. 2.

51 Unofficial translation available at: http://www.flevin.com/id/lgso/translations/JICA%20Mirror/english/3002_UU_25_2007_e.html.

market value.[52] Crucially, Article 7(3) of the Investment Law provides that if there is no consensus on the amount of compensation among the parties, the dispute shall be settled by arbitration.

Article 14 of the Investment Law sets out certain rights granted to investors. It states that each investor is entitled to: (a) certainty of rights, law and protection; (b) transparent information on the business sectors being operated; (c) rights to service; and (d) all facilities under prevailing laws and regulations.

Article 32 of the Investment Law sets out provisions on the settlement of disputes between investors and the Indonesian Government. Article 32(1) provides that capital investment disputes between the Government and investors which cannot be settled amicably may be settled by arbitration or by alternative dispute settlement or in court in accordance with the prevailing laws and regulations.[53] If the dispute is between the Government and a foreign investor, it shall be settled through international arbitration based upon agreement between the parties.[54] However, if the dispute is between the Government and a domestic investor, it shall be settled through arbitration based on an agreement between the parties. If such arbitration fails, the settlement of dispute shall be conducted in court.[55]

Article 12 permits the Government, based on a Presidential Regulation, to determine certain business sectors closed to foreign investment, or open to foreign investment, subject to certain conditions. The Presidential Regulation in which this is done is known as the "Negative List" and is updated typically every three or four years.[56] As at the date of writing, the latest Negative List was Presidential Regulation No. 39 of 2014.[57] Under Presidential Regulation No. 39 of 2014, more restrictions have been placed on foreign capital ownership of small scale power plants (1–10MW), oil and gas drilling and support services, construction and installation of electricity services and telecommunication value-added services.[58] Further, under Presidential Regulation No. 39 of 2014, there are 15 business sectors that are closed to foreign investment, with the majority of them in the transportation industry.[59] Overall, there are fewer

52 Article 7(2) of the Investment Law.

53 *Ibid.*, Article 32(2).

54 *Ibid.*, Article 32(4).

55 *Ibid.*, Article 32(3).

56 Oentoeng Suria & Partners, Investing in Indonesia, An introduction of investors, 2014, at p. 9, available at: https://www.ashurst.com/page.aspx?id_Content=10473.

57 BKPM, Presidential Regulation Number 39 of Year 2014 on List of Business Fields Closed to Investment and Business Fields Open, with Condition, to Investment, 16 May 2014, available at: https://www5.jetro.go.jp/newsletter/jkt/2014/140516BKPM_English.pdf.

58 *Ibid.*, pp. 14–16.

59 *Ibid.*, p. 30.

business sectors that are closed or open with conditions to foreign investment under Presidential Regulation No. 39 of 2014, compared with the preceding Negative List,[60] which reflects an increased openness to foreign investment.

Indonesia also has industry-specific regulations that may apply, depending on the industry in which the investment is made. For instance, in 2014, Indonesia issued a new regulation to tighten controls on the export of coal and coal products.[61] Under this regulation, a company must be recognized by the Minister of Trade as a Registered Coal Exporter before it may export coal and coal products. As regards Indonesia's capital markets, they are regulated by Law No. 8 of 1995.[62]

III Indonesia's Bilateral Investment Treaties

1 *Overview*

Indonesia signed its first Bilateral Investment Treaty ("BIT") on 30 January 1968, with Denmark.[63] Since then, at the time of writing, Indonesia has signed at least 70 other BITs,[64] of which at least 52 have entered into force.[65]

---

60 *Ibid.*, p. 30.

61 Minister of Trade Regulation No. 39/M-DAG/PER/7/2014 of 2014, see Oentoeng Suria & Partners, Indonesian Mining Law – New Regulation Exporting Coal, August 2014, available at: https://www.ashurst.com/publication-list.aspx?id_Content=1362&expandOfficeList=true&id_queryContent=6579&page=4.

62 Oentoeng Suria & Partners, Investing in Indonesia, An introduction of investors, 2014, at p. 14, available at: https://www.ashurst.com/page.aspx?id_Content=10473.

63 Investment Policy Hub, Indonesia, available at: http://investmentpolicyhub.unctad.org/IIA/CountryBits/97.

64 Indonesia has signed BITs with Algeria, Argentina, Australia, Bangladesh, Belgium-Luxembourg Economic Union, Bolivarian Republic of Venezuela, Bulgaria, Cambodia, Chile, China, Croatia, Cuba, Czech Republic, Denmark, Egypt, Finland, France, Germany, Guyana, Hungary, India, Islamic Republic of Iran, Italy, Jamaica, Jordan, Kyrgyzstan, Lao People's Democratic Republic, Libya, Malaysia, Mauritius, Mongolia, Morocco, Mozambique, Netherlands, Norway, Pakistan, People's Democratic Republic of Korea, Philippines, Poland, Qatar, Republic of Korea, Romania, Russian Federation, Saudi Arabia, Serbia, Singapore, Slovakia, Spain, Sri Lanka, Sudan, Suriname, Sweden, Switzerland, Syrian Arab Republic, Tajikistan, Thailand, Tunisia, Turkey, Turkmenistan, Ukraine, United Kingdom, Uzbekistan, Vietnam, Yemen, and Zimbabwe; see: http://investmentpolicyhub.unctad.org/IIA/CountryBits/97.

65 UNCTAD reports that Indonesia's BITs with the following States have entered into force: Argentina, Australia, Bangladesh, Belgium-Luxembourg Economic Union, Bolivarian Republic of Venezuela, Bulgaria, China, Cuba, Czech Republic, Denmark, Egypt, Finland, France, Germany, Hungary, India, Islamic Republic of Iran, Italy, Jordan, Kyrgyzstan, Lao

The English text of 34 BITs to which Indonesia is a party, and which have not been terminated, are publicly available at this time.[66] This Chapter only discusses these treaties. Six of them also have signed protocols, namely the Indonesia-Belgium, Indonesia-Chile, Indonesia-Denmark, Indonesia-Germany, Indonesia-Switzerland and Indonesia-Syria BITs. In each case, the protocol was signed at the same time as the respective BIT was signed.

2 *Definition of Investment*

Most of the publicly available BITs define an investment in relatively broad terms to include any kind of asset as long as the investment is made in accordance with the laws and regulations of the host State.[67] For instance, Article 1, paragraph 1 of the Indonesia-Jamaica BIT provides:

People's Democratic Republic, Malaysia, Mauritius, Mongolia, Morocco, Mozambique, Netherlands, Norway, Pakistan, Poland, Republic of Korea, Romania, Russian Federation, Saudi Arabia, Singapore, Slovakia, Spain, Sri Lanka, Sweden, Switzerland, Syrian Arab Republic, Thailand, Tunisia, Turkey, Ukraine, United Kingdom, Uzbekistan, and Vietnam; see: http://investmentpolicyhub.unctad.org/IIA/CountryBits/97.

66 Indonesia-Algeria BIT, Indonesia-Australia BIT, Indonesia-Bangladesh BIT, Indonesia-Belgium-Luxembourg Economic Union BIT, Indonesia-Chile BIT, Indonesia-Croatia BIT, Indonesia-Cuba BIT, Indonesia-Czech Republic BIT, Indonesia-Denmark BIT (1968), Indonesia-Finland BIT (2006), Indonesia-Germany BIT (2003), Indonesia-India BIT, Indonesia-Jamaica BIT, Indonesia-Jordan BIT, Indonesia-Korea BIT, Indonesia-Kyrgyzstan BIT, Indonesia-Mauritius BIT, Indonesia-Morocco BIT, Indonesia-Mongolia BIT, Indonesia-Mozambique BIT, Indonesia-Pakistan BIT, Indonesia-Singapore BIT (2005), Indonesia-Spain BIT, Indonesia-Sri Lanka BIT, Indonesia-Sudan BIT, Indonesia-Sweden BIT, Indonesia-Switzerland BIT, Indonesia-Syria BIT, Indonesia-Thailand BIT, Indonesia-Ukraine BIT, Indonesia-UK BIT, Indonesia-Uzbekistan BIT, Indonesia-Yemen BIT and Indonesia-Zimbabwe BIT: see Investment Policy Hub, Indonesia, available at: http://investmentpolicyhub.unctad.org/IIA/CountryBits/97.

67 Article I, paragraph 1 of Indonesia-Algeria BIT, Article 1, paragraph 1 of Indonesia-Bangladesh BIT, Article 1(2) of Indonesia-Chile BIT, Article 1, paragraph 1 of Indonesia-Croatia BIT, Article I, paragraph 1 of Indonesia-Cuba BIT, Article 1, paragraph 1 of Indonesia-Czech Republic BIT, Article 1(1) of Indonesia-Finland BIT, Article 1, paragraph 1 of Indonesia-Germany BIT, Article 1, paragraph 1 of Indonesia-India BIT, Article 1, paragraph 1 of Indonesia-Jamaica BIT, Article I, paragraph 1 of Indonesia-Jordan BIT, Article 1, paragraph 1 of Indonesia-Kyrgyzstan BIT, Article 1, paragraph 1 of Indonesia-Mauritius BIT, Article I, paragraph 1 of Indonesia-Mongolia BIT, Article I, paragraph 1 of Indonesia-Morocco BIT, Article 1, paragraph 1 of Indonesia-Mozambique BIT, Article I, paragraph 1 of Indonesia-Pakistan BIT, Article 1 of Indonesia-Singapore BIT, Article I, paragraph 1 of Indonesia-Spain BIT, Article 1(1) of Indonesia-Sri Lanka BIT, Article I, paragraph 1 of Indonesia-Sudan BIT, Article 1(1) of Indonesia-Sweden BIT, Article I, paragraph 1 of Indonesia-Syria BIT, Article I, paragraph 1 of Indonesia-Thailand BIT, Article I, paragraph 1

> The term "investment" shall mean any kind of asset invested by investors of one Contracting Party in the territory of the other Contracting Party, in conformity with the laws and regulations of the latter, including, but not exclusively:
>
> a. movable and immovable property as well as other rights such as mortgages, privileges, and any other similar rights;
> b. rights derived from shares, bonds or any other form of interest in companies or joint venture in the territory of the other Contracting Party;
> c. claims to money or to any performance having a financial value;
> d. intellectual property rights, technical processes, goodwill and know-how;
> e. business concessions conferred by law or under contract related to the investment including concessions to search for or exploit natural resources.

The Indonesia-Korea BIT, Indonesia-Switzerland BIT and Indonesia-UK BIT define "investment" as "every kind of asset",[68] without reference to the investment being in conformity with the laws and regulations of the host State. However, these BITs contain other provisions that specify that only investments that are made in accordance with the relevant investment laws of the host State enjoy treaty protection.[69]

The Indonesia-Denmark BIT, which is the first BIT signed by Indonesia, does not define "investment".

The Indonesia-Australia BIT defines investment to mean "every kind of asset owned or controlled and invested by investors of one Party and admitted by the other Party in its territory in conformity with the laws, regulations and investment policies of the latter applicable from time to time".[70] The reference to "investment policies" is unusual. Difficulty may arise in determining what the "investment policies" of the host State are and whether these policies are likely to remain the same, which potentially creates uncertainty for investors.

---

of Indonesia-Ukraine BIT, Article I, paragraph 1 of Indonesia-Uzbekistan BIT, Article I, paragraph 1 of Indonesia-Yemen BIT and Article I, paragraph 1 of Indonesia-Zimbabwe BIT.

68 Article 1(1) of the Indonesia-Korea BIT, Article 3(c) of the Indonesia-Switzerland BIT and Article 1(a) of the Indonesia-UK BIT.

69 Article 2, paras. 1 and 2 of the Indonesia-UK BIT, Article 2 of the Indonesia-Switzerland BIT and Article 3 of the Indonesia-Korea BIT.

70 Article 1, para. 1(a) of the Indonesia-Australia BIT.

An uncommon definition of "investment" is found in Article 3 of the Indonesia-Belgium BIT, which defines "investments" as "every direct and indirect contribution of capital and any other kind of assets, invested or reinvested in enterprises in the field of agriculture, industry, mining, forestry, communications and tourism" industries. Unlike the Indonesia-Belgium BIT, the other publicly available BITs do not restrict the definition of "investment" to specified industry sectors.

3 *Definition of Investor*

A majority of the publicly available BITs define an "investor" as a national of a Contracting Party, who is either a natural person having the nationality of that Contracting Party or a legal person constituted under the law of that Contracting Party.[71] For instance, Article 2 of the Indonesia-Mongolia BIT states: "[t]he term 'investor' means national of one Contracting Party who invests in the territory of the other Contracting Party. The term 'national' shall comprise with regard to either Contracting Party: (i) natural person having the nationality of that Contracting Party; (ii) legal person constituted under the law of that Contracting Party".

As regards the definition of "investor" in relation to natural persons, an interesting example is provided by the Indonesia-Finland BIT, which stipulates that the provisions of that BIT shall not apply to investments made by natural persons who are nationals of one contracting party if such persons have, at the time of the investment, been domiciled in the latter contracting party for more than two years, unless it is proved that the investment was admitted into its territory from abroad.[72]

As regards the definition of "investor" for legal persons, some of the other publicly available BITs contain different definitions of investors depending on

71 Article I, para. 2 of Indonesia-Algeria BIT, Article I, para. 2 of Indonesia-Bangladesh BIT, Article I, para. 2 of Indonesia-Cuba BIT, Article I, para. 2 of Indonesia-India BIT, Article I, para. 2 of Indonesia-Jamaica BIT, Article I, para. 2 of Indonesia-Jordan BIT, Article I, para. 2 of Indonesia-Kyrgyzstan BIT, Article I, para. 2 of Indonesia-Mauritius BIT, Article I, para. 2 of Indonesia-Mongolia BIT, Article I, para. 2 of Indonesia-Mozambique BIT, Article I, para. 2 of Indonesia-Pakistan BIT, Article I, para. 2 of Indonesia-Sri Lanka BIT, Article I, para. 2 of Indonesia-Sudan BIT, Article I, para. 2 of Indonesia-Syria BIT, Article I, para. 2 of Indonesia-Thailand BIT, Article 1(c) and Article 1(d) of Indonesia-UK BIT, Article I, para. 2 of Indonesia-Ukraine BIT, Article I, para. 2 of Indonesia-Uzbekistan BIT, Article I, para. 2 of Indonesia-Yemen BIT and Article I, para. 2 of Indonesia-Zimbabwe BIT.

72 Article 1(4) of the Indonesia-Finland BIT.

their home States.[73] Usually, in these BITs, the definition of investor is broader for investors from Indonesia's counterparty than for investors from Indonesia. A notable example is the Indonesia-Australia BIT, which defines an "investor" to include, in respect of Indonesia, any company with a limited liability incorporated in Indonesia or any juridical person constituted in accordance with its laws.[74] In respect of Australian investors, the Indonesia-Australia BIT defines an investor as "any corporation, association, partnership, trust or other legally recognized entity that is duly incorporated, constituted, set up or otherwise duly organized: (i) under the law of Australia, or (ii) under the law of a third country and owned or controlled by a natural person [who is a citizen or permanent resident of Australia] or by [any corporation, association, partnership, trust or other legally recognized entity that is duly incorporated, constituted, set up or otherwise duly organized under the law of Australia] regardless of whether or not the entity is organized for pecuniary gain, privately or otherwise owned, or organized with limited or unlimited liability".[75]

Another example is the Indonesia-Sweden BIT, which defines "companies" to be "[i]n respect of the Kingdom of Sweden: any legal person having its seat in the territory of the Kingdom of Sweden, or in a third country with a predominant interest of an investor of the Kingdom of Sweden."[76] By contrast, the same BIT provides that "companies" mean, "in respect of the Republic of Indonesia, any company with a limited liability incorporated in the territory of the Republic of Indonesia, or any juridical persons lawfully constituted in accordance with its legislation."[77]

There are also some BITs that define an "investor" by reference to whether or not it has genuine business activities in the host State. For instance, the Indonesia-Chile BIT defines a "national" to comprise "legal entities, including companies, corporations, business associations and other legally recognized entities, which are constituted or otherwise duly organized under the law of that Contracting Party and have their seat together with effective economic activities in the territory of that same Contracting Party."[78] Similarly, the Indonesia-Croatia BIT provides that the term "investor" means a "legal person

73 Article 1, para. 1(b)(i)(B) of Indonesia-Australia BIT, Article 1, para. 3 of Indonesia-Germany BIT, Article 1(4) of Indonesia-Korea BIT, Article 1(4) of Indonesia-Sweden BIT and Article 3(b) of Indonesia-Switzerland BIT.

74 Article I, para. 1(b)(i)(B) of the Indonesia-Australia BIT.

75 *Ibid.*, Article I, para. 1(b)(ii)(B)Indonesia-Australia.

76 Article 1(4)(a) of the Indonesia-Sweden BIT.

77 Article 1(4)(b) of the Indonesia-Sweden BIT.

78 Article 1(1)(b) of the Indonesia-Chile BIT.

incorporated, constituted or otherwise duly organized in accordance with the laws and regulations of one Contracting Party, having its seat and performing real business activity in the territory of the same Contracting Party and making an investment in the territory of the other Contracting Party."[79] While it is not common, States sometimes do limit the definition of corporate "investor" in their BITs to those that conduct genuine business activities in the host State.[80] Such a limitation has the effect of disqualifying shell companies that have no economic activity in the host State from protection under the relevant BITs.

The Indonesia-Czech Republic BIT defines an "investor" as comprising a "legal person constituted or incorporated in accordance with the laws of one of the Contracting Parties having the permanent seat in the territory of that Contracting Party and investing in the territory of the other Contracting Party."[81] The reference to a "permanent seat" is highly unusual. At the time of writing, there are only 16 other publicly available BITs in the world that contain such a reference,[82] and the Czech Republic is a party to most of these BITs.

4 *Scope*

Most of Indonesia's publicly available BITs apply to investments made before and after the entry into force of the BIT, which have been admitted under the respective laws and regulations of the host State.[83] In the case of investments in Indonesia, the BITs typically apply to investments that have been admitted under Law No. 1 of 1967 concerning Foreign Investment and subsequent law

---

79 Article 1, para. 2(b) of the Indonesia-Croatia BIT.

80 Dolzer and Schreuer, *Principles of International Investment Law*, 2nd ed, (Oxford University Press, 2012) at 49.

81 Article 1, para. 2(b) of the Indonesia-Czech Republic BIT.

82 Based on a search on Investment Policy Hub at: http://investmentpolicyhub.unctad.org/IIA/AdvancedSearchBIT.

83 Article X, para. 1 of Indonesia-Algeria BIT, Article X of Indonesia-Bangladesh BIT, Article II(1) of Indonesia-Chile BIT, Article 12 of Indonesia-Croatia BIT, Article X of Indonesia-Cuba BIT, Article 11 of Indonesia-Finland BIT, Article 7 of Indonesia-Germany BIT, Article 2 of Indonesia-India BIT, Article X of Indonesia-Jamaica BIT, Article X of Indonesia-Jordan BIT, Article 3 of Indonesia-Korea BIT, Article X of Indonesia-Kyrgyzstan BIT, Article II, para. 1 of Indonesia-Mauritius BIT, Article X of Indonesia-Mongolia BIT, Article X of Indonesia-Morocco BIT, Article XI, para. 1 of Indonesia-Mozambique BIT, Article X of Indonesia-Pakistan BIT, Article X of Indonesia-Singapore BIT, Article III of Indonesia-Spain BIT, Article X of Indonesia-Sri Lanka BIT, Article X of Indonesia-Sudan BIT, Article 10 of Indonesia-Sweden BIT, Article X of Indonesia-Syria BIT, Article II of Indonesia-Thailand BIT, Article X of Indonesia-Ukraine BIT, Article X of Indonesia-Uzbekistan BIT and Article X of Indonesia-Yemen BIT.

amending or replacing it, including the Investment Law mentioned above.[84] For instance, Article 12 of the Indonesia-Croatia BIT provides as follows:

> 1. This Agreement shall apply to investments made prior to or after the entry into force of this Agreement, but shall not apply to any investment dispute that may have arisen or any claim, which was settled before its entry into force.
>
> 2. This Agreement shall apply to investments by investors of the Republic of Croatia in the territory of the Republic of Indonesia which have been previously granted admission in accordance with the Law No. 1 of 1967 concerning Foreign Investment and any law amending or replacing it.

As stated above, Article 12, paragraph 1 of the Indonesia-Croatia BIT does not apply to disputes that arose before the entry into force of that BIT. The same exclusion from applicability is found in several other BITs, namely the Indonesia-Finland BIT,[85] Indonesia-Jamaica BIT,[86] Indonesia-Mauritius BIT,[87] Indonesia-Mongolia BIT[88] and Indonesia-Morocco BIT.[89]

The Indonesia-Syria BIT is notable, applying only to investments made after the entry into force of that BIT.[90] Interestingly, the Indonesia-Morocco BIT provides that the treaty applies to "investments made in convertible currencies before its entry into force".[91]

Another interesting example is Article X of the Indonesia-Jamaica BIT, which provides that "with respect to investments made prior to this Agreement, the period of applicability shall be ten years". Such language is not found in the other publicly available BITs.

With the exception of the Indonesia-Belgium and Indonesia-Switzerland BITs, all the Indonesian BITs contain subrogation rights.

Under most of the publicly available BITs, where there are rules more favourable to the investor that exist under either international law or the

84 See Section II.

85 Article 11 of the Indonesia-Finland BIT.

86 Article X of the Indonesia-Jamaica BIT.

87 Article II, para. 2 of the Indonesia-Mauritius BIT.

88 Article X, para. 2 of Indonesia-Mongolia BIT.

89 Article X, para. 2 of Indonesia-Morocco BIT.

90 Article X of the Indonesia-Syria BIT.

91 Article X, para. 2 of the Indonesia-Morocco BIT.

law of the Contracting States, such rules would prevail.[92] The Indonesia-Denmark, Indonesia-Syria, Indonesia-Thailand, Indonesia-United Kingdom and Indonesia-Zimbabwe BITs, however, do not contain such a provision.

Under the Indonesia-Belgium BIT and Indonesia-Korea BIT, where more favourable rules exist under another international agreement between the Contracting Parties, such rules would prevail over the provisions in these BITs.[93] Under the Indonesia-Spain BIT and the Indonesia-Switzerland BIT, where more favourable rules exist under an agreement between one of the contracting parties and investors of the other Party, such rules would prevail over these BITs.[94]

The Indonesia-Australia BIT provides that where there are more favourable rules under "any applicable law, regulation or policy",[95] such rules would prevail over the BIT. This provision preserves a wide scope of rights for investors, allowing them to benefit not only from more favourable rules set out in international or domestic laws, but also more favourable rules found in regulations or policies. This is a unique provision and, at the time of writing, is not found in any other BITs in the world.[96]

5 *Substantive Protections*

Fair and Equitable Treatment

With the exception of the Indonesia-Denmark BIT, which was the first BIT signed by Indonesia, all the publicly available BITs require that the host State accord investments "fair and equitable treatment". For instance, Article IV of the Indonesia-Spain BIT states: "[e]ach Party shall guarantee in its territory

92 Article XI of Indonesia-Algeria BIT, Article XI of Indonesia-Bangladesh BIT, Article XI of Indonesia-Chile BIT, Article 9 of Indonesia-Croatia BIT, Article Xi of Indonesia-Cuba BIT, Article 11 of Indonesia-Czech Republic BIT, Article 8 of Indonesia-Finland BIT, Article 8(1) of Indonesia-Germany BIT, Article 13 of Indonesia-India BIT, Article XI of Indonesia-Jamaica BIT, Article XI of Indonesia-Jordan BIT, Article XI of Indonesia-Kyrgyzstan BIT, Article Xi of Indonesia-Mauritius BIT, Article XI of Indonesia-Mongolia BIT, Article XI of Indonesia-Morocco BIT, Article X, para. 1 of Indonesia-Mozambique BIT, Article XI of Indonesia-Pakistan BIT, Article XI of Indonesia-Singapore BIT, Article XI of Indonesia-Sri Lanka BIT, Article XI of Indonesia-Sudan BIT, Article 9 of Indonesia-Sweden BIT, Article XI of Indonesia-Ukraine BIT, Article XI of Indonesia-Uzbekistan BIT and Article XI of Indonesia-Yemen BIT.

93 Article 8 of the Indonesia-Belgium BIT; Article 11 of the Indonesia-Korea BIT.

94 Article VIII of the Indonesia-Spain BIT; Article 8 of the Indonesia-Switzerland BIT.

95 Article II, para. 4 of the Indonesia-Australia BIT.

96 Based on a search on Investment Policy Hub at: http://investmentpolicyhub.unctad.org/IIA/AdvancedSearchBIT.

fair and equitable treatment for the investments made by investors of the other Party."

Non-Discrimination

A majority of Indonesia's publicly available BITs contain provisions that prohibit the contracting parties from taking arbitrary or discriminatory measures against investments.[97] As regards the prohibition against "arbitrary" measures, these BITs employ the terms "unjustified", "unreasonable" and "arbitrary" measures, which are interchangeable terms under international law.[98] For instance, Article II, paragraph 2 of the Indonesia-Zimbabwe BIT states *inter alia* that: "[n]either Contracting Party shall impair, by unreasonable or discriminatory measures, the operation, management, maintenance, use, enjoyment or disposal thereof by those investors". The Indonesia-Spain BIT provides that each Contracting Party "shall not hamper, by means of unjustified or discriminatory measures, the management, maintenance, use, enjoyment, expansion, sale and if appropriate, the liquidation of such investments".[99]

Article 2(2) of the Indonesia-Sweden BIT prohibits arbitrary measures, but is silent on discriminatory measures. It states: "[e]ach Contracting Party ... shall not impair the management, maintenance, use, enjoyment or disposal thereof as well as the acquisition of goods, by unreasonable measures." This is a unique exception as all other Indonesian BITs which prohibit arbitrary measures also prohibit discriminatory measures.

A significant minority of Indonesia's BITs, namely those with Australia, Belgium, Czech Republic, Denmark, India, Republic of Korea, Mauritius,

97 Article III, para. 1 of Indonesia-Algeria BIT, Article III, para. 1 of Indonesia-Bangladesh BIT, Article IV(1) of Indonesia-Chile BIT, Article 3, para. 1 of Indonesia-Croatia BIT, Article III, para. 1 of Indonesia-Cuba BIT, Article 2(2) of Indonesia-Finland BIT, Article 2(3) of Indonesia-Germany BIT, Article III, para. 1 of Indonesia-Jamaica BIT, Article III, para. 1 of Indonesia-Jordan BIT, Article III, para. 1 of Indonesia-Kyrgyzstan BIT, Article III, para. 1 of Indonesia-Mongolia BIT, Article III, para. 1 of Indonesia-Mozambique BIT, Article III, para. 1 of Indonesia-Pakistan BIT, Article II, para. 2 of Indonesia-Spain BIT, Article III(1) of Indonesia-Sri Lanka BIT, Article 4(1) of Indonesia-Switzerland BIT, Article III, paragraph 1 of Indonesia-Syria BIT, Article 3(2) of Indonesia-UK BIT, Article III, para. 1 of Indonesia-Ukraine BIT, Article III, para. 1 of Indonesia-Uzbekistan BIT, Article III, para. 1 of Indonesia-Yemen BIT and Article II, para. 2 of Indonesia-Zimbabwe BIT.

98 Rudolf Dolzer and Christoph Schreuer, *Principles of International Investment Law*, 2nd ed, (Oxford University Press, 2012) at 191.

99 Article II, para. 4 of the Indonesia-Spain BIT.

Morocco, Singapore, Sudan and Thailand, do not contain provisions on arbitrary and discriminatory measures.

Full Protection and Security

Most of Indonesia's publicly available BITs require the host State to provide "adequate protection and security" to investments.[100] For instance, Article II, paragraph 2 of the Indonesia-Zimbabwe BIT states *inter alia*: "[i]nvestments of investors of either Contracting Party shall at all times be accorded fair and equitable treatment and shall enjoy adequate protection and security in the territory of the other Contracting Party."

The Indonesia-Germany, Indonesia-Thailand and Indonesia-UK BITs provide that "full protection and security" shall be accorded to investments.[101] The Indonesia-Australia BIT provides that "protection and security"[102] shall be accorded to investments. The Indonesia-Belgium and Indonesia-Sweden BITs provide that investments shall enjoy the "full protection under the respective BITs[103] and the Indonesia-Spain BIT merely requires that the host State "protect"[104] investments.

The Indonesia-Morocco BIT requires the host State to accord "adequate protection and security" to investments, which is "subject to the strictly necessary measures to maintain the public order".[105] This is an unusual provision and, at the time of writing, is only found in one other BIT between Morocco and Turkey.[106]

---

100 Article II, para. 2 of Indonesia-Algeria BIT, Article II, para. 2 of Indonesia-Bangladesh BIT, Article III(2) of Indonesia-Chile BIT, Article 3, para. 1 of Indonesia-Croatia BIT, Article II, para. 2 of Indonesia-Cuba BIT, Article 2, para. 2 of Indonesia-Czech Republic BIT, Article II, para. 2 of Indonesia-Jamaica BIT, Article II, para. 2 of Indonesia-Jordan BIT, Article 2(2) of Indonesia-Korea BIT, Article II, para. 2 of Indonesia-Kyrgyzstan BIT, Article II, para. 2 of Indonesia-Mongolia BIT, Article II, para. 2 of Indonesia-Mozambique BIT, Article II, para. 2 of Indonesia-Pakistan BIT, Article II(2) of Indonesia-Sri Lanka BIT, Article II, para. 2 of Indonesia-Sudan BIT, Article II, para. 2 of Indonesia-Syria BIT, Article II, para. 2 of Indonesia-Ukraine BIT, Article II, para. 2 of Indonesia-Uzbekistan BIT and Article II, para. 2 of Indonesia-Zimbabwe BIT.

101 Article 3(2) of the Indonesia-UK BIT, Article 4(1) of the Indonesia-Germany BIT and Article II, para. 2 of the Indonesia-Thailand BIT.

102 Article II, para. 3 of the Indonesia-Australia BIT.

103 Article 1, para. 2 of the Indonesia-Belgium BIT and Article 2(6) of the Indonesia-Sweden BIT.

104 Article II, para. 2 of the Indonesia-Spain BIT.

105 Article II, para. 2 of the Indonesia-Morocco BIT.

106 Based on a search on Investment Policy Hub at: http://investmentpolicyhub.unctad.org/IIA/AdvancedSearchBIT.

The Indonesia-Denmark BIT, Indonesia-Finland BIT, India-Indonesia BIT and Indonesia-Switzerland BIT do not contain provisions according investments full protection and security.

Expropriation

All of Indonesia's publicly available BITs require that expropriation or measures having the effects of expropriation not be taken unless certain conditions are met.

More than half (18) of these BITs contain very similar provisions on expropriation, requiring that the expropriation be pursuant to a public purpose or lawful purpose, under process of law, non-discriminatory and against prompt, adequate and effective compensation, which shall amount to the fair market value before the expropriation became public knowledge.[107] For instance, Article IV of the Indonesia-Mongolia BIT states:

> Each Contracting Party shall not take any measures of expropriation, nationalization or any other dispossession, having effect equivalent to nationalization or expropriation against the investments of an investor of the other Contracting Party except under the following conditions:
>
> (a) the measures are taken for a lawful purpose or public purpose and under process of law;
> (b) the measures are non-discriminatory;
> (c) the measures are accompanied by provisions for the payment of prompt, adequate and effective compensation. Such compensation shall amount to the fair market value without delay before the measure of dispossession became public knowledge. Such market value shall be determined in accordance with internationally acknowledged practices and methods or, where such fair market value

107 Article IV of the Indonesia-Algeria BIT, Article IV of the Indonesia-Bangladesh BIT, Article IV of the Indonesia-Cuba BIT, Article IV of the Indonesia-Jamaica BIT, Article IV of the Indonesia-Jordan BIT, Article IV of the Kyrgyz Republic-Indonesia BIT, Article IV of the Indonesia-Mongolia BIT, Article IV of the Indonesia-Mozambique BIT, Article IV of the Indonesia-Pakistan BIT, Article IV of the Indonesia-Singapore BIT, Article IV of the Indonesia-Sri Lanka BIT, Article IV of the Indonesia-Sudan BIT, Article IV of the Indonesia-Syria BIT, Article VI of the Indonesia-Thailand BIT, Article IV of the Indonesia-Ukraine BIT, Article IV of the Indonesia-Uzbekistan BIT, Article IV of the Indonesia-Yemen BIT and Article IV of the Indonesia-Zimbabwe BIT.

> cannot be determined, it shall be such reasonable amounts as may be mutually agreed between the Contracting Parties hereto, and it shall be freely transferable in freely usable currencies from the Contracting Party.

As regards the other publicly available BITs, most of them require that the expropriation be taken pursuant to some "public purpose",[108] "public interest"[109] or "public benefit",[110] under due process of law or in accordance with law,[111] be non-discriminatory[112] and be against "prompt, adequate and effective compensation".[113]

Notably, the Indonesia-Australia, Indonesia-Korea and Indonesia-UK BITs require that the "public purpose" be related "to the internal needs" of the

108 Article VI, para. 1(a) of the Indonesia-Australia BIT, Article 4, para. 1(a) of the Indonesia-Czech Republic BIT, Article 5, para. 1 of the Indonesia-India BIT, Article 6(1) of the Indonesia-Korea BIT, Article VI, para. 1 of the Indonesia-Mauritius BIT, Article IV, para. 1 of the Indonesia-Morocco BIT, Article 5(1) of the Indonesia-UK BIT.

109 Article 5(a) of the Indonesia-Belgium BIT, Article 4(1)(a) of the Indonesia-Finland BIT, Article VI of the Indonesia-Spain BIT, Article 4(1)(a) of the Indonesia-Sweden BIT, Article 6(1) of the Indonesia-Switzerland BIT.

110 Article VI(1)(a) of the Indonesia-Chile BIT, Article 5, para. 1(a) of the Indonesia-Croatia BIT, Article IV(1) of the Indonesia-Denmark BIT, Article 4(2) of the Indonesia-Germany BIT.

111 Article VI, para. 1(a) of the Indonesia-Australia BIT, Article 5(a) of the Indonesia-Belgium BIT, Article VI(1)(a) of the Indonesia-Chile BIT, Article 5(c) of the Indonesia-Croatia BIT, Article 4, para. 1(a) of the Indonesia-Czech Republic BIT, Article 5, para. 1 of the Indonesia-India BIT, Article 4(1)(a) of the Indonesia-Finland BIT, Article VI, para. 1 of the Indonesia-Mauritius BIT, Article IV of the Indonesia-Spain BIT, Article 4(1)(a) of the Indonesia-Sweden BIT, Article 6(1) of the Indonesia-Switzerland BIT.

112 Article VI, para. 1(b) of the Indonesia-Australia BIT, Article 5(b) of the Indonesia-Belgium BIT, Article VI(1)(b) of the Indonesia-Chile BIT, Article 5, para. 1(b) of the Indonesia-Croatia BIT, Article 4, para. 1(b) of the Indonesia-Czech Republic BIT, Article 4(b) of the Indonesia-Finland BIT, Article VI, para. 1 of the Indonesia-Mauritius BIT, Article IV, para. 1 of the Indonesia-Morocco BIT, Article VI of the Indonesia-Spain BIT, Article 4(1)(b) of the Indonesia-Sweden BIT.

113 Article VI, para. 1(c) of the Indonesia-Australia BIT, Article VI(1)(c) of the Indonesia-Chile BIT, Article 5, para. 1(d) of the Indonesia-Croatia BIT, Article 4, para. 1(c) of the Indonesia-Czech Republic BIT, Article 4(c) of the Indonesia-Finland BIT, Article 5, para. 1 of the Indonesia-India BIT, Article VI, para. 1 of the Indonesia-Mauritius BIT, Article 4(1)(c) of the Indonesia-Sweden BIT.

expropriating Party.[114] Such a requirement restricts the host State from invoking foreign policy reasons to justify its expropriation.[115]

The Indonesia-UK BIT, Indonesia-Morocco BIT, Indonesia-Korea BIT, Indonesia-Germany BIT and Indonesia-Denmark BIT do not contain provisions that require expropriation to be pursuant to due process of law. However, with the exception of the Indonesia-Morocco BIT, all of these BITs grant investors a right of review by "due process of law" of the legality of the expropriation.[116]

The Indonesia-Germany, Indonesia-Denmark, Indonesia-Korea, Indonesia-Switzerland and Indonesia-UK BITs do not contain provisions that require expropriations to be non-discriminatory.

Apart from those BITs that use the Hull formula of "prompt, adequate and effective" compensation, the other publicly available BITs contain a variety of formulations of the compensation payable. The treaties with Denmark, Germany and the UK require that expropriation be "against compensation",[117] while the Indonesia-Belgium BIT requires that expropriation be against "just compensation".[118] The Indonesia-Morocco and India-Indonesia BITs require that "fair and equitable compensation"[119] be made. The Indonesia-Switzerland BIT requires that "effective and adequate compensation"[120] be made, the Indonesia-Spain BIT requires that an "adequate indemnity"[121] be paid, and the Indonesia-Korea BIT requires that expropriation be made against "full, prompt and effective compensation".[122]

Some of the BITs impose additional conditions if expropriation is to be carried out. The Indonesia-Belgium BIT requires that the expropriation not be "contrary to a specific engagement".[123] This is similar to the Indonesia-

114 Article VI, para. 1(a) of the Indonesia-Australia BIT, Article 6(1) of the Indonesia-Korea BIT and Article 5(1) of the Indonesia-UK BIT.

115 Newcombe and Paradell, *Law and Practice of Investment Treaties: Standards of Treatment* (Kluwer Law International, 2009) at para. 7.32.

116 Article IV of the Indonesia-Denmark BIT, Article 4(2) of the Indonesia-Germany BIT, Article 6(1) of the Indonesia-Korea BIT, Article 5(1) of the Indonesia-UK BIT.

117 Article 5(1) of the Indonesia-UK BIT, Article 4(2) of the Indonesia-Germany BIT and Article IV(1) of the Indonesia-Denmark BIT.

118 Article 5(c) of the Indonesia-Belgium BIT.

119 Article 5, para. 1 of the Indonesia-India BIT and Article IV, para. 2 of the Indonesia-Morocco BIT.

120 Article 6(1) of the Indonesia-Switzerland BIT.

121 Article VI of the Indonesia-Spain BIT.

122 Article 6(1) of the Indonesia-Korea BIT.

123 Article 5(b) of the Indonesia-Belgium BIT.

Denmark BIT, which requires that the expropriation not be "contrary to existing obligations".[124] The Indonesia-Morocco BIT requires that compensation be paid "without delay and at the latest within three months of the date"[125] of the expropriation. The Indonesia-Singapore BIT requires that "any measure of expropriation relating to land, which shall be as defined in its domestic legislation of each Contracting Party, shall be for a purpose and upon payment of compensation in accordance with the aforesaid legislation and any subsequent amendment thereto".[126]

The India-Indonesia BIT, Indonesia-Korea BIT, Indonesia-Mauritius BIT and Indonesia-UK BIT extend the application of the provisions on expropriation to the extent necessary to guarantee compensation to shareholders who are nationals of the other contracting State party, where they are shareholders of a company that is incorporated in the expropriating State. For instance, Article 5(2) of the Indonesia-UK BIT provides:

> Where a Contracting Party expropriates the assets of a company which is incorporated or constituted under the law in force in any part of its territory, and in which nationals or companies of the other Contracting Party own shares, it shall ensure that the provisions of paragraph (1) of this Article are applied to the extent necessary to guarantee the compensation provided for in that paragraph to the owners of these shares.

As regards valuation of the compensation, almost all the publicly available BITs require that compensation amount to the "market value"[127] or "fair market value"[128] of the investment. The Indonesia-Sweden, Indonesia-Spain and

124 Article IV(1) of the Indonesia-Denmark BIT.

125 Article IV, para. 3 of the Indonesia-Morocco BIT.

126 Article IV, para. 3 of the Indonesia-Singapore BIT.

127 Article VI, para. 2 of the Indonesia-Australia BIT, Article VI(2) of the Indonesia-Chile BIT, Article 4(2) of the Indonesia-Finland BIT, Article IV(c) of the Indonesia-Jamaica BIT, Article 6(1) of the Indonesia-Korea BIT, Article IV, para. 3 of the Indonesia-Morocco BIT, Article IV(c) of the Indonesia-Sudan BIT, Article 5(1) of the Indonesia-UK BIT.

128 Article IV(c) of the Indonesia-Algeria BIT, Article IV(c) of the Indonesia-Bangladesh BIT, Article 5, para. 3 of the Indonesia-Croatia BIT, Article IV(c) of the Indonesia-Cuba BIT, Article 4, para. 1(c) of the Indonesia-Czech Republic BIT, Article 5, para. 1 of the Indonesia-India BIT, Article IV, para. c of the Indonesia-Jordan BIT, Article IV(c) of the Kyrgyz Republic-Indonesia BIT, Article VI, para. 1 of the Indonesia-Mauritius BIT, Article IV(c) of the Indonesia-Mongolia BIT, Article IV of the Indonesia-Mozambique BIT, Article IV(c) of the Indonesia-Pakistan BIT, Article IV, para. c of the Indonesia-Singapore BIT, Article IV(c) of the Indonesia-Sri Lanka BIT, Article IV(c) of the

Indonesia-Germany BITs do not contain provisions on how compensation is to be valued. The Indonesia-Belgium BIT provides that the compensation shall amount to the "actual value of the affected goods",[129] the Indonesia-Denmark BIT provides that the "compensation shall represent the commercial value of the investment"[130] and the Indonesia-Switzerland BIT requires that the amount of compensation be fixed at the time of expropriation.[131]

Umbrella Clauses

Three of Indonesia's publicly available BITs contain provisions that require the contracting States to observe any other obligations they had undertaken with regard to investments by investors from the other State,[132] which are commonly known as "umbrella clauses" because they bring contractual obligations and other commitments under the protective umbrella of the treaty. For instance, Article 8(2) of the Indonesia-Germany BIT provides that "[e]ach Contracting Party shall observe any other obligation it has assumed with regard to investments in its territory by investors of the other Contracting Party".

Most Favoured Nation and National Treatment

All of Indonesia's BITs require that the host State accord investments treatment no less favourable than that accorded to investments of investors from any third State. For instance, the Indonesia-Ukraine BIT provides that "each Contracting Party shall accord to such investments treatment which in any case shall not be less favourable than that accorded to investments of nationals of any third State."[133] Such provisions are commonly known as "Most-Favoured-Nation Provisions" ("MFN") provisions and can have the effect of extending to its beneficiaries substantive treaty guarantees such as "fair and equitable treatment" granted to a third State or its nationals.

With the exception of the Indonesia-Denmark and Indonesia-Switzerland BITs, all the BITs explicitly provide that the MFN provisions do not apply to more favourable treatment arising out of customs unions, economic unions or

---

Indonesia-Syria BIT, Article VI, para. 1(c) of the Indonesia-Thailand BIT, Article IV(c) of the Indonesia-Ukraine BIT, Article IV(c) of the Indonesia-Uzbekistan BIT, Article IV(c) of the Indonesia-Yemen BIT and Article IV(c) of the Indonesia-Zimbabwe BIT.

129 Article 5 of the Indonesia-Belgium BIT.

130 Article IV(3) of the Indonesia-Denmark BIT.

131 Article 6(2) of the Indonesia-Switzerland BIT.

132 Article 8(2) of the Indonesia-Germany BIT, Article X, para. 2 of the Indonesia-Mozambique BIT and Article 3(2) of the Indonesia-UK BIT.

133 Article III, para. 2 of the Indonesia-Ukraine BIT.

monetary unions or similar institutions or interim agreements leading to such unions or institutions.

A significant number of the publicly available BITs provide that the MFN provisions do not apply to more favourable treatment arising out of trade agreements or a free trade area.[134]

There is also a significant number of BITs which provide that the MFN provisions do not apply to benefits or advantages arising out of taxation agreements or arrangements.[135]

In terms of national treatment, only a minority of the treaties contain provisions requiring the host State to accord investments of the other contracting State a treatment no less favourable than that accorded to its own investors.[136] For instance, Article 4, paragraph 3 of the India-Indonesia BIT states: "[e]ach Contracting Party shall, subject to its laws and regulations, accord to investment of investors of the other Contracting Party treatment no less favourable than that which is accorded to investments of its investors".

Some of these BITs modify the national treatment requirement. For instance, the Protocol to the Indonesia-Belgium BIT, which was signed at the same time as the BIT, provides that "[f]or the purpose of protecting the Indonesian national economy, the Government of the Republic of Indonesia may grant some facilities to Indonesian concerns which do not fully apply to Belgium concerns, without prejudice to the principle that Belgian investment

134 Article IV, para. 1(a) of the Indonesia-Australia BIT, Article IV(3) of the Indonesia-Chile BIT, Article 4, para. 3(a) of the Indonesia-Croatia BIT, Article 3(2) of the Indonesia-Finland BIT, Article 3(3) of the Indonesia-Germany BIT, Article 4, para. 2(a) of the Indonesia-India BIT, Article 4(4) of the Indonesia-Korea BIT, Article IV, para. 3a of the Indonesia-Mauritius BIT, Article IV, para. 3(a) of the Indonesia-Morocco BIT, Article III, para. 3a of the Indonesia-Mozambique BIT, Article III, para. 2 of the Indonesia-Singapore BIT, Article IV, para. 3 of the Indonesia-Spain BIT, Article 3(2)(a) of the Indonesia-Sweden BIT and Article IV, para. 3(a) of the Indonesia-Thailand BIT.

135 Article IV, para. 1(b) of the Indonesia-Australia BIT, Article IV(3) of the Indonesia-Chile BIT, Article 4, para. 3(b) of the Indonesia-Croatia BIT, Article 3, para. 3 of the Indonesia-Czech Republic BIT, Article 3(3) of the Indonesia-Finland BIT, Article 3(4) of the Indonesia-Germany BIT, Article 4, para. 2(b) of the Indonesia-India BIT, Article III, para. 4 of the Indonesia-Jamaica BIT, Article 4(4) of the Indonesia-Korea BIT, Article IV, para. 3b of the Indonesia-Mauritius BIT, Article III, para. 3(b) of the Indonesia-Morocco BIT, Article III, para. 3b of the Indonesia-Mozambique BIT, Article IV, para. 4 of the Indonesia-Spain BIT, Article III(3) of the Indonesia-Sri Lanka BIT, Article 3(4) of the Indonesia-Sweden BIT and Article IV, para. 3(c) of the Indonesia-Thailand BIT.

136 Indonesia-Belgium BIT, Indonesia-Czech Republic BIT, Indonesia-Denmark BIT, Indonesia-Germany BIT, Indonesia-India BIT, Indonesia-Korea BIT, Indonesia-Singapore BIT and Indonesia-Switzerland BIT.

shall be accorded a treatment no less favourable than that which is accorded to nationals or legal persons of third States."

Similarly, the Protocol to the Indonesia-Switzerland BIT, which was also signed at the same time as the treaty, provides that certain derogations from the requirement of national treatment is permitted with respect to the Indonesian Government's treatment of Swiss investments "in view of the present stage of development of the Indonesian national economy". Pursuant to paragraph 2 of that Protocol, Indonesia reserved its right to accord domestic investments governed by the Domestic Investment Law (Law No. 6 of 1968) as amended by Law No. 12 of 1970 a more advantageous treatment compared to foreign investments governed by the Foreign Investment Law (Law No. 1 of 1967) as amended by Law No. 11 of 1970.

6 *Repatriation of Capital and Compensation for Losses*

All Indonesian BITs contain provisions requiring the contracting States to allow the repatriation or transfer of capital invested and investment returns out of their territories. For instance, the Jordan-Indonesia BIT provides that "[e]ither Contracting Party shall guarantee within the scope of its laws and regulations in respect to investments by nationals of the other Contracting Party grant to those nationals without delay, after duely paying its legal financial and tax commitments if there is any, the transfer of: a. profits, interests, dividends and other current income; b. funds necessary (i) for the acquisition of raw or auxiliary materials, semi-fabricated or finished products, or (ii) to replace capital assets in order to safeguard the continuity of an investment; c. additional funds necessary for the development of an investment; d. funds in repayment of loans; e. royalties or fees; f. earnings of natural persons; g. the proceeds of sale or liquidation of the investment; h. compensation for losses; i. compensation for expropriation."[137]

With the exception of the Indonesia-Switzerland BIT, all Indonesian BITs require the host State to accord to investors, whose investments suffer losses due to armed conflicts, riots, national emergencies and similar situations, a treatment no less favourable than that accorded to nationals of a third State or its own investors. For instance, Article V of the Indonesia-Algeria BIT states: "[i]nvestors of one Contracting Party, whose investments in the territory of the other Contracting Party suffer losses owing to war or other armed conflict, revolution, a state of national emergency, revolt, insurrection or riot in the territory of the latter Contracting Party, shall be accorded by the latter Contracting Party treatment, as regards restitution, indemnification, compensation or

137 Article VI, para. 1 of the Indonesia-Jordan BIT.

other settlement, no less favourable than that which the latter Contracting Party accords to investors of any third state."

Notably, the Indonesia-Spain BIT requires that such compensation be "prompt, adequate, effective and freely transferable."[138]

7 *Investor-State Dispute Settlement*

Almost half of the publicly available BITs contain largely similar provisions on disputes between an investor and the host State, allowing the investor, six months after an attempt to settle the dispute amicably via consultation or negotiations, to submit the dispute to domestic judicial procedures in the host State or to international arbitration or conciliation under the auspices of ICSID.[139] For instance, Article VIII of the Indonesia-Mongolia BIT states:

> 1. Any dispute between a Contracting Party and an investor of the other Contracting Party, concerning an investment of the latter in the territory of the former, be settled amicably through consultations and negotiations.
>
> 2. If such a dispute cannot be settled within a period of six months from the date of a written notification either party requested amicable settlement, the dispute shall, at the request of the investor concerned, be submitted either to the judicial procedures provided by the Contracting Party concerned or to international arbitration or conciliation.
>
> 3. Each Contracting Party hereby consents to submit any dispute arising between that Contracting Party and an investor of the other Contracting Party concerning an investment of that investor in the territory of the former Contracting Party to the International Center for Settlement of Investment Disputes for settlement by conciliation or arbitration under the Convention on the Settlement of Investment Disputes between States

---

138 Article V of the Indonesia-Spain BIT.

139 Article VIII of Indonesia-Algeria BIT, Article VIII of Indonesia-Bangladesh BIT, Article 10 of Indonesia-Germany BIT, Article VIII of Indonesia-Jordan BIT, Article VIII of Indonesia-Kyrgyzstan BIT, Article VIII of Indonesia-Mongolia BIT, Article VIII of Indonesia-Morocco BIT, Article VIII of Indonesia-Pakistan BIT, Article VIII of Indonesia-Sri Lanka BIT, Article VIII of Indonesia-Sudan BIT, Article VIII of Indonesia-Syria BIT, Article VIII of Indonesia-Ukraine BIT, Article VIII of Indonesia-Uzbekistan BIT, Article VIII of Indonesia-Yemen BIT and Article VIII of Indonesia-Zimbabwe BIT.

and Nationals of other States opened for signature at Washington, D.C. on 18 March 1965.

The Indonesia-Chile BIT allows the investor to submit the dispute to international arbitration under ICSID or to the domestic tribunals of the host State four months after the date of the written notification of a settlement if no solution has been reached.[140]

Some of the publicly available BITs provide for the possibility of the investor submitting the dispute, after an attempt at settling the dispute amicably, to international arbitration under either ICSID or to an *ad hoc* tribunal under UNCITRAL Rules.[141] The Indonesia-Singapore BIT provides an additional option for the investor to submit the arbitration to any regional center for arbitration in ASEAN.[142]

The Indonesia-Cuba BIT does not provide for the option of arbitration under ICSID. Rather, it provides that the investor may, after a period of six months of attempting an amicable settlement, submit the dispute to international arbitration or settlement to the Court of Arbitration of the ICC in Paris or an arbitrator or an *ad hoc* tribunal set up under the UNCITRAL Rules.[143]

Notably, however, the Indonesia-Switzerland and Indonesia-Denmark BITs do not contain provisions on investor-State dispute resolution.

There are three BITs that require the investor to pursue local remedies before it may submit the dispute to arbitration. Article 8(3) of the Indonesia-Sweden BIT provides that the investor may submit the dispute to ICSID if the dispute cannot be finally disposed of within 6 months between the parties to the dispute through the pursuit of local remedies. Under the Indonesia-Korea BIT and Indonesia-Spain BIT, the investor may only submit the dispute to arbitration if the dispute cannot be settled after the pursuit of local remedies for 12 months.[144]

By contrast, the Indonesia-Belgium BIT and Indonesia-Croatia BIT contain provisions that specify that the Contracting State's "consent implies renun-

---

140 Article IX(2) of the Indonesia-Chile BIT.

141 Article 10, para. 2 of the Indonesia-Croatia BIT, Article 8, para. 2 of the Indonesia-Czech Republic BIT, Article IX, para. 5 of the Indonesia-Jamaica BIT, Article 9, para. 3 of the Indonesia-India BIT, Article VII, para. 3 of the Indonesia-Mozambique BIT, Article VIII, para. 2 of the Indonesia-Singapore BIT, Article X, para. 2 of the Indonesia-Spain BIT, Article VIII, para. 3 of the Indonesia-Syria BIT and Article X, para. 3 of the Indonesia-Thailand BIT.

142 Article VIII, para. 2b of the Indonesia-Singapore BIT.

143 Article VIII, para. 3 of the Indonesia-Cuba BIT.

144 Article X, para. 2 of the Indonesia-Spain BIT and Article 9(2) of the Indonesia-Korea BIT.

ciation of the requirement that the internal administrative or judicial resorts should be exhausted".

The Indonesia-Morocco BIT, Indonesia-Mauritius BIT, Indonesia-Jamaica BIT, India-Indonesia BIT, Indonesia-Chile BIT contain "fork-in-the-road" provisions that state that once an investor chooses a mode of dispute resolution, such as to submit the dispute to the domestic courts of the host State, that election is final and the investor may not then submit the same dispute to another mode of dispute resolution, such as international arbitration. However, even where such "fork-in-the-road" provisions are not explicitly set out, choice of one mode of dispute resolution may nonetheless preclude resort to other modes.

Notably, the Indonesia-Sweden BIT and Indonesia-UK BIT contain provisions that deem a company incorporated in the host State as a company of the other contracting State where the majority of the company's shareholders are from the other contracting State.[145]

8 *State-to-State Disputes Settlement*

Most of the publicly available BITs provide that where a dispute arises between the contracting States, the States should first seek to settle the dispute amicably, through consultations, negotiations or diplomatic channels, failing which, the dispute may be submitted to arbitration by a tribunal consisting of 3 members.[146] Some of these BITs prescribe a time limit of 6 months for attempted settlement, after the expiry of which a State may then submit a request for arbitration.[147]

---

145 Article 8(2) of the Indonesia-Sweden BIT and Article 7(2) of the Indonesia-UK BIT.

146 Article IX of Indonesia-Algeria BIT, Article XII of Indonesia-Australia BIT, Article 11 of Indonesia-Belgium BIT, Article X of Indonesia-Chile BIT, Article 11 of Indonesia-Croatia BIT, Article 9 of Indonesia-Czech Republic BIT, Article VIII of Indonesia-Denmark BIT, Article 10 of Indonesia-Finland BIT, Article 9 of Indonesia-Germany BIT, Article 10 of Indonesia-India BIT, Article VIII of Indonesia-Jamaica BIT, Article IX of Indonesia-Jordan BIT, Article 10 of Indonesia-Korea BIT, Article X of Indonesia-Mauritius BIT, Article IX of Indonesia-Mongolia BIT, Article IX of Indonesia-Morocco BIT, Article VIII of Indonesia-Mozambique BIT, Article IX of Indonesia-Singapore BIT, Article XI of Indonesia-Spain BIT, Article 7 of Indonesia-Sweden BIT, Article 9 of Indonesia-Switzerland BIT, Article XI of Indonesia-Thailand BIT, Article 8 of Indonesia-UK BIT, Article IX of Indonesia-Ukraine BIT, Article IX of Indonesia-Uzbekistan BIT and Article 10 of Indonesia-Zimbabwe BIT.

147 Article IX, para. 2 of the Indonesia-Algeria BIT, Article XII, para. 2 of the Indonesia-Australia BIT, Article VIII, para. 2 of the Indonesia-Bangladesh BIT, Article 11 of the Indonesia-Belgium BIT, Article X(2) of the Indonesia-Chile BIT, Article 11, para. 2 of

Notably, the Indonesia-Belgium BIT provides that the tribunal may at any stage of the proceedings before rendering its decision, propose to the parties that the dispute be settled amicably.[148] The Indonesia-Australia BIT is also notable, providing that the tribunal may render an award on the default of a party.[149]

The Indonesia-Syria BIT, Indonesia-Sudan BIT, Indonesia-Sri Lanka BIT, Indonesia-Pakistan BIT, Kyrgyz Republic-Indonesia BIT and Indonesia-Bangladesh BIT do not provide for the dispute to be submitted to arbitration if the dispute cannot be settled by diplomatic channels. The Indonesia-Yemen BIT provides that if the disputes between the parties cannot be settled, then it shall at the request of either party be submitted to an arbitration tribunal "acceptable to both Contracting Parties."[150]

9 *Additional Provisions*

Article 10 of the Indonesia-UK BIT extends the provisions of that BIT to "such territories, for whose international relations the Government of the United Kingdom are responsible, as may be agreed upon by the Contracting Parties in an Exchange of Notes". In this regard, in an Exchange of Notes which entered into force on 30 July 1999, the UK and Indonesia extended the provisions of the Indonesia-UK BIT to Bermuda, the Isle of Man and the Bailiwicks of Guernsey and Jersey.[151]

Also concerning the territorial application of the BITs, Article IX of the Indonesia-Denmark BIT specifies that BIT shall not apply to the Faroe Islands and Greenland.

---

the Indonesia-Croatia BIT, Article 9, para. 2 of the Indonesia-Czech Republic BIT, Article VIII of the Indonesia-Denmark BIT, Article 10(2) of the Indonesia-Finland BIT, Article IX, paragraph 2 of the Indonesia-Jordan BIT, Article X, para. 2 of the Indonesia-Mauritius BIT, Article IX, para. 2 of the Indonesia-Morocco BIT, Article VIII, para. 2 of the Indonesia-Mozambique BIT, Article XI, para. 2 of the Indonesia-Spain BIT, Article 7(2) of the Indonesia-Sweden BIT, Article XI, para. 2 of the Indonesia-Thailand BIT, Article IX, para. 2 of the Indonesia-Uzbekistan BIT and Article 10, para. 2 of the Indonesia-Zimbabwe BIT.

148 Article 11 of the Indonesia-Belgium BIT.

149 Article XII, para. 5 of the Indonesia-Australia BIT.

150 Article IX, para. 2 of the Indonesia-Yemen BIT.

151 Exchange of Notes extending the Agreement between the Government of the United Kingdom of Great Britain and Northern Ireland and the Government of the Republic of Indonesia for the Promotion and Protection of Investments signed at London on 27 April 1976 to Bermuda, the Isle of Man and the Bailiwicks of Guernsey and Jersey, Treaty Series No. 75 (2000), available at: http://treaties.fco.gov.uk/docs/pdf/2000/TS0075.pdf.

Most of Indonesia's BITs provide that either contracting party may request that consultations be held on any matter concerning the BIT and the other party shall accord sympathetic consideration to the proposal and to afford adequate opportunity for such consultations.

10 *Notable Trends*

The majority of Indonesia's BITs were signed in the 1990s. Since 2000, only 18 new BITs have been signed, out of which, at the time of writing, only 7 are in force.[152] The last BIT signed by Indonesia to date, was signed in 2011 with Serbia and it has not entered into force.

The decline in Indonesia's enthusiasm in BITs was made apparent in March 2014, when Indonesia announced that it intends to terminate its BITs by letting them expire. Since then, at the time of writing, the Indonesia-Netherlands BIT, Indonesia-France BIT, the Indonesia-Italy BIT and the Indonesia-Hungary BIT have expired and are terminated.[153]

It has been suggested that Indonesia's stance with regard to its BITs was motivated by a desire to renegotiate these with better terms.[154] It was also argued that Indonesia's announcement was made in response to the Decision on Jurisdiction issued by the tribunal in *Churchill Mining Plc v Republic of Indonesia*[155] on 24 February 2014, in which the tribunal found that it has jurisdiction over the claims submitted by the Claimant, in excess of US$1 billion.

In conjunction with the announcement that it intends to terminate its existing BITs, it has been reported that Indonesia is intending to issue a new model BIT.[156] At the time of writing, however, the text of such a new model BIT has not been made publicly available.

---

152 Investment Policy Hub at: http://investmentpolicyhub.unctad.org/IIA/CountryBits/97#iiaInnerMenu.

153 Oentoeng Suria & Partners, "BIT by BIT: Indonesia's move away from Bilateral Investment Treaties continues", July 2015, available at https://www.ashurst.com/publication-list.aspx?id_Content=1362&expandOfficeList=true&id_queryContent=6579&page=1. See also: http://investmentpolicyhub.unctad.org/IIA/CountryBits/97.

154 *Ibid.* See also: "Revamping Bilateral Treaties", *The Jakarta Post*, 7 July 2014.

155 ICSID Case No. ARB/12/14 and 12/40, Decision on Jurisdiction, 24 February 2015.

156 Prof. Michael Ewing-Chow and Mr Junianto James Losari, *Indonesia is letting its bilateral treaties lapse so as to negotiate better ones*, Financial Times, available at: http://www.ft.com/intl/cms/s/0/20c6c518-c16c-11e3-97b2-00144feabdc0.html#axzz4301GWTNS.

IV Multilateral Investment Related Treaties and Organizations to which Indonesia is a Party

1 *ASEAN – ACIA*

Indonesia is one of the founding members of ASEAN, which was established in August 1967.[157] The most significant treaty relating to investment protection within ASEAN is arguably the ASEAN Comprehensive Investment Agreement (the "ACIA").

Indonesia signed the ACIA on 26 February 2009 and the ACIA entered into force on 29 March 2012.[158] Investors from other ASEAN States that have also ratified the ACIA can therefore look to the ACIA for protection of their investments in Indonesia.

The ACIA contains substantive investment protections commonly found in BITs, such as provisions on MFN treatment,[159] fair and equitable treatment,[160] full protection and security,[161] and rules on expropriation.[162] Article 3(3) of the ACIA states that the ACIA is applicable to several sectors including manufacturing, agriculture, fishery, forestry, mining and quarrying, services incidental to these above-mentioned industries and other sectors that may be agreed upon by all member States.

Article 32 of the ACIA provides an investor wishing to submit a claim against a Member State with six different choices: (i) the courts or administrative tribunals of the disputing Member State; (ii) under the ICSID Convention and ICSID Rules of Procedure for Arbitration Proceedings if both the disputing Member State and the non-disputing Member State are parties to the ICSID Convention; (iii) under the ICSID Additional Facility Rules if either the disputing Member State or the non-disputing Member State is a party to the ICSID Convention; (iv) under UNCITRAL Arbitration Rules; (v) to the Regional Centre for Arbitration at Kuala Lumpur or any other regional centre for arbitration in ASEAN; or (vi) any other arbitration institution if the disputing parties agree. Resort to any of the above choices will exclude resort to the other options.

157 History, The Founding of ASEAN, ASEAN's website, available at: http://www.asean.org/asean/about-asean/history/.

158 ASEAN Comprehensive Investment Agreement, Investment Policy Hub, available at: http://investmentpolicyhub.unctad.org/IIA/country/97/treaty/3273.

159 Article 6 of ACIA.

160 *Ibid.*, Article 11.

161 *Ibid.*, Article 11.

162 *Ibid.*, Article 14.

Further discussion on investment protection under the ACIA can be found in the ASEAN chapter of this book.

2 *APEC*

Indonesia became a member State of the Asia-Pacific Economic Cooperation ("APEC") on 7 November 1989.[163] Three key APEC investment-related instruments are the Non-Binding Investment Principles ("NBIP"), the Menu of Options, and the Transparency Standards on Investment.

The NBIP sets out 12 investment principles that are broadly similar to the core elements of international investment agreements concluded between APEC Member States, including provisions on transparency, national treatment, fair and equitable treatment, full protection and security, protection from strife, the transfer of funds, and the entry of key personnel.

The Menu of Options (or the Options for Investment Liberalization and Business Facilitation to Strengthen the APEC Economies) lists policies for liberalization and business facilitation.

The Transparency Standards on Investment cover the publication, awareness and availability of investment laws and measures. For instance, paragraph 1 of the Transparency Standards on Investment provides that each Economy will "ensure that its investment laws, regulations and progressively procedures and administrative rulings of general application ('investment measures') are promptly published or otherwise made available in such a manner as to enable interested persons and other economies to become acquainted with them."[164]

3 *APPGI*

Indonesia signed the Agreement on Promotion, Protection and Guarantee of Investments among Member States of the Organization of the Islamic Conference ("APPGI") on 5 June 1981.[165] The APPGI entered into force on 23 September 1986.[166]

The APPGI seeks to provide and develop a favourable climate for investments. Under the APPGI, contracting parties agree to, *inter alia*, permit the

---

163 http://www.apec.org/about-us/about-apec/member-economies.aspx.

164 "Identifying core elements in investment agreements in the APEC region", UNCTAD Series on International Investment Policies for Development, United Nations (New York and Geneva: 2008), Annex 2, available at http://unctad.org/en/Docs/diaeia20083_en.pdf.

165 Investment Policy Hub, available at: http://investmentpolicyhub.unctad.org/IIA/country/97/treaty/3092.

166 *Ibid.*

transfer of capital among them and its utilization therein in the fields permitted for investment, guarantee adequate protection and security over any capital invested, and provide treatment to investors of any contracting party which is not less favourable than the treatment accorded to investors belonging to any other State not party to the APPGI (the equivalent of a MFN clause).

Under Article 16 of the APPGI, the Host State undertakes to allow the investor the right to resort to its national judicial system to (i) complain against a measure adopted by its authorities against him, (ii) to contest the extent of its conformity with the provisions of the regulations and laws in force in its territory, or (iii) to complain against the non-adoption by the Host State of a certain measure which is in the interest of the investor, and which the State should have adopted.

Article 17 of the APPGI provides that until an organ for the settlement of disputes arising under that agreement is established, disputes shall be settled by conciliation or arbitration in accordance with the APPGI. Under Article 17, paragraph 2(a) of the APPGI, if the parties to the dispute do not reach an agreement after conciliation, or if the conciliator is unable to issue the report within the prescribed period, or if the parties do not accept the proposed solutions, then either party has the right to commence arbitration. This provision was invoked by the Claimant in *Al Warraq v Republic of Indonesia*,[167] alleging breaches by Indonesia of several provisions of the APPGI. Further details on this case are set out under the section "International Investment Arbitration Jurisprudence" below.

Article 9 of the APPGI is a unique provision which binds an investor to observe certain norms of conduct, and is potentially potent. Article 9 states: "[t]he investor shall be bound by the laws and regulations in force in the host state and shall refrain from all acts that may disturb public order or morals or that may be prejudicial to the public interest. He is also to refrain from exercising restrictive practices and from trying to achieve gains through unlawful means". In the *Al Warraq v Indonesia* case mentioned above, the Claimant was found by the Tribunal to have acted contrary to this provision, which rendered his claims inadmissible.

167 *Hesham Talaat M. Al-Warraq v. Republic of Indonesia*, UNCITRAL, available at: http://www.italaw.com/cases/1527.

V Multilateral Dispute Settlement Related Treaties

1 *ICSID Convention*

Indonesia signed the ICSID Convention on 16 February 1968 and deposited its notice of ratification on 28 September 1968. The ICSID Convention entered into force in Indonesia on 28 October 1968.[168]

As at the time of writing, Indonesia has not issued a notification that any part of its territory is excluded from the application of the ICSID Convention pursuant to Article 70 of the ICSID Convention.

Pursuant to Article 25(1) and Article 25(3) of the ICSID Convention, Indonesia has designated the Government of the Regency of East Kutai on 27 September 2012 to ICSID.[169] This has the effect of giving the Government of the Regency of East Kutai *locus standi* under the ICSID Convention in principle, provided the other ICSID Convention requirements are also met.[170] In the Award on Jurisdiction rendered on 28 December 2009 in the case of *Government of the Province of East Kalimantan v. PT Kaltim Prima Coal et al*, ICSID Case No. ARB/07/03, the Tribunal found that the claimant, the Government of East Kalimantan had no right to bring claims under the ICSID Convention because it was not a designated constituent subdivision of the Indonesian Government. This case will be discussed below under the section, "International Investment Arbitration Jurisprudence".

Pursuant to Article 54(2) of the ICSID Convention, Indonesia has also designated its Supreme Court as the court competent for the purpose of recognizing and enforcing awards rendered pursuant to the ICSID Convention.[171]

As at the time of writing, Indonesia has been the respondent in 6 ICSID cases.[172] Further details on these cases will be set out below.

---

168 ICSID's website, available at: https://icsid.worldbank.org/apps/ICSIDWEB/about/Pages/Database-of-Member-States.aspx?tab=FtoJ&rdo=BOTH.

169 ICSID's website, available at: https://icsid.worldbank.org/apps/ICSIDWEB/about/Pages/MembershipStateDetails.aspx?state=ST65.

170 Schreuer et al., *The* ICSID *Convention: A Commentary*, 2nd ed, (Cambridge University Press, 2009) at para. 232.

171 ICSID's website, available at: https://icsid.worldbank.org/apps/ICSIDWEB/about/Pages/MembershipStateDetails.aspx?state=ST65.

172 ICSID's website, available at: https://icsid.worldbank.org/apps/ICSIDWEB/cases/Pages/AdvancedSearch.aspx?gE=s&rspndnt=Republic%20of%20Indonesia.

2 *New York Convention*

Indonesia acceded to the New York Convention on 7 October 1981.[173] Pursuant to Article I(3) of the New York Convention, Indonesia issued a declaration that it will apply the New York Convention on the basis of reciprocity, to the recognition and enforcement of awards made only in the territory of another Contracting State of the New York Convention, and that it will apply the New York Convention only to differences arising out of legal relationships, whether contractual or not, which are considered as commercial under Indonesian law.[174]

A notable case relating to the application – or more accurately, non-application – of the New York Convention is *Navigation Maritime Bulgare v. P. T. Nizawar Mahkamah Agung*, Supreme Court, 20 August 1984.[175] In this case, the Indonesian Supreme Court held that the London arbitral award, being a foreign award, was not enforceable in Indonesia even though Indonesia had already ratified the New York Convention at that time because it was still necessary for the Indonesian Government to promulgate implementing regulations concerning whether a request to enforce a foreign award should be made to a District Court (and if so, which District Court) or whether such request should be made directly to the Supreme Court. This was because a determination as to whether the award is contrary to the Indonesian legal order was necessary. This issue is likely to have been resolved at the latest by the promulgation of Law No. 30 of 1999 relating to Arbitration and Alternative Dispute Resolution, which clarifies that the application for the enforcement of foreign arbitral awards is to be made to the Central Jakarta District Court.[176]

VI International Investment Arbitration Jurisprudence

At the time of writing, there have been 7 investor-State arbitration proceedings commenced against Indonesia,[177] out of which 6 were commenced under the

---

173 New York Convention's website, available at: http://www.newyorkconvention.org/list+of+contracting+states.

174 *Ibid.*

175 An English excerpt of the decision is available at: http://www.kluwerarbitration.com/CommonUI/document.aspx?id=ipn2759.

176 Article 65 of Law No. 30 of 1999.

177 Based on a search on italaw at: http://www.italaw.com/browse/respondent-state?field_case_type_tid%5B%5D=1090&field_respondent_state_tid=631&=Filter and ICSID's website at: https://icsid.worldbank.org/apps/ICSIDWEB/cases/Pages/AdvancedSearch.aspx?gE=s&rspndnt=Republic%20of%20Indonesia.

auspices of ICSID. The remaining case, *Al Warraq v Indonesia* was governed by the 2010 UNCITRAL Arbitration Rules.

Cases Involving Indonesia as the Respondent State

Awards

Amco Asia Corporation (U.S.), Pan American Development Limited (British), PT Amco (Indonesian) v Republic of Indonesia, ICSID Case No. ARB/81/1

First Tribunal: Berthold Goldman (President, France)
Isi Foighel (Denmark)
Edward W. Rubin (Canada)

Ad Hoc Committee: Ignaz Seidl-Hohenveldern (President, Austria)
Florentino Feliciano (Philippines)
Andrea Giardina (Italy)

Second Tribunal: Rosalyn Higgins (President, United Kingdom)
Per Magid (Denmark)
Marc Lalonde (Canada)

Case Initiated: 15 January 1981

Key Awards Rendered:

1. Decision on Jurisdiction, 25 September 1983 (not publicly available)
2. Award on the Merits, 21 November 1984 (not publicly available)
3. Decision on Annulment, 16 May 1986 (not publicly available)
4. Decision on Jurisdiction in Resubmitted Proceedings of 10 May 1988
5. Award on the Merits in Resubmitted Proceedings of 5 June 1990 (not publicly available)
6. Decision on Supplemental Decisions and Rectification of the Award of 17 October 1990 (not publicly available)

7. Decision rejecting the parties' application for annulment of the Award and annulling the Decision on Supplemental Decisions and Rectification issued of 17 December 1992 (not publicly available)

Background Facts

On 15 January 1981, Amco Asia Corporation ("Amco Asia"), Pan American Development Limited ("Pan American") and PT Amco Indonesia ("PT Amco") (together, the "Claimants") filed a Request for Arbitration against Indonesia with the Secretary General of ICSID. The Claimants alleged that, in 1980, Indonesia had seized their investment in the building and management of a hotel complex and had then unjustifiably cancelled their investment license. The Jakarta courts had rescinded a Lease and Management Agreement relating to the hotel. The Claimants instituted ICSID arbitration proceedings against Indonesia based on an arbitration clause included in the investment license.

Indonesia instituted counterclaims against PT Amco, alleging that it was obliged to return tax and other concessions granted by Indonesia.

Overview of the Procedural History

This case took almost 10 years to conclude and multiple awards and decisions were issued by three different bodies constituted over those 10 years. The protracted procedural history of this case can be summarised as follows:

- On 15 January 1981, the Claimants filed a Request for Arbitration;
- On 25 September 1983, the Tribunal issued its Decision on Jurisdiction;
- On 9 December 1983, the Tribunal issued its Decision on Request for Provisional Measures;
- On 21 November 1984, the Tribunal rendered its Award on the Merits;
- On 18 March 1985, Indonesia filed an application for the annulment of the Award on the Merits of 21 November 1984;
- On 7 September 1985, the *Ad Hoc* Committee issued its Decision on the Application for Stay of Enforcement of the Award under Article 52(5) of the ICSID Convention;
- On 16 May 1986, the *Ad Hoc* Committee issued its decision on the Application for annulment, annulling the Award of 21 November 1984 subject to the qualification that the annulment did not extend to all of the tribunal's findings;
- On 12 May 1987, the Claimants filed the Request for Resubmission of the dispute;

- On 20 October 1987, the second Tribunal was constituted;
- On 10 May 1988, the second Tribunal rendered a Decision on Jurisdiction of the Resubmitted Case;
- On 5 June 1990 the second Tribunal rendered its Final Award;
- On 17 October 1990, the second Tribunal issued a Decision on Supplemental Decisions and Rectification;
- On 2 March 1991, the Tribunal issued Interim Order No. 1 Concerning the Stay of Enforcement of Award; and
- On 17 December 1992, the Tribunal issued its Decision on the Application by Parties for Annulment and Partial Annulment of the Arbitral Award of June 5, 1990 and the Application by Respondent for Annulment of the Supplemental Award of October 17, 1990.

Key Legal Outcomes

The First Tribunal found in favour of the Claimants and awarded US 3.2 million plus interest to the Claimants and rejected Indonesia's counterclaim.[178] The Tribunal found that Indonesia had failed to protect PT Amco's right to manage the hotel in breach of a host State's duty under international law to protect foreign investors' rights and interests.[179] The Tribunal also found that the revocation of PT Amco's license to do business in Indonesia was in violation of the principle of due process because no prior warning was given and PT Amco was given no more than one hour's hearing at the revocation proceedings.[180]

Indonesia filed an application for the annulment of the First Tribunal's award under Article 52 of the ICSID Convention, alleging that the First Tribunal had manifestly exceeded its powers, seriously departed from a fundamental rule of procedure and had failed to state the reasons upon which the award was based in various aspects.[181] The *ad hoc* Committee found that the First Tribunal had manifestly exceeded its powers by failing to apply the relevant provisions of Indonesian law. In this regard, the *ad hoc* Committee found that PT Amco had failed to invest the required amounts of foreign capital in conformity with the provisions of Indonesia's foreign investment law.[182] The *ad hoc* Committee therefore annulled the finding of the First Tribunal that the revocation of PT Amco's license was not justified and its finding on

178 Decision on Jurisdiction of the Resubmitted Case, paragraph 4.
179 *Ibid.*, para. 8.
180 *Ibid.*, para. 8.
181 *Ibid.*, para. 9.
182 *Ibid.*, para. 13.

the amount of damages.[183] The *ad hoc* Committee also annulled the First Tribunal's rejection of Indonesia's counterclaim.[184]

However, the *ad hoc* Committee did not annul certain findings made by the First Tribunal, including the findings that the actions taken by the Indonesian army and police personnel were illegal[185] and that the procedures for the revocation of the license were unlawful.[186]

The Second Tribunal found that the findings of the First Tribunal that were not annulled by the *ad hoc* Committee remained *res judicata* for the resubmitted proceedings before the Second Tribunal,[187] one of them being that the procedure for the license revocation was unlawful. On the basis of this finding, the Second Tribunal found that while not every procedural irregularity constitutes a denial of justice under international law, Indonesia had committed a denial of justice in this case.[188] The Second Tribunal found that the denial of justice had effectively deprived PT Amco of its contractual rights and awarded it non-speculative profits under that contract, in order to place PT Amco in the position it would have been in had it received the benefits of the profit-sharing agreement until its end in 1999.[189]

Cemex Asia Holdings Ltd (Singapore) v Republic of Indonesia, ICSID Case No. ARB/04/3

Tribunal:	L. Yves Fortier (President, Canada) Robert Von Mehren (United States) Brigitte Stern (France)
Case Initiated:	27 January 2004
Award:	Award embodying the parties' settlement agreement rendered on 23 February 2007, pursuant to Arbitration Rule 43(2).

183 *Ibid.*, para. 13.
184 *Ibid.*, para. 13.
185 *Ibid.*, para. 15.
186 *Ibid.*, para. 15.
187 *Ibid.*, paras. 28 and 29.
188 Irmgard Marboe, *Amco v Indonesia Case*, Max Planck Encyclopedia of Public International Law, available at: http://opil.ouplaw.com/view/10.1093/law:epil/9780199231690/law-9780199231690-e1781?rskey=nQQ5xp&result=1&prd=EPIL.
189 *Ibid.*

Background Facts

Cemex Asia Holdings, a Singaporean company, instituted ICSID proceedings against Indonesia for claims arising out of the non-execution of its contractual option to buy a majority shareholding in a State-owned entity in which it had invested, due to alleged local opposition by workers and politicians to a foreign takeover of the company.[190] The claim was brought under the ACIA and the sum claimed was US$ 400 million.[191] This case was settled for an award of US$ 337 million.[192] However, the award is not publicly available.

Rafat Ali Rizvi (UK) v Republic of Indonesia (ICSID Case No. ARB/11/13)

Tribunal:	Gavan Griffith QC (President, Australian) Joan E. Donoghue (United States) Muthucumaraswamy Sornarajah (Australian)
Ad Hoc Committee:	Andrés Rigo Sureda (President, Spain) Teresa Cheng (China) Rolf Knieper (Germany)
Case Initiated:	5 April 2011
Award Rendered:	Award on Jurisdiction of 16 July 2013

Key Legal Outcomes

- Jurisdiction

On 5 April 2011, the Claimant, Mr Rafat Ali Rizvi, a British citizen, filed a Request for Arbitration with ICSID, instituting arbitration proceedings against Indonesia under the Indonesia-UK BIT. The Claimant had, together with Mr Hesham al-Warraq, who was the Claimant in a separate arbitration against Indonesia, through a Bahamas company, Chinkara Capital Limited, acquired shares in three Indonesian banks from early 2000.

Indonesia objected to the Tribunal's jurisdiction on the basis that the Claimant's investments fell outside the protection of the Indonesia-UK BIT. Indonesia argued that pursuant to Article 2(1) of the Indonesia-UK BIT, only investments that were granted admission in a process administered by

190 Investment Policy Hub at: http://investmentpolicyhub.unctad.org/ISDS/Details/171.

191 *Ibid.*

192 *Ibid.*

the Indonesian Investment Coordinating Board (BKPM) were covered by the Indonesia-UK BIT.[193]

The Tribunal did not agree with the Respondent that only investments granted admission by the BKPM would fall within the scope of Article 2(1) of the Indonesia-UK BIT. Rather, Article 2(1) of the Indonesia-UK BIT is wide enough to encompass investments granted admission pursuant to conditions imposed by Indonesia where the relevant sector is open to investment but not governed by the BKPM procedures.[194]

However, in that case, the Tribunal found that there was insufficient evidence that the Claimant's investment was granted admission in accordance with Indonesia's Foreign Capital Investment Law, which was required under Article 2(1) of the Indonesia-UK BIT in order for the investment to come under the protection of that BIT. In particular, the Tribunal found that there was insufficient evidence that the Claimant's investments had been approved by Bank Indonesia.[195] The Tribunal also found that the Claimant could not rely on the MFN provision in the Indonesia-UK BIT to establish jurisdiction of the Tribunal because the investment did not even come within the scope of the Indonesia-UK BIT.[196] For these reasons, the Tribunal held that it had no jurisdiction over the claim.

- Annulment

By way of an application dated 11 November 2013, the Claimant filed an application to annul the Tribunal's Award on Jurisdiction alleging that the Tribunal had manifestly exceeded its powers, that there had been a serious departure from a fundamental rule of procedure and that the Award had failed to state the reasons on which it is based.[197]

The annulment proceedings were discontinued. On 4 May 2015, the *ad hoc* Committee issued an Order taking note of the discontinuance of the proceedings pursuant to ICSID Arbitration Rules 53 and 44.

193 Paragraph 52(1) of the Award on Jurisdiction, 16 July 2013.

194 *Ibid.*, para. 139.

195 *Ibid.*, para. 196.

196 *Ibid.*, para. 223.

197 Application for Annulment and Stay of Enforcement of Award on Jurisdiction, 11 November 2013, para. 5.

Hesham Talaat M. Al-Warraq (Saudi Arabia) v Republic of Indonesia (UNCITRAL Rules)

Tribunal:	Bernardo Cremades (President, Spain) Michael Hwang, S.C. (Singapore) Fali Nariman, S.C. (India)
Case Initiated:	1 August 2011
Awards Rendered:	1. Award on Respondent's Preliminary Objections to Jurisdiction and Admissibility of the Claims of 21 June 2012 2. Final Award of 15 December 2014

Background Facts

On 1 August 2011, the Claimant, Hesham Talaat M. Al-Warraq, a Saudi Arabian national, filed a Notice of Arbitration with ICSID, alleging that Indonesia had breached certain provisions of the Agreement on Promotion, Protection and Guarantee of Investments among Member States of the Organization of the Islamic Conference ("APPGI").

The Claimant had, personally and through a Bahamas company Chinkara Capital Ltd. (later renamed to First Gulf Asia Holdings Ltd. ("FGAH")), invested in shares of an Indonesian bank, Bank Century. On 21 November 2008, Bank Century was placed under the administration of Indonesia's Deposit Insurance Agency, which the Claimant argued was a breach of various standards of protection under the APPGI, and various BITs by virtue of the MFN clause in the APPGI and customary international law.[198]

After the nationalisation of Bank Century, the Claimant was convicted of various offences relating to alleged banking irregularities. The Claimant argued that the prosecution of those offences were so fundamentally unfair it amounted to a denial of justice and a breach of the fair and equitable treatment standard.

198 Award on Respondent's Preliminary Objections to Jurisdictions and Admissibility of the Claims of 21 June 2012, para. 46.

Key Legal Outcomes

- Preliminary Objections

Indonesia objected to the jurisdiction of the Tribunal on several grounds.

First, Indonesia argued that Article 17 of the APPGI does not contain Indonesia's consent to arbitration with a private individual because the APPGI focuses on inter-State relations. The Tribunal rejected this argument, reasoning that it is implicit in Articles 16 and 17 of the APPGI, and is consistent with the object and purpose of the APPGI, to interpret Article 17 to provide for investor-State arbitration.[199]

Second, Indonesia argued that arbitration was no longer an option for the investor under Article 17 of the APPGI because the International Court of Justice has been established, which thereby excluded the arbitration option under Article 17. The Tribunal also rejected this argument because the ICJ is a judicial organ and does not provide conciliation or arbitration services,[200] unlike the organ contemplated in Article 17 of the APPGI.

Third, Indonesia argued that the Claimant is denied the protection of the APPGI because of his illegal conduct. Fourth, Indonesia argued that the Claimant did not have any "investment" within the meaning of the APPGI because it was not clear whether he owned shares in FGAH. The Tribunal reserved its decision on this issue to the merits phase of the proceedings.

- Final Award

At the merits phase, the Tribunal held that it had jurisdiction over the claims because the Claimant was an investor within the meaning of Article 1(6) of the APPGI by virtue of his indirect shareholding in Bank Century through FGAH.[201]

With regard to the Claimant's expropriation claim, the Tribunal held that the nationalisation of Bank Century was a bailout that was allowed as a permissible preventive measure under Article 10(2)(b) of the APPGI.[202]

The Tribunal held that Indonesia's conduct in the prosecution and conviction of the Claimant breached the fair and equitable treatment standard, which the Claimant was entitled to by operation of the MFN clause in Article 8 of the APPGI. However, the Tribunal, by a majority, found that the Claimant had carried out illegal activity which constituted acts prejudicial to public

199 *Ibid.*, para. 75.

200 *Ibid.*, para. 88.

201 Final Award, para. 517.

202 *Ibid.*, para. 539.

interest and pursuant to Article 9 of the APPGI, and was therefore disentitled from any damages in respect of Indonesia's breaches of the fair and equitable standard as his claims were inadmissible.[203]

Churchill Mining PLC and Planet Mining Pty Ltd v Republic of Indonesia (ICSID Case No. ARB/12/14 and 12/40)

Tribunal:	Gabrielle Kaufmann-Kohler (President, Switzerland) Albert Jan Van den Berg (Netherlands) Michael Hwang, S.C. (Singapore)
Case Initiated:	22 May 2012
Award Rendered:	Decision on Jurisdiction (*Churchill Mining v Indonesia*), 24 February 2014 Decision on Jurisdiction (*Planet Mining v Indonesia*), 24 February 2014

Background Facts

The background facts to the *Churchill Mining* and *Planet Mining* cases are largely identical.[204]

In 2006, an Indonesian group of companies, the Ridlatama group introduced the East Kutai Coal Project in the Regency of East Kutai to Churchill Mining and Planet Mining, which then acquired 95% (Churchill) and 5% (Planet) of the shares in an Indonesian foreign direct investment company, PT ICD, in furtherance of their investment plans.[205] PT ICD was authorised by the BKPM to be incorporated as an Indonesian foreign direct-investment company and to conduct business in the mining industry in Indonesia on 23 November 2005 (the "2005 BKPM Approval").

On 12 January 2009, Indonesia promulgated Law No. 4 of 2009 concerning Mining of Mineral and Coal, together with the implementing Regulation No. 23 of 2009 of 1 February 2009. This law adopted a new system of licensing and abolished the previous regime of licenses.[206]

On 4 May 2010, the Regent of East Kutai issued four Revocation Decrees of the exploitation licenses held by four companies within the Ridlatama group.

203 *Ibid.*, para. 647.

204 *Planet Mining v Indonesia*, Decision on Jurisdiction, para. 6.

205 *Ibid.*, para. 16.

206 *Ibid.*, para. 31.

On 22 May 2012, Churchill Mining filed a Request for Arbitration against Indonesia under the Indonesia-UK BIT, alleging that Indonesia had "violated its international legal obligations" under that BIT.[207] On 26 November 2012, Planet Mining filed a Request for Arbitration against Indonesia under the Indonesia-Australia BIT alleging breaches of the fair and equitable treatment, protection and security and MFN provisions.[208] Pursuant to the Tribunal's Procedural Order No. 4 of 18 March 2013, these two cases were consolidated.

Key Legal Outcomes

The Tribunal rendered two decisions on jurisdiction on the same day, 24 February 2014, one pertaining to each Claimant.

- Planet Mining

With regard to Planet Mining, Indonesia objected to the Tribunal's jurisdiction on two bases. First, Indonesia had not provided its consent to ICSID arbitration. Second, Planet Mining's investments fell outside the scope of the Indonesia-Australia BIT because Planet Mining violated the terms of the investment approvals, the Indonesian Civil Code and the 2007 Investment Law.[209]

On Indonesia's first objection, the Tribunal found that Indonesia did not, in its BIT with Australia, consent in advance to ICSID arbitration.[210] Article XI, paragraph 4a of the Indonesia-Australia BIT provides that where an investor had submitted a request for arbitration to ICSID, the Respondent State "shall consent in writing to the submission of the dispute to the Centre within forty-five days of receiving such a request". Indonesia did not provide such consent in this case.

Notably, the Tribunal compared all the 64 BITs signed by Indonesia at that time and found that Indonesia had given advance consent to ICSID arbitration in 60 of those BITs, but the Indonesia-Australia BIT was not one of them.[211]

However, the Tribunal found that the 2005 BKPM Approval contained an expression of consent by Indonesia to ICSID proceedings, which extended to PT ICD's shareholders, including Planet Mining.[212] Section IX(4) of the 2005 BKPM Approval reads as follows: "[i]n the event of a dispute between the company and the Government of the Republic of Indonesia which cannot be settled by consultation/deliberation, the Government of Indonesia is [prepared/

207 *Churchill Mining v Indonesia*, Decision on Jurisdiction, para. 50.
208 *Planet Mining v Indonesia*, Decision on Jurisdiction, para. 51.
209 *Ibid.*, para. 77.
210 *Ibid.*, para. 198.
211 *Ibid.*, para. 186.
212 *Ibid.*, para. 217.

ready to follow/ willing to follow][213] settlement according to the provisions of the Convention on the settlement of disputes between States and Foreign Citizen regarding investments in accordance with Law Number 5 Year 1968".[214] On this basis, the Tribunal rejected Indonesia's first objection to jurisdiction.

On Indonesia's second objection to jurisdiction, the Tribunal found that BKPM had approved the change in shareholding, specifically Planet Mining's acquisition of shares, in PT ICD in 2006.[215] The Tribunal found that this was sufficient to satisfy the requirement of approval under Article III(1)(a) of the Indonesia-Australia BIT and consequently rejected Indonesia's second objection.[216]

Having rejected Indonesia's objections to jurisdiction, the Tribunal decided that it had jurisdiction over the dispute submitted by Planet Mining.

- Churchill Mining

Indonesia raised the same two objections to jurisdiction in this case. First, that Indonesia had not consented to ICSID arbitration. Second, that the investment had not been granted approval in accordance with Indonesia's 1967 Investment Law.

With regard to Indonesia's first objection, the Tribunal found that Article 7(1) of the Indonesia-UK BIT contains a standing offer to arbitrate any dispute that may arise in connection with an investment before ICSID.[217] In particular, contrary to Indonesia's position that the language "shall assent" in Article 7(1) of the Indonesia-UK BIT denotes that subsequent consent from Indonesia is required, the Tribunal concluded that the language "shall assent" was "functionally equivalent" to "hereby consents" or similar wording and constituted consent in advance to arbitration.[218]

The Tribunal held that in any event, it would also have found consent to ICSID arbitration in the approvals given by BKPM.[219]

213 The Parties disagreed on the translation of the Indonesian word "*bersedia*" but the Tribunal found the Parties' differences in translations irrelevant to its conclusion, see *Planet Mining v Indonesia*, Decision on Jurisdiction, paragraph 208.

214 *Planet Mining v Indonesia*, Decision on Jurisdiction, paragraphs 203 and 204.

215 *Ibid.*, para. 292.

216 *Ibid.*, para. 292.

217 *Ibid.*, para. 231.

218 *Ibid.*, para. 230.

219 *Ibid.*, para. 232.

With regard to Indonesia's second objection, the Tribunal found that BKPM had approved the change in shareholding, specifically Churchill Mining's acquisition of shares, in PT ICD in 2006.[220] The Tribunal found that this was sufficient to satisfy the requirement of approval under Article 2(1) of the Indonesia-UK BIT and consequently rejected Indonesia's second objection.[221]

Since Indonesia's jurisdictional objections in both cases were rejected, these cases proceeded to the merits phase. At the time of writing, the latest development in these cases that is publicly available[222] is that on 20 August 2015, the Tribunal issued Procedural Order No. 20 concerning post-hearing briefs on the authenticity of certain documents.[223]

Nusa Tenggara Partnership B.V. and PT Newmont Nusa Tenggara, ICSID Case No. ARB/14/15

Tribunal:	Not constituted
Case Initiated:	15 July 2014
Award Rendered:	Case discontinued, no award rendered.

On 15 July 2014, the Secretary-General of ICSID registered the Claimants' request for the institution of arbitration proceedings against Indonesia, alleging breaches of the now-terminated 1994 Netherlands-Indonesia BIT. The claim arose out of the introduction of export restrictions on copper, including an export duty and a ban on the export of copper concentrate which allegedly stalled production at copper and gold mines operated by the Claimants.[224] On 25 August 2014, slightly more than a month after the case was registered, the Claimants filed a request for the discontinuance of the proceedings.

A few days later, on 29 August 2014, the Secretary-General issued a procedural order taking note of the discontinuance of the proceedings. The reason for the discontinuance is not clear from publicly available information.

220 *Ibid.*, para. 313.

221 *Ibid.*, para. 314.

222 Available at: http://www.italaw.com/cases/1479.

223 Procedural Order No. 20, available at: http://www.italaw.com/sites/default/files/case-documents/italaw6358.pdf.

224 Investment Policy Hub, at: http://investmentpolicyhub.unctad.org/ISDS/Details/584.

Cases involving Indonesia as the Claimant

Government of the Province of East Kalimantan v PT Kaltim Prima Coal, Rio Tinto plc, BP P.L.C., Pacific Resources Investments Limited, BP International Limited, Sangatta Holdings Limited, Kalimantan Coal Limited, ICSID Case No. ARB/07/3

Tribunal:	Gabrielle Kaufmann-Kohler (President, Switzerland) Albert Jan van den Berg (Netherlands) Michael Hwang, S.C. (Singapore)
Case Initiated:	5 April 2006
Award Rendered:	Decision on Jurisdiction, 28 December 2009

Background Facts

On 8 April 1982, PT Kaltim Prima Coal (PT KPC) entered into an agreement with a State-owned entity, Peruskan Negara Tambang Batubura, to conduct coal mining operations for a duration of 30 years in Sangatta, East Kalimantan, Regency of East Kutai (the "Contract").[225] PT KPC was an Indonesian joint venture company originally owned by Rio Tinto Limited and BP P.l.c. in equal shares. Under the Contract, PT KPC was to sell its shares from 1996 to 2001 to Indonesian buyers.

In 2001, PT Kaltim Prima Coal, pursuant to discussions with the Indonesian Government, agreed to offer 51% of its shares subject to agreement on the price.[226] The Claimant, the Government of East Kalimantan, argued that it had priority rights over these shares. The Respondents, who are PT Kaltim Prima Coal and its original shareholders, Rio Tinto Limited and BP P.l.c. and their subsidiaries, argued that they had discretion to decide to whom they would sell its shares, subject to the approval of the Indonesian Government.[227] On 16 July 2003, all the shares in PT KPC were sold to an Indonesian company, PT Bumi Resources Tbk.[228]

On 5 April 2006, the Claimant filed a Request for Arbitration at ICSID, alleging that the Respondents had breached their obligations under the Contract and the Law on Foreign Investment and Decisions of the Indonesian Government

225 Award on Jurisdiction, 28 December 2009, para. 9.
226 *Ibid.*, para. 20.
227 *Ibid.*, para. 21.
228 *Ibid.*, para. 54.

by failing to sell to the Claimant 51% of the shares in PT KPC.[229] The Claimant alleged that as a result of the Respondents' breaches, the Claimant incurred losses in the form of lost revenue and income from dividends which would have been received by the Claimant.[230]

Key Legal Outcomes

The Respondents argued that the ICSID Tribunal had no jurisdiction because the Claimant, the Government of East Kalimantan, is not a Contracting State under the ICSID Convention or a designated subdivision of a Contracting State.[231] The Tribunal found that it had no jurisdiction because the Claimant had no right to bring the case.

The Claimant had sought to rely on two grounds to assert a right to rely on the ICSID Convention to bring a case before an ICSID Tribunal. First, the Claimant argued that pursuant to Article 2 of Indonesian Law No. 5 of 1968, it had stepped into the shoes of the Indonesian Government.[232] The Tribunal found that that Article had provided the Indonesian Government with the power to consent to ICSID arbitration and to designate a third party to represent it in ICSID proceedings.[233] However, the Tribunal found that Indonesia had not given such consent in this case.[234]

Second, the Claimant argued that it had been designated by the Indonesian Government as a constituent subdivision to the ICSID.[235] The Tribunal found that while the form and channel of communicating a designation do not matter, an intention to designate must be clearly established.[236] In this case, the Tribunal found that the Indonesian Government had not designated the Claimant as a constituent subdivision to ICSID.[237] On the contrary, the Indonesian Government had clearly denied the Claimant's authority to act as a party to ICSID arbitration.[238]

---

229 *Ibid.*, para. 69.
230 *Ibid.*
231 *Ibid.*, para. 109.
232 *Ibid.*, para. 180.
233 *Ibid.*, paras. 182 and 183.
234 *Ibid.*, para. 185.
235 *Ibid.*, para. 188.
236 *Ibid.*, para. 192.
237 *Ibid.*, para. 200.
238 *Ibid.*, para. 200.

VII Outlook: Anticipated Developments

Indonesia announced in March 2014 that it intends to let its existing BITs expire. Since then, at the time of writing, 16 of the Indonesian BITs have been terminated.[239] In conjunction with this development, it has been reported that Indonesia is intending to issue a new model BIT.[240] Taking these developments into consideration, it is likely that Indonesia will continue to let its existing BITs lapse[241] while preparing a new model BIT that will form the basis of negotiations for future BITs.

That said, Indonesia's attitude is rendered less clear by the fact that it is negotiating a FTA with Australia and has also announced its intention to sign the Trans-Pacific Partnership Agreement ("TPP").[242] At the time of writing, the TPP has been signed by 12 Pacific Rim countries, namely the US, Japan, Malaysia, Vietnam, Singapore, Brunei, Australia, New Zealand, Canada, Mexico, Chile and Peru. The TPP is intended to create a free trade area among these countries, focused on reducing tariffs, imposing stricter safeguards for patents and levelling the playing field for companies that compete with government-backed businesses.[243] Some requirements under the TPP may prove particularly challenging for Indonesia to comply with, such as allowing greater competition against State-owned entities, loosening restrictions on foreign ownership and allowing investor-State arbitration to bypass its domestic courts system.[244]

---

239 The Indonesia-Bulgaria BIT, Indonesia-Cambodia BIT, Indonesia-China BIT, Indonesia-Egypt BIT, Indonesia-France BIT, Indonesia-Hungary BIT, Indonesia-India BIT, Indonesia-Italy BIT, Indonesia-Lao People's Democratic Republic BIT, Indonesia-Malaysia BIT, Indonesia-Netherlands BIT, Indonesia-Romania BIT, Indonesia-Slovakia BIT, Indonesia-Switzerland BIT, Indonesia-Turkey BIT and Indonesia-Viet Nam BIT. See: http://investmentpolicyhub.unctad.org/IIA/CountryBits/97#iiaInnerMenu (last accessed on 17 June 2016).

240 Prof. Michael Ewing-Chow and Mr Junianto James Losari, *Indonesia is letting its bilateral treaties lapse so as to negotiate better ones*, Financial Times, available at: http://www.ft.com/intl/cms/s/0/20c6c518-c16c-11e3-97b2-00144feabdc0.html#axzz4301GWTNS.

241 As an example, at the time of writing, the Indonesia-Singapore BIT will expire on 21 June 2016 if notice is provided to terminate the BIT. It is unclear if Indonesia has or will provide such notice to terminate the BIT.

242 The Guardian, "Indonesia will join Trans-Pacific Partnership, Jokowi tells Obama", 27 October 2015, available at: http://www.theguardian.com/world/2015/oct/27/indonesia-will-join-trans-pacific-partnership-jokowi-tells-obama.

243 Bloomberg Business, "Here's Why Indonesia Joining the TPP is Easier Said than Done", 29 October 2015, available at: http://www.bloomberg.com/news/articles/2015-10-28/here-s-why-indonesia-joining-the-tpp-is-easier-said-than-done.

244 *Ibid.*

CHAPTER 5

Lao People's Democratic Republic[1]

I Introduction

The Lao People's Democratic Republic ("Laos") is a constitutional socialist republic,[2] which gained independence from France in October 1953.[3] Laos is a landlocked country bordered by Myanmar and China to the northwest, Vietnam to the east, Cambodia to the south and Thailand to the west. The population of Laos is relatively small at approximately 7 million people.[4]

Laos has a civil law system, which was modelled on the Soviet and Chinese systems.[5] The legal system has developed relatively recently and faces a number of challenges, including inconsistency in laws and regulations and weak training and independence of the judiciary.[6] Therefore, the US Department of State advises foreign investors to seek arbitration outside Laos.[7] However, Laos has adopted a Law on Making Legislation in order to strengthen the rule of law and transparency in the country.[8]

Although the country remains a one-party socialist State, in 1986 Laos began to liberalize and open its economy to trade and private investment.[9] Laos is working with the World Bank and other partners to increase its regional and global economic integration. In 1997, Laos became a member State of the

1 This chapter has been drafted by Ms Natasha Harrington, Eversheds LLP, Paris, with assistance from Mr Alvin Yap, Eversheds LLP, Singapore.

2 Constitution of the Lao People's Democratic Republic, No. 25/NA, 6 May 2003, available at: http://www.mfa.gov.sg/content/dam/mfa/images/om/vientiane/Lao%20Law/Amended%20Constitution%20of%20the%20Lao%20PDR.pdf.

3 France granted independence to Laos on 22 October 1953. However, the First Indochina War continued until the signing of the Geneva Accord in 1954.

4 See, the CIA World Factbook figures from July 2015: https://www.cia.gov/library/publications/the-world-factbook/geos/la.html.

5 U.S. Department of State, 2015 Investment Climate Statement, June 2015, p. 8.

6 *Ibid.* See also, *Lao PDR Investment Climate Assessment 2014: Policy uncertainty in the midst of a natural resources boom*, December 2014, pp. 9 and 74–76.

7 U.S. Department of State, 2015 Investment Climate Statement, June 2015, pp. 8–9.

8 Law on Making Legislation, No. 19/NA, 12 July 2012. Note that under Article 8 both domestic and foreign individuals are entitled to provide comments on draft legislation.

9 See, *An investment guide to the Lao People's Democratic Republic, Opportunities and Conditions*, 2010, United Nations, New York and Geneva, pp. 7–8.

 | DOI 10.1163/9789004335257_007

Association of Southeast Asian Nations ("ASEAN"). On 2 February 2013, Laos also became a member of the World Trade Organization ("WTO").[10]

Laos is currently classified as a Least Developed Country ("LDC"). In 2015 it ranked 148th out of 189 economies in the World Bank's Ease of Doing Business scale.[11] Nevertheless, over the last ten years the country has enjoyed economic growth of 7–8%.[12] According to the World Bank, Laos is likely to continue to experience growth, enabling Laos to achieve its target of graduating from LDC status by 2020.[13]

Increasing trade and foreign direct investment into Laos is a key part of the country's plans for economic development.[14] Most foreign investment has been in the hydroelectric and mining sectors, reflecting Laos' rich mineral resources.[15] Sustainable tourism and agribusiness are target areas for growth in foreign investment in Laos. Currently, the largest sources of foreign direct investment are from China, Vietnam, Thailand, Korea, France and Japan.[16]

II Laos' National Arbitration and Investment Legislation

1 *Laos' Arbitration Legislation and Institutions*

Laos' Arbitration Law

Laos has not adopted legislation based on the UNCITRAL Model Law on International Commercial Arbitration.[17] However, arbitration is supported by

---

10 See the list of World Trade Organization members, available at: https://www.wto.org/english/thewto_e/whatis_e/tif_e/org6_e.htm.

11 World Bank, Doing Business Economy Rankings, available online at: http://www.doingbusiness.org/rankings.

12 U.S. Department of State, 2015 Investment Climate Statement, June 2015, p. 3. The sources of economic growth are shown in the Asia Development Bank's Asian Development Outlook 2013, available at: http://www.adb.org/sites/default/files/publication/30205/ado2013-lao-pdr.pdf.

13 See, http://www.worldbank.org/en/country/lao/overview. See also, the World Bank's projections for future growth: http://www.worldbank.org/en/publication/global-economic-prospects/data?region=EAP.

14 U.S. Department of State, 2015 Investment Climate Statement, June 2015, pp. 3–4.

15 *Ibid.*, Approximately 80% of foreign direct investment is currently in the mining and hydropower sectors.

16 *Ibid.*, p. 4.

17 The List of States adopting legislation based on the UNCITRAL Model Law is available at: http://www.uncitral.org/uncitral/en/uncitral_texts/arbitration/1985Model_arbitration_status.html.

Laos' Law on Resolution of Economic Disputes and the Law on Investment Promotion. The Government of Laos has established the Centre for Economic Dispute Resolution ("CEDR") as an institution to oversee arbitration in Laos, and the Courts of Laos should recognise and enforce foreign arbitral awards pursuant to the New York Convention. However, there is currently limited practice or precedent regarding domestic or international arbitration in Laos.

Dispute Resolution Under the Law on Resolution of Economic Disputes

The Laos Law on Resolution of Economic Disputes (the "Economic Disputes Law") governs the submission of an "economic dispute" to arbitration in Laos or to international arbitration, and the recognition and enforcement of domestic and international arbitration awards. The Economic Disputes Law was first adopted by Presidential Decree in July 1994,[18] and then made into legislation in May 2005,[19] and amended in 2010.[20]

The Economic Disputes Law provides for dispute resolution by arbitration or mediation in Laos.[21] It established a Lao institution for arbitration, the CEDR, under the supervision of the Ministry of Justice and the Lao courts, (see below).

The Economic Disputes Law applies to "economic disputes", which is defined as "a conflict of interest" arising from a breach of contract, or from a dispute related to production or business operations, between legal entities or individuals or legal entities and individuals, whether domestic or foreign.[22] Thus, the Law does not distinguish between domestic and international arbitration on the basis of the nationality or location of the parties to a dispute.

However, Article 5 of the Economic Disputes Law provides that any person engaged in international trade or foreign investment has the right to choose to submit a dispute to an international or foreign institute for dispute resolution, and to choose the arbitrators, the governing law, the rules of procedure, the location and language of the arbitration, in accordance with the agreement of the disputing parties. Further, one of the stated purposes of the Law,

18 Decree No. 106/PM On the Resolution of Economic Disputes, 15 July 1994.

19 Law No. 02/NA On the Resolution of Economic Disputes, 19 May 2005.

20 Law on Resolution of Economic Disputes No. 06/NA, 17 December 2010 – (official language) – http://www.vlaw.la/lawlist/2010-12-17_Economic_Dispute_Resolution_Law.pdf; English translation available at http://www.laoftpd.com/index.php?option=com_docman&task=cat_view&gid=65&Itemid=86&lang=en, Article 2.

21 *Ibid.*, Article 15.

22 *Ibid.*, Article 2.

as amended in 2010, was to ensure that disputes are resolved peacefully, fairly and promptly, such as to promote the growth of business and international integration by creating a favourable environment for domestic and foreign investors.[23]

Under the Economic Disputes Law, a dispute may be submitted if:

a. "the dispute relates to economics or trade;
b. the disputing parties have agreed to submit disputes to arbitration in a contract;
c. the disputing parties agreed to dispute resolution voluntarily;
d. the dispute has not been submitted to the Lao courts, or subject to a final decision of the Lao courts; and
e. the dispute "is not related to the violation of laws and regulations concerning the stability of the State, social security and public order and the environment".[24]

In addition to the exclusion of disputes relating to the stability of the State and other matters set out above, the Lao courts may also refuse to recognise or enforce an arbitral award on similar grounds (see below).

Article 8 of the Economic Disputes Law sets out the basic principles according to which disputes must be resolved, including justice and compliance with the law; voluntary agreement of the disputing parties; equality of the disputing parties; independence and impartiality of the arbitrator(s); the language used and confidentiality. Article 11 provides that the parties to a dispute must have equal rights before the law without discrimination, and that foreign parties engaged in business in Laos have equal rights to Lao citizens "unless otherwise determined by law".

Dispute Resolution Under the Law on Investment Promotion

The Law on Investment Promotion 2009 provides that dispute resolution related with investment can be performed by (i) mediation; (ii) administrative dispute resolution; (iii) arbitration by the Committee [*or* Centre] for Economic Dispute Settlement; and (iv) litigation before the Lao courts.[25] This is an hierarchical list, which means that dispute settlement should be attempted by following these four steps in order.

23 *Ibid.*, Article 1.

24 *Ibid.*, Article 16.

25 Article 78 of the Law on Investment Promotion No. 02/NA, 8 July 2009.

However, the Law on Investment Promotion 2009 also states that disputes related to an investment agreement with the Laos Government should be settled according to the dispute resolution provision in the investment agreement.[26] In practice, this means that the above list only applies in the absence of a specific agreement in an investment agreement regarding dispute resolution.

Further, as noted above, the Economic Disputes Law 2010 also provides foreign investors with the right to submit disputes to a foreign or international dispute resolution institution.[27] Thus, foreign investors may agree to submit disputes regarding their investment directly to international arbitration.

Administrative dispute resolution involves submitting a dispute to the relevant industry sector, which for foreign investors is usually the Ministry of Planning and Investment or the Ministry of Industry and Trade.

Commercial Law in Laos

Contract and commercial law in Laos is still developing. As discussed below, the commercial court system in Laos is a relatively recent development.

Under the Lao Law on Contract and Tort, contracts can be voided by the Lao courts if they disadvantage one party,[28] or if they conflict with State or public interests. A contract that disadvantages one of the contract parties can be either voided or affirmed by the party that is disadvantaged.[29] A contract that is in conflict with State or public interests is absolutely null and cannot be affirmed by either party.[30]

Further, if a contract is nullified because it disadvantages one of the parties, then any assets transferred under the contract shall be returned to the relevant party.[31] However, if a contract is null because it is in conflict with national security, peace or social order, then the Law states that "all applied assets shall be confiscated and transferred into the property of the State".[32]

With such serious consequences for the nullification of a contract, it is important to obtain good legal advice before entering into a contract under Lao law.

26 *Ibid.*, Article 82(2).

27 Article 5 of the Law on Resolution of Economic Disputes No. 06/NA, 17 December 2010.

28 Article 10 of the Law on Contract and Tort No. 01/NA, 8 December 2008, requires that the parties to a contract should enter into the contract voluntarily; and Article 11 provides a voluntary act requires the giving of consent without, *inter alia*, disadvantage of any contracting parties, meaning "when the benefits resulting from the contract are unfair".

29 Article 19 of the Law on Contract and Tort No. 01/NA, 8 December 2008.

30 *Ibid.*, Article 20.

31 *Ibid.*, Article 23(1).

32 *Ibid.*, Article 23(3).

Further, the Economic Disputes Law requires that in order to submit a dispute to the CEDR, the disputing parties must have agreed to arbitration in a contract.[33] The above rules on the validity of contracts will apply to an agreement to arbitrate or to a contract containing an agreement to arbitrate. The laws of Laos do not expressly recognise the autonomy and separability of an agreement to arbitrate in a contract.[34] Therefore, if a contract is void under the Law on Contract and Tort, there is a risk that it may not be possible to rely on an arbitration agreement in the contract.

Laos' Arbitral Institutions and Rules

As noted above, the Economic Disputes Law establishes the CEDR, a State organization, which is under the instruction and supervision of the Ministry of Justice.[35] There are also four provincial Offices for Economic Dispute Resolution (the "OEDR"), which are under the supervision of the provincial Departments of Justice.[36]

The CEDR and the OEDR have a broad mandate to create and maintain favourable conditions for the resolution of economic disputes. Their powers and duties include the administration and facilitation of dispute resolution through arbitration.[37] In addition, the CEDR may propose and draft new laws and regulations on dispute resolution.[38]

According to the Economic Disputes Law, an arbitration tribunal should be composed of at least three arbitrators, and must include an odd number of arbitrators.[39]

Arbitrators must be appointed from the list of arbitrators maintained by the CEDR. Arbitrators are appointed to, and removed from, the list of arbitrators by the Minister of Justice of Laos, on the recommendation of the CEDR.[40] Foreign nationals as well as Lao nationals can be included on the list of arbitrators.[41]

If the disputing parties agree to have three arbitrators, they should each select an arbitrator from the list of arbitrators within fifteen days, and the two

33 Article 16 of the Law on Resolution of Economic Disputes No. 06/NA, 17 December 2010.

34 Moser, *Arbitration in Asia*, Juris Publishing Inc., 2008, section 3.2.6, LAO PDR-10.

35 Article 61 of the Law on Resolution of Economic Disputes No. 06/NA, 17 December 2010.

36 *Ibid.*, Article 62.

37 *Ibid.*, Articles 41 and 42.

38 *Ibid.*, Article 41.

39 *Ibid.*, Article 30.

40 *Ibid.*, Articles 42(2) and 43(2).

41 *Ibid.*, Article 47.

party-appointed arbitrators should select the third arbitrator, who will act as chairperson, within fifteen days. If either of the parties fails to appoint an arbitrator or the party-appointed arbitrators fail to select a chairperson, the CEDR shall make the relevant selection from the list of arbitrators within ten days.[42]

Arbitrators are required to be independent and impartial in the resolution of disputes.[43] A party may challenge an arbitrator if he/she has an interest in the dispute, is related to or has a dispute with either party, or is otherwise unable to perform his/her duties.[44]

According to Article 14 of the Law, arbitral proceedings shall be confidential. The law does not expressly allow the disputing parties to agree otherwise in order to provide greater transparency. The language of the arbitration will be Lao unless the parties agree otherwise.[45] Chapters 3 and 5 of the Economic Disputes Law provide further rules of procedure for the resolution of disputes by the CEDR and the OEDR.

According to Article 33 of the Economic Disputes Law, the resolution of disputes should be "successfully completed" (and an arbitral award rendered) within three months of the appointment of the arbitral tribunal. However, this very short period can be extended by the CEDR or the OEDR if the dispute is particularly complicated in terms of the collection of evidence, or for any other reason.

The arbitral award should be made unanimously, or if a unanimous decision is not possible, by a majority vote.[46] The disputing parties are obliged to implement an arbitral award issued pursuant to the Economic Disputes Law within 15 days of the date when the award was rendered, or when the disputing parties were informed of the award.[47] The enforcement of, and challenges to, arbitral awards before the Lao courts are dealt with below.

Laos' Courts and Arbitration

The court system in Laos is developing. In 2003, courts with jurisdiction over civil and commercial matters were established, and they started hearing cases in 2005.[48] The hierarchy of courts in Laos is the People's Courts, the Appellate

42 *Ibid.*, Article 30 (referring to Article 23, paras. 3–5).

43 *Ibid.*, Articles 8, 12 and 46.

44 *Ibid.*, Article 31, referring to Article 24.

45 *Ibid.*, Article 13.

46 *Ibid.*, Article 36.

47 *Ibid.*, Article 49.

48 *An investment guide to the Lao People's Democratic Republic, Opportunities and Conditions*, 2010, United Nations, New York and Geneva, p. 53.

Courts and the Supreme Court of Laos.[49] The Appellate and Supreme Courts have specialised civil and commercial chambers.

The Courts and the CEDR

The Lao courts have the power to support arbitration by the CEDR or the OEDR by ordering the seizure or confiscation of any property in order to protect the rights and interests of the parties to a dispute.[50] The party making the application must first apply to the arbitral tribunal, which may request such an order from the People's Court at any time during the arbitral process. The Economic Disputes Law does not expressly provide the Lao courts with any other powers to support the arbitration process during the proceedings.

As mentioned above, the disputing parties are obliged to implement an award of the CEDR or the OEDR within 15 days. A party who suffers any disadvantage due to the non-implementation of an arbitral award may apply to the Laos courts to enforce the award.[51]

The court must issue a decision on an application for enforcement within 15 days.[52] The court must verify that the award was properly conducted in accordance with relevant laws, regulations and international treaties to which Laos is a party, and that it does not endanger the stability of the nation, the peacefulness of society and the environment.[53] If all of the necessary conditions are met, then the court will decide to enforce the award. Such a decision is final and there is no appeal from a decision to grant enforcement.[54]

On the other hand, if the court finds that any of the conditions for enforcement are not satisfied, the court will refuse to enforce the award.[55] If the court refuses enforcement, the disputing parties may re-submit the dispute to the CEDR for arbitration. Alternatively, they may submit the dispute to the People's Court for resolution.

Arbitral awards issued pursuant to arbitration under the Economic Disputes Law may be challenged before the Laos courts within 45 days of the date of receipt of the award.[56] The grounds for challenge include: (i) the invalidity of the agreement to arbitrate; (ii) improper composition of the arbitration

49 Law on the People's Court, No. 05/PSA, 21 October 2003.

50 Article 34 of the Law on Resolution of Economic Disputes No. 06/NA, 17 December 2010.

51 *Ibid.*, Article 50.

52 *Ibid.*, Article 51(1).

53 *Ibid.*, Article 51(2).

54 *Ibid.*, Article 51(2).

55 *Ibid.*, Article 51(3).

56 *Ibid.*, Article 38.

tribunal; (iii) procedural impropriety (including failure to apply the rules agreed by the parties in the agreement to arbitrate); (iv) fraud or bribery in the making of the award; (v) the dispute was outside the scope of the Economic Disputes Law; and (vi) the arbitral award "exceeded or was less than the claim of the disputing parties".

The Courts and International Arbitration Awards

Laos is a State party to the New York Convention.[57] The Economic Disputes Law provides that a foreign or international arbitral award will be recognised and enforced if it is certified by a Laos court. According to Article 52(2) of the Law, the Laos court "will consider certifying" a foreign or international arbitral award if the following conditions are met:

a. the parties to the dispute must be nationals of countries that are parties to the New York Convention;
b. the decision must not be in conflict with the Constitution of Laos or rules relating to stability, peace and the environment; and
c. the award debtor must have property, business operations, equity, bank deposits or other assets in Laos.[58]

Therefore, the grounds for refusing to enforce a foreign arbitral award under the Economic Disputes Law differ from the grounds under Article V of the New York Convention. Further, because the Law states that the Lao courts "will consider" certifying an award if the above conditions are met, the scope of the courts' discretion to refuse enforcement is unclear.[59]

2 *Laos' Investment Laws*

The Investment Promotion Law 2009 has been heralded as levelling the playing field between domestic and foreign investors in Laos.[60] The Investment Promotion Law introduced uniform business registration requirements and

57 Laos acceded to the New York Convention on the Recognition and Enforcement of Foreign Arbitral Awards 1958 in 1998. See the list of member States: http://www.uncitral.org/uncitral/en/uncitral_texts/arbitration/NYConvention_status.html.

58 Article 52 of the Law on Resolution of Economic Disputes No. 06/NA, 17 December 2010.

59 The author was not able to find any examples of decisions of the Lao courts on the enforcement of a foreign arbitral award.

60 See, e.g., *An investment guide to the Lao People's Democratic Republic, Opportunities and Conditions*, 2010, United Nations, New York and Geneva, p. iii. Note that the law entered into force in 2011.

tax incentives that apply to both domestic and foreign investors, and allowed for the establishment of special economic zones with incentives to encourage investment.[61] The Investment Promotion Law also introduced the right for foreign nationals to acquire rights in land akin to ownership, whereas in the past such rights were restricted to Lao nationals.

However, there are some controls and restrictions on foreign investment under Lao law that investors will need to comply with. In particular, foreign investors in Laos require an investment licence.

Investment Forms and Licences

Three forms of investment are recognised under the Investment Promotion Law:

- a business enterprise established in Laos;
- a joint venture established in Laos; and
- business cooperation in Laos by contract.[62]

Business enterprises established in Laos: Foreign investors in Laos may own up to 100% of the shares in a business enterprise established in Laos.[63]

Joint ventures established in Laos: Foreign investors may also form a joint venture with domestic investors. The foreign investors in a joint venture must contribute at least 10% of the total capital.[64]

Business cooperation in Laos by contract: Business cooperation by contract allows foreign investors to do business in Laos without establishing a business enterprise in the country.[65] However, this form of investment is less common because it does not provide the investor with the same tax incentives as other forms of investment.

Before commencing operations, an investment must be registered. The Lao Government has introduced measures to speed up the process of enterprise registration through a "one-stop-shop" model.

The Law on Enterprises governs the requirements for registration of an enterprise in Laos.[66] The Law on Enterprises simplified the registration process

61 U.S. Department of State, 2015 Investment Climate Statement, June 2015, p. 5.
62 Article 8 of the Investment Promotion Law 2009 No. 02/NA, 8 July 2009.
63 *Ibid.*, Article 9.
64 *Ibid.*, Article 10.
65 *Ibid.*, Article 11.
66 Law on Enterprises 2005 No. 11/NA. Available at: http://www.investlaos.gov.la/index.php/start-up/laws-and-regulations/enterprise-law.

for all businesses except those in particularly sensitive sectors, such as national security, public order, cultural traditions and the environment.[67] The registration requirements are the same for foreign and domestic companies.[68]

However, the registration and licensing requirements and processes differ according to the type of investment made by an investor. The Investment Protection Law recognises three types of investment:

- general business activities;
- a concession business; and
- development of Special Economic Zones and Specific Economic Zones in Laos.[69]

Investment in general business activities: The investor must apply for an Enterprise Registration Certificate from the "one-stop shop" service of the Ministry of Industry and Commerce. The Enterprise Registration Certificate includes the investment licence, applicable investment promotion incentives and tax registration for the business entity.[70] Once an Enterprise Registration Certificate is received the investor can immediately start business operations.

An Enterprise Registration Certificate should be issued within ten working days of the submission of an application, unless the business activities in question are controlled activities included on the "Negative List".[71] The Negative List includes a range of activities such as mining, energy, transportation, telecommunications and broadcasting, healthcare, finance and gambling.[72] Business activities on the Negative List are not prohibited, but require approval by the Government Ministry concerned. An Enterprise Registration Certificate for a business on the Negative List should be issued within 13 working days, within

---

67 See, e.g., *An investment guide to the Lao People's Democratic Republic, Opportunities and Conditions*, 2010, United Nations, New York and Geneva, p. 50.

68 Article 12 of the Law on Enterprises No. 11/NA, 9 November 2005 (entered into force in 2007).

69 Articles 14–16 of the Investment Promotion Law 2009 No. 02/NA, 8 July 2009.

70 Article 19(2) of the Investment Promotion Law 2009 No. 02/NA, 8 July 2009 and Article 8 of the Decree on the Implementation of the Investment Promotion Law, 20 April 2011 No. 119/PM, available at: http://www.investlaos.gov.la/index.php/start-up/laws-and-regulations/investment-law (last accessed on 1 September 2015).

71 Article 18 of the Investment Promotion Law 2009 No. 02/NA, 8 July 2009.

72 Table 2, Report of the Working Party on the Accession of Lao PDR to the World Trade Organization, 1 October 2012, WT/ACC/LAO/45, based on Decree On Controlled Business (Negative List) No. 68/PM of 28 April 2008.

which time the relevant Ministry has an opportunity to provide comments on the application.[73]

Investment in a concession business: Concession businesses are investment activities authorised by the Lao Government to use State assets, such as mining, power and infrastructure construction.[74] The list of concession activities is set out in Annex 3 to the Decree on the Implementation of the Investment Promotion Law.[75]

The Ministry of Planning and Investment and the Committee for Investment Promotion are responsible for considering and approving applications for investments in concession activities.[76] If the Committee approves an application for investment, it is responsible for signing a memorandum of understanding or agreement with the investor.[77] The Chair of the Committee is the Minister for Investment Promotion, and representatives of other Government ministries are members of the Committee.[78]

A Concession Registration Certificate must be obtained from the Ministry of Planning and Investment.[79] A Concession Registration Certificate includes enterprise registration, investment licence, applicable investment promotion incentives and tax registration for the business entity.[80] An investor must start operations within 90 days of the issuance of a Concession Registration Certificate.[81]

Investment in Special Economic Zones and Specific Economic Zones: Special incentives for the development of infrastructure and commercial facilities

---

73 Article 18(1) of the Investment Promotion Law 2009 No. 02/NA, 8 July 2009; and Article 14(2) of the Law on Enterprises No. 11/NA, 9 November 2005, which allows for an extension of the review period "in the case of certain businesses that require a longer technical review process".

74 Article 15 of the Investment Promotion Law 2009 No. 02/NA, 8 July 2009.

75 Decree No. 119/PM, English translation available at: http://www.investlaos.gov.la/index.php/start-up/laws-and-regulations/investment-law.

76 Article 13 of the Decree on the Implementation of the Investment Promotion Law, 20 April 2011 No. 119/PM.

77 Article 23 of the Decree on the Implementation of the Investment Promotion Law, 20 April 2011 No. 119/PM.

78 Article 22 of the Decree on the Implementation of the Investment Promotion Law, 20 April 2011 No. 119/PM. Note that there are also provincial Committees for Investment Promotion.

79 Article 24 of the Investment Promotion Law 2009 No. 02/NA, 8 July 2009.

80 *Ibid.*, Article 25.

81 *Ibid.*, Article 26.

apply in Special Economic Zones and Specific Economic Zones.[82] A higher level of incentives apply to Special Economic Zones than to Specific Economic Zones.[83] A list of the incentives applicable to such zones is set out in the Decree on Specific and Special Economic Zones No. 443/PM.[84]

Applications for investment in Special or Specific Economic Zones must be submitted to the Secretariat to the Lao National Committee on Special Economic Zone and Specific Economic Zone Management, in the Office of the Prime Minister.[85]

Incentives for Investment

The Investment Promotion Law provides for investment incentives, which are equal for domestic and foreign investors.

Profit Tax: Exemptions from profit tax are accorded to investments for certain durations based on the activities in question and the area where the investment is made.[86]

a. Article 49 of the Investment Promotion Law identifies three promoted sectors: agriculture, industry and services. Annex 1 to the Decree on the Implementation of the Investment Promotion Law sets out a detailed list of promoted activities. There are three levels of promoted activities, which are organised according to the level of priority accorded by the Government to the activity in question. For example, primary, secondary and high school education are Level 1 activities, whereas the manufacture of items such as refined petroleum products is a Level 3 activity.
b. Article 50 of the Investment Promotion Law also identifies three promoted zones based on the extent to which investment is supported by good socio-economic infrastructure and the geography of the area. A list of investment promoted zones is set out in Annex 2 to the Decree on the Implementation of the Investment Promotion Law.[87]

---

82 *Ibid.*, Article 33.

83 U.S. Department of State, 2015 Investment Climate Statement, June 2015, pp. 15–16.

84 See, Section V of the Decree on Specific and Special Economic Zones No. 443/PM, 26 October 2010.

85 U.S. Department of State, 2015 Investment Climate Statement, June 2015, p. 16.

86 Article 51 of the Investment Promotion Law 2009 No. 02/NA, 8 July 2009. For discussion, see *An investment guide to the Lao People's Democratic Republic, Opportunities and Conditions*, 2010, United Nations, New York and Geneva, p. 54.

87 Decree No. 119/PM, English translation available at: http://www.investlaos.gov.la/index.php/start-up/laws-and-regulations/investment-law.

The greatest profit tax incentives are offered to the most highly promoted sectors in remote areas with limited economic infrastructure (exemption from profit tax is available for ten years).

Other incentives: There are also incentives for investment such as exemption from import and export duties and other taxes.[88] In addition, investments in the construction of hospitals, kindergartens, schools, colleges and research centres benefit from exemptions from land lease/concession fees and additional exemptions from profit tax.[89]

Rights in Land: Under the Land Law and the Constitution of Laos, land belongs to the "national community" of Laos. As a result, Laos and foreign nationals cannot "own" land. Instead, individuals and entities may hold rights in land, the main rights are "land-use rights", which are similar to ownership rights, and "usufructs", which are lesser rights to use land for productive activities. Under Article 58 of the Investment Promotion Law, foreign investors with registered investment capital of over US$ 500,000 may acquire land-use rights.

Special and Specific Economic Zones: Further investment incentives for Special and Specific Economic Zones are defined in regulations for each Zone. For example, the Savan-Seno Special Economic Zone is developing as a production, supply and distribution centre. Investment incentives in Savan-Seno include exemptions from leasing fees, exemptions from VAT and excise tax on imported goods, and tax exemptions for the industrial and service sector, subject to certain limitations.

For investments in Special and Specific Economic Zones, there are exemptions from turnover, excise and land taxes. Certain materials, such as construction material and machinery, are exempt from customs duty. In addition, reductions or exemptions from profit tax are granted for between two and ten years.[90]

Investment Protection

Part IV, Chapter 3 of the Investment Promotion Law establishes protections for investments in Laos.

88 Further information on investment incentives is available on the website of the Ministry of Planning and Investment: http://www.investlaos.gov.la/index.php/tax-and-duty-incentives.

89 Article 54 of the Investment Promotion Law 2009 No. 02/NA, 8 July 2009.

90 See, Report of the Working Party on the Accession of Lao PDR to the World Trade Organization, 1 October 2012, WT/ACC/LAO/45, para. 155.

Article 61 of the Investment Promotion Law provides that investors enjoy protection against the seizure, confiscation or nationalization of their investments. Paragraph 2 of Article 61 provides that if the Government needs to take control over a public utility, the investor shall be compensated for the market value of the investment at the time of the transfer.

Article 62 of the Investment Promotion Law states that the intellectual property of investors is protected in accordance with the Law on Intellectual Property.

Part V of the Investment Promotion Law sets out the rights and obligations of investors.

The rights granted to investors under the Investment Promotion Law include the following:

- the right to invest in accordance with the laws of Laos;
- the right to establish a representative office or branch in Laos;
- the right to own assets;
- the right to "protection of their rights and legitimate interests from investment";
- the right to manage the business investment;
- the right to hire workers in Laos;
- the right to reside for foreign investors, technicians and experts; and
- the right to repatriate capital, assets and income.[91]

The obligations of investors include the following:

- the payment of duties, taxes and other fees in a timely manner;
- respect for Lao law regarding insurance and social security for employees;
- facilitation of trade unions within a business investment;
- the coordination of business activities with local authorities and payment of compensation for the impact of the business operation, community development and the alleviation of poverty; and
- the protection of the environment.[92]

91 See Article 64 of the Investment Promotion Law 2009 No. 02/NA, 8 July 2009 for the complete list of investors' rights.

92 See Articles 69–70 of the Investment Promotion Law 2009 No. 02/NA, 8 July 2009 for the complete list of investors' rights.

III Laos' Bilateral Investment Treaties

1 *Overview*

Laos is reported to have concluded 28 bilateral investment treaties ("BITs"),[93] of which 19 are currently in force.[94] Laos does not have a BIT with the USA, although the two countries have concluded a bilateral trade agreement (see below).

Most, although not all, of Laos' BITs are publicly available in the English language. Laos does not currently have a model BIT. The following outline of Laos' BITs is based on a survey of the texts of those BITs that are readily available.

2 *Definition of Investment*

The notion of "Investment" is broadly defined under Laos' BITs as including "every kind of asset", together with a non-exhaustive list of the types of assets that will constitute investments. The non-exhaustive list generally includes tangible and intangible rights in property; shares in a company and other forms of participation in a company; claims to money or other performance with economic value; intellectual property rights; and rights conferred by a concession, which are expressly stated to include concessions in relation to natural resources.[95]

The Laos-Japan BIT was signed and entered into force in 2008, making it the most recent of Laos' BITs in force. In many respects it is more detailed than Laos' other BITs, including with respect to the definition of "investment".

---

93 UNCTAD lists BITs with the following countries: Australia, Belarus, Cambodia, China, Cuba, Denmark, France, Germany, India, Indonesia, Japan, Malaysia, Mongolia, Myanmar, Netherlands, Pakistan, Russian Federation, Singapore, South Korea, Sweden, Switzerland, Thailand, United Kingdom and Vietnam. (http://investmentpolicyhub.unctad.org/IIA/CountryBits/114#iiaInnerMenu).

In addition, Laos reportedly signed a BIT with the Philippines in June 2007 (http://www.bilaterals.org/?trade-accord-with-laos-signed), and is also reported to have BITs with Kuwait and North Korea (U.S. Department of State, 2015 Investment Climate Statement, June 2015, pp. 13–14).

94 According to UNCTAD, Laos' BITs with the following countries are not in force: Belarus, Cambodia, Malaysia, Myanmar and Pakistan. The status of Laos' BITs with North Korea, the Philippines and Kuwait is unknown.

95 The Laos-Australia BIT (1994) includes a longer list of concessions "conferred by law or under a contract, including rights to engage in agriculture, forestry, fisheries and animal husbandry, to search for, extract or exploit natural resources and to manufacture, use and sell products" (Article 1(1)(5)).

The Laos-Japan BIT expressly states that an "investment" is an asset that is "owned or controlled, directly or indirectly" by an investor.[96] It also defines "owned" to mean owning over 50% of the equity in an enterprise, and "controlled" to mean holding the power to appoint a majority of the directors or otherwise legally direct the actions of an enterprise.[97]

As noted above, some of Laos' BITs specifically include legal entities established in a third State and owned or controlled by a natural or legal person from a contracting party within the meaning of "investor", which allows investments to be made indirectly through a third State.

A number of Laos' BITs expressly state that investments must be made in accordance with the law of the host State of the investment.[98] The Laos-China BIT and the Laos-Thailand BIT also contain approval requirements for investments.[99] The Laos-Indonesia BIT refers to specific laws governing admission for each contracting State.[100]

In some of Laos' BITs, returns on investment are expressly stated to enjoy the same protection as the investment itself, or to benefit from particular standards of protection under the BIT.[101]

3 *Definition of Investors*

Most of Laos' BITs apply to natural persons who are nationals of a contracting party[102] and to companies or other juridical entities established or constituted under the law of the relevant contracting party.

---

96 Article 1(1) of the Laos-Japan BIT (2008).

97 Article 1(3) of the Laos-Japan BIT.

98 For example, Article 1(a) of the Laos-Australia BIT defines investments as assets "admitted... subject to [the host State's] laws and investment policies applicable from time to time".

99 Article 10 of the Laos-China BIT (1993) provides that investments "shall be approved in accordance with the laws and regulations" of the host State. Article 2(1) of the Laos-Thailand BIT provides that the "investment of capital must be approved in writing" by the host State. The Laos-India BIT also states that it applies to investments "accepted as such" in accordance with the laws and regulations of the host State.

100 Article X of the Laos-Indonesia BIT (1994), which refers to the Law on the Promotion and Management of Foreign Investment of 14 March 1994. However, this law was replaced in 2004, and the 2004 law was replaced by the Investment Protection Law 2009 (Article 99).

101 For example, the Laos-Denmark BIT (1998) and the Laos-Germany BIT (1996) and the Protocol to the BIT. Article 3(2) of the Laos-India BIT (2000) specifies that fair and equitable treatment shall apply to investments and returns on investment.

102 A number of Laos' BITs expressly stated that nationality is to be determined according law of the relevant State.

As regards natural persons, the Laos-Australia BIT and the Laos-Denmark BIT also apply in respect of persons with rights of permanent residence in a contracting party, in addition to the nationals of a contracting party.[103]

With respect to legal persons, the Laos-France BIT and the Laos-Switzerland BIT, require the relevant entity to have its seat in a contracting party. The Laos-Switzerland BIT also requires a legal entity to conduct real economic activities in the contracting party where it has its seat.[104]

A number of Laos' BITs include legal persons that are not established in one of the contracting parties, if they are controlled by a national of a contracting party or a legal person established in a contracting party. For example, the Laos-Netherlands BIT applies to "legal persons ... controlled, directly or indirectly, by natural persons ... or by legal persons [constituted under the law of a Contracting Party]."[105]

4 *Scope*

Most of Laos' BITs state that they apply to investments made before or after the entry into force of the BIT. A number also expressly state that the BIT does not apply to disputes or claims arising prior to the entry into force of the BIT.[106] For example, the Laos-Sweden BIT provides that:

> This Agreement shall apply to all investments, whether made before or after its entry into force but shall not apply to any dispute concerning an investment which arose, or any claim concerning an investment which was settled, before its entry into force.[107]

All of the BITs surveyed stated that they would remain in force for an initial period (most often ten years, but up to twenty years), after the expiry of which they would remain in force either for further renewable periods or indefinitely unless terminated by one of the contracting parties, on prior notice to the

103 Article 1(c) of the Laos-Australia BIT (1995) includes natural persons "whose residence in a Contracting Party is not limited as to time under its law"; and Article 1(5) of the Laos-Denmark BIT (1998) includes natural persons "who are permanently residing" in a Contracting Party in accordance with its laws.

104 Article 1(1)(b) of the Laos-Switzerland BIT (1996).

105 Article 1(b)(iii) of the Laos-Netherlands BIT (2003). Article 1(2)(b) of the Laos-Sweden BIT (1996) includes legal persons with their seat in a third State "with a predominant interest of an investor of either Contracting Party".

106 For example, the Laos-Denmark BIT (Article 12), the Mongolia-Laos BIT (Article 11), the Laos-Netherlands BIT (Article 10) and the Laos-Sweden BIT (Article 9).

107 Article 9(1) of the Laos-Sweden BIT.

other contracting party. The notice periods for termination vary between six and twelve months.

5 *Substantive Protections*

Fair and Equitable Treatment

All of the BITs surveyed contain a guarantee of fair and equitable treatment. Some, but not all, also include protection from the impairment of an investment by unreasonable or discriminatory measures. For example, Article 2 of the Laos-Germany BIT provides as follows:

> (1) Each Contracting Party ... shall in any case accord such investments fair and equitable treatment.
>
> (2) Neither Contracting Party shall in any way impair by arbitrary or discriminatory measures the management, maintenance, use or enjoyment of investments in its territory of nationals or companies of the other Contracting Party.

Full Protection and Security

A number of Laos' BITs also contain a "full protection and security" standard, although there are differences in the way in which this standard is described in the text of the different treaties. The Laos-France and Laos-Germany BITs both refer to "full protection and security", whereas the Laos-Indonesia BIT refers to "adequate protection and security". On the other hand, the Laos-Australia BIT refers simply to "protection and security", and the Laos-China BIT to "protection in the territory".

The Laos-Netherlands BIT was the only BIT surveyed that referred to "full *physical* protection and security", such that the standard is limited to "physical", rather than "legal", protection and security.[108]

Most of Laos' BITs do not define the scope of "fair and equitable treatment" or "full protection and security". The Laos-Japan BIT is the exception, in that it explicitly links these standards to the minimum standard of treatment of aliens under customary international law. Note 1 to Article 5 states that the article "prescribes the international law minimum standard of treatment of aliens" and that the "concepts of 'fair and equitable treatment' and 'full protection and security' do not require treatment in addition to or beyond that which is required by the customary international law minimum standard of treatment of aliens".

---

108 Article 3(1) of the Laos-Netherlands BIT.

Expropriation

All of Laos' BITs provide protection from the expropriation or nationalization of an investment, or measures having an equivalent effect to expropriation or nationalization (referred to as "expropriation").[109] In general, expropriation is unlawful under Laos' BITs unless four conditions are met: the expropriation must be (i) for a public purpose; (ii) in accordance with due process of law; (iii) non-discriminatory;[110] and (iv) accompanied by the payment of compensation.

Some of Laos' BITs do not include "due process" as a condition for lawful expropriation, although almost all of these BITs do include a right to a review by an independent authority of the expropriation and the value of the investment.[111] Some of Laos' BITs include both a requirement that the expropriation shall be conducted in accordance with due process of law and a right for the investor to a review of the expropriation and the valuation of their investment.[112]

The Laos-Netherlands BIT and the Laos-France BIT expressly prohibit expropriation if it is contrary to a specific undertaking made by the State concerned in respect of an investment.[113]

Various terms are used to describe the compensation that must be paid for the expropriation of an investment, such as "fair and equitable,"[114] "just"[115] and

---

109 Article 5(1) of the Laos-Switzerland BIT also expressly refers to both direct and indirect expropriation in the following terms: "Aucune des Parties Contractantes ne prendra, directement ou indirectement, des mesures d'expropriation, de nationalisation ou toute autre mesure ayant le même caractère ou le même effet, à l'encontre des investissements d'investisseurs de l'autre Partie Contractante".

110 Note that the Laos-Thailand BIT (1995) does not expressly state that expropriatory measures must not be discriminatory. However, it does provide that nationals and companies shall be accorded fair and equitable treatment in relation to expropriatory measures, which would seem to include a guarantee of non-discrimination.

111 Article 4(2) of the Laos-Germany BIT; Article 5(1) of the Laos-UK BIT (1995); Article 6(1)(b) of the Laos-Thailand BIT; and Article 5(1) of the Laos-India BIT. Article 5 of the Laos-France BIT (1989) is an exception in that it does not expressly provide a right to an independent review of the expropriation or the valuation of the investment.

112 For example, the Article 12(4) of the Laos-Japan BIT, which is expressly stated to be without prejudice to dispute settlement under Article 17 of the treaty.

113 Article 5(2) of the Laos-France BIT; Article 6(b) of the Laos-Netherlands BIT states that neither Contracting Party may take measures depriving, directly or indirectly, nationals of the other Contracting Party of their investments if such measures are "contrary to any undertaking which the Contracting Party which takes such measures may have given".

114 Article 5(1) of the Laos-India BIT.

115 Article 6(c) of the Laos-Netherlands BIT.

"prompt, adequate and effective".[116] However, the measure of compensation is subject to the same requirements in most cases, including:

- compensation for the "market value,"[117] "fair market value"[118] or "genuine value"[119] of the investment;
- the date of valuation is immediately before the expropriation, or before the expropriation became public knowledge;
- payment without delay, or "unreasonable" delay;
- compensation must be "effectively realizable", "freely transferrable" and "convertible"; and
- a commercial rate of interest must be paid.

A number of Laos' BITs also expressly require the contracting parties to pay compensation for the expropriation of the assets of a locally incorporated company when investors of the other contracting party hold an investment in the shares of the local company.[120] The Protocol to the Laos-Germany BIT provides that a claim to compensation exists "when, as a result of State intervention in the company in which the investment is made, its economic substance is severely impaired".[121]

Umbrella Clauses

Some of the BITs signed by Laos include an obligation on the Contracting Parties to observe any obligation they have undertaken with regard to investments of an investor of the other Contracting Party.[122] This is commonly known as an "umbrella clause". This means that State obligations such as those

116 For example, Article 7(1)(c) of the Laos-Australia BIT and Article 5(1) of the Laos-Denmark BIT.

117 Article 7(2) of the Laos-Australia BIT provides that compensation shall be based on the market value of the investment, or if that value cannot be readily ascertained compensation shall be determined "in accordance with generally recognised principles of valuation and equitable principles taking into account factors including the capital invested, depreciation, capital already repatriated, replacement value and currency exchange rate movements."

118 Article 12(2) of the Laos-Japan BIT.

119 Article 5(1) of the Laos-India BIT and Article 5(1) of the Laos-UK BIT.

120 See, for example, Article 5(5) of the Laos-Denmark BIT; Article 5(3) of the Laos-India BIT; Article 5(4) of the Laos-Mongolia BIT; and Article 5(2) of the Laos-UK BIT.

121 Article 4 of the Protocol to the Laos-Germany BIT.

122 Such as the Laos-Netherlands BIT, the Laos-Switzerland BIT, the Laos-Thailand BIT and the Laos-UK BIT.

contained in contracts between investors and the host State can potentially be elevated to treaty obligations.

Most-Favoured Nation and National Treatment

All of the BITs surveyed contain a most-favoured nation ("MFN") clause, and most but not all BITs contain a national treatment clause. For example, the Laos-Australia BIT and the Laos-Switzerland BIT include an MFN clause, but not a national treatment clause.

Furthermore, in some of Laos' BITs MFN and national treatment are expressly linked to other standards of treatment such as fair and equitable treatment and full protection and security. Thus, the protection provided by the MFN or national treatment clause may be limited by the scope of the standard to which it is linked. For example, Article 3(2) of the Laos-China BIT states that:

> The treatment and protection as mentioned in paragraphs 1 of this Article [fair and equitable treatment and protection] shall not be less favorable than that accorded to investments and activities associated with such investments of investors of a third State.[123]

As discussed below, this has been interpreted to mean that the MFN clause only applies to matters falling within the scope of fair and equitable treatment and protection.

In the Laos-Netherlands BIT, the MFN and national treatment standards follow the fair and equitable treatment, non-impairment and full physical protection and security standards, and are introduced by the words "More particularly, each Contracting Party shall . . ."[124]

Most of Laos' BITs exclude customs unions, free trade areas, common markets, and international agreements or domestic legislation relating mainly or wholly to taxation from the scope of application of the MFN and national treatment provisions. In addition, the protocol to the Laos-Germany BIT gives examples of the types of unequal treatment that violate the MFN standard, and expressly excludes certain measures, as follows:

---

123 Also, Article 3(1) of the Laos-Mongolia BIT provides that investments and returns of investors "shall be accorded treatment which is fair and equitable and not less favourable than that accorded to the investments and returns of investors of the latter Contracting Party or of any third State."

124 Article 3(2) of the Laos-Netherlands BIT.

Measures that have to be taken for reasons of public security and order, public health or morality shall not be deemed 'treatment less favourable' within the meaning of Article 3.

6 *Repatriation of Capital and Compensation for Losses*

All of the BITs surveyed contain provisions guaranteeing the free transfer of funds.

In addition, all of the BITs surveyed contain provision for compensation for losses resulting from war, armed conflict, revolution and other similar events in the territory of the host State. The compensation payable must be no less favourable than that provided to investors of the host State or any other third State.[125]

7 *Investor-State Dispute Settlement*

All of Laos' publicly available BITs contain a provision concerning the settlement of disputes between investors and the contracting States, except the Laos-Thailand BIT concluded in 1990.

All of the BITs with an investor-State dispute settlement ("ISDS") clause provide that disputes should, in the first instance and if possible, be settled amicably. For the most part, amicable settlement under an ISDS clause relates to "any dispute" in connection with an investment. However, the ISDS clause in the Laos-Japan BIT (Article 17) defines an investment dispute more narrowly as a dispute between an investor "that has incurred loss or damage by reason of, or arising out of, an alleged breach of any right conferred by this Agreement..." and the host State.[126]

Most BITs then provide a right to submit disputes to international arbitration after a "cooling off period" of three or six months. There is a difference between the language used in Laos' BITs in relation to the "cooling off period". Some BITs refer to disputes that "cannot be settled" within three or six months,[127] whereas others refer to disputes that continue to exist after the specified period.[128]

The Laos-Australia BIT does not specify any particular "cooling off period", although the right to submit a dispute to third party adjudication applies

125 Such as Article 13(1) of the Laos-Japan BIT and Article 8 of the Laos-Australia BIT.

126 Similarly, Article 8 of the Laos-UK BIT refers to disputes "concerning an obligation of the latter [the host State] under this Agreement".

127 For example, the Laos-Germany BIT, the Laos-Sweden BIT and the Laos-Switzerland BIT.

128 For example, the Laos-Denmark BIT and the Laos-India BIT.

in respect of a dispute that "cannot be resolved through consultations or negotiations".[129]

The Laos-China BIT contains a so-called "Chinese style" ISDS clause, which provides that any dispute in connection with an investment shall be settled amicably, and may be submitted to the host State's courts, but limits access to international arbitration to disputes "involving the amount of compensation for expropriation".[130] The scope of this ISDS clause has been interpreted by an arbitral tribunal and by the Singapore High Court, as explained below.

The form and options for arbitration offered in Laos' BITs differ. Most of Laos' BITs provide for ICSID arbitration. For example, both the Laos-France and Laos-Indonesia BITs provide that disputes that cannot be settled amicably within six months shall be submitted to ICSID arbitration.

However, Laos is not a State Party to the ICSID Convention, and therefore the Centre has no jurisdiction in respect of disputes brought by investors against Laos.[131] A number of Laos' BITs expressly provide that if both of the contracting parties are not parties to the ICSID Convention then the dispute may be submitted to arbitration before the ICSID Additional Facility or to *ad hoc* arbitration under UNCITRAL Rules. The choices offered to investors differ in that:

a. Some of Laos' BITs appear to establish a hierarchy of dispute settlement options, with ICSID arbitration at the top and *ad hoc* arbitration, or any other form of arbitration mutually agreed by the disputing parties, permitted if ICSID arbitration is not available.[132]
b. It is more common to find a choice for the investor between ICSID and *ad hoc* arbitration under UNCITRAL Rules (although several BITs provide for ICSID arbitration only if both of the contracting parties are party to the ICSID Convention).[133]
c. The Laos-Japan BIT and the Netherlands-Laos BIT offer investors a choice, which includes arbitration before the ICSID Additional Facility in case only one of the contracting parties is a party to the ICSID Convention.

129 Article 12(2) of the Laos-Australia BIT.
130 Article 7(3) of the Laos-China BIT.
131 Article 25(1) of the ICSID Convention.
132 For example, the Laos-Australia BIT and the Laos-Germany BIT.
133 For example, the Laos-India BIT, the Laos-Japan BIT, the Laos-Sweden BIT and the Laos-Switzerland BIT.

d. The Laos-China BIT and the Laos-UK BIT provide for *ad hoc* arbitration and do not include ICSID arbitration, although the Laos-China BIT states that the arbitral tribunal may base its procedural rules on the ICSID Rules of Arbitration.

A right to submit the dispute to the local courts of the host State is provided in a number of Laos' BITs. In most cases, the right to submit a dispute to the local courts appears to be additional to the right to submit the dispute to arbitration,[134] or appears as one of a series of dispute resolution options.[135] However, under the Laos-China and the Laos-Japan BITs the submission of a dispute to the local courts excludes the right to submit the dispute to arbitration. This is a so-called "fork in the road" provision, which requires the investor to choose between adjudication by the local courts and international arbitration.

The ISDS provision in the Laos-Japan BIT is uniquely detailed, and provides rules on matters such as the notice of intent that must be submitted by the investor, the nationality of the arbitrators and the location of the arbitration (which should be a country that is party to the New York Convention). It also includes a limitation provision, according to which no claim may be submitted to conciliation or arbitration if more than three years have elapsed since the date on which the investor first knew or should have known of the loss or damage caused by the alleged breach of the BIT.[136]

8 *State-to-State Dispute Settlement*

As regards State-to-State disputes, all of the BITs surveyed provided for the amicable settlement of such disputes. Most of the Laos' BITs also provide for the submission of such disputes to arbitration, if they cannot be settled amicably. The Laos-Indonesia BIT is a notable exception in that regard, because it provides only for the amicable settlement of disputes through diplomatic negotiation.[137]

Most of Laos' BITs provide that State-to-State disputes relating to the interpretation or application of the BIT may be submitted to *ad hoc* arbitration,

134 For example, Article 9(2) of the Laos-Mongolia BIT. Under the Laos-India BIT, a dispute may be referred to arbitration if the disputing parties fail to agree on submission to the local courts or to international conciliation.

135 For example, the Laos-Australia BIT and Article VIII(2) of the Laos-Indonesia BIT.

136 Article 17(8) of the Laos-Japan BIT.

137 Article IX of the Laos-Indonesia BIT.

and that the President of the International Court of Justice shall act as the appointing authority.

9 *Additional Provisions*

The Laos-Australia BIT includes two notable provisions. First, Article 6 contains a transparency obligation, which requires contracting parties to publish their laws relating to investments.[138] Second, Article 13 contains rights in respect of disputes between nationals of the two contracting parties. An investor must be given access to the courts of the host State, and the contracting parties agree to permit their own nationals to choose how to settle disputes regarding investments with nationals of the other contracting party, including by arbitration conducted in a third country.

The Laos-Sweden BIT includes a provision on the sojourn of individuals working for an investor and members of their household, which requires the host State to allow such persons to enter, remain on and leave their territory for the purpose of carrying out activities associated with investments, subject to the laws and regulations of the host State.[139] Similarly, the Laos-Germany BIT and the Laos-Japan BIT provide that the contracting parties should give "favourable" or "sympathetic" consideration to applications to enter and sojourn in their territory in connection with an investment.[140]

The Laos-Japan BIT also prohibits certain performance requirements under Article 7. However, new[141] or existing[142] measures in relation to certain sectors of activity are not subject to the prohibition in Article 7 or to the MFN and national treatment standard under Articles 2 and 3 of the BIT.[143] Exceptions are provided in Articles 18 and 19 of the Laos-Japan BIT for "General and Security Measures" and "Temporary Safeguard Measures" respectively. The former include measures necessary for the preservation of the essential security interests of the State in times of armed conflict or other emergency, "any measure necessary to protect human, animal or plant life or health", measures necessary for the maintenance of public order and measures imposed

138 There is a similar provision in Article 9 of the Laos-Japan BIT.

139 Article 2(2) of the Laos-Sweden BIT. Article 11 of the Laos-India BIT includes a similar obligation to allow experts to enter and remain.

140 Article 3(c) of the Laos-Germany BIT and Article 11 of the Laos-Japan BIT.

141 Annex II sets out the sectors in relation to which new measures may be taken and existing measures may be maintained.

142 Annexes I set out sectors in which existing measures may be maintained, continued, renewed, amended or modified.

143 Article 8, paragraphs 8 and 9 also exclude measures covered by exceptions or derogations from the TRIPS Agreement and measures relating to government procurement.

for the protection of "national treasures" of artistic, historic or archaeological value. The latter include measures to address serious financial problems.

Similarly, the Laos-India BIT states that nothing in the treaty "precludes the host Contracting Party from taking action for the protection of its essential security interests or in circumstances of extreme emergency in accordance with its laws normally and reasonably applied on a non-discriminatory basis".[144]

10 *The Laos-US Bilateral Trade Agreement*

The Laos-US bilateral trade agreement is intended to promote trade, protect intellectual property rights and eliminate non-tariff barriers to trade.[145] As such, it does not expressly contain measures to promote and protect investments. Notably, Article 10 of the Agreement provides that both parties will encourage the settlement of commercial disputes between their respective nationals by way of arbitration, which may be conducted pursuant to any internationally recognised arbitral rules, including the UNCITRAL Rules.

IV Multilateral Investment Related Treaties and Organizations to which Laos is a Party

1 *ASEAN – ACIA*

Laos became a member of ASEAN in 1997. Laos took on the rotating chair of ASEAN in 2016.

Laos is a member of the ASEAN Comprehensive Investment Agreement (the "ACIA"), which entered into force on 29 March 2012. As explained in the ASEAN Chapter, the ACIA aims to create a free and open investment environment through the consolidation and expansion of existing agreements between ASEAN Member States.[146]

The ACIA contains substantive investment protections commonly found in BITs, such as provisions on non-discrimination, MFN treatment, fair and equitable treatment, full protection and security, and expropriation. Where a dispute arises between an investor and a Member State, the ACIA provides for various dispute resolution options, including the submission of a claim to arbitration under the ICSID Convention, under the UNCITRAL Arbitration

---

144 Article 12(2).

145 See the Preamble to the Laos-US bilateral trade agreement.

146 http://www.aseanbriefing.com/news/2013/04/12/introduction-to-the-asean-comprehensive-investment-agreement.html.

Rules, to the Regional Centre for Arbitration at Kuala Lumpur or to any other regional centre for arbitration in ASEAN.[147]

Beyond the usual provisions found in BITs, the ACIA also contains provisions aimed at enhancing cooperation between ASEAN States in the promotion[148] and facilitation of investment,[149] and to enhance ASEAN integration.[150]

2 *ASEAN Investment Agreements with Third States*

As a member of ASEAN, Laos is also a party to ASEAN's international investment agreements with third States. These investment agreements relate to broader framework agreements on economic cooperation,[151] or free trade agreements.[152] The ASEAN investment agreements include the ASEAN-China Investment Agreement, the ASEAN-India Investment Agreement, the ASEAN-South Korea Investment Agreement and the investment chapter of the ASEAN-Australia-New Zealand Free Trade Agreement.[153]

ASEAN's investment agreements with third States contain substantive protections such as national treatment, MFN treatment,[154] fair and equitable treatment, full protection and security and protection from expropriation.[155] In addition, they include transparency requirements to ensure that laws, regulations and other measures affecting investment are publicly available.[156]

The ASEAN investment agreements also provide the right for investors to submit investment disputes to arbitration before a choice of different forums, including under the ICSID Convention or under the UNCITRAL Rules.[157]

147 Article 33 of Section B of the ACIA.

148 *Ibid.*, Article 24.

149 *Ibid.*, Article 25.

150 *Ibid.*, Article 26.

151 The Framework Agreements recognised the different stages of development of different ASEAN Member States and provided for differential treatment and flexibility for newer ASEAN Member States, including Laos.

152 For example, the ASEAN-Australia-New Zealand Free Trade Agreement, and its Chapter 11 on Investment.

153 See Investment Policy Hub for further information: http://investmentpolicyhub.unctad.org/IIA/CountryOtherIias/114#iiaInnerMenu.

154 The ASEAN-India Investment Agreement includes the option to consider the inclusion of an MFN clause in Article 5.

155 Note that the ASEAN-Korea Investment Agreement and the ASEAN-India Agreement include certain characteristics that an "investment" must have to benefit from protection under the Agreement (e.g. Article 1(j) of the ASEAN-Korea Investment Agreement).

156 See, e.g. Article 8 of the ASEAN-Korea Investment Agreement.

157 See, e.g. Article 14 of the ASEAN-China Investment Agreement; Article 18(5) of the ASEAN-Korea Investment Agreement. Note that the ASEAN-India Investment

As such, investor-State dispute settlement under the ASEAN-China Investment Agreement is broader than under the Laos-China BIT.

However, there are certain exclusions and limitations contained in ASEAN's investment agreements with third States.[158] For example, limitations of the scope of application of the agreements to taxation measures,[159] and exceptions for: the protection of public morals, order and essential security interests; the protection of human, animal or plant life or health; and the conservation of exhaustible natural resources,[160] among other matters.[161]

3 *MIGA*

Laos is a party to the Convention Establishing the Multilateral Investment Guarantee Agency (the "MIGA") of 1985. MIGA is a part of the World Bank Group and a multilateral investment insurance system against political risks, which offers investment protection for cross-border investments against losses resulting from, *inter alia*, currency transfer restrictions, expropriation and a government's (or, in certain circumstances, a State-owned enterprise's[162]) breach or repudiation of a contract with an investor.

V Multilateral Dispute Settlement Related Treaties

1 *ICSID Convention*

As noted above, Laos is not a member State of the International Centre for the Settlement of Investment Disputes (the "ICSID Convention"). Therefore, investment disputes between Laos and foreign investors are not within the

Agreement includes an explicit fork-in-the-road provision requiring investors to choose between dispute resolution before local courts and arbitration (Article 20(7)).

158 For example, a limitation period of three years (Article 14(6)(a) of the ASEAN-China Investment Agreement).

159 e.g., Article 4(a) of the ASEAN-China Investment Agreement provides that it does not apply to any taxation measure, except, *inter alia*, as regards expropriation, transfers and repatriation of profits and investor-State dispute settlement "only when the dispute arises from Article 8 (Expropriation)"; and Article 2(1)(c) of the ASEAN-Korea Investment Agreement.

160 However, such measures must be "made effective in conjunction with restrictions on domestic protection or consumption" (Article 16(1)(f) of the ASEAN-China Investment Agreement).

161 See, e.g. Articles 20 and 21 of the ASEAN-Korea Investment Agreement.

162 http://www.miga.org/documents/IGGenglish.pdf at p. 7.

jurisdiction of the Centre.[163] However, the ICSID Additional Facility offers an alternative forum for arbitration or conciliation where Laos has concluded a BIT or an International Investment Agreement ("IIA") with a State Party to the ICSID Convention and the relevant BIT or IIA provides for recourse to the Additional Facility.

2 *The New York Convention*

The New York Convention is an international treaty for the recognition and enforcement of arbitral awards. Membership of the New York Convention has important implications for the enforcement of an arbitral award.

Laos has been a State Party to the New York Convention since 1998.[164] Laos has not made any reservations to the Convention.

VI International Investment Arbitration Cases Involving Laos

Sanum Investments v Laos (UNCITRAL, PCA Case No. 2013–13)

Tribunal:	Andres Rigo Sureda (President, Spain) Prof. Bernard Hanotiau (Belgium) Prof. Brigitte Stern (France)
Case Initiated:	14 August 2013
Awards Rendered:	

- Award on Jurisdiction: 13 December 2013
- Judgment of Singapore High Court: 20 January 2015

Background and Summary

The claimant, Sanum Investments Ltd. (Sanum), invested through a joint venture with a local Lao entity in the development of two casinos and five slot clubs in Laos. Sanum commenced arbitration under the Laos-China BIT, alleging breaches of a number of the treaty standards of protection including fair and equitable treatment, protection from expropriation and MFN treatment.

---

163 Article 25(1) of the ICSID Convention.

164 See http://www.uncitral.org/uncitral/en/uncitral_texts/arbitration/NYConvention_status.html.

This case was closely related to the Lao Holdings arbitration discussed below, which was commenced on the same day, under the Laos-Netherlands BIT by the Dutch company that owned 100% of the shares in Sanum.

Both cases related to changes in the tax regime applicable to the claimants' gambling investments, including the refusal to renew a flat tax agreement and the imposition of a new 80% tax on revenues.

However, because the two arbitration cases were commenced under different BITs, different legal issues arose in the tribunals' decisions on jurisdiction. The two cases were settled before any decision on the merits of the BIT claims could be made.

Sanum was an entity established in the Macao Special Administrative Region of China. One of the key issues of jurisdiction in the *Sanum* case was whether or not the Laos-China BIT applied to the territory of Macao.

A further issue was the scope of Laos' consent to arbitrate under the Laos-China BIT. As noted above, Article 8(3) of the Laos-China BIT contains an investor-State dispute settlement clause that limits the contracting parties' consent to arbitration to disputes "involving the amount of compensation for expropriation".

The *Sanum* arbitration was conducted under the UNCITRAL 2010 Rules, and was seated in Singapore. In the Decision on Jurisdiction, the arbitral tribunal upheld its jurisdiction over the dispute.

However, the Government of Laos referred the issue of jurisdiction to the High Court of Singapore under Article 10(3)(a) of the Singapore International Arbitration Act, which allows a party to apply to the Court for a decision on the jurisdiction of the arbitral tribunal within 30 days of a preliminary ruling from the tribunal upholding its own jurisdiction. As explained below, the High Court of Singapore found that the arbitral tribunal had no jurisdiction over the dispute, although the case was settled before the Court's judgment was issued.

Key Legal Outcomes

- The Arbitral Tribunal's Award on Jurisdiction

The arbitral tribunal upheld its jurisdiction over the dispute in the Award of 13 December 2013. The tribunal found that: (1) the Laos-China BIT did apply to the territory of Macao; and (2) the tribunal had jurisdiction under Article 8(3) of the BIT to determine whether or not Laos had expropriated the claimant's investment and the amount of compensation, if any, to be paid for the alleged expropriation of the investment.

The arbitral tribunal also dismissed Laos' objections to the competence of the tribunal on a number of other grounds, including that Sanum was not a qualifying "investor" with a qualifying "investment" and that Sanum's claims were barred by the principles of *lis pendens* and abuse of process. However, the arbitral tribunal did not accept that Sanum could rely on the MFN clause in the Laos-China BIT to broaden the scope of Laos' consent to arbitrate.

- Territorial Scope of the BIT

The Laos-China BIT was concluded in 1993, at a time when Macao was considered a "Chinese territory" under the administration of Portugal. In 1999, China resumed the exercise of sovereignty over Macao, which was designated as a special administrative region of China. Thus, the question was whether the Laos-China BIT applied to Macao once China had resumed full sovereignty over the territory in 1999.

The tribunal found that under customary international law a treaty applies to the expanded territory of a State from the moment of the State's succession to that territory, unless an exception to the general rule applies. The tribunal found that customary rules regarding State succession were relevant even though China's position was that it merely "resumed" full sovereignty over Macao.[165] The tribunal also found that Article 29 of the Vienna Convention on the Law of Treaties 1969 (VCLT) and Article 15 of the Vienna Convention on the Succession of States in respect of Treaties 1978 (VCST) reflect customary international law in that regard.

The BIT does not expressly state whether or not it applies to Macao. Therefore, the tribunal found that the BIT would, *prima facie*, apply unless it could be established that an exception to the rules concerning the territorial scope of a treaty applied. The tribunal found that no exception applied because the application of the BIT to Macao would be consistent with the treaty's object and purpose and would not "radically change the conditions for its operation".[166] However, the tribunal noted with regret the lack of evidence on the record concerning the intentions of the States parties to the BIT with regard to its application to Macao.[167]

- Scope of Laos' Consent to Arbitrate

Sanum argued that under Article 8(3) of the Laos-China BIT, Laos had consented to submit to arbitration disputes concerning whether or not

---

165 See, *Sanum Investments Ltd. v Laos*, PCA Case No. 2013–13, Award on Jurisdiction, 13 December 2013, paras. 237–238.

166 *Ibid.*, paras. 239–269.

167 *Ibid.*, para. 232.

an expropriation had occurred and the amount of compensation due for such expropriation.

In addition, Sanum argued that it was entitled to invoke the MFN clause in the Laos-China BIT in order to rely on the broader investor-State dispute settlement provisions in Laos' BITs with third States. On this basis, Sanum sought to persuade the tribunal that it had jurisdiction over its expropriation claims and its claims for the violation of other treaty provisions, including fair and equitable treatment.

In contrast, Laos argued that its consent to arbitrate was limited under Article 8(3) of the Laos-China BIT to disputes concerning only the "amount of compensation for expropriation". According to Laos, all other disputes including disputes over whether or not an expropriation had occurred should be submitted to Laos' local courts under Article 8(2) of the Laos-China BIT.[168] Laos further argued that the scope of its consent to arbitrate could not be expanded by relying on the MFN clause in the BIT.

The tribunal found that, although the "first impression" given by Article 8(3) was that the jurisdiction of the tribunal was limited to disputes related to the amount of compensation due for expropriation, the proper interpretation of the text of the BIT was that the tribunal had jurisdiction over whether or not an expropriation had occurred.

The tribunal relied, in particular, on the use of the words "disputes *involving* the amount of compensation for expropriation", rather than a more clearly limiting form of words such as "disputes *limited to*".[169] The tribunal also explained the different conclusions reached by arbitral tribunals on such "Chinese style" arbitration clauses by the existence or absence of fork-in-the-road clauses. The tribunal found that the presence of a broadly worded fork-in-the-road clause in the Laos-China BIT meant that a more restrictive interpretation of the scope of Article 8(3) would deprive that provision of any effect because it would be impossible for an investor to submit a dispute over whether or not an expropriation had occurred to the local courts of Laos without losing the right to submit a dispute over the amount of compensation due to arbitration.[170]

The tribunal found that the MFN clause in Article 3(2) of the Laos-China BIT could not be invoked to give the tribunal jurisdiction over expropriation

---

168 Article 8(2) provides that either party "shall be entitled to submit the dispute to the competent court of the Contracting State accepting the investment".

169 *Sanum Investments Ltd. v Laos*, PCA Case No. 2013–13, Award on Jurisdiction, 13 December 2013, para. 329.

170 *Ibid.*, paras. 340–342.

claims. Article 3(2) of the Laos-China BIT provides MFN treatment in respect of "treatment and protection as mentioned in Paragraph 1 of this Article", which relates to fair and equitable treatment and "protection" in the territory of the host State. The tribunal found that this meant that the "treatment" to which the MFN clause related did not extend to access to arbitration.[171]

- The Respondent's Other Objections to the Competence of the Tribunal

The tribunal found that Sanum was a qualifying "investor", established under the laws of China. It rejected Laos' argument that the Laos-China BIT requires an economic entity to perform some economic activities in the State of its establishment in order to qualify as an "investor".[172] The tribunal also found that the Laos-China BIT applies to indirect investments, and that the treaty did not impose limitations on the form in which "contributions" in respect of an investment must be made. Thus, loans made in respect of shares and the provision of know-how might constitute "contributions".[173]

The tribunal found no abuse of process or issue of *lis pendens* arising from the concurrent Lao Holdings arbitration.[174] In particular, the tribunal observed that Sanum had offered to consolidate the two cases, but that Laos had refused that offer and was therefore precluded from arguing that it had suffered any prejudice from the concurrent proceedings.

The Judgment of the Singapore High Court

Following the tribunal's ruling on jurisdiction, Sanum, Lao Holdings (see below) and Laos entered into a deed of settlement on 15 June 2014. Therefore, the *Sanum* tribunal did not have the opportunity to rule on the merits of the dispute.

However, on 10 January 2014 Laos applied to the High Court of Singapore for a jurisdictional ruling following the arbitral tribunal's Award on Jurisdiction. The High Court's decision was rendered on 20 January 2015, and it found that the arbitral tribunal did not have jurisdiction over the claims.[175]

171 *Ibid.*, para. 358.

172 *Ibid.*, paras. 306–315.

173 *Ibid.*, para. 320. The tribunal did not address whether or not a "contribution" is a necessary aspect of an "investment", and did not need to do so as the dispute was not whether or not Sanum had made any "contributions", but the form in which those "contributions" were made.

174 *Ibid.*, paras. 365–367.

175 *Government of the Lao People's Republic v Sanum Investments Ltd.* [2015] SGHC 15.

(a) Territorial Scope of the BIT

The High Court of Singapore agreed with the arbitral tribunal that there was a general presumption under international law that the Laos-China BIT applied to the entire territory over which China exercises sovereignty, including Macao.[176] However, the Court found that the general presumption did not apply because the evidence proved that the States parties to the BIT did not intend for the BIT to apply to Macao.[177]

The Court's decision relied on two new pieces of evidence that were not before the arbitral tribunal. First, two letters exchanged in 2014 between Laos' Ministry of Foreign Affairs and the Chinese Embassy in Laos, which the Court found evidenced a common understanding between the two States that the BIT did not apply to Macao. Second, a World Trade Organization Trade Policy Report of 2001, which said that Macao was only a party to one BIT, the China-Portugal BIT.[178]

However, the Singapore Court also found that there was sufficient evidence before the Tribunal to conclude that the Laos-China BIT did not apply to Macao. The Court relied, in particular, on the 1987 China-Portugal Joint Declaration, which suggested that treaties to which China was a party would not automatically be applied to Macao. The Joint Declaration affirms the application of the "one country, two systems" principle to Macao, and Macao's competence to conclude international treaties on its own behalf.

The arbitral tribunal did consider the Joint Declaration in its Award, but had found that, as an agreement between China and Portugal, the Declaration did not bind Laos insofar as it established different rules to those existing under customary international law.[179]

(b) Scope of Laos' Consent to Arbitrate

Having determined that the Laos-China BIT did not apply to Macao, the Singapore Court did not need to decide whether or not the tribunal had jurisdiction over the question of whether or not an expropriation had occurred under Article 8(3) of the Laos-China BIT. However, the Court nonetheless

---

176 [2015] SGHC 15, para. 62.

177 [2015] SGHC 15, paras. 110–111.

178 The Court said that this report was relevant but "by no means conclusive": [2015] SGHC 15, para. 109.

179 See, *Sanum v Investments Ltd. v Laos*, PCA Case No. 2013-13, Award on Jurisdiction, 13 December 2013, paras. 265–269. The Singapore High Court dismissed this argument, see [2015] SGHC 15, paras. 92–93.

proceeded to find that the tribunal lacked jurisdiction over whether or not an expropriation had occurred.[180]

The Court reasoned that a restrictive interpretation of the scope of consent to arbitration was appropriate given the context of an agreement between two communist regimes with a certain degree of distrust over foreign private capital and international arbitration. As regards the fork-in-the-road provision, the tribunal rejected a restrictive interpretation proposed by Laos that the provision would not apply if an investor submitted a dispute concerning *liability* to the local courts, whilst seeking to reserve issues of *quantum* for arbitration.[181] Nevertheless, and despite finding that the fork-in-the-road would apply whenever the investor submitted an expropriation dispute to the local courts, the Court found that this did not mean that a restrictive interpretation of Article 8(3) would deny any effect to the consent to arbitration contained therein. The tribunal reasoned that Article 8(2) gives both the investor and the host State the right to submit a dispute to the host State's courts. Therefore, an investor would be able to submit a dispute concerning the amount of compensation for expropriation to arbitration where the expropriation dispute had been submitted to the host State's courts by the authorities of the host State itself.[182]

Conclusions on the *Sanum v Laos* Case

While the arbitral tribunal's findings in respect of the scope of "investor", "investment" and the MFN clause under the Laos-China BIT provide useful guidance, the conflicting decisions of the arbitral tribunal and the High Court of Singapore concerning the scope of consent to arbitration under Article 8(3) of the BIT and the territorial application of the BIT are causes for concern. The High Court's decision on the territorial scope of the BIT was primarily based on new evidence that was not before the arbitral tribunal. However, the Court also found that there was sufficient evidence before the arbitral tribunal to support its conclusion that the BIT did not apply to the territory of Macao.

Laos Holdings v Laos (ICSID Case No. ARB (AF)/12/6)

Tribunal:	Ian Binnie C.C., Q.C. (President, Canada), Prof. Bernard Hanotiau (Belgium), Prof. Brigitte Stern (France)
Case Initiated:	14 August 2012

180 [2015] SGHC 15, para. 121.

181 *Ibid.*, para. 127.

182 *Ibid.*, para. 122.

Awards Rendered:

- Decision on Jurisdiction: 21 February 2014
- Interim Ruling on Issues Arising Under the Deed of Settlement: 19 December 2014
- Decision on Merits: 10 June 2015

Background and Summary

The claimant, Lao Holdings N.V., a company established in the Netherlands, filed proceedings before ICSID requesting arbitration under the ICSID Additional Facility, and alleging multiple violations of the Laos-Netherlands BIT by the Government of Laos.

Lao Holdings indirectly owned gambling assets in Laos through Sanum Investments (see above), in a strategic location close to the border with Thailand, including the Savan Vegas Hotel and Casino Complex. It argued that the introduction of a new 80% tax on casino revenues and what it alleged were unfair and oppressive audits violated the Laos-Netherlands BIT.

As noted above in respect of the *Sanum* case, the parties to the dispute signed a deed of settlement in June 2014, resolving the dispute over the alleged breaches of the BIT. Subsequently, Lao Holdings sought to revive the arbitral proceedings by claiming that Laos had committed a material breach of the deed of settlement. The arbitral tribunal rejected Laos' allegations of material breach in the Decision on Merits of 10 June 2015.

Key Legal Outcomes

- Decision on Jurisdiction

The Government of Laos objected to the jurisdiction *ratione temporis* of the tribunal on the basis that the investment had been restructured through the Netherlands to gain protection under the Laos-Netherlands BIT after the dispute arose.

The tribunal found that the dispute arose approximately two months after the restructuring took place, and that therefore the tribunal had jurisdiction *ratione temporis* over the dispute.[183] The tribunal's decision was based on a close analysis of the facts giving rise to the dispute. It found that the dispute crystallised when the Government of Laos made the final decision not to grant a new tax agreement in respect of Lao Holdings' investment. Prior to that date,

183 *Lao Holdings N.V. v Laos*, ICSID Case No. ARB(AF)/12/6, Decision on Jurisdiction, 21 February 2014, para. 146.

there remained at least a realistic possibility that the new tax law would not be applied to the claimant's investment.

In so finding, the tribunal highlighted the distinction between an objection to jurisdiction *ratione temporis*, which requires a finding that the dispute arose before the BIT applied to the investment, and an objection that the tribunal should decline jurisdiction due to the claimant's abuse of process in "forum shopping" at a time when a dispute was likely to arise. The tribunal emphasized that Laos' objection was based on jurisdiction *ratione temporis*, and not on an alleged abuse of process.[184] Accordingly, the tribunal found that it need only determine whether or not the dispute had already arisen before the investment was restructured through the Netherlands.

- Award on Merits

Under the settlement agreement, Lao Holdings was allowed to revive the arbitration proceedings if Laos was in material breach of the settlement agreement and failed to remedy such breach within 45 days after receiving notice of the breach.

Lao Holdings alleged that the Government of Laos had breached the settlement agreement by granting permission for other rival casinos within its area of exclusivity. This dispute related directly to the establishment of a Special Economic Zone ("SEZ") adjacent to Lao Holdings' casino investment. Following the declaration of the SEZ, a group of private and public investors signed an agreement for a major development project, which would include a financial centre, a resort, shopping centre and casino.

On the facts, the tribunal found that the Government had not granted permission for a rival casino in Lao Holdings' area of exclusivity. The fact that the new investors in the SEZ had announced their intention to include a casino in their development did not prove that the Government of Laos had approved or granted permission for the casino. Importantly, the tribunal found that the Government of Laos' 30% minority interest in the new development project did not mean that the developer's acts could be attributed to Laos.[185]

Further, the tribunal found that, even if Laos had breached the settlement agreement by tacitly giving approval to rival investors, it remedied the breach within 45 days by making clear that rival casino projects would not be approved.

---

184 *Ibid.*, para. 68.

185 *Lao Holdings N.V. v Laos*, ICSID Case No. ARB(AF)/12/6, Decision on the Merits, 10 June 2015, paras. 64–65 and 81–85.

VII Conclusion

While investment protection in Laos remains in a state of development, the country has been taking progressive steps to improve the business climate and develop the necessary legal infrastructure to support foreign investment. While it remains to be seen how ease of doing business in the country will improve, Laos remains an exciting jurisdiction in which to invest and explore opportunities.

CHAPTER 6

Malaysia[1]

I Introduction

Malaysia is a federal democratic constitutional monarchy which gained independence in 1963. It has adopted a common law adversarial legal system based on binding precedents. The judicial system in Malaysia is federal and operates uniformly throughout its territory. Parallel to the common law system, Malaysia also applies Sharia principles regarding matters involving the Muslim faith.[2]

Although Foreign Direct Investment ("FDI") inflow to Malaysia continues to recover from the effects of the 2008–2009 global financial crises, Malaysia's performance in attracting FDI relative to both earlier decades and other States of the Association of Southeast Asian Nations ("ASEAN") has slowed. The Malaysian Government through the National Economic Advisory Council is working to improve Malaysia's competitiveness as a foreign investment destination and to meet the country's goal of becoming a high-income economy by 2020.

Inflows of actual FDI to Malaysia in 2014 decreased to USD 10.8 billion, from USD 12.1 billion in 2013.[3] The US, Japan, and Singapore are the largest sources of FDI into Malaysia, with the largest source of newly approved investments in 2013 coming from Saudi Arabia.[4] The UNCTAD World Investment Report in 2012 listed Malaysia as the 15th "top prospective host economy" for transnational corporations between 2015 and 2017.[5]

---

1 This chapter has been drafted by Ms Laura Zielinski of Eversheds LLP, Paris and reviewed by Skrine, Kuala Lumpur, Malaysia.

2 "Doing business in Malaysia", Practical Law Company, 1 June 2013: http://us.practicallaw.com/7-504-4991?source=relatedcontent#a133971.

3 UNCTAD World Investment Report 2015, Country fact sheet Malaysia, available at: http://unctad.org/sections/dite_dir/docs/wir2015/wir15_fs_my_en.pdf.

4 2015 Investment Climate Statement: http://www.state.gov/e/eb/rls/othr/ics/2015/241648.htm. *See* the WTO website for more information on trade with Malaysia: https://www.wto.org/english/thewto_e/countries_e/malaysia_e.htm.

5 UNCTAD World Investment Report 2015, Chapter 1 p. 26:http://unctad.org/en/PublicationsLibrary/wir2015_en.pdf.

 | DOI 10.1163/9789004335257_008

Malaysia has a high level of trade with other States, reaching 165% of annual GDP.[6] In the World Bank's global Doing Business 2016 report, Malaysia placed 18th overall among the 189 economies covered.[7]

Investment protection for foreign investors and investments is granted at the national level in Malaysia and accorded to investors from States with which Malaysia has entered into bilateral or multilateral investment treaties. Investment protection encompasses substantive provisions as well as dispute settlement mechanisms and *fora* for the resolution of investment disputes.

II Malaysia's National Arbitration and Investment Legislation

1 *Malaysia's Arbitration Legislation and Institutions*

Malaysia's Arbitration Law

The law governing arbitration proceedings seated in Malaysia is the Arbitration Act 2005 (as revised in 2011),[8] which is based on the UNCITRAL Model Law of 1985 and was modelled on the New Zealand Arbitration Act of 1969.

The Act applies to both domestic and international arbitrations, but draws some distinctions between them. International arbitrations are defined in section 2(1) of the Arbitration Act 2005; broadly, they are arbitrations which are also connected to another State other than Malaysia. For example, where one of the parties to an arbitration agreement has its place of business outside Malaysia at the time the arbitration agreement is concluded, the arbitration will be an international arbitration. Similarly, where the parties have expressly agreed that the subject matter of the arbitration agreement relates to more than one State, the arbitration will be an international arbitration.[9]

A domestic arbitration is any arbitration which is not an international arbitration.[10] It is noteworthy that unless otherwise agreed by the parties, where a domestic arbitration is seated in Malaysia, the arbitral tribunal is to apply the substantive law of Malaysia to determine the substance of the dispute.[11]

---

6 2015 Investment Climate Statement: http://www.state.gov/e/eb/rls/othr/ics/2015/241648.htm.

7 World Bank Group Doing Business 2016 data for Malaysia, available at http://www.doingbusiness.org/data/exploreeconomies/malaysia/.

8 http://klrca.org/downloads/rules/english/klrca_arbitration_act_2005_en.pdf.

9 Laws of Malaysia, Act 646, Arbitration Act 2005 as at 1 December 2011, Section 2(1). This is similar to the corresponding provision in the UNCITRAL Model Law of 1985.

10 *Ibid.*

11 *Ibid.*, Section 30.

While many of the provisions apply equally to both domestic and international arbitrations, some of the provisions that apply by default to domestic arbitrations do not apply to international arbitrations unless the parties agree otherwise in writing.[12] For instance, Sections 41 and 42 of the Arbitration Act 2005 apply by default to domestic arbitrations unless parties agree otherwise in writing. Section 41 allows for a party to apply to the Malaysian High Court to determine any question of law arising in the course of the arbitration, provided that the arbitral tribunal consents, or all other parties consent. Section 42 allows for any party to refer to the Malaysian High Court any question of law arising out of an award. The position is the opposite for international arbitrations, and Sections 41 and 42 do not apply unless parties agree otherwise in writing.

The Arbitration Act 2005 replaced the Arbitration Act 1952, which was based on the English Arbitration Act 1950. The Arbitration Act 2005 only applies to arbitrations commenced after 15 March 2006. Arbitrations commenced prior to that date continue to be governed by the Arbitration Act 1952.

The Arbitration Act 2005 was amended on 1 July 2011: Section 11 of the Arbitration Act 2005 was amended to clarify that, in order to secure the amount in dispute, the court may order the arrest of property, bail or other security before or during the proceedings; Section 11(3) now empowers courts to make orders for interim measures even if the seat of arbitration is outside Malaysia.[13]

The Arbitration Act 2005 did not repeal the Reciprocal Enforcement of Judgments Act 1958, which provides for the enforcement of an arbitral award from Commonwealth countries and scheduled countries as if it were a foreign judgment, provided that it is first registered in the courts of the country in which the arbitral award was given.[14]

Malaysia's Arbitral Institutions and Rules

The main arbitral institutions in Malaysia are the Kuala Lumpur Regional Centre for Arbitration ("KLRCA")[15] and the Malaysian Institute for Arbitrators.[16] The KLRCA administers most of its cases under its own Rules, the latest version

12 *Ibid.*, Section 3.

13 Practical Law Company, Q&A Guide to Arbitration in Malaysia, 1 August 2011; Chong Yee Leon, Choi Fuh Mann, "The Asia-Pacific Arbitration Review 2013 – Malaysia", *Global Arbitration Review*, 2013.

14 Chong Yee Leon, Choi Fuh Mann, "The Asia-Pacific Arbitration Review 2013 – Malaysia", *Global Arbitration Review*, 2013.

15 See http://www.klrca.org.my.

16 See http://www.miarb.com.

of which was revised in 2013.[17] International arbitration may also be carried out under *ad hoc* rules, and the KLRCA may administer arbitrations under any rules agreed on by the parties, such as the UNCITRAL Rules.[18] Foreign arbitral institutions can also operate in Malaysia subject to the agreement between the parties.[19]

A reported advantage of the KLRCA compared to other arbitral institutions in the region is its lower costs.[20] The KLRCA is also actively marketing itself and its services, for example, through measures such as the publication of Fast Track Arbitration Rules in 2013[21] and of arbitration rules for disputes arising out of Shariah-based banking and/or financial contracts in 2007.[22] The KLRCA also published Mediation/Conciliation Rules in 2013 and promotes mediation and conciliation as an alternative to arbitration.[23]

Malaysia's Courts and Arbitration

There is no court in Malaysia which hears only arbitration-related cases and applications, but the High Court of Malaysia is familiar with the law and practice of international arbitration and the enforcement of arbitration awards. Section 11 of the Arbitration Act 2005 provides that a party may apply to the High Court for interim measures and the High Court may make an order for security for costs, discovery of documents and interrogatories, giving of evidence by affidavit, appointment of a receiver, securing the amount in dispute, the preservation, interim custody or sale of any property which is the subject matter of the dispute, ensuring that any award which may be made in the arbitral proceedings is not rendered ineffectual by the dissipation of assets by a party, and an interim injunction or any other interim measure.[24] In addition, Section 29 of the Arbitration Act 2005 provides that a party may apply to the High Court for assistance in taking evidence with the approval of the arbitral tribunal.

17 The KLRCA Rules can be downloaded at: http://klrca.org/downloads/rules/english/klrca_arbitration_en.pdf.

18 Sanjay Mohanasundram, "Commercial Arbitration – Malaysia", *Global Arbitration Review*, First published on 25 July 2011 and last verified on 28 February 2012.

19 *Ibid.*

20 Risen Jayaseelan, "New life for arbitration", *The Star Online*, 1 January 2011.

21 http://klrca.org/downloads/rules/english/klrca_fast_track_arbitration_en.pdf.

22 "Malaysia introduces Shariah banking and financial arbitration", *ADR Resources*; Risen Jayaseelan, "New life for arbitration", *The Star Online*, 1 January 2011.

23 The Mediation/Conciliation Rules can be downloaded at: http://klrca.org/downloads/rules/english/klrca_mediation_en.pdf.

24 Sunil Abraham, "Arbitration Guide – Malaysia", *IBA Arbitration Committee*, April 2012.

Unless the parties agree otherwise, challenges to international arbitral awards can only be made on the limited grounds set out in the Arbitration Act 2005. The grounds for refusing recognition or enforcement of an award under the Arbitration Act 2005 follow closely Article 36 of the UNCITRAL Model Law.[25]

Section 37 of the Arbitration Act 2005 sets out the grounds for setting aside an arbitral award. Under Section 39 of the Arbitration Act 2005, the grounds for denying recognition and/or enforcement of an award are limited, and are *in pari materia* to the grounds stated in Article 36 of the UNCITRAL Model Law of 1985 and Article V of the New York Convention 1958. Many of the grounds on which an award can be set aside are also grounds for denying recognition or enforcement of an award.

The trend appears to be that the courts in Malaysia are increasingly supportive of the recognition and enforcement of awards.[26] In January 2013, however, the Malaysian High Court set aside a USD 57 million award that an *ad hoc* UNCITRAL tribunal had awarded to two coal-mining companies against Laos. The judge found that the tribunal had simultaneously adjudicated claims under a mining agreement governed by Laotian law and a separate New York law-governed agreement, and by doing so had exceeded its jurisdiction under section 37 of the Arbitration Act 2005. This decision ran contrary to the enforcement decisions already reached by the High Court of England and Wales and the US District Court for the Southern District of New York.[27]

2 *Malaysia's Investment Laws*

Malaysia can be said proactively to encourage foreign direct investment in Malaysia, although it maintains restrictions or limits on investment in some sectors.[28]

There are generally limited restrictions on foreign investment in Malaysia. Foreign investors can hold 100% equity in investments in new projects, in expanding investments and in diversification of projects in existing companies.[29] This liberal approach does not, however, extend to all sectors. Specific guidelines, policies and licensing requirements apply to certain regulated sectors,

25 http://www.uncitral.org/pdf/english/texts/arbitration/ml-arb/07-86998_Ebook.pdf.

26 Sunil Abraham, "Arbitration Guide – Malaysia", *IBA Arbitration Committee*, April 2012.

27 Clemmie Spalton, "Laos award set aside in Malaysia", *Global Arbitration Review*, 9 January 2013.

28 2015 Investment Climate Statement: http://www.state.gov/e/eb/rls/othr/ics/2015/241648.htm.

29 "Doing business in Malaysia", Practical Law Company, 1 January 2014: http://uk.practicallaw.com/cs/Satellite/resource/7-504-4991.

such as high-tech manufacturing, energy, information technology, telecommunications, and other sectors of strategic importance to Malaysia. In general, foreign companies must not hold more than 30% of a company's equity, unless the company is in the manufacturing or multimedia technology sector.[30]

Under the Strategic Trade Act of 2010, the export of strategic items and technology relating to arms and material connected with the design, development, production and delivery of weapons of mass destruction is subject to controls. Malaysia restricts or prohibits trade with the following countries: The Democratic Republic of Korea, The Islamic Republic of Iran, The Democratic Republic of Congo, Ivory Coast, Lebanon, Sudan, Libya, Afghanistan, Iraq, Liberia, Rwanda, Somalia and Eritrea.[31]

Malaysia's exchange transactions are regulated by the Central Bank of Malaysia – the Bank Negara Malaysia. The Malaysian foreign exchange administration rules have been progressively liberalised to create a competitive business environment. This means that the Exchange Control Act of 1953, as amended, currently allows for the extension of a domestic credit facility to non-resident controlled companies, for payments to non-residents for the import of goods and services, and for the repatriation of a foreign direct investor's investments including capital, profits, dividends and interest.[32]

The Federal Territory of Labuan was declared an International Offshore Financial Centre in October 1990. Businesses incorporated in this centre receive preferential tax treatment for offshore banking activities, trust and fund management, offshore insurance and offshore insurance-related businesses, and offshore investment.[33]

In 2012, the Malaysian Parliament passed legislation to update the regulatory framework for Islamic Financial Services as the Malaysian Government hopes to turn Malaysia into a global hub for Islamic financial services.[34]

Investors investing in certain industries, such as manufacturing, biotechnology, environmental management and protection, tourism, agriculture, research and development, and Islamic financial services, benefit from direct and indirect tax incentives. While such direct tax incentives grant partial or total relief from income tax for a specified period, indirect tax incentives provide exemptions from, or refunds of, import duty, sales tax and excise duty. Moreover,

---

30 *Ibid.*

31 *Ibid., See also* http://www.miti.gov.my/cms/index.jsp.

32 *Ibid.*

33 http://www.mida.gov.my/home/invest-in-malaysia/posts/.

34 http://etp.pemandu.gov.my/Financial_Services-@-Financial_Services_-_EPP_10-;_Becoming_the_Indisputable_Global_Hub_for_Islamic_Finance.aspx.

incentives are available to foreign companies setting up regional distribution centres, international procurement centres, operational headquarters or pioneer status industries in Malaysia. Tax allowance and tax exemption incentives are also available to investors in promoted areas and regional multimedia and development corridors.

Direct and indirect tax incentives in Malaysia are provided for in the Promotion of Investments Act 1986, the Income Tax Act 1967, the Customs Act 1967, the Sales Tax Act 1972, the Excise Act 1976 and the Free Zones Act 1990. These Acts cover investments in the manufacturing, agriculture, tourism and approved services sectors, as well as research and development, training and environmental protection activities.[35]

III Malaysia's Bilateral Investment Treaties

1 *Overview*

Malaysia signed its first Bilateral Investment Treaty ("BIT") with Germany on 22 December 1960. Over the last 53 years it has signed at least 68 BITs,[36] of which at least 53 have entered into force.[37] At least 39 of these BITs are publicly available at the time of writing.[38]

35 http://www.mida.gov.my/env3/index.php?page=incentives-for-investments.

36 Malaysia has signed BITs with Albania, Algeria, Argentina, Austria, Bahrain, Bangladesh, Belgium and Luxemburg, Bosnia and Herzegovina, Botswana, Burkina Faso, Cambodia, Chile, China, Croatia, Cuba, the Czech Republic, Denmark, Djibouti, Egypt, Ethiopia, Finland, France, Germany, Ghana, Guinea, Hungary, India, Indonesia, Iran, Italy, Jordan, Kazakhstan, the Republic of Korea, the Democratic People's Republic of Korea, Kuwait, Kyrgyzstan, Lao, Lebanon, Macedonia, Malawi, Mongolia, Morocco, Namibia, the Netherlands, Norway, Pakistan, Papua New Guinea, Peru, Poland, Romania, Saudi Arabia, Senegal, Spain, Sri Lanka, Sudan, Sweden, Switzerland, Syria, Taiwan, Turkey, Turkmenistan, the United Arab Emirates, the United Kingdom, Uruguay, Uzbekistan, Vietnam, Yemen and Zimbabwe.

37 UNCTAD reflects that Malaysia's BITs with the following States have entered into force: Albania, Argentina, Austria, Bahrain, Bangladesh, Belgium and Luxemburg, Bosnia and Herzegovina, Chile, China, Croatia, Cuba, the Czech Republic, Denmark, Egypt, Ethiopia, Finland, France, Germany, Ghana, Guinea, Hungary, India, Indonesia, Iran, Italy, Jordan, Kazakhstan, the Republic of Korea, the Democratic People's Republic of Korea, Kyrgyzstan, Lebanon, Macedonia, Mongolia, Morocco, the Netherlands, Norway, Pakistan, Peru, Poland, Romania, Saudi Arabia, Spain, Sri Lanka, Sweden, Switzerland, Syria, Taiwan, Turkey, the United Arab Emirates, the United Kingdom, Uruguay, Uzbekistan and Vietnam. http://investmentpolicyhub.unctad.org/IIA/CountryBits/127#iiaInnerMenu.

38 Malaysia's BITs with the following States are available on the UNCTAD website: Argentina, Austria, Belgium and Luxemburg, Bosnia and Herzegovina, Cambodia, Chile,

2 *Definition of Investment*

The publicly available BITs signed by Malaysia generally provide for a relatively broad definition of investment. The majority of these BITs define investment to include any kind of asset and in particular, though not exclusively, movable and immovable property rights and any other rights *in rem*, shares, stocks and debentures of or interests in the property of companies, claims to money or any performance having a financial value, intellectual and industrial property rights and business concessions.[39]

Unusually, the BIT between Malaysia and Jordan does not contain any definition of "investment". However, it provides that investments must be made in accordance with the laws, regulations and national policies of the Contracting States.

A number of Malaysia's BITs require that in respect of investments in the territory of Malaysia, the investment must be made in a project that has been approved by the relevant governmental authorities in Malaysia.[40] Some of those BITs also contain mirror provisions in respect of investments in the territory of the other Contracting Party.[41] For instance, under the Malaysia-United Arab Emirates BIT, an investment has to be "made in projects classified by the appropriate Ministry of Malaysia in accordance with its legislation and administrative practices as 'approved projects' ".[42] Some of Malaysia's BITs are even more specific and refer to specific national legislation with respect to qualifying investments. For example, the BIT between Malaysia and Indonesia contains a specific requirement limiting its application "to investments by investors of Malaysia in the territory of the Republic of Indonesia which have

---

China, Croatia, the Czech Republic, Denmark, Egypt, Ethiopia, Finland, France, Germany, Ghana, Hungary, India, Indonesia, Italy (only in Italian and therefore not part of the analysis), Jordan, Kazakhstan, the Republic of Korea, Kyrgyzstan, Lebanon, Mongolia, the Netherlands, Norway, Pakistan, Peru, Saudi Arabia, Spain, Sweden, Switzerland, Turkey, the United Arab Emirates, the United Kingdom, Uruguay and Vietnam. http://investmentpolicyhub.unctad.org/IIA/CountryBits/127#iiaInnerMenu.

39 The inclusion of business concessions as qualifying investments may be limited, for instance, in the case of the Malaysia-Netherlands BIT, to those concession that give their holder a legal position of some duration.

40 Such as those concluded with Austria, Belgium and Luxemburg, Chile, China, Denmark, Finland, Germany, the Republic of Korea, The Netherlands, Norway, Sweden, Switzerland, the United Arab Emirates, the United Kingdom and Vietnam.

41 Such as the BITs concluded with Chile, China, Indonesia, the United Arab Emirates and Vietnam.

42 BIT between Malaysia and the United Arab Emirates, Article 1(1)(b)(i).

been previously granted admission in accordance with the Law No. 1 of 1967 concerning Foreign Investment and any law amending or replacing it".[43]

The majority of Malaysia's publicly available BITs stipulate that the investments shall be made in accordance with the laws and regulations of the State in which they are made.

3 *Definition of Investor*

The definition of "investor" in Malaysia's BITs most commonly includes "nationals" and "companies", as respectively defined, of a Contracting State. The former are generally defined as nationals of a State pursuant to the laws or Constitution of that State and the latter as companies duly incorporated or constituted in accordance with the laws of that State. In some cases the definition is broader, also including associations and partnerships in which a national or company of one of the Contracting States has a predominant interest,[44] or individuals permanently residing in one of the Contracting States. Sometimes an investor is defined as a company having its seat and conducting its business in one of the Contracting States.

Generally, the BITs signed by Malaysia include as "investors" companies with or without legal personality and with or without limited liability.

The Malaysia-Saudi Arabia BIT extends the notion of "investor" to the Government of the Kingdom of Saudi Arabia and its financial institutions and authorities such as the Saudi Arabian Monetary Agency, public funds and other similar governmental institutions existing in Saudi Arabia. The Malaysia-United Arab Emirates BIT also defines the United Arab Emirates Government as a qualifying "investor".

4 *Scope*

Malaysia's BITs characteristically apply to investments made prior as well as after the entry into force of the treaty.[45] Several of Malaysia's BITs specify that they shall not apply to disputes that have arisen before their entry into force,[46] while other BITs are silent on this issue. All of Malaysia's publicly available BITs, except for the Malaysia-United Arab Emirates BIT, contain subrogation

43 BIT between Malaysia and Indonesia, Article X.

44 For example the BITs signed with Austria, Finland, Norway, Sweden and the United Arab Emirates.

45 However, in the case of the BITs concluded with Hungary and Vietnam, the BITs only apply to investments made after the entry into force of the treaty.

46 Examples include Malaysia's BITs with Argentina, Chile, Ethiopia, Lebanon, Mongolia and Uruguay.

rights and a number of Malaysia's BITs provide that where more favourable rules exist either under international law and/or under the law of the Contracting States, then the more favourable rules shall prevail.[47]

5 *Substantive Protections*

Fair and Equitable Treatment

All of Malaysia's publicly available BITs at the time of writing, except for the Malaysia-France and Malaysia-Germany BITs, contain a "fair and equitable treatment" provision as an obligation on the Contracting State *vis-à-vis* qualifying investors and/or investments. However, the Malaysia-Cambodia and the Malaysia-Finland BITs restrict this standard to fair and equitable treatment which is in accordance with the laws, regulations and national policies of the Contracting States.

Non-Discrimination

Some of Malaysia's BITs prohibit arbitrary and discriminatory treatment of qualifying investors and/or investments by Contracting States. The Malaysia-United Arab Emirates BIT entitles investors to apply to the competent authorities in the Contracting State in which they have invested to ensure that appropriate measures be taken and appropriate facilities be granted to promote and protect their investments.[48]

Full Protection and Security

All of Malaysia's publicly available BITs at the time of writing, except for the Malaysia-France, Malaysia-Germany, Malaysia-Netherlands, Malaysia-Sweden and Malaysia-Switzerland BITs, provide for "full protection and security" of the investments of the other Contracting State. The Malaysia-United Arab Emirates BIT specifies that full protection and security granted to investments of investors of the other Contracting State shall be consistent with international law.[49]

---

47 Such as those concluded by Malaysia with Argentina, Austria, Belgium and Luxemburg, China, the Czech Republic, Denmark, Germany, Hungary, Indonesia, Kyrgyzstan, The Netherlands, Saudi Arabia, Spain, Switzerland and the United Arab Emirates.

48 Such as the Malaysia-Argentina, Malaysia-Austria, Malaysia-Belgium and Luxemburg, Malaysia-Denmark, Malaysia-Netherlands, Malaysia-Saudi Arabia, Malaysia-Switzerland and Malaysia-United Arab Emirates BITs.

49 Article 2(2).

Expropriation

All BITs signed by Malaysia that are publicly available at the time of writing contain a provision generally prohibiting the expropriation, nationalization and any other measure having an effect equivalent to expropriation or nationalization except if such a measure taken by the host State serves a public purpose, is taken under due process of law, in a non-discriminatory manner (the non-discrimination requirement is lacking in the Malaysia-France BIT and the Malaysia-Germany BIT) and is accompanied by the payment of a prompt, adequate and effective compensation (the Malaysia-France BIT mentions the payment of such compensation as the only requirement accompanying an expropriatory measure taken by the host State).

The Malaysia-Croatia BIT provides furthermore that the measure has to be taken "in accordance with the laws and regulations of the Contracting Party" while the BITs with Norway, Sweden and the United Arab Emirates stipulate that the provision in question applies to direct and indirect measures of expropriation. The Malaysia-United Arab Emirates BIT provides, moreover, that investments of either Contracting State or its nationals and juridical persons shall not be subject to sequestration, confiscation or any similar measures save with the order of a competent court issued in accordance with the laws in force in that State. Most of Malaysia's BITs indicate how the compensation shall be calculated and paid, specify the treatment of company shares and the BITs signed with several States, provide for a review by a judicial or other independent authority of the host State of the investor's case and the valuation of its investment.[50]

Umbrella Clauses

Some of the BITs signed by Malaysia include an obligation on the Contracting Parties to observe any obligation they have undertaken with regard to investments of an investor of the other Contracting Party.[51] This is commonly known as an "umbrella clause". This means that State obligations such as those contained in the agreements between investors and the host State that fall under the protection of the BIT can potentially be elevated to treaty obligations.

Most Favoured Nation and National Treatment

All of Malaysia's publicly available BITs require that the treatment of the investments of investors from the other Contracting State be no less favourable than

50 Such as the Malaysia-Germany, the Malaysia-Czech Republic, Malaysia-India, the Malaysia-Republic of Korea, Malaysia-Kyrgyzstan and Malaysia-Mongolia BITs.

51 Such as the Malaysia-United Kingdom, Malaysia-Denmark and Malaysia-Netherlands BITs.

that granted to nationals or companies of third states. The Malaysia-Austria and Malaysia-Belgium and Luxemburg BITs add that the treatment shall in no case be less favourable than that recognized by international law. This is commonly known as a "Most Favoured Nation" or "MFN" provision. By contrast, the Malaysia-Germany BIT restricts its MFN provision to situations in which no specific stipulations made in the document of admission provide otherwise. The Malaysia-Netherlands BIT specifically applies the MFN provision to, *inter alia,* taxes, fees, and the protection of industrial property, but exempts special tax advantages on the basis of reciprocity. The Malaysia-France BIT also includes tax matters within the scope of the National Treatment and MFN provisions. The Malaysia-Saudi Arabia BIT excludes the banking and insurance sectors from the National Treatment provision and the Malaysia-Republic of Korea BIT provides that in the banking and insurance sectors, MFN treatment shall be accorded in compliance with the relevant laws and regulations of each Contracting State. Most of Malaysia's BITs specify the application of the MFN provisions to compensation for losses.

Many of Malaysia's BITs exclude from the MFN provision, *inter alia*, customs unions, free trade areas, common markets, and international agreements or domestic legislation relating mainly or wholly to taxation (France, however, explicitly includes taxation). The Malaysia-Austria BIT moreover exempts membership of ASEAN with respect to Malaysia and arrangements concerning "traffic in frontier areas" or "Kleiner Grenzverkehr" with respect to Austria, the Malaysia-Lebanon BIT exempts the treatment granted to investors who are nationals of Arab countries and the Malaysia-China BIT exempts arrangements concerning frontier trade.

Some of Malaysia's BITs also contain explicit National Treatment provisions requiring the Contracting State to treat qualifying investors and/or investments at least as favourably as their national investors and/or their investments.[52]

6 *Repatriation of Capital and Compensation for Losses*

All BITs signed by Malaysia publicly available at the time of writing contain provisions allowing for the repatriation by the investor of capital invested and investment returns. Moreover, except for a handful of treaties, Malaysia's BITs contain a provision providing for the compensation for losses resulting from

52 Such as the Malaysia-Denmark, Malaysia-France, Malaysia-Germany, Malaysia-India, Malaysia-Saudi Arabia, Malaysia-Switzerland, Malaysia-United Arab Emirates and Malaysia-United Kingdom BITs.

war or other armed conflict, revolution, a state of national emergency, revolt, insurrection or riot in the territory of the host State.[53]

7 *Investor-State Dispute Settlement*

The vast majority of publicly available BITs signed by Malaysia provide that a dispute arising between a Contracting State and an investor shall as far as possible be resolved amicably.[54] If this is not possible through negotiations and consultations, or through the pursuit of local remedies as stipulated in the Malaysia-Finland BIT and the Malaysia-Norway BIT, after a specified period (generally three[55] or six[56] months), the dispute shall be submitted to arbitration or to the courts or tribunals of the Contracting State.

Some of Malaysia's BITs provide for the requirement of consent by the host State before commencement of conciliation and arbitration proceedings under ICSID but the vast majority[57] provide for the submission of the dispute to ICSID for conciliation or arbitration proceedings, by either the investor, or the host State (in the event that the investor consents in writing to submit the dispute to ICSID for settlement under the ICSID Convention). In case of disagreement with regard to the choice between conciliation and arbitration, most of Malaysia's BITs specify that the investor's opinion shall take priority over the choice by the host State.

Many Malaysian BITs also provide the investor with the choice of *ad hoc* arbitration under the UNCITRAL Rules.[58] The Malaysia-India and Malaysia-Vietnam BITs provide for conciliation under the UNCITRAL Rules and foresee submission to arbitration only in case the conciliation proceedings remain

53 This includes Malaysia-France, Malaysia-Germany, Malaysia-Netherlands, Malaysia-Sweden and Malaysia-United Kingdom BITs.

54 Notable exceptions are those signed with France, Germany, Sweden and Switzerland.

55 BITs signed with Austria, Belgium and Luxemburg, Bosnia and Herzegovina, Chile, Croatia, Denmark, Egypt, Finland, Ghana, Jordan, Kazakhstan, Republic of Korea, Kyrgyzstan, Mongolia, Pakistan, Spain, the United Arab Emirates and the United Kingdom.

56 BITs signed with Argentina, Cambodia, China, the Czech Republic, Ethiopia, Hungary, India, Indonesia, Lebanon, Saudi Arabia, Turkey, Uruguay and Vietnam.

57 Except for the BITs signed with China, Germany, Switzerland and Vietnam.

58 For instance, this is provided for under the Malaysia-Argentina, Malaysia-Cambodia, Malaysia-China, Malaysia-Czech Republic, Malaysia-Ethiopia, Malaysia-Ghana, Malaysia-Hungary, Malaysia-India, Malaysia-Lebanon, Malaysia-Spain, Malaysia-Uruguay and Malaysia-Vietnam BITs. In fact, under the Malaysia-Ghana BIT, if there is no agreement after three months, the default choice is arbitration under the UNCITRAL Rules. Under the Malaysia-India BIT, the Appointing Authority is the President of the ICJ.

fruitless. The Malaysia-Ethiopia and Malaysia-India BITs also provide for arbitration under the ICSID Additional Facility (for the Malaysia-India BIT only in case both parties agree) and the Malaysia-India BIT stipulates that the award shall state the basis of the decision and give reasons. The Malaysia-China BIT provides only for *ad hoc* arbitration but indicates that, when deciding on its own procedure, the arbitral tribunal can refer either to the ICSID or UNCITRAL Rules. This same BIT designates the Chairman of the International Arbitration Institute of the Stockholm Chamber of Commerce as the default appointing authority.

While the Malaysia-Austria and Malaysia-Belgium and Luxemburg BITs provide for the renunciation of the exhaustion of local remedies by the Contracting States, other treaties[59] leave the investor with the option of submitting the dispute to the national courts and tribunals of the host State instead of submitting it to international arbitration. The Malaysia-Finland and Malaysia-Norway BITs consider the pursuit of local remedies as a first step before the submission of the dispute to conciliation or arbitration and the Malaysia-Netherlands BIT provides for the exhaustion of local remedies before a dispute can be submitted to ICSID conciliation or arbitration.

A number of Malaysia's BITs[60] contain (implicitly or explicitly) "fork in the road clauses", which preclude initial arbitration for disputes which have previously been submitted for resolution to the local courts.

Malaysian BITs generally exclude the recourse to diplomatic channels unless the arbitral tribunal is found not to have jurisdiction or in case of non-compliance with an award by a Contracting State.

It is noteworthy that the Malaysia-Germany and the Malaysia-Switzerland BITs, concluded in 1960 and 1978 respectively, do not contain any provision dealing with the resolution of investment disputes. The Malaysia-France BIT only indicates that disputes shall be submitted to ICSID arbitration without further specifying the procedure.

8 *State-to-State Dispute Settlement*

All of Malaysia's publicly available BITs stipulate that disputes between the Contracting States shall be resolved as far as possible through recourse to

---

59 Such as the Malaysia-Argentina, Malaysia-Chile, Malaysia-China, Malaysia-Croatia, Malaysia-Ethiopia, Malaysia-India, Malaysia-Indonesia, Malaysia-Jordan, Malaysia-Lebanon, Malaysia-Saudi Arabia, Malaysia-Turkey and Malaysia-Uruguay BITs.

60 For instance, the BITs signed by Malaysia with Argentina, Bosnia and Herzegovina, Chile, Croatia, Egypt, Kazakhstan, the Republic of Korea, Kyrgyzstan, Lebanon, Mongolia, Pakistan, Peru, Saudi Arabia, the United Arab Emirates and Uruguay.

diplomatic channels. In the event that diplomatic settlement fails, a dispute shall be submitted to an arbitral tribunal. The Malaysia-Croatia, Malaysia-France, Malaysia-Hungary and Malaysia-Peru BITs foresee arbitral proceedings if the dispute cannot be solved diplomatically within six months.

The BITs require the establishment of an *ad hoc* arbitral tribunal constituted by two arbitrators each appointed by one of the Contracting States and a chairman appointed by the two co-arbitrators. The BIT between Malaysia and Austria requires the agreement of the Contracting States to the appointment of the chairman, while the others either leave it completely to the co-arbitrators or only require the approval by the Contracting States.

In case a Contracting State fails to appoint its arbitrator, generally this task shall be conferred on the President of the International Court of Justice.[61]

Malaysia's BITs generally allow the thus constituted *ad hoc* tribunal to determine its own rules and procedure, except for the repartition of the costs which is detailed in the BITs, and stipulate that the tribunal shall decide by majority and that the arbitral award shall be final and binding. The Malaysia-Netherlands BIT allows the *ad hoc* tribunal to decide *ex aequo et bono* if necessary.

9 *Additional Provisions*

The Malaysia-Germany BIT contains an additional provision relating to further cooperation with regard to the interchange of the use of, *inter alia*, science and technical knowledge. The Malaysia-Netherlands BIT contains several provisions dealing specifically with issues relating to vessels and shipping. The Malaysia-Ghana, Malaysia-Indonesia, Malaysia-Kazakhstan, Malaysia-Kyrgyzstan, Malaysia-Lebanon, Malaysia-Mongolia and the Malaysia-Saudi Arabia BITs contain provisions relating to the amendment of the BIT in question. The Malaysia-United Arab Emirates BIT provides for periodic consultation on investment opportunities between the Contracting States.

10 *Notable Trends*

A notable trend is that the bulk of the BITs entered into by Malaysia were signed and/or ratified in the 1990s. In fact, about two-thirds of Malaysia's publicly-known BITs were concluded in the 1990s. Comparatively, relatively few of Malaysia's known BITs were concluded in the 2000s.

---

61 Or the Secretary General of the United Nations in the case of the Malaysia-France BIT.

IV Multilateral Investment Related Treaties and Organizations to which Malaysia is a Party

1 *ASEAN – ACIA*

Malaysia is one of the Founding Members of ASEAN together with Indonesia, The Philippines, Singapore and Thailand. As recalled in detail in the ASEAN chapter, ASEAN was established on 8 August 1967 with the signing of the ASEAN Declaration in Bangkok and has the aims and purposes of, *inter alia*, accelerating economic growth, social progress and cultural development in the region, promoting regional peace and stability and promoting active collaboration and mutual assistance on matters of common interest.[62] Malaysia is a party to the ASEAN Comprehensive Investment Agreement (the "ACIA") which entered into force on 29 March 2012. It aims to create a free and open investment environment through the consolidation and expansion of existing agreements between ASEAN Member States.[63]

The ACIA contains substantive investment protections commonly found in BITs, such as provisions on non-discrimination, MFN treatment, fair and equitable treatment, full protection and security, and expropriation. Where a dispute arises between an investor and a Member State, the ACIA provides for various dispute resolution options, including the submission of a claim under the ICSID Convention, under the UNCITRAL Arbitration Rules, or to the KLRCA or any other regional centre for arbitration in ASEAN.[64]

Beyond the usual provisions found in BITs, the ACIA also contains provisions aimed at enhancing cooperation between ASEAN States in the promotion[65] and facilitation of investment,[66] and to enhance ASEAN integration.[67]

2 *APEC*

Malaysia is a Member State of the Asia-Pacific Economic Cooperation ("APEC") since 7 November 1989.[68] APEC's aim is to promote sustainable growth and prosperity in the Asia-Pacific region.[69] Among other APEC initiatives for free

62 http://www.asean.org/asean/about-asean/overview.

63 http://www.aseanbriefing.com/news/2013/04/12/introduction-to-the-asean-comprehensive-investment-agreement.html.

64 Article 33 of the ACIA.

65 *Ibid.*, Article 24.

66 *Ibid.*, Article 25.

67 *Ibid.*, Article 26.

68 http://www.apec.org/about-us/about-apec/member-economies.aspx.

69 http://www.apec.org/About-Us/About-APEC/Mission-Statement.aspx.

and open trade and investment, three key APEC investment-related instruments are the Non-Binding Investment Principles ("NBIP"), the Menu of Options, and the Transparency Standards on Investment.

The NBIP sets out 12 investment principles that are broadly similar to the core elements of international investment agreements concluded between APEC Member States, including provisions on transparency, national treatment, fair and equitable treatment, full protection and security, protection from strife, the transfer of funds, and the entry of key personnel. The Menu of Options (or the Options for Investment Liberalization and Business Facilitation to Strengthen the APEC Economies) lists policies for liberalization and business facilitation. The transparency Standards on investment cover the publication, awareness and availability of investment laws and measures.[70]

3 *OIC-APPGI*

Malaysia signed the Agreement on Promotion, Protection and Guarantee of Investments (the "APPGI") among Member States of the Organization of the Islamic Conference (the "OIC") of 1981 on 30 September 1987 but as at the date of writing has not yet ratified it.[71]

The OIC, of which Malaysia has been a member since 1969, was established in 1969 and aims to enhance and consolidate the links between Member States and to strengthen economic and trade cooperation between them.[72]

4 *Multilateral Investment Guarantee Agency*

Malaysia is a party to the Convention Establishing the Multilateral Investment Guarantee Agency (the "MIGA") of 1985. MIGA is a part of the World Bank Group and a multilateral investment insurance system against political risks, which offers investment protection for cross-border investments against losses resulting from, *inter alia*, currency transfer restrictions, expropriation and a government's (or, in certain circumstances, a State-owned enterprise's)[73] breach or repudiation of a contract with an investor. Malaysia has been a member of MIGA since 6 December 1991.[74]

---

70 "Identifying core elements in investment agreements in the APEC region", UNCTAD Series on International Investment Policies for Development, United Nations (New York and Geneva: 2008), available at http://unctad.org/en/Docs/diaeia20083_en.pdf.

71 http://www.oic-oci.org/english/convenion/Accords_Eng_31_01.pdf.

72 http://www.oic-oci.org/oicv2/page/?p_id=52&p_ref=26&lan=en.

73 http://www.miga.org/documents/IGGenglish.pdf at p. 7.

74 http://www.miga.org/whoweare/index.cfm?stid=1695.

V Multilateral Dispute Settlement Related Treaties

1 *ICSID Convention*

Malaysia is a party to the ICSID Convention, also called the Washington Convention of 1966, which established ICSID. Malaysia signed the ICSID Convention on 22 October 1965 and deposited its ratification on 8 August 1966. The ICSID Convention entered into force in Malaysia on 14 October 1966.[75]

2 *New York Convention*

Although the New York Convention is not a convention which specifically addresses the issue of investment protection, its importance cannot be overstated with respect to the enforcement of arbitral awards including in certain cases, those arising out of investments. Recognizing the growing importance of international arbitration as a means of settling international commercial disputes, the New York Convention seeks to provide common legislative standards for the recognition of arbitration agreements and court recognition and enforcement of foreign and non-domestic arbitral awards. It obliges parties to ensure that foreign and non-domestic arbitral awards will not be discriminated against but will be recognized and enforced in the same way as domestic awards in each of the signatory States.[76] Malaysia has been a contracting State to the New York Convention since 3 February 1986.

Investment disputes can be resolved through arbitration under a variety of arbitral rules, for example the UNCITRAL Arbitration Rules, International Chamber of Commerce (the "ICC") Rules and the Stockholm Chamber of Commerce (the "SCC") Rules, whether administered by arbitral institutions such as the Permanent Court of Arbitration (the "PCA") or on an *ad hoc* basis. While ICSID awards benefit from the specific enforcement framework offered under the Washington Convention, the New York Convention plays a very important role in the enforcement of these other arbitral awards.

In terms of reservations, Malaysia will apply the Convention only to recognition and enforcement of awards made in the territory of a Contracting State

---

75 See the ICSID website for more detailed information on this institution: https://icsid.worldbank.org/ICSID/Index.jsp.

76 As stated by the United Nations Commission on International Trade Law (UNCITRAL): http://www.uncitral.org/uncitral/uncitral_texts/arbitration/NYConvention.html.

and only to differences arising out of legal relationships (whether contractual or not) that are considered commercial under national law.[77]

VI International Investment Arbitration Jurisprudence

With regard to the practical application of the investment protection provisions for international investors mentioned above, at the time of writing, Malaysia has been a party to two international investment disputes that are in the public domain and Malaysian investors have been involved in at least two other of such disputes. Each of these four cases is considered in more detail below.

1 *Cases involving Malaysia as the Respondent State*

Philippe Gruslin v. Malaysia (ICSID Case No. ARB/99/3)

Tribunal:	Gavan Griffith QC (Australia)
Case Initiated:	16 March 1999
Award Rendered:	27 November 2000

Background Facts

In the ICSID Case *Gruslin v. Malaysia* under the Belgium and Luxembourg-Malaysia BIT, a Belgian investor sued Malaysia after losing money on portfolio investments in the Kuala Lumpur Stock Exchange. He claimed that his losses resulted from Malaysia's introduction of exchange controls in 1998 in the context of the Asian financial crisis.

Key Legal Outcomes

- Jurisdiction

The claimant tried to establish jurisdiction under the applicable BIT and Article 25(1) of the ICSID Convention. The sole arbitrator rejected the claimant's claim on the basis that it fell outside of the scope of the relevant BIT. He held that the treaty only applied to investments in approved projects, given a specific provision to that effect in the Belgian and Luxembourg-Malaysia BIT, and he found that the investor's assets did not qualify as an approved project.

77 Sanjay Mohanasundram, "Commercial Arbitration – Malaysia", *Global Arbitration Review*, First published on 25 July 2011 and last verified on 28 February 2012.

The respondent also objected to jurisdiction on the basis that the treaty required that the investment be made in the territory of the host State, and in this case, the claimant had not made an investment in Malaysia. While the sole arbitrator also dealt with this territorial requirement, he did not conclude on it and based his finding of a lack of jurisdiction on the absence of an approved investment.

Malaysian Historic Salvors SDN BHD v. The Government of Malaysia (ICSID Case No. ARB/05/10)

Sole Arbitrator:	Michael Hwang, S.C. (Singapore)
Case Initiated:	30 September 2004
Award Rendered:	17 May 2007

Background Facts

The ICSID claim was brought under the UK-Malaysia BIT and concerned a dispute that resulted out of a 1990s salvaging operation conducted off the shores of Malaysia.

The claimant entered into a contract with the Malaysian Government on a "no finds-no pay" basis, under which the claimant was required to use its expertise, labour and equipment to determine the location, and salvage the cargo, of a British vessel that sank off the coast of Malacca in 1817.

The claimant was required to expand its financial and other resources and to assume all risks of the salvage operation. Under a later contract, the claimant was obliged to, and did arrange for, the auction of the recovered items. The items were auctioned in 1995 for approximately USD 2.98 million, out of which the claimant was paid 40% instead of the 70% it alleged it should have received under the contract.

The claimant further alleged that the respondent withheld from sale salvaged items valued at over USD 400,000 and did not pay the claimant its share of the best attainable value of such items.

Key Legal Outcomes

- Jurisdiction

The sole arbitrator declined jurisdiction based on the finding that the project in question failed to make a significant contribution to the host country's economy – one of the characteristics he found to be essential for a project to fall under the scope of the definition of an "investment" under Article 25 of the ICSID Convention. He analysed relevant jurisprudence to establish "hallmarks" which were required for a project to fall under the definition of an "investment" within the Convention. In the sole arbitrator's view, in order for an investment to benefit from the provisions of the ICSID Convention, a project had to pass a two-stage test: it had to qualify as an investment under the applicable bilateral investment treaty and under Article 25 of the ICSID Convention. Having found that the project in question did not qualify as an investment under Article 25 of the ICSID Convention, he did not proceed to analyse the provisions of the applicable bilateral investment treaty, but declined jurisdiction on the basis that the project was not an investment under the ICSID Convention.

Annulment

Members of the Committee:	Judge Stephen M. Schwebel (President, United States) Judge Mohamed Shahabuddeen (Guyana) Judge Peter Tomka (Slovakia)
Decision Rendered:	16 April 2009

Two members of the annulment committee, Judges Stephen Schwebel and Peter Tomka, held by a majority decision that the award declining jurisdiction should be annulled. In their view, the hallmarks set out by the sole arbitrator are not mandatory.

The majority found that the reason why the ICSID Convention does not specify the definition of an investment is to allow for the broadest definition possible so as not to preclude jurisdiction if a project qualifies as an investment under the applicable bilateral investment treaty. They held that the sole arbitrator manifestly exceeded his powers by not construing jurisdiction as broadly as required by the applicable BIT.

Judge Mohamed Shahabuddeen disagreed with the majority's holding. In his view, the annulment committee should not act as a court of appeal and he stated that there should be outer limits to jurisdiction under the ICSID Convention. In his dissenting opinion, he stated that the definition of investment under the Convention is controlling and that the sole arbitrator correctly used it as the starting point of his analysis and was right to stop after finding that the project did not qualify as an investment under the ICSID Convention. Moreover, he stated that he agreed with the sole arbitrator's finding that a significant contribution to the host State's economic development is a condition of ICSID jurisdiction.

2 *Cases involving Malaysia's Investors*

MTD Equity Sdn. Bhd. and MTN Chile S.A. v. Republic of Chile (ICSID Case No. ARB/01/7)

Tribunal:	Andrés Rigo Sureda (President, Spain) Marc Lalonde (Canada) Rodrigo Oreamuno Blanco (Costa Rica)
Case Initiated:	26 June 2001
Award Rendered:	25 May 2004

Background Facts

MTD Equity Sdn, a Malaysia company, and MTD Chile S.A., a Chilean company (collectively "MTD") initiated ICSID proceedings against the Republic of Chile in 2001 invoking the 1992 Agreement between the Government of Malaysia and the Government of the Republic of Chile for the Promotion and Protection of Investments. After the joint resignation of the first set of arbitrators (James H. Carter, Professor Michael Reisman and Guillermo Aguilar Alvarez as presiding arbitrator), a new tribunal was constituted (Marc Lalonde, Rodrigo Oreamuno Blanco and Andrés Rigo Sureda as presiding arbitrator).

The dispute was related to MTD's non-realisation of an investment project of developing a satellite city in the Chilean municipality of Pirque. The land acquired by MTD had originally been destined for agricultural use and needed to be rezoned before MTD could start building the self-sufficient city following the Malaysian model. The Chilean Government had previously assured MTD that the rezoning of the land would take place in due course. Moreover, the Chilean Foreign Investment Commission (FIC) had also signed a contract generally approving MTD's investment in Chile without, however, explicitly approving the relevant rezoning. MTD invested USD 17 million into the project before learning that the responsible government agency refused to rezone the land now owned by it on the grounds that it would be inconvenient and contrary to Chilean law.

MTD started ICSID proceedings alleging breaches of the BIT including expropriation, unreasonable and discriminatory measures and breaches of the fair and equitable treatment obligation as well as breaches of obligations under the foreign investment contracts that MTD had concluded with the FIC. MTD requested compensation for the damages it had allegedly sustained, including compound interest and costs.

Key Legal Outcomes

- Merits

The tribunal dismissed MTD's claims relating to expropriation, unreasonable and discriminatory measures, and the obligations under the foreign investment contracts but found that Chile had breached its fair and equitable treatment obligation.

The tribunal drew a "distinction between permits to be granted in accordance with the laws and regulations of the country concerned and those actions that require a change of said laws and regulations."[78] It stated that:

> To the extent that the application for a permit meets the requirements of the law, then … the investor should be granted such permit. On the other hand, said provision does not entitle an investor to a change of the normative framework of the country where it invests. All that the investor may expect is that the law be applied.[79]

While the tribunal thus decided that the claimants had no right to expect the Government of Chile to change its laws to render the proposed project possible, it found that Chile had breached its fair and equitable treatment obligation when Chile's FIC approved the investment for a project that was against the urban policy of the Government.[80]

The tribunal decided that the claimants and the respondent should each bear 50% of the damages because it decided that part of the claimants' losses resulted from their own lack of diligence and investigation prior to making the investment.

Annulment

Members of the Committee: Judge Gilbert Guillaume (France)
Prof. James Crawford (Australia)
Dr. Sara Ordóñez Noriega (Colombia)

Decision Rendered: 21 March 2007

78 Award, 25 May 2004, para. 205.
79 Award, 25 May 2004, para. 205.
80 Award, 25 May 2004, para. 166.

On 30 December 2004, Chile applied for the annulment of the award. On 21 March 2007, the *Ad Hoc* Annulment Committee denied the request for annulment.

Telekom Malaysia Bhd. v. Government of Ghana (*UNCITRAL* Rules)

Tribunal: Prof. Albert Jan van den Berg (President, Netherlands)
Prof. Emmanuel Gaillard (France)
Robert Layton (USA)

Background Facts

In 1996, Telekom Malaysia Berhad ("TMB"), a Malaysian telecommunications company, invested USD 38 million in Ghana Telecommunications Company Limited ("Ghana Telecom") to acquire a 30% interest in, and control over the management of, Ghana Telecom, the national telecoms company. In 2001, a dispute arose between TMB and the Government of Ghana concerning TMB's shareholding in Ghana Telecom.[81]

TMB brought arbitration proceedings against Ghana, in accordance with the terms of the Malaysia-Ghana BIT, under the UNCITRAL Rules of Arbitration at the Permanent Court of Arbitration in the Hague.[82]

Key Legal Outcomes

In 2005, TMB and the Government of Ghana reached a settlement under which the Government agreed to pay an undisclosed sum over a period of two years, after which the Government would acquire TMB's minority stake in Ghana Telecom.[83]

81 *The Republic of Ghana v Telekom Malaysia Berhad*, Decision of 18 October 2004, HA/RK 2004.667, District Court of the Hague.

82 "Telekom Malaysia and Ghana look to settle UNCITRAL arbitration", Luke Eric Peterson, Investment Law and Policy News Bulletin, 27 May 2005, available at http://www.iisd.org/pdf/2005/investment_investsd_may27_2005.pdf.

83 "Telekom Malaysia and Ghana look to settle UNCITRAL arbitration", Luke Eric Peterson, Investment Law and Policy News Bulletin, 27 May 2005, available at http://www.iisd.org/pdf/2005/investment_investsd_may27_2005.pdf.

VII Outlook: Anticipated Developments

Malaysia is a party to the Trans-Pacific Partnership ("TPP") which was concluded in Atlanta, Georgia, USA on 5 October 2015, after five and a half years of negotiations. The TPP is a comprehensive, high standard regional trade agreement that is widely expected to create new trade and investment opportunities for Malaysia in the Asia-Pacific region. The TPP brings together 12 economies from both sides of the Pacific, namely, Australia, Brunei Darussalam, Canada, Chile, Japan, Malaysia, Mexico, New Zealand, Peru, Singapore, the United States and Vietnam. Collectively, these countries represent 40% of global GDP, one-third of world trade, and comprise a population of 800 million, making the TPP the largest regional trade agreement at the time of writing.[84] Apart from offering new market access for Malaysian goods and services producers exporting to and investing in TPP markets, the TPP also reinforces the region's commitment to a rules-based trading system by updating international rules that apply to cross-border trade and investment.[85]

Malaysia already has existing bilateral Free Trade Agreements ("FTAs") with 6 of the 11 TPP partners and 5 regional FTAs.[86] The TPP represents Malaysia's first preferential trade agreement with Canada, Mexico, Peru and the US.[87] While the TPP has been concluded, it will only enter into force when at least six original signatories, accounting for at least 85% of the GDP across the TPP economies, have ratified the agreement. When the TPP comes into force, it will be interesting to see how this agreement will fit with Malaysia's treaty arrangements, such as its existing FTAs, BITs, regional investment agreements such as the ASEAN Comprehensive Investment Agreement, as well as the widely anticipated Regional Comprehensive Economic Partnership Agreement ("RCEP") where negotiations are expected to be concluded soon.[88] While the TPP and RCEP might open doors to vast investment opportunities and a jump in FDI inflows to Malaysia, these agreements at the same time afford investors in

84 Singapore Ministry of Trade and Industry, *Trans Pacific Partnership Free Trade Agreement (TPP) 7 Things You Should Know*, available at https://www.mti.gov.sg/MTIInsights/SiteAssets/Pages/TPP/Seven%20things%20you%20should%20know%20about%20the%20TPP%20(Final).pdf.

85 *Ibid.*

86 Malaysian Ministry of International Trade and Industry, *Brief on the Trans-Pacific Partnership (TPP)* http://www.miti.gov.my/miti/resources/fileupload/TPP%20-%20Briefing%20Notes%20-%20Website%20(FINALrev1).pdf.

87 http://fta.miti.gov.my/.

88 http://fta.miti.gov.my/index.php/pages/view/60?mid=39.

Malaysia with greater protection when investing in economies which did not previously have investment agreements with Malaysia.[89]

In view of the efforts of KLRCA, arbitration and other means of alternative dispute resolution are likely to become more frequently used in the coming years in Malaysia. As part of the move towards increasing visibility of arbitration, the Malaysian branch of the Chartered Institute for Arbitrators held, for example, a major international arbitration conference in Malaysia in August 2013.

---

89 Institute of Strategic and International Studies (ISIS) Malaysia, *National Interest Analysis of Malaysia's Participation in the Trans-Pacific Partnership*, available at http://fta.miti.gov.my/miti-fta/resources/ISIS_The_Grand_Finale.pdf.

CHAPTER 7

Myanmar[1]

I Introduction

After decades of isolation, Myanmar is going through a process of political transition toward democracy. Since 2011, the Government of Myanmar has been trying to tackle poverty and promote sustainable and equitable growth by liberalizing the economy. This liberalization process also extends to the investment and arbitration framework. Given Myanmar's rich natural resources, its young labour force and its strategic location between India and China, Myanmar has a lot to gain from greater global and regional economic integration.[2]

II Myanmar's National Arbitration and Investment Legislation

1 *Myanmar's Arbitration Legislation and Institutions*

Myanmar's Arbitration Law[3]

On 5 January 2016, Myanmar enacted its new Arbitration Law, under the Union Parliament Act No. 5 of 2016, thereby repealing and replacing the Myanmar Arbitration Act of 1944, which had been in force since 1946.

The new Arbitration Law is largely based on the UNCITRAL Model Law and represents an important step forward in creating an attractive legal environment for foreign investors. Notably, it gives effect to the New York Convention on the Recognition and Enforcement of Foreign Arbitral Awards (the "New York Convention") that Myanmar signed in 2013. Going forward, foreign arbitral awards from more than 150 New York Convention States shall be enforceable in Myanmar – subject, however, to the Myanmar courts' interpretation of the limited exceptions stated in the New York Convention.

1 This chapter has been drafted by Ms Laura Zielinski, Eversheds LLP, Paris and reviewed by Ms Hnin Ei Ei Aung of U Tin Yu & Associates in Yangon, Myanmar.

2 OECD Investment Policy Reviews: Myanmar 2014, 1 March 2014, pp. 17–19.

3 The analysis is based on an unofficial translation of 14 January 2016 produced by Myanmar's Legal Services, available at: http://www.myanmarlegalservices.com/wp-content/uploads/pdf/Myanmar-Arbitration-Law%28Unofficial-English-Translation-140116%29_%2818 27166_1%29.PDF.

 | DOI 10.1163/9789004335257_009

The provisions of the Arbitration Law on interim relief, the appointment of arbitrators, the jurisdiction of the arbitral tribunal, the conduct of the proceedings, as well as on the making of the award are also substantially compliant with those of the UNCITRAL Model Law.

The new Arbitration Law distinguishes between domestic and international arbitration and subjects them to different regimes of court oversight (Chapter 9). International arbitration occurs when: i) at the time of the arbitration agreement, one of the parties' place of business and trading activity is situated in a country other than Myanmar; ii) where the place stated in the arbitration agreement, or the place where the arbitration is conducted in accordance with the arbitration agreement, is situated outside the country in which the parties have their place of business; or iii) where among the commercially related business obligations, any place where a substantial part of the obligations is to be performed, or the closest place connected to the subject-matter of the dispute, is situated outside the country in which the parties have their place of business (Chapter 1, Section 3(i)).

An explanatory note to Chapter 1, Section 3 of the Arbitration Law states that, if the place of business of a party is located in more than one place, the place of business of the party shall be that which is the closest to the place of execution of the arbitration agreement. If a party does not have a place of business, reference to its place of business shall be construed by reference to its permanent residence.

Parties can opt into international arbitration but the Arbitration Law does not allow them to opt out of it (Chapter 1, Section 3(i)(4)).

While parties to international arbitration proceedings can choose the applicable law, domestic arbitrations are governed by Myanmar law (Chapter 8, Section 32).

Myanmar's Arbitral Institutions and Rules

Myanmar currently does not have any arbitral institutions, either domestic or international, but it has been reported that a Myanmar Arbitration Centre is in the process of formation.[4] The future establishment of an arbitral institution was also anticipated in the 2016 Arbitration Law to the extent that it allows the Chief Justice of the Union of Myanmar to request "an institution" to appoint an arbitrator and allows parties or the arbitral tribunal to seek assistance from any "suitable institution" (Chapter 3, Section 8).

---

4 Christopher Chuah, Goh Wanjing, "The Asia-Pacific Arbitration Review 2016 – Myanmar", *Global Arbitration Review*, available at: http://globalarbitrationreview.com/reviews/71/sections/238/chapters/2886/myanmar/.

Myanmar's Courts and Arbitration

Applying the UNCITRAL Model Law, the new Arbitration Law requires a court before which an action is brought to refer the parties to arbitration unless it finds that the arbitration agreement is null and void, inoperative or incapable of being performed. This provision applies irrespective of whether the seat of the arbitration is in Myanmar or not.[5]

However, the Arbitration Law specifically confers large powers upon the courts to obtain testimony, issue subpoenas for the examination of witnesses and the production of documents (Chapter 7, Section 30) as well as relating to interim measures (Chapter 4, Section 11).[6]

As explained above, the amount of permissible court intervention differs depending on whether an arbitration qualifies as domestic or international (Chapter 9). Thus, when dealing with domestic arbitrations, and unless otherwise agreed by the parties, courts may determine any issue of law arising in the course of the proceedings which they are satisfied substantially affects the rights of one or more of the parties (Chapter 9, Section 39). Moreover, unless otherwise agreed, a party to a domestic arbitration in Myanmar may, for example, also appeal to a court on an issue of law arising out of an award made in domestic arbitral proceedings (Chapter 9, Section 42).

2 *Myanmar's Investment Law*

Myanmar's Investment Law

The Foreign Investment Law ("Law No. 21/2012"), which is currently in force, offers some improvements compared to the earlier 1988 Foreign Investment Law but still leaves many questions unanswered.[7] According to the OECD, one of the most pressing problems of the current regulatory framework is its complexity resulting from a multiplicity of different laws as well as of the convoluted process for the approval of investments.[8]

Chapter II of Law 21/2012 states that the Law applies to economic activities "prescribed by the Commission ["Myanmar Investment Commission" established by the same law], by notification from time to time with the prior approval of the Union Government." Certain investment activities are prescribed as restricted or outright prohibited. These are:

5 Minn Niang Oo, Ankit Goyal, Vivekananda N., "Myanmar joins the UNCITRAL MAL Asian Vanguard, *YSIAC Newsletter*, February 2016, available at: http://kluwerarbitrationblog.com/2016/02/05/myanmar-joins-the-uncitral-model-law-asian-vanguard/.

6 *Ibid.*

7 OECD Investment Policy Reviews: Myanmar 2014, 1 March 2014, p. 84.

8 *Ibid.*

a) businesses which can affect the traditional culture and customs of the national races within the State;
b) businesses which can affect the public health;
c) businesses which can affect the natural environment and ecosystem of the people;
d) businesses which can import hazardous and poisonous waste into the State;
e) manufacturing activities which use or produce hazardous chemicals according to international conventions;
f) manufacturing activities and services which can only be carried out by Myanmar citizens in accordance with prescribed rules and regulations;
g) businesses which import utensils, medicines and technologies that are still experimental and not yet approved for use in a foreign country;
h) long-term and short-term agricultural activities prescribed by the State that can only be carried out by citizens;
i) livestock breeding activities prescribed by the State that may only be carried out by citizens;
j) fishing activities in Myanmar's maritime waters which may only be carried out by citizens, as prescribed by relevant regulations; and
k) any foreign investment activities within 10 miles of the State's boundary with another State, unless the area is prescribed by the Union Government as an economic zone.[9]

However, Chapter II also provides that the Commission may allow restricted and prohibited activities if they are "for the benefits of the State and the People, especially the National Races by [obtaining] prior approval from the Union Government." This chapter adds that the Commission "shall submit to the Union Parliament through the Union Government [applications] relating to large foreign investments which shall be of huge benefits for the State and Citizens' security status, [economic] status, environmental status and social status." The Commission thus seems to have discretion over the approval of foreign investments.

Chapter XIII provides investors with certain guarantees. It states that the Government guarantees that an economic enterprise formed under a permit shall not be nationalized during the term of the contract or during an extended

9 The wording of this clause as well as the other quotes from the Investment Law is taken from the draft translation of the 21/2012 Investment Law by Myanmar Legal Services Limited; the English draft translation is available here: http://www.myanmarlegalservices.com/wp-content/uploads/2012/11/Myanmar-Foreign-Investment-Law-FIL-Draft-081112-v6_781979_2.pdf.

term, if so extended. It also states that the investment activities operating under a permit of the Commission shall not be terminated before the expiration of the term of the permit without sufficient cause. Additionally, on the expiry of the term of the contract, the Government guarantees a foreign investor the right to payment in the foreign currency in which such investment was made.

Chapter IX sets out the procedure for foreign investors to obtain a permit for foreign investment from the Commission. According to the May 2015 Report by the US Bureau of Economic and Business Affairs on the Investment Climate in Myanmar, investors have complained that the Government's investment approval process is opaque, complex, onerous with regard to the paperwork required, and lengthy.[10] Investors have also noted an increase in the Government's level of scrutiny of foreign investors, and it appears that the recent increase in the number of investment proposals being submitted has over-burdened the Government.

Law 21/2012 expressly recognizes that disputes can be settled in accordance with the mechanism specified by the parties in the "investment agreement" but does not go so far as to provide for a dispute resolution mechanism or to set out a framework for the recognition and enforcement of arbitral awards (Chapter XIX).

The Draft Investment Law

To remedy the remaining issues of the regulatory framework, a new draft Investment Law has been prepared, and was released on 24 February 2015. It consolidates Law 21/2012 and other existing investment laws, and aims to provide a transparent, equitable and non-discriminatory legal framework for both domestic and foreign investors.[11]

Pursuant to Section 8 of the draft Investment Law, any investor may invest in any legitimate form of enterprise, in any economic sector within Myanmar, with some exceptions mentioned in Section 9 of the Law. The section also specifies that investment into the economy of Myanmar is to be realized through the regular process of registration of enterprises. Additionally, this is complemented by the requirement to obtain licenses and permits for investments in certain sectors.

10 Burma Investment Climate Statement 2015, US Department of State, p. 5, available at: http://www.state.gov/documents/organization/241712.pdf.

11 Christopher Chuah, Goh Wanjing, "The Asia-Pacific Arbitration Review 2016 – Myanmar", *Global Arbitration Review*; an English draft translation is available at: http://www.burmalibrary.org/docs21/2015-Myanmar-Investment-Bill-V2-24-02-2015.pdf.

As mentioned, Section 9 lists a limited number of sectors and business activities where restrictions to investment are maintained. These restrictions concern: i) sectors where both domestic and foreign investments are prohibited; ii) sectors where only foreign investment is prohibited; iii) sectors where foreign investment is allowed but only in joint ventures with an entity or citizen of Myanmar; and iv) sectors where domestic or foreign investment requires prior approval of the Myanmar Investment Commission that will be established pursuant to the same law. Any investor investing into a sector from this last category may only transfer control of the investment to another investor with the express approval of the Commission. Schedules listing the sectors falling into each of these categories will be provided for in the implementing regulations of the Investment Law. The draft law also states that it is the intention of the Government to reduce or remove these restrictions to investments over time.

With regard to dispute resolution, Section 89 of Chapter 19 of the draft Investment Law states that in the event of any dispute between the Government or any Government entity and an investor in relation to its investment, the disputing parties shall initially seek to resolve the dispute amicably. If the dispute cannot be so resolved, the investor shall have access to a dispute settlement mechanism. According to Sections 86 to 88 of Chapter 19, the disputing foreign investor may submit a claim to domestic courts, to alternative dispute resolution, or to arbitration. In the event that an award is made by a foreign arbitral tribunal, such award shall be recognized and enforceable in the Republic of the Union of Myanmar according to international law, and pursuant to the New York Convention.

The draft Investment Law provides for other core investor guarantees, such as non-discrimination (Chapter 10), regulatory transparency and fair and equitable treatment (Chapter 11), protection against expropriation (Chapter 14), and the right to transfer funds (Chapter 15). It also provides for access to land (Chapter 12) and the right to employ (Chapter 13). On the downside for investors, the draft Investment Law provides for general exceptions for certain necessary Government actions, including actions taken to protect the Government's essential security interests (Chapter 22).

Another relevant law is the Myanmar Companies Act of 1914, which remains in force but is acknowledged by the authorities to be outdated.[12]

---

12 OECD Investment Policy Reviews: Myanmar 2014, 1 March 2014, p. 87.

III Myanmar's Bilateral Investment Treaties

1 *Overview*

Myanmar signed its first Bilateral Investment Treaty ("BIT") with the Philippines on 17 February 1998.[13] Since that date, it has signed additional BITs with China,[14] India,[15] Israel,[16] Japan,[17] Korea,[18] the Lao People's Democratic Republic,[19] Thailand[20] and Vietnam.[21] However, only the BITs concluded with China, India, Japan, the Philippines and Thailand are currently in force. The remaining ones have yet to be ratified. The last one to have been signed is the Myanmar-Israel BIT on 5 October 2014. All the BITs in force are publicly available at the time of writing and constitute the subject of the following analysis.[22]

2 *Definition of Investment*

Myanmar's BITs generally provide for a relatively broad definition of investment. The term "investment" is usually defined to include any kind of assets and in particular, though not exclusively, movable and immovable property and any other property rights such as mortgages, liens and pledges; shares, stocks and debentures of a company and any other similar forms of participation in a company; claims to money and any other rights to performance under contracts having an economic value; intellectual property and industrial property rights as recognized by the law of the contracting party in whose territory the investment is made, know-how and goodwill; business concessions, licenses, authorizations, and permits conferred pursuant to laws and regulations or

13 Entered into force on 11 September 1998, available at: http://investmentpolicyhub.unctad.org/Download/TreatyFile/2059.

14 Signed on 12 December 2001, entered into force on 21 May 2002, available at: http://investmentpolicyhub.unctad.org/Download/TreatyFile/762.

15 Signed on 24 June 2008, entered into force on 8 February 2009, available at: http://investmentpolicyhub.unctad.org/Download/TreatyFile/1582.

16 Signed on 5 October 2014, not in force, available at: http://investmentpolicyhub.unctad.org/Download/TreatyFile/3161.

17 Signed on 15 December 2013, entered into force on 7 August 2014, available at: http://investmentpolicyhub.unctad.org/Download/TreatyFile/3113.

18 Signed on 5 June 2014, not in force, not publicly available.

19 Signed on 5 May 2003, not in force, not publicly available.

20 Signed on 14 March 2008, entered into force on 8 June 2012, available at: http://investmentpolicyhub.unctad.org/Download/TreatyFile/2060.

21 Signed on 15 February 2000, not in force, not publicly available.

22 The BITs are available here: http://investmentpolicyhub.unctad.org/IIA/CountryBits/144.

contracts, including concessions to search for, cultivate, extract, or exploit natural resources.

It is generally also stipulated that any alteration of the form in which assets are invested should not affect their nature as an investment, provided that such alteration is consistent with the laws and regulations of the contracting party in whose territory the investments were made. The Myanmar-Japan BIT adds that investments include the amounts yielded by investments, in particular, profit, interest, capital gains, dividends, royalties and fees.

The BITs Myanmar concluded with China, India and Thailand also require that investments be made in accordance with the laws and regulations of the State in which they were made. The Myanmar-Thailand BIT also contains annexes detailing a specific procedure for approval of investments. Indeed, the Myanmar-Thailand BIT restricts its scope to cases where the investment by an investor of one contracting party in the territory of the other contracting party has been specifically approved in writing, if so required by the competent authorities of the latter contracting party.[23] This would be the case under the current investment law in force in Myanmar, as explained above.

The newly-signed Myanmar-Israel BIT (that has not yet entered into force) includes a provision stating that for the avoidance of doubt, the term "investment" does not include public debt operations, "claims to money arising solely from commercial contracts for the sale of goods and services by a national or a legal entity in the territory of a home contracting party to a national or a legal entity in the territory of the host contracting party", or credit granted in relation to a commercial transaction. This means that mere contracts for the sale of goods or the provision of services do not amount to an "investment" under the BIT. The same BIT does, however, expand the definition of "investment" to include reinvestment of the returns of an investment.

3 *Definition of Investor*

The BITs signed by Myanmar commonly extend the definition of "investor" to natural persons who have the nationality of either contracting party to the investment treaty in accordance with the law of the contracting party in question, and to legal persons incorporated or constituted under the laws and regulations of the respective contracting party.

Under the Myanmar-China BIT, a company must also have its seat in the contracting party in question in order to qualify as an investor (Article 1(2)). According to the Myanmar-Philippines BIT, legal entities qualify as investors

23 Article 2 of the Myanmar-Thailand BIT, available at: http://investmentpolicyhub.unctad.org/Download/TreatyFile/2060.

if they are incorporated in the territory of a contracting party, or are properly organized and are actually doing business under the laws of the respective contracting party and have their headquarters where management is carried out in the territory of that contracting party (Article I(b)). The same BIT defines the term "companies" as corporations, partnerships or other associations, incorporated and constituted and actually doing business under the laws in force in any part of the territory of the contracting party wherein a place of effective management is situated. This treaty further provides that any particular company may be excluded from the foregoing definition by mutual agreement between the contracting parties on the grounds of the need to maintain public order, to protect essential security interests or to fulfil commitments relating to peace and security (Article II). The Myanmar-Thailand BIT only defines juridical persons as investors if they are constituted or otherwise duly organised under the law of the contracting party in question and have their seat, together with real economic activities, in the territory of that same contracting party (Article 1(2)).

The Myanmar-Japan BIT restricts the definition of legal persons even further. Under Article I(b), the term "investor" extends to an enterprise of a contracting party that seeks to make, is making or has made investments in the territory of the other contracting party. The same article specifies that "[i]t is understood that an investor of a Contracting Party seeks to make investments in the Area of the other Contracting Party only when the investor has taken concrete steps necessary to make investments, such as when the investor has made an application for a permit or license which authorises the establishment of investments".

The newly signed Myanmar-Israel BIT defines a legal entity as an investor if the entity in question was: (i) incorporated, constituted or otherwise duly organized under the legislation of the home State; (ii) is controlled, directly or indirectly, by persons who are nationals or permanent residents of the home State and its registered office, centre of management or practical management is located in the territory of either contracting party; or (iii) a substantial part of its economic activity is located in the territory of either contracting party. The Myanmar-Israel BIT also excludes citizens of dual nationality from the definition of "investor" (Article I(d)).

A significant proportion of Myanmar's BITs appear to require the headquarters of a company to be located in the host State in order for the company to qualify as an investor. This seems to be in line with the inclusion of "Denial of Benefit" clauses in many of Myanmar's BITs – the aim of which appears to be to exclude pure "shell companies" from the investment protections offered by the BITs.

4 *Scope*

Myanmar's BITs typically apply to investments which are made prior to or after their entry into force but do not cover disputes that arose before the entry into force of the agreement in question.

The Myanmar-India BIT applies to all investments made by investors of either contracting party in the territory of the other contracting party, accepted as such in accordance with its laws and regulations, whether made before or after the coming into force of the BIT. It does not explicitly exclude disputes that arose before its entry into force, though that may nonetheless be the position under general international law. The Myanmar-Philippines BIT is entirely silent on its scope of application.

The Myanmar-China BIT states that it shall apply irrespective of the existence of diplomatic or consular relations between the contracting parties (Article 12).

All of Myanmar's BITs in force at the time of writing contain subrogation rights.

The Myanmar-Thailand BIT also contains a "Preservation of Rights" clause stipulating that the BIT shall in no way restrict the rights and benefits conferred on an investor of one contracting party by the provisions of the national law of the other contracting party, or on the basis of commitments made in international agreements which both contracting parties have entered into (Article 13). Myanmar's BITs concluded with China, India and Thailand, provide that where more favourable rules exist either under international law and/or under the law of the contracting States, then the more favourable rules shall prevail.

5 *Substantive Protections*

Fair and Equitable Treatment

All of Myanmar's BITs in force at the time of writing contain a fair and equitable treatment ("FET") (labelled as "equitable and reasonable treatment" under the Myanmar-Philippines BIT) provision as an obligation on the contracting State towards the investor and/or investments. For example, the Myanmar-India BIT provides that "[i]nvestments and returns of investors of each Contracting Party shall at all times be accorded fair and equitable treatment in the territory of the other Contracting Party." Similarly, the Myanmar-Thailand BIT provides that "[i]nvestments of investors of either Contracting Party shall at all times be accorded fair and equitable treatment". The exact wording of the Myanmar-Philippines BIT is that investments "shall be accorded equitable and reasonable treatment."

Investors should carefully analyse the FET clause in the applicable BIT, as slight differences in the wording of such clauses can result in substantial interpretative differences. This same comment also applies to the other protections offered by Myanmar's BITs.

Non-Discrimination

The BITs that Myanmar concluded with China, the Philippines and Thailand prohibit arbitrary or unreasonable and discriminatory treatment of qualifying investors and/or investments by contracting States. For instance, the Myanmar-China BIT provides that "[w]ithout prejudice to its laws and regulations, neither Contracting Party shall take any unreasonable or discriminatory measures against the management, maintenance, use, enjoyment and disposal of the investments by the investors of the other Contracting Party." In substantially similar terms, the Myanmar-Philippines BIT states that a contracting party "shall in no way by unreasonable or discriminatory measures impair the management, maintenance, use, enjoyment, or disposal of investments by investors of the other Contracting Party."

Full Protection and Security

The BITs in force between Myanmar and China, Japan, the Philippines and Thailand provide for "Full Protection and Security" of the investments of investors from the other contracting State. The China-Myanmar BIT states that "[i]nvestments of the investors of either Contracting Party shall enjoy the constant protection and security in the territory of the other Contracting Party." The Myanmar-Japan BIT provides for "treatment in accordance with international law", which is stated to include fair and equitable treatment and "full protection and security".

Expropriation

All of Myanmar's BITs in force at the time of writing contain a provision generally prohibiting the expropriation or nationalization of investments as well as any other measure having an effect equivalent to expropriation or nationalization, unless such measure taken by the host State serves a public purpose, is taken under due process of law, in a non-discriminatory manner and is accompanied by the payment of prompt, adequate and effective compensation.

Such compensation shall amount to the market value ("fair market value" under the Myanmar-Japan BIT) of the expropriated investment immediately before the impending expropriation or before the expropriation becomes public knowledge, whichever is earlier, and shall be made without unreasonable delay and be freely transferable. The Myanmar-China BIT does not refer to the market value but instead to "generally recognized principles of valuation". It further specifies that compensation shall include interest at a normal commercial rate from the date of the expropriation until the date of payment

(Article 4(2)). The Myanmar-Japan BIT also provides for "interest at a commercially reasonable rate" (Article 13(3)).

Under the Myanmar-Thailand and Myanmar-India BITs, the investor affected shall have the right, under the law of the contracting party making the expropriation, to seek a review, by a judicial or other independent authority of that contracting party, of his or its case (Article 6(3)). Similarly, the Myanmar-Japan BIT provides for a right of access to the courts of justice or administrative tribunals or agencies of the contracting party making the expropriation to seek a prompt review of the investors' case and the amount of compensation without prejudice to the applicable dispute settlement provisions (Article 13(4)).

Umbrella Clauses

The BITs in force between Myanmar and China (Article 10(2)), Myanmar and Japan (Article 4(2)) and Myanmar and Thailand (Article 10(2)) contain an obligation on the contracting parties to observe any obligation they have undertaken with regard to investments of an investor of the other contracting party. This "umbrella clause" implies that State obligations such as those contained in contracts between investors and the host State that fall under the protection of the BIT can potentially be elevated to treaty obligations. As an example, Article 10(2) of the Myanmar-Thailand BIT states that "[e]ach Contracting Party shall observe any other obligation it may have entered into with regard to investments of investors of the other Contracting Party."

Most Favoured Nation and National Treatment

All of Myanmar's BITs that are in force at the time of writing require that the treatment of investments of investors from the other contracting State be no less favourable than that granted to nationals or companies of third States (i.e. "Most Favoured Nation" or "MFN" clause).

The BITs in force between Myanmar and China, India, the Philippines and Thailand exclude from the scope of the MFN provision any treatment arising out of customs unions, free trade areas, common markets, similar international agreements leading to such unions or other forms of regional cooperation and international agreements or domestic legislation relating mainly or wholly to taxation. Surprisingly, the Myanmar-Japan BIT does not contain such a limitation.

Myanmar's BITs with China, India, Japan and Thailand also contain explicit "National Treatment" provisions requiring the contracting States to treat qualifying investors and/or investments at least as favourably as their national investors and/or their investments. The Myanmar-Japan BIT limits the application of this obligation by providing that it should not be construed to prevent a contracting party from adopting or maintaining a measure that prescribes special formalities in connection with investment activities of investors of the other contracting party in its territory, provided that such special formalities do not impair the substance of the rights of such investors under the agreement in question (Article 2(2)). The Myanmar-Philippines BIT does not provide for National Treatment.

The Myanmar-Japan BIT explicitly provides for MFN and National Treatment for investors with respect to access to the courts of justice and administrative tribunals and agencies at all levels of jurisdiction, both in pursuit and in defence of such investors' rights (Article 5). It is, however, highly unlikely that this provision could be used to incorporate a basis for jurisdiction outside of the host State's domestic legal system, as the wording specifically refers to "access to the courts of justice".

It is interesting to note that the newly signed Myanmar-Israel BIT (not yet in force) explicitly excludes from the scope of the MFN and National Treatment clauses all provisions relating to definitions and to mechanisms for dispute settlement between one contracting party and an investor of the other contracting party, as well as any other matter not specifically mentioned in those clauses (Article 3(3)). The MFN and National Treatment provisions are, however, specifically stated to apply to investments and returns of investments, and to the management, use, enjoyment and disposal of investments.

6 *Repatriation of Capital and Compensation for Losses*

All BITs signed by Myanmar and in force at the time of writing contain provisions allowing for the repatriation by the investor of capital invested and investment returns. They also all contain a clause providing for the compensation for losses resulting from war, other armed conflicts, a revolution, a state of national emergency, a revolt, insurrection or riot in the territory of the host State.

The Myanmar-China, Myanmar-India and Myanmar-Japan BITs expressly extend the application of the MFN and National Treatment clauses to compensation for losses (Article 14).

The Myanmar-Philippines BIT contains a clause providing for compensation for losses, but it is formulated in a conditional manner stating that "if a Contracting Party makes restitution [...]", the MFN standard applies. The clause does not state the criteria which determine whether or not a contracting State will provide compensation.

The BITs in force between Myanmar and the Philippines and Myanmar and Thailand, as well as the newly signed Myanmar-Israel BIT, limit the transfer obligations by the host State by making them subject to the host State's right to impose, equitably and in good faith, such measures as may be necessary to safeguard the integrity and independence of its currency, its external financial position and balance of payments.

The Myanmar-Thailand BIT, as well as the Myanmar-Israel BIT (which is not yet in force), further expand the compensation obligation to include losses suffered by the investor resulting from requisitioning of their property by the latter contracting party's forces or authorities, or from destruction of their property by the latter contracting party's forces or authorities, which is not caused in combat action or is not required by the necessity of the situation.

7 *Investor-State Dispute Settlement*

All of Myanmar's BITs, except for the Myanmar-Philippines BIT, provide that any legal dispute between an investor of one contracting State and the other contracting State in connection with an investment in the territory of the other contracting party shall, as far as possible, be settled amicably through negotiations or consultations between the parties to the dispute.

Under the Myanmar-India BIT, any dispute which has not been amicably settled within a period of six months may, if both parties agree, be submitted for resolution, in accordance with the law of the contracting party which has admitted the investment, to that contracting party's competent judicial, arbitral or administrative bodies, or to international conciliation under the Conciliation Rules of the United Nations Commission on International Trade Law ("UNCITRAL"). If the parties fail to agree on one of these procedures, or where a dispute is referred to conciliation but conciliation proceedings are terminated other than by the signing of a settlement agreement, the dispute may be referred to arbitration under the ICSID Convention, the ICSID Additional Facility Rules or an *ad hoc* tribunal in accordance with the 1976 UNCITRAL Arbitration Rules, subject to a number of modifications.

Under the Myanmar-China BIT, if the dispute cannot be settled through negotiations within six months, the investor of one contracting party may submit the dispute to the competent court of the other contracting party. Any dispute, if it cannot be settled within six months after resort to negotiations has been made, shall be submitted at the request of either party to ICSID arbitration or an *ad hoc* tribunal, subject to the contracting State's power to require the investor to exhaust local remedies.

The Myanmar-Thailand BIT provides that, if the mandatory consultations between the parties do not result in a resolution within six months, the investor may submit the dispute, at the investor's choice, to the competent courts of the contracting State in the territory of which the investment has been made, to an arbitrator or international *ad hoc* tribunal established under the UNCITRAL Arbitration Rules, or to ICSID arbitration.

Pursuant to the Myanmar-Japan BIT, if a dispute cannot be settled through consultations within three months, the disputing investor may submit the dispute to ICSID arbitration, arbitration under the ICSID Additional Facility Rules, arbitration under the UNCITRAL Arbitration Rules, or, if agreed with the disputing contracting party, arbitration in accordance with other arbitration rules. The BIT contains, however, a time limit of three years for the commencement of arbitration proceedings: no investment disputes may be submitted to arbitration if more than three years have elapsed since the date on which the disputing investor acquired or should have first acquired, whichever is earlier, the knowledge that it had incurred loss or damage (Article 18(6)). Further, the BIT provides for the involvement of a non-disputing contracting State in the proceedings. The contracting State which is not the disputing party may, upon written notice to the disputing parties, make submissions to the arbitral tribunal on a question of interpretation of the BIT (Article 18(10)). The same BIT allows the disputing contracting State to make available to the public all documents, including an award, subject to redaction of certain confidential elements (Article 18(12)).

On the other hand, the Myanmar-Philippines BIT does not contain any investor-State dispute settlement provisions. Concerned investors might, however, try to resort to the BIT's MFN clause to incorporate a dispute resolution clause from another BIT. While the debate on whether MFN clauses can be used to incorporate dispute resolution provisions is not yet settled,[24] the restrictive wording of the clause in question renders it rather unlikely that such an attempt by investors would be successful. The relevant clauses provide:

> 1. Each Contracting Party shall in its territory accord investments of nationals or companies of the other Contracting Party treatment not less favourable than that which accords to investments or return[*sic*] of investments of nationals or companies of any third State.
> 2. Each Contracting Party shall in its territory accord the nationals or companies of the other Contracting Party, as regard[*sic*]

24 See, *inter alia*, Yas Banifatemi, "The Emerging Jurisprudence on the Most-Favoured-Nation Treatment in Investment Arbitration," *Investment Treaty Law: Current Issues III*, A. Bjorklund, I. Laird, S. Ripinsky eds., BIICL, 2009, at p. 241; Rudolf Dolzer and Christoph Schreuer, *Principles of International Investment Law*, Oxford University Press, second edition, 2012, pp. 270–275.

> management, maintenance, use, enjoyment, or disposal of their investments, treatment not less favourable that [*sic*] which [*sic*] accords to nationals or companies of any third State.[25]

8 *State-to-State Dispute Settlement*

The Myanmar-China, Myanmar-India, Myanmar-Japan and the Myanmar-Thailand BITs stipulate that disputes between the contracting States shall be resolved as far as possible through recourse to diplomatic channels. In the event that diplomatic settlement fails, a dispute shall be submitted to an arbitral tribunal. The BITs provide for arbitral proceedings if the dispute cannot be solved diplomatically within six months (though the Myanmar-Japan and the Myanmar-Thailand BITs do not specify a time frame).

The BITs require that an *ad hoc* arbitral tribunal be established, constituted by two arbitrators each appointed by one of the contracting States, and a chairman appointed by the two co-arbitrators. In case a contracting party fails to appoint its arbitrator, generally the task is conferred on the President of the International Court of Justice, or to the next most senior Judge if the President is a national of either contracting party. Less commonly, the newly signed Myanmar-Israel BIT confers the task upon the Secretary General of the Permanent Court of Arbitration in The Hague.

Myanmar's BITs allow the *ad hoc* tribunal to determine its own rules and procedure, save that the Myanmar-Japan BIT does not mention any procedural rules and the Myanmar-Israel BIT refers to the 2010 UNCITRAL Arbitration Rules. However, the sharing of the costs of arbitration is detailed in the BITs, under which each contracting party bears its own costs (sometimes subject to the limited discretionary power of the Tribunal). It is also usually stipulated that the tribunal shall decide by majority and that the final award shall be final and binding.

The Myanmar-Philippines BIT does not contain a State-to-State dispute settlement clause. Instead it provides for consultations between the contracting States: the parties agree to consult each other at the request of either contracting party on any matters relating to an investment falling within the scope of the agreement or any other issue affecting the agreement's implementation (Article VIII). The Myanmar-China BIT provides for a dispute settlement mechanism for disputes between the contracting States, but also provides for regular consultations between China and Myanmar (Article 13). The Myanmar-Thailand BIT allows for the possibility to request consultations (Article 9), and

25 Myanmar-Philippines BIT, Article III, available at: http://investmentpolicyhub.unctad.org/Download/TreatyFile/2059.

the newly signed Myanmar-Israel BIT arranges for the establishment of a Joint Committee on Investments (Article 15).

9 *Additional Provisions*

The Myanmar-China, Myanmar-Thailand, Myanmar-India BITs contain a ten-year (fifteen years for the Myanmar-India BIT) "Sunset Clause" stipulating that in respect of investments made prior to the date when the termination of the Agreement becomes effective, the provisions of the agreement shall remain in force for a period of ten/fifteen years in respect of investments made prior to the effective termination. Termination is stated to become effective one year after notice of termination has been received by the other contracting party under the Myanmar-Thailand BIT. The date when termination becomes effective is not specified in the Myanmar-China and the Myanmar-India BITs.

The Myanmar-Japan BIT contains several provisions aimed at protecting public interests such as provisions on transparency (Article 8), public comment procedures (Article 9), anti-corruption measures (Article 11), general and security exceptions (Article 19), scope for the host States to enact measures relating to financial services for prudential reasons (Article 21) and health, safety and environmental measures and labour standards (Article 25). It also contains, however, a prohibition of performance requirements (Article 6).

The Myanmar-India and the Myanmar-Japan BITs contain "Denial of Benefits" clauses allowing a contracting State to deny the benefits of the relevant BIT to an investor (which is an enterprise) of the other contracting State if the enterprise is owned or controlled by an investor of a non-contracting party, and the denying contracting party does not maintain diplomatic relations with such non-contracting party. Benefits may also be denied if the contracting party has adopted or maintains measures with respect to the non-contracting party that prohibit transactions with the enterprise, or that would be violated or circumvented if the benefits of the BIT in question were accorded to the investor or its investments.

Such clauses also allow contracting States to deny the benefits of the BIT to an investor of the other contracting party and to its investments if the enterprise is owned or controlled by an investor of a non-contracting party and the enterprise has no substantial business activities in the territory of the other contracting party (under the Myanmar-Japan BIT there must be a prior notification and consultation for this provision to apply, but the exact procedure to be followed is not specified (Article 26(2)).

As mentioned above, the motivation behind these clauses seems to be partly explained by the desire to exclude pure "shell companies" from the protections offered by the BITs in question.

10 *Notable Trends*

It is interesting to note that, despite increasing economic liberalisation, Myanmar has so far signed very few bilateral investment treaties, with only five BITs in force. According to the US Bureau of Economic and Business Affairs' May 2015 Investment Climate Report on Myanmar, Myanmar has, however, engaged in investment treaty negotiations with Russia, Mongolia, Bangladesh, Iran, Serbia, Hong Kong and the European Union.[26]

In this context, it should also be mentioned that the more recently concluded BIT with Japan goes further in terms of protecting public interests than earlier agreements.

IV Multilateral Investment Related Treaties and Organizations to which Myanmar is a Party

Myanmar has been a member of the Association of Southeast Asian Nations ("ASEAN") since 23 July 1997 and is notably a signatory to the ASEAN Investment and the ASEAN Services Agreements. As a member of ASEAN, Myanmar is also a party to Trade or Services and Investment agreements that ASEAN concluded with China, India (signed in 2014 but not yet in force), Japan, Korea, the United States and Australia and New Zealand ("AAZNFTA") as well as to Framework Agreements concluded between ASEAN and China, Korea, India, Japan and the Bay of Bengal Initiative for Multi-Sectoral Technical and Economic Cooperation ("BIMSTEC"). Myanmar is also a party to the ASEAN-EU Cooperation Agreement and has signed a Bilateral Trade and Investment Framework Agreement with the United States in May 2013 that has not, however, entered into force to date.

1 *ASEAN*

As discussed in the relveant Chapter, ASEAN's purpose is, among others, to accelerate economic growth, social progress and cultural development in the region and to promote regional peace and stability through the promotion of active collaboration and mutual assistance on matters of common interest.[27]

Myanmar is also a party to the ASEAN Comprehensive Investment Agreement ("ACIA") which entered into force on 29 March 2012. The ACIA aims to create a free and open investment environment through the consolidation and expansion of existing agreements between ASEAN Member States.

---

26 OECD Investment Policy Reviews: Myanmar 2014, 1 March 2014, p. 119.

27 http://www.asean.org/asean/about-asean/overview.

It was drafted with the intent of creating a freer and more open investment regime towards the achievement of ASEAN economic integration, based on international best practices. ACIA was envisioned to facilitate the transformation of ASEAN into an investment hub that would be able to compete effectively with other emerging economies.[28]

The ACIA contains substantive investment protections commonly found in BITs, such as provisions on non-discrimination, MFN treatment, fair and equitable treatment, full protection and security, and expropriation. Where a dispute arises between an investor and a Member State, the ACIA provides for various dispute resolution options, including the submission of a claim under the ICSID Convention, under the UNCITRAL Arbitration Rules, or to one of the regional centres for arbitration in ASEAN.[29]

In addition to the usual provisions found in BITs, the ACIA also contains provisions aimed at enhancing cooperation between ASEAN States in the promotion[30] and facilitation of investment,[31] and to enhance ASEAN integration.[32]

2 *MIGA*

Myanmar is a party to the Convention Establishing the Multilateral Investment Guarantee Agency (the "MIGA") of 1985. MIGA is a part of the World Bank Group and a multilateral investment insurance system against political risks, which offers investment protection for cross-border investments against losses resulting from, *inter alia*, currency transfer restrictions, expropriation and a government's breach or repudiation of an investor. Myanmar became MIGA's 180th member on 17 December 2013.[33]

3 *OPIC*

On 21 May 2013, the Overseas Private Investment Corporation ("OPIC") signed an Investment Incentive Agreement with Myanmar. In 2014, OPIC announced that its financing and insurance programs are available for Myanmar.

---

28 http://www.asean.org/asean-comprehensive-investment-agreement-acia-enters-into-force-creating-a-stable-and-predictable-business-investment-environment/.

29 Article 33 of the ACIA.

30 *Ibid.*, Article 24.

31 *Ibid.*, Article 25.

32 *Ibid.*, Article 26.

33 http://www.worldbank.org/en/news/press-release/2013/12/17/miga-myanmar-member-country.

V Multilateral Dispute Settlement Related Treaties

1 *ICSID Convention*

To date, Myanmar has not yet signed the ICSID Convention. ICSID arbitration is only available where both the home and the host State are members of the ICSID Convention. This means that any provision for ICSID arbitration in Myanmar's bilateral or multilateral investment treaties may, in so far as such an interpretation is possible, only be understood to refer to proceedings under the ICSID Additional Facility Rules.

Notably, the reference to ICSID arbitration in the new draft Investment Law discussed above might suggest that Myanmar intends to accede to the ICSID Convention in the future.

2 *New York Convention*

On 15 July 2013, Myanmar formally acceded to the New York Convention, which is now enabled by the new 2016 Arbitration Law that gives effect to Myanmar's obligations to enforce arbitration agreements and to recognize and enforce foreign arbitral awards.

VI International Investment Arbitration Jurisprudence

At the time of writing and based on the information that is publicly available, Myanmar has only been a respondent in one treaty arbitration case so far. No treaty arbitration cases involving claimants from Myanmar could be found in the public domain at the time of writing.

1 *Cases Involving Myanmar as the Respondent State*

Yaung Chi Oo Trading Pte Ltd. v. Government of the Union of Myanmar, ASEAN I.D., Case No. ARB/01/1.

Tribunal:	Sompong Sucharitkul (President, Thailand) James Crawford (Australia) Francis Delon (France)
Case Initiated:	29 June 2000
Award Rendered:	31 March 2003

Background Facts

The proceedings were brought by Yaung Chi Oo Trading Pte. Ltd., ("YCO" or the "Claimant") a family enterprise incorporated in Singapore, against Myanmar under the ASEAN Agreement for the Promotion and Protection of Investments of 1987 ("ASEAN IGA") and the 1998 Framework Agreement for the ASEAN Investment Area ("AIA Agreement"). The dispute arose out of the interim seizure and a judicial winding up order of a joint venture company. The proceedings were conducted under the ICSID Additional Facility Arbitration Rules.

On 29 November 1993, a joint venture agreement was concluded between Myanmar Foodstuff Industries ("MFI"), the State Industrial Organization of Myanmar and Yaung Chi Oo Trading Pte. Ltd. The agreement provided for the creation of a joint venture company, Myanmar Yaung Chi Oo Company Ltd. ("MYCO"), that would own and operate a brewery in Myanmar. MFI was to contribute machinery and other items and the use of the land comprising the beer factory whilst YCO was to contribute capital as well as expertise, marketing and the provision of foreign raw materials for the purposes of operating the brewery and promoting and distributing its products.[34]

The parties were to apply to the competent authorities of the Myanmar Government for a permit for MYCO to manufacture and distribute beer and soft drinks in Myanmar and abroad for an initial term of five years. The issuing of this permit was a condition precedent to the entry into force of the joint venture agreement and the incorporation of the joint venture company.[35]

The relevant permits and approvals having been obtained, MYCO began its operations, which were, according to the Claimant, highly successful and resulted in significant profits.[36]

At the time of the conclusion of the joint venture agreement, Myanmar was not yet a member of ASEAN but had applied for membership. Pursuant to the Protocol of Admission, on 23 July 1997 Myanmar acceded to a number of ASEAN treaties, including the ASEAN IGA and Jakarta Protocol of 12 September 1996. Myanmar then also became a party to the AIA Agreement, which came into force for all ASEAN Member States on 21 June 1999.[37]

By the end of 1997, a number of problems had occurred between the parties to the joint venture agreement. The Claimant alleged that armed agents of Myanmar seized the brewery and that certain bank accounts of the Claimant and its managing director and principal shareholder, Mme Win Win Nu, were

34 Award, 31 March 2003, para. 4.

35 *Ibid.*, para. 4.

36 *Ibid.*, para. 5.

37 *Ibid.*, para. 6.

frozen. On 28 November 1998, the initial five-year contract term for the joint venture agreement expired without having been renewed. On 11 February 1999, the Union of Myanmar Foreign Investment Commission appointed an inspector and manager of MYCO. On 29 September 1999, winding-up proceedings were commenced before the Yangon Divisional Court in respect of the joint venture company and, although opposed by the Claimant, a winding up order was issued on 24 December 1999. The Claimant appealed against this order to the Supreme Court but was unsuccessful.[38]

Negotiations failed and YCO initiated arbitration proceedings under Article X of the ASEAN IGA. The Claimant claimed that Myanmar's conduct amounted to expropriation and that the court proceedings were only an attempt to legalize the expropriation after the fact. The Claimant alleged that Myanmar's conduct breached the ASEAN IGA, in particular Articles III, IV and VI on fair and equitable treatment, full protection and compensated expropriation.[39]

Key Legal Outcomes

The Tribunal concluded that it lacked jurisdiction.[40] While it did not accept the Respondent's objections based on an alleged lack of privity and the alleged failure by the investor to exhaust local remedies,[41] it concluded that the investment did not qualify for protection under the 1987 ASEAN Agreement or the AIA Agreement.

In its analysis, the Tribunal considered that the core jurisdictional issues before it centred on the interpretation of Articles I and II of the ASEAN IGA and their application to the facts of the dispute. Since Myanmar became a party to the 1987 ASEAN Agreement only on 23 July 1997, after the conclusion of the joint venture agreement, the relevant provision was Article II(3).[42] Under Article II(3) investments made before the ASEAN IGA entered into force for the host State must have been "specifically approved in writing and registered by the host country and upon such conditions as it deems fit for purposes of this Agreement subsequent to its entry into force." In addition, pursuant to Article I(2), a company investing in the host State must not only be incorporated in or constituted under the laws in force in the territory of another State

38 *Ibid.*, para. 7.

39 *Ibid.*, para. 8.

40 *Ibid.*, para. 85.

41 *Ibid.*, paras. 36–41.

42 *Ibid.*, para. 42.

party, but it must also have its "place of effective management" in that State.[43] A number of distinct issues were raised in this regard: first, whether there was a foreign investment originating from or made by the Claimant; second, whether Singapore was "the place of effective management" of the Claimant, as required by Article I(2) of the ASEAN IGA; and third, whether the investment was specifically approved and registered in writing for the purposes of the 1987 ASEAN Agreement after 23 July 1997, as required by Article II(3).[44]

On the first issue,[45] the Tribunal held that the relevant question for the purpose of jurisdiction under the ASEAN IGA was whether there was an investment brought into Myanmar by a Singapore corporation. The Tribunal noted that the parties to the joint venture agreement accepted the existence of capital contributions made by the Claimant over a period of time, although there may have been unresolved questions regarding the full extent and form of these contributions. There was also no doubt that both equipment and supplies were shipped from Singapore to Myanmar and paid for from the Claimant's resources. On this basis, the Tribunal ruled that an investment had been brought into Myanmar by the Claimant such as to qualify as an "investment" within the meaning of that term as broadly defined in Article I(3) of the ASEAN IGA and that it was not necessary for the purposes of jurisdiction precisely to quantify the amount of the investment.

As regards the second issue,[46] the Tribunal held that, for companies to qualify as investors under the ASEAN IGA, both local incorporation and effective management were required. In the Tribunal's opinion, there was no justification for ignoring either requirement. The Tribunal took the view that, since the test of effective management was used to define a company making an investment, it was logical to apply it, in the first place at least, at the time the investment was made. The Tribunal explained that, where the investment was made over a period of time (as in the case before it), effective management of the investing company at the place of incorporation may be required throughout this period. On the other hand, although satisfaction of the legal requirements of the State of incorporation would not necessarily be sufficient, there was no reason to ignore those requirements in assessing whether there was effective management. The Tribunal cautioned that it should be slow to hold that a company which was effectively managed from the place of incorporation at the time an investment was made had subsequently lost treaty

43 *Ibid.*, para. 42.

44 *Ibid.*, para. 42.

45 *Ibid.*, paras. 43–45.

46 *Ibid.*, paras. 46–52.

protection, and especially so in the case before it when key personnel had been engaged to give effect to the investment in accordance with the terms of the joint venture agreement. The Tribunal considered that such a finding could lead to arbitrary results and would disfavour small investors who may play a significant role in intra-ASEAN investment. On the basis of the foregoing, the Tribunal held that the Claimant was effectively managed from Singapore.

With regard to the third issue, the Tribunal held that the investment had not been specifically approved in writing after 23 July 1997 as required by Article II(3) of the ASEAN IGA.[47] The investment had been approved under domestic law before 1997, but an express written act would have been required to make the investment protected under the ASEAN IGA. Based on the language of Article II(3), an express subsequent act amounting at least to written approval, and eventually to registration of the investment, after the Agreement entered into force, was required. This was necessary even if the investments had been approved in writing and registered under the law of the host State when they were made. The Tribunal rejected the Claimant's arguments that the decisions taken by MYCO's board of directors after the entry into force of the ASEAN IGA satisfied the requirements of Article II(3). This was because, firstly, it was very difficult to accept that either MYCO through its board of directors or individual directors, could have acted on behalf of the respondent, and secondly, the decisions taken by the board of directors were managerial in character and could not be construed as entailing the official approval of the investment by Myanmar itself, let alone as substituting for the written registration of the investment. In the circumstances, no such subsequent written approval had been given with regard to the investment in question. The Tribunal considered that the mere fact that the approval and registration granted earlier by the host State continued to be operative after the entry into force of the ASEAN IGA was not sufficient to satisfy the requirements of Article II(3). It therefore concluded that the Claimant's investment did not qualify as such under Article II(3) of the 1987 ASEAN Agreement.[48]

The Tribunal similarly held that the investment was not protected under the AIA Agreement. In the Claimant's view, the AIA Agreement extended both the substantive protections and arbitral jurisdiction under the ASEAN IGA by introducing a new, general and more extensive definition of "ASEAN investor" and of "direct investment" in place of the more restrictive definitions contained in Articles I and II of the ASEAN IGA. The Tribunal held, however, that the AIA Agreement did not provide the Claimant with any new rights

47 *Ibid.*, paras. 53–62.

48 *Ibid.*, para. 63.

in relation to the claim before the Tribunal because the definitions of "investment" under both agreements were distinct and there was no intention to substitute one for the other, or to merge the two.[49]

The Tribunal also rejected the Claimant's argument that jurisdiction could be attracted on the basis of the MFN clause contained in Article 8 of the AIA Agreement read in conjunction with the Myanmar-Philippines BIT for a number of reasons.[50] Firstly, the ASEAN IGA and AIA Agreement provided for arbitration of investment disputes under different arbitration rules and with different appointing authorities. Secondly, there was no indication that there would be arbitral jurisdiction on the facts under any BIT entered into by Myanmar which was in force at the relevant time, and therefore there could be no corresponding basis for such jurisdiction under Article 8 of the AIA Agreement.

Although the award involves the interpretation and application of provisions in the ASEAN IGA and the AIA Agreement, both of which have been terminated pursuant to the entry into force of the ACIA, the decision sheds light on what may amount to a qualifying investment in relation to similar provisions which may be found in other investment guarantee agreements or BITs.[51]

Following the concluding remarks of the Tribunal, where it was noted that the system of investment protection established by the ASEAN IGA and the AIA Agreement raised difficult questions,[52] the conclusion of the ACIA six years after this case was perhaps a timely one which sought to build on the objectives of, and at the same time resolve any dichotomy which existed between, its two predecessors.

2 *Cases Involving Myanmar Investors*

There are no reported Investment Treaty cases involving investors from Myanmar.

VII Outlook: Anticipated Developments

Myanmar seems to be engaged in a process of liberalization of its investment regime. To what extent this will be successful will depend on whether the Government has the political will to enact the necessary national laws

49 *Ibid.*, para. 64.
50 *Ibid.*, para. 83.
51 See, for example, the chapter on Brunei.
52 *Ibid.*, para. 86.

and enter into further bilateral and multilateral treaties, such as the ICSID Convention.

In this regard, it can be added that in March 2014, the European Commission received a mandate from EU member States to begin negotiations for an investment treaty with Myanmar.[53] Acting upon the mandate, two rounds of negotiations on the EU-Myanmar Investment Protection Agreement took place between February 2015 and September 2015 culminating in a European Commission sponsored Sustainability Impact Assessment ("SIA").[54]

The EU-Myanmar SIA, negotiations and consultations have not been without opposition. In January 2016 a combination of over 500 Myanmar Civil Society Organisations expressed their concerns about the EU-Myanmar Investment Protection Agreement in an open letter to the European Commissioner for Trade, specifically highlighting their concerns in relation to the impact on the developing Myanmar legal system.[55]

In March 2016 the European Commission published its draft final report on the SIA in support of the Investment Protection Agreement with the final deadline for comments on the draft final report expected April 2016.[56] In response to the draft final report the Myanmar Civil Society Organisations released a further open letter in April 2016 opposing the Investment Protection Agreement.[57] At the time of writing the European Commission final report has not been published.

53 According to a press release by the European Commission of 20 March 2014, available at: http://europa.eu/rapid/press-release_IP-14-285_en.htm.

54 http://www.eu-myanmarsia.com/index.php.

55 The text of the open letter is available at: http://www.burmapartnership.org/2016/01/investment-protection-agreement-myanmar-eu/.

56 The European Commission Sustainability Impact Assessment (SIA) in support of an investment protection agreement between the European Union and the Republic of the Union of Myanmar, Draft Final Report of 18 March 2016, available at: http://www.eu-myanmarsia.com/data/info/20160318093538 5856pic.pdf.

57 Available at: http://www.s2bnetwork.org/myanmar-sia/.

CHAPTER 8

The Philippines[1]

I Introduction

The Philippines is a democratic republic with a presidential form of government. It initially declared independence from Spain on 12 June 1898 and subsequently achieved full independence from the United States on 4 July 1946.[2] Geographically, it comprises an archipelago of approximately 7,100 islands and spans circa 300,000 km^2. The Philippines has a population of around 100 million.[3]

The GDP of the Philippines has been increasing in recent years, the percentage growth having been most significant between 2011 and 2012.[4] However, according to World Bank forecasts, this growth is expected to stabilise at around 6.5% between 2015 and 2017.[5] In 2013, the rating agencies Fitch, Standard & Poor's and Moody's upgraded the Philippines' sovereign credit ratings to investment grade, on the basis of robust economic performance, continued fiscal and debt consolidation efforts, and improved governance.[6]

In early 2015, Foreign Direct Investment ("FDI") in the Philippines represented 1.24% of the country's nominal GDP.[7] According to FDI statistics published by the World Bank,[8] net inflows of investment in the Philippines

1 This chapter has been drafted by Ms Natalie Limbasan, formerly of Eversheds LLP, Paris, and reviewed by Mr Agustin Mantilla IV of Romulo Mabanta Buenaventura Sayoc & De Los Angeles, Manila, Philippines.

2 See http://www.gov.ph/about/philippines/.

3 See http://data.worldbank.org/country/philippines.

4 Whereas GDP was at 3.6% in 2011, it increased to 6.8% in 2012; and to 7.2% in 2013. However, in 2014, it was at approximately 6% – *World Bank, Global Economic Prospects, Regional Outlooks, East Asia and Pacific*, available at http://www.worldbank.org/en/publication/global-economic-prospects/regional-outlooks/Global-Economic-Prospects-June-2015-East-Asia-and-Pacific-analysis.

5 *Ibid.*, it is expected to increase to 6.5% in 2015 and 2016, and to drop to 6.3% in 2017.

6 United States Department of State, Investment Climate Statement 2014 for the Philippines, available at http://www.state.gov/e/eb/rls/othr/ics/2014/index.htm, p. 4.

7 CEIC, "Philippines Economic Data & Statistics", available at http://www.ceicdata.com/en/statistics/Philippines. In mid-2014, this figure was 2.43%.

8 These statistics are based on data collected by the IMF and supplemented by data from UNCTAD and from national sources.

 | DOI 10.1163/9789004335257_010

totalled USD 6.2 billion in 2014 and USD 3.7 billion in 2013, compared with USD 3.2 billion the year prior, and USD 2 billion in 2011.[9]

The majority of investment inflows have been in the manufacturing, construction, retail, real estate, mining (gold and copper industries have been identified as high potential sectors),[10] renewable energy, agriculture and information and communication sectors.[11]

A large part of the Philippines' population speaks English, a factor that the country publicises to encourage investment and which has driven growth in the "business process outsourcing" and in the tourism sectors, both of which have accelerated in recent years. The Philippines has also marketed itself as a gateway to a wider Asian market and to the ASEAN Free Trade Area.[12]

In order to stimulate investment, the Philippines has taken steps to open its economy by removing restrictions to foreign investment in a variety of industries, such as infrastructure, insurance, banking, telecommunications and energy.[13] The government's role in a number of sectors was also redefined through a policy of privatisation.[14] This thrust is expected to continue.[15]

There are special economic zones and free ports,[16] and fiscal incentives including a six-year income tax holiday for "pioneer" firms, a four-year one for non-pioneer firms and tax credits on certain materials.[17]

9 See http://data.worldbank.org/indicator/BX.KLT.DINV.CD.WD. These figures are largely corroborated by those in the UNCTAD World Investment Report 2015: http://unctad.org/en/PublicationsLibrary/wir2015_en.pdf.

10 Santander Trade Portal, *Foreign investment in the Philippines*, available at https://en.santandertrade.com/establish-overseas/philippines/foreign-investment.

11 United States Department of State, Investment Climate Statement 2014 for the Philippines, available at http://www.state.gov/e/eb/rls/othr/ics/2014/index.htm, p. 4; SyCip Gorres Velayo & Co, *Doing Business in the Philippines*, 2013, pp. 10–12, available at http://www.ey.com/Publication/vwLUAssets/Doing_business_in_the_Philippines/$FILE/Doing-business-in-the-Philippines.pdf.

12 See, for example, the 2013 PWC report *Explore opportunities – How to invest in the Philippines* at p. 1, available at http://www.pwc.com/en_PH/ph/business-guides/assets/documents/htip-2013.pdf.

13 SyCip Gorres Velayo & Co, *Doing Business in the Philippines*, 2013, p. 4, available at http://www.ey.com/Publication/vwLUAssets/Doing_business_in_the_Philippines/$FILE/Doing-business-in-the-Philippines.pdf.

14 *Ibid.*

15 PWC, *Explore opportunities – How to invest in the Philippines*, 2013, p. 19, available at http://www.pwc.com/en_PH/ph/business-guides/assets/documents/htip-2013.pdf.

16 *Ibid.*, p. 2.

17 *Ibid.*, pp. 19–20.

Only Filipinos persons and domestic companies that are at least 60% owned by Filipinos are permitted to own land.[18] However, leasing terms are liberal: pursuant to the Investors Lease Act of 1994, the maximum allowable lease to foreign companies was extended from 25 years to 50 years, renewable once for 25 years.[19] Under the Mining Act of 1995, full foreign ownership of a project under a financial and technical assistance agreement ("FTAA") approved by the government is permitted, provided that specific minimum requirements are met in order to qualify as a FTAA. The term of a FTAA is for 25 years, with the possibility of renewal for another 25 years subject to mutual agreement.[20]

The remaining restrictions on foreign ownership, poor infrastructure and corruption are areas of risk and concern for investors.[21] An inefficient judicial system is a factor in the country's low rating by the World Bank in the area of enforcement of contracts. The courts are criticised for their poor record in terms of the timely and fair resolution of commercial disputes.[22]

II Philippines' National Arbitration and Investment Legislation

1 *Philippines' Arbitration Laws and Institutions*

Philippines' Arbitration Law

The recognition of arbitration as a means of dispute resolution in the Philippines dates back to the application of the Spanish Law of Civil Procedure (*Ley de Enjuiciamiento Civil*). This law was superseded by the passage of Republic Act No. 386 in 1949, the Civil Code of the Philippines, which contained a short chapter on arbitration. Four years later, in 1953, the Philippines passed Republic Act No. 876, the Arbitration Law.

Republic Act No. 876 provided the legal framework for arbitration until 2004. It made no distinction between domestic and international arbitration. Moreover, there was no indication that foreign arbitral awards would be recognised in the Philippines until the country acceded to the Convention on the Recognition and Enforcement of Foreign Arbitral Awards, referred to as the New York Convention, in 1965 via Senate Resolution No. 71.

---

18 Article XII, Sections 2 and 7 of the Philippines Constitution.

19 Section 4(1) of the Investors Lease Act 1994.

20 Section 32 of the Mining Act 1995.

21 See United States Department of State, Investment Climate Statement 2015 for the Philippines: http://www.state.gov/documents/organization/241916.pdf.

22 *Ibid.*

In 2004, Republic Act No. 9285, also known as the Alternative Dispute Resolution Act, was enacted. This law has served to modernise the arbitration framework. It is aimed at encouraging alternative dispute resolution, particularly arbitration, for the resolution of disputes of an international character. Republic Act No. 9285 declared that the Philippines' policy is to "actively promote party autonomy in the resolution of disputes or the freedom of the parties to make their own arrangements to resolve their disputes" and to "encourage and actively promote the use of Alternative Dispute Resolution (ADR) as an important means to achieve speedy and impartial justice and declog court dockets."[23] It also specifically provided that "in interpreting the Act, the court shall have due regard to the policy of the law in favor of arbitration."[24]

Republic Act No. 9285 introduced a distinction between domestic and international arbitration. Arbitration is classified as international if it falls within the definition of international arbitration under Article 1(3) of the UNCITRAL Model Law on International Commercial Arbitration (the "Model Law").

As such, arbitration is considered international if:

(a) the parties to an arbitration agreement have, at the time of the conclusion of such agreement, their places of business in different States; or
(b) one of the following places is situated outside the State in which the parties have their places of business:
    (i) the place of arbitration if determined in, or pursuant to, the arbitration agreement;
    (ii) any place where a substantial part of the obligations of the commercial relationship is to be performed or the place with which the subject matter of the dispute is most closely connected; or
(c) the parties have expressly agreed that the subject matter of the arbitration agreement relates to more than one country.

Domestic arbitration is simply defined as arbitration that is not international. Therefore, it is likely that, if the dispute is between parties who have their place of business in the Philippines, their obligations are to be performed in the Philippines, and there is no stipulation in their arbitration agreement that the subject matter or seat of the arbitration agreement relates to another country, the arbitration will be considered domestic.

23 Section 2 of Republic Act No. 9285.

24 *Ibid.*, Section 25.

Mirroring developments in international trade, Republic Act No. 9285 has ensured that international commercial arbitration is governed by the Model Law. Section 19 of the law accordingly incorporates the Model Law.[25]

Domestic arbitration meanwhile continues to be governed by the old law, Republic Act No. 876, as amended by Republic Act No. 9285.

In addition, Articles 2028 to 2046 of the Philippine Civil Code apply to both domestic and international commercial arbitration,[26] as does, with regard to the application and interpretation of laws, settled jurisprudence and judicial decisions of the Supreme Court.

It is noteworthy that Republic Act No. 876 has however been amended by Republic Act No. 9285 so as to include several Model Law provisions in Republic Act No. 876. This latter Act and Republic Act No. 9285 will be discussed in more detail under the corresponding subtitles below.

All types of commercial disputes may be referred to arbitration pursuant to Philippine laws. The word "commercial" is broadly defined as "matters arising from all relationships of a commercial nature, whether contractual or not."[27]

---

25 Section 19 of Republic Act No. 9285 provides:

"***Adoption of the Model Law on International Commercial Arbitration.*** – International commercial arbitration shall be governed by the Model Law on International Commercial Arbitration (the 'Model Law') adopted by the United Nations Commission on International Trade Law on June 21, 1985 (United Nations Document A/40/17) and recommended approved on December 11, 1985, copy of which is hereto attached as Appendix 'A'."

26 Articles 2028 to 2041 relate to compromises, *i.e.* "a contract whereby the parties, by making reciprocal concessions, avoid a litigation or put an end to one already commenced" (Article 2028). The court is accordingly required to "endeavor to persuade the litigants in a civil case to agree upon some fair compromise" (Article 2029). Article 2043 specifies that the provisions of the chapter concerning compromises are also applicable to arbitrations. Articles 2042 to 2046, which concern arbitration, read as follows:

"CHAPTER 2

ARBITRATIONS

Art. 2042. The same persons who may enter into a compromise may submit their controversies to one or more arbitrators for decision.

Art. 2043. The provisions of the preceding Chapter upon compromises shall also be applicable to arbitrations.

Art. 2044. Any stipulation that the arbitrators' award or decision shall be final, is valid, without prejudice to Articles 2038, 2039, and 2040.

Art. 2045. Any clause giving one of the parties power to choose more arbitrators than the other is void and of no effect.

Art. 2046. The appointment of arbitrators and the procedure for arbitration shall be governed by the provisions of such rules of court as the Supreme Court shall promulgate."

27 Section 3(g) of Republic Act No. 9285.

Disputes which cannot be submitted to arbitration are those relating to:

(a) labour disputes covered by the Labour Code of the Philippines,[28] as amended, and its Implementing Rules and Regulations;
(b) the civil status of persons;
(c) the validity of a marriage;
(d) any ground for the legal separation of persons;
(e) the jurisdiction of courts;
(f) future legitime;[29]
(g) criminal liability; and
(h) those which by law cannot be compromised or which cannot be the subject of a contract, for example those that are contrary to law, morals or good custom.[30]

The domestic and international arbitration regimes are discussed in more detail below.

Domestic Arbitration

As noted above, domestic arbitration is governed by Republic Act No. 876, as supplemented by Republic Act No. 9285, and, consequently, Articles 8, 10, 11, 12, 13, 14, 18, 19 and 29 to 32 of the Model Law.

The Arbitration Agreement

The Philippine Civil Code treats arbitration agreements like any other contract. Consequently, provided that the parties agree to be bound by the terms of the arbitration agreement and those terms are not contrary to law, morals, good custom, public order, or public policy, the agreement is binding.[31]

According to Republic Act No. 876, an arbitration agreement must be in writing and subscribed by the party or by his lawful agent.[32]

---

28 Officially Presidential Decree No. 442.

29 "Legitime" refers to the future inheritance of compulsory heirs, *i.e.* heirs that a testator cannot deprive of their inheritance. Legitime is defined in Article 886 of the Philippine Civil Code as "that part of the testator's property which he cannot dispose of because the law has reserved it for certain heirs who are, therefore, called compulsory heirs."

30 Articles 2035 and 2043 of the Philippine Civil Code and Section 6 of Republic Act No. 9285.

31 Articles 1305 and 1306 of the Philippine Civil Code.

32 Section 4 of Republic Act No. 876.

Constitution of the Arbitral Tribunal

Parties are free to determine the number of arbitrators, except for the limitation provided by Article 2045 of the Philippine Civil Code. In the absence of an agreement on the number of arbitrators, three arbitrators are to be appointed.[33]

Where the parties refuse or fail to appoint an arbitrator, the default appointing authority, which is the same for both domestic and international arbitration, is defined as "the person or institution named in the agreement as the appointing authority; or the regular arbitration institution under whose rules the arbitration is agreed to be conducted."[34] In an *ad hoc* arbitration, the default appointing authority is the National President of the Integrated Bar of the Philippines or his duly authorised representative.[35] If the appointing authority fails or refuses to act within thirty days, an application may be filed with the Regional Trial Court.[36]

Philippines arbitration law requires that an arbitrator must possess certain qualifications in order to be appointed: he/she must be of legal age, in full enjoyment of his/her civil rights and must know how to read and write. No disqualifications should apply either, *i.e.*, he/she should not be related by blood or marriage within the sixth degree to either party to the dispute, and he/she should not have a financial, fiduciary or other interest in the dispute, or any personal bias which might prejudice the right of any party to a fair and impartial arbitral award.[37]

The law prohibits an arbitrator from "championing" or "advocating" the cause of either party.

Provisional Relief and Interim Measures

It is possible for a party to apply for provisional relief or interim measures with the courts prior to the constitution of the arbitral tribunal or even during the arbitration proceedings to the extent that the arbitral tribunal has no power to act or is unable to act effectively.

The Arbitral Award

A tribunal is to render the award within the period agreed upon by the parties. In the absence of such agreement, the tribunal must render a written award

33 Article 10 of the Model Law, as made applicable to domestic arbitration by Section 33 of Republic Act No. 9285.

34 Section 26 of Republic Act No. 9285.

35 *Ibid.*

36 Section 27 of Republic Act No. 9285 and Article 6 of the Model Law.

37 Section 10 of Republic Act No. 876.

within 30 days of closing the hearing, a period that is subject to extension by mutual consent of the parties.[38]

Enforcement of the Arbitral Award

Unless the parties agree to comply voluntarily with a domestic arbitral award, either party may file a petition for confirmation with the Regional Trial Court at any time after a period of 30 days from receipt by the petitioner of the award. The court is required to order confirmation of the award unless the award is vacated, modified or corrected.[39]

Section 41 of Republic Act No. 9285 provides that:

> A party to a domestic arbitration may question the arbitral award with the appropriate regional trial court in accordance with rules of procedure to be promulgated by the Supreme Court only on those grounds enumerated in Section 25 of Republic Act No. 876. Any other ground raised against a domestic arbitral award shall be disregarded by the regional trial court.[40]

A petition to vacate a domestic arbitral award can be filed before the Regional Trial Court having jurisdiction within 30 days from receipt of the award. A petition to vacate filed later than this will be dismissed.

The grounds that can be invoked to vacate an arbitral award include that it was procured by corruption, fraud, or other undue means; that there was evident partiality or corruption on the part of the arbitrators; that the arbitrators were guilty of certain forms of misconduct; that one or more of the arbitrators was disqualified to act as such under the law and wilfully refrained from disclosing such disqualification; or that they exceeded their powers or so imperfectly executed them, such that a complete, final and definite arbitral award on the subject matter was not made.

---

38 *Ibid.*, Section 19.

39 *Ibid.*, Section 23. See also Section 40 of Republic Act No. 9285.

40 The reference to Section 25 of Republic Act No. 876 appears to be a clerical error, since this Section actually refers to the grounds for modification or correction of an award, and does not include grounds that may be employed to vacate an award. It is Section 24 of Republic Act No. 876 that relates to the grounds for vacation of an award. The proposed Implementing Rules and Regulations of Republic Act No. 9285 re-link the grounds for vacating an award with Section 24 of Republic Act No. 876.

Where an arbitral award is vacated, the court may direct a new hearing either before the same arbitrators or before a new arbitrator(s) to be appointed in accordance with the arbitration agreement.

International Arbitration

As noted above, Republic Act No. 9285 stipulates that international arbitration is to be governed by the Model Law, together with relevant Philippine laws, such as Articles 2028 to 2046 of the Philippine Civil Code, and settled jurisprudence or decisions of the Philippine Supreme Court.

The Policy behind Republic Act No. 9285

Given that the primary goal of Republic Act No. 9285 is to encourage arbitration and other alternative forms of dispute settlement, the law directs courts to give due regard to an arbitration agreement, notwithstanding any action commenced before the courts:

> Where action is commenced by or against multiple parties, one or more of whom are parties who are bound by the arbitration agreement, the court shall refer to arbitration those parties who are bound by the arbitration agreement although the civil action may continue as to those who are not bound by such arbitration agreement.[41]

In addition, the Model Law provides that, where an action is brought in a matter that is the subject of an arbitration agreement, the court must refer the parties to arbitration unless it finds that the agreement is "null and void, inoperative or incapable of being performed".[42]

Interpretation of Republic Act No. 9285

With regard to interpretation, Republic Act No. 9285 provides that, in interpreting the Model Law, regard is to be had to its international origin and the need for uniformity in its interpretation. It also provides that resort may be made to the *travaux préparatoires* and the report of the Secretary General of UNCTAD dated 25 March 1985, entitled "International Commercial Arbitration: Analytical Commentary on Draft Text identified by reference number a/CN. 9/264".[43]

---

41 Section 25 of Republic Act No. 9285.

42 Article 8 of the Model Law.

43 Available at: https://documents-dds-ny.un.org/doc/UNDOC/GEN/V85/244/18/PDF/V8524418.pdf?OpenElement.

Key Aspects of Republic Act No. 9285

The following are some of the key aspects of international arbitrations under Republic Act No. 9285 and the Model Law:

- The Model Law provides that an arbitration agreement must be in writing. The Model Law stipulates what will be considered an agreement in writing:

  (3) An arbitration agreement is in writing if its content is recorded in any form, whether or not the arbitration agreement or contract has been concluded orally, by conduct, or by other means.

  (4) The requirement that an arbitration agreement be in writing is met by an electronic communication if the information contained therein is accessible so as to be useable for subsequent reference; "electronic communication" means any communication that the parties make by means of data messages; "data message" means information generated, sent, received or stored by electronic, magnetic, optical or similar means, including, but not limited to, electronic data interchange (EDI), electronic mail, telegram, telex or telecopy.

  (5) Furthermore, an arbitration agreement is in writing if it is contained in an exchange of statements of claim and defence in which the existence of an agreement is alleged by one party and not denied by the other.

  (6) The reference in a contract to any document containing an arbitration clause constitutes an arbitration agreement in writing, provided that the reference is such as to make that clause part of the contract.[44]

- The Model Law provides that the parties are free to determine the number of arbitrators. In the absence of an agreement on the number of arbitrators, the number of arbitrators shall be three.[45] A clause that gives one of the parties the power to choose more arbitrators than the other will be void and of no effect.[46]
- The Model Law provides that the arbitral tribunal may rule on its own jurisdiction, including any objections with respect to the existence or validity of the arbitration agreement.[47]

---

44 Article 7 of the Model Law.

45 Article 10 of the Model Law and Section 19 of Republic Act No. 9285.

46 Article 2045 of the Philippine Civil Code.

47 Article 16 of the Model Law.

- Republic Act No. 9285 allows a party in an international arbitration to apply for provisional relief or interim measures with the courts prior to the constitution of the arbitral tribunal or even during the arbitration proceedings to the extent that the arbitral tribunal has no power to act or is unable to act effectively.[48] The principle behind this provision is in line with the Model Law, which provides that "[i]t is not incompatible with an arbitration agreement for a party to request, before or during arbitral proceedings, from a court an interim measure of protection and for a court to grant such measure."[49] However, Republic Act No. 9285 provides that once the arbitral tribunal is constituted, an application for an interim measure of protection or a modification thereof may be made to the arbitral tribunal, unless the arbitral tribunal has no power to act or is unable to act effectively, in which case the application may be made to the appropriate branch of the Regional Trial Court.[50]
- Republic Act No. 9285 provides that arbitration proceedings, including the records, evidence and the arbitral award, shall be considered confidential. No comparable provision is contained within the Model Law.[51]
- The Model Law provides that a party may petition the court to set aside the arbitral award on the grounds enumerated in Article 34(2), among which are the incapacity of a party to the arbitration agreement, invalidity of the arbitration agreement and public policy.[52]
- Republic Act No. 9285 confirms that the New York Convention shall govern the recognition and enforcement of foreign arbitral awards. A party to a foreign arbitral proceeding may ask the appropriate branch of the Regional Trial Court that the recognition and enforcement of an award be refused only on the grounds listed in Article V of the New York Convention, mirrored in Article 36 of the Model Law. Foreign arbitral awards not covered by the New York Convention, on the other hand, may, upon grounds of comity and reciprocity, be recognised and enforced in accordance the Special Rules of Court on Alternative Dispute Resolution promulgated by the Philippine Supreme Court.[53]

---

48 Section 28 of Republic Act No. 9285.

49 Article 9 of the Model Law.

50 Section 28(a) of Republic Act No. 9285.

51 Section 23 of Republic Act No. 9285. Section 33 of Republic Act No. 9285 also makes Section 23 applicable to domestic arbitration.

52 Article 34 of the Model Law.

53 Section 43 of Republic Act No. 9285.

- A foreign arbitral award, when confirmed by the Regional Trial Court, is to be enforced in the same manner as final and executory decisions of the courts of law of the Philippines. However, a foreign arbitral award that has been confirmed by a court of a foreign country will be recognised and enforced as a foreign arbitral award, and not as a judgment of a foreign court.[54]

Philippines' Arbitral Institutions and Rules

In both domestic arbitration and international arbitration, parties are free to decide on the rules of procedure that are to apply to their arbitration.

In the absence of agreement, the arbitrators may conduct the arbitration in such manner as they consider appropriate.[55]

The Special Rules of Court on Alternative Dispute Resolution promulgated by the Supreme Court in September 2009 govern the procedure to be followed when recourse is made to the courts on any matter subject to arbitration or other forms of alternative dispute resolution.[56]

The Philippine Dispute Resolution Center, Inc. and the Construction Industry Arbitration Commission are two of the leading arbitral institutions in the Philippines that have been in existence even before the passage of Republic Act No. 9285.[57]

Philippines' Courts and Arbitration

The Philippines' judiciary is an independent branch of the government and comprises the Supreme Court, which is the highest court, and several lower courts.[58]

The lower courts are composed of the Court of Appeals (an appellate court) and several trial courts with limited jurisdictions, such as the Regional Trial Courts, Municipal Trial Courts, and Shari'ah District Courts (Muslim courts). There are also special courts, such as the "Sandiganbayan" (anti-graft court for public officials) and the Court of Tax Appeals.[59]

---

54 *Ibid.*, Section 44.

55 Sections 33 and 19 of Republic Act No. 9285 together with Article 19 of the Model Law; Article 4.19(b) of the IRR to Republic Act No. 9285.

56 The rules took effect on 30 October 2009 and are available at http://www.lawphil.net/courts/supreme/am/am_07-11-08-sc_2009.html.

57 The websites of these institutions are accessible, respectively, at http://www.pdrci.org/ and https://ciap.dti.gov.ph/.

58 See the website of the Supreme Court, available at http://sc.judiciary.gov.ph.

59 See http://www.judiciary.gov.ph/.

The heavy workload and complex nature of the judicial system, which persist despite the efforts of the Supreme Court to streamline the judiciary,[60] means that the timely resolution of disputes is often inhibited. This contributes to the encouragement of the use of arbitration even on a domestic level.

For the recognition and enforcement of foreign arbitral awards, a petition must be filed with the appropriate branch of the Regional Trial Court, attaching: (1) the duly authenticated original arbitral award or a duly certified copy thereof; and (2) the original arbitration agreement or a duly certified copy thereof. If the award or arbitration agreement is not in an official language of the Philippines, *i.e.* English or Filipino, then the party applying for recognition and enforcement must produce a translation that is duly certified by an official, sworn or prepared by a diplomatic or consular agent.[61]

Moreover, although Philippine law recognises that an arbitral award shall be final, this does not mean that it is beyond judicial review. As noted above, the recognition and enforcement of a foreign arbitral award may be refused on any of the grounds enumerated under Article V of the New York Convention, while an arbitral award issued in an international commercial arbitration seated in the Philippines may be set aside under any of the grounds listed under Article 34 of the Model Law.

Finally, pursuant to Republic Act No. 9285, a decision of a Regional Trial Court confirming, vacating, setting aside, modifying, or correcting a domestic or international arbitral award may be appealed to the Court of Appeals in accordance with the Special Rules of Court on Alternative Dispute Resolution.[62]

2 *Philippines' Investment Laws*

Two principal pieces of legislation governing foreign investment in the Philippines are: the 1987 Omnibus Investments Code;[63] and the 1991 Philippine Foreign Investment Act.[64]

---

60 See http://www.americanbar.org/advocacy/rule_of_law/where_we_work/asia/philippines/news/news_philippines_supreme_court_launches_pilot_process_management_project_0111.html.

61 Section 42 of Republic Act No. 9285.

62 *Ibid.*, Section 46.

63 Also known as Executive Order No. 226, as amended, available at http://invest.cfo.gov.ph/pdf/part2/omnibus-investment-code-of-1987.pdf.

64 Also known as the Republic Act No. 7042, as amended, available at http://www.wipo.int/wipolex/en/details.jsp?id=13845.

The 1987 Omnibus Investments Code

The Omnibus Investments Code ("OIC") provides a range of incentives available to domestic and foreign investors engaged in activities considered as a priority by the Government.

The incentives comprise certain tax and non-tax measures. The non-tax measures focus around import facilitation and family reunifications, and do not grant rights that attach specifically to the investment itself.

To qualify for OIC incentives, an investor must either engage in an area of activity listed in the current Investment Priorities Plan (the "IPP", referred to further below). Alternatively, for enterprises with more than 40% foreign equity, at least 70% of the production of such enterprises must be for purposes of export.[65]

In addition, an investor must apply for registration with the Board of Investments ("BOI").[66] The BOI was established by the OIC and is responsible for regulating and promoting investment in the Philippines.

The 1991 Philippine Foreign Investment Act

The Foreign Investment Act ("FIA") is "an act to promote foreign investments, prescribe the procedures for registering enterprises doing business in the Philippines, and for other purposes".[67] Investment is defined as "equity participation in any enterprise organized or existing under the laws of the Philippines".[68]

> "[F]oreign investment" is defined as "an equity investment made by a non-Philippine national in the form of foreign exchange and/or other assets actually transferred to the Philippines and duly registered with the Central Bank which shall assess and appraise the value of such assets other than foreign exchange".[69]

65 For Filipino-owned enterprises, the threshold is 50%.

66 Note that export-oriented manufacturing and service enterprises within the economic zones must register with the Philippine Economic Zone Authority.

67 Preamble, Philippines Foreign Investments Act of 1991.

68 *Ibid.*, Section 3(b).

69 *Ibid.*, Section 3(c).

The term Philippine national is defined in the FIA,[70] and foreign nationals are referred to as non-Philippine nationals.[71]

The FIA grants no substantive protections to investors.

According to the FIA, foreign investors are generally allowed to do business in the Philippines, subject to restrictions contained in the Foreign Investments Negative List ("FINL").

The FINL is published bi-annually and lists sectors in which foreign investment is either prohibited or limited to a specified maximum percentage by the Philippine Constitution or other laws (Part A of the FINL), or for reasons of national security, defence, public health, morals and the protection of small and medium enterprises (Part B of the FINL).[72]

At the time of writing, the FINL prohibited, *inter alia*, foreign equity in: the mass media (except recording); retail trade enterprises with a paid-up share capital of less than USD 2.5 million; small-scale mining; and the utilisation of marine resources in sovereign territory.[73]

Investment in certain areas is limited to a specific percentage. The following areas are subject to restrictions: private radio communications networks; contracts for the construction and repair of locally-funded public works; contracts for the construction of defence-related structures; advertising; exploration, development and utilisation of natural resources; operation of public utilities; operation of commercial deep sea fishing vessels; and contracts for the supply

70 Section 3(a) of the Philippines Foreign Investments Act of 1991 provides that:

"The term 'Philippine national' shall mean a citizen of the Philippines or a domestic partnership or association wholly owned by citizens of the Philippines; or a corporation organized under the laws of the Philippines of which at least sixty percent (60%) of the capital stock outstanding and entitled to vote is owned and held by citizens of the Philippines; or a trustee of funds for pension or other employee retirement or separation benefits, where the trustee is a Philippine national and at least sixty (60%) of the fund will accrue to the benefit of the Philippine nationals: Provided, That where a corporation and its non-Filipino stockholders own stocks in a Securities and Exchange Commission (SEC) registered enterprise, at least sixty percent (60%) of the capital stocks outstanding and entitled to vote of both corporations must be owned and held by citizens of the Philippines and at least sixty percent (60%) of the members of the Board of Directors of both corporations must be citizens of the Philippines, in order that the corporations shall be considered a Philippine national."

71 See, for example, Section 5 of the Philippines Foreign Investments Act of 1991.

72 The relevant activities are defined as: "the manufacture and distribution of dangerous drugs; all forms of gambling; nightclubs, bars, beerhouses, dance halls; sauna and steam bathhouses and massage clinics" (Section 8 of the FIA).

73 At the time of writing, the tenth FINL was the most recent, published in May 2015. It is available at http://www.gov.ph/downloads/2015/05may/20150529-EO-0184-BSA.pdf.

of materials, goods and commodities to Government-owned or controlled corporations, companies, agencies or municipal corporations; and financing companies and investment houses. Foreign investors are prohibited from owning stock in lending, financing or investment companies unless the investor's home country affords the same reciprocal rights to Filipino investors.[74]

In addition, certain licensed professions can only be practiced by Philippine citizens, such as pharmacy, criminology and law. Other specified professions, including engineering, medicine and accountancy, can be practiced by foreigners provided that their countries allow Philippine citizens to practice the same professions.[75]

Small and medium-sized domestic market enterprises, with paid-up equity capital of less than the equivalent of USD 200,000, are also reserved to Philippine nationals, unless they involve advanced technology or they directly employ at least 50 employees, in which case a minimum paid-in capital of USD 100,000 is allowed for non-Philippine nationals.[76]

There is a registration requirement for investments in domestic enterprises and for doing business, but there is no approval requirement. However, where a non-Philippine national intends to engage in the same line of business as an existing joint venture between non-Philippine national(s) and Philippine national(s), this must be disclosed and the registration disallowed if the existing joint venture can reasonably prove that it is capable of making the investment needed for the domestic market activities to be undertaken by the competing applicant.[77]

The Commonwealth Act No. 108 as Amended

The Commonwealth Act No. 108 or "Anti-Dummy" law[78] was adopted in order to punish evasion of the laws which safeguard rights, franchises or privileges for Filipino nationals. It imposes criminal and civil penalties on persons violating foreign equity limitations.

---

74 Section 6 of Republic Act No. 9474 and Section 6 of Republic Act No. 5980, as amended by Republic Act No. 8556, available at http://www.lawphil.net/statutes/repacts/ra1969/ra_5980_1969.html and http://www.bsp.gov.ph/downloads/laws/RA8556.pdf, respectively.

75 Part A.2 and footnote 1 of the FINL.

76 Section 8 of the Philippines Foreign Investments Act of 1991.

77 *Ibid.*, Section 5.

78 The Anti-Dummy Law is available at http://www.lawphil.net/statutes/comacts/ca_108_1936.html.

The Investment Priorities Plan

In addition to the OIC and the FIA, the Investment Priorities Plan ("IPP"), published on an annual basis, identifies preferred economic activities that are approved by the President. The 2014 IPP identified as preferred activities those pertaining to four broad sectors: manufacturing, agribusiness and fishery, services and infrastructure and logistics.[79] Government agencies are encouraged to adopt policies and implement programs consistent with the IPP.

Other Domestic Laws Relevant to Foreign Investors

Foreign investors are prohibited from owning land pursuant to the Philippine Constitution. The most far-reaching land right for foreign investors is a 50-year lease of a contiguous parcel of up to 1,000 hectares of land, renewable once for 25 additional years, as permitted pursuant to the 1993 Investors' Lease Act. The land concerned must be intended for a specific investment purpose, such as for manufacturing facilities or industrial sites.

The Philippine Constitution provides that private property shall not be taken for public use without just compensation.[80] To this end, the government is required to ensure that owners of real property acquired for national government infrastructure projects are promptly paid just compensation for the expeditious acquisition of the required right-of-way for the projects.[81]

With regard to capital movements, amounts above the equivalent of USD 10,000 must be declared upon physical entry into the country. Investors may register their investment with the Bangko Sentral ng Pilipinas ("BSP") if they wish to ensure that dividend and profit remittances from the return of capital in local currency can be exchanged into foreign currency sourced from the banking system.[82] However, investors are free to remit profits from their own foreign exchange sourced from outside the domestic banking system.[83]

79 The 2014 IPP is available at http://rboi.armm.gov.ph/uploads/DOC_FILES/2014%20IPP.pdf?bcsi_scan_571fca99b36dc46b=1.

80 Article III, Section 9 of the Philippine Constitution.

81 Section 2 of Republic Act 10752. See also Article 1488 of the Philippine Civil Code.

82 2013 PWC report "Explore opportunities – How to invest in the Philippines" at p. 27, available at http://www.pwc.com/en_PH/ph/business-guides/assets/documents/htip-2013.pdf. Funds remitted outside the banking system cannot be registered as foreign equity investment with the SEC or the BSP. Also, an investor is required to convert inward remittances of foreign investment to Philippine pesos for purposes of registration with the BSP.

83 *Ibid.* at p. 28.

III Philippines' Bilateral Investment Treaties

1 *Overview*

The Philippines concluded its first BIT in December 1980, with the UK. It entered into its next BIT in June 1988, with Italy, and into numerous others as of 1992.

At the time of writing, the Philippines is a party to 38 BITs,[84] of which at least 32 have entered into force.[85] At least 34 of the Philippines' BITs are currently publicly available.[86] The BITs that are not publicly available, namely those entered into with Indonesia, Kuwait, Saudi Arabia and Syria, have consequently not been taken into account in the below analysis.

Worthy of mention is also an agreement concluded by the Philippines with Japan for an "Economic Partnership" (the "EPA"), which includes an investment chapter.[87]

---

84 The Philippines has signed BITs with Argentina, Australia, Austria, Bahrain, Bangladesh, Belgium (together with Luxembourg), Cambodia, Canada, Chile, China, the Czech Republic, Denmark, Finland, France, Germany, India, Indonesia, Iran, Italy, Luxembourg (together with Belgium), Korea, Kuwait, Mongolia, Myanmar, Netherlands, Islamic Republic of Pakistan, Portugal, Romania, Russian Federation, Saudi Arabia, Spain, Sweden, Switzerland, Syria, Taiwan, Thailand, Turkey, the United Kingdom and Vietnam.

85 UNCTAD reflects that the Philippines' BITs with the following States have entered into force: Argentina, Australia, Austria, Bangladesh, Belgium (together with Luxembourg), Canada, Chile, China, the Czech Republic, Denmark, Finland, France, Germany, India, Italy, Luxembourg (together with Belgium), Korea, Mongolia, Myanmar, Netherlands, Portugal, Romania, Russian Federation, Saudi Arabia, Spain, Switzerland, Syria, Taiwan, Thailand, Turkey, the United Kingdom and Vietnam (http://investmentpolicyhub.unctad.org/IIA/CountryBits/166#iiaInnerMenu). Kluwer Arbitration reflects that the Philippines' BITs with Bahrain has also entered into force (http://www.kluwerarbitration.com/CommonUI/BITs.aspx?country=Philippines). Kluwer Arbitration is a subscription-only website.

86 This includes the BITs that have been signed but are not yet in force. The Philippines' BITs with the following States are publicly available: Argentina, Australia, Austria, Bahrain, Bangladesh, Belgium (together with Luxembourg, as the Belgo-Luxembourg Economic Union or BLEU), Cambodia, Canada, Chile, China, the Czech Republic, Denmark, Finland, France, Germany, India, Iran, Italy, Luxembourg (together with Belgium as the BLEU), Korea, Mongolia, Myanmar, Netherlands, Islamic Republic of Pakistan, Portugal, Romania, Russian Federation, Spain, Sweden, Switzerland, Taiwan, Thailand, Turkey, the United Kingdom and Vietnam.

87 The EPA is different in nature to the Philippines' BITs, and is therefore considered separately in this footnote.

Investments are defined as "every kind of asset owned or controlled, directly or indirectly, by an investor" and include a juridical person (*i.e.* a company itself may be

2 *Definition of Investment*

The publicly available BITs entered into by the Philippines generally include a relatively broad definition of investment.

The majority of these BITs define investment to include "any" or "every" kind of asset and include a non-exhaustive list of examples.[88] These typically encompass movable and immovable property and any other rights *in rem*, shares, debentures and other forms of participation in companies, claims to money or any performance having an economic value, intellectual and industrial property rights and business concessions.

The majority of the publicly available BITs require that the investment is undertaken in accordance with, or in conformity with, the laws of the host State,[89] or refer to the investment being "accepted" or "admitted" pursuant to domestic law.[90] It is questionable whether this latter stipulation adds to the substance of the requirement, given how it is expressed,[91] but government or

---

an investment), shares, loans and other forms of debt, rights under contracts, claims to money, IP rights, concessions, other tangible and intangible properties. In addition, income from investments is also defined as an investment – Article 88(b) of the EPA. An investor is defined as a national of one party and not a national of the other party (Article 88(c) of the EPA); for juridical persons, there is a seat as well as a constitution or organisation requirement (Article 88(e) of the EPA). Moreover, branches of juridical persons of a non-party are expressly excluded (Article 88(c) of the EPA).

The EPA provides for various substantive protections (Articles 89 to 91 inclusive of the EPA); grants national treatment and MFN as regards access to the courts (Article 92 of the EPA); includes a standard protection against expropriation, providing that compensation equivalent to the fair market value of the property is to be awarded (Article 91 of the EPA; it is noteworthy that taxation measures are expressly included within the scope of the expropriation provision by virtue of Article 104); and provides for the free transfer of capital and income, subject to certain exceptions (Article 97 of the EPA; there are certain exclusions to the scope of application of the protections, and a (albeit fairly limited) denial of benefits provision at Article 104). However, although a menu of dispute resolution options is available for disputes between the contracting parties at Chapter 15 of the EPA, no direct recourse is provided to investors who feel that the obligations under the EPA have not been honoured.

88 The Philippines-China BIT varies from the rest in that the list of examples of what will constitute an investment is expressed not as non-exhaustive, but as "including mainly" the listed items (Article I(a)).

89 The BITs concerned are those entered into with Argentina; Canada; Finland; France; India; the Netherlands; Portugal; Romania; Russia; Taiwan; Thailand; Turkey; and Vietnam.

90 The BITs concerned are those entered into with Australia; Bahrain; Bangladesh; the BLEU; Cambodia; Chile; China; the Czech Republic; Germany; Italy; Iran; Mongolia; Myanmar; Pakistan; and Spain.

91 These provisions are generally worded along the lines of "assets … admitted by the other Party subject to its law and investment policies applicable from time to time" (Article 1(1)

regulatory approvals may be required in order for an investment to be permitted in the Philippines. The type of approval required will depend on factors such as the nature of the investment and the amount of the investment.

The language contained in the Philippines-China BIT seems to impose a higher threshold than the majority of Philippines BITs to the extent that it refers to "the Contracting Party accepting the investment in its territory".[92] The Philippines-Taiwan BIT contains an important limitation as it provides that it only applies to "investments of investors who have been granted admission".[93] No further specification is however provided as to the type of admission required, or the conditions for such admission. On the other hand, the Philippines-Iran BIT specifies that "admitted investment refers to an investment for which an Admission Certificate ... has been issued",[94] and the Philippines-Vietnam BIT requires investments to have been "specifically approved in writing".[95]

A large number of Philippines' BITs stipulate that any alteration in the form in which assets are invested shall not affect their classification as investments.[96]

The Philippines-Canada BIT also expressly includes indirect investments made "through an investor of a third State".[97]

The Philippines-Czech Republic BIT includes an additional test, providing that investment shall mean "any kind of asset invested in connection with economic activities".[98]

(a) of the Philippines-Australia BIT) and "asset[s] ... accepted in accordance with the respective laws and regulations of either Contracting Party" (Article I(1) of the Philippines-Bangladesh BIT). The verbs "admit" and "accept" therefore seem to be alternatives to verbs used in a number of other BITs, notably "invested", "owned" (Philippines-Romania BIT) or "owned or controlled" (BITs entered by the Philippines into with Argentina; Australia; Canada) or "established or acquired" (BITs entered into by the Philippines with Finland, India, Turkey).

92 Article I(a) of the Philippines-China BIT.

93 Article III of the Philippines-Taiwan BIT.

94 Article 1(5) of the Philippines-Iran BIT.

95 Article III(1) of the Philippines-Taiwan BIT.

96 The BITs concerned are those entered into with Argentina; Bahrain; the BLEU; Cambodia; Canada; the Czech Republic; France; Italy; Myanmar; Pakistan; Portugal; Romania; Russia; Spain and Thailand.

97 Article I(f) of the Philippines-Canada BIT.

98 Article I(1) of the Philippines-Czech Republic BIT. Article II(1) of the Philippines-Pakistan BIT also provides that investment means "any kind of asset connected with business investment".

3 *Definition of Investor*

The definition of investor in all but one of the Philippines' publicly available BITs includes both natural and legal persons, as respectively labelled and defined, of a contracting State.[99] In the majority of the BITs, the definition varies depending on which contracting State is concerned.[100]

Natural persons are generally defined as nationals or citizens of a State pursuant to the laws or constitution of that State. In two BITs, the definition includes individuals permanently residing in one of the contracting States.[101]

Legal persons are generally defined as entities duly incorporated or constituted in accordance with the laws of a contracting State. In most BITs, the definition includes associations of companies and, albeit in fewer instances, partnerships.[102]

However, the majority of publicly available BITs contain at least one additional requirement that needs to be met with regard to legal persons. These additional requirements may be that: (1) the seat, headquarters or head or main office of the company is located in the territory of the respective contracting State;[103] and/or[104] (2) that it is "actually doing business" under the

99 The Philippines-Cambodia BIT provides that nationals of the Philippines constitute only natural persons – Article I(2). This treaty is not however in force.

100 This applies to the BITs entered into with Australia; Austria; Bahrain; Bangladesh; the BLEU; Cambodia; Canada; China; the Czech Republic; Germany; India; Korea; Myanmar; Portugal; Russia; Portugal; Spain; Switzerland; Thailand; Turkey; and the UK. In a limited number of instances, the distinction is made only to reflect the different national instruments governing nationality or citizenship. For example, according to the Philippines-Bahrain BIT, investors "with respect to the State of Bahrain are natural persons deriving their status as nationals of either Contracting Party according to its applicable law; and individuals who, with respect to the Republic of the Philippines, are citizens of the Philippines within the meaning of its Constitution".

101 This applies to the BITs entered into with Australia and Canada, but only with regard to Canadian residents in the case of the latter.

102 This applies to the BITs entered into with Argentina; Austria; Bahrain; Bangladesh; China, but only with regard to Philippine entities; the Czech Republic; Finland; Germany; Italy; Korea; Myanmar; Pakistan; Portugal, but only with regard to Philippine legal entities; Spain; and Taiwan.

103 This applies to the BITs entered into with Austria, but only with regard to Austrian juridical persons; Bangladesh; the BLEU; Finland; France; Germany, but only with regard to German juridical persons; Iran; Portugal, but only with regard to Portuguese legal persons; and Turkey.

104 The following BITs contain both types of additional requirements (and in several instances two of the second type): Canada, but only with regard to Philippine enterprises;

laws of that State; that it has "effective economic activities" in the territory of the State; and/or that has its "place of effective management" there.[105]

In some cases, the definition includes corporations organised abroad, but effectively controlled by nationals of one of the contracting parties.[106] The Philippines-Sweden BIT provides protection to legal entities "in a third country with a predominant interest of an investor of either Contracting Party".[107]

At least four publicly available BITs provide provisions along the lines of the following: "any particular company may be excluded from the foregoing definition by mutual agreement between the Contracting Parties on the grounds of the need to maintain public order, to protect essential security interest or to fulfil commitments relating to international peace and security."[108]

4 *Scope*

The majority of the Philippines' publicly available BITs apply to investments made prior as well as after the entry into force of the treaty.[109] Less than one

---

Argentina; Chile; the Czech Republic; India; Italy; Korea, but only with regard to Philippine entities; Mongolia; Myanmar; Pakistan; Portugal, but only with regard to Philippine legal entities; Spain; and Taiwan.

For example, the BIT entered into with Argentina reads as follows at Article I(2)(b):

"[L]egal entities, including companies, associations of companies, trading corporate entities and other organisations that are incorporated or, in any event are properly organised and actually doing business under the laws of the respective Contracting Party and have their headquarters in the territory of the respective Contracting Party where effective management is carried out."

105 This applies to the BITs entered into with Austria, but only with regard to Philippine legal entities; Bahrain; China, but only with regard to Philippine entities; Germany, but only with regard to Philippine entities; Switzerland, but only with regard to Philippine entities; the UK and Vietnam. All of these, with the exception of the Philippines-Austria BIT with regard to Philippine legal entities, include the requirement of "place of effective management".

106 This applies to the BITs entered into with Austria, but only with regard to Philippine legal entities; the BLEU; France; Russia, but only with regard to Philippine entities; and Switzerland, but only with regard to Swiss companies.

107 Article I(2)(b) of the Philippines-Sweden BIT.

108 Article I(b) of the Philippines-China BIT. A similar provision is contained in the Philippines-India BIT at Article 1(3)(b); in the Philippines-UK BIT at Article 1(4) and in the Philippines-Vietnam BIT at Article 1(4).

109 This is the case for the BITs entered into with Argentina; Australia; Austria; Bahrain; Bangladesh; the BLEU; Cambodia; Canada; Chile; China; the Czech Republic; Denmark; Finland; Germany; India; Mongolia; Portugal; Romania; Sweden; and Switzerland.

third of the Philippines' BITs specify that they shall not apply to disputes that have arisen before their entry into force, while other BITs are silent on this issue.[110]

All of the BITs contain subrogation rights. The BITs entered into with the Netherlands and with Portugal go one step further by extending subrogation rights to third party insurers.[111]

A number of the Philippines' BITs provide that, where more favourable rules exist either under international law and/or under the national law of the contracting States, then the more favourable rules shall prevail.[112]

5 *Substantive Protections*

Fair and Equitable Treatment

With the exception of the Philippines-Korea BIT, all of the Philippines' publicly available BITs contain the obligation for host States to ensure fair and equitable treatment ("FET").

The scope of this provision varies somewhat, ranging from an FET obligation without any reference to international law or any further criteria;[113] an FET obligation linked to international law;[114] and FET with additional substantive content (such as denial of justice, unreasonable/discriminatory measures, breach of other treaty obligations, accounting for the level of development).[115]

---

110 This is the case for the BITs entered into with Argentina; Bahrain; Cambodia; Chile; Denmark; Finland; Portugal; and Romania.

111 See Article 6 of the Philippines-Netherlands BIT; Article 7 of the Philippines-Portugal BIT; and Article 7 of the Philippines-Bahrain BIT.

112 This is the case for the BITs entered into with Argentina; Australia; Austria; Bahrain; Bangladesh; the BLEU; Cambodia; China; the Czech Republic; Finland, France, Germany, India, Mongolia; Portugal; Romania; and Switzerland.

113 This is the case for the BITs entered into with Australia; Austria; the BLEU; Chile; Czech Republic; Finland; Germany; India; Italy; Myanmar; the Netherlands; Pakistan; Spain; Taiwan; Thailand; Turkey; the UK; and Vietnam.
With regard to Italy and Pakistan, see footnote 110.

114 This is the case for the BITs entered into with Canada and France.

115 This is the case for the BITs entered into with Argentina; Bahrain; Bangladesh; Cambodia; Denmark; Mongolia; Portugal; Romania; Russia; and Switzerland.

The Philippines-China BIT and the Philippines-Iran BIT refer only to equitable treatment,[116] whilst the Philippines-Italy BIT and the Philippines-Pakistan BIT refer to fair and reasonable treatment.[117]

In most cases, the FET provision takes the form of a requirement in relation to qualifying investments. In a handful of BITs, it is also expressed as relating to investment returns.[118]

Furthermore, the Philippines-France BIT provides, with regard to the definition of FET, that:

> *Toute restriction injuste à l'achat et au transport de matières premières et de matières auxiliaires, d'énergie et de combustibles, ainsi que de moyens de production et d'exploitation de tout genre, toute entrave à la vente et au transport des produits à l'intérieur du pays et à l'étranger, ainsi que toutes autres mesures ayant un effet analogue sont considérées comme des entraves de droit ou de fait au traitement juste et équitable.*[119]

Non-Discrimination

Almost half of the publicly availably BITs prohibit arbitrary and discriminatory treatment of the management, maintenance, use, enjoyment or disposal of qualifying investments by contracting States.[120]

---

116 Article 3(1) of the Philippines-China BIT ("Investments and activities associated with investments of investors of either Contracting Party shall accorded equitable treatment [...]") and Article 4(1) of the Philippines-Iran BIT ("Admitted Investments of investors of one Contracting Party effected within the territory of the other Contracting party in accordance with the laws and regulations of the latter, shall receive in the other Contracting Party full legal protection and fair treatment not less favourable than that accorded to its own investor or investors of any third state which are in a comparable situation").

117 Article I of the Philippines-Italy BIT ("Each Contracting Party shall [...] accord such investments equitable and reasonable treatment") and Article 1 of the Philippines-Pakistan BIT ("[...] Such investment shall be accorded equitable and reasonable treatment").

118 This is the case for the BITs entered into with Austria; Bangladesh; Canada; and Thailand.

119 Article 3 of the Philippines-France BIT. Unofficial translation: "Any unfair restriction to the purchase and transportation of raw and auxiliary materials, of energy and fuels, as well as means of production and exploitation of any kind, any obstacle to the sale and transportation of products within the country and abroad, as well as any other measures having an analogous effect, are considered as legal and factual obstacles to fair and equitable treatment."

120 This is the case for the BITs entered into with Argentina; Bahrain; Bangladesh; the BLEU; Cambodia; Denmark; Finland; Germany; Mongolia; Myanmar; Portugal; Romania; Russia; Sweden; Switzerland; and Turkey.

Full Protection and Security

Eighteen of the Philippines' publicly availably BITs provide for "full protection and security" of the investments of the other contracting State.[121] In many of these, the common "full protection and security" language is used; in others, the wording varies. For example, "continuous protection and security" is used in the Philippines-Belgo-Luxembourg Economic Union (or "BLEU") BIT, and "full legal protection" is used in the Philippines-Iran BIT.[122]

Expropriation

All of the publicly available BITs to which the Philippines is a party prohibit direct expropriation as well as measures having equivalent effect. The exception to this prohibition in 29 of the 34 publicly available BITs is when the measure in question meets the customary international law requirements for expropriation: *i.e.*, the measure serves a public purpose; the measure is not arbitrary or discriminatory; the procedure employed follows principles of due process; and the measure is accompanied by prompt, adequate and effective compensation. In the five other publicly available BITs, expropriation is prohibited unless the measure in question serves a public purpose and is compensated.[123]

All of the publicly available BITs, with the exception of the BIT with Mongolia, specify what the compensation shall amount to. This is normally stipulated to be the "fair market value", "market value" or the "value" of the investment,[124] immediately before the expropriation became public

121 These are the BITs entered into with Bahrain, Bangladesh, the BLEU, Cambodia, Canada, Czech Republic, Denmark, Finland, France, Germany, Myanmar, Netherlands, Portugal, Russia, Switzerland, Thailand, UK, Vietnam.

122 Article III(2) of the Philippines-BLEU BIT and Article 4(1) of the Philippines-Iran BIT.

123 These are the BITs entered into with Finland, Germany, India, Taiwan and the UK, in which no reference is made to the non-arbitrary or non-discriminatory nature of measures.

In addition, the BITs entered into with Thailand and with Vietnam do not refer to a requirement for the expropriation procedure to follow principles of due process. However, due process is an expression of the minimum standard under customary international law and of the requirement of fair and equitable treatment. In the context of expropriation, the inclusion of such a stipulation may therefore not add an independent requirement for the legality of an expropriation. See R. Dolzer and C. Schreuer, *Principles of International Investment Law*, Oxford (2012), Second Edition, p. 100.

124 The only exception is the BIT entered into with India, according to which compensation is to equate to the genuine value of the investment.

knowledge, or, in some instances, immediately before the expropriation measure occurred,[125] or "whichever is the earlier" of the two.[126]

Seven of the Philippines' publicly available BITs specify that, when the market value cannot be determined, compensation shall amount to the actual loss sustained,[127] that it shall be calculated based on generally recognised and/or equitable principles of valuation,[128] or that "it shall correspond to a reasonable amount".[129]

Approximately two thirds of the publicly available BITs provide that compensation in case of expropriation should be paid without delay,[130] or promptly. Most also stipulate that compensation should be "effectively realizable", "freely transferrable" and in a "freely convertible currency".[131]

Around one third of the publicly available BITs encourage payment of the compensation without delay by providing that interest is to be paid from the date of the expropriation to the date of payment.[132] The interest rates, where stipulated,[133] vary. The range of interest rates includes "the appropriate market rate of interest", "the prevailing commercial rate", "a commercial rate", "the LIBOR rate", "a fair and equitable rate" and "a commercial rate established on a market basis".

Interestingly, the BITs concluded with Austria, Germany, and Taiwan impose an obligation on the host State to make provision at, or prior to, the time of expropriation for the determination and payment of the compensation.

---

125 This is the case for the BITs entered into with Austria; the Netherlands; and Portugal.

126 This is the case for the BITs entered into with Canada; India; Iran; and Switzerland. The BIT entered into with Romania does not contain a specification concerning timing of the valuation.

127 This is the case for the BITs entered into with the Netherlands, the UK and Vietnam. The BIT entered into with Vietnam also refers to the actual loss sustained being calculated in accordance with a method agreed upon by the parties that is in conformity with internationally acknowledged evaluation methods.

128 This is the case for the BITs entered into with Argentina, Australia and Chile.
The BIT entered into with Romania stipulates that the compensation equivalent to the value of the investment is to be determined in accordance with recognised principles of valuation.

129 This is the case for the BIT entered into with Cambodia.

130 In some BITs, it is stipulated that compensation should be paid without "unreasonable" or "undue" delay.

131 Article 4(2) of the Philippines-Austria BIT; Article 4(2) of the Philippines-Germany BIT; and Article VI(1) of the Philippines-Taiwan BIT.

132 This is the case for the Philippines' BITs with Argentina; Austria; Chile; Denmark; Finland; India; Mongolia; Portugal; Romania; Russia; Switzerland; and Turkey.

133 The BITs entered into with Mongolia; Romania; and Switzerland do not specify a rate.

Finally, half of the publicly available BITs provide that the investor may have "its case", "the legality of the expropriation" or "the amount and the payment of its compensation" promptly reviewed by the host State's judicial bodies or competent authorities.[134]

Umbrella Clauses

Over half of the publicly available BITs include an obligation on the contracting parties to observe any obligation they have undertaken with regard to investments of an investor of the other contracting party, known as "umbrella clauses".[135]

Most Favoured Nation and National Treatment

All of the Philippines' publicly available BITs contain a "Most Favoured Nation" ("MFN") provision, *i.e.* they require that the treatment of the investments of investors from the other contracting State be no less favourable than that granted to nationals or companies of third States.

The MFN requirement extends to investments of foreign investors in all the relevant BITs, with the exception of the Philippines-Russia BIT.[136] In the vast majority of the BITs, such protection covers investors in addition to investments.[137]

The Philippines-BLEU BIT adds that the treatment shall in no case be less favourable than that recognised by international law.[138]

---

134 This is the case for the BITs entered into with Canada; Chile; China; the Czech Republic; Denmark; Finland; Germany; India; the Netherlands; Portugal; Romania; Taiwan; Thailand; Turkey; UK; Vietnam; and Austria. The latter BIT can be distinguished from the others in the sense that it is the only one which provides for review by an international arbitral tribunal in the expropriation clause itself.

135 This is the case for the BITs entered into with Austria; Bahrain; the BLEU, Denmark; Finland; Germany; Iran; Mongolia; Netherlands; Portugal; Switzerland; Thailand; and the UK.

136 Article III(2) of the Philippines-Russia BIT provides: "Each Contracting Party shall in its territory accord the investors of the other Contracting Party, as regards management, maintenance, use, enjoyment, or disposal of their investments, treatment not less favourable than that which it accords to investors of any third State."

137 This is the case for the BITs entered into with Australia; Austria; Bangladesh; Canada; the Czech Republic; Denmark; Finland; Germany; India; Italy; Korea; Myanmar; Pakistan; Portugal; Romania; Spain; Sweden; Switzerland; Thailand; the UK; and Vietnam.

138 Article III(3) of the Philippines-BLEU BIT.

Many of the Philippines' publicly available BITs exclude from the MFN provision, *inter alia*, benefits from international economic agreements and international agreements on taxation.[139]

Eight of the publicly available BITs require the host State to grant National Treatment to qualifying investments and, in certain cases, also specifically to the investors.[140] In other words, the host State is thereby required to treat qualifying investors and/or investments at least as favourably as their national investors and/or their investments.

6 *Repatriation of Capital and Compensation for Losses*

All the publicly available BITs signed by the Philippines at the time of writing contain provisions allowing for the free transfer of money by the investor, notably the repatriation by the investor of capital invested and investment returns, in freely convertible currency.

Moreover, except for a handful of them,[141] the Philippines' BITs contain a provision providing for the compensation for losses resulting from war or other armed conflict, revolution, a state of national emergency, revolt, civil disturbances, insurrection or riot or similar events in the territory of the host State.

7 *Investor-State Dispute Settlement*

The scope of the investor-State dispute resolution clauses in the Philippines' publicly available BITs is generally broad.

With the exception of the Philippines-Netherlands BIT and the Philippines-UK BIT, all publicly available BITs specifically state that disputes should be resolved amicably where possible. The majority of these BITs also impose a cooling off period of six months or, in fewer instances, three months,[142] before a claim may be brought.[143]

---

139 Certain BITs include other exceptions too, namely the BITs entered into with Argentina; Canada; Finland; the Netherlands; and Russia. Many of these relate to the Philippines' membership in the ASEAN.

140 This is the case for the BITs entered into with Austria; Canada; Chile; the Czech Republic; France; India; Iran; and Thailand.

141 The exceptions are the BITs entered into with Chile; China; and the Netherlands.

142 This is the case with regard to the BITs entered into with Bahrain; Chile; Finland; Thailand; and Turkey.

143 The exceptions, in addition to the Philippines-Netherlands BIT and the Philippines – UK BIT, are the BITs entered into with Australia and Taiwan.

All BITs provide for investment disputes to be referred to either the local courts of the host State, or to international arbitration.[144] As customary, the choice is normally that of the investor, though in some instances the clause is expressed to apply to either party to the dispute.

A few BITs include a fork-in-the-road provision, whereby the investor is required to select one recourse over, and at the exclusion of, any other.[145]

The BITs entered into with China, Denmark, Finland, Iran, the Netherlands, Taiwan, and the UK refer only to recourse to international arbitration, as opposed to domestic courts.

The BIT with Korea provides for a three-month period of time during which local remedies must be pursued before the dispute may be submitted to ICSID arbitration.[146] The Philippines-Austria BIT contains a similar provision, except that disputes may also be referred to "any applicable, previously agreed dispute-settlement procedures"[147] upon failure of amicable negotiations. A later provision of the same BIT stipulates that "[e]ach Contracting Party, by this Agreement irrevocably and unconditionally consents in advance to submit any such disputes to international arbitration, if the investor so chooses."[148]

The Philippines-Canada BIT is the only publicly available BIT that imposes objective conditions on the investor's right to arbitration, these conditions being that:

(a) the investor has consented in writing thereto;
(b) the investor has waived its right to initiate or continue any other proceedings in relation to the measure that is alleged to be in breach of this Agreement before the courts or tribunals of the Contracting Party concerned or in a dispute settlement procedure of any kind;
(c) if the matter involves taxation, the conditions specified in paragraph 5 of Article XII have been fulfilled; and
(d) not more than three years have elapsed from the date on which the investor first acquired, or should have first acquired, knowledge of

144 The Philippines-Taiwan BIT provides that disputes may be submitted to arbitration "on such terms and conditions as the disputing parties may agree" – Article X.

145 This applies to the BITs entered into with Argentina; the BLEU; Canada; Chile; and Turkey.

146 Article 9(2) of the Philippines-Korea BIT.

147 Article 9(2)(b) of the Philippines-Austria BIT.

148 Article 9(4) of the Philippines-Austria BIT.

> the alleged breach and knowledge that the investor has incurred loss or damage.[149]

The BIT with China limits the types of disputes that may submitted to arbitration (absent agreement of the parties) to disputes concerning matters of compensation due as a result of an expropriation. The relevant provision reads as follows:

> [T]he investor may submit the following dispute to international arbitration:
> a) a dispute on the matter of compensation mentioned in Article 4 of this Agreement and other matters related thereto;
> b) any other dispute on the matter of this Agreement agreed by the two parties to the dispute for submission to international arbitration.[150]

Recourse to international arbitration mostly consists of a choice between ICSID and UNCITRAL arbitration. Some BITs provide for only UNCITRAL arbitration, or UNCITRAL or ICSID in addition to another choice of arbitration.

Seven of the publicly available BITs also include the possibility of referring the dispute to conciliation.[151]

The dispute resolution clauses also sometimes contain other residual provisions, for example:

- stipulating the place of arbitration;
- regarding the costs of arbitration; and
- authorising the arbitral tribunal to order interim measures.

However, none of these provisions appear frequently, nor do they constitute a noticeable trend.

8 *State-to-State Dispute Settlement*

Provisions relating to State-to-State dispute resolution are fairly uniform across the Philippines' publicly available BITs.

149 Article XIII(3) of the Philippines-Canada BIT.

150 Article 10(2) of the Philippines-China BIT.

151 This is the case with regard to the BITs entered into with Australia; Cambodia; Germany; France; India; Italy; and the Netherlands.

All of the publicly available BITs encourage such disputes to be resolved in the first instance through negotiation or consultation through diplomatic channels.

Most of the publicly available BITs (the exceptions being the BITs entered into with Cambodia, Canada and the UK) impose a cooling-off period before the dispute may be submitted to arbitration. In most BITs, this cooling-off period is six months. The Philippines-Bahrain BIT and the Philippines-Iran BIT provide for a twelve-month cooling-off period.

All BITs provide that an inter-State dispute be referred to an *ad hoc* arbitral tribunal, and provide the rules and schedule for the appointment of the arbitrators.[152]

The relevant clause also often refers to the costs of arbitration, stating in some cases that they shall be borne equally by each party, and in others, such as the Philippines-Pakistan BIT, that whilst this is the general principle, the arbitral tribunal can decide otherwise.

9 *Additional Provisions*

A number of the Philippines' BITs include provisions concerning the right to employ foreign employees and consultants in connection with investment-related activities.[153]

In addition, a small number of the BITs contain a requirement for the host State to ensure transparency with regard to investment-related domestic laws.[154]

---

152 For instance, Article 10(3) and (4) of the Philippines-Korea BIT provides as follows:

"3. Such an arbitral tribunal shall be constituted for each individual case in the following way: Within two (2) months of the receipt of the request for arbitration, each Contracting Party shall appoint one member of the tribunal. Those two members shall then select a national of a Third State who, on approval by two Contracting Parties, shall be appointed Chairman of the tribunal. The Chairman shall be appointed within two (2) months from the date of appointment of the other two members.

4. If within the period specified in paragraph 3 of this Article the necessary appointments have not been made, either Contracting Party may, in the absence of any other Agreement, invite the President of the International Court of Justice to make any necessary appointments. If the President is a national of either Contracting Party, or if he is otherwise prevented from discharging the said function, the Vice-President shall be invited to make the necessary appointments. If the Vice-President is a national of either Contracting Party, or if he too is prevented from discharging the said function, the member of the International Court of Justice next in seniority who is not a national of either Contracting Party, shall be invited to make the necessary appointments."

153 See the BITS entered into with Australia; Bangladesh; Finland; France, Germany; India; Mongolia; Romania; Russia; Sweden; Switzerland; and Turkey.

154 See the BITS entered into with Australia; Canada; and Russia.

Certain BITs contain provisions relating to the amendment of the BIT in question, and the majority include a provision that provides for the contracting States to consult each other on matters affecting the implementation of the BIT.

10 *Notable Trends*

The majority of the Philippines BITs were entered into between the mid- and late-1990s. The most recently signed BIT dates back to November 2009, whilst the second most recent BIT was signed in November 2002.

Notable trends with regard to specific provisions of the BITs are detailed above. However, the hurdles associated with the definition of investors who are legal persons in the majority of the Philippines' BITs, and the strong tendency of a choice between domestic court proceedings and international arbitration in investor-State disputes, warrant particular attention. In addition, it is noteworthy that only the EPA contains a denial of benefits provision.[155]

IV **Multilateral Investment Related Treaties and Organizations to which Philippines is a Party**

1 *ASEAN*

The Philippines is a founding member of ASEAN, alongside Indonesia, Malaysia, Singapore and Thailand. At the time of writing, the Philippines is consequently a member of the following four regional free trade agreements that include an investment chapter:

- The ASEAN Comprehensive Investment Agreement;
- The ASEAN-Australia-New Zealand Free Trade Agreement;
- The Agreement on Investment under the Framework Agreement on Comprehensive Economic Cooperation among Governments of ASEAN and Republic of Korea; and
- The Agreement on Investment under the Framework Agreement on Comprehensive Economic Cooperation among Governments of ASEAN and China.

In addition, an Agreement on Comprehensive Economic Cooperation among Japan and Member States of the ASEAN was signed in April 2008, but is not

155 See Article 104 of the EPA.

yet in force. Similarly, an ASEAN-India Service Investment Agreement was signed in September 2014, but is not yet in force.[156]

2 *APEC*

The Philippines has been a member of the Asia-Pacific Economic Cooperation (APEC) since November 1989.

3 *MIGA*

The Philippines has been a member of the Multilateral Investment Guarantee Agency (MIGA) since February 1994.

V Multilateral Dispute Settlement Related Treaties

1 *ICSID Convention*

The Philippines signed the ICSID Convention on 26 September 1978, and it entered into force on 17 December 1978.

2 *The Convention on the Recognition and Enforcement of Foreign Arbitral Awards*

The Philippines signed the New York Convention on 10 June 1958, and ratified it on 11 October 1965, the instrument of ratification having been deposited on 6 July 1967. Nevertheless, the US Department of State has noted that "Philippine courts have shown a reluctance to abide by the process or its resulting decisions, meaning enforcing an arbitral award in the Philippines can take years."[157]

VI International Investment Arbitration Jurisprudence

With regard to the practical application of the investment protections available to foreign investors mentioned above, at the time of writing, the Philippines has been a party to four international investment disputes that are in the public domain. There are no known cases involving Filipino investors.

Of the four disputes involving the Philippines as the respondent host State, one is currently pending. Two of the four cases are related, the second

156 These agreements have been discussed in the chapter dedicated to ASEAN.

157 See United States Department of State, Investment Climate Statement 2014 for the Philippines, p. 7, available at http://www.state.gov/e/eb/rls/othr/ics/2014/index.htm.

claim brought by *Fraport AG Frankfurt Airport Services Worldwide* against the Philippines having resulted from a previously annulled arbitral award.

The cases are summarized below.

Baggerwerken Decloedt En Zoon v. Republic of the Philippines (ICSID Case No. ARB/11/27) (*"Baggerwerken v. Philippines"*)

Tribunal:	Pierre Tercier (President, Switzerland) Stanimir A. Alexandrov (Bulgaria) Christopher Thomas (Canada)
Case Initiated:	11 October 2011
Award:	n/a

Background Facts

The ICSID Case *Baggerwerken v. Philippines*, brought under the Philippines-BLEU BIT, involves a claim by a Belgian investor against the Philippines on the basis of the cancellation of a contract for the dredging and rehabilitation of Laguna de Bay, the largest lake in the Philippines. The case is pending, with each party filing observations to the other's statement of costs in June 2015.[158]

Fraport AG Frankfurt Airport Services Worldwide v. Republic of the Philippines (ICSID Case No. ARB/03/25) (*"Fraport v. Philippines"*)

Tribunal:	Yves Fortier (President, Canada) Bernardo M. Cremades (Spain) Michael Reisman (United States)
Case Initiated:	9 October 2003
Award:	16 August 2007
Annulment Committee:	Peter Tomka (President, Slovakia) Dominique Hascher (France) Campell Alan McLachlan (New Zealand)
Annulment Request Issued:	8 January 2008 (by claimants)
Decision on Annulment Rendered:	23 December 2010

158 See https://icsid.worldbank.org/apps/ICSIDWEB/cases/pages/casedetail.aspx?CaseNo=ARB/11/27&tab=PRD.

Background Facts

The first *Fraport* case, brought under the Philippines-Germany BIT, concerned the alleged expropriation of an investment in the Ninoy Aquino International Airport Passenger Terminal III.[159]

Fraport invested in a Philippine consortium, PIATCO, which had won a concession in 1997 to build and operate the airport terminal. It was PIATCO that was a party to the 25-year concession contract.[160]

Prior to the completion of the terminal, disputes arose between Fraport and PIATCO and the Philippine government. Following a ruling in 2003 from the Philippine Supreme Court that PIATCO's concession contract and related agreements were null and void under Philippine law, Fraport commenced ICSID arbitration, alleging expropriation of its investment.[161]

Annulment Proceedings

Fraport sought annulment of this decision, and was successful. The ICSID annulment committee annulled the arbitral award in its entirety on the basis that the First Tribunal had seriously departed from a fundamental rule of procedure pursuant to Article 52(1)(d) of the ICSID Convention by denying the applicant the right to be heard.[162]

Key Legal Outcomes

- Jurisdiction

The Philippines argued that Fraport had openly sought to evade nationality restrictions found in the Philippine Constitution and in the Anti-Dummy Law by means of "indirect" ownership and a series of secret shareholder agreements.[163]

The tribunal decided that Fraport "was consistently aware that the way it was structuring its investment in the Philippines was in violation of the Anti-Dummy Law and accordingly sought to keep those arrangements secret" on the basis of Fraport's own internal and contemporaneous documents.[164] It held that "Fraport knowingly and intentionally circumvented the Anti-

159 Para. 2 of the Fraport I Award.

160 *Ibid.*, para. 28.

161 *Ibid.*, para. 149 *et seq.* and para. 217.

162 Paras. 218 and Section VI of the Decision on Annulment.

163 Para. 287 of the Fraport I Award.

164 *Ibid.*, para. 332.

Dummy Law by means of secret shareholder agreements", and that "it cannot claim to have made an investment 'in accordance with law.'"[165]

The tribunal hence concluded that it lacked jurisdiction *ratione materiae* and dismissed the case accordingly.[166]

The arbitral award was accompanied by a dissenting opinion of one of the arbitrators, Dr. Bernardo Cremades, who found that the majority's approach to illegality was incorrect as a matter of principle, because PIATCO's shareholding remained "an asset accepted in accordance with Philippine law", and that "[a]s a matter of principle [...] the proper question is whether the kind of asset is legal under domestic law and, if so, the tribunal has jurisdiction and should move on to consider the merits."[167]

- Annulment

The *ad hoc* committee annulled the award on the basis of a serious departure from a fundamental rule of procedure as a result of denying the applicant the right to be heard.

Specifically, the annulment committee concluded that the First Tribunal had disregarded a domestic law finding in the form of a legal opinion from the Philippines Special Prosecutor from domestic court proceedings that was presented to the First Tribunal after the close of proceedings, together with other documentation that provided specific evidence on relevant municipal law issues for the first time in the proceedings.[168] According to this legal opinion, Fraport had not breached the terms of the Anti-Dummy Law.

The annulment committee found it to be of particular significance that the First Tribunal failed to order the parties to comment on the scope and implications of the factual evidence used by the Special Prosecutor. It held that this failure alone constituted a serious departure of a fundamental rule of procedure, triggering grounds for annulment under Article 52(1)(d) of the ICSID Convention.[169]

It also found it to be compelling that the First Tribunal did not invite comments on the legal effect of the domestic legal opinion. The committee noted that under international law, the First Tribunal was bound to give consideration

165 *Ibid.*, para. 401.
166 *Ibid.*, paras. 401 and 404.
167 Paras. 13 and 40 of the Dissenting Opinion.
168 Paras. 211 and 218 of the Decision on Annulment.
169 *Ibid.*, paras. 225, 227–230.

to domestic decisions interpreting the Anti-Dummy Law, particularly given that none of the tribunal members was an expert in Philippine law.[170]

The committee concluded that the "departure was one which materially prejudiced Fraport, in view of the Tribunal's adverse findings both as to the question of fact relating to the record before the Prosecutor and as to the relevance of the Prosecutor's Resolution for the question of law concerning the construction of the Anti-Dummy Law (irrespective of what the proper construction of that law might finally be). Each of these related specifically to evidence which had been tendered to the Tribunal after its closure of the proceedings. Each was an essential step in the Tribunal's reasoning, leading to the decision in its Award to accept the Philippines' objection to ICSID jurisdiction and to dismiss Fraport's claim".[171]

Fraport's secondary claims for annulment, based on the alleged manifest excess of power and failure to state reasons of the First Tribunal, were rejected.[172]

The decision of the annulment committee, in addition to being one of only a few successful ICSID annulment requests to date, highlights the importance of inviting the parties to comment on new evidence that is pertinent to the ultimate decision of the tribunal, even if this new evidence has arisen after the formal close of proceedings.

Fraport AG Frankfurt Airport Services Worldwide v. Republic of the Philippines (ICSID Case No. ARB/11/12) (*"Fraport v. Philippines II"*)

Tribunal:	Piero Bernardini (President, Italy) Stanimir A. Alexandrov (Bulgaria) Albert Jan Van Den Berg (Netherlands)
Case Initiated:	27 April 2011
Award:	10 December 2014

Background Facts

This case, brought under the Philippines-Germany BIT, constitutes the second claim brought by the German multinational Fraport against the Philippines.

The dispute concerned the same alleged expropriation of a concession contract for the construction and operation of a new terminal at the Ninoy Aquino

170 *Ibid.*, paras. 236 and 244–245.

171 *Ibid.*, para. 246.

172 *Ibid.*, paras. 118 and 280.

International Airport Passenger Terminal III in Manila, further to the first airport privatisation in Asia.[173]

Procedural Background

The claim was brought following the annulment, in 2010, of an arbitral award rendered against Fraport in 2007 in relation to a first claim concerning the same project.[174]

As discussed, the first claim had been dismissed by the majority of the tribunal (the "First Tribunal") on the basis of lack of jurisdiction *ratione materiae*. This finding centred on the conclusion of the First Tribunal that Fraport's investment fell outside of the scope of the BIT because there had been no investment "in accordance with law", as required by the treaty. Specifically, the First Tribunal held that Fraport had acted to circumvent the Philippines Anti-Dummy Law, which limits foreign ownership of the capital of a public utility to 40%.[175]

In 2010, an ICSID *ad hoc* annulment committee decided that the 2007 award should be annulled on the ground that the First Tribunal had seriously departed from a fundamental rule of procedure by denying Fraport the right to be heard on new evidence submitted on Philippines law.

Key Legal Outcomes

- Award

The arbitral award in the second case was rendered on 10 December 2014. Like the First Tribunal, the tribunal hearing the second case (the "Second Tribunal") rejected jurisdiction over the claim on the basis of lack of jurisdiction *ratione materiae*, holding that the underlying investment had not been made in compliance with Philippine law because Fraport was in breach of the Anti-Dummy Law. The Philippines was awarded USD 5 million for costs.[176]

In particular, the Second Tribunal agreed with the Philippines' interpretation of Article 1 of the Philippines-Germany BIT by considering that it limits the scope of protected investments to investments that are lawful in accordance with the host State's laws and regulations at the time the investments

173 ICSID Case No. ARB/11/12, *Award*, 10 December 2014 ("Fraport II Award"), para. 6.

174 ICSID Case No. ARB/03/25, *Decision on the Application for Annulment of Fraport AG Frankfurt Airport Services Worldwide*, 23 December 2010 ("Decision on Annulment").

175 ICSID Case No. ARB/03/25, *Award*, 16 August 2007 ("Fraport I Award"), para. 332.

176 Para. 530 of the Fraport II Award.

were made.[177] The Second Tribunal therefore analysed the legality of the Fraport's investment at the time it was made.[178]

The Second Tribunal disagreed with Fraport's objection that the Anti-Dummy Law was not applicable because the project did not concern the operation of a public utility, on the basis that, even if the construction itself was not of public utility, the companies investing in it were subject to the Anti-Dummy Law as proponents of a Build-Operate-Transfer ("BOT") project.[179] The Second Tribunal recalled the wide scope of the Anti-Dummy Law, according to which it applies to the intervention by any person in the management, operation, administration or control of an activity subject to nationality restrictions,[180] as well as to any person freely and consciously engaging in an act which constitutes aiding, assisting, planning or carrying out a prohibited act.[181]

The Second Tribunal furthermore considered that all three required elements to the violation of the Anti-Dummy Law were fulfilled: (1) the investment vehicle, PIATCO, was a person or entity possessing the right to engage in an activity subject to nationality restrictions; (2) this entity permitted an unqualified person, Fraport, to intervene in the management, operation, administration or control of that nationalised activity; and (3) Fraport aided PIATCO in planning and carrying out such an intervention.[182] The Second Tribunal found that, as a matter of fact, Fraport thus knowingly and intentionally violated the Anti-Dummy Law at the time of its initial investment by entering into agreements securing its powers of decision and by appointing selected persons to managerial positions.[183]

The Second Tribunal thus found that Fraport's investment violated the Anti-Dummy Law and that it was therefore illegal and could not benefit from protection offered by the BIT. Hence, it concluded that it had no jurisdiction *rationae materiae*.[184]

The Second Tribunal however dismissed the Philippines' contentions that Fraport had proceeded to the investment via fraud and/or corruption[185] and that Fraport knew of the misrepresentation made by PIATCO to obtain the concession award.[186]

---

177 *Ibid.*, para. 331.
178 *Ibid.*, para. 333.
179 *Ibid.*, paras. 399–400.
180 *Ibid.*, paras. 410 and 412.
181 *Ibid.*, paras. 420–423 and 427.
182 *Ibid.*, paras. 442–443.
183 *Ibid.*, paras. 444, 458 and 462–463.
184 *Ibid.*, paras. 467–468.
185 *Ibid.*, paras. 479 and 481.
186 *Ibid.*, para. 519.

- Procedural Order No. 1

Another interesting legal outcome in relation to this case is embodied in the first procedural order that was issued by the Second Tribunal.[187] In Procedural Order No. 1, the Second Tribunal considered, *inter alia*, the effect of the annulment of an arbitral award in a previous arbitration between the parties.

Fraport argued that the annulled arbitral award was void in its entirety, whilst the Philippines argued that the scope of the annulment was limited to the parts of the annulled award "tainted by an alleged procedural violation".[188] The central questions were therefore whether any portions of the annulled award remained binding on the parties and how the records in the first case should be treated.

The Second Tribunal found that the annulled award had been annulled in its entirety, and denied the Philippines' request to consider certain paragraphs binding.[189] It concluded that, in the absence of any qualifications in the *dispositif* of the Annulment Decision, attempts to determine which issues were *res judicata* and which issues may be re-litigated, would be likely to expose its own decision to a request for annulment.[190] It also found that the records in the first case should be admitted into the records of the second case, subject to certain provisos, and established guidelines for the treatment of the evidence of witnesses and experts who gave testimony in the first case.[191]

SGS Société Générale de Surveillance SA v. Republic of the Philippines (ICSID Case No. ARB/02/6) (*"SGS v. Philippines"*)

Tribunal:	Ahmed Sadek El-Kosheri (President, Egypt) Antonio Crivellaro (Italy) James Crawford (Australia)
Case Initiated:	6 June 2002
Award Rendered:	11 April 2008

187 ICSID Case No. ARB/11/12, *Procedural Order No. 1*, 17 May 2012 ("Procedural Order No. 1"), available at http://opil.ouplaw.com/view/10.1093/law:iic/551-2012.case.1/IIC551(2012)D.pdf.

188 *Ibid.*, paras. 16–17 and 18–19.

189 *Ibid.*, para. 85.

190 *Ibid.*, para. 56.

191 *Ibid.*, para. 74 and 76–78.

Background Facts

In August 1991, the Swiss company SGS Société Générale de Surveillance S.A. ("SGS") concluded an agreement with the Philippines regarding the provision of comprehensive import supervision services aimed at improving the customs clearance and control processes of the Philippines (the "Contract").[192]

The Contract was extended three times, the final extension running from 31 December 1999 to 31 March 2000, when the Philippines government discontinued SGS's services under the Contract.[193]

SGS subsequently claimed for unpaid sums under the Contract, amounting to approximately USD 140 million plus interest.[194]

After unsuccessful settlement discussions, SGS commenced ICSID proceedings on the basis of the Switzerland – Philippines BIT. SGS alleged that the Philippines had breached the treaty by refusing to pay the amounts claimed under the Contract; by failing to accord SGS fair and equitable treatment; by unlawfully expropriating SGS's property; and by breaching the umbrella clause contained in the treaty,[195] according to which: "Each Contracting Party shall observe any obligation it has assumed with regard to specific investments in its territory by investors of the other Contracting Party."[196]

The Philippines' position was that the tribunal lacked jurisdiction over the matter, because there was no "investment" in its territory as required by the BIT; that the dispute was purely contractual in character; and that the issues in dispute were governed by the contractual dispute resolution clause, which referred the parties to Philippines courts, and not to international arbitration.[197]

The tribunal held that SGS had made an investment in the territory of the Philippines and that both the umbrella clause and the broad dispute resolution clause in the BIT gave it jurisdiction to hear the contract claims. However, the tribunal also held that the contract claims were inadmissible because priority was to be given to the forum selection clause in the Contract. The tribunal hence stayed the proceedings in favour of the dispute resolution forum specified in the Contract.[198]

---

192 ICSID Case No. ARB/02/6, Decision of the Tribunal on Objections to Jurisdiction, 29 January 2004 ("SGS Decision on Jurisdiction"), para. 13.

193 *Ibid.*, para. 14.

194 *Ibid.*, para. 15.

195 *Ibid.*, para. 16.

196 Article X(2) of the Switzerland – Philippines BIT.

197 Para. 17 of the SGS Decision on Jurisdiction.

198 *Ibid.*, para. 169. The stay was lifted on 17 December 2007 by order of the tribunal (*Order of the Tribunal on Further Proceedings*).

A settlement was then agreed by the parties and recorded at their request in the form of an arbitral award dated 11 April 2008, pursuant to ICSID Arbitration Rule 43(2).[199]

Key Legal Outcomes

SGS argued that the Philippines breached the umbrella clause contained in the BIT by failing to pay for SGS's services under the Contract.

The tribunal agreed with SGS. It held, with regard to the wording of the umbrella clause, that it meant what it said:

> [The umbrella clause] uses the mandatory term "shall", in the same way as substantive Articles III–VI. The term "any obligation" is capable of applying to obligations arising under national law, for example those arising from a contract; indeed, it would normally be under its own law that a host State would assume obligations "with regard to specific investments in its territory by investors of the other Contracting Party". Interpreting the actual text of Article X(2), it will in the future assume, with regard to specific investments covered by the BIT. Article X(2) was adopted within the framework of the BIT, and has to be construed as intended to be effective within that framework. The object and purpose of the BIT supports an effective interpretation of Article X(2). The BIT is a treaty for the promotion and reciprocal protection of investments.[200]

Critics of *SGS v. Philippines* argue that wide interpretations of umbrella clauses risk elevating commitments made by States to investors under contracts or national laws to commitments enforceable under international law.[201]

However, as noted above, although the tribunal accepted jurisdiction under the umbrella clause over the contract claims, it decided to give effect to the

199 ICSID Case No. ARB/03/25, Award embodying the parties' settlement agreement, 11 April 2008. See https://icsid.worldbank.org/apps/icsidweb/cases/Pages/casedetail.aspx?caseno=ARB/02/6&tab=PRO.

200 Para. 115 of the SGS Decision on Jurisdiction. The tribunal also set out a number of other arguments to support its findings. See, for example, also paras. 119 and 120 of the SGS Decision on Jurisdiction.

201 See, for example, James Crawford, *Treaty and Contract in Investment Arbitration*, (2008) 24(3) Arbitration International 351; Jonathan Potts, *Stabilizing the Role of Umbrella Clauses in Bilateral Investment Treaties: Intent, Reliance, and Internationalization*, (2011) 51:4 Virginia Journal of International Law 1005; and Stephan Schill, "Enabling Private Ordering: Function, Scope and Effect of Umbrella Clauses in International Investment Treaties", (2009) 18 *Minnesota Journal of International Law* 1.

forum selection clause in the Contract, according to which the local Philippine courts had exclusive jurisdiction over contractual disputes. The tribunal noted that "a binding exclusive jurisdiction clause in a contract should be respected, unless overridden by another valid provision".[202]

The tribunal found that the BIT did not override the forum selection clause in the Contract, on the basis that generic provisions such as the umbrella clause are generally not interpreted as overriding specific provisions of particular contracts freely negotiated between the parties.[203] In a dissenting opinion, arbitrator Professor Antonio Crivellaro disagreed with this part of the decision, finding instead that the tribunal should have proceeded to issue a decision on the merits, based on the broad scope of both the umbrella clause and the dispute resolution provision in the BIT.[204]

The decision is classed as a landmark one, and is one of the main cases relied on by investors seeking to bring a claim on the basis of an umbrella clause. It came not long after the arbitral award in *SGS v. Pakistan*, another claim brought by SGS on the basis of the Switzerland-Pakistan BIT, based on similar facts and legal issues, and involving SGS performing the same type of services for Pakistan.[205] However, the tribunal in that case took a more restrictive approach to the umbrella clause and the dispute resolution clause. This has led to some uncertainty as to the scope and effect of umbrella clauses in investment treaties, and both decisions have since been relied on in different subsequent awards.

In addition, the tribunal applied a broad interpretation to the term "investment", holding that the Contract, which was for the provisions of services performed mostly outside of the Philippines, qualified as an investment

---

202 Para. 138 of the SGS Decision on Jurisdiction.

203 The tribunal thereby also addressed concerns voiced by the tribunal in *SGS v. Pakistan*, referred to further below, regarding the impact of broad interpretations of umbrella clauses on existing forum selection clauses in investor-State contracts.

204 Antonio Crivellaro, Para. 11 of the Declaration (Dissenting Opinion) accompanying the *SGS* Decision on Jurisdiction.

The broad scope of the dispute resolution provision in the BIT was recognised by the tribunal as a whole. In the award, the majority held that the phrase "disputes with respect to investments" could apply to an expropriation claim under the BIT as well as to a dispute arising from an investment contract such as the SGS-Philippines Contract. Notably, the tribunal stated that "the phrase 'disputes with respect to investments' naturally includes contractual disputes" (para. 132 of the *SGS* Decision on Jurisdiction).

205 *SGS Société Générale de Surveillance S.A. v. Islamic Republic of Pakistan*, ICSID Case No. ARB/01/13, Decision of the Tribunal on Objections to Jurisdiction, 6 August 2003.

made in the territory of the host State. This was because SGS's liaison offices in the Philippines were considered by the tribunal to be a "substantial and non-severable aspect of the overall service".[206] The tribunal also found that there "was no distinct or separate investment elsewhere than in the territory of the Philippines but a single integrated process of inspection arranged through the Manila Liaison Office, itself unquestionably an investment 'in the territory of' the Philippines".[207] In other words, according to the tribunal's interpretation of the wording of the BIT, even activities that are primarily carried out abroad may be covered under a similarly worded BIT, provided they are connected to activities in the host State's territory.

VII Outlook: Anticipated Developments

Critics of the Philippines' national investment framework continue to comment that, over time, reform to allow increased international direct investment has been blocked by different private interests and that, as a result, the Philippines has fallen behind the long list of other Asian economies attracting substantial foreign direct investment. Further, it is reported that the government of Benigno S. Aquino III had ruled out any attempts at constitutional change to lift constitutionally-enshrined limitations to foreign investment, such as those prohibiting ownership of land by foreign citizens.[208]

However, legislative developments during the period prior to the time of writing indicate that at least several aspects of the national framework in the Philippines are in flux.

Furthermore, 2013 saw negative press with regard to new rules on foreign investment drafted by the Securities and Exchange Commission upon request of the Supreme Court of the Philippines. These new rules would limit access by foreign investors to the Philippine economy because the foreign ownership provisions contained therein will require entities with foreign ownership to reorganise their corporate structures by either creating a new class for shares that are held by foreigners, or by reducing the holdings of foreign

---

206 Para. 102 of the *SGS* Decision on Jurisdiction.

207 *Ibid.*, para. 112.

208 *Philippines Could Be Crippled by New FDI Rules*, Asia Sentinel, available at http://www.asiasentinel.com/econ-business/philippines-could-be-crippled-by-new-fdi-rules/.

shareholders.[209] There is no evidence on the website of the Securities and Exchange Commission that these rules have been promulgated however.[210]

As such, the current climate indicates that investors should continue to monitor closely national developments in particular.

---

209 *Ibid.*

210 See http://www.sec.gov.ph/laws/laws.html.

CHAPTER 9

Singapore[1]

I Introduction

The World Bank's Doing Business 2015 report ranked Singapore as the easiest country in which to do business. The Global Competitiveness Report 2014–2015 by the World Economic Forum ranked Singapore as the second-most competitive economy globally and first on its enabling trade index.[2] Singapore also topped the Asia Pacific Investment Climate Index[3] in 2014 for the third consecutive year.

Singapore's foreign direct investment ("FDI") amounted to SGD853.3 billion as at end 2013, an increase of 12.9 percent from 2012. Financial and insurance services, manufacturing and wholesale and retail trade were the sectors with the highest amount of FDI. Nearly half of all FDI in Singapore were in the financial and insurances services. The corresponding share in manufacturing and wholesale and retail trade were 17.7 percent and 17.1 percent respectively. Europe and Asia have been the top sources of FDI in Singapore. As at end 2013, European investors contributed 34.8 percent (or SGD296.7 billion) of total FDI while Asian investors accounted for 24.8 percent (or SGD212 billion). There were also significant direct investments from South and Central America and the Caribbean (22.2 percent or SGD189.1 billion) and North America (14.2 percent or SGD120.8 billion).[4]

The Singapore government is strongly committed to maintaining a free market but also takes a leadership role in planning Singapore's economic development, with a combination of both foreign investments and investments

---

1 This chapter has been drafted by Ms Charis Tan and Ms Kate Lan, Eversheds LLP, Singapore. The editors are also grateful to Ms Davinia Aziz of Singapore's Attorney General Chambers for her valuable comments.

2 United States of America Department of State, *Singapore Investment Climate Statement 2015* (June 2015), available at http://www.state.gov/documents/organization/241949.pdf.

3 Which evaluates and ranks 20 Asia Pacific countries according to six criteria: rule of law, openness to international trade and business, taxation, corruption, political stability, and fiscal and monetary administration; see http://www.vrienspartners.com/wp-content/uploads/2014/04/VP-Asia-Pacific-Investment-Climate-Index-2014.pdf.

4 Department of Statistics Singapore, *Foreign Equity Investment in Singapore 2013*, available at: http://www.singstat.gov.sg/docs/default-source/default-document-library/publications/publications_and_papers/investment/fei2013.pdf.

 | DOI 10.1163/9789004335257_011

through government-linked corporations underpinning Singapore's open and heavily trade-dependent economy.[5] Singapore has undertaken a number of international obligations concerning foreign investment by virtue of its membership in various bilateral and multilateral treaties with investment protection provisions. The protection afforded to investors under these agreements, coupled with the established legal and judicial regime in Singapore, provide a stable investment climate, as a consequence of which investors have propelled Singapore to be one of the top investment destinations for foreigners both in the region and globally.

II Singapore's National Arbitration and Investment Legislation

1 *Singapore's Arbitration Legislation and Institutions*

Singapore's Arbitration Law[6]

Two separate regimes govern international and domestic arbitrations in Singapore under the International Arbitration Act (Chapter 143A) ("IAA") and the Arbitration Act (Chapter 10) ("AA") respectively.

Part II of the IAA and the UNCITRAL Model Law on International Commercial Arbitration[7] ("Model Law") apply to all international arbitrations seated in Singapore, unless parties to an arbitration agreement have expressly agreed that the Model Law or Part II of the IAA shall not apply to the arbitration, or that the AA shall apply to the arbitration instead.[8]

Briefly, an arbitration is international if at least one of the parties to the arbitration agreement has its place of business outside Singapore, the place of arbitration is different from the State in which the parties have their places of business, the obligations to be performed or subject-matter of the dispute is most closely connected to a place different from where the parties have their places of business, or the parties have expressly agreed that the subject-matter of the arbitration agreement relates to more than one country.[9] In short,

5 United States of America Department of State, *Singapore Investment Climate Statement 2015* (June 2015), available at http://www.state.gov/documents/organization/241949.pdf.

6 See also *Arbitration in Singapore, A Practical Guide* (Sweet & Maxwell, 2014) ("*Arbitration in Singapore*") at pp. 40–41.

7 As adopted by the United Nations Commission on International Trade Law on 21st June 1985. It is incorporated in the IAA as the First Schedule of the IAA, and with the exception of Chapter VIII thereof, has the force of law in Singapore under section 3 of the IAA.

8 IAA, section 15.

9 IAA, section 5(2).

besides those arbitrations where the parties are located in Singapore, the transaction took place in Singapore and all dealings between the parties were carried out in Singapore, most arbitrations would be international and the IAA would apply.

A number of rules for the conduct of international arbitral proceedings are set out in Chapter V of the Model Law. Subject to the provisions of the Model Law, parties are free to agree on the procedure to be followed by the tribunal in conducting the proceedings, including the adoption of institutional rules.[10] Such rules agreed to or adopted by the parties, whether before or after the commencement of the arbitration, shall apply and be given effect to the extent that they are not inconsistent with relevant provisions of the Model Law or Part II of the IAA which the parties cannot derogate from.[11]

On the other hand, the AA is applicable to any arbitration where the place of arbitration is Singapore and where the arbitration is not an "international" arbitration as defined in section 5(2) of the IAA. Part VII of the AA sets out the general duties and power of the tribunal as well as the rules of procedure in the arbitration (*e.g.* pleadings, hearings and written proceedings, consolidation of proceedings and concurrent hearings, appointment of experts, witnesses and the court's powers exercisable in support of arbitral proceedings). Subject to the provisions set out in the AA, parties are free to agree on the procedure to be followed by the tribunal in conducting the domestic arbitral proceedings,[12] including the adoption of institutional rules.

The key difference between the IAA and AA regimes relates to the extent of court intervention in the arbitral proceedings, with the court retaining more discretion and powers in domestic arbitrations as compared to international arbitrations, for example, in applications for stay of court of proceedings in favour of arbitration and recourse against awards.

Singapore's Arbitral Institutions and Rules[13]

The main arbitral institution in Singapore is the Singapore International Arbitration Centre ("SIAC"). That being so, it is also common for arbitrations seated in Singapore to be administered by other institutions such as the International Chamber of Commerce International Court of Arbitration ("ICC") and the London Court of International Arbitration ("LCIA"). Apart from administering arbitrations under its own arbitration rules, SIAC also

10 Model Law, Article 19.

11 IAA, section 15A(1).

12 IAA, section 23(1).

13 See also *Arbitration in Singapore* at pp. 241–243.

administers arbitrations conducted under other rules, such as the UNCITRAL Arbitration Rules. The SIAC arbitration rules can be used for both international and domestic arbitrations.[14]

SIAC administered arbitrations have gained momentous popularity in the last decade, particularly in the region. The total number of new cases handled by SIAC more than doubled from 78 in 2004 to 222 in 2014.[15] The tremendous growth in SIAC administered arbitrations is marked by multiple revisions to the SIAC arbitration rules since its first edition was published in 1991.

The current version of the rules came into force on 1 April 2013, and constitutes the 5th edition of the SIAC rules.[16] Some of the more significant changes to the SIAC arbitration rules include provisions for an expedited procedure, the appointment of an emergency arbitrator, and the establishment of a new Court of Arbitration charged with oversight of case administration and the appointment of arbitrators. With this change in its structure, the SIAC has separated the body responsible for conduct of its business functions from that responsible for the conduct of its substantive legal functions. The primary changes in the 2013 edition of the SIAC arbitration rules relate to the powers and duties of the new Court of Arbitration. It bears noting that the revisions made to the SIAC arbitration rules often reflect changes made in the prevailing legislation (*i.e.* IAA or AA) or significant judicial pronouncements relating to arbitration in Singapore. For example, pursuant to Rule 24(n) of the SIAC Arbitration Rules,[17] the tribunal has the power to decide any issue not expressly or impliedly raised in the parties' submissions, as long as such issue was clearly brought to the notice of the other party and that other party had been given adequate opportunity to respond. This amendment was possibly inserted in light of the case of *PT Prima International Development v Kempinski*

14 Note that on 1 February 2016 the SIAC commenced public consultation on draft SIAC Investment Arbitration Rules, see: http://siac.org.sg/images/stories/press_release/Public%20Consultation%20on%20Draft%20SIAC%20Investment%20Arbitration%20Rules_1February2016.pdf (last accessed on 1 June 2016). However, at the time of writing, SIAC has yet to formally release its Investment Arbitration Rules and the text of the final version of such rules is not publicly available.

15 See http://www.siac.org.sg/2014-11-03-13-33-43/facts-figures/statistics.

16 Note that the SIAC released the sixth edition of its Arbitration Rules on 27 May 2016 ("SIAC Rules 2016"), see: http://siac.org.sg/images/stories/press_release/SIAC%20Announces%20Release%20of%20its%20Arbitration%20Rules%202016_27%20May%202016.pdf (last accessed on 1 June 2016). However, the text of the SIAC Rules 2016 was not publicly available at the time of writing.

17 Arbitration Rules of the Singapore International Arbitration Centre SIAC Rules (5th Edition, 1 April 2013).

Hotels SA and other appeals,[18] where the Court of Appeal held that it was within the tribunal's jurisdiction to decide the points in contention, notwithstanding that they were not specifically pleaded, particularly since the parties had had notice of those points and had ample opportunity to address them. This example is reflective of the pro-arbitration policy in Singapore, that has led to the significant development of arbitration in the country, particularly in the last few years.

Singapore's Courts and Arbitration

Arbitration-related cases are handled by the Supreme Court of Singapore, before the High Court at first instance or the apex Court of Appeal on appeal. In general, Singapore has adopted a very supportive environment for enforcement of international arbitration agreements and arbitral awards in line with its pro-arbitration philosophy and the Singapore courts' recognition of the principle of the finality of the arbitral process.

The Singapore courts have powers to stay court proceedings in favour of arbitration,[19] to grant interim measures[20] and to enforce or set aside arbitral awards,[21] among others. However, the extent of the courts' powers are much more limited in international arbitrations as compared to domestic arbitrations. As an example, when an application is made to stay court proceedings to enforce an international arbitration agreement, it is mandatory for the court to stay the proceedings in favour of arbitration unless it is satisfied that the arbitration agreement is null and void, inoperative or incapable of being performed.[22] In contrast, the court is accorded far greater discretion under the AA when determining whether to stay court proceedings in favour of a domestic arbitration.[23] As another example, while a party to domestic arbitral proceedings may appeal to the court on a question of law arising out of an award made in the proceedings, an award arising out of an international arbitration may only be set aside by the court based on the limited grounds set out in the IAA[24] and Model Law.[25]

18 [2012] 4 SLR 98.

19 See IAA, section 6 and AA, section 6.

20 See IAA, section 12A and AA, section 31.

21 See IAA, sections 19 and 24; Model Law, Article 34; and AA, Part IX.

22 IAA, section 6.

23 AA, section 6.

24 Section 24.

25 Article 34.

Awards made in international arbitrations are also enforceable under the Convention on the Recognition and Enforcement of Foreign Arbitral Awards Concluded at New York on 10 June 1958 ("New York Convention"). There are broadly speaking two types of arbitral awards enforceable in Singapore: international arbitral awards made in Singapore ("domestic international awards") and foreign awards.

A domestic international award can be enforced through section 19 of the IAA. An application under section 19 of the IAA to enforce a domestic international award can be made pursuant to Order 69A Rule 6 of the Rules of Court. The grounds upon which the court can refuse enforcement of a domestic international arbitral award were considered by the Court of Appeal in the case of *PT First Media TBK (formerly known as PT Broadband Multimedia TBK) v Astro Nusantara International BV and others and another appeal.*[26] The Court of Appeal held that a losing party in an arbitration can either take active or positive steps to invalidate the award or, passively resist the enforcement of an award where and when the award is sought to be enforced. In other words, a party can actively challenge the award pursuant to Article 34 of the Model Law and/or section 24 of IAA and/or Article 16(3) of the Model Law (for a ruling on jurisdiction), or wait for the enforcement stage to resist enforcement of the award under Article 36 of the Model Law.

Foreign arbitral awards (*i.e.*, awards rendered by tribunals seated outside Singapore) may be enforced in Singapore pursuant to Part III of the IAA. A foreign award may be enforced in a Singapore court in the same manner as a domestic international award. The losing party may resist enforcement of the award on the grounds set out in section 31 of the IAA (which encapsulates Article 36 of the Model Law). Section 30 of the IAA sets out the evidential burden of a party who seeks to enforce a foreign award in the Singapore High Court.

2 *Singapore's Investment Laws*

Singapore aggressively pursues foreign investors, both individuals and corporates, through the Economic Development Board ("EDB"), the lead government agency set up under the auspices of the Ministry of Trade and Industry charged with planning and executing strategies to enhance Singapore's position as a global business centre. In recent years, EDB has been focussing on securing major investments in high value-added manufacturing and

---

26 [2014] 1 *SLR* 372.

service activities as part of a strategy to replace labour-intensive, low value-added activities that have migrated offshore.[27]

Singapore's proactive strategy in attracting foreign investment is evident in the various schemes and incentives that have been put in place to encourage foreign individuals and businesses to invest in Singapore. Foreign individuals who wish to set up and operate a business in Singapore may do so via the Global Investor Scheme which has been designed to facilitate and streamline the process for foreigners who are keen on setting up business operations in Singapore.[28] EDB also works with partners such as business associations, country chambers, banks, accounting and legal firms, to attract international companies to expand their footprints to Singapore.[29] Eligible businesses with substantive plans to grow through conducting high value activities in Singapore may also apply for various programmes and schemes to obtain grants, allowances and tax incentives.[30]

With the exception of restrictions in the financial services, professional services and media sectors, Singapore maintains a predominantly open investment regime. Singapore's legal framework and public policies are generally favourable toward foreign investors. Foreign investors are not required to enter into joint ventures or cede management control to local interests, and local and foreign investors are subject to the same laws in Singapore. Apart from regulatory requirements in some sectors, the government screens investment proposals only to determine eligibility for various incentives programmes.[31] Singapore places no restrictions on reinvestment or repatriation of earnings or capital.[32] It has an efficient judicial system which upholds the sanctity of

---

27 Ministry of Trade and Industry, *Report of the Economic Strategies Committee* (1 February 2010), available at https://www.mti.gov.sg/ResearchRoom/Pages/Report-of-the-Economic-Strategies-Committee.aspx; Ministry of Finance, *Committee on the Future Economy Sets Up Five Subcommittees* (January 2016), available at http://www.mof.gov.sg/newsreader/articleid/1570/parentId/59/year/2016?category=Press%20Releases; United States of America Department of State, *Singapore Investment Climate Statement 2015* (June 2015), available at http://www.state.gov/documents/organization/241949.pdf.

28 See https://www.edb.gov.sg/content/edb/en/why-singapore/ready-to-invest/setting-up/entering-singapore.html.

29 See https://www.edb.gov.sg/content/edb/en/why-singapore/ready-to-invest/partners.html.

30 See https://www.edb.gov.sg/content/edb/en/why-singapore/ready-to-invest/incentives-for-businesses.html.

31 United States of America Department of State, *Singapore Investment Climate Statement 2015* (June 2015), available at http://www.state.gov/documents/organization/241949.pdf.

32 *Ibid.*

contracts and enforces decisions effectively.[33] Exceptions to Singapore's general openness to foreign investment exist in telecommunications, broadcasting, the domestic news media, financial services, legal, and other professional services and property ownership.[34] Special licences are needed for some businesses such as banking, insurance and stock broking, as well as for the manufacture of goods such as cigars and firecrackers.[35] Any individual, firm or corporation that carries out business for a foreign company must be registered with the Accounting & Corporate Regulatory Authority in Singapore.[36] Singapore law generally does not prohibit articles of incorporation of a company to include shareholding limits that restrict ownership in corporations by foreign persons.

III Singapore's Bilateral Investment Treaties

1 *Overview*

Since 1966 when Singapore concluded its first investment guarantee agreement with the United States, the island-State has signed at least 48 agreements related to foreign investment.[37]

Based on publicly available information at the time of writing, of those 48 agreements, two have been terminated,[38] seven are not in force,[39] and 39 are in force.[40]

---

33 *Ibid.*

34 See https://www.edb.gov.sg/content/edb/en/why-singapore/ready-to-invest/incentives-for-businesses.html.

35 See https://www.edb.gov.sg/content/edb/en/why-singapore/ready-to-invest/setting-up/registration.html.

36 *Ibid.*

37 See the analysis of Singapore's bilateral investment treaties in: Chester Brown (ed.), *Commentaries on Selected Model Investment Treaties*, Jean Ho, "Singapore", p. 623, (Oxford University Press, 2013).

38 The Singapore-Indonesia BIT, dated 28 August 1990, and the Singapore-Peru BIT, dated 27 February 2003, have been terminated. Another Singapore-Indonesia BIT, dated 16 February 2005, has since been concluded and is in force.

39 The Singapore-Burkina Faso BIT, the Singapore-Colombia BIT, the Singapore-Côte d'Ivoire BIT, the Singapore-Ukraine BIT, the Singapore-United Arab Emirates BIT ("Singapore-UAE BIT"), the Singapore-Zimbabwe BIT and the Singapore-Iran BIT. The latest BIT to be signed, the Singapore-Iran BIT was signed on 29 February 2016 in Tehran, Iran. The text of the BIT was not publicly available at the time of writing.

40 The BITs concluded with Bahrain, Bangladesh, Belarus, the Belgium-Luxembourg Economic Union ("BLEU"), Bulgaria, Cambodia, Canada, China, Czech Republic, Egypt,

It should also be noted that investment protection in Singapore can consist of a relatively complex web of rights and obligations, depending on the range of instruments that may be relevant to that investor and investment. In addition to Bilateral Investment Treaties ("BITs"), Singapore has actively negotiated and entered into a number of free trade agreements ("FTAs") and multilateral investment agreements, such as those involving ASEAN Member States and ASEAN Dialogue Partners,[41] or the Trans-Pacific Partnership ("TPP"), a proposed treaty that has been generating headlines globally.

Where Singapore has entered into both a BIT and a FTA with another State, the investment and services chapters of the FTA and the BIT may co-exist, impact upon the understanding of the other, or even entirely supersede the other. For instance, the Singapore-Peru BIT was superseded by the investment chapter of the Singapore-Peru FTA, and the BIT has since been terminated; on the other hand, the Singapore-Jordan BIT and FTA should be considered in tandem.[42]

Additionally, FTAs, multilateral investment agreements, ASEAN-related regional arrangements and other BITs are relevant when most favoured nation ("MFN") clauses (which are contained in most of Singapore's BITs) are considered. The extent to which any other provisions, protections or standards of treatment may be relied upon will depend on the scope of the MFN clause. Further, Singapore's BITs commonly provide that where investments are entitled to more favourable treatment under legislation or other international agreements, that position will not be affected by the BIT. Finally, a careful reading of the schedules to the relevant FTA chapters, where parties list their reservations and non-conforming measures with respect to investment obligations, is also necessary in order to work out the precise scope of

---

France, Germany, Hungary, Indonesia, Jordan, Democratic People's Republic of Korea ("North Korea"), Kuwait, Laos, Latvia, Libya, Mauritius, Mexico, Mongolia, Netherlands, Oman, Pakistan, Poland, Russia, Saudi Arabia, Slovak Republic, Slovenia, Sri Lanka, Switzerland, Taiwan, Turkey, United Kingdom, United States, Uzbekistan and Vietnam. This information is available on UNCTAD's website at: http://investmentpolicyhub.unctad.org/IIA/CountryBits/190#iiaInnerMenu and on the Singapore Ministry of Trade and Industry website at: http://www.mti.gov.sg/MTIInsights/Pages/IGAs.aspx (last accessed 25 June 2015).

41 For more information, see the Chapter on ASEAN.

42 The preamble of the Singapore-Jordan BIT states: "Pursuant to Article 8.7 of the Agreement between the Government of the Hashemite Kingdom of Jordan and the Government of the Republic of Singapore on the Establishment of a Free Trade Area (hereafter, "the Agreement") which provides that, subject to Chapter 4 of the Agreement, the rights and obligations of the Parties in respect of investments shall be governed by this Treaty".

the obligation in question. Thus, while a comprehensive examination of the interaction between all FTAs, BITs and other types of investment agreements would go beyond the scope of this chapter, the potential impact of other agreements on investment protection should be recognized. Accordingly, this section is based on an analysis of the 39 BITs officially available in English from the Singapore Ministry of Trade and Industry, including two that are not yet in force.[43]

In considering Singapore's BITs, it is interesting to note certain broad (though by no means definitive) trends depending on when the BIT was signed. The BITs agreed in the 1960s and 1970s are distinctive and often entirely different creatures; the BITs from the 80s start to demonstrate consolidation and signs of consistency; by the 90s, BITs reflect strong trends of consistent practice, with less variation, and that continues into the 2000s, though in some BITs signed after 2000, there appears to be a greater sophistication in the language adopted; from the 2000s and onwards, possibly in line with increasing adoption of FTAs with investment-related obligations, there is again greater variation among BITs. The vast majority of BITs were concluded by Singapore after 1990, possibly a reflection of its own economic priorities and policies.

While perhaps not unique to BITs entered into by Singapore, there are certain phrases which recur repeatedly in the preamble of these BITs. Common preambular language contains references to "greater economic co-operation" between the two State parties based on "principles of equality and mutual benefit", and the recognition that "the encouragement and reciprocal protection" of investments will be conducive to "stimulating business initiative and increasing prosperity" in both States.

An example of a typical preamble is found in the Singapore-Bahrain BIT:

> The Government of the Republic of Singapore and the Government of the Kingdom of Bahrain (each hereinafter referred to as a "Contracting Party");
>
> DESIRING to create favourable conditions for greater economic co-operation between them and in particular for investments by investors of one State in the territory of the other State based on the principles of equality and mutual benefit;
>
> RECOGNISING that the encouragement and reciprocal protection of such investments will be conducive to stimulating business initiative and increasing prosperity in both States;
>
> HAVE AGREED AS FOLLOWS…

43 The Singapore-Ukraine and Singapore-UAE BITs.

Materially similar preambles are also found in 20 other BITs concluded by Singapore.[44]

More uniquely, the Singapore-Turkey BIT appears to be the only BIT that refers to fair and equitable treatment ("FET") in its preamble, stating that "fair and equitable treatment of investments is desirable in order to maintain a stable framework for investments . . .".

2 *Definition of Investment*

There are three aspects of the definition of "investment" that bear mentioning. The first is in respect of the kinds of assets usually identified as being included in the definition. "Investment" commonly includes:

(a) movable and immovable property and other property rights such as mortgages, liens or pledges;
(b) shares, stocks, debentures and similar interests in companies;
(c) claims to money or to any performance under contract having an economic value;
(d) intellectual property rights, including industrial property rights, know-how and goodwill;
(e) concessions conferred by law or under contract, including any concession to search for, cultivate, extract or exploit natural resources.[45]

These five categories are similarly identified in almost all BITs signed by Singapore, though with differences in expression,[46] at times more significant, which could indicate differences in scope. For instance:

---

44 The BITs concluded with Belarus, BLEU, Bulgaria, Cambodia, China, Czech Republic, Egypt, Hungary, North Korea, Laos, Latvia, Libya, Mongolia, Pakistan, Poland, Slovak Republic, Slovenia, Ukraine, UAE and Vietnam.

45 Singapore-Belarus BIT, Article 1(1).

46 Singapore-Bahrain BIT, Article 1(1); Singapore-Bangladesh BIT, Article 1(1)(a); Singapore-Belarus BIT, Article 1(1) (cited above); Singapore-BLEU, Article 1(1); Singapore-Bulgaria BIT, Article 1(1); Singapore-Cambodia BIT, Article 1(1); Singapore-China BIT, Article 1(1); Singapore-Czech Republic BIT, Article 1(1); Singapore-Egypt BIT, Article 1(1); Singapore-France BIT, Article 1(1); Singapore-Germany BIT, Article 1(1); Singapore-Hungary BIT, Article 1(1); Singapore-Indonesia BIT, Article I; Singapore-Jordan BIT, Article 1(1); Singapore-North Korea BIT, Article 1(1); Singapore-Kuwait BIT, Article 1(1); Singapore-Laos BIT, Article 1(1); Singapore-Latvia BIT, Article 1(1); Singapore-Libya BIT, Article 1(1); Singapore-Mauritius BIT, Article 1(1); Singapore-Mongolia BIT, Article 1(1); Singapore-Netherlands BIT, Article I; Singapore-Oman BIT, Article 1(1); Singapore-Pakistan BIT, Article 1; Singapore-Poland BIT, Article 1(1); Singapore-Russia BIT, Article 1(2);

- In respect of shares, stocks and debentures, the Singapore-Kuwait BIT refers more comprehensively to "shares, stocks, and other forms of equity participation, and bonds, debentures, and other forms of debt interests in a company, and other debts and loans and securities issued by any investor of a Contracting Party;"[47]
- In respect of claims to money or performance, the Singapore-Czech Republic BIT ties it to an investment, stating "claims to money or to any performance under contract having an economic value associated with an investment;"[48]
- In respect of intellectual property rights, the Singapore-China BIT refers to "copyright, industrial property rights (such as patents for inventions, trademarks, industrial design), know-how, technical processes, trade names and goodwill"[49] and the Singapore-Slovak Republic BIT identifies the fields from which those rights are generated, stating "intellectual property rights, which relate to the output which results from intellectual activity in the industrial, scientific, literary and artistic fields, and comprises, inter alia, industrial property including inventions, trademarks, industrial designs, trade secrets, geographical indications and copyright;"[50] and
- In respect of concessions, the Singapore-Germany BIT states "such business concessions under public law, including concessions regarding the prospecting for, or the extraction or winning of, natural resources, as give their holder a legal position of some duration"[51] and the Singapore-Jordan BIT more broadly mentions "rights to engage in economic and commercial activities conferred by law or by virtue of a

---

Singapore-Saudi Arabia BIT, Article 1(1); Singapore-Slovak Republic BIT, Article 1(1); Singapore-Slovenia BIT, Article 1(1); Singapore-Sri Lanka BIT, Article 1(1); Singapore-Switzerland BIT, Article 8(c); Singapore-Turkey BIT, Article 1(2); Singapore-Ukraine BIT, Article 1(1); Singapore-UK BIT, Article 1(a); Singapore-Uzbekistan BIT, Article 1(1); and Singapore-Vietnam BIT, Article 1(1).

47 Singapore-Kuwait BIT, Article 1(1)(a); the Singapore-Switzerland BIT, Article 8(c) also refers to "securities".

48 Singapore-Czech Republic BIT, Article 1(1)(c); see also the Singapore-Libya BIT, Article 1(1), which adopts a similar formulation.

49 Singapore-China BIT, Article 1(1)(d).

50 Singapore-Slovak Republic BIT, Article 1(1)(d).

51 Singapore-Germany BIT, Article 1(1)(e); see also the Singapore-Netherlands BIT, Article I, which adopts a similar formulation.

> contract, including concessions to search for, cultivate, extract or exploit natural resources."[52]

For examples of Singapore's BITs that have adopted significantly different formulations for the definition of "investment", see the Singapore-Mexico[53] and the Singapore-UAE[54] BITs.

The second aspect of the definition of "investment", found in just over half of Singapore's BITs, is a reference to assets having been "permitted by each Contracting Party in accordance with its laws and regulations."[55] A few BITs only require assets to have been invested "in accordance with the laws and regulations of the Contracting Party in whose territory the investment is made,"[56] while others appear to set a more limiting standard, requiring that assets are also "owned or controlled directly or indirectly by an investor."[57]

---

52 Singapore-Jordan BIT, Article 1(1)(e).

53 Article 1(7).

54 Article 1(1).

55 This is found in the Singapore-Bahrain BIT, Article 1(1); Singapore-Bangladesh BIT, Article 1(1)(a); Singapore-Belarus BIT, Article 1(1); Singapore-Cambodia BIT, Article 1(1); Singapore-China BIT, Article 1(1); Singapore-Czech Republic BIT, Article 1(1); Singapore-Egypt BIT, Article 1(1); Singapore-Hungary BIT, Article 1(1); Singapore-Laos BIT, Article 1(1); Singapore-Latvia BIT, Article 1(1); Singapore-Libya BIT, Article 1(1); Singapore-Mauritius BIT, Article 1(1); Singapore-Mongolia BIT, Article 1(1); Singapore-Pakistan BIT, Article 1; Singapore-Poland BIT, Article 1(1); Singapore-Slovak Republic BIT, Article 1(1); Singapore-Slovenia BIT, Article 1(1); Singapore-Turkey BIT, Article 1(2); Singapore-Ukraine BIT, Article 1(1); Singapore-Uzbekistan BIT, Article 1(1); and Singapore-Vietnam BIT, Article 1(1).

56 See the Singapore-Bulgaria BIT, Article 1(1); for other examples, see the Singapore-Indonesia BIT, Article I; Singapore-Oman BIT, Article 1(1); and Singapore-Russia BIT, Article 1(2).

57 Singapore-Kuwait BIT, Article 1(1); for instance, the Singapore-Mexico BIT, Article 1(7) refers to assets "owned or controlled, directly or indirectly by investors of one Contracting Party and established or acquired in accordance with the laws and regulations of the other Contracting Party"; the Singapore-North Korean BIT, Article 1(1) provides for assets that an investor "owns or controls, directly or indirectly, in the territory of the other Contracting Party in accordance with the laws and regulations of the latter"; the Singapore-Saudi Arabia BIT, Article 1(1) refers to assets "owned or controlled by an investor... in accordance with its legislation"; and the Singapore-UAE BIT, Article 1(1) mentions assets that an investor "owns or controls, directly or indirectly, that was made in accordance with the laws and regulations of the other Contracting Party".

The Singapore-Turkey BIT also restricts investments to "all direct investments" made in accordance with applicable laws and regulations.[58]

The third aspect, found in the minority of Singapore's BITs, is explicit reference to how any change in the form of investments will not affect their character as investments. As an example, Article 1(2)(ii) of the Singapore Bangladesh BIT states:

> Any change in the form of the investments shall not affect their character as investments if such change is in line with the applicable procedure in Article 2.

This is similarly provided for under the Singapore-Bulgaria BIT,[59] Singapore-France BIT,[60] Singapore-Germany BIT,[61] Singapore-Indonesia BIT,[62] Singapore-Jordan BIT,[63] Singapore-Kuwait BIT,[64] Singapore-Libya BIT,[65] Singapore-Oman BIT,[66] Singapore-Russia BIT,[67] Singapore-Saudi Arabia BIT,[68] Singapore-Slovak Republic BIT,[69] and Singapore-UAE BIT.[70]

3 *Definition of Investor*

The definition of "investor" in Singapore's BITs is generally fairly consistent. Where natural persons are concerned, citizens or nationals of Singapore and the other Contracting Party are included in practically all BITs.[71] More rarely,

58 Singapore-Turkey BIT, Article 1(2).
59 Article 1(1).
60 *Ibid.*
61 *Ibid.*
62 Article I.
63 Article 1(1).
64 *Ibid.*
65 *Ibid.*
66 *Ibid.*
67 Article 1(2).
68 Article 1(1).
69 *Ibid.*
70 Article 1(8).
71 Singapore-Bahrain BIT, Article 1(3); Singapore-Bangladesh BIT, Article 1(1)(c); Singapore-Belarus BIT, Article 1(3); Singapore-BLEU, Article 1(2); Singapore-Bulgaria BIT, Article 1(3); Singapore-Cambodia BIT, Article 1(3); Singapore-China BIT, Article 1(3); Singapore-Czech Republic BIT, Article 1(3); Singapore-Egypt BIT, Article 1(3); Singapore-France BIT, Article 1(2); Singapore-Germany BIT, Article 1(3); Singapore-Hungary BIT, Article 1(3); Singapore-Indonesia BIT, Article I(2); Singapore-Jordan BIT, Article 1(2); Singapore-Laos

permanent residents of Singapore are also expressly stated to fall within the category of "investors."[72]

Sometimes, an "investor" with respect to a Contracting Party is also specified to include the Government of that Contracting Party.[73]

The degree of variation increases where the definition concerns non-natural persons. A typical provision for an "investor" of Singapore stipulates that bodies "with or without legal personality" are included, such as in Article 1(4)(b) of the Singapore-Laos BIT:

> [A]ny company, firm, association or body, with or without legal personality, incorporated, established or registered under the laws in force in the Republic of Singapore.[74]

Other BITs do not explicitly include bodies "without legal personality", though the clauses in some instances are arguably sufficiently broad to encompass

BIT, Article 1(3); Singapore-Latvia BIT, Article 1(3); Singapore-Libya BIT, Article 1(3); Singapore-Mauritius BIT, Article 1(3); Singapore-Mexico BIT, Article 1(8); Singapore-Mongolia BIT, Article 1(3); Singapore-Netherlands BIT, Article I; Singapore-Oman BIT, Article 1(3); Singapore-Pakistan BIT, Article 1(3); Singapore-Poland BIT, Article 1(3); Singapore-Russia BIT, Article 1(1); Singapore-Saudi Arabia BIT, Article 1(3); Singapore-Slovak Republic BIT, Article 1(3); Singapore-Slovenia BIT, Article 1(4); Singapore-Sri Lanka BIT, Article 1(3); Singapore-Switzerland BIT, Article 8(a); Singapore-Turkey BIT, Article 1(1); Singapore-Ukraine BIT, Article 1(3); Singapore-UK BIT, Article 1(c); Singapore-Uzbekistan BIT, Article 1(3); and Singapore-Vietnam BIT, Article 1(3).

72 Singapore-North Korea BIT, Article 1(3)(b)(i); Singapore-Kuwait BIT, Article 1(2)(b); and Singapore-UAE BIT, Article 1(2)(c)(ii).

73 See, for instance, the Singapore-Kuwait BIT, Article 1(2)(a); Singapore-Saudi Arabia BIT, Article 1(3)(b)(iii); and Singapore-UAE BIT, Article 1(2)(a).

74 This is similarly provided for under the Singapore-Bahrain BIT, Article 1(3)(a)(ii); Singapore-Belarus BIT, Article 1(3)(b)(ii); Singapore-BLEU, Article 1(2)(b); Singapore-Bulgaria BIT, Article 1(3)(b); Singapore-Cambodia BIT, Article 1(4)(a); Singapore-China BIT, Article 1(4)(b); Singapore-Czech Republic BIT, Article 1(4); Singapore-Hungary BIT, Article 1(4); Singapore-Indonesia BIT, Article I(2)(b); Singapore-North Korea BIT, Article 1(3)(b)(ii); Singapore-Latvia BIT, Article 1(4)(a); Singapore-Mongolia BIT, Article 1(4)(b); Singapore-Pakistan BIT, Article 1(4)(a); Singapore-Poland BIT, Article 1(4)(b); Singapore-Saudi Arabia BIT, Article 1(3)(a)(ii); Singapore-Slovenia BIT, Article 1(5)(a); Singapore-Sri Lanka BIT, Article 1(4)(b); Singapore-Ukraine BIT, Article 1(3)(b); and Singapore-Vietnam BIT, Article 1(4)(b).

unincorporated bodies.[75] On the other hand, some clauses appear to exclude non-legal persons from the definition of "investor."[76]

The BITs signed with a few States, such as Jordan, Libya and the UAE, expressly include legal persons "whether or not for profit, and whether private or government owned or controlled."[77] While uncommon, a few BITs have also extended the definition of "investor" beyond legal persons constituted or incorporated in that Contracting Party, to include "legal persons controlled directly or indirectly by nationals of that Contracting Party and constituted in accordance with the laws of the other Contracting Party"[78] (which means that a Dutch company controlled by a Singaporean could seek protection as a Singaporean "investor" under the Singapore-Netherlands BIT), or legal persons majority owned by citizens of that Contracting Party[79] (which means that a Swiss company majority owned by a Singaporean could seek protection as a Singaporean investor under the Singapore-Switzerland BIT).

Some BITs provide for different meanings of "investor" in respect of non-natural persons from Singapore and its State counterparty. Where a separate definition is stipulated, a company from the other State is usually an entity incorporated or constituted under that State's laws.[80] Some of these

---

75 As an example, the Singapore-Egypt BIT, Article 1(4)(a) provides that the term "company" means, "[i]n respect of the Republic of Singapore, any company, firm, association or body, incorporated, established or registered under the laws in force in the Republic of Singapore". While there is no mention of bodies "without legal personality", associations or bodies, such as those registered in Singapore, given a registration number, but with no legal personality, potentially fall within the definition. See also the Singapore-France BIT, Article 1(3)(b); Singapore-Germany BIT, Article 1(4)(b); Singapore-Mauritius, Article 1(3)(ii); Singapore-Russia BIT, Article 1(1)(b); Singapore-Slovak Republic BIT, Article 1(3)(b); Singapore-Turkey BIT, Article 1(1)(b); Singapore-UK BIT, Article 1(d)(ii); and Singapore-Uzbekistan BIT, Article 1(3)(b).

76 For instance, the Singapore-Kuwait BIT, Article 1(2)(c) states that "investor" shall mean "any legal person constituted or incorporated under the laws and regulations of that Contracting Party"; see also the Singapore-Bangladesh BIT, Article 1(1)(c).

77 Singapore-Jordan BIT, Article 1(2)(b). The relevant provisions of other BITs vary slightly: see the Singapore-Libya BIT, Article 1(3)(b); and Singapore-UAE BIT, Article 1(3).

78 Singapore-Netherlands BIT, Article I(c).

79 The definition of "Companies" under the Singapore-Switzerland BIT, Article 8(b) includes companies and associations "in which Swiss nationals have at all times directly or indirectly a majority interest" or "in which citizens of Singapore have at all times directly or indirectly a majority interest."

80 See, for instance, the BITs concluded with Bahrain, Cambodia, China, Egypt, Laos, Latvia, Mongolia, Pakistan, Slovenia, Sri Lanka, UK, Uzbekistan and Vietnam.

definitions also include bodies "with or without legal personality."[81] Less commonly, though noteworthy, some BITs contain additional requirements that the entity has its "seat"[82] and "economic activities,"[83] "head office"[84] or "substantive business operations"[85] in the host State.[86]

As a final note, it bears mentioning that some old BITs, such as Government-to-Government treaties that provide for both States to issue investment guarantees, do not contain definitions of "investor" and "investment."[87]

4 *Scope*

This section deals with a range of provisions and issues, including the conditions to be satisfied for applicability of Singapore's BITs, the temporal scope of the BITs, provisions in respect of entry into force, duration and termination of the BITs, and rights of subrogation.

Specific Approval in Writing

The majority of Singapore's BITs stipulate that the treaty will only apply to investments in Singapore "specifically approved in writing by the competent authority" of Singapore and upon "conditions, if any". By way of illustration, Article 2(1)(a) of the Singapore-Latvia BIT provides that it will only apply:

> [I]n respect of investments in the territory of the Republic of Singapore, to all investments made by nationals and companies of the Republic of Latvia, which are specifically approved in writing by the competent

81 See, for instance, the BITs concluded with BLEU, Bulgaria, Czech Republic, Hungary and Poland.

82 Singapore-Germany BIT, Article 1(4)(a).

83 The Singapore-Belarus BIT, Article 1(3)(a)(ii) requires that legal persons constituted or organised under the law of Belarus "have their seat, together with economic activities" in the territory of Belarus; and Singapore-North Korea BIT, Article 1(3)(a)(ii) requires that legal entitles "have their seat, together with real economic activities" in the territory of North Korea.

84 Singapore-France BIT, Article 1(3)(a); and Singapore-Saudi Arabia BIT, Article 1(3)(b)(ii).

85 The Singapore-Mexico BIT, Article 1(8)(b) refers to enterprises "engaged in substantive business operations" in the territory of that Contracting Party; see also Singapore-Jordan BIT, Article 1(2)(b); Singapore-Libya BIT, Article 1(3)(b); and Singapore-Oman BIT, Article 1(3)(b).

86 This is usually in relation to companies incorporated in Singapore's counterparty to the BIT, although it has also been used in relation to companies incorporated in Singapore, such as in the Singapore-Mexico BIT.

87 See, for instance, the Singapore-United States Investment Guarantee Agreement, 25 March 1966 ("Singapore-US BIT"); and the Canada-Singapore Bilateral Agreement on Foreign Investment Insurance, 30 July 1971 ("Singapore-Canada BIT").

> authority designated by the Government of the Republic of Singapore and upon such conditions, if any, as it shall deem fit.

Numerous other BITs contain provisions that are *in pari materia* to the clause cited above.[88] Some BITs specify that the competent authority in Singapore is the EDB, although in those cases, allowance is made for the Government to designate any other body or authority.[89] This is likely because the EDB was the agency with primary responsibility for the negotiation of investment treaties until a few years ago, when this responsibility was transferred to the Ministry of Trade and Industry. In contrast, the Singapore-Turkey BIT requires that investments be made in accordance with the national laws and regulations of the host State "or" be specifically approved in writing by the designated competent authority.[90]

As a general observation, Singapore's BITs often contain a number of references to the requirement that investments shall be made "in accordance with the laws and regulations" of the host State,[91] "permitted" by the host

---

88 Singapore-Bahrain BIT, Article 2(1)(a); Singapore-Bangladesh BIT, Article 2(1)(a); Singapore-Belarus BIT, Article 2(1)(a); Singapore-Bulgaria BIT, Article 2(1)(a); Singapore-Cambodia BIT, Article 2(1)(a); Singapore-China BIT, Article 2(1)(b); Singapore-Czech Republic BIT, Article 2(b); Singapore-Egypt BIT, Article 2(1)(a); Singapore-Hungary BIT, Article 2(1)(b); Singapore-Indonesia BIT, Article X(a); Singapore-Laos BIT, Article 2(b); Singapore-Latvia BIT, Article 2(1)(a); Singapore-Mauritius BIT, Article 2(1)(a); Singapore-Mongolia BIT, Article 2(1)(b); Singapore-Pakistan BIT, Article 2(1)(a); Singapore-Poland BIT, Article 2(1)(b); Singapore-Saudi Arabia BIT, Protocol, Article 2(1); Singapore-Slovenia BIT, Article 2(1)(a); Singapore-Sri Lanka BIT, Article 2(1)(b); Singapore-Ukraine BIT, Article 2(1); Singapore-Uzbekistan BIT, Article 2(1); and Singapore-Vietnam BIT, Article 2(1)(b). While in different formulations, approval in writing is also required in other BITs, such as the Singapore-Canada BIT, Article (6), Singapore-France BIT, Article 9, Singapore-Germany BIT, Article 1(ii), Singapore-Netherlands BIT, Article XII(1)(a) and Singapore-UK BIT, Article 12.

89 Singapore-North Korea BIT, Article 2(1)(b); Singapore-Kuwait BIT, Article 2(a); Singapore-Oman BIT, Article 2(1)(a); and Singapore-Slovak Republic BIT, Article 3(1)(b).

90 Singapore-Turkey BIT, Article 2.

91 For instance, the Singapore-Slovenia BIT, Article 10 provides: "For the avoidance of any doubt, it is declared that all investments shall, subject to this Agreement, be governed by the laws in force in the territory of the Contracting Party in which such investments are made." This is similarly found in the Singapore-Bahrain BIT, Article 10; Singapore-Belarus BIT, Article 10; Singapore-Bulgaria BIT, Article 9; Singapore-Cambodia BIT, Article 10; Singapore-China BIT, Article 10; Singapore-Czech Republic BIT, Article 10; Singapore-Egypt BIT, Article 10; Singapore-Hungary BIT, Article 10; Singapore-North Korea BIT, Article 9; Singapore-Laos BIT, Article 10; Singapore-Latvia BIT, Article 10; Singapore-Mauritius BIT, Article 10; Singapore-Mongolia BIT, Article 10; Singapore-Pakistan BIT,

State,[92] or "approved" by the host State.[93] These are indicative of requirements for admission, and additionally, "in accordance with the laws and regulations" of the host State implies that any investments made in violation of national laws could be excluded from the scope of the treaty.

Temporal Scope

Approximately a third of Singapore's BITs are stated to apply to all investments, whether made before or after the coming into force of the relevant treaty, and additionally, only to disputes which arose after its entry into force. Many such provisions are *in pari materia* to Article 13 of the Singapore-Kuwait BIT, which provides:

> The provisions of this Agreement shall apply to all investments made by investors of either Contracting Party in the territory of the other Contracting Party, whether made before or after the coming into force of this Agreement, but shall not apply to any dispute concerning an investment which arose, or any claim which was settled, before its entry into force.[94]

This is not particularly unique in light of the general position under bilateral investment treaties in existence, but approximately another one-third of Singapore's BITs explicitly state that the treaty applies to investments made before or after the coming into force of the agreement, without stipulating the position in respect of disputes that arose after entry into force.[95]

Article 10; Singapore-Poland BIT, Article 10; Singapore-Slovenia BIT, Article 10; Singapore-Sri Lanka BIT, Article 8; Singapore-Turkey BIT, Article 9; Singapore-Ukraine BIT, Article 8; Singapore-Uzbekistan BIT, Article 10; and Singapore-Vietnam BIT, Article 10.

92 As explained under the definition of "investment" above, the definition is often limited to those "permitted by each Contracting Party in accordance with its laws and regulations".

93 For example, the Singapore-Mexico BIT, Article 2 provides that "Each Contracting Party shall admit the entry of investments made by investors of the other Contracting Party pursuant to its applicable laws and regulations." The Singapore-Saudi Arabia BIT, Article 2(1) states that "Each Contracting Party shall in its territory … admit or approve such investments in accordance with its laws, regulations and policies. …"

94 Singapore-Bahrain BIT, Article 2(2); Singapore-Indonesia BIT, Articles X(2) and X(3); Singapore-Jordan BIT, Article 2(1); Singapore-North Korea BIT, Article 2(2); Singapore-Kuwait BIT, Article 13; Singapore-Latvia BIT, Article 2(2); Singapore-Libya BIT, Article 2(2); Singapore-Mexico, Article 27; Singapore-Oman BIT, Article 2(2); Singapore-Saudi Arabia BIT, Article 2(2); Singapore-Slovak Republic BIT, Article 2; Singapore-Turkey BIT, Article 2; Singapore-Ukraine BIT, Article 2(2); and Singapore-UAE BIT, Article 2(2).

95 Singapore-Belarus BIT, Article 2(2); Singapore-BLEU, Article 3; Singapore-Bulgaria BIT, Article 2(3); Singapore-Cambodia BIT, Article 2(2); Singapore-China BIT, Article 2(2); Singapore-Egypt BIT, Article 2(2); Singapore-France BIT, Article 9; Singapore-Germany

The remainder of Singapore's BITs either contain no provision in this respect,[96] refer to coverage of investments made after a specific date,[97] or are unique in other aspects.[98]

Entry Into Force, Duration and Termination

Singapore's BITs commonly provide for the treaty to enter into force a certain number of days (e.g., 30 days) after the later contracting party gives notification that its internal legal procedures required for the bringing into force of the treaty have been fulfilled.[99]

Usually, the treaty then enters into force for an initial period of 5, 10 or 15 years, after which it is stated to continue in force,[100] or is renewed for subsequent periods of 5, 10 or 15 years,[101] unless terminated.

BIT, Article 1(1)(ii); Singapore-Laos BIT, Article 2(2); Singapore-Mauritius BIT, Article 2(2); Singapore-Mongolia BIT, Article 2(2); Singapore-Netherlands BIT, Article XII(2); Singapore-Poland BIT, Article 2(2); Singapore-Slovenia BIT, Article 2(2); Singapore-Sri Lanka BIT, Article 2(2); Singapore-Switzerland BIT, Article 5; and Singapore-Vietnam BIT, Article 2(2).

96 See for instance, the Singapore-Bangladesh BIT, Singapore-Czech Republic BIT, and Singapore-UK BIT.

97 For example, the Singapore-Hungary BIT, Article 2(2) refers to investments made after 1 January 1973; the Singapore-Pakistan BIT, Article 2(2) refers to investments made after 1 September 1954; and the Singapore-Russia BIT, Article 2 refers to investments made on or after 1 January 1990, but states that the treaty will not apply to any dispute that arose before its entry into force.

98 As an example, besides stating that it applies to all investments made before or after the entry into force of the agreement, Article 2(2) of the Singapore-Uzbekistan BIT continues to provide that: "No claim under this Agreement may be made in respect to any act or fact that took place or any situation that ceased to exist before the date of entry into force of this Agreement."

99 As an example, Article 15(1) of the Singapore-Bahrain BIT provides: "Each Contracting Party shall notify the other Contracting Party of the fulfilment of its internal legal procedures required for the bringing into force of this Agreement. This Agreement shall enter into force on the thirtieth day from the date of notification of the later Contracting Party."

100 As an example, Article 15(2) of the Singapore-Bahrain BIT provides: "This Agreement shall remain in force for a period of fifteen years and shall continue in force thereafter unless, after the expiry of the initial period of fourteen years, either Contracting Party notifies in writing the other Contracting Party of its intention to terminate this Agreement. The notice of termination shall become effective one year after it has been received by the other Contracting Party."

101 As an example, Article 12(3) of the Singapore-BLEU BIT provides: "Unless either of the Contracting Parties notifies the other Contracting Party through diplomatic channels the former's confirmation of the expiry of this Agreement at least six months before the

In respect of termination, Singapore's BITs often state that either contracting party may notify the other party of its intention to terminate the agreement, and the termination becomes effective one year after receipt of that notice.[102]

The BITs also usually contain a sunset clause, providing that the treaty will remain in force in respect of investments made prior to the date the notice of termination becomes effective,[103] for a further period from that date.

Subrogation

All of Singapore's BITs contain rights of subrogation, providing for a Contracting State Party to exercise the rights and assert the claims of its own investors where the State had, as a result of an indemnity it gave in respect of an investment, made payment to its own investors in respect of their claims. The formulation of these clauses usually do not differ significantly among the BITs concluded by Singapore after the 1980s, compared to subrogation provisions in earlier BITs.

Article 8 of the Singapore-Oman BIT provides:

> SUBROGATION
>
> 1. In the event that either Contracting Party (or any agency, institution, statutory body or corporation designated by it) as a result of an indemnity it has given in respect of an investment or any part thereof makes payment to its own investors in respect of any of their claims under this Agreement, the other Contracting Party acknowledges that the former Contracting Party (or any agency, institution, statutory body or corporation designated by it) is entitled by virtue of subrogation to exercise the rights and assert the claims of its own investors. The subrogated rights or claims shall not be greater than the original rights or claims of the said investor.

---

end of the said ten years, this Agreement shall be automatically renewed for further periods of ten years at a time. Either Contracting Party may, by giving at least six months' notice, terminate this Agreement in respect of any ten year period subsequent to the first ten years mentioned in paragraph (2) of this Article."

102 As an example, Article 15(2) of the Singapore-Bahrain BIT provides: "... The notice of termination shall become effective one year after it has been received by the other Contracting Party."

103 As an example, Article 15(3) of the Singapore-Bahrain BIT provides: "In respect of investments made prior to the date when the notice of termination of this Agreement becomes effective, the provisions of Articles 1 to 14 shall remain in force for a further period of fifteen years from that date."

2. Any payment made by one Contracting Party (or any agency, institution, statutory body or corporation designated by it) to its investors shall not affect the right of such investors to make their claims against the other Contracting Party in accordance with Article 9.[104]

Comparatively, some of the BITs concluded before the 1980s have starkly different provisions in respect of rights of subrogation, possibly a reflection that such clauses were more crucial in older investment guarantee agreements where the basis of investment protection was, at times, provided by the guarantees given by the investor's own State. For example, the Singapore-Canada BIT was concluded on the basis that the Government of Canada, through its agent the Export Development Corporation, would guarantee investments in Singapore. Clause (1) of that agreement proceeds to provide that in the event of payment by the Export Development Corporation under a contract of insurance for any loss by reason of, among others, any action by the Government in Singapore that deprives the investor of any right in an investment, the Export Development Corporation shall be authorized by the Singapore Government to exercise the rights having devolved on it by law or having been assigned to it by the predecessor in title.[105] The Singapore-US BIT also contemplated that guarantees would be issued pursuant to that agreement, and thus if the guaranteeing government made payment to any investor under a guarantee, the

104 Most other BITs concluded by Singapore contain similar clauses in respect of subrogation rights, with varying degrees of deviation: Singapore-Bahrain BIT, Article 11; Singapore-Bangladesh BIT, Article 9; Singapore-Belarus BIT, Article 12; Singapore-BLEU, Article 7; Singapore-Bulgaria BIT, Article 10; Singapore-Cambodia BIT, Article 12; Singapore-China BIT, Article 12; Singapore-Czech Republic BIT, Article 12; Singapore-Egypt BIT, Article 12; Singapore-France BIT, Article 7; Singapore-Hungary BIT, Article 11; Singapore-North Korea BIT, Article 10; Singapore-Laos BIT, Article 12; Singapore-Latvia BIT, Article 12; Singapore-Libya BIT, Article 9; Singapore-Mauritius BIT, Article 12; Singapore-Mexico BIT, Article 8; Singapore-Mongolia BIT, Article 12; Singapore-Pakistan BIT, Article 12; Singapore-Poland BIT, Article 12; Singapore-Russia BIT, Article 8; Singapore-Saudi Arabia BIT, Article 7; Singapore-Slovak Republic BIT, Article 8; Singapore-Slovenia BIT, Article 11; Singapore-Sri Lanka BIT, Article 9; Singapore-Turkey BIT, Article 10; Singapore-Ukraine BIT, Article 9; Singapore-UAE BIT, Article 8; Singapore-Uzbekistan BIT, Article 12; and Singapore-Vietnam BIT, Article 12. Some BITs, though concluded after the 1980s have clauses which are slightly more unique, for example, the Singapore-Indonesia BIT, Article VII, Singapore-Jordan BIT, Article 11, Singapore Kuwait BIT, Article 8.

105 Singapore-Canada BIT, Article (1). See also SG-Germany Art 6; Singapore-Netherlands BIT, Article X; Singapore-Switzerland BIT, Article 7; Singapore-UK BIT, Article 10; SG-US (3) and (4).

host government would recognize the transfer to the guaranteeing government of any investment on account of which payment was made, as well as the succession of the guaranteeing government to any right or cause of action that may arise in connection therewith.[106]

5 *Substantive Protections*

Turning to substantive protections commonly included in the BITs signed by Singapore, while it will be impossible to consider in detail the precise scope of individual clauses in every BIT, this section will touch upon a broad review of the substantive provisions.

Fair and Equitable Treatment

Almost all of Singapore's BITs provide for "fair and equitable treatment" of investments.[107] Exceptionally, the Singapore-Bangladesh BIT accords "equitable treatment."[108] A common clause provides:

> Investments approved ... shall be accorded fair and equitable treatment and protection in accordance with this Agreement.[109]

---

106 See Singapore-US BIT, Articles 1, 3 and 4. For other examples, see Singapore-Germany BIT, Article 6; Singapore-Netherlands BIT, Article X; Singapore-Switzerland BIT, Article 7; and Singapore-UK BIT, Article 10.

107 Singapore-Bahrain BIT, Article 3(2); Singapore-Belarus BIT, Article 3(2); Singapore-BLEU, Article 2(2); Singapore-Bulgaria BIT, Article 3(2); Singapore-Cambodia BIT, Article 3(2); Singapore-China BIT, Article 3(2); Singapore-Czech Republic BIT, Article 3(2); Singapore-Egypt BIT, Article 3(2); Singapore-France BIT, Article 2(1); Singapore-Hungary BIT, Article 3(2); Singapore-Indonesia BIT, Article II(2); Singapore-Jordan BIT, Article 4; Singapore-North Korea BIT, Article 3(2); Singapore-Kuwait BIT, Article 3(2); Singapore-Laos BIT, Article 3(2); Singapore-Latvia BIT, Article 3(2); Singapore-Libya BIT, Article 3(2); Singapore-Mauritius BIT, Article 3(2); Singapore-Mexico BIT, Article 4(1); Singapore-Mongolia BIT, Article 3(2); Singapore-Netherlands BIT, Article VII(1); Singapore-Oman BIT, Article 4(1); Singapore-Pakistan BIT, Article 3(2); Singapore-Poland BIT, Article 3(2); Singapore-Russia BIT, Article 4(1); Singapore-Saudi Arabia BIT, Article 3(1); Singapore-Slovak Republic BIT, Article 3(3); Singapore-Slovenia BIT, Article 3(2); Singapore-Sri Lanka BIT, Article 3(2); Singapore-Switzerland BIT, Article 2(2); Singapore-Turkey BIT, Article 3(3); Singapore-Ukraine BIT, Article 3(2); Singapore-UAE BIT, Article 3(1); Singapore-UK BIT, Article 2(2); Singapore-Uzbekistan BIT, Article 3(2); and Singapore-Vietnam BIT, Article 3(2).

108 Singapore-Bangladesh BIT, Article 3(2).

109 Singapore-China BIT, Article 3(2).

Full Protection and Security

Often, FET is coupled with protection, "fair and equitable treatment and protection,"[110] though there is much greater variation amongst Singapore's BITs in respect of protection and security. Some BITs refer to "protection and security,"[111] "full protection and security,"[112] "full and adequate protection and security,"[113] and "continuous protection and security."[114] Interestingly, the Singapore-Netherlands BIT pegs the standard of security and protection to that accorded to its own nationals or nationals of third countries.[115]

Singapore's BITs also often provide that each contracting party will "encourage and create favourable conditions" for investors of the other contracting party to invest in its territory.[116] In some BITs, this obligation is only in respect of investments that are "in line with its general economic policy."[117]

---

110 Singapore-Bahrain BIT, Article 3(2); Singapore-Belarus BIT, Article 3(2); Singapore-Bulgaria BIT, Article 3(2); Singapore-Cambodia BIT, Article 3(2); Singapore-China BIT, Article 3(2); Singapore-Czech Republic BIT, Article 3(2); Singapore-Egypt BIT, Article 3(2); Singapore-North Korea BIT, Article 3(2); Singapore-Laos BIT, Article 3(2); Singapore-Latvia BIT, Article 3(2); Singapore-Libya BIT, Article 3(2); Singapore-Mauritius BIT, Article 3(2); Singapore-Mongolia BIT, Article 3(2); Singapore-Pakistan BIT, Article 3(2); Singapore-Poland BIT, Article 3(2); Singapore-Slovenia BIT, Article 3(2); Singapore-Sri Lanka BIT, Article 3(2); Singapore-Turkey BIT, Article 3(3); Singapore-Ukraine BIT, Article 3(2); Singapore-Uzbekistan BIT, Article 3(2); and Singapore-Vietnam BIT, Article 3(2).

111 Singapore-France BIT, Article 2(1); Singapore-Hungary BIT, Article 3(2); and Singapore-Indonesia BIT, Article II(2).

112 Singapore-Jordan BIT, Article 4; Singapore-Kuwait BIT, Article 3(2); Singapore-Mexico BIT, Article 4(1); Singapore-Oman BIT, Article 4(1); Singapore-Saudi Arabia BIT, Article 3(1); Singapore-Slovak Republic BIT, Article 3(3); Singapore-UAE BIT, Article 3(1); and Singapore-UK BIT, Article 2(2).

113 Singapore-Bangladesh BIT, Article 3(2).

114 Singapore-BLEU, Article 2(2).

115 The Singapore-Netherlands BIT, Article VII(2) states: "…[E]ach Contracting Party shall accord to such investments the same security and protection as it accords to those of its own nationals or to those of nationals of third countries, whichever is more favourable to the investor."

116 See, for instance, the Singapore-Bulgaria BIT, Article 3(1) which states: "Each Contracting Party shall encourage and create favourable conditions for investors of the other Contracting Party to make investments in its territory."

117 For example, Article 3(1) of the Singapore-Belarus BIT provides that: "Each Contracting Party shall encourage and create favourable conditions for investors of the other Contracting Party to make in its territory investments that are in line with its general economic policy", and Article 3(1) of the Singapore-Hungary BIT states: "Each Contracting

Non-Discrimination

Only about seven of the BITs concluded by Singapore contain a provision prohibiting arbitrary and discriminatory measures.[118] For instance, the Singapore-Kuwait BIT provides that neither contracting party shall in any way "impair by unreasonable or discriminatory measures"[119] the management, maintenance, use, enjoyment or disposal of investments. Other BITs refer to, e.g., "unjustified or discriminatory measures"[120] and "arbitrary or unjustifiable measures."[121]

Expropriation

All of Singapore's BITs, save for the old investment guarantee agreements which are very different creatures from the modern BITs,[122] and are therefore excluded from consideration in this chapter, contain provisions prohibiting expropriation. There are four aspects of the expropriation clauses that are worth noting.

The first is, as is commonly provided in BITs, that expropriation or measures having effect equivalent to expropriation (indirect expropriation) is prohibited unless the measures are taken for:

a) a public purpose;
b) on a non-discriminatory basis;
c) in accordance with the State's laws; and
d) against prompt, adequate and effective compensation.

Party shall encourage and create favourable conditions for nationals and companies of the other Contracting Party to make in its territory investments that are in conformity with its general economic policy."

118 Singapore-Czech Republic BIT, Article 4(2); Singapore-Kuwait BIT, Article 3(2); Singapore-Netherlands BIT, Article VII(1); Singapore-Switzerland BIT, Article 2(1); Singapore-Turkey BIT, Article 4(3); Singapore-UAE BIT, Article 3(2); and Singapore-UK BIT, Article 2(2).

119 Singapore-Kuwait BIT, Article 3(2). This is also used in the Singapore-Switzerland BIT, Article 2(1), Singapore-UAE BIT, Article 3(2), and Singapore-UK BIT, Article 2(2).

120 Singapore-Netherlands BIT, Article VII(1).

121 Singapore-Turkey BIT, Article 4(3).

122 Most notably, the Singapore-US investment guarantee agreement and the Singapore-Canada investment guarantee agreement.

In reference to (a), a few BITs state "public purposes,"[123] most refer to "any purpose authorised by law,"[124] and a few require "for the public benefit"[125] or "in the public interest."[126] Uniquely, the Singapore-Switzerland BIT provides that measures must be taken "in the public interest" or must be "authorised by an Act of Parliament in force at the time of approval of the investment,"[127] and the Singapore-UK BIT specifies that it must be "for a public purpose related to the internal needs of the expropriating Party."[128]

The requirement of a non-discriminatory basis is provided in almost all of Singapore's BITs,[129] except for, for instance, the Singapore-UK BIT and the Singapore-Sri Lanka BIT.

---

123 For example, Singapore-BLEU BIT, Article 4(1); Singapore-France BIT, Article 4(1). The Singapore-Mexico BIT, Article 6(1), Singapore-UAE BIT, Article 5(1)(a) and Singapore-Russia BIT, Article 5(1)(a) refer to "a public purpose".

124 For example, the Singapore-Bahrain BIT, Article 6(1); Singapore-Bangladesh BIT, Article 5(1); Singapore-Belarus BIT, Article 6(1); Singapore-Bulgaria BIT, Article 5(1); Singapore-Cambodia BIT, Article 6(1); Singapore-China BIT, Article 6(1); Singapore-Egypt BIT, Article 6(1); Singapore-Hungary BIT, Article 6(1); Singapore-North Korea BIT, Article 6(1); Singapore-Laos BIT, Article 6(1); Singapore-Latvia BIT, Article 6(1); Singapore-Libya BIT, Article 5(1); Singapore-Mongolia BIT, Article 6(1); Singapore-Oman BIT, Article 5(1); Singapore-Slovenia BIT, Article 6(1); Singapore-Sri Lanka BIT, Article 6(1); Singapore-Ukraine BIT, Article 5(1); and Singapore-Vietnam BIT, Article 6(1).

125 Singapore-Germany BIT, Article 4(1); Singapore-Saudi Arabia BIT, Article 4(1).

126 Singapore-Jordan BIT, Article 7(1)(a); Singapore-Mexico BIT, Article IX(a).

127 Singapore-Switzerland BIT, Article 4.

128 Singapore-UK BIT, Article 5(1).

129 Singapore-Bahrain BIT, Article 6(1); Singapore-Bangladesh BIT, Article 5(1); Singapore-Belarus BIT, Article 6(1); Singapore-BLEU, Article 4(1); Singapore-Bulgaria BIT, Article 5(1); Singapore-Cambodia BIT, Article 6(1); Singapore-China BIT, Article 6(1); Singapore-Czech Republic BIT, Article 6(1); Singapore-Egypt BIT, Article 6(1); Singapore-France BIT, Article 4(1); Singapore-Hungary BIT, Article 6(1); Singapore-Indonesia BIT, Article IV(b); Singapore-Jordan BIT, Article 7(1); Singapore-North Korea BIT, Article 6(1); Singapore-Kuwait BIT, Article 6(1)(a); Singapore-Laos BIT, Article 6(1); Singapore-Latvia BIT, Article 6(1); Singapore-Libya BIT, Article 5(1); Singapore-Mauritius BIT, Article 6(1); Singapore-Mexico BIT, Article 6(1); Singapore-Mongolia BIT, Article 6(1); Singapore-Oman BIT, Article 5(1); Singapore-Pakistan BIT, Article 6(1); Singapore-Poland BIT, Article 6(1); Singapore-Russia BIT, Article 5(1)(b); Singapore-Saudi Arabia BIT, Article 4(1); Singapore-Slovak Republic BIT, Article 5(1); Singapore-Slovenia BIT, Article 6(1); Singapore-Switzerland BIT, Article 4; Singapore-Turkey BIT, Article 6(1); Singapore-Ukraine BIT, Article 5(1); Singapore-UAE BIT, Article 5(1)(b); Singapore-Uzbekistan BIT, Article 6(1); and Singapore-Vietnam BIT, Article 6(1).

With regard to the measure having to be in accordance with the State's laws, a few BITs refer to "under due process of law,"[130] though most simply require that the measure must be "in accordance with its laws."[131]

In respect of compensation, the Hull formula of "prompt, adequate and effective"[132] compensation is often, though not always used. For instance, a large number of BITs refer to compensation which shall be "effectively realisable" and made "without unreasonable delay."[133] Other BITs use formulations

130 Singapore-Indonesia BIT, Article IV(a); Singapore-Indonesia BIT, Article IV(a); Singapore-Mexico BIT, Article IX(a); Singapore-Switzerland BIT, Article 4; and Singapore-Ukraine BIT, Article 5(1). The Singapore-Jordan BIT, Article 7(1)(c), Singapore-Kuwait BIT, Article 6(1)(a); Singapore-Mexico BIT, Article 6(1), Singapore-Russia BIT, Article 5(1)(c) and Singapore-UAE BIT, Article 5(1)(c) refer to "in accordance with due process of law".

131 Singapore-Bahrain BIT, Article 6(1); Singapore-Bangladesh BIT, Article 5(1); Singapore-Belarus BIT, Article 6(1); Singapore-Bulgaria BIT, Article 5(1); Singapore-Cambodia BIT, Article 6(1); Singapore-China BIT, Article 6(1); Singapore-Czech Republic BIT, Article 6(1); Singapore-Egypt BIT, Article 6(1); Singapore-Hungary BIT, Article 6(1); Singapore-North Korea BIT, Article 6(1); Singapore-Laos BIT, Article 6(1); Singapore-Latvia BIT, Article 6(1); Singapore-Libya BIT, Article 5(1); Singapore-Mauritius BIT, Article 6(1); Singapore-Mongolia BIT, Article 6(1); Singapore-Oman BIT, Article 5(1); Singapore-Pakistan BIT, Article 6(1); Singapore-Poland BIT, Article 6(1); Singapore-Slovak Republic BIT, Article 5(1); Singapore-Slovenia BIT, Article 6(1); Singapore-Turkey BIT, Article 6(1); Singapore-Uzbekistan BIT, Article 6(1); and Singapore-Vietnam BIT, Article 6(1). The Singapore-Saudi Arabia BIT, Article 4(1) provides that the measures shall be "in accordance with domestic laws of general application".

132 For instance, see the Singapore-BLEU BIT, Article 4(1); Singapore-Indonesia BIT, Article IV(c); Singapore-Jordan BIT, Article 7(1)(d); Singapore-Kuwait BIT, Article 6(1)(a); Singapore-Russia BIT, Article 5(2); Singapore-Saudi Arabia BIT, Article 4(1); Singapore-Sri Lanka BIT, Article 6(1); Singapore-UAE BIT, Article 5(2); and Singapore-UK BIT, Article 5(1).

133 Singapore-Bahrain BIT, Article 6(1); Singapore-Bangladesh BIT, Article 5(1); Singapore-Belarus BIT, Article 6(1); Singapore-Bulgaria BIT, Article 5(1); Singapore-Cambodia BIT, Article 6(1); Singapore-China BIT, Article 6(1); Singapore-Czech Republic BIT, Article 6(1); Singapore-Egypt BIT, Article 6(1); Singapore-Hungary BIT, Article 6(1); Singapore-North Korea BIT, Article 6(1); Singapore-Laos BIT, Article 6(1); Singapore-Latvia BIT, Article 6(1); Singapore-Libya BIT, Article 5(1); Singapore-Mauritius BIT, Article 6(1); Singapore-Mongolia BIT, Article 6(1); Singapore-Oman BIT, Article 5(1); Singapore-Poland BIT, Article 6(1); Singapore-Slovak Republic BIT, Article 5(1); Singapore-Slovenia BIT, Article 6(1); Singapore-Turkey BIT, Article 6(1); Singapore-Uzbekistan BIT, Article 6(1); and Singapore-Vietnam BIT, Article 6(1).

such as "just and equitable compensation,"[134] "just compensation"[135] and "fair and equitable."[136]

As for valuation of the assets taken, the notion of "market value"[137] or "fair market value"[138] has been used. One of the most detailed provisions, Article 6(2)(a) of the Singapore-Mexico BIT, states explicitly that "[v]aluation criteria may include the going concern value, asset value, including declared tax value of tangible property, and other criteria, as appropriate, to determine the fair market value", though such terms are rare. In respect of the date of valuation, Singapore's BITs have pegged the valuation to, among others, "the date of expropriation,"[139] the date when (or before) the expropriation becomes known[140] or immediately before the expropriation.[141] Other BITs, such as the Singapore-Czech Republic BIT,[142] do not expressly address valuation.

Some BITs specifically provide that any measure may be reviewed by a judicial authority. For instance, Article 6(2) of the Singapore-Bahrain BIT states

134 Singapore-Germany BIT, Article 4(1).

135 Singapore-Netherlands BIT, Article IX(c).

136 Singapore-Pakistan BIT, Article 6(1).

137 Singapore-Bahrain BIT, Article 6(1); Singapore-BLEU BIT, Article 4(2); Singapore-Oman BIT, Article 5(2); Singapore-Sri Lanka BIT, Article 6(2); Singapore-Turkey BIT, Article 6(1); and Singapore-Ukraine BIT, Article 5(1).

138 Singapore-Germany BIT, Article 4(1); Singapore-Indonesia BIT, Article IV(c); Singapore-Jordan BIT, Article 7(3); Singapore-Mexico BIT, Article 6(2)(a); Singapore-Russia BIT, Article 5(2); and Singapore-UAE BIT, Article 5(2).

139 Singapore-BLEU BIT, Article 4(2) and Singapore-Sri Lanka BIT, Article 6(2).

140 Singapore-Bangladesh BIT, Article 5(1); Singapore-Indonesia BIT, Article IV(c); Singapore-Kuwait BIT, Article 6(1)(b); Singapore-Russia BIT, Article 5(2); Singapore-Saudi Arabia BIT, Article 4(1); Singapore-Slovenia BIT, Article 6(1); Singapore-UAE BIT, Article 5(2); and Singapore-UK BIT, Article 5(1).

141 Singapore-Bahrain BIT, Article 6(1); Singapore-Belarus BIT, Article 6(1); Singapore-Bulgaria BIT, Article 5(1); Singapore-Cambodia BIT, Article 6(1); Singapore-China BIT, Article 6(1); Singapore-Egypt BIT, Article 6(1); Singapore-Hungary BIT, Article 6(1); Singapore-Jordan BIT, Article 7(3); Singapore-North Korea BIT, Article 6(1); Singapore-Kuwait BIT, Article 6(1)(b); Singapore-Laos BIT, Article 6(1); Singapore-Latvia BIT, Article 6(1); Singapore-Libya BIT, Article 5(1); Singapore-Mauritius BIT, Article 6(1); Singapore-Mexico BIT, Article 6(2)(a); Singapore-Mongolia BIT, Article 6(1); Singapore-Pakistan BIT, Article 6(1); Singapore-Poland BIT, Article 6(1); Singapore-Russia BIT, Article 5(2); Singapore-Saudi Arabia BIT, Article 4(1); Singapore-Slovak Republic BIT, Article 5(1); Singapore-Turkey BIT, Article 6(1); Singapore-Ukraine BIT, Article 5(1); Singapore-UAE BIT, Article 5(2); Singapore-UK BIT, Article 5(1); Singapore-Uzbekistan BIT, Article 6(1); and Singapore-Vietnam BIT, Article 6(1).

142 Singapore-Czech Republic BIT, Article 6.

that "[a]ny measure of expropriation or valuation may, at the request of the investors affected, be reviewed by a judicial or other independent authority of the Contracting Party taking the measures in the manner prescribed by its laws." Other BITs, such as the Singapore-Cambodia BIT,[143] Singapore-Egypt BIT,[144] and Singapore-Hungary BIT[145] contain similar provisions.

Two other unique aspects of expropriation clauses of Singapore's BITs are of note. The first is that some BITs state that, where assets of a company are expropriated, the host State will guarantee compensation to investors of the other contracting party who are owners of those shares.[146] This makes specific provision for the protection of shareholders, importantly, including minority shareholders, where the company is not in a position to seek investment protection. The second aspect is the exception where expropriation of land is concerned. Some BITs, like the Singapore-Indonesia BIT, provide for a different standard of protection in respect of land, stating that notwithstanding the provision in respect of expropriation, "any measure of expropriation relating to land, which shall be as defined in its domestic legislation of each Contracting Party, shall be for a purpose and upon payment of compensation in accordance with the aforesaid legislation and any subsequent amendments thereto."[147]

Umbrella Clauses

Provisions that guarantee the observance of obligations assumed by the host State to the investor are commonly referred to as "umbrella clauses"; such clauses are found in the majority of Singapore's BITs. One example is Article 11(2) of the Singapore-Slovak Republic BIT, which states:

> Each Contracting Party shall observe any commitment in accordance with its laws additional to those specified in this Agreement, entered into by the Contracting Party with investor of the other Contracting Party as regards their investments.

143 Singapore-Cambodia BIT, Article 6(2).

144 Singapore-Egypt BIT, Article 6(2).

145 Singapore-Hungary BIT, Article 6(2).

146 For example, Article 6(3) of the Singapore-North Korea BIT provides: "Where a Contracting Party expropriates the assets of a company which is incorporated or constituted under the laws in force in any part of its own territory, and in which investors of the other Contracting Party own shares, it shall ensure that the provisions of paragraph 1 of this Article are applied to the extent necessary to guarantee compensation as specified therein to such investors of the other Contracting Party who are owners of those shares."

147 Article IV(3).

Approximately half of the BITs containing umbrella clauses include similar clauses under which the host State commits to observing any commitment undertaken by the host State to the investor of the other contracting party as regards the investment.[148]

In a broader formulation, the other half of those BITs contain umbrella clauses that guarantee the observance of commitments entered into by the host State or its investors with investors of the other contracting party as regards the investment,[149] such as the Singapore-Belarus BIT:

> Each Contracting Party shall observe lawful commitments, additional to those specified in this Agreement, entered into by the Contracting Party, or its investors with investors of the other Contracting Party as regards their investments.[150]

Of particular note is the umbrella clause in the Singapore-Czech Republic BIT, which only extends to commitments undertaken by the State, but then goes on to state that in respect of commitments entered into by its investors, the State will not interfere with those obligations.[151]

Most Favoured Nation and National Treatment

Most Favoured Nation ("MFN") clauses generally require that the host State treats investors of the other contracting party as favourably as it treats any

148 Singapore-Bahrain BIT, Article 14(2); Singapore-Czech Republic BIT, Article 15(2); Singapore-Germany BIT, Article 8; Singapore-Hungary BIT, Article 14; Singapore-North Korea BIT, Article 13; Singapore-Libya BIT, Article 12; Singapore-Oman BIT, Article 11(2) (though this clause is rather unique); Singapore-Slovak Republic BIT, Article 11(2); Singapore-Turkey BIT, Article 13; Singapore-Ukraine BIT, Article 12; and Singapore-UK BIT, Article 2(2).

149 Singapore-Belarus BIT, Article 15; Singapore-Bulgaria BIT, Article 4(4); Singapore-Cambodia BIT, Article 15; Singapore-China BIT, Article 15; Singapore-Egypt BIT, Article 15; Singapore-Laos BIT, Article 15; Singapore-Latvia BIT, Article 15; Singapore-Mauritius BIT, Article 15; Singapore-Mongolia BIT, Article 15; Singapore-Pakistan BIT, Article 15; Singapore-Poland BIT, Article 15; Singapore-Slovenia BIT, Article 14; Singapore-Uzbekistan BIT, Article 15; and Singapore-Vietnam BIT, Article 15.

150 Singapore-Belarus BIT, Article 15.

151 Article 15(2) of the Singapore-Czech Republic BIT states: "Each Contracting Party shall observe commitments, additional to those specified in this Agreement, it has entered into with respect to the investments of the investors of the other Contracting Party. Each Contracting Party shall not interfere with any commitments, additional to those specified in this Agreement, entered into by its nationals or companies with the nationals or companies of the other Contracting Party as regards their investments."

other third State. In comparison, national treatment provisions require that the host State treats investors of the other contracting party as favourably as it treats its own nationals. MFN treatment and national treatment are commonly provided for under Singapore's BITs, although some BITs only provide for one and not the other. For instance, the Singapore-Jordan BIT only contains provisions on national treatment,[152] and the Singapore-Mongolia BIT only contains terms on MFN treatment.[153]

While MFN treatment provisions differ, an example of a MFN clause is Article 4 of the Singapore-Pakistan BIT:

> Neither Contracting Party shall in its territory subject investments admitted in accordance with the provisions of Article 2 or returns of nationals and companies of the other Contracting Party to treatment less favourable than that which it accords to investments or returns of nationals and companies of any third State.

The BITs concluded with Bahrain, Belarus, Cambodia, China, Czech Republic, Egypt, Hungary, Laos, Latvia, Mauritius, Mongolia, Pakistan, Poland, Slovenia, Uzbekistan and Vietnam contain materially similar clauses.[154]

On the other hand, a few BITs, such as the Singapore-BLEU BIT and the Singapore-France BIT, specifically use the term "most favoured nation" or "most favoured State."[155] Article 11 of the Singapore-BLEU BIT provides that "the treatment, protection and guarantee accorded to investments under the provisions of this Agreement including the returns, management, use, enjoyment and liquidation of such investments, shall be at least as favourable as that accorded to nationals of the most favoured nation."

Notably, the standard of treatment and level of protection granted under BITs can differ significantly. For instance, the Singapore-Sri Lanka BIT contains an Article 4(1) which is *in pari materia* to Article 4 of the Singapore-Pakistan BIT cited above, but Article 4(2) then goes on to state that investments

152 Singapore-Jordan BIT, Article 5.

153 Singapore-Mongolia BIT, Article 4.

154 Singapore-Bahrain BIT, Article 4; Singapore-Belarus BIT, Article 4; Singapore-Cambodia BIT, Article 4; Singapore-China BIT, Article 4; Singapore-Czech Republic BIT, Article 4(1); Singapore-Egypt BIT, Article 4; Singapore-Hungary BIT, Article 4; Singapore-Laos BIT, Article 4; Singapore-Latvia BIT, Article 4; Singapore-Mauritius BIT, Article 4; Singapore-Mongolia BIT, Article 4; Singapore-Pakistan BIT, Article 4; Singapore-Poland BIT, Article 4; Singapore-Slovenia BIT, Article 4; Singapore-Uzbekistan BIT, Article 4;); and Singapore-Vietnam BIT, Article 4.

155 See Singapore-France BIT, Articles 2(2) and 3.

of either contracting party and the returns therefrom shall not be entitled to any treatment or privilege which is not available, "on a reciprocal basis", to investments or returns of investors of the other contracting party. In effect, it appears to impose a condition of reciprocity, and the host State could thus justify withholding MFN treatment where the relevant treatment or privilege was not available in the other contracting State. This concept of reciprocity is also reflected in Article 4(2) of the Singapore-Turkey BIT, though in a different manner.

A few BITs, such as that concluded with Russia, link fair and equitable treatment and MFN treatment. For instance, the Singapore-Russia BIT provides for fair and equitable treatment, and states that such treatment "shall be at least as favourable as that provided by a contracting party to investments of its own investors, or to investments of investors of any third State, whichever is more favourable."[156]

An example of a national treatment clause is that found in Article 5(1) of the Singapore-Jordan BIT:

> Each Party shall accord to investors of the other Party and their investments, in relation to the establishment, acquisition, expansion, management, conduct, operation, sale or other disposition of investments, treatment no less favourable than it accords in like circumstances to its own investors and their investments.

More commonly, however, where a BIT provides for national treatment, it also provides for MFN treatment, and states that whichever is more favourable to the investor shall apply.[157]

There are also three common exceptions to MFN and national treatment. Singapore's BITs often state that the provisions to accord MFN and/or national treatment will not oblige either contracting party to extend to the investors of the other contracting party the benefit of any treatment, preference or privilege resulting from: (1) any customs union, free trade area, free trade arrangement or other forms of regional cooperation; and (2) any arrangement with a third State or States in the same geographical region designed to promote

---

156 Singapore-Russia BIT, Article 4(2).

157 See Singapore-Indonesia BIT, Article III(1); Singapore-North Korea BIT, Article 4; Singapore-Kuwait BIT, Article 4; Singapore-Libya BIT, Article 4(1); Singapore-Oman BIT, Article 4(2); Singapore-Saudi Arabia BIT, Article 3(2), (3) and (4); Singapore-Slovak Republic BIT, Article 4(1); Singapore-Switzerland BIT, Article 2(2); Singapore-Turkey BIT, Article 4(1); and Singapore-UAE BIT, Article 4(1).

regional cooperation. Additionally, (3) the provisions of the BIT do not apply to matters of taxation, any such matters will be governed by any treaty for the avoidance of double taxation between the two parties and their domestic laws.[158] In the context of Singapore, this means that MFN and national treatment provisions cannot be used to extend benefits granted under ASEAN-related arrangements to investors under most BITs.

Similarly, it could be said that concessions and privileges granted under free trade agreements will not be extended under most BITs. However, interestingly, a handful of BITs only exclude benefits or privileges resulting from "any regional arrangement for customs, monetary, tariff or trade matters (including a free trade area) or any agreement designed to lead in future to such a regional arrangement."[159] This raises the question of whether it could be argued that arrangements between a contracting party and a third State outside its region (say, for instance, the free trade agreement between Singapore and the United States, or the free trade agreement between Singapore and Peru) may be "imported" by way of a MFN provision.

More rarely, a few BITs exclude benefits or privileges resulting from other bilateral investment agreements from MFN or national treatment. For instance, the Singapore-North Korea and Singapore-UAE BITs provide that MFN treatment shall not oblige a contracting party to extend to investors of the other contracting party the benefit of any treatment, preference or privilege resulting from "any existing bilateral investment agreements,"[160] and the Singapore-Oman BIT states that with respect to Singapore, it is not obliged to extend the benefits of "any Investment Guarantee Agreement entered into prior to 1991."[161]

Separately, the Singapore-Mexico and Singapore-UAE BITs also specifically state that the MFN and national treatment clause "shall not be construed as granting to investors options or procedures for the settlement of disputes other than those set out in this Agreement,"[162] while most BITs are silent on this point.

---

158 For examples, see Singapore-Bahrain BIT, Article 5; Singapore-Belarus BIT, Article 5; Singapore-Kuwait BIT, Article 4(2); Singapore-Latvia BIT, Article 5; and Singapore-Mauritius BIT, Article 5.

159 Singapore-Cambodia BIT, Article 5(1)(a). Similar provisions can also be found in, e.g., the Singapore-Hungary BIT, Article 5(1)(a), Singapore-Laos BIT, Article 5(1)(a), Singapore-Mongolia BIT, Article 5(1)(a), and Singapore-Pakistan BIT, Article 5(1)(a).

160 Singapore-North Korea BIT, Article 5(1)(b); and Singapore-UAE BIT, Article 4(2)(b). See also Singapore-Kuwait BIT, Article 4(2)(a).

161 Singapore-Oman BIT, Article 4(5). See also Singapore-Mexico BIT, Article 3(3)(a).

162 Singapore-Mexico BIT, Article 3(4); and Singapore-UAE BIT, Article 4(3).

6 *Repatriation of Capital and Compensation for Losses*

Generally, the BITs concluded by Singapore provide for compensation for losses suffered due to war or other armed conflict, revolution and other like circumstances, but the majority of those BITs peg it to the compensation accorded to investors of any third State.[163] Slightly less commonly, in respect of compensation, a few BITs accord both national and MFN treatment,[164] for example, the Singapore-Jordan BIT provides that the compensation shall be "not less favourable than the treatment that [the Contracting Party] accords in like circumstances to its own investors or to investors of any non-Party, whichever is more favourable to the investors concerned."[165]

As for repatriation, almost all of Singapore's BITs guarantee to investors the free transfer of their capital and the returns from any investments.[166] The

163 Singapore-Bahrain BIT, Article 7; Singapore-Bangladesh BIT, Article 4(4); Singapore-Belarus BIT, Article 7; Singapore-Bulgaria BIT, Article 6; Singapore-Cambodia BIT, Article 7; Singapore-China BIT, Article 7; Singapore-Czech Republic BIT, Article 7; Singapore-Egypt BIT, Article 7; Singapore-Hungary BIT, Article 7(1); Singapore-Indonesia BIT, Article V; Singapore-Laos BIT, Article 7; Singapore-Latvia BIT, Article 7; Singapore-Mauritius BIT, Article 7(1); Singapore-Mongolia BIT, Article 7; Singapore-Pakistan BIT, Article 7; Singapore-Poland BIT, Article 7; Singapore-Slovenia BIT, Article 7; Singapore-Ukraine BIT, Article 6; Singapore-Uzbekistan BIT, Article 7; and Singapore-Vietnam BIT, Article 7.

164 Singapore-Germany BIT, Article 4(2) and (3); Singapore-Jordan BIT, Article 8; Singapore-North Korea BIT, Article 7; Singapore-Kuwait BIT, Article 5(1); Singapore-Libya BIT, Article 6; Singapore-Mexico BIT, Article 5; Singapore-Oman BIT, Article 6(1); Singapore-Russia BIT, Article 6; Singapore-Saudi Arabia BIT, Article 5; Singapore-Slovak Republic BIT, Article 6; Singapore-Turkey BIT, Article 7; Singapore-UAE BIT, Article 6; and Singapore-UK BIT, Article 4(1).

165 Singapore-Jordan BIT, Article 8.

166 Singapore-Bahrain BIT, Article 8; Singapore-Bangladesh BIT, Article 6; Singapore-Belarus BIT, Article 8; Singapore-BLEU, Article 5; Singapore-Bulgaria BIT, Article 7; Singapore-Cambodia BIT, Article 8; Singapore-China BIT, Article 8; Singapore-Czech Republic BIT, Article 8; Singapore-Egypt BIT, Article 8; Singapore-France BIT, Article 5; Singapore-Germany BIT, Article 5; Singapore-Hungary BIT, Article 8; Singapore-Indonesia BIT, Article VI; Singapore-Jordan BIT, Article 9; Singapore-North Korea BIT, Article 8; Singapore-Kuwait BIT, Article 7; Singapore-Laos BIT, Article 8; Singapore-Latvia BIT, Article 8; Singapore-Libya BIT, Article 7; Singapore-Mauritius BIT, Article 8; Singapore-Mexico BIT, Article 7; Singapore-Mongolia BIT, Article 8; Singapore-Netherlands BIT, Article VIII; Singapore-Oman BIT, Article 7; Singapore-Pakistan BIT, Article 8; Singapore-Poland BIT, Article 8; Singapore-Russia BIT, Article 7; Singapore-Saudi Arabia BIT, Article 6; Singapore-Slovak Republic BIT, Article 7; Singapore-Slovenia BIT, Article 8; Singapore-Sri Lanka BIT, Article 7; Singapore-Switzerland BIT, Article 3; Singapore-Turkey BIT,

clause commonly stipulates that the transfers will be made in a freely convertible currency, without any restriction or undue delay.

7 *Investor-State Dispute Settlement*

Almost all of the BITs concluded by Singapore contain dispute resolution provisions for the settlement of disputes between the host State and the investor,[167] except for a few exceptions such as the Singapore-Germany and Singapore-Switzerland BITs that only provide for dispute resolution at a State-to-State level.

Commonly, the clauses first require that written notice be given by a disputing party,[168] and an attempt be made by both parties to settle the dispute amicably through negotiations.[169] If the dispute cannot be resolved within (usually)

Article 8; Singapore-Ukraine BIT, Article 7; Singapore-UAE BIT, Article 7; Singapore-UK BIT, Article 6; Singapore-Uzbekistan BIT, Article 8; and Singapore-Vietnam BIT, Article 8.

167 Singapore-Bahrain BIT, Article 12; Singapore-Bangladesh BIT, Article 7; Singapore-Belarus BIT, Article 13; Singapore-BLEU, Article 9; Singapore-Bulgaria BIT, Article 11; Singapore-Cambodia BIT, Article 13; Singapore-China BIT, Article 13; Singapore-Czech Republic BIT, Article 13; Singapore-Egypt BIT, Article 13; Singapore-France BIT, Article 6; Singapore-Hungary BIT, Article 12; Singapore-Indonesia BIT, Article VIII; Singapore-Jordan BIT, Article 13; Singapore-North Korea BIT, Article 11; Singapore-Kuwait BIT, Article 9; Singapore-Laos BIT, Article 13; Singapore-Latvia BIT, Article 13; Singapore-Libya BIT, Article 10; Singapore-Mauritius BIT, Article 13; Singapore-Mexico BIT, Articles 9–19; Singapore-Mongolia BIT, Article 13; Singapore-Netherlands BIT, Article XI; Singapore-Oman BIT, Article 9; Singapore-Pakistan BIT, Article 13; Singapore-Poland BIT, Article 13; Singapore-Russia BIT, Article 9; Singapore-Saudi Arabia BIT, Article 9; Singapore-Slovak Republic BIT, Article 9; Singapore-Slovenia BIT, Article 12; Singapore-Sri Lanka BIT, Article 10; Singapore-Turkey BIT, Article 11; Singapore-Ukraine BIT, Article 10; Singapore-UAE BIT, Articles 9–10; Singapore-UK BIT, Article 8; Singapore-Uzbekistan BIT, Article 13; and Singapore-Vietnam BIT, Article 13.

168 See, for instance, Singapore-Bahrain BIT, Article 12; Singapore-Bangladesh BIT, Article 7; Singapore-Belarus BIT, Article 13; Singapore-Bulgaria BIT, Article 11; Singapore-Cambodia BIT, Article 13; Singapore-Czech Republic BIT, Article 13; Singapore-Egypt BIT, Article 13; Singapore-Indonesia BIT, Article VIII; Singapore-North Korea BIT, Article 11; Singapore-Kuwait BIT, Article 9; Singapore-Laos BIT, Article 13; Singapore-Latvia BIT, Article 13; Singapore-Libya BIT, Article 10; Singapore-Mauritius BIT, Article 13; Singapore-Mongolia BIT, Article 13; Singapore-Oman BIT, Article 9; Singapore-Oman BIT, Article 9; Singapore-Russia BIT, Article 9; Singapore-Saudi Arabia BIT, Article 9; Singapore-Slovak Republic BIT, Article 9; Singapore-Slovenia BIT, Article 12; Singapore-Turkey BIT, Article 11; Singapore-Ukraine BIT, Article 10; and Singapore-Uzbekistan BIT, Article 13.

169 See, for instance, Singapore-Bahrain BIT, Article 12; Singapore-Bangladesh BIT, Article 7; Singapore-Belarus BIT, Article 13; Singapore-Bulgaria BIT, Article 11; Singapore-Cambodia BIT, Article 13; Singapore-China BIT, Article 13; Singapore-Czech Republic BIT, Article 13;

a six-month period, either party may then submit the dispute to one of the dispute resolution procedures available under that BIT.[170] Singapore's BITs often list one or more of the following options: (1) the competent local courts of the host State, (2) arbitration under the ICSID Convention or the ICSID Additional Facility Rules, and (3) *ad hoc* arbitration under the UNCITRAL Arbitration Rules.[171] Sometimes, the clause also explicitly states that the procedure adopted shall be at the option of the investor,[172] or expressly contains a "fork-in-the-road" provision.[173]

A few BITs also provide for the applicable law for determination of the issues in dispute, but this is not commonplace.[174]

Singapore-Egypt BIT, Article 13; Singapore-Hungary BIT, Article 12; Singapore-Indonesia BIT, Article VIII; Singapore-Jordan BIT, Article 13; Singapore-North Korea BIT, Article 11; Singapore-Laos BIT, Article 13; Singapore-Latvia BIT, Article 13; Singapore-Libya BIT, Article 10; Singapore-Mauritius BIT, Article 13; Singapore-Mongolia BIT, Article 13; Singapore-Oman BIT, Article 9; Singapore-Oman BIT, Article 9; Singapore-Poland BIT, Article 13; Singapore-Russia BIT, Article 9; Singapore-Slovak Republic BIT, Article 9; Singapore-Slovenia BIT, Article 12; Singapore-Turkey BIT, Article 11; Singapore-Ukraine BIT, Article 10; Singapore-Uzbekistan BIT, Article 13; and Singapore-Vietnam BIT, Article 13.

170 See, for instance, Singapore-Bahrain BIT, Article 12; Singapore-Bangladesh BIT, Article 7; Singapore-Belarus BIT, Article 13; Singapore-Bulgaria BIT, Article 11; Singapore-Cambodia BIT, Article 13; Singapore-China BIT, Article 13; Singapore-Czech Republic BIT, Article 13; Singapore-Egypt BIT, Article 13; Singapore-Hungary BIT, Article 12; Singapore-Indonesia BIT, Article VIII; Singapore-North Korea BIT, Article 11; Singapore-Kuwait BIT, Article 9; Singapore-Laos BIT, Article 13; Singapore-Latvia BIT, Article 13; Singapore-Libya BIT, Article 10; Singapore-Mauritius BIT, Article 13; Singapore-Mongolia BIT, Article 13; Singapore-Oman BIT, Article 9; Singapore-Poland BIT, Article 13; Singapore-Russia BIT, Article 9; Singapore-Saudi Arabia BIT, Article 9; Singapore-Slovak Republic BIT, Article 9; Singapore-Slovenia BIT, Article 12; Singapore-Turkey BIT, Article 11; Singapore-Ukraine BIT, Article 10; Singapore-Uzbekistan BIT, Article 13; and Singapore-Vietnam BIT, Article 13.

171 See, for instance, Singapore-Bahrain BIT, Article 12; Singapore-Bulgaria BIT, Article 11; Singapore-Indonesia BIT, Article VIII; Singapore-North Korea BIT, Article 11; Singapore-Libya BIT, Article 10; Singapore-Oman BIT, Article 9; Singapore-Russia BIT, Article 9; Singapore-Slovak Republic BIT, Article 9; and Singapore-Turkey BIT, Article 11.

172 See, for instance, Singapore-Bahrain BIT, Article 12; Singapore-Saudi Arabia BIT, Article 9(2); and Singapore-Slovak Republic BIT, Article 9(2).

173 For example, the Singapore-Bulgaria BIT, Article 11(4), Singapore-Oman BIT, Article 9(3), and Singapore-Saudi-Arabia BIT, Article 9(3) make it clear that "[a] dispute shall be submitted to only one forum."

174 See, for instance, Singapore-Mexico BIT, Article 17.

8 *State-to-State Dispute Settlement*

All the BITs reviewed provide for dispute resolution between the State parties.[175] The degree of variation from BIT to BIT in respect of the substance of such clauses is also not large; most clauses first state that disputes should be settled, as far as possible, through negotiation or diplomatic channels.[176] If it cannot be settled, arbitration is often provided for, and the process of appointment of the tribunal is set out.[177] Where a party fails to make its appointment of an

175 Singapore-Bahrain BIT, Article 13; Singapore-Bangladesh BIT, Article 8; Singapore-Belarus BIT, Article 14; Singapore-BLEU, Article 10; Singapore-Bulgaria BIT, Article 12; Singapore-Cambodia BIT, Article 14; Singapore-Canada BIT, Article (7); Singapore-China BIT, Article 14; Singapore-Czech Republic BIT, Article 14; Singapore-Egypt BIT, Article 14; Singapore-France BIT, Article 10; Singapore-Germany BIT, Article 9; Singapore-Hungary BIT, Article 13; Singapore-Indonesia BIT, Article IX; Singapore-Jordan BIT, Article 14; Singapore-North Korea BIT, Article 12; Singapore-Kuwait BIT, Article 10; Singapore-Laos BIT, Article 14; Singapore-Latvia BIT, Article 14; Singapore-Libya BIT, Article 11; Singapore-Mauritius BIT, Article 14; Singapore-Mexico BIT, Articles 20–26; Singapore-Mongolia BIT, Article 14; Singapore-Netherlands BIT, Article XV; Singapore-Oman BIT, Article 10; Singapore-Pakistan BIT, Article 14; Singapore-Poland BIT, Article 14; Singapore-Russia BIT, Article 10; Singapore-Saudi Arabia BIT, Article 10; Singapore-Slovak Republic BIT, Article 10; Singapore-Slovenia BIT, Article 13; Singapore-Sri Lanka BIT, Article 11; Singapore-Switzerland BIT, Article 9; Singapore-Turkey BIT, Article 12; Singapore-Ukraine BIT, Article 11; Singapore-UAE BIT, Articles 11–12; Singapore-UK BIT, Article 9; Singapore-US BIT, Article (6); Singapore-Uzbekistan BIT, Article 14; and Singapore-Vietnam BIT, Article 14.

176 See, for instance, Singapore-Bahrain BIT, Article 13; Singapore-Bangladesh BIT, Article 8; Singapore-Belarus BIT, Article 14; Singapore-BLEU, Article 10; Singapore-Bulgaria BIT, Article 12; Singapore-Cambodia BIT, Article 14; Singapore-China BIT, Article 14; Singapore-Czech Republic BIT, Article 14; Singapore-Egypt BIT, Article 14; Singapore-France BIT, Article 10; Singapore-Hungary BIT, Article 13; Singapore-Indonesia BIT, Article IX; Singapore-Jordan BIT, Article 14; Singapore-North Korea BIT, Article 12; Singapore-Kuwait BIT, Article 10; Singapore-Laos BIT, Article 14; Singapore-Latvia BIT, Article 14; Singapore-Libya BIT, Article 11; Singapore-Mauritius BIT, Article 14; Singapore-Mongolia BIT, Article 14; Singapore-Netherlands BIT, Article XV; Singapore-Oman BIT, Article 10; Singapore-Pakistan BIT, Article 14; Singapore-Poland BIT, Article 14; Singapore-Russia BIT, Article 10; Singapore-Saudi Arabia BIT, Article 10; Singapore-Slovak Republic BIT, Article 10; Singapore-Slovenia BIT, Article 13; Singapore-Sri Lanka BIT, Article 11; Singapore-Switzerland BIT, Article 9; Singapore-Turkey BIT, Article 12; Singapore-Ukraine BIT, Article 11; Singapore-UK BIT, Article 9; Singapore-Uzbekistan BIT, Article 14; and Singapore-Vietnam BIT, Article 14.

177 See, for instance, Singapore-Bahrain BIT, Article 13; Singapore-Bangladesh BIT, Article 8; Singapore-Belarus BIT, Article 14; Singapore-BLEU, Article 10; Singapore-Bulgaria BIT,

arbitrator or the tribunal is not constituted for any other reason (e.g., failure of parties to reach agreement on appointment of the Chairman of the tribunal), it is often provided that either contracting party may invite the President of the International Court of Justice or if he is unable to do so (or is a national of either contracting party), the Member of the International Court of Justice next in seniority to make the necessary appointments.[178]

9 *Additional Provisions*

A few BITs contain denial of benefits clauses, such as the BITs concluded with Kuwait, Mexico and the UAE.[179] Under Article 14 of the Singapore-Kuwait BIT,

---

Article 12; Singapore-Cambodia BIT, Article 14; Singapore-China BIT, Article 14; Singapore-Czech Republic BIT, Article 14; Singapore-Egypt BIT, Article 14; Singapore-France BIT, Article 10; Singapore-Germany BIT, Article 9; Singapore-Hungary BIT, Article 13; Singapore-Indonesia BIT, Article IX; Singapore-Jordan BIT, Article 14; Singapore-North Korea BIT, Article 12; Singapore-Kuwait BIT, Article 10; Singapore-Laos BIT, Article 14; Singapore-Latvia BIT, Article 14; Singapore-Libya BIT, Article 11; Singapore-Mauritius BIT, Article 14; Singapore-Mexico BIT, Article 22; Singapore-Mongolia BIT, Article 14; Singapore-Netherlands BIT, Article XV; Singapore-Oman BIT, Article 10; Singapore-Pakistan BIT, Article 14; Singapore-Poland BIT, Article 14; Singapore-Russia BIT, Article 10; Singapore-Saudi Arabia BIT, Article 10; Singapore-Slovak Republic BIT, Article 10; Singapore-Slovenia BIT, Article 13; Singapore-Sri Lanka BIT, Article 11; Singapore-Switzerland BIT, Article 9; Singapore-Turkey BIT, Article 12; Singapore-Ukraine BIT, Article 11; Singapore-UAE BIT, Article 12; Singapore-UK BIT, Article 9; Singapore-Uzbekistan BIT, Article 14; and Singapore-Vietnam BIT, Article 14.

178 See, for instance, Singapore-Bahrain BIT, Article 13; Singapore-Bangladesh BIT, Article 8; Singapore-Belarus BIT, Article 14; Singapore-BLEU, Article 10; Singapore-Bulgaria BIT, Article 12; Singapore-Cambodia BIT, Article 14; Singapore-China BIT, Article 14; Singapore-Czech Republic BIT, Article 14; Singapore-Egypt BIT, Article 14; Singapore-Germany BIT, Article 9; Singapore-Hungary BIT, Article 13; Singapore-Indonesia BIT, Article IX; Singapore-Jordan BIT, Article 14; Singapore-North Korea BIT, Article 12; Singapore-Kuwait BIT, Article 10; Singapore-Laos BIT, Article 14; Singapore-Latvia BIT, Article 14; Singapore-Libya BIT, Article 11; Singapore-Mauritius BIT, Article 14; Singapore-Mexico BIT, Article 22; Singapore-Mongolia BIT, Article 14; Singapore-Netherlands BIT, Article XV; Singapore-Oman BIT, Article 10; Singapore-Pakistan BIT, Article 14; Singapore-Poland BIT, Article 14; Singapore-Russia BIT, Article 10; Singapore-Saudi Arabia BIT, Article 10; Singapore-Slovak Republic BIT, Article 10; Singapore-Slovenia BIT, Article 13; Singapore-Sri Lanka BIT, Article 11; Singapore-Switzerland BIT, Article 9; Singapore-Turkey BIT, Article 12; Singapore-Ukraine BIT, Article 11; Singapore-UAE BIT, Article 12; Singapore-UK BIT, Article 9; Singapore-Uzbekistan BIT, Article 14; and Singapore-Vietnam BIT, Article 14.

179 Singapore-Kuwait BIT, Article 14; Singapore-Mexico BIT, Article 29; and Singapore-UAE BIT, Article 14.

the contracting parties can decide jointly to deny the benefits of the BIT to an investor where it is owned or controlled by persons of a third State (i.e., a non-contracting party to the BIT) and has no substantive business operations in the territory of the host State.

Many of Singapore's BITs also contain a "national security" exception, providing that the BIT shall not limit the right of either contracting party to apply prohibitions or restrictions directed to the protection of essential security interests or the protection of public health.[180]

Preservation of Rights

Most of Singapore's BITs contain preservation of rights clauses,[181] which work by essentially confirming that the investor will receive the most favourable treatment it is entitled to, although it does not add any new substantive treaty obligation. For instance, the Singapore-Kuwait BIT, Article 12 states:

> If the legislation of either Contracting Party or international obligations existing at present or established hereafter between the Contracting Parties, in addition to this Agreement, contain rules, whether general or specific, entitling investments by investors of the other Contracting Party to a treatment more favourable than is provided for by this Agreement, such rules shall to the extent that they are more favourable to the investor prevail over this Agreement.

180 See, for instance, Singapore-Latvia BIT, Article 11; Singapore-Pakistan BIT, Article 11; and Singapore-Uzbekistan BIT, Article 11.

181 Singapore-Bahrain BIT, Article 14(1); Singapore-Belarus BIT, Article 15; Singapore-BLEU, Article 8; Singapore-Bulgaria BIT, Article 4(4); Singapore-Cambodia BIT, Article 15; Singapore-China BIT, Article 15; Singapore-Czech Republic BIT, Article 15(1); Singapore-Egypt BIT, Article 15; Singapore-Germany BIT, Article 8; Singapore-Hungary BIT, Article 14; Singapore-Indonesia BIT, Article XI; Singapore-Jordan BIT, Article 12; Singapore-North Korea BIT, Article 13; Singapore-Kuwait BIT, Article 12; Singapore-Laos BIT, Article 15; Singapore-Latvia BIT, Article 15; Singapore-Libya BIT, Article 12; Singapore-Mauritius BIT, Article 15; Singapore-Mongolia BIT, Article 15; Singapore-Netherlands BIT, Article XIV; Singapore-Oman BIT, Article 11(1); Singapore-Pakistan BIT, Article 15; Singapore-Poland BIT, Article 15; Singapore-Russia BIT, Article 11; Singapore-Slovak Republic BIT, Article 11(1); Singapore-Slovenia BIT, Article 14; Singapore-Switzerland BIT, Article 6; Singapore-Turkey BIT, Article 13; Singapore-Ukraine BIT, Article 12; Singapore-UAE BIT, Article 13; Singapore-Uzbekistan BIT, Article 15; and Singapore-Vietnam BIT, Article 15.

Thus, whichever is more favourable to the investor, whether domestic legislation, customary international law, other treaties entered into by the Contracting Parties, or the BIT itself, will prevail.

IV Multilateral Investment Related Treaties and Organizations to which Singapore is a Party

1 *ASEAN – ACIA*

Singapore is one of the Founding Members of ASEAN together with Indonesia, Malaysia, the Philippines and Thailand. Under the auspices of ASEAN, Singapore entered into a number of investment-related agreements[182] with the other Member States of ASEAN. This culminated in the conclusion of the ASEAN Comprehensive Investment Agreement ("ACIA"), which was signed on 26 February 2009 and entered into force on 29 March 2012.

The ACIA contains a number of substantive investment protections, including provisions on national treatment, MFN treatment, fair and equitable treatment and expropriation, in addition to providing for the resolution of investment disputes between an investor and a Member State. The ACIA applies to a number of specific sectors, including manufacturing, agriculture, fishery, forestry, mining and quarrying, and services incidental to these sectors,[183] while application is excluded in certain areas, such as taxation measures (with exceptions), subsidies or grants provided by a Member State, government procurement, services supplied in the exercise of governmental authority by a Member State, and measures adopted or maintained by a Member State affecting trade in services under the ASEAN Framework Agreement on Services.[184]

Notably, the ACIA recognises the importance of according special and differential treatment to the newer ASEAN Member States, including through recognising that commitments by such a Member State may be made in accordance with its individual stage of development.[185] While this clause has not been tested judicially, it raises an interesting question of whether, and if so,

182 These include the Agreement on Promotion and Protection of Investment in ASEAN signed by Brunei, Indonesia, Malaysia, the Philippines, Singapore and Thailand in 1987, and by Vietnam in 1996, as well as the Framework Agreement on the ASEAN Investment Area signed in 1998.

183 Article 3(3).

184 Article 3(4).

185 Article 23(c).

how such special and differential treatment may impact upon the standard of substantive protections provided under the ACIA.

2 *APEC*

Singapore has been a Member Economy of APEC since November 1989.[186] APEC's primary goal is to support sustainable economic growth and prosperity in the Asia-Pacific region.[187] In line with this aim, trade and investment liberalisation and facilitation is one of the cornerstones of APEC's mission and activities.[188]

Among other initiatives, three key APEC investment-related instruments are the Non-Binding Investment Principles ("NBIP"), the Menu of Options, and the Transparency Standards on Investment. The NBIP sets out 12 investment principles that are broadly similar to the core elements of international investment agreements concluded between APEC Member States, including provisions on transparency, national treatment, fair and equitable treatment, full protection and security, protection from strife, the transfer of funds, and the entry of key personnel. The Menu of Options (or the Options for Investment Liberalization and Business Facilitation to Strengthen the APEC Economies) lists policies for liberalization and business facilitation. The Transparency Standards on Investment cover the publication, awareness and availability of investment laws and measures.[189]

3 *Others*

As referenced above, Singapore has actively negotiated and entered into a number of FTAs. While a comprehensive review of Singapore's FTAs would be beyond the scope of this chapter, a few comments may be in order.

First, it is noteworthy that Singapore has an extensive network of 20 implemented FTAs with 31 trading partners, including the China-Singapore FTA, India-Singapore Comprehensive Economic Cooperation Agreement, Japan-Singapore Economic Partnership Agreement, United States-Singapore FTA, and under the auspices of ASEAN, the ASEAN-Australia-New Zealand FTA, ASEAN-China FTA, ASEAN-India FTA, ASEAN-Japan Comprehensive Economic Partnership and ASEAN-Korea FTA. These numbers do not

---

186 See http://www.apec.org/About-Us/About-APEC/Member-Economies.aspx.

187 See http://www.apec.org/About-Us/About-APEC/Mission-Statement.aspx.

188 See http://www.apec.org/About-Us/How-APEC-Operates/Scope-of-Work.aspx.

189 "Identifying core elements in investment agreements in the APEC region", *UNCTAD Series on International Investment Policies for Development, United Nations* (New York and Geneva: 2008), available at http://unctad.org/en/Docs/diaeia20083_en.pdf.

include the European Union-Singapore FTA, which is the first FTA concluded between the EU and an ASEAN country, or the Trans Pacific Partnership ("TPP"). At the time of writing, Singapore is also party to negotiations on the Regional Comprehensive Economic Partnership Agreement ("RCEP"), which are underway among the ASEAN Member States, Australia, China, India, South Korea, Japan and New Zealand.[190]

Many of these concluded FTAs contain investment chapters that cover substantive protections, such as provisions on national treatment, MFN treatment, fair and equitable treatment and expropriation, as well as dispute resolution mechanisms for investor-State disputes. See, for instance, the Singapore-Peru FTA[191] and the United States-Singapore FTA.[192]

Where there is more than one investment protection agreement in force between two trading partners, the protection of an investment may have to be considered under more than one instrument. For instance, as between Singapore and China, the China-Singapore FTA, ASEAN-China FTA and Singapore-China BIT could potentially cover the same investment. In that regard, an investor may wish to consider the interactions between the relevant instruments and the standard of protection under each agreement.

V Multilateral Dispute Settlement Related Treaties

1 *ICSID Convention*

Singapore has been a party to the ICSID Convention since 13 November 1968, and the Convention is implemented by way of the Arbitration (International Investment Disputes) Act.[193] Singapore has not lodged any notifications on exclusion of territories (under Article 70) or designated any constituent subdivisions or agencies under Article 25. Under Article 54(2) of the Convention, the competent court designated for the recognition and enforcement of an award is the High Court of Singapore.[194]

---

190 See the ASEAN chapter.

191 See Chapter 10 of the Singapore-Peru FTA, available at http://www.sice.oas.org/TPD/PER_SGP/Final_Texts_PER_SGP_e/index_e.asp.

192 See Chapter 15 of the United States-Singapore FTA, available at https://ustr.gov/sites/default/files/uploads/agreements/fta/singapore/asset_upload_file708_4036.pdf.

193 The Act is available at http://statutes.agc.gov.sg/aol/search/display/view.w3p;page=0;query=DocId%3A958b5af6-3d93-4898-8c20-b9e3f9543794%20%20Status%3Ainforce%20Depth%3A0;rec=0.

194 See https://icsid.worldbank.org/apps/ICSIDWEB/about/Pages/MembershipStateDetails.aspx?state=ST122.

2 *New York Convention*

Singapore ratified the New York Convention on 21 August 1986, and the Convention is given effect to under the IAA. Thus, as mentioned above, awards made in international arbitrations are enforceable under the New York Convention.

VI International Investment Arbitration Jurisprudence

While there has been a case brought by a Singaporean investor against the Government of the Union of Myanmar under the ASEAN treaties,[195] as at the date of writing, there has yet to be a publicly available case concerning investment claims against Singapore. The US Department of State 2015 Investment Climate Statement states that Singapore has not expropriated foreign owned property and there is no history of incidents involving politically motivated damage to foreign investments in Singapore.[196]

VII Outlook: Anticipated Developments

Singapore is a party to the TPP which was concluded in Atlanta, Georgia, USA on 5 October 2015, after five and a half years of negotiations. The TPP is a comprehensive, high standard regional trade agreement that is widely expected to create new trade and investment opportunities for Singapore in the Asia-Pacific region. The TPP brings together 12 economies from both sides of the Pacific, namely, Australia, Brunei Darussalam, Canada, Chile, Japan, Malaysia, Mexico, New Zealand, Peru, the United States, Vietnam and Singapore. Collectively, these countries represent 40% of global GDP, one-third of world trade, and comprise a population of 800 million, making the TPP the largest regional trade agreement at the time of writing.[197] Apart from offering new market access for Singapore goods and services producers exporting to and

---

195 See *Yaung Chi Oo Trading Pte Ltd., v. Government of the Union of Myanmar* (ASEAN I.D. Case No. ARB/01/1); this case has been discussed in the ASEAN chapter.

196 United States of America Department of State, "Singapore Investment Climate Statement 2015" (June 2015), available at http://www.state.gov/documents/organization/241949.pdf.

197 Singapore Ministry of Trade and Industry, "Trans Pacific Partnership Free Trade Agreement (TPP) 7 Things You Should Know", available at https://www.mti.gov.sg/MTIInsights/SiteAssets/Pages/TPP/Seven%20things%20you%20should%20know%20about%20the%20TPP%20(Final).pdf.

investing in TPP markets, the TPP also reinforces the region's commitment to a rules-based trading system by updating international rules that apply to cross-border trade and investment.[198]

Singapore already has existing FTAs with 9 of the 11 TPP partners. The TPP represents Singapore's first preferential trade agreement with Canada and Mexico. While the TPP has been concluded, it will only enter into force when at least six original signatories, accounting for at least 85% of the GDP across the TPP economies, have ratified the agreement. In Singapore, ratification will take place once the agreement is approved by the Cabinet, and any legislative changes that may be required are approved by the Parliament. When the TPP comes into force, it will be interesting to see how this agreement will fit into Singapore's complex web of treaty arrangements in its existing FTAs, BITs, regional investment agreements such as the ASEAN Comprehensive Investment Agreement, as well as the widely anticipated Regional Comprehensive Economic Partnership Agreement ("RCEP") where negotiations are expected to be concluded soon.[199] While the TPP and RCEP might open doors to vast investment opportunities and a jump in FDI inflows to Singapore, these agreements at the same time afford investors in Singapore with greater protection when investing in economies which did not previously have investment agreements with Singapore.[200] With the rapid proliferation of such agreements, and investors (as well as their advisors) becoming increasingly savvy in the area of investment treaty law, it may only be a matter of time before significant jurisprudence involving Singaporean investors (or even the Singapore government as a respondent State) emerges.

---

198 *Ibid.*

199 Singapore Ministry of Trade and Industry, "Factsheet: What You Need To Know About Regional Comprehensive Economic Partnership (RCEP)" (Updated in June 2014), available at https://www.mti.gov.sg/MTIInsights/SiteAssets/Pages/FACTSHEET-WHAT-YOU-NEED-TO-KNOW-ABOUT/Factsheet%20on%20RCEP%20(June%202014).pdf.

200 See, for example, "Summary Of The Trans-Pacific Partnership Agreement", available at https://www.mti.gov.sg/MTIInsights/SiteAssets/Pages/TPP/Summary%20of%20TPP%20Agreement.pdf, at para. 9.

CHAPTER 10

Thailand[1]

I Introduction

Thailand has been a democratic constitutional monarchy since the Siamese revolution of 1932, with a Prime Minister as the head of a parliamentary government, and the King as the Head of State. Before this, Thailand had been subject to absolute monarchical rule for more than 700 years.[2]

Since Thailand's first written constitution was issued in 1932, there have been, at the time of writing, 18 different constitutions and charters, reflecting the political transitions in Thailand. Following the military coup d'état led by General Prayuth Chan-Ocha in May 2014, the 2007 Constitution[3] was abandoned and replaced by an interim constitution on 22 July 2014,[4] paving the way for political reforms, including the establishment of a new national legislature.

Thailand has a codified legal system, introduced at the end of the 19th Century during the reign of King Chulalongkorn (Rama V). The main legislative codes are drawn from the codes in European civil law jurisdictions such as France, Switzerland and Germany, but are also influenced by common law systems such as the laws applied in England, and also by the principles of traditional Thai law.[5] The Thai Civil and Commercial Code came into force in 1925.[6] There is a dual court system, with separate administrative courts, and a number of specialized courts, such as the Central and Regional Intellectual Property and International Trade Courts.

1 This chapter has been drafted by Mr Steve Gibson and Ms Kate Lan of Eversheds LLP, Singapore, and reviewed by Mr Alastair Timblick of Timblick and Partners, Bangkok, Thailand.

2 Information on the history of Thailand, made available via Tourism Thailand at http://www.tourismthailand.org/Thailand/politics.

3 Constitution of the Kingdom of Thailand B.E. 2550 (2007), available at http://www.asianlii.org/th/legis/const/2007/1.html.

4 Puanthong Pawakapan, "The Thai Junta's Interim Constitution: Towards an Anti-Electoral Democracy", 12 August 2014, in *ISEAS Perspective*.

5 Prior to legal reforms under King Chulalongkorn (Rama V) a body of traditional rules – the *Thammasat* – formed the basis of Thai law for almost 500 years.

6 See Alastair Henderson, "Commercial Arbitration in Thailand", *Asian International Arbitration Journal*, Kluwer Law International 2009, Volume 5 Issue 1, pp. 46–49, at p. 47.

 | DOI 10.1163/9789004335257_012

Thailand has welcomed and encouraged investment and continues to attract significant inflows of foreign direct investment ("FDI"). The Board of Investment for Thailand ("BOI") has reported that in 2014, a total of 3,469 projects worth more than 2 trillion baht applied for investment promotion, the most in almost 50 years.[7] This was a significant increase on the 1,584 FDI projects in Thailand in 2012.[8] In 2013, inflows of FDI amounted to US $13 billion despite about 400 projects being shelved due to the political transition.[9] A large proportion of the FDI in Thailand has been from other Asian countries, such as Japan, Taiwan, Singapore and Hong Kong. Significant investments have also originated from the U.S. and Europe. Japanese investors are particularly active, accounting for more than 50% of the total investment into Thailand in 2013,[10] mostly in the manufacturing sector.[11] On the World Bank's "Ease of Doing Business" scale, Thailand was ranked 49th out of 189 countries, ranking it fifth in the East Asia & Pacific region.[12]

Thailand's economy has been focused on its manufacturing sector. From 1960 until the Asian financial crisis in 1997, the Thai economy grew at a rate of nearly 8% per year.[13] Despite a subsequent slowdown, it has continued to grow, driven by FDI and the Thai government's export-friendly policies. As of 2013, approximately 73% of Thailand's GDP resulted from the export of goods and services, a higher share than the pre-1997 crisis level of 50%.[14]

As a founder member of ASEAN, Thailand has promoted and encouraged trade and investment with its regional neighbours, and much of Thailand's incoming and outgoing FDI is with ASEAN economies. In 2015, Thailand

7 Press Release No.14/2015 (0.8) of The Board of Investment, 26 January 2015, available at http://www.boi.go.th/upload/content/2014-01-23.applications.Exceed.2.Trillion.Baht_38646.pdf.

8 Thailand Board of Investment 2013 Statistics: http://www.boi.go.th/upload/content/TFDI13_73036.pdf (where foreign capital is at least 10% of the total investment).

9 UNCTAD World Investment Report 2014, Chapter II, page 48: http://unctad.org/en/PublicationsLibrary/wir2014_en.pdf, although a slight reduction in FDI inflow has been seen in 2014 to US $12.5 billion, UNCTAD World Investment Report 2015: http://unctad.org/en/PublicationsLibrary/wir2015_en.pdf.

10 Statistics published by the BOI, available at: http://www.boi.go.th/index.php?page=statistics_foreign_direct_investment.

11 Pisit Puapan, "Assessment of FDI impact on Thailand's Production Sectors: Implications for Investment Promotion Activities," *IDE Discussion Paper No. 443*, February 2014, p. 5.

12 World Bank Group, "Doing Business 2016 – Thailand", 13th ed., http://www.doingbusiness.org/data/exploreeconomies/thailand/.

13 Pisit Puapan, *op. cit.*, p. 2.

14 *Ibid.*, p. 3.

formed part of the newly established ASEAN Economic Community, a single market promoting the free movement of goods, services and labour amongst member States.[15]

II Thailand's National Arbitration and Investment Legislation

1 *Thailand's Arbitration Legislation and Institutions*

Arbitration Law in Thailand

The Arbitration Act B.E. 2545 (2002) (the "Arbitration Act") governs both domestic and international arbitration in Thailand. It is based on the UNCITRAL Model Law ("Model Law"), but with some differences and local adaptation. Unlike the Model Law, which is intended to apply only to international arbitration, no distinction between domestic and international arbitration is made in the Arbitration Act. In contrast, the preceding legislation, the Arbitration Act of 1987, was not based on the Model Law, a conscious decision by the Thai drafters who considered the Model Law to be "too modern" for Thailand.[16]

The Arbitration Act affirms, without qualification, that in a contract made between a government agency and a private party, the parties may agree to settle any dispute by arbitration, and such arbitration agreement shall bind the parties. This applies regardless of whether or not the contract is an administrative contract.[17] That said, it appears that arbitration has not been accepted ubiquitously in the public sector in Thailand, and arbitration clauses may be resisted in some public sector contracts. Under a resolution of the Thai Cabinet in 2009, which updated a 2004 resolution (that was passed following a number of adverse rulings against Government entities), it was stated that a contract between a Government entity and a private company shall not contain an arbitration clause unless approved by the Thai Cabinet on a case-by-case basis.[18] The 2009 resolution was amended by a further Cabinet resolution that was passed in 2015. Under the 2015 resolution, Cabinet approval for arbitration clauses will only be required for three types of contracts involving Thai

---

15 Information available on the website of the Association of Southeast Asian Nations, at: http://www.asean.org/communities/asean-economic-community.

16 Henderson *op. cit.*, p. 51.

17 Section 15, Arbitration Act.

18 See Kluwer Arbitration blog, 9 October 2014, Vanina Sucharitkul: http://kluwerarbitrationblog.com/blog/2014/10/09/thai-administrative-court-overturns-an-arbitration-award-against-the-government/.

government agencies. These are contracts involving partnerships between the public and private sector, concession agreements and contracts that require Cabinet approval under Royal Decree 2005. Although Cabinet resolutions do not have the same binding legal status of a legislation or decree in Thailand, they must be complied with by government agencies and are generally observed by those affected in the private sector as well. Further issues around the enforcement of arbitration awards against public sector parties are discussed below.

The Arbitration Act emphasises the contractual aspect of arbitration more than earlier legislation in Thailand.[19] The tribunal is obliged to decide disputes in accordance with the governing law which is chosen by the parties. If the parties have not designated a governing law, the tribunal will apply Thai law to the dispute, unless there is a conflict of laws, in which case the tribunal will apply the law determined by the conflict of laws rules that it considers applicable.[20]

To be recognised under the Arbitration Act, an arbitration agreement must be in writing.[21] The Arbitration Act requires Thai courts to strike out cases initiated in court in respect of any dispute that is the subject of an arbitration agreement, unless the arbitration agreement is found to be void, inoperative or incapable of being performed by the relevant court after it has completed its inquiry.[22] The arbitration agreement is recognised as being independent of the contract in which it is found under Section 24 of the Arbitration Act, enshrining the principle of separability.[23] Thus, even if the contract is found to be void, invalid or unenforceable, the validity and enforceability of the arbitration clause will not be affected. There are no explicit obligations of confidentiality in arbitration under Thai law, but in practice, arbitral tribunals usually require parties to maintain the confidentiality of proceedings, whether or not specified in the arbitration agreement.

Since the Arbitration Act was passed into law in 2002, arbitration agreements have generally been respected in Thailand, as evidenced by more than 90 per cent of cases before the courts concerning arbitration agreements being decided in favour of recognizing or upholding the arbitration agreements.[24]

---

19 Saowanee Asawaroj, "National Report for Thailand" (2013) in Jan Paulsson and Lise Bosman (eds), *ICCA International Handbook on Commercial Arbitration* (Kluwer Law International; Kluwer Law International 1984, Supplement No. 77, December 2013).

20 Section 34, Arbitration Act.

21 Section 11, Arbitration Act.

22 Section 14, Arbitration Act.

23 Section 24, Act.

24 Saowanee Asawaroj *op. cit.*

But the picture is not quite so rosy for investors in other respects. Under Thai law, State property is immune from judicial execution, conferring wide immunities on the assets of State entities, including assets which are used for commercial purposes.[25]

In order to afford more assurances to private parties, regulations were introduced in 2001 providing that where an arbitration award is made against a State agency, the agency must comply with the award without requiring enforcement proceedings, unless the award: is contrary to the law governing the dispute; is the result of an unjust act or process; or is outside the scope of the arbitration agreement.[26] However, compliance with these regulations has been limited, and it remains common that parties will have to follow and exhaust court procedures for enforcement before a public sector entity will make payment following an arbitration award.[27]

Thailand's Arbitral Institutions and Rules

Two main arbitral institutions exist in Thailand, together with a number of specialized institutions operating in specific sectors.[28] The Thai Commercial Arbitration Committee of the Board of Trade of Thailand (the "BOT"), was established in 1967, and the Thai Arbitration Institute (the "TAI") was established in 1990. While there has been limited usage of BOT proceedings, the TAI, which is part of the Office of the Judiciary, a constitutionally independent body, has become the main arbitral institution in Thailand and has contributed significantly to the growth of arbitration as a form of dispute resolution in Thailand.[29]

The TAI facilitates the arbitration process and assists with the appointment of arbitrators. Unusually, when compared with most arbitral institutions around the world, the TAI does not charge for its services, except for a small fee for the use of its facilities. TAI has published the Rules on Arbitration of the Thai Arbitration Institute,[30] which came into force on 2 May, 2003. TAI's

25 Section 1307 Civil and Commercial Code.

26 Regulation of the Prime Minister's Office on Compliance with Arbitral Awards BE 2544 (2001).

27 Henderson *op. cit.*, p. 65.

28 For example, insurance disputes may be heard by the Office of Insurance Commission, Ministry of Commerce or the Arbitration Office of the Insurance Association, or intellectual property disputes by the Office of Intellectual Property Dispute Prevention and Resolution, the Department of Intellectual Property.

29 Henderson *op. cit.*, p. 55.

30 Available at http://www.adro.coj.go.th/userfiles/file/TAI/en/Law_Regulations/Arbitration%20Rules_en.pdf.

arbitration rules follow the UNCITRAL Rules in many respects, particularly in relation to arbitration awards, and do not contain detailed procedural requirements. Unless agreed otherwise by the parties, and subject to the consent of the Director of the Alternative Dispute Resolution Office of the Thai Office of the Judiciary, the TAI arbitration rules will apply to all arbitrations administered by the TAI.[31]

The TAI arbitration rules also provide for the following model arbitration clause:

> Any dispute, controversy or claim arising out of or relating to this contract or the breach, termination or invalidity thereof, shall be settled by arbitration in accordance with the Arbitration Rules of the Thai Arbitration Institute, Office of the Judiciary applicable at the time of submission of the dispute to arbitration and the conduct of the arbitration thereof shall be under the auspices of the Thai Arbitration Institute.[32]

Briefly, the rules provide for the party initiating recourse to arbitration to submit a statement of claim, following which the respondent will file a defence or counterclaim.[33] The rules expressly provide for the appointment of arbitrators (Rules 10 to 14), the challenge of arbitrators (Rules 15 to 19) and the conduct of arbitral proceedings (Rules 20 to 26). While the rules do not provide for confidentiality, Rule 22(3) states that "arbitral proceedings shall be held *in camera*". In respect of the rendering of the award, the award must be made within 180 days after the appointment of the last arbitrator (Rule 27). Under Rule 29, the arbitral tribunal is to make its decision "in accordance with legal principle and the rule of justice", though parties may request that the tribunal decide the dispute *ex aequo et bono*.[34]

Other arbitration institutions and rules may be used in Thailand, and in practice are. The ICC has an arbitration commission in Thailand and administers cases seated in Thailand or with Thai parties. The ICC Rules of Arbitration have been published in the Thai language. Other neutral venues and rules, such as SIAC and HKIAC, as well as *ad hoc* arbitration under the UNCITRAL rules may be selected by the parties.

---

31 Rule 2, Rules on Arbitration of the Thai Arbitration Institute.

32 *Ibid.*, Rule 5.

33 *Ibid.*, Rules 6 to 8.

34 *Ibid.*, Rule 29.

Thailand's Courts and Arbitration

Prior to the introduction of the 2002 Arbitration Act, the approach of the Thai courts was not consistently supportive of arbitration, as arbitration agreements were not always respected and the enforcement of awards was not assured.[35] However, more recently, the Thai courts have shown a much greater willingness to uphold and enforce awards, and order provisional measures in support of arbitration.

As arbitral tribunals are not empowered under Thai law to order provisional measures,[36] any applications for provisional measures must be made to a competent court under section 16 of the Arbitration Act. The court may award such interim measures, such as a temporary injunction or requiring a party to pay a deposit of money for security, as it would be entitled to do in pending litigation, in accordance with the Code of Civil Procedure.[37]

Enforcement of Arbitration Awards

The Arbitration Act makes no distinction between domestic and foreign arbitral awards with regards to the challenging and setting aside of such awards. Section 41 sets out the general principle that an award shall be recognized as binding, irrespective of the country in which it was made, and shall be enforced. Section 42 sets out the procedure for enforcement, which requires that a party apply to a competent court within 3 years of "the date on which the award became enforceable". This wording was deliberately chosen by the drafters of the Arbitration Act to encompass more than one situation. It will usually refer to the date on which the award is served on the parties. If the parties enter into a settlement agreement and request that the tribunal render an award on the agreed terms, a grace period may be given for a party to pay an amount of money. The award then only becomes enforceable at the expiry of the grace period.[38] The party seeking to enforce must produce a duly authenticated original award or duly certified copy thereof. He must also file a certified translation of the award if it is not made in the Thai language. Documents

---

35 Henderson *op. cit.*, p. 60.

36 Indeed, the TAI arbitration rules make no reference to provisional measures.

37 Provisional measures under the Civil Procedure Code include orders for deposit of money as security; seizure of property or funds; temporary injunctions to restrain a party from continuing or repeating any act, transferring or disposing of property; and orders directing public officials to register, modify or cancel registrations relating to property.

38 See Sorawit Limparangsri, "Improving on Enforcement of International Commercial Arbitral Awards in ASEAN: A Thai Perspective", a paper for the 10th General Assembly of the ASEAN Law Association, at p. 4.

must be certified by a sworn translator or an officer of the Ministry of Foreign Affairs, or diplomatic delegate or Thai consul in the country where they were made.

The only competent court for the enforcement of foreign arbitral awards is the Central Intellectual Property and International Trade Court,[39] though it should be noted that that court is not a specialised arbitration court. Applications for the enforcement of domestic awards may be made in the competent court where the arbitration proceedings were conducted, the court with jurisdiction over the place where a party is domiciled or the Administrative Court of Thailand. First instance decisions in enforcement proceedings may be appealed to the Supreme Court of Thailand. As there is no time limit for appeals provided in the Arbitration Act, a period of one month from the pronouncement of the judgment, which is specified at Section 229 of the Code of Civil Procedure will apply.

Thailand is a party to the New York Convention, without reservation.[40] The Arbitration Act specifies that foreign arbitral awards will only be enforced to the extent of Thailand's obligations under international conventions or treaties.[41] The grounds on which the court may set aside (Section 40 of the Arbitration Act) or refuse to enforce (Section 43 of the Arbitration Act) an arbitration award are effectively the same as those which are set out under Article V of the New York Convention and Articles 34 and 36 of the UNCITRAL Model Law. In addition, the Act also provides for awards to be set aside or enforcement refused where the award is "contrary to public order or good morals".[42] An example of an award not being enforced on this basis was in *Expressway* and *Rapid Transit Authority v. Joint Venture*,[43] where the Supreme Court held that an arbitral award could not be enforced as the underlying contract was unlawful and the claimants did not exercise their rights in good faith.

However, the overall picture shows that Thai courts generally will enforce most foreign arbitral awards that come before them. For instance, in a case heard by the Supreme Court,[44] the claimant sought the enforcement of an award rendered by an arbitral tribunal in London. The defendant argued that the appointment of the tribunal had not been properly carried out because it had been done by the claimant without the defendant's participation. The

39 *Ibid.*, at p. 5.

40 See below for further details.

41 Section 41, Arbitration Act.

42 *Ibid.*, Sections 40(2)(b) and 44.

43 Decision of the Supreme Court, Case no. 7277 of BE 2549 (2006).

44 Supreme Court Case No. 2562/2540, as referred to in Limparangsri, *op. cit.*, at p. 9.

court found in favour of the claimant, and enforced the award, finding the defendant had been given proper notice of the arbitration and had chosen not to participate in the appointment of the tribunal.[45] In *Canada Packers Co. v. T.K. Food Industry Co.*,[46] the fact that the defendant did not attend the arbitration proceedings (due to the high cost of doing so) did not render the award contrary to public order or good morals, and the Supreme Court held that the award could be enforced. Additionally, while the time taken to enforce arbitration awards has been the subject of criticism in the past, recent cases have shown an improvement, with enforcement decisions being obtained within six to eight months of the initiation of proceedings.[47]

In Thailand, a judgment enforcing an arbitration award is itself enforceable according to the normal procedures of the Thai courts for enforcing judgments. The judgment creditor can then initiate further proceedings at court in order to obtain available relief, such as court examination of the debtor or any third party believed to have information about the debtor's assets, the attachment of debts or other property owed or to be transferred to the debtor by third parties, and the issuance of an execution decree empowering officials of the Legal Execution Department to seize the debtor's property and sell it through public auction.[48]

2 *Thailand's Investment Laws*

There are several laws and regulations applicable to foreign investment in Thailand. The Foreign Business Act[49] (the "FBA") limits the types of investments which a "foreigner" may engage in within Thailand. Under the FBA, a "foreigner" is defined as a natural person not of Thai nationality, a juristic person not registered in Thailand, or a juristic person where 50% or more of the share capital is held by a non-Thai national or company.[50]

45 Limparangsri *op. cit.* at p. 9.

46 Decision of the Supreme Court, Case no. 8151 of BE 2542 (1999).

47 "Thailand, Towards an Arbitration-Friendlier Jurisdiction," Herbert Smith Freehills, 8 January 2014, available at: http://hsfnotes.com/arbitration/2014/01/08/thailand-towards-an-arbitration-friendlier-jurisdiction.

48 Alastair Henderson, "Enforcement of Arbitral Awards in Indochina – Law, Practice, and Alternatives," *Journal of International Arbitration*, pp. 841–857, at p. 843.

49 Foreign Business Act B.E. 2542 (1999), available at the website of the Thailand Department of Business Development, Ministry of Commerce (http://www.dbd.go.th/dbdweb_en/more_news.php?cid=271).

50 *Ibid.*, Section 4.

The FBA sets out three categories (or lists) of business activities in Thailand in which the participation of foreigners is subject to restrictions.[51]

List One consists of business activities in which foreigners are prohibited from participating for "special reasons". While it is not specified what "special reasons" are, the prohibited activities are clearly listed. These include newspapers, radio broadcasting stations, radio and television broadcasting businesses, rice farming and growing plantations or crops, livestock farming, fishery in Thai territorial waters and specific economic zones, and land trading.

List Two contains business activities which relate to national security or safety, art, culture, customs, native manufacturing or handicraft production, natural resources or the environment. Foreigners can only operate businesses falling under List Two with permission from the Minister of Commerce, and a resolution of the Thai cabinet is required.[52] Furthermore, Thai nationals must hold at least 40% of the share capital in the foreign juristic person, and two-fifths of the directors must be Thai. The Minister of Commerce may reduce the shareholding requirement, with approval from the Thai cabinet, but not below 25%.[53] Exceptions to the restrictions imposed on List Two business activities are businesses which have received "investment promotion" status under the Investment Promotion Act or have been authorised by the Industrial Estate Authority,[54] or where an exception applies under a treaty by which Thailand is bound.[55]

List Three contains business activities in which there are economic protections for Thai nationals. Those include professional services such as legal and accountancy services, architectural services, engineering services, and brokerage and construction activities. Foreigners may only engage in such businesses with permission from the Director-General at the Department of Business Development at the Ministry of Commerce, with approval from the Foreign Business Committee.[56] However, provided permission is granted, there is no

---

51 See, in general, "A Business Guide To Thailand 2014", published by the Thailand Board of Investment, at pp. 70–75.

52 Section 8(2), Foreign Business Act.

53 *Ibid.*, Section 15.

54 *Ibid.*, Section 12.

55 Section 10, FBA. As considered in paragraphs 3 and 4 below, Thailand is party to a number of bilateral, multilateral and regional treaties concerning trade and investment. The U.S. – Thailand Treaty of Amity and Economic Relations grants the broadest exemptions to the provisions of the FBA, giving U.S. investors the right to engage in business on the same basis as Thai nationals except in certain specified fields (see paragraph 4.1.1 below).

56 Section 8(3), FBA.

minimum Thai shareholding or directors required.[57] Exceptions to the restrictions on List Three business activities are businesses receiving "investment promotion" under the Investment Promotion Act, authorised by the Industrial Estate Authority, or that have obtained a Foreign Business Certificate from the Director-General at the Department of Business Development at the Ministry of Commerce,[58] or where an exception applies under a treaty by which Thailand is bound.[59]

A foreigner operating a business in breach of the restrictions imposed by the FBA may be liable to criminal sanctions, including imprisonment of up to three years.[60]

Separately, the Investment Promotion Act,[61] last amended in 2001, established the BOI and created a legal framework covering investment incentives granted in Thailand. It provides the BOI with significant discretionary powers to promote investment. Section 16 of the Investment Promotion Act states that:

> The activities which are eligible for promotion by the Board are those which are important and beneficial to the economic and social development, and security of the country, activities which involve production for export, activities which have high content of capital, labour or service or activities which utilise agricultural produce or natural resources as raw materials, provided that in the opinion of the Board, they are non-existent in the Kingdom, or existent but inadequate, or use out-of-date production processes.
>
> The Board shall make an announcement designating the types and sizes of investment activity eligible for promotion and may stipulate there in the conditions under which promotion is to be granted and may amend or abolish these conditions at any time.

57 Note, however, that there are other requirements which may be applicable, such as minimum capital, number of foreign director(s) or representative(s) required to be resident in Thailand, transfer of technology to local staff and capital-to-loan ratio. The licence holder is also required to comply with the obligations set out in the relevant Foreign Business Licence (in addition to statutory obligations imposed on the company) (*e.g.* filing of annual reports).

58 Section 11, FBA.

59 Alastair Henderson, "Enforcement of Arbitral Awards in Indochina – Law, Practice, and Alternatives," *Journal of International Arbitration*, pp. 841–857, at p. 843.

60 Section 34, FBA.

61 The Investment Promotion Act, B.E. 2520 (1977) (as amended), available at: http://www.boi.go.th/english/download/boi_forms/proact_eng.pdf.

> In case where the Board is of the opinion that any activity announced to be eligible for promotion under paragraph two no longer requires to be promoted, it may announce a temporary or permanent cancellation of promotion for that activity.

The current seven categories of activities eligible for investment promotion are agriculture and agricultural products; mining, ceramics and basic metals; light industry; metal products, machinery and transport equipment; electronic industry and electric appliances; chemicals, paper and plastics; services and public utilities.[62] Announcement of the Board of Investment No. 2/2557[63] sets out a complete list of activities which are eligible for investment promotion, together with the conditions to be met in order to qualify for such status.

The Investment Promotion Act permits the BOI to grant incentives and privileges for promoted investments, such as State guarantees, business protection,[64] the relaxation of restrictions on participation in business activities which would otherwise apply under Thai legislation (for example, the FBA),[65] and taxation incentives and reliefs. Importantly, the Investment Promotion Act also grants foreigners permission to own land in Thailand[66] which, as discussed below, is otherwise not permissible under Thai law.

Chapter 5 of the Investment Promotion Act provides investors with certain guarantees and protections in respect of promoted investments. Significantly, there is an express prohibition on the State nationalizing the activity of a promoted person,[67] i.e., investors who hold a certificate for promoted investments. Further, under Section 44, an investor is guaranteed that the State will not undertake a new activity in competition with it. Investors are also protected against the State's monopolization of products or commodities similar to any promoted investments,[68] the imposition of price controls and export bans on promoted products,[69] except where those are necessary for the economic and

62 Published on the website of the BOI at http://www.boi.go.th/index.php?page=eligible_activities.

63 Which is applicable from January 2015.

64 Examples include the imposition of a surcharge on the import of competing products, banning the import of competing products, ordering actions necessary to assist the promoted projects and the provision of tax relief for promoted projects.

65 The BOI grants privileges to investors which provide exceptions to the restrictions in the FBA on a case-by-case basis.

66 Section 27, Investment Promotion Act.

67 *Ibid.*, Section 43.

68 *Ibid.*, Section 45.

69 *Ibid.*, Section 46.

social development and the national security of Thailand.[70] Other measures protect the promoted investment from the foreign dumping of imported goods in Thailand, such as by enabling the BOI to impose a special fee on imported goods that compete with promoted products at a rate of up to 50% of the price of the imported product or commodity, for a maximum period of one year.[71] Where the imposition of special fees on imports is considered inadequate by the BOI, the Ministry of Commerce may impose an import ban on such products.[72]

The Investment Promotion Act also seeks to encourage the industrial development of Thailand's provinces by granting special privileges to projects established in "investment promotion zones". The BOI periodically identifies and specifies zones which are eligible for investment incentives,[73] and specifies the privileges that will apply in such zones. Currently, the eligible zones include 20 provinces of Thailand with low per capita incomes and science and technology parks approved by the BOI.

The general criteria for the approval of projects for investment promotion is specified in Chapter 2 of the Investment Promotion Act. Specific criteria are set out in the decisions and Announcements of the BOI. At the time of writing, the criteria for project approval applied by the BOI is specified in Announcement No. 2/2557. Two different sets of criteria are employed to determine whether a proposed project is economically and technologically eligible for investment promotion. The first set of criteria applies to general investment projects, the second set applies to concession projects or the privatization of State enterprises.[74] Some examples of the conditions to be met are: modern production processes must be used; new machinery must be used; and ISO certification must be achieved in certain instances.[75]

Investment incentives are also provided for under other Thai legislation. The Industrial Estate Authority of Thailand Act[76] confers preferential treatment upon BOI promoted businesses located in industrial estates falling under the

---

70 *Ibid.*, Section 47.

71 *Ibid.*, Section 49.

72 *Ibid.*, Section 50.

73 See for example paragraph 7 of Announcement No. 2/2557, available at: http://www.boi.go.th/upload/content/newpolicy-announcement%20as%20of%2020_12_57_33650.pdf.

74 Pursuant to the Thai Cabinet's decision on 25 May 1998.

75 See paragraph 6.1 of Announcement No. 2/2557, available at http://www.boi.go.th/upload/content/newpolicy-announcement%20as%20of%2020_3_58_23499.pdf.

76 The Industrial Estate Authority of Thailand Act, B.E. 2522 (1979), unofficial translation available at http://www2.austlii.edu.au/~graham/AsianLII/Thai_Translation/Industrial%20Estate%20Authority%20of%20Thailand%20Act.pdf.

Act and also grants tax privileges to non-BOI promoted foreign or Thai investors establishing commercial operations in an approved export processing zone. The tax privileges are similar to those provided by the BOI under the Investment Promotion Act, including exemptions from import and export duties, as well as exemptions from VAT on machinery, equipment, tools, raw materials and goods. Another statute, the Petroleum Act,[77] offers concession holders privileges similar to those conferred by the BOI under the Investment Promotion Act. Under Section 64 of the Petroleum Act, investors holding a concession for the exploration and production of petroleum are provided with a guarantee that the State will not nationalize the investor's properties or rights to conduct petroleum operations, nor will the State restrict the export of petroleum, except for reasons of national security or in order to meet domestic demand.

One important piece of legislation relating to foreign investment in Thailand is the Land Code.[78] Pursuant to Section 86 of the Land Code, non-nationals may only acquire land ownership rights where permitted to do so under the provisions of a treaty. Where no treaty granting the foreign investor the right to own land applies, the investor is effectively prohibited from owning land in Thailand, unless he falls within one of the stated exceptions under other legislation. For instance, foreigners investing more than 40,000 baht in specified Thai businesses may own up to one *rai* (1,600 square meters) of land for residential purposes with permission from the Ministry of the Interior.[79] Foreign investors are also entitled to own land in Thailand if they are promoted by the BOI under the Investment Promotion Act, or if the business activity is caught by the exceptions under the Industrial Estate Authority of Thailand Act or Petroleum Act. If none of these circumstances exist, non-Thai investors will not be entitled to own land.

---

77 The Petroleum Act, B.E. 2514 (1971), available at http://law.dmf.go.th/sub_main.php?lan=en&main_no=M935502387.

78 Land Code Promulgating Act, B.E. 2497 (1954), translation available at http://library.siam-legal.com/land-act-2497-2008/.

79 Section 96 bis Land Code added by the Land Code Amendment Act (No. 8), B.E. 2542 (1999).

III Thailand's Bilateral Investment Treaties

1 *Overview*

Thailand is a party to more than 40 bilateral and multilateral agreements for the protection of investments. Such protection dates back to a treaty signed with the United States of America in 1833.[80] It has signed 39 Bilateral Investment Treaties ("BIT"),[81] of which 36 are currently in force.[82] The majority of BITs signed by Thailand are publicly available in the English language.[83] Thailand has a Model BIT, adopted in 2002. Thailand has introduced a new Model BIT in 2013. However, it is unclear if Thailand has officially adopted and implemented the 2013 Model BIT as the revised provisions were still being discussed within the Thai government in 2015.[84] Based on publicly available information at the time of writing, Thailand has not yet entered into any BITs based on the 2013 Model BIT. Discussions relating to Thailand's Model BIT in this Chapter are therefore based only on provisions in the 2002 Model BIT.

---

80 The Treaty of Amity and Commerce between Siam and the United States (Roberts Treaty) of 1833; see 2012 Investment Climate Statement – Thailand, published by the U.S. Bureau of Economic and Business Affairs, June 2012. Available at: http://www.state.gov/e/eb/rls/othr/ics/2012/191248.htm. See below, section IV, which considers the successor to the Roberts treaty, the 1966 U.S.-Thailand treaty, and its provisions.

81 Thailand has signed agreements with (in alphabetical order) Argentina, Bahrain, Belgium-Luxembourg Economic Union (BLEU), Bulgaria, Cambodia, Canada, China, Croatia, Czech Republic, Egypt, Finland, Germany, Hong Kong, Hungary, India, Indonesia, Israel, Jordan, Democratic People's Republic of Korea, Republic of Korea, Laos, Myanmar, Netherlands, Peru, Philippines, Poland, Romania, Russia, Slovenia, Sri Lanka, Sweden, Switzerland, Taiwan, Tajikistan, Turkey, United Kingdom, Vietnam, Zimbabwe. Note that while the agreement between Thailand and the Netherlands has been included in this section as it provides for the protection of investments between the contracting States, it is an Agreement on Economic Co-operation, not a BIT, and unlike most BITs, it does not contain provisions granting recourse to arbitration or other forms of dispute settlement.

82 The following BITs are not in force at the time of writing: Russia, Tajikistan, Zimbabwe.

83 UNCTAD Investment Policy Hub at http://investmentpolicyhub.unctad.org/IIA/CountryBits/207. The BIT signed with Tajikistan is not publicly available.

84 See http://investmentpolicyhub.unctad.org/Download/TreatyFile/2874, and Nottage, Luke R., *The TPP Investment Chapter and Investor-State Arbitration in Asia and Oceania: Assessing Prospects for Ratification* (April 20, 2016). Sydney Law School Research Paper No. 16/28. Available at SSRN: http://ssrn.com/abstract=2767996).

2 *Definition of Investment*

The Model BIT provides for a broad definition of "investment", which is defined as "any kind of asset", and enumerates specific categories of investments as examples. These are: movable and immovable property and other property rights such as mortgages and liens; shares, stocks, debentures and other interests in a company; claims to money and other rights; intellectual property and industrial property rights (as recognised by the law of the contracting State in which the investment is made); and business concessions (including those concerned with natural resources).[85] The majority of Thailand's BITs define "investment" in a similar way to the Model BIT, including the same categories of investments.

All of Thailand's BITs provide protection for investments only once written approval has been given by the competent authority.[86] Without such written approval, investments will not *prima facie* be afforded protection under the relevant BIT. Under some of the BITs, approval of an investment may be subject to conditions set by the approving State.[87] Many of the BITs expressly provide that an investment must be in accordance with the laws and regulations of the contracting State in which it is made.[88] The Thailand-China BIT defines investments as "assets as permitted by each Contracting Party in accordance with its laws and regulations."[89] In addition to the requirement that investments are to be made in accordance with a contracting State's laws and regulations, the Thailand-Egypt BIT further provides that to obtain protection, an investment must accord to the "general economic policy" of the Contracting State.[90] The Netherlands-Thailand agreement,[91] unlike other BITs, offers no definition of "investment".

Thailand's BITs provide little guidance on the ownership of investments which will be given protection. Almost all of the BITs make no express reference to whether assets must be directly owned or controlled by a qualifying investor, or whether they can be indirectly controlled (e.g., shares held through

---

85 Article 1(1) Thailand Model BIT.

86 For Thailand, this is the Committee for Approval of Investment under the Agreement for the Promotion and Protection of Investments between the Kingdom of Thailand and other countries (or its successor), established by the Ministry of Foreign Affairs.

87 See the BITs with China (Article 2(3)), the Republic of Korea (Article 2(3)), Peru (Article 2(3)), Sri Lanka (Article II(1)) and the United Kingdom (Article 3(3).

88 See the BITs with Argentina, Canada, Croatia, Czech Republic, Egypt, India, Indonesia, Israel, Philippines, Romania, Russia, Slovenia, Sweden, Taiwan and Turkey.

89 BIT between Thailand and China, Article 1(3).

90 BIT between Thailand and Egypt, Article 2(1).

91 See note above.

a series of shareholdings) and still be afforded BIT protection. An exception is the Thailand-Canada BIT, which explicitly extends coverage to investments indirectly controlled by an investor of a contracting State through an investor of a third State.[92] It is the only BIT entered into by Thailand which specifically provides protection for indirect investments. The Thailand-Turkey BIT, by contrast states that "'investment'… shall refer to all direct investments made in accordance with the laws and regulations of the territory of the Party where the investments are made."[93]

The Thailand-Canada BIT excludes from its protection real estate or other property "not acquired in the expectation or used for the purposes of economic benefit or other business purposes."[94]

Several of Thailand's BITs expressly provide that an alteration or change in the form of investment shall not affect its character as investment under the BIT. However, in some treaties, alterations or changes to investments are made subject to the further approval of the contracting State in which the investment has been made.[95] In the Thailand-Germany BIT, such approval is only necessary where required by the laws of the State in which the investment is made.[96] Other BITs permit alterations or changes to investments provided they are in accordance with the laws and regulations of the contracting State in which the investment has been made.[97] The Thailand-Canada BIT allows for changes to the form of investments, but states that in respect of investments made in Thailand, it shall not relieve investors of the need to obtain approvals from the competent authorities in Thailand.[98]

The Thailand-Bulgaria BIT explicitly confers protection on the reinvestments of returns from an investment, and returns on such reinvestments, by providing that they shall enjoy the same protection as the initial investment.[99]

---

92 BIT between Canada and Thailand, Article I(f).

93 BIT between Turkey and Thailand, Article I(2).

94 *Ibid.*

95 See the BITs with BLEU, Finland, Hong Kong, Indonesia and the Philippines.

96 BIT between Thailand and Germany, Article 1(1).

97 See the BITs with Cambodia, Jordan, Democratic People's Republic of Korea, Myanmar, Russia and Slovenia.

98 BIT between Canada and Thailand, Article I(f). This refers to approvals as may be required from the competent authorities of Thailand as established under the Thai Cabinet's decision of 26 July (as contained in the Secretariat of the Cabinet's Note No. 0201/9549 dated 28 July 1994), a copy of which is attached to the BIT.

99 BIT between Thailand and Bulgaria, Article 2(2).

3 *Definition of Investor*

Model BIT

Thailand's Model BIT defines an "investor" as the following:[100]

(a) natural persons who, according to the law of that Contracting Party, are considered to be its nationals;
(b) juridical persons, including companies, corporations, business associations and other organisations, which are constituted or otherwise duly organised under the law of that Contracting Party and have their seat, together with real economic activities, in the territory of that same Contracting Party;
(c) juridical persons established under the law of that Contracting Party which are, directly or indirectly, controlled by nationals of that Contracting Party.

"Investor" under Thailand's BITs

"Investor" is typically defined in Thailand's BITs in the same terms as the Model BIT. In several cases, reference is instead made to "nationals" and "companies", which are given the same meaning as investors under the Model BIT. As per Thailand's Model BIT, a number of its BITs afford protection to "companies" or "juridical persons" incorporated or established under the law of a contracting State, which are seated in that State or controlled by nationals of such State (even if they are not seated in that State). Some only cover "companies" which are both established and seated in a contracting State.[101] The Thailand-BLEU, Thailand-Sweden and Thailand-Switzerland BITs extend protection to juridical persons established in a third State where such investor is controlled by a national or company of the contracting State.

Typically, the BITs entered into by Thailand explicitly extend protection to investments made by not-for-profit organisations. In several BITs, this applies only in respect of Thai investors.[102] The Thailand-Canada BIT extends protection to government-owned and controlled enterprises and State enterprises in Canada.[103] Other BITs do not make this distinction.

The Thailand-Argentina BIT excludes from its protection investors of one contracting State which have been domiciled in the other State for more than

100 Thailand Model BIT, Article 1(2).

101 See the BITs with Argentina, Bangladesh (in respect of Bangladeshi investors), Bulgaria, Croatia, Finland, Germany and Myanmar.

102 See the BITs with Bangladesh, Hong Kong, India, Philippines and the United Kingdom.

103 BIT between Canada and Thailand, Article I(a).

two years prior to the investment, unless it can be proven that the investment was made from abroad.[104]

4 *Scope*

Thailand's Model BIT, and the majority of the BITs it has entered into, provide that they shall remain in force for an initial period of 10 years following the date on which the BIT was ratified by both contracting States.[105] Some BITs provide for an initial period of 15 years,[106] while the Thailand-Sweden BIT remains in force for an initial period of 20 years.

The BITs cannot be denounced by contracting States during the initial period.[107] Thereafter, the BITs continue in force indefinitely or on a rolling basis,[108] until terminated by either State providing one year's written notice.[109] A number of the BITs provide that written notice may be given in the penultimate year of the initial period.[110] The Thailand-Bahrain BIT is an exception in that it has an initial validity period of 5 years, after which it will continue for successive periods of one year.

Where terminated, all of Thailand's BITs provide that the agreement shall remain in force for a specified period to afford protection to investments made before the date of termination. Generally, this will be a period of time equivalent to the initial validity period of the BIT.[111]

With the exception of the Thailand-Cambodia BIT and Netherlands-Thailand agreement which are silent on the issue, Thailand's BITs explicitly state that they shall apply to investments made both before and after their

---

104 BIT between Thailand and Argentina, Article 2(3).

105 Thailand Model BIT, Article 14.

106 The BITs with Finland, Hong Kong and Russia.

107 With the exception of the BIT between Cambodia and Thailand, which may be terminated by either State giving 1 year's notice to the other within the initial 10 year period (Article 12(3)).

108 See, for example, Article 13(1) of the BIT between the Philippines and Thailand.

109 With the exception of the Thailand-Bahrain and Thailand-Egypt BITs, which each may be terminated by a contracting State providing 6 months' notice.

110 See the BITs with Argentina, Bangladesh, BLEU, China, Republic of Korea, Laos, Peru, Switzerland, Taiwan, United Kingdom and Vietnam.

111 The BITs with Canada, Czech Republic, Germany, India and the Democratic People's Republic of Korea provide that they shall remain in force for a period of 15 years after the date of termination in respect of investments made before such termination, notwithstanding that each of these BITs had an initial validity period of 10 years.

entry into force.[112] Several treaties specify that disputes which have arisen prior to their entry into force will not fall under the scope of it.[113] In the absence of such wording, BITs are unlikely to have retroactive application in respect of disputes arising before the effective date of the BIT, an issue which was considered by the tribunal in the *Walter Bau* arbitration,[114] where the tribunal looked at previous cases on this issue.

All of Thailand's publicly available BITs include rights of subrogation,[115] meaning that where a contracting State or its agent has made a payment to an investor under an insurance policy or indemnity, the other contracting State recognises the rights of that State to "step into the shoes" of the investors, and enforce any rights or claims it may have.

5 *Substantive Protections*

Fair and Equitable Treatment

All of Thailand's BITs[116] provide that each contracting State shall afford "fair and equitable" treatment to the investments and returns of investors of the other contracting State. In some of the BITs, it is linked to the requirements of international law.[117] For example, the Thailand-Canada BIT states that each contracting State shall accord investments "fair and equitable treatment in accordance with the principles of international law."[118] Some BITs qualify the fair and equitable treatment standard, for example in the Thailand-India BIT, fair and equitable treatment is afforded "under the laws of the other Contracting Party."[119]

Non-Discrimination

Some of Thailand's BITs also contain a prohibition on the discriminatory treatment of protected investors or investments by the contracting States. For instance, Thailand's Model BIT includes the following provision:

---

112 The BITs between Thailand and the Czech Republic, and Thailand and Hungary provide that they shall not apply to investments made before 1 January 1950 and 1 January 1973, respectively.

113 See Thailand's Model BIT and BITs with Argentina, Indonesia, Jordan, Myanmar, Romania, Russia, Slovenia, Sweden, Switzerland and Turkey.

114 As discussed in paragraph 5.

115 See, for example, Article 8 of Thailand's Model BIT.

116 With the exception of the agreement between the Netherlands and Thailand.

117 See the BITs with Canada, Croatia and Laos.

118 Article II(2)(a).

119 The BIT between Thailand and India, Article 3(2).

> Neither Contracting Party shall in any way impair by unreasonable or discriminatory measures the management, use, enjoyment or disposal of investments in its territory of investors of the other Contracting Party.

The same clause can be found in the BITs between Thailand and Cambodia, BLEU, Bahrain, Germany, Hong Kong, Israel, Jordan, Democratic People's Republic of Korea, Myanmar, Slovenia, Sweden and Switzerland. The Thailand-Croatia BIT also extends such protection to the "liquidation" of investments.

Full Protection and Security

The obligation for contracting States to afford "full protection and security" in respect of qualifying investments is included in the majority of Thailand's BITs, but the scope and standard of the protection differs from BIT to BIT. For example, this is sometimes expressed as the "most constant protection and security",[120] under the Thailand-Bangladesh BIT it is "protection and security", the Thailand-BLEU BIT refers to "protection", the Thailand-Egypt BIT grants "legal protection", and the Thailand-India BIT provides for "protection and security".

Expropriation

Article 6(1) of Thailand's Model BIT states that:

> Investments of investors of either Contracting Party shall not be expropriated, nationalised or subjected to measures having effect equivalent to nationalisation or expropriation in the territory of the other Contracting Party except for public purposes, under due process of law, on a non-discriminatory basis and against prompt, effective and adequate compensation.

All of the BITs entered into by Thailand prohibit expropriation, or equivalent measures, unless it is for "public purposes" or in the "public interest", and on a non-discriminatory basis. Some of the BITs add further qualification by referring to a public purpose "related to the internal needs" of a contracting State,[121] while the Indonesia-Thailand BIT permits expropriation more broadly, for any "lawful purpose or public purpose."[122]

---

120 See, for example, the BITs with Argentina, China, the Czech Republic, Hungary, Republic of Korea, Laos, Peru, the United Kingdom, Taiwan and Vietnam.

121 See the BITs with Hong Kong, Israel, Republic of Korea, Laos and Sri Lanka.

122 The BIT between Indonesia and Thailand, Article VI.

A number of BITs expand on what amounts to expropriation of an investment, such as the Thailand-Canada BIT, which provides that "taxation measures" amounting to measures which have an effect equivalent to expropriation or nationalization are prohibited.[123] More substantively, the Thailand-Egypt BIT appears to lift the threshold of protection by providing in the relevant Article on "Nationalization or Expropriation" that qualifying investments "shall not be subject to any measures limiting the right of ownership, control or enjoyment of the investments, whether permanent or temporary except for specific provisions of the laws in force or an order issued by a competent court."[124]

Almost all of Thailand's BITs follow Article 6(1) of the Model BIT and require expropriation to be carried out in accordance with "due process of law,"[125] or provide that the legality of the expropriation will be subject to review in accordance with the due process of law. Several BITs grant investors the right to a review by a judicial body or other independent authority of the expropriation and the State's valuation of the expropriated assets.[126]

A number of Thailand's BITs also explicitly confer protection on the shareholders of companies (not just the companies) whose assets are expropriated. For instance, the Thailand-India BIT provides:

> Where a Contracting Party expropriates the assets of a company which is incorporated or constituted under the law in force in any part of its own territory, and in which investors of the other Contracting Party own shares, it shall ensure that the provisions of [the relevant clause on expropriation] are applied to the extent necessary to ensure fair and equitable compensation in respect of their investment to such investors of the other Contracting Party who are owners of those shares.[127]

---

123 The BIT between Canada and Thailand, Article VII.

124 The BIT between Thailand and Egypt, Article 5(1)(a).

125 See the BITs with Argentina, BLEU, Bulgaria, Canada, Croatia, Finland, Hungary, Jordan, Democratic People's Republic of Korea, Myanmar, Netherlands, Romania, Slovenia, Sweden and Turkey.

126 Article 6(3) Thailand's Model BIT, and the BITs with Croatia, Hong Kong, India, Indonesia, Israel, Jordan, Democratic People's Republic of Korea, Republic of Korea, Myanmar, Russia, Sri Lanka, Sweden and Turkey.

127 The Thailand-India BIT, Article 6(3). See also the Thailand-Argentina BIT, Article 6(2); Thailand-Bahrain BIT, Article 6(2); Thailand-Bangladesh BIT, Article 5(2); Thailand-BLEU BIT, Article 5(2); Thailand-China BIT, Article 5(2); Thailand-Egypt BIT, Article 5(2); Thailand-China BIT, Article 5(3); Thailand-Republic of Korea BIT, Article 5(2); Thailand-Laos BIT, Article 6(2); Thailand-Peru BIT, Article 6(2); Thailand-Philippines

Thailand's BITs require payment of prompt, adequate and effective compensation in the event of expropriation. The formulation of what amounts to adequate compensation varies between the BITs. As per the Model BIT, several BITs specify that the measure of compensation shall be the "market value" of the investments,[128] others refer to "fair market value",[129] the Thailand-China BIT specifies that compensation shall be equal to the "appropriate value" of the expropriated asset, the "real value" of the investment in the Thailand-Hong Kong BIT, and the "genuine market value" in the Thailand-India BIT. The Thailand-Netherlands BIT requires that "just compensation in accordance with international law" shall be paid. Other BITs do not provide a measure of compensation, other than the requirement that the compensation paid by the expropriating State is "adequate".

Finally, while many of Thailand's BITs are silent as to whether compensation for expropriation carries interest, some BITs expressly provide for the payment of interest. The Model BIT states that interest is payable "at the rate applicable in the territory of that Contracting Party from the date the payment was due until the date of actual payment",[130] and several of Thailand's BITs require interest to be paid at the rate applicable under the law of the contracting State where the investment was expropriated.[131] Under other BITs, interest shall be paid at a "commercial rate",[132] "market lending rate"[133] and a "fair and equitable rate".[134]

BIT, Article 7(2); Thailand-Sri Lanka BIT, Article VI(2); Thailand-Sweden BIT, Article 5(3); Thailand-UK BIT, Article 6(2); and Thailand-Vietnam BIT, Article 6(2).

128 See the BITs with Argentina, BLEU, Bulgaria, Czech Republic, Egypt, Finland, Israel, Jordan, Republic of Korea, Myanmar, Philippines, Poland, Russia, Slovenia, Sri Lanka and Zimbabwe.

129 See the BITs with Canada, Croatia and Indonesia.

130 Thailand's Model BIT, Article 6(2).

131 See the BITs with Israel, Jordan, Democratic People's Republic of Korea, Myanmar, Slovenia and Canada, Article VIII (2)(b) (however this applies only in respect of compensation which is payable in Thailand, and the BIT specifies that in the case of immovable property, interest will be paid from the date compensation is determined by the committee established under Article 23 of the Immovable Property Expropriation Act at the highest rate of interest for the fixed deposit of the Government Savings Bank, whereas for movable property, interest will be paid as determined by the Thai Civil and Commercial Code).

132 The BITs between Thailand and BLEU, Art. 5(1); Canada and Thailand, Article VIII(2)(a) (but in respect of payments made in Canada only); Croatia and Thailand, Article 5(4); Thailand and Zimbabwe, Article 4(4).

133 The BIT between Thailand and Germany, Article 4(2).

134 The BIT between Thailand and India, Article 6(1).

Umbrella Clauses

Approximately two-thirds of Thailand's BITs presently in force include an obligation that the contracting States observe any obligation in addition to those under the BIT that they have entered into with regards to an investment of an investor of the other contracting State.[135] Such clauses are more commonly known as "umbrella clauses" and mean that obligations in agreements between investors and the host contracting State may be elevated to the status of treaty obligations.

Most Favoured Nation and National Treatment

All of Thailand's BITs presently in force contain Most Favoured Nation ("MFN") and national treatment provisions, requiring each contracting State to afford treatment to investors which is no less favourable than that which is granted to a national of the contracting State, or of a third State. These obligations apply to both investments and returns on investments.

Several of Thailand's BITs (though not its Model BIT) state that treatment shall be afforded "immediately and unconditionally,"[136] whereas the BITs with Sri Lanka, Taiwan and Vietnam make the conferral of MFN and national treatment conditional upon reciprocity. For instance, Article IV(3) of the Thailand-Sri Lanka BIT states:

> Investments of nationals or companies of either Contracting Party and the returns therefrom shall not be entitled to any treatment which is not available on a reciprocal basis, to investments or returns of nationals or companies of the other Contracting Party.

Slightly less commonly, some BITs allow for a contracting party to have the choice between MFN or national treatment, where both are provided for.[137] One such example is Article 4(1)(d) of the Thailand-Bahrain BIT:

> Wherever this Agreement makes alternative provision for the grant of national treatment or of treatment not less favourable than that accorded

135 The exceptions, which do not have an umbrella clause, are the BITs with Bulgaria, Canada, Croatia, Egypt, Finland, India, Indonesia, Israel, Netherlands, Romania, Slovenia, Sri Lanka and Taiwan.

136 See the BITs with Argentina, Bahrain, Bangladesh, BLEU, Republic of Korea, Laos, Peru, the United Kingdom and Vietnam.

137 See the BITs with Bahrain, Bangladesh, Republic of Korea, Laos, Peru and the United Kingdom.

> to the investors of any third State in respect of any matter, the option as between these alternatives shall rest with the Contracting Party beneficiary in each particular case.

This is particularly interesting as the option is granted to the contracting party beneficiary. As a hypothetical scenario, a dispute could arise between an investor of the beneficiary State and the host State, where the host State would be held liable under national treatment, but not MFN treatment, and the beneficiary State is called upon to elect between the two. In that situation, the beneficiary State may choose not to get involved, or if it does, its election could necessarily determine the success or failure of its investor's claim, or the tribunal could consider that the election is to be made by the investor on behalf of the beneficiary State.

All of Thailand's BITs state that the provisions of national treatment and MFN treatment do not extend to the benefits of: (a) membership of a customs union or free trade area, regional association or arrangements for economic cooperation,[138] or other international agreements to which either of the contracting States are, or may become, party to;[139] and (b) any international agreement or arrangement, or any domestic legislation relating wholly or mainly to taxation.

In addition, a number of BITs exclude from the scope of the national treatment and MFN treatment clauses the benefits derived from the status of a "promoted person"[140] (or its equivalent) under Thailand's investment laws,[141]

---

138 Most of Thailand's BITs refer to the exclusion of regional arrangements/ cooperation agreements in economic, social, labour, industrial or monetary fields, including those within the framework of specific projects.

139 In some BITs the exclusion of future unions, arrangements and agreements is restricted to those which are adopted "within a reasonable length of time." See, for example, the BIT between Thailand and Cambodia, Article 5(b).

140 As defined pursuant to Article [X] of the Investment Promotion Act.

141 See the BITs with Argentina, Bangladesh, Cambodia, China, Czech Republic, Egypt, Finland, Hong Kong, Hungary, Republic of Korea, Peru, Poland, Romania, Sri Lanka and the United Kingdom. For example, Article 5 of the Thailand-Argentina BIT states, under the heading of "Exceptions", that "The provisions of this Agreement relating to the grant of treatment not less favourable than that accorded to the investors of either Contracting Party or of any third State shall not be construed so as to oblige one Contracting Party to extend to the investors of the other Contracting Party the benefit of any treatment, preference or privilege which may be extended by the former Contracting Party by virtue of: ... (c) the grant to a particular person or company of the status of a 'promoted person' under the law of Thailand on the promotion of investment".

or under the investment laws of both contracting States.[142] The Thailand-Bulgaria BIT explicitly confers a right on both States to make further exceptions from national treatment, but provides that any such exceptions will not apply retroactively to investments.[143]

The Thailand-Canada BIT contains additional exclusions on MFN treatment, including existing or future bilateral or multilateral agreements which are: (a) negotiated within the framework of the General Agreement on Tariffs and Trade ("GATT");[144] or (b) relating to aviation, telecommunications transport networks and telecommunications transport services, fisheries, maritime matters and financial services.[145] A contracting party may also maintain measures inconsistent with national treatment, such as where they are existing measures, or where they result from the continuation or prompt renewal of existing measures.[146] Further, a contracting party is allowed to "make or maintain measures" (not merely to maintain pre-existing measures) inconsistent with national treatment in certain sectors or matters listed in an annex to the BIT, which include business in agriculture, commerce and services, construction, and industry and handicrafts.

The BIT with Germany is Thailand's only agreement that gives specific examples of less favourable treatment, which include "unequal treatment in the case of restrictions on the purchase of raw or auxiliary materials" and "unequal treatment in the case of impeding the marketing of products inside or outside the country", while measures taken for reasons of public security

142 See the BITs with Bahrain, China, Laos, Taiwan and Vietnam.

143 The BIT between Thailand and Bulgaria, Article 3(3).

144 The BIT between Canada and Thailand, Article III(3)(b).

145 *Ibid.*, Article III(3)(d).

146 Article IV(2) of the Thailand-Canada BIT provides that "[a] Contracting Party may maintain, within its territory, measures that are inconsistent with the provisions of", among others, national treatment "if such measures are in accordance with the following: (a) such measures are existing measures; or (b) such measures are maintained or adopted after the date of entry into force of this Agreement at the time of sale or other disposition of a government's equity interests in, or the assets of, an existing state enterprise or an existing governmental entity, and which prohibit or impose limitations on the ownership of equity interests or assets or impose nationality requirements relating to senior management or members of the board of directors; (c) such measures result from the continuation or prompt renewal of any existing measures; or (d) such measures are an amendment to any existing measures, to the extent that the amendment does not decrease the conformity of the measures, as they existed immediately before the amendment, with the obligations in paragraphs (a), (b) and (c) above and paragraphs (1) and (2) of Article V."

and order, public health or morality will not be considered less favourable treatment within the meaning of the MFN and national treatment provisions.[147]

6 *Repatriation of Capital and Compensation for Losses*

Article 5(1) of Thailand's Model BIT states that investors shall be entitled to compensation where they suffer losses as a result of "war or other armed conflict, revolution, a state or national emergency, revolt, insurrection, riot or other such similar activity" in a contracting State. All of Thailand's BITs provide a right to compensation for investors in the event of war, armed conflict and civil disturbance and similar events, with some minor variations between the BITs in the drafting of such obligations. The Thailand-Canada BIT explicitly affords a right to compensation for natural disasters in a contracting State. Some of Thailand's BITs also contain an explicit right to compensation for the requisition or destruction of an investor's property by a contracting State.[148] However, where the amount of compensation is large, some BITs confer the right on a contracting State to effect payment in reasonable instalments.[149]

As per Thailand's Model BIT, almost all BITs include a requirement for treatment no less favourable than that accorded to the contracting State's own nationals or investors of a third State, as regards restitution, indemnification or other settlement for such events.

Separately, while the expression of the right is not uniform, all of Thailand's BITs contain provisions requiring contracting States to guarantee the free transfer of investments, investment returns, compensation and other proceeds. In some cases, this is made subject to a contracting State's right to exercise in good faith powers conferred by its laws, consistent with its status as a member of the International Monetary Fund.[150]

7 *Investor-State Dispute Settlement*

Almost all of Thailand's BITs provide that in the event of a dispute arising between an investor and a contracting State, consultations or negotiations

147 The BIT between Thailand and Germany, Article 3(2).

148 See the BITs with Croatia, Hong Kong, Israel, Jordan, Democratic People's Republic of Korea and Myanmar.

149 See the BITs with Bangladesh, the United Kingdom, China, Laos, Netherlands and Vietnam.

150 The BITs between Thailand and Bangladesh, Article 6(1) and the United Kingdom and Thailand, Article 7(1).

shall take place to resolve the dispute amicably.[151] If resolution cannot be reached, then most of the BITs contain a "cooling off" period of 3 months[152] or 6 months,[153] before an investor may submit the dispute to a local court or tribunal, or to arbitration. Of the BITs containing provisions for the settlement of investment disputes, only those between Thailand and the Czech Republic, Peru and Poland do not provide for a cooling off period.

A handful of the BITs signed by Thailand do not contain any provisions for compulsory resolution of investment disputes. The treaties which do not provide a mechanism for the resolution of investments disputes are the BITs concluded with Bangladesh, China, Laos, the United Kingdom and Vietnam, and Thailand's agreement with the Netherlands. It should be noted, however, that as Laos and Vietnam are, together with Thailand, Member States of the ASEAN Comprehensive Investment Agreement, that agreement could provide an alternative jurisdictional basis for the resolution of investment disputes involving those States or investors of those States. As for the rest of the States where there is no compulsory dispute resolution procedure for investment disputes under the BIT, an investor's recourse in the event of a dispute is likely to be limited to requesting its own government to pursue diplomatic action, which it may be unwilling to do, or if the investor has entered into a contract directly with the State in respect of the investment, to bring proceedings under the dispute resolution clause of such contract. However, the latter more likely would be an action for breach of contract, not a claim under international law, and accordingly, may not be as attractive to an investor, particularly where there are concerns as to the enforcement of a judgment or arbitration award against a State.

Amongst the BITs that contain provisions for dispute settlement, most offer an investor the options of pursuing a remedy in a court or tribunal of the contracting State in which the investment was made, and arbitration. A few provide for only arbitration, and confer no explicit right to submit disputes to local courts.[154] Only the Thailand-Argentina BIT contains an explicit

---

151 The exceptions are the BITs with Hungary, Republic of Korea and Switzerland, and the BITs with Bangladesh, China, Laos, the United Kingdom and Vietnam, and Agreement with the Netherlands, which do not contain any provisions relating to investor disputes.

152 Article 11(2) of Thailand's Model BIT, and see the BITs with Bahrain, Bulgaria, Cambodia, Finland, Indonesia, Democratic People's Republic of Korea, Philippines, Romania, Slovenia and Sri Lanka.

153 The BITs with Argentina, BLEU, Canada, Croatia, Egypt, Germany, Hong Kong, India, Israel, Jordan, Myanmar, Russia, Sweden, Taiwan, Turkey and Zimbabwe.

154 The BITs with BLEU, Canada, Czech Republic, Germany, Hong Kong, Korea, Peru, Poland, Sweden, Switzerland and Taiwan.

"fork-in-the-road" provision, precluding an investor from submitting a dispute to arbitration where it has already been submitted to the local courts, or vice versa.[155] The Thailand-Canada BIT provides a partial restriction, stating that an investor can only submit a dispute to arbitration where it has "waived its right to initiate or continue any other proceedings in relation to the measure that is alleged to be in breach of this [BIT] before the courts or tribunals of the Contracting Party concerned or in a dispute settlement procedure of any kind."[156] None of Thailand's BITs that provide for investment treaty arbitration require that local remedies are exhausted first. However, recourse to arbitration in the Thailand-India BIT is limited to where the parties fail to agree to settle the dispute in local courts or by conciliation, or where conciliation fails to resolve the dispute.[157]

The majority of Thailand's BITs, including its Model BIT, provide for ICSID arbitration proceedings or conciliation where both States are Contracting Parties to the ICSID Convention. However, it should be highlighted at this juncture that Thailand has signed but has not yet ratified the ICSID Convention.[158] Therefore, unless and until Thailand does so, recourse to proceedings under the ICSID Convention will not be available, as this is only possible where both contracting States have ratified the Convention.[159] Only some BITs provide for disputes to be submitted under the ICSID Additional Facility Rules where only one contracting State has ratified the ICSID Convention.[160] In such cases, disputes may be heard under the auspices of the Additional Facility for the administration of proceedings by the Secretariat of ICSID, provided that the other party to the BIT has ratified the ICSID Convention.

Many of the BITs provide the option of pursuing arbitration through an *ad hoc* tribunal constituted under the UNCITRAL Rules.[161] The Thailand-Hong

155 The BIT between Thailand and Argentina, Article 9(4).

156 The BIT between Canada and Thailand, Article XIII(3)(b).

157 The BIT between Thailand and India, Article 9(3).

158 See the list of signatories and Contracting States at: https://icsid.worldbank.org/apps/ICSIDWEB/about/Pages/Database-of-Member-States.aspx?tab=PtoT&rdo=BOTH.

159 Article 25(1) ICSID Convention.

160 The BITs with Argentina, BLEU, Canada, India and Sweden.

161 Article 11(2)(b) of Thailand's Model BIT, and the BITs with Argentina, Bahrain, BLEU, Bulgaria, Cambodia, Canada, Croatia, India, Israel, Jordan, Democratic People's Republic of Korea, Myanmar, Philippines, Russia, Slovenia, Sweden, Turkey and Zimbabwe. The Thailand-India BIT provides for some modifications to the UNCITRAL Rules, at Article 9(3)(c) of the BIT) and specifies the President of the ICJ as the Appointing Authority. The Thailand-Israel BIT provides for the tribunal to be constituted as per the provisions of the BIT referring to State-to-State disputes (Article 8(2)(c)) of that BIT.

Kong BIT provides for recourse to *ad hoc* arbitration under the UNCITRAL Rules only where the parties have not agreed on other procedures to resolve the dispute.[162] The Thailand-Romania BIT provides for *ad hoc* arbitration, but does not specify the applicable rules; the Thailand-Taiwan BIT provides for *ad hoc* arbitration only "if agreed by the parties."[163] The Thailand-Germany BIT provides for *ad hoc* arbitration, with the tribunal to be appointed in accordance with the procedures in the BIT relating to State-to-State disputes,[164] failing which the President of the Court of International Arbitration of the ICC is to appoint the tribunal.[165] The Thailand-Sweden BIT provides that the Secretary-General of ICSID is to be the Appointing Authority for *ad hoc* arbitration proceedings. A few of the BITs state that arbitration proceedings shall be held in a state which is a party to the New York Convention,[166] to seek to ensure that any award rendered is capable of enforcement.

Only the Thailand-Canada BIT provides a time limit within which claims must be brought by an investor, being 3 years from when it acquired, or should have acquired, knowledge of the alleged breach and loss or damage incurred.[167]

As regards the law which is to be applied where there is a dispute, Article 11(3) of Thailand's Model BIT states:

> The arbitral tribunal established under this Article shall reach its decision on the basis of national laws and regulations of the Contracting Party, which is a party to the dispute, the provisions of the present Agreement, as well as applicable rules of international law.

This has been adopted in several of Thailand's BITs.[168] The Thailand-Argentina and Thailand-BLEU BITs also provide that the terms of the agreement pursuant to which the investment is made shall be applied by the tribunal;[169] as

162 The BIT between Thailand and Hong Kong, Article 8.

163 The BIT between Thailand and Taiwan, Article 10.

164 Where each State appoints an arbitrator, who agree on the name of a Chairman to be appointed by the States (see the BIT between Germany and Thailand, Article 10(2).

165 *Ibid.*

166 The BITs with BLEU, Canada and Sweden.

167 The BIT between Canada and Thailand, Article XIII(3).

168 See the BITs with Bulgaria, Canada, Jordan, Democratic People's Republic of Korea, Myanmar.

169 See the BITs with Argentina and BLEU. For instance, Article 11(7) of the Thailand-BLEU BIT provides that "[t]he arbitral tribunal shall decide on the basis of the national law, including the rules relating to conflicts of law, of the Contracting Party involved in the dispute in whose territory the investment has been made, as well as on the basis of the

both those BITs contain umbrella clauses, it is possible that this was included to reflect the presence of umbrella clauses. The Thailand-India BIT provides that the law of the contracting State in which the investment is made shall be applied where the dispute is before local courts. The remaining BITs are silent as to the applicable law.

Most of the BITs provide that arbitral awards are final and binding, and shall be enforced in accordance with the national laws and regulations of the contracting State. Some BITs provide that awards shall be carried out without delay by the contracting State against which it is made.[170]

8 *State-to-State Dispute Settlement*

All of Thailand's BITs provide that disputes between contracting States shall be resolved, as far as possible, through consultation or negotiation between the States. Where this fails to resolve the dispute, usually after a specified period of time,[171] all of the BITs provide for recourse to arbitration.

The BITs require the establishment of an *ad hoc* arbitral tribunal, constituted of three arbitrators of which two will be appointed by each contracting State, and a Chairman selected by the other two arbitrators, whose appointment is confirmed upon the approval of both Contracting States.[172] The BITs generally include a time period for the arbitrators and Chairman to be appointed,[173] failing which an appointing body may be requested to make the appointments. In almost all of Thailand's BITs this will be the President of the ICJ, or Vice-President, or next most senior person in case the President is a national of either contracting State.[174] In the Thailand-Israel BIT, the arbitrators will be

provisions of this Agreement, of the terms of the specific agreement which may have been entered into regarding the investment, and of the principles of international law."

170 See the BITs with BLEU and Sweden.

171 A period of 6 months is specified in the BITs with Argentina, Bahrain, Bangladesh, BLEU, Bulgaria, Cambodia, China, Croatia, Czech Republic; Egypt, Finland, Hungary, India, Indonesia, Israel, Jordan, Democratic People's Republic of Korea, Republic of Korea, Laos, Peru, Philippines, Poland, Romania, Slovenia, Sweden, Switzerland, Taiwan, Turkey, the United Kingdom, Vietnam and Zimbabwe. No time period is specified in the BITs with Canada, Germany, Hong Kong, Myanmar, Netherlands, Russia, Sri Lanka, or in the Model BIT.

172 See Article 12(3) of Thailand's Model BIT.

173 It is 2 months in the Model BIT.

174 The BIT between Taiwan and Thailand provides only that State-to-State disputes shall be submitted to an arbitral tribunal on "such terms and conditions as the parties may agree" (Article 9(2)).

appointed by the Secretary-General of the Permanent Court of Arbitration if not done by the parties.[175]

Thailand's BITs provide that the *ad hoc* arbitral tribunal shall determine its own procedure,[176] and that it shall reach its decision, which will be binding on the parties, by a majority of votes. The BITs also provide that each party shall be responsible for its own costs and the costs of the member of the tribunal appointed by it, and that the costs of the Chairman and remaining costs shall be borne equally, subject to the tribunal being entitled to direct that one party pays a higher proportion of costs.[177] The Thailand-China BIT also explicitly states that the tribunal shall give reasons for its award.[178]

The BITs are silent on enforcement of the tribunal's award, a position which is not unheard of under international law where awards determining State-to-State disputes are concerned. The sole exception among Thailand's BITs is the Thailand-Canada BIT, which provides for the parties to reach an agreement on the resolution of the dispute within 60 days of the tribunal's decision, otherwise the contracting State bringing the dispute is entitled to compensation or to suspend benefits granted to the other contracting State to the value of the tribunal's award.[179] The BITs are generally also silent as to the law which the tribunal should apply when making its decision[180], though presumably, international law would be applied by the tribunals, at least to some extent.

9 *Additional Provisions*

A number of the BITs entered into by Thailand contain provisions requiring contracting States to treat favourably, in compliance with their laws and regulations, questions relating to the entry, stay, movement and employment of

175 BIT between Thailand and Israel, Article 9(4).

176 The BIT between Turkey and Thailand states that the tribunal may request that the President of the ICJ determines the procedure of the arbitration if it is unable to do so (Article X(5)).

177 With the exception of the Thailand-Hong Kong BIT, and Thailand-Israel BIT, and Netherlands-Thailand Agreement.

178 The BIT between Thailand and China, Article 9(5)(d).

179 The BIT between Canada and Thailand, Article XV(7).

180 Exceptions are the Thailand-Croatia BIT, which states that the tribunal is to reach its decision in accordance with the BIT and the rules of international law, and the Netherlands-Thailand Agreement which allows the tribunal to reach its decision *ex aequo et bono*, if the parties agree.

nationals and their families of the other contracting State in connection with qualifying investments.[181]

The Thailand-Canada BIT contains a number of provisions not found in Thailand's other BITs, including a transparency clause, requiring sharing of information between the contracting States,[182] and restrictions on conditions which a contracting State is entitled to attach to its approval of investments.[183]

Separately, several of Thailand's BITs contain provisions explicitly permitting the amendment of the BIT.[184]

IV Multilateral Investment Related Treaties and Organizations to which Thailand is a Party

1 *U.S. – Thailand Treaty of Amity and Economic Relations*

A treaty providing for reciprocal investment benefits was first entered into between the United States and Thailand in 1833. The present treaty (the "1966 Treaty") was signed on 29 May 1966, and entered into force on 8 June 1968.[185] The 1966 Treaty exempts investors protected by it from most of the restrictions in the FBA, and contains many of the investment protection provisions found in Thailand's BITs. The 1966 Treaty affords fair and equitable treatment to protected investors, includes a prohibition on discrimination, and provides for the "most constant security and protection" for investors' interests.[186] The treaty also appears to include a prohibition on expropriation without due process of law or the payment of compensation.[187] Further, it contains a national

181 See the BITs with Bulgaria, Germany, Croatia, India, Jordan, Democratic People's Republic of Korea, Myanmar, Russia, Slovenia and Turkey.

182 Article XVI.

183 Article V.

184 See, for example, the BIT between Thailand and Indonesia, Article IX, and the BIT between Turkey and Thailand, Article XI(3).

185 1966 Treaty available at http://tcc.export.gov/trade_agreements/all_trade_agreements/exp_005404.asp.

186 *Ibid.*, Article III.

187 *Ibid.*, Article III(2), although the term "expropriation" is not expressly used. Article III(2) provides that "[p]roperty of nationals and companies of either Party, including direct or indirect interests in property, shall receive the most constant protection and security within the territories of the other Party. Such property shall not be taken without due process of law or without payment of just compensation in accordance with the principles of international law."

treatment requirement, subject to exceptions similar to those found in Thailand's other BITs, such as advantages afforded under customs unions or in free trade areas, but unlike other BITs, national treatment is granted in respect of taxation. However, excluded from national treatment protection under the 1966 Treaty are investments in the fields of communications, transport, fiduciary functions, banking involving depository functions, the exploitation of land or other natural resources and domestic trade in agricultural products.[188]

Unlike most BITs entered into by Thailand, there is no provision for investor-State dispute resolution in the 1966 Treaty, though it does provide that State-to-State disputes may be submitted to *ad hoc* arbitration for settlement in accordance with the principles of international law.[189] In addition, the 1966 Treaty includes other provisions not typically found in BITs, such as a reciprocal guarantee of freedom of commerce and navigation.

2 *International Investment Agreements and Free Trade Agreements*

Thailand is a party to Economic Partnership Agreements ("EPA") with Japan[190] and New Zealand.[191] These EPAs contain most of the investment protections commonly found in Thailand's BITs, and also afford mechanisms for the resolution of investment disputes between nationals and companies of a contracting State and the other State. In addition, the EPAs include a number of other provisions not usually found in BITs, which cover, *inter alia*, trade in goods and services between the Contracting States, the movement of persons, customs procedures, intellectual property, competition and government procurement.

The Thailand-Japan EPA provides for the fair and equitable treatment of investments, and accords full protection and security.[192] It contains MFN[193] and national treatment[194] requirements, a prohibition on expropriation, provisions for the payment of compensation,[195] and provides for rights of free

188 *Ibid.*, Article IV(2).

189 1966 Treaty, Article XIII(2).

190 Agreement Between Japan And The Kingdom of Thailand For An Economic Partnership, signed 3 April 2007, entered into force on 1 November 2007, available at http://www.mofa.go.jp/region/asia-paci/thailand/epa0704/agreement.pdf.

191 Thailand-New Zealand Closer Economic Partnership Agreement, signed 19 April 2005, entered into force 1 July 2005, available at http://www.mfat.govt.nz/downloads/trade-agreement/thailand/thainzcep-december2004.pdf.

192 Thailand-Japan EPA, Article 95.

193 *Ibid.*, Article 96.

194 *Ibid.*, Article 93.

195 *Ibid.*, Article 102.

transfer of capital[196] and subrogation.[197] Investment disputes not settled within a six month cooling off period may be referred to conciliation or arbitration under the ICSID Convention or ICSID Additional Facility Rules, or to *ad hoc* arbitration under the UNCITRAL Rules.[198] There are, however, some restrictions on the use of arbitration under the EPA to resolve investment disputes. A tribunal constituted under the arbitration clause may only make an award for the payment of damages or the restitution of property,[199] and the disputes which may be referred to arbitration are restricted to those relating to the management, conduct, operation, maintenance, use, enjoyment and sale or disposition of investments, and must have arisen after the Thailand-Japan EPA came into force.[200]

The Thailand-New Zealand EPA provides similar investment protections as the Thailand-Japan EPA and other BITs, although it does not include an explicit requirement for fair and equitable treatment and full protection and security for investments. Investment disputes under the EPA may, after a cooling off period of three months, be submitted to *ad hoc* arbitration under the UNCITRAL Rules, to national courts, or arbitration or conciliation under the ICSID Convention.[201] Once proceedings have been commenced under the arbitration clause, the parties are no longer entitled to seek to resolve the dispute through diplomatic channels.[202]

Thailand has also entered into Free Trade Agreements ("FTAs") with Australia,[203] Peru[204] and Chile.[205] and has signed a framework agreement for establishing a free trade area with India.[206]

196 *Ibid.*, Article 104.

197 *Ibid.*, Article 105.

198 *Ibid.*, Article 106.

199 *Ibid.*, Article 106(12).

200 *Ibid.*, Article 106(15).

201 Thailand-New Zealand EPA, Article 9.16.

202 *Ibid.*, Article 9.16(3).

203 Australia-Thailand Free Trade Agreement, signed 5 July 2004, entered into force 1 January 2005.

204 Framework Agreement On Closer Economic Partnership Between The Government Of The Republic Of Peru And The Government Of The Kingdom Of Thailand, signed 16 November 2005, entered into force 31 December 2011.

205 See information on UNCTAD Investment Policy Hub, available at http://investmentpolicyhub.unctad.org/IIA/country/41/treaty/3402 (a full text version of the FTA is not publicly available).

206 Framework Agreement For Establishing Free Trade Area Between The Republic Of India And The Kingdom Of Thailand, signed 9 October 2003.

As an example, the Thailand-Australia FTA contains a number of provisions for the protection of investments, including requirements of fair and equitable treatment, full protection and security, MFN, the prohibition of expropriation and requirement for compensation, the free transfer of capital and subrogation rights. Investment disputes may be submitted to competent national judicial or administrative bodies, or for *ad hoc* arbitration under the UNCITRAL Rules.[207]

3 *ASEAN*

Thailand was a founding member of ASEAN, together with Indonesia, Malaysia, the Philippines and Singapore. The ASEAN declaration, or Bangkok Declaration, was signed on 8 August 1967, in Bangkok, Thailand. ASEAN was founded to promote peace and stability, and accelerate economic growth, social progress and cultural development in South East Asia.[208] The ASEAN Charter, an institutional framework codifying the norms, rules and values amongst ASEAN members, was entered into in 2008, under Thailand's chairmanship of ASEAN.

Thailand is a party to the ASEAN Comprehensive Investment Agreement (the "ACIA"), which entered into force on 29 March 2012 and provides investment protections throughout the Member States of ASEAN. The ACIA contains similar protections to those found in Thailand's other BITs, including provisions on non-discrimination, fair and equitable treatment, full protection and security, MFN treatment and prohibition of expropriation. In the event of a dispute between an investor protected under the ACIA and a Member State, the ACIA affords several options for dispute resolution, following a 180-day cooling off period,[209] including a submission of a claim to national courts or tribunals, arbitration under the ICSID Convention or ICSID Additional Facility Rules,[210] *ad hoc* arbitration under the UNCITRAL Arbitration Rules, or institutional arbitration under the Kuala Lumpur Regional Centre for Arbitration ("KLRCA") or any other regional centre for arbitration in ASEAN.[211]

207 Australia-Thailand Free Trade Agreement, signed 5 July 2004, entered into force 1 January 2005, Article 917.

208 'Thailand and ASEAN,' available via the website of the Thai Ministry of Foreign Affairs (http://www.mfa.go.th/asean/contents/files/other-20121207-114514-431514.pdf).

209 Article 32 of the ACIA.

210 See paragraph 3.6 above, as Thailand has not ratified the ICSID Convention, an investor will not be able to initiate proceedings against Thailand pursuant to the ICSID Convention, however a claim may be brought within the scope of the ICSID Additional Facility.

211 Article 33 of the ACIA.

In addition to the usual provisions found in BITs, the ACIA includes provisions for the enhancement of cooperation between Member States with regards to investment promotion,[212] the facilitation of investment[213] and integration between Member States.[214]

4 *APEC*

Thailand became one of the founding Member States of the Asia-Pacific Economic Cooperation in 1989.[215] The Member States of APEC have developed instruments for the promotion and facilitation of investment. In 1994, the Non-Binding Investment Principles[216] ("NBIP") were unanimously adopted, and in 2003 the Investment Transparency Standards were adopted. The NBIP provide a basis for the region's international commitments as they set out 12 principles covering the key elements of BITs and International and Investment Agreements ("IIAs"), including MFN treatment, national treatment, fair and equitable treatment, expropriation and compensation, repatriation of capital and convertibility, the settlement of disputes and regulatory principles regarding conduct in and physical entry into host economies. The NBIP do not provide any substantive obligations or protections, or dispute settlement mechanisms.

V Multilateral Dispute Settlement Related Treaties

1 *ICSID Convention*

While Thailand is a signatory to the ICSID Convention,[217] it has not yet ratified it, being one of the most prominent States in a small group of countries not to have done so.[218] Under Article 25(1) of the Convention, disputes will only fall under the jurisdiction of the Centre where both States have ratified the Convention, therefore, the ICSID Convention does not presently provide a

---

212 *Ibid.*, Article 24.

213 *Ibid.*, Article 25.

214 *Ibid.*, Article 26.

215 See http://www.apec.org/About-Us/About-APEC/History.aspx.

216 Available at: http://www.apec.org/Press/News-Releases/2010/~/media/965E37FDA6D848B4A0350D68D2A4BE1C.ashx.

217 Thailand signed the ICSID Convention on 6 December 1985 (https://icsid.worldbank.org/apps/ICSIDWEB/about/Pages/Database-of-Member-States.aspx?tab-PtoT&rdo=BOTH).

218 Another notable State to have signed but not ratified the ICSID Convention is Russia. States which have neither signed nor ratified the ICSID Convention include Brazil, India, Mexico, South Africa and Vietnam.

basis of jurisdiction for disputes involving Thailand or Thai investors. However, the ICSID Additional Facility Rules offers an alternative where the relevant BIT or IIA provides for the option and the other contracting State is a party to the ICSID Convention.

2 *New York Convention*

The New York Convention obliges its Contracting States to ensure that foreign and non-domestic arbitration awards will be recognised and enforced in the same way as domestic awards. Thailand was one of the earliest contracting parties to adopt the New York Convention,[219] and did so without any reservations. The New York Convention therefore applies to the recognition and enforcement of foreign arbitral awards in Thailand, even if the country in which the award was made is not a party to the New York Convention. In practice, Thai courts have generally recognised and enforced awards rendered outside of Thailand.[220]

VI International Investment Arbitration Jurisprudence

At the time of writing, Thailand has been a party to only one investment dispute in the public domain, as the Respondent State in an arbitration brought by Walter Bau AG, a German investor. The dispute was brought under the provisions of the Thailand-Germany BIT, under the UNCITRAL Arbitration Rules 1976, in Geneva. This case, which has been described as a "real test for Thailand's loosely non-institutionalized investment dispute management and prevention mechanism,"[221] is considered below.

---

219 It did so on 21 December 1959 (http://www.newyorkconvention.org/contracting-states/list-of-contracting-states).

220 As discussed at paragraph 2.3.2. See also Saowanee Asawaroj, "National Report for Thailand" (2013) in Jan Paulsson and Lise Bosman (eds), *ICCA International Handbook on Commercial Arbitration*, (Kluwer Law International; Kluwer Law International 1984, Supplement No. 77, December 2013).

221 Vilawan Mangklatanakul, "Thailand's First Treaty Arbitration: Gain From Pain", published in 'Investor-State Disputes: Prevention and Alternatives to Arbitration II', UNCTAD, *Proceedings of the Washington and Lee University and UNCTAD Joint Symposium on International Investment and Alternative Dispute Resolution*, held on 29 March 2010 in Lexington, Virginia, United States of America.

Walter Bau AG (In Liquidation) v. The Kingdom of Thailand (UNCITRAL)[222]

Tribunal:	The Hon. Sir Ian Barker, Q.C. (President, New Zealand) The Hon. Marc Lalonde, P.C., O.C., Q.C. (Canada) Mr. Jayavadh Bunnag (Thailand)

Case Initiated:	21 September 2005
Award (Jurisdiction) Rendered:	5 October 2007 (not public)
Award (Merits) Rendered:	1 July 2009

Background Facts

The case was brought by the insolvency administrator of Walter Bau AG (In Liquidation), following Walter Bau's purchase of shares in Dong Muang Tollway Co. Ltd. ("DMT"), a Thai Company. In 1989, DMT entered into a concession agreement with the Thai Government for the design, construction, operation and maintenance of the Don Muang Tollway, near Bangkok. The concession agreement granted DMT the right to collect tolls for a period of 25 years. However, the project was beset by a number of problems, including changes to the initial plans and severe delays to progress. Additionally, after financing had been secured, the Government entered into a concession agreement for the construction of a competing toll road, a controversial project which was later abandoned. These issues and others led to disputes between DMT and the Government, and an amendment of DMT's concession agreement was entered into in 1996 which provided for a settlement of DMT's existing claims against the Government in return for, *inter alia*, agreements concerning the refinancing of the project, the 25-year concession period being restarted, agreed increases in the toll rates set out in the concession agreement and the provision for 5-yearly increases in toll fees during the concession period. Despite the amendment, however, toll rates were not increased as agreed. Further, as part of DMT's refinancing, Walter Bau's shareholding in DMT was diluted, while the Government's was increased, and the Government exerted greater influence over DMT. In 2004, shareholder and board meetings of DMT approved reductions in toll fees, despite opposition to these plans from the Walter Bau directors and shareholdings. Such actions were considered by Walter Bau to be against its interests, and several attempts were made to resolve these issues,

222 *Werner Schneider, acting in his capacity as insolvency administrator of Walter Bau AG (In Liquidation) v. The Kingdom of Thailand, UNCITRAL (formerly Walter Bau AG (In Liquidation) v. The Kingdom of Thailand)*, Award available at http://italaw.com/cases/123; Award on Jurisdiction dated 5 October 2007 (not publicly available).

including through diplomatic channels before it ultimately agreed to sell its shareholding in DMT in December 2006.

In bringing a BIT claim against Thailand, Walter Bau alleged various breaches of the Thailand-Germany BIT, including claims relating to (1) the fair and equitable treatment (FET) provision, (2) impairment of its enjoyment of its investment, (3) expropriation, and (4) the national treatment provision.

Key Legal Outcomes

- Jurisdiction

Walter Bau claimed that it was entitled to relief as an investor with a qualifying investment pursuant to the BIT between Germany and Thailand, signed on 24 June 2002, and entered into force on 20 October 2004 (the "2002 BIT"). It relied on a provision of the 2002 BIT which extended protection to "approved investments" made in Thailand before the entry into force of the 2002 BIT, on the basis it had an investment approved under the terms of a prior treaty between Germany and Thailand signed on 13 December 1961 (the "1961 BIT"). The proceedings were bifurcated, and an award on jurisdiction was made by the Tribunal on 5 October 2007. The main issue The tribunal ruled on was whether Walter Bau's shareholding of 9.87% in DMT (which had been reduced during the course of execution of the project) was a protected investment under the 2002 BIT. The Tribunal found that the shareholding was an investment within the meaning of the 2002 BIT, and that it had jurisdiction *ratione materiae* to hear the claim, based on Article 8 of the BIT, which provided that:

> This Treaty shall also apply to approved investments made prior to its entry into force by investors of either Contracting Party in the territory of the other Contracting Party consistent with the latter's laws and regulations.[223]

Subsequently, the Respondent also argued that the Tribunal had no jurisdiction *ratione temporis* in respect of disputes arising before the 2002 BIT came into force, relying on, *inter alia*, the presumption against retroactivity found in Article 28 of the Vienna Convention on the Law of Treaties.[224] The Tribunal agreed with the Respondent and held that it did not have jurisdiction *ratione temporis* to consider disputes in existence prior to the 2002 BIT coming into

223 See Award, 1 July 2009, paras. 9.1–9.2.

224 Award, 1 July 2009, para. 9.16.

force.[225] Whilst Article 8 of the 2002 BIT made it clear that it would apply to "investments" made before the entry into force of the 2002 BIT, this did not mean that investors could claim damages for matters giving rise to disputes prior to that date.[226] The Tribunal also considered that the decision of the ICSID tribunal in *Impregilo SpA v. Islamic Republic of Pakistan*[227] was persuasive, in which the jurisdictional provision was of similar effect. Thus, in the absence of specific provision for retroactivity, the inference was that disputes that may have arisen before the entry into force of the BIT were not covered.[228] Accordingly, the Claimant had no basis on which it could claim damages for events prior to 20 October 2004, the date when the 2002 BIT entered into force. The Tribunal noted, however, that since the provisions of the 1961 BIT inured until October 2014, theoretically, claims could be made on the investor's behalf by Germany on a State-to-State basis under the 1961 BIT (which did not provide for investor-state arbitration), in respect of the Government's conduct prior to October 2004.[229] Separately, the Tribunal discussed the issue of continuing or composite acts, where a series of acts preceded the date of entry into force of the treaty but which achieved consummation as a treaty breach after that date.[230] The Tribunal found that it had to distinguish between "breaches which crystallised before October 2004", and "ongoing conduct before that date which crystallised into a dispute after that date".[231] While the Tribunal did not have jurisdiction to consider the former, the 2002 BIT would apply to acts that fell within the latter category, in accordance with the reasoning of the tribunal in *Société Générale v Dominican Republic*.

- Merits

The investor's arguments centred on claims that Thailand's conduct amounted to a "creeping" expropriation of its investment and that Thailand had acted in breach of the investor's legitimate expectations. The Claimant's arguments were based on the various actions or inactions of Thailand, including failures to adjust the toll rates upwards and failed negotiations, which it contended amounted to an indirect expropriation of its investment.

225 *Ibid.*, para. 9.67.
226 *Ibid.*, para. 9.68.
227 *Impregilo SpA v. Islamic Republic of Pakistan* ICSID Case No. ARB/03/3.
228 Award, 1 July 2009, paras. 9.21 and 9.72.
229 *Ibid.*, para. 9.69.
230 *Ibid.*, para. 9.83.
231 *Ibid.*, para. 9.91.

The investor's submission that the conduct of Thailand amounted to "creeping" expropriation was rejected by the Tribunal, as it considered that:

> None of the actions of the Respondent reaches the level described in *PSEG Global*[232] above. More than *'many things wrongly handled'* is required to justify a finding of expropriation. A strong interference with contractual rights needs to be shown – see *Sempra Energy International v Argentina*. Many of the alleged misdeeds of the Respondent were inaction rather than affirmative action.[233]

However, the Tribunal found in favour of the Claimant on its argument that a reasonable rate of return of the project was part of its legitimate expectations, and Thailand's failure to meet that reasonable expectation was a breach of the FET obligation under the 2002 BIT.[234] The Tribunal also recognised the limited protection the investor had under Thai company law as a minority shareholder in DMT, finding it was protected as an "investor" under the 2002 BIT. While the Respondent may have acted within domestic company law in taking the decisions (through its representatives on the board of DMT) in relation to DMT, that did not mean that it could justify the violation of the Claimant's international law rights. In so finding, the Tribunal made an important distinction between domestic law and international law. Conduct which was legitimate under domestic law could nonetheless be in breach of a State's international law obligations.

The Tribunal also found that Thailand's failure to increase tolls over an extended period, changes to the road network, and short-term closure of Don Muang Airport amounted to a series of wrongful acts, which although they commenced prior to the 2002 BIT coming into force, fell within the jurisdiction of the Tribunal under the principles espoused in *Société Générale v Dominican Republic*.[235] As the Tribunal found that such disputes had not crystallised prior to October 2004, but continued after such date, it had jurisdiction to hold that there was a breach of the FET obligations under the 2002 BIT as

232 Referring to *PSEG Global Inc. and Konya Ilgin Elektrik Üretim ve Ticaret Limited Sirketi v Republic of Turkey*, ICSID Case No. ARB/02/5 available at http://www.italaw.com/cases/880.

233 Award, 1 July 2009, para. 10.17.

234 Award, 1 July 2009, para. 12.3.

235 *Société Générale v. Dominican Republic*, UNCITRAL Arbitration, Decision on Jurisdiction of 18 September 2008.

a consequence of such acts, originating well before the 2002 BIT came into force, but continuing after the relevant date.[236]

Consequently, the Tribunal awarded Walter Bau EUR 29.21 million in damages for the breach of Thailand's treaty obligations.

Subsequent Developments

The Government of Thailand has not complied with the Award rendered by the Tribunal, prompting Walter Bau's insolvency administrator to commence parallel enforcement proceedings in Germany and in the US. The ongoing dispute has even resulted in a Boeing 737 belonging to the Thai crown prince being impounded in Germany, following a court order for its seizure.[237]

In the US, the District Court of the Southern District of New York[238] considered, among others, Thailand's argument that the arbitrators had improperly asserted jurisdiction as Walter Bau's investment was not an "approved investment" and therefore did not qualify for treaty protection under the 2002 BIT.[239] The District Court found that the question of whether an approved investment had been made was an issue of the scope of the arbitration agreement and adopted a deferential review of the Tribunal's jurisdiction, accepting its findings on jurisdiction. Thailand appealed on the basis that the court should have independently adjudicated the Tribunal's jurisdiction, but the US Court of Appeals, Second Circuit, upheld the decision of the District Court.

In Germany, the Berlin Court of Appeal rejected Thailand's objections and declared the Award enforceable,[240] finding that Thailand had waived its right to sovereign immunity from jurisdiction by entering into the 2002 BIT, so enforcement would not be contrary to public policy. On 30 January 2013, the German Federal Court of Justice found the Berlin court had not dealt with the question of whether the investment was protected by the 2002

236 Award, 1 July 2009, para. 12.37.

237 See news article at http://www.nytimes.com/2011/07/14/business/global/thai-princes-plane-impounded-in-germany.html?_r=0.

238 US No. 777, *Werner Schneider, acting in his capacity as insolvency administrator of Walter Bau AG (In Liquidation) v. The Kingdom of Thailand*, United States Court of Appeals, Second Circuit, Docket No. 11–1458-cv, 8 August 2012, available at: http://www.italaw.com/sites/default/files/case-documents/ita0069.pdf.

239 US No. 777, *Werner Schneider, acting in his capacity as insolvency administrator of Walter Bau AG (In Liquidation) v. The Kingdom of Thailand*, United States Court of Appeals, Second Circuit, Docket No. 11–1458-cv, 8 August 2012, p. 16.

240 Germany No. 147, *Werner Schneider as liquidator of Walter Bau A.G. v. The Kingdom of Thailand*, Higher Regional Court of Berlin, Case No. 20 Sch 10/11, 4 June 2012 and Federal Court of Justice of Germany, Case No. III ZB 40/12, 30 January 2013.

BIT, and whether the Tribunal had jurisdiction, as Thailand could not have waived its sovereign immunity if the Tribunal had wrongly accepted its own competence. The case was referred back to the Berlin court to decide whether the dispute was covered by the arbitration clause in the 2002 BIT.[241]

In its decision on 23 February 2015 the Berlin Court, in fulfilment of the review requirements set out by the Federal Court of Justice, decided that Thailand had waived its sovereign immunity and that the UNCITRAL tribunal therefore had jurisdiction to issue the award, thereby reaffirming the EUR29 million award in favour of Walter Bau.[242]

Thailand has also unsuccessfully moved to set aside the award in proceedings in Switzerland.[243]

VII Conclusion

It is perhaps surprising that, given the number of BITs which Thailand is party to, *Walter Bau* remains the only known investment dispute involving Thailand at the time of writing. This may be a sign of the pro-investor approach which has been favoured by successive administrations in Thailand. However, it remains to be seen whether this position will change, with an increasing number of investment disputes involving Thailand, and how, if at all, the FDI flow will be affected.

241 Germany No. 147, *Werner Schneider as liquidator of Walter Bau A.G. v. The Kingdom of Thailand*, Higher Regional Court of Berlin, Case No. 20 Sch 10/11, 4 June 2012 and Federal Court of Justice of Germany, Case No. III ZB 40/12, 30 January 2013.

242 See, http://globalarbitrationreview.com/news/article/33613/thailand-award-confirmed-germany-files-amicus-brief/?utm_source=Law%20Business%20Research&utm_medium=email&utm_campaign=5461451_GAR%20Briefing&dm_i=1KSF%2C3922Z%2CIRRWX5%2CBN1IN%2C1, at the time of writing it is understood that this decision remains on appeal with the German Federal Court of Justice.

243 Reported L.E. Peterson and J. Hepburn, Noose Tightens on Thailand as Swiss Court Declines to Set Aside a Still-Unpaid 2009 BIT Award, IA Reporter, 2 September 2012.

CHAPTER 11

The Democratic Republic of Timor-Leste[1]

I Introduction

The Democratic Republic of Timor-Leste, formerly known as "East Timor", has a population of 1.2 million and a size of approximately 15,000 km^2.[2] Its official currency is the U.S. dollar.[3] Timor-Leste gained independence in May 2002, and underwent parliamentary and presidential elections in 2012.[4]

Timor-Leste is a civil law country. Its legal system, which has continued to evolve following independence, is based on a combination of Indonesian law and regulations, acts passed by the UN Transitional Administration and post-independence Timorese legislation.

Following independence, Timor-Leste experienced an intense period of economic growth in a short period of time, driven largely by oil and gas revenues, the sector that accounts for the vast majority of Foreign Direct Investment ("FDI").[5] The country's development goals, as laid out in the Strategic Development Plan 2011–2030, include using its petroleum revenue to support economic development and a transition to a middle-income country by 2030.[6] Investment opportunities outside of the oil and gas sector are also increasing, particularly in the telecommunications,[7] construction and agricultural sectors, the latter particularly with regard to wood and coffee.

1 This chapter has been drafted by Ms Natalie Limbasan, formerly of Eversheds LLP, Paris.

2 This information, based on the United Nations' data, is available at http://www.bbc.co.uk/news/world-asia-pacific-14952878.

3 See the Government of Timor-Leste's website, at http://timor-leste.gov.tl/?p=547&lang=en.

4 Those elections are further described in the European Parliament's Report on Legislative Elections in Timor-Leste, prepared by the Election Observation Delegation, available at http://www.europarl.europa.eu/intcoop/election_observation/missions/2009-2014/2012_07_07_east_timor_en.pdf.

5 At the time of writing, international investors included ConocoPhillips, Shell, BHP Petroleum and Eni.

6 *The Strategic Development Plan 2011–2030* is available at http://timor-leste.gov.tl/wp-content/uploads/2011/07/Timor-Leste-Strategic-Plan-2011-20301.pdf?bcsi_scan_1daa8b70d81d7bd8=0&bcsi_scan_filename=Timor-Leste-Strategic-Plan-2011-20301.pdf.

7 At the time of writing, international investors included Portugal Telecom, Indonesia's Telin and Vietnam's Viettel.

 | DOI 10.1163/9789004335257_013

Timor-Leste's economic growth has been accompanied by important legislative changes facilitating business and foreign investment. In 2005, the Government established TradeInvest Timor-Leste, an agency aimed at promoting foreign investment and assisting investors.[8] In 2008, a new tax law came into force which transformed the tax regime for businesses.[9] This prompted the World Bank to refer to it as one of the top twenty tax laws in the world in its *Doing Business Report 2009*.[10] The Government also offers investment incentives such as periods of tax exemption and import duty exemptions.

Foreign investors may invest in any sector other than those reserved specifically for the State, namely postal services, public communications, protected natural areas, and weapons production and distribution. Investors are also prohibited from investing in activities otherwise prohibited by law, such as criminal and immoral activities.[11]

Importantly, Section 54 of Timor-Leste's Constitution grants the right of land ownership exclusively to Timorese nationals.[12] However, foreigners may conclude long-term (up to 50-year) leases. There is no national legislation governing land ownership and investors who wish to lease property may have to sort through competing claims from the Portuguese colonial administration, the Indonesian occupation era, and the post-independence period.

II Timor-Leste's National Arbitration and Investment Legislation

1 *Timor-Leste's Arbitration Legislation and Institutions*

Timor-Leste's judicial system is still evolving. Courts of first instance and a Court of Appeal have been established and other tribunals, such as specialised tax courts, are foreseen in the Constitution and legislation, but have not yet been created.

---

8 See the U.S. Department of State's Report, "2014 Investment Climate Statement – Timor-Leste", available at http://www.state.gov/e/eb/rls/othr/ics/2014/227292.htm.

9 The Taxes and Duties Act, 2008, is available on the Timor-Leste Ministry of Finance's website, at https://www.mof.gov.tl/taxes-duties-act-2008/?lang=en.

10 "Doing Business Report 2009", World Bank Group, available at www.doingbusiness.org/reports/global-reports/doing-business-2009, see also the World Bank Group "Doing Business Report 2016 – Economy Profile 2016", available at: http://www.doingbusiness.org/data/exploreeconomies/timor-leste for updated commentary on taxation.

11 See the U.S. Department of State's Report, "2015 Investment Climate Statement – Timor-Leste", available at http://www.state.gov/documents/organization/241976.pdf.

12 Timor-Leste's Constitution is available at http://www.constitution.org/cons/east_timor/constitution-eng.htm.

Given the still developing legislative and judicial framework, there is no arbitration law. Moreover, with regard to foreign arbitral awards, Timor-Leste is not party to the New York Convention and the Court of Appeal must recognise a foreign judgment or arbitral award in order for it to be enforced in the country.[13]

2 *Timor-Leste's Investment Law*

Law No. 14/2011: Private Investment Law

In 2005, Timor-Leste enacted its first investment law, Law No. 5/2005, entitled the "Foreign Investment Law".[14] The preamble to the law stressed the need to improve economic performance and acknowledged the paramount importance of a legal framework that would attract and promote foreign investment in the country. The Foreign Investment Law was replaced in 2011 with Law No. 14/2011, the "Private Investment Law".[15]

The Private Investment Law, like the previous Foreign Investment Law, establishes a set of guarantees and incentives for foreign investments in Timor-Leste. Its main provisions are recalled below.

Preamble

The Preamble recognises that the private sector "is an essential partner in the development of the Country" and that "current legislation should be revised in order to produce a clear legal framework, by bringing together into one single diploma those regimes applicable to national and foreign investment." The Preamble further states as follows:

> [A]ll investors have the right to access courts in order to defend their legally protected rights and interests, to private property in accordance with the limits set out by the Constitution, to import capital goods and equipment, to export products produced according to legally established procedures and restrictions, to credit, to the free transfer of funds abroad,

13 See the U.S. Department of State's Report, "2015 Investment Climate Statement – Timor-Leste", available at http://www.state.gov/documents/organization/241976.pdf.

14 The Foreign Investment Law is available at http://www.jornal.gov.tl/lawsTL/RDTL-Law/RDTL-Laws/Law%205-2005.pdf.

15 An English version of this law has been made publicly available by the Government of Timor-Leste at http://www.jornal.gov.tl/lawsTL/RDTL-Law/RDTL-Laws/Law%2014-2011.pdf. The English version has been cited for the purposes of this chapter. However, this English version should be used with caution, as it sometimes differs from the original versions of the law, published in the official languages of Timor-Leste, namely Portuguese and Tetum.

to free employment of foreign workers, to protect intellectual property and to the respect for professional, banking and commercial secrecy.

The current Law also proposes the definition of a process of benefits and incentives of a fiscal and customs nature, aimed at creating favourable conditions to investment and greater flexibility in terms of adjusting to investors' requirements.

Scope of Application

Pursuant to Article 2(1), the law regulates "investments and re-investments made in Timor-Leste by a national or foreign, resident or non-resident, individual or company".

The law applies to all sectors of the economy, with the following exceptions:

a) Prospection, research and production of oil and natural gas, as well as the mining industry of mineral resources, both the object of specific legislation;
b) Developments geared to the direct sale of goods and equipment to the final consumer;
c) All developments geared to the commercialisation of property (Article 2(2)).

Definition of Investor

Three different categories fall under the definition of investor: at Article 3(h), "Private Investor" or "Investor" "means a national or foreign, resident or non-resident individual or legal person, holder of an Investor's Certificate"; at Article 3(i), "National Investor", "means an individual of Timorese citizenship or a legal person, of which at least 75% of shares with voting rights belong to individuals of Timorese citizenship or other legal persons who are also nationals according to the present definition"; and, at Article 3(j), "Foreign Investor", "means an individual whose nationality is any but Timorese or a legal person, of which at least 75% of shares with voting rights do not belong to individuals of Timorese citizenship or other legal persons who are also nationals."

Definition of "Investment" and "Re-investment"

"Investment" is defined as follows in Article 3(l):

> [A]ny direct or indirect investment in the Country undertaken on behalf of and at the risk of the private investor with cash or other goods, quantifiable in money terms, such as;

i. Capital goods or equipment or others;
ii. Financial resources originating from bank loans;
iii. Capital shares and restricted shares in commercial companies, as well as increases or supplementary inputs of capital;
iv. Patented technology, technical processes, industrial secrets and utility models, franchising and transfer of know-how, brands, logos, names or insignias of registered establishments, as well as any other form of intellectual property;
v. All rights recognised by law or contract and all licences or authorisations issued in accordance with the law.

A "Re-investment", under Article 3(m), is "any investment made in the same business development by resorting to the profits and dividends resulting from the economic activity of such business development."

General Principles

Pursuant to Article 4, an investment must comply with the following "general principles":

a) Free initiative, with the exceptions set out in no. 1 of article 8;
b) Equal treatment between national and foreign investors, with the exceptions set out in articles 10 and 14;
c) Guaranteeing protection for the investment;
d) Respect for international agreements or others of an economic nature which have already been entered into, as well as for Investor's Certificates already issued, in accordance with articles 5 and 6.

Forms of Investment

Article 7 provides a non-exhaustive list of activities that may comprise investments and re-investments, namely:

a) Incorporation of a company under the terms of the applicable law of the Country;
b) Acquisition of part or all the shares of a company or participation in the increase of its capital;
c) Entering into or amending consortium agreements, partnerships, joint ventures or any other form of permissible contract of association, even if not set out in the applicable law of the Country;
d) Entering into or amending agreements involving the property or the management of companies, establishments of an agricultural,

industrial or commercial nature, real estate compounds and other installations or facilities geared to the development of economic activities;

e) Loans taken out or supplementary inputs of capital made by an investor vis-à-vis a company in which such investor has shares, or any loans related to re-investment in the company or participation in profits;

f) Purchase, leasing or acquisition of any other rights in rem over property on national territory, when the acquisition is part of a private investment project, in compliance with the applicable legislation of the Country.

Rights and Protection Afforded to Investors

Investors are accorded the following rights and protections with regard to their investment or re-investment pursuant to the Private Investment Law:

Equal Treatment (Article 12)

1. All investors shall enjoy non-discriminatory treatment in relation to nationality in terms of rights and guarantees, except as regards land ownership, as defined in the Constitution and in the legislation.
2. All investors shall have equal opportunities in terms of accessing benefits and incentives, in relation to criteria for granting such benefits and incentives and to the minimum investment or re-investment values defined in article 10.

Right to Access Courts (Article 13)

All investors shall be guaranteed access to courts to defend their legally protected rights and interests, as set out in the Constitution and legislation.

Land Ownership and Use (Article 14)

1. The State shall grant the right to private property in order that investment or re-investment projects be undertaken, subject to the limits set out in the Constitution and in legislation on land and commercial companies.
2. For the purposes of the provisions in paragraph 1 above, the nationality of the investor shall be defined based on the criteria established in the legislation regarding land and commercial companies, and the definition set out in article 3 shall not be applied.

3. The State shall undertake not to adopt a nationalisations or land policy which would deliberately harm the property of the investors on national territory.
4. Should it be necessary to requisition or expropriate for public use part or all of the investor's property, the State shall give fair compensation to the investor, under the terms to be approved by Law.

Transferring Funds Abroad (Article 17)

1. All investors shall, in accordance with the applicable legislation, be guaranteed the right to freely transfer funds abroad which result from any investment in Timor-Leste, notably:
   a) Distributed profits and dividends resulting from the realisation of an investment;
   b) Capital resulting from the sale, liquidation and extinction of shares or companies which constitute the investment, as well as the sales of company assets which belong to the investor;
   c) Capital resulting from the reduction of share capital of a company which constitutes the investment;
   d) Amounts due resulting from contracts which constitute an investment, in accordance with sub-paragraph d), Article 7;
   e) Inputs due resulting from depreciation or payment of financial interest which constitute the investment, in accordance with sub-paragraph e), Article 7;
   f) Personal income obtained from the performance of management or administration positions vis-à-vis economic activities in which such person participates as investor;
   g) Income obtained from the transfer of intellectual property rights which constitute the investment;
   h) Compensation due under the terms of no. 3, Article 14;
   i) Payments resulting from disputes over the investment.
2. All investors may request that the values be converted into foreign currency through the banking system, as well as transfer those values abroad to fulfil the financial obligations resulting from investments realised, such as:
   a) Payment of imports;
   b) Payment of capital or interest on loans taken out abroad;
   c) Payment of rights and management services.
3. The right to freely transfer funds abroad shall be only limited by way of the application of legislation of a general nature, such as

tax and environmental legislation, and the fulfilment of all legal obligations.

Obligations of Investors

The Private Investment Law also stipulates certain obligations for investors, in the following terms:

General and Specific Duties (Article 27)

1. All investors shall be obliged to comply with the applicable legislation in Timor-Leste, as well as the obligations set out in the Investor's Certificate, and shall be subject to the penalties established therein.
2. The investor shall fulfil the following, especially:
   a) Observing the time limits for the commencement, implementation and completion of the investment or re-investment projects, in accordance with terms set out in the Investor's Certificate;
   b) Employing Timorese workers and promoting their vocational training for the performance of skilled technical or management positions;
   c) Implementing the rules and procedures regarding environmental protection, health and safety at the workplace, under the terms of the applicable legislation of the Country;
   d) Complying with the applicable rules and procedures in terms of setting up funds and reserves, realisation of provisions, organised bookkeeping and accountability instruments, notably by considering the provisions set out in the Law of Commercial Companies and the other applicable legislation of the Country;
   e) Fulfilling the applicable rules and procedures concerning the transfer of funds, under the terms of the applicable legislation of the Country;
   f) Providing the Specialised Investment Agency and other competent authorities with data on such investor's business development, by way of a request made under the terms of the applicable legislation of the Country.

Obtaining an Investor's Certificate (Article 28)

1. The Specialised Investment Agency issues an Investor's Certificate to qualified investors, thus regulating the investment or re-investment to be made in relation to each business development.

2. The Investor's Certificate shall describe the investment or re-investment project and shall contain the following data:
   a) Investor's obligations, such as the date of commencement and conclusion, as well as implementation deadlines and project costs, requested location and infrastructures, capital goods and equipment to be imported, jobs to be created, corresponding vocational empowerment plans for permanent Timorese workers, the necessary residence permits and work visas already obtained and other necessary records and licences already granted, notably tax, commercial, intellectual property, construction or environmental, among others, and all duly annexed.
   b) Tax benefits and customs incentives to be granted by the State, as well as possible terms under which lease agreements of State property have been entered into or costs for training;
   c) Conditions under which the Investor's Certificate has been repealed, in the event investors do not fulfil part or all of their obligations.
3. The Investor's Certificate shall be the document supporting the rights and duties of the investor and shall serve as the basis for all operations undertaken within the scope of the private investment, notably access to benefits and incentives, the settlement of disputes and other facts resulting from the investment or re-investment project.

Special Investment Agreements

For foreign investments of particular import for the national development strategy, special investment agreements may be entered into pursuant to Article 29 of the Private Investment Law.[16] These need to be authorised by the Council of Ministers and provide the possibility of tax reductions or exemptions, customs incentives, leases of state property, and up to a 100-percent cost sharing in the

16 Article 29 of the Private Investment Law reads:

"1. The State may enter into special investment agreements with the investor, by defining special legal regimes for investment or re-investment projects which, given their scale or nature or their corresponding economic, social, environmental or technological impact, may be of great interest to the Country within the framework of the strategy of the National Development Plan, which justifies the adoption of incentives not considered under the provisions set out in Articles 21, 22, 24 and 25 of this Law.

2. The special investment agreements set out in paragraph 1 above must be authorised by Government resolution, expressly indicating the causes justifying such agreement and the special regime governing it."

training of employees. However, the Private Investment Law does not set out criteria for determining which investments may qualify. At the time of writing, two such projects have been authorised: the South Coast Project, aimed at developing refineries and infrastructure for the petroleum industry along Timor-Leste south coast, and the Oecusse Special Economic Zone (ZEESM) Project.[17]

Promotion, Authorisation and Registration of Investments

The Private Investment Law provides, at Article 30, that "[t]he State shall, by Decree-Law, establish a Specialised Investment Agency, a public institute responsible for the promotion and registration of the private investment and for the promotion of exports, as well as the centralisation of the administrative procedures leading to the granting of the Investor's Certificate."

The authorisation of investment and re-investment projects is dealt with in Article 31, according to which:

1. As set out in paragraph 1 of Article 28, all investment and re-investment projects authorised under the terms of this Law shall be granted an Investor's Certificate, in accordance with an administrative procedure to be defined by Government Decree.
2. The administrative procedure granting the Investor's Certificate shall contemplate the obtaining and granting of all authorisations, visas, registrations and licences required to pursue the business development, to be requested from the competent government authorities under the terms of the applicable legislation of the Country.
3. The Investor's Certificate shall be valid as long as the investor does not give any cause for justifying its repeal or invalidity, in accordance with the terms set put in the Investor's Certificate and other applicable legislation.

Pursuant to Article 32, there is a single rate for completion for investors' certificates:

1. For the processing and completion of the request for an Investor's Certificate to be granted a single rate of USD$500 (five hundred

17 U.S. Department of State's Report, "2015 Investment Climate Statement – Timor-Leste", available at http://www.state.gov/documents/organization/241976.pdf.

U.S. dollars) shall be charged national investors upon the submission of such request to Investe Timor-Leste.

2. In relation to foreign investors, the single rate for the processing and completion of the request for an Investor's Certificate to be granted shall be of USD$2,000 (two thousand U.S. dollars) to be charged upon the submission of such request to Investe Timor-Leste.
3. The rate to which paragraphs 1 and 2 above refer shall be considered State revenue and shall be paid in the competent services of the Finance Ministry or in its bank account to be indicated, and the receipt of such payment shall be shown at the time of submission of request for an Investor's Certificate to Investe Timor-Leste.

Article 33 in turn provides for a registration requirement:

1. Once the investment or re-investment project has been authorised, it shall be registered at the Specialised Investment Agency, under the terms to be defined by Government Decree.
2. The registration to which paragraph 1 above refers shall be independent of the commercial company registration, under the terms of the applicable commercial legislation.

Settlement of Disputes

Article 34 deals with the settlement of disputes arising between the State and an investor in relation to the interpretation or application of the Private Investment Law "and respective regulations".

Pursuant to Article 34(1), such disputes are to be "settled by reconciliation, under the terms to be defined by Government Decree, if no other procedure has been established in international agreements to which the Democratic Republic of Timor-Leste is [a] party, or in an agreement between the State and the Investor".

Where reconciliation is unsuccessful, Article 34(2) provides that the dispute is to be submitted to arbitration, "in accordance with the rules of the International Chamber of Commerce, unless there is a convention to the contrary".[18]

---

18 This is a modification from the previous Foreign Investment Law, which provided for disputes between the State and foreign investors arising from the interpretation and application of the law to be resolved by conciliation and, failing that, ICSID arbitration, in the absence of an agreement to the contrary (Article 23 (1) and (2) of the Foreign Investment Law).

Finally, Article 34(3) stipulates that "[t]he terms and provisions set out in paragraphs 1 and 2 above shall not preclude the right to appeal to the competent courts of the Democratic Republic of Timor-Leste, whenever the parties so decide."

3 *Other Laws*

Other major laws affecting incoming foreign investment include the Companies Code of 2004, the Commercial Registration Code and the Taxation Act of 2008.

III Timor-Leste's Bilateral Investment Treaties

1 *Overview*

At the time of writing, Timor-Leste has entered into three Bilateral Investment Treaties ("BITs"): with Qatar (signed on 21 January 2012), Germany (signed on 10 August 2005)[19] and Portugal (signed on 20 May 2002).[20]

Only the BIT entered into with Portugal is in force at the time of writing.[21]

The text of the treaty signed with Qatar has not yet been made publicly available. Thus, for purposes of this review, only the content of the BITs signed with Germany and Portugal shall be considered.

2 *Definition of Investment*

Pursuant to Article 1(1) of the Timor-Leste-Germany BIT, investments comprise every kind of asset, including, but not limited to: movable and immovable property and other rights *in rem*; shares in companies and other kinds of interests in companies; claims to money or claims to any performance having an economic value; intellectual property rights including technical processes, know-how and goodwill; and business concessions, including in relation to the

---

19 Treaty between the Federal Republic of Germany and the Democratic Republic of Timor-Leste concerning the Encouragement and Reciprocal Protection of Investments (the "Timor-Leste-Germany BIT"). An official version of the Timor-Leste-Germany BIT is available in German, Portuguese and English and can be accessed via the UNCTAD website at http://investmentpolicyhub.unctad.org/IIA/country/208/treaty/1767.

20 Agreement between the Portuguese Republic and the Democratic Republic of Timor-Leste concerning the Reciprocal Promotion and Protection of Investments (free translation into English) (the "Timor-Leste-Portugal BIT"). The Timor-Leste-Portugal BIT is available only in Portuguese and can be accessed via the UNCTAD website at http://investmentpolicyhub.unctad.org/IIA/country/208/treaty/2800.

21 The Timor-Leste-Portugal BIT entered into force on 7 April 2004.

exploration, extraction and exploitation of natural resources.[22] The BIT specifies that any alteration in the form in which assets are invested shall not affect their classification as an investment.[23]

Pursuant to Article 1(1) of the Timor-Leste-Portugal BIT, investments comprise all types of properties and rights invested by investors of one of the parties to the BIT in the territory of the other, in accordance with the law of the latter. The examples of covered investments are worded widely and include: movable and immovable property; shares, stocks and other forms of participation in companies, including economic interests resulting from the respective activity; claims to money or any other rights of economic value; intellectual property rights including technical processes, know-how and clientele (goodwill); business concessions, including in relation to the exploration of natural resources; and leasehold properties.[24] The definition of investments in the

---

22 It is noteworthy that whilst the Portuguese version also refers to exploration, extraction and exploitation ("prospeccão, extraccão e exploracão"), the German version refers simply to exploration and exploitation concessions ("Aufsuchungs- und Gewinnungskonzessionen").

23 Article 1(1) *in fine* of the Timor-Leste-Germany BIT provides that "any alteration of the form in which assets are invested shall not affect their classification as investment".

24 Article 1(1) of the Timor-Leste-Portugal BIT defines "investments" as follows: "O termo «investimentos» compreende toda a espécie de bens e direitos investidos por investidores de uma das Partes no território da outra Parte, nos termos da legislação da última, incluindo em particular, mas não exclusivamente: *a*) Propriedade sobre móveis e imóveis, bem como quaisquer outros direitos reais, tais como hipotecas, garantias, penhores e direitos análogos; *b*) Acções, quotas ou outras partes sociais que representem o capital de sociedades ou quaisquer outras formas de participação e ou interesses económicos resultantes da respectiva actividade; *c*) Direitos de crédito ou quaisquer outros direitos com valor económico; *d*) Direitos de propriedade intelectual, tais como direitos de autor, patentes, modelos de utilidade e desenhos industriais, marcas, denominações comerciais, segredos comerciais e industriais, processos técnicos, *know-how* e clientela (aviamento); *e*) Concessões conferidas por força de lei, nos termos de contrato ou acto administrativo emanado por uma autoridade pública competente, incluindo concessões para prospecção, pesquisa e exploração de recursos naturais; *f*) Bens que, no âmbito e em conformidade com a legislação e respectivos contratos de locação, sejam colocados à disposição de um locador no território de uma Parte, em conformidade com a sua legislação."

Translated freely into English, this reads:

"The term "investments" includes all kinds of properties and rights invested by investors of one of the Parties in the territory of the other Party, in accordance with the law of the latter, including in particular, but not exclusively: a) Movable and immovable property, as well as any other property rights such as mortgages, liens, pledges and similar rights; b) Shares, stocks or other securities that represent the capital of companies or

Timor-Leste-Portugal BIT is therefore slightly broader than that in the Timor-Leste-Germany BIT.

Similar to the Timor-Leste-Germany BIT, the treaty with Portugal specifies that any alteration in the form in which an investment is made shall not affect its classification as an investment, provided the alteration is done in accordance with the law.[25]

3 *Definition of Investor*

Article 2 of the Timor-Leste-Germany BIT defines investors in respect of Germany as:

- Germans within the meaning of the Basic Law of the Federal Republic of Germany,
- any juridical person as well as any commercial or other company or association with or without legal personality having its seat in the territory of the Federal Republic of Germany, irrespective of whether or not its activities are directed at profit.

Investors in respect of Timor-Leste are defined as:

- natural persons having the nationality of the Democratic Republic of Timor-Leste in accordance with its laws,

---

any other forms of participation and or economic interests resulting from the respective activity; c) Claims to money or any other rights of economic value; d) Intellectual property rights such as copyrights, patents, utility models and industrial designs, trademarks, trade names, commercial and industrial secrets, technical processes, know-how and clientele (goodwill); e) Concessions conferred by law, under contract or administrative act issued by a competent public authority, including concessions for prospection, exploration and exploitation of natural resources; f) Goods that, within the scope of and in accordance with the law and respective lease agreements, are made available to a lessor in the territory of one Party in accordance with its legislation."

25 Article 1(1) *in fine* of the Timor-Leste-Portugal BIT provides that "Qualquer alteração na forma de realização dos investimentos não afectará a sua qualificação como investimentos desde que essa alteração seja feita de acordo com a legislação da Parte no território da qual os investimentos tenham sido realizados."

Translated freely into English, this reads:

"Any change in the form in which the investments are made will not affect their character as investments provided that such change is in accordance with the laws of the Party in the territory of which the investments have been made."

– legal persons constituted under the laws of the Democratic Republic of Timor-Leste.

In other words, the definition of legal persons with regard to Timorese nationals is wider than that applicable to German legal persons, because in the former case there is no corporate seat requirement.

The Timor-Leste-Portugal BIT also defines investors as either:

(i) natural persons with the nationality of either contracting State pursuant to the laws of the respective State; and
(ii) legal persons including corporations, commercial companies or associations.

However, this BIT also requires that legal persons have their seat in the territory of one of the State parties, are incorporated and operating in accordance with the laws of that State.[26]

4 *Scope*

Once in force, the Timor-Leste-Germany BIT is to apply to investments made prior and subsequent to its entry into force "consistent with" the legislation of the host State.[27]

The Timor-Leste-Portugal BIT applies to investments made prior as well as after its entry into force. However, disputes concerning investments that arose prior to the entry into force of the BIT are not covered.[28]

---

26 Article 1(3) of the Timor-Leste-Portugal BIT provides that "O termo «investidores» designa: *a*) Pessoas singulares, com a acionalidade de qualquer das Partes, nos termos da respectiva legislação; e *b*) Pessoas colectivas, incluindo empresas, sociedades comerciais ou outras sociedades ou associações que tenham sede no território de uma das Partes, estejam constituídas e funcionem de acordo com a legislação dessa Parte."

Translated freely into English, this reads:

"The term "investors" means: a) Natural persons with the nationality of either Party in accordance with the laws of that Party; and b) Legal persons, including corporations, commercial companies or other companies or associations that have their seat in the territory of one of the Parties, are incorporated in and operate in accordance with the laws of that Party."

27 Article 9 of the Timor-Leste-Germany BIT provides that "This Treaty shall also apply to investments made prior to its entry into force by investors of either Contracting State in the territory of the other Contracting State consistent with the latter's legislation."

28 Article 2 of the Timor-Leste-Portugal BIT provides that "O presente Acordo aplica-se a todos os investimentos realizados por investidores de uma das Partes no território da

5 *Substantive Protections*

Fair and Equitable Treatment

Article 2(2) of the Timor-Leste-Germany BIT provides that each contracting State will accord investments by investors of the other contracting State fair and equitable treatment (as well as full protection).[29]

Article 4(1) of the Timor-Leste-Portugal BIT goes further as it extends the fair and equitable treatment of investments to the income resulting from those investments.[30] Similarly, the management, maintenance, use, enjoyment or disposal of investments made in the territory of one of the contracting States are also afforded fair and equitable treatment under Article 4(2) of the BIT.[31] However, Article 4(3) contains a carve out with regard to free trade areas,

---

outra Parte, antes e após a sua entrada em vigor, em conformidade com as respectivas disposições legais, com excepção dos diferendos relativos a investimentos emergentes antes da respectiva entrada em vigor."

Translated freely into English, this reads:

"This Agreement applies to all investments made by investors of one of the Parties in the territory of the other Party, before and after its entry into force, in accordance with their laws, with the exception of disputes concerning investments that arose before its entry into force."

29 Article 2(2) of the Timor-Leste-Germany BIT provides that "Each Contracting State shall in its territory in any case accord investments by investors of the other Contracting State fair and equitable treatment as well as full protection under the Treaty."

30 Article 4(1) of the Timor-Leste-Portugal BIT provides that "Os investimentos realizados por investidores de uma das Partes no território da outra Parte, bem como os rendimentos deles resultantes, são objecto de tratamento justo e equitativo e não menos favorável do que o concedido pela última Parte aos investimentos dos seus próprios investidores ou aos investimentos de investidores de terceiros Estados."

Translated freely into English, this reads:

"Investments made by investors of one of the Parties in the territory of the other Party, as well as the income arising therefrom, are subject to fair and equitable treatment and treatment no less favourable than that accorded by the latter Party to investments of its own investors or to investments of investors from third States."

31 Article 4(2) of the Timor-Leste-Portugal BIT provides that "Ambas as Partes concedem aos investidores da outra Parte, no que respeita à gestão, manutenção, uso, fruição ou disposição dos investimentos realizados no seu território, um tratamento justo e equitativo e não menos favorável do que o concedido aos seus próprios investidores ou a investidores de terceiros Estados."

Translated freely into English, this reads:

"Both Parties grant investors of the other Party, as regards the management, maintenance, use, enjoyment or disposal of investments in its territory, fair and equitable treatment and treatment no less favourable than that accorded to its own investors or to investors from third States."

customs unions, common markets that are in existence or to be established and other similar international agreements or forms of economic cooperation, as well as bilateral or multilateral agreements of regional character or not, relating wholly or partially to fiscal matters.[32]

Non-Discrimination

Article 2(3) of the Timor-Leste-Germany BIT provides that neither contracting State shall in any way impair by arbitrary or discriminatory measures the management, maintenance, use, enjoyment or disposal of investments in its territory of investors of the other Contracting State.[33]

The Timor-Leste-Portugal BIT contains similar wording. Its Article 3(3) provides that the management, maintenance, use, enjoyment or disposal of investments made in the territory of either of the contracting States is not to be subjected to unjustified, arbitrary or discriminatory measures.[34]

---

32 Article 4(3) of the Timor-Leste-Portugal BIT provides that "As disposições deste artigo não implicam a concessão de tratamento de preferência ou privilégio por uma das Partes a investidores da outra Parte que possa ser outorgado em virtude de: *a*) Participação em zonas de comércio livre, uniões aduaneiras, mercados comuns existentes ou a criar e em outros acordos internacionais similares, incluindo outras formas de cooperação económica a que qualquer das Partes tenha aderido ou venha a aderir; e *b*) Acordos bilaterais, multilaterais, com carácter regional ou não, de natureza total ou parcialmente fiscal."

Translated freely into English, this reads:

"The provisions of this Article shall not imply the granting of preferential treatment or privilege by one of the Parties to investors of the other Party that may be granted by virtue of: a) Participation in free trade areas, customs unions, common markets, whether existing or to be established, and in other similar international agreements, including other forms of economic cooperation to which either Party has adhered or may adhere; and b) Bilateral, multilateral agreements, of regional character or not, that are wholly or partially of a fiscal nature."

33 Article 2(3) of the Timor-Leste-Germany BIT provides that "Neither Contracting State shall in any way impair by arbitrary or discriminatory measures the management, maintenance, use, enjoyment or disposal of investments in its territory of investors of the other Contracting State."

34 Article 3(3) of the Timor-Leste-Portugal BIT provides that "As Partes não sujeitarão a gestão, manutenção, uso, fruição ou disposição dos investimentos realizados no seu território por investidores de outra Parte a medidas injustificadas, arbitrárias ou de carácter discriminatório."

Translated freely into English, this reads:

"The Parties shall not subject the management, maintenance, use, enjoyment or disposal of investments made in their territory by investors of the other Party to unjustified, arbitrary or discriminatory measures."

Full Protection and Security

Both treaties expressly provide for full protection and security of investments of investors of a contracting State in the territory of the other contracting State.[35] The Timor-Leste-Portugal Treaty contains the limitation that such investments be made "in accordance with the legal provisions in force" in the Territory of the State where the investment is made (Article 3(2)).

Expropriation

Article 4(2) of the Timor-Leste-Germany BIT prohibits direct or indirect expropriation, nationalisation or subjection to measures the effect of which would be tantamount to expropriation or nationalisation, "except for the public benefit and against compensation".[36]

The compensation is to be equivalent to the value of the expropriated investment immediately before the date on which the actual or threatened expropriation, nationalisation or comparable measure became publicly known.

---

35 Article 4(1) of the Timor-Leste-Germany BIT provides that "Investments by investors of either Contracting State shall enjoy full protection and security in the territory of the other Contracting State" and Article 3(2) of the Timor-Leste-Portugal BIT provides that "Os investimentos realizados por investidores de uma das Partes no território da outra Parte, em conformidade com as disposições legais vigentes nesse território, gozam de plena protecção e segurança no território da última."

Translated freely into English, this reads:

"Investments made by investors of one of the Parties in the territory of the other Party in accordance with the legal provisions in force in that territory, shall enjoy full protection and security in the territory of the latter."

36 Article 4(1) of the Timor-Leste-Germany BIT provides that "Investments by investors of either Contracting State shall not directly or indirectly be expropriated, nationalized or subjected to any other measure the effects of which would be tantamount to expropriation or nationalization in the territory of the other Contracting State except for the public benefit and against compensation. Such compensation shall be equivalent to the value of the expropriated investment immediately before the date on which the actual or threatened expropriation, nationalization or comparable measure has become publicly known. The compensation shall be paid without delay and shall carry the usual bank interest until the time of payment; it shall be effectively realizable and freely transferable. Provision shall have been made in an appropriate manner at or prior to the time of expropriation, nationalization or comparable measure for the determination and payment of such compensation. The legality of any such expropriation, nationalization or comparable measure and the amount of compensation shall be subject to review by due process of law."

The compensation is to be paid without delay and is to carry the usual bank interest until the time of payment. Moreover, it is to be effectively realisable and freely transferable.

The legality of any such expropriation, nationalisation or comparable measure and the amount of compensation due are to be subject to review by due process of law.

The Timor-Leste-Portugal BIT also prohibits expropriation, nationalisation and measures with equivalent effect (referred to together as "expropriation"), unless such a measure is taken by operation of law, in the public interest, on a non-discriminatory basis and against prompt compensation.[37]

The Timor-Leste-Portugal BIT specifies that the amount of compensation is to correspond to the market value of the expropriated investment immediately before the expropriation, or the date on which the future expropriation became public knowledge, whichever the earlier.[38]

---

37 Article 6(1) of the Timor-Leste-Portugal BIT provides that "Os investimentos efectuados por investidores de uma das Partes no território da outra Parte não podem ser expropriados, nacionalizados ou sujeitos a outras medidas com efeitos equivalentes à expropriação ou nacionalização (adiante designadas como «expropriação»), excepto por força da lei, no interesse público, sem carácter discriminatório e mediante pronta indemnização."

Translated freely into English, this reads:

"Investments made by investors of either Party in the territory of the other Party shall not be expropriated, nationalised or subjected to other measures having effects equivalent to expropriation or nationalisation (hereinafter referred to as 'expropriation'), except by operation of law, in the public interest, on a non-discriminatory basis and against prompt compensation."

38 Article 6(2) of the Timor-Leste-Portugal BIT provides that "A indemnização deve corresponder ao valor de mercado que os investimentos expropriados tinham à data imediatamente anterior ao momento em que a expropriação tenha ocorrido ou ao momento em que a futura expropriação seja do conhecimento público, contando, para o efeito, a primeira das datas. A indemnização deve ser paga sem demora, vence juros à taxa bancária usual, desde a data da expropriação até à data da sua liquidação, e deve ser pronta, efectiva, adequada e livremente transferível."

Translated freely into English, this reads:

"The compensation shall correspond to the market value of the expropriated investment at the date immediately preceding the moment the expropriation occurred or the moment the future expropriation became public knowledge, relying, for that purpose, on the earlier of these dates. The compensation shall be paid without delay, bear interest at the usual bank rate from the date of the expropriation until the date of payment, and should be prompt, effective, adequate and freely transferable."

Compensation is to be paid without delay, and interest is to be paid at the usual banking rate applicable from the date of the expropriation to the time of payment. It is also to be prompt, effective, adequate and readily transferable.[39]

Unlike in the Timor-Leste-Germany BIT, the expropriation provision in the Timor-Leste-Portugal BIT expressly provides that the investor has the right, in accordance with the laws applicable in the territory of the contracting State in which the investment was expropriated, to prompt review of its claim in judicial or other proceedings, and to valuation of its investments according to the principles defined in the same article of the BIT.[40]

Umbrella Clauses

Both treaties contain umbrella clauses. The Timor-Leste-Germany BIT provides that each contracting State "shall observe any other obligation it has assumed with regard to investments in its territory by investors of the other Contracting State."[41] The Timor-Leste-Portugal BIT stipulates that the contracting States are required to comply with obligations not covered by the BIT, but undertaken in relation to investments made by investors of the other contracting State in the territory of the host State.[42]

---

39 *Ibid.*

40 Article 6(3) of the Timor-Leste-Portugal BIT provides that "O investidor cujos investimentos tenham sido expropriados terá o direito, de acordo com a legislação da Parte no território da qual os bens tiverem sido expropriados, à pronta revisão do seu caso, em processo judicial ou outro, e à avaliação dos seus investimentos, de acordo com os princípios definidos neste artigo."

Translated freely into English, this reads:

"The investor whose investments have been expropriated shall have the right, in accordance with the laws of the territory in which the assets have been expropriated, to prompt review of his case, in judicial or other proceedings, and to the valuation of his investments, in accordance with the principles set out in this Article."

41 Article 8(2) of the Timor-Leste-Germany BIT provides that "Each Contracting State shall observe any other obligation it has assumed with regard to investments in its territory by investors of the other Contracting State."

42 Article 5(2) of the Timor-Leste-Portugal BIT provides that "Ambas as Partes devem cumprir eventuais obrigações, não incluídas no presente Acordo, assumidas em relação aos investimentos realizados por investidores da outra Parte no seu território."

Translated freely into English, this reads:

"Both parties shall comply with any obligations, not included in this agreement, undertaken in relation to investments made by investors of the other Party in its territory."

Most Favoured Nation and National Treatment

The Timor-Leste-Germany BIT contains various provisions obliging the contracting States to provide Most Favoured Nation ("MFN") treatment. In particular, it provides that each contracting State should not subject investors or investments of the other State to treatment less favourable than that accorded to its own investors or those of any third State, or to investments of its own investors or those of any third State.[43] Excluded from these provisions are privileges accorded on account of customs or economic unions, common markets or free trade areas, as well as advantages accorded by virtue of a double taxation agreement or other agreements regarding matters of taxation.[44]

MFN treatment is also extended to matters covered by Article 4, namely full protection and security, expropriation and MFN/national treatment with regard to compensation for losses.[45]

Finally, the Timor-Leste-Germany BIT provides that, if the legislation of either contracting State or obligations under international law (existing or established after the date of the treaty) provide for more favourable treatment than the BIT, then those more favourable provisions shall prevail.[46]

---

43 Article 3(1) and 3(2) of the Timor-Leste-Germany BIT provide that "(1) Neither Contracting State shall subject investments in its territory owned or controlled by investors of the other Contracting State to treatment less favourable than it accords to investments of its own investors or to investments of investors of any third State. (2) Neither Contracting State shall subject investors of the other Contracting State, as regards their activity in connection with investments in its territory, to treatment less favourable than it accords to its own investors or to investors of any third State."

44 Article 3(3) and 3(4) of the Timor-Leste-Germany BIT provide that "(3) Such treatment shall not relate to privileges which either Contracting State accords to investors of third States on account of its membership of, or association with, a customs or economic union, a common market or a free trade area. (4) The treatment granted under this Article shall not relate to advantages which either Contracting State accords to investors of third States by virtue of a double taxation agreement or other agreements regarding matters of taxation."

45 Article 4(4) of the Timor-Leste-Germany BIT provides that "(4) Investors of either Contracting State shall enjoy most-favoured-nation treatment in the territory of the other Contracting State in respect of the matters provided for in this Article."

46 Article 8(1) of the Timor-Leste-Germany BIT provides that "If the legislation of either Contracting State or obligations under international law existing at present or established hereafter between the Contracting States in addition to this Treaty contain a regulation, whether general or specific, entitling investments by investors of the other Contracting State to a treatment more favourable than is provided for by this Treaty, such regulation shall to the extent that it is more favourable prevail over this Treaty."

The Timor-Leste-Portugal BIT requires that the treatment of all investments and resulting income of investors from the other contracting State is no less favourable than that granted to nationals of that State or investors from third States.[47] The same applies to the management, maintenance, use, enjoyment or disposal of investments made in the territory of one of the contracting States.[48] However, as with regard to fair and equitable treatment, the treaty contains a carve out with regard to free trade areas, customs unions, common markets that are in existence or to be established and other similar international agreements or forms of economic cooperation, as well as bilateral or multilateral agreements, whether or not they are of a regional character, relating wholly or partially to fiscal matters.[49]

---

47 Article 4(1) of the Timor-Leste-Portugal BIT provides that "Os investimentos realizados por investidores de uma das Partes no território da outra Parte, bem como os rendimentos deles resultantes, são objecto de tratamento justo e equitativo e não menos favorável do que o concedido pela última Parte aos investimentos dos seus próprios investidores ou aos investimentos de investidores de terceiros Estados."

Translated freely into English, this reads:

"Investments made by investors of one of the Parties in the territory of the other Party, as well as the resulting income arising therefrom, are subject to fair and equitable treatment and treatment no less favourable than that accorded by the latter Party to investments of its own investors or to investment of investors from third States."

48 Article 4(2) of the Timor-Leste-Portugal BIT provides that "Ambas as Partes concedem aos investidores da outra Parte, no que respeita à gestão, manutenção, uso, fruição ou disposição dos investimentos realizados no seu território, um tratamento justo e equitativo e não menos favorável do que o concedido aos seus próprios investidores ou a investidores de terceiros Estados."

Translated freely into English, this reads:

"Each Party grants investors of the other Party, as regards the management, maintenance, use, enjoyment or disposal of investments made in its territory, fair and equitable treatment and treatment not less favourable than that accorded to its own investors or to investors from third States."

49 Article 4(3) of the Timor-Leste-Portugal BIT provides that "As disposições deste artigo não implicam a concessão de tratamento de preferência ou privilégio por uma das Partes a investidores da outra Parte que possa ser outorgado em virtude de: *a*) Participação em zonas de comércio livre, uniões aduaneiras, mercados comuns existentes ou a criar e em outros acordos internacionais similares, incluindo outras formas de cooperação económica a que qualquer das Partes tenha aderido ou venha a aderir; e *b*) Acordos bilaterais, multilaterais, com carácter regional ou não, de natureza total ou parcialmente fiscal."

Translated freely into English, this reads:

"The provisions of this Article shall not imply the granting of preferential treatment or privilege by one of the Parties to investors of the other Party that may be granted by virtue

The Timor-Leste-Portugal BIT also provides that, to the extent that the domestic law of one of the contracting States or obligations arising under international law provide more favourable treatment than foreseen by the BIT, the more favourable regime shall prevail.[50]

6 *Repatriation of Capital and Compensation for Losses*

According to Article 4(3) of the Timor-Leste-Germany BIT, investors suffering losses as a result of armed conflict, revolution, a state of national emergency or revolt are to be accorded treatment no less favourable than that accorded to nationals of the host State with regard to restitution, indemnification, compensation or other valuable consideration for such losses. This also applies with regard to treatment accorded to third States by virtue of the MFN provision at Article 4(4) of the Treaty. Moreover, any compensation is to be freely transferable.

A similar provision is found in the Timor-Leste-Portugal BIT. According to Article 7 of the treaty, investors are to receive treatment no less favourable than that accorded to nationals of the host State or those of third Sates, with regard to restitution, compensation or other relevant factors relating to losses resulting from war or other armed conflict, revolution, state of national emergency or other events considered equivalent to this under international law.[51]

---

of: a) Participation in free trade areas, customs unions, common markets, whether existing or to be established, and in other similar international agreements, including other forms of economic cooperation to which either Party has adhered or may adhere; and b) Bilateral, multilateral agreements, of regional character or not, that are wholly or partially of a fiscal nature."

50 Article 5(1) of the Timor-Leste-Portugal BIT provides that "Se, para além do presente Acordo, as disposições da lei interna de uma das Partes ou as obrigações emergentes do direito internacional em vigor ou que venha a vigorar entre as duas Partes estabelecerem um regime, geral ou especial, que confira aos investimentos efectuados por investidores da outra Parte um tratamento mais favorável do que o previsto no presente Acordo, prevalecerá sobre este o regime mais favorável."

Translated freely into English, this reads:

"If, in addition to this Agreement, the provisions of the domestic law of one of the Parties or current or future obligations under international law between the two parties establish a regime, whether general or specific, which confers investments made by investors of the other Party with more favourable treatment than that provided for in this Agreement, the more favourable regime will prevail."

51 Article 7(1) of the Timor-Leste-Portugal BIT provides that "Os investidores de uma das Partes que venham a sofrer perdas nos investimentos realizados no território da outra Parte em virtude de guerra ou outros conflitos armados, revolução, estado de emergência nacional ou outros eventos considerados equivalentes pelo direito internacional receberão

Such compensation is to be freely transferable, without delay, in convertible currency.[52]

The Timor-Leste-Germany BIT grants the free transfer of payments in connection with an investment including the principal and additional amounts to maintain or increase the investment; the returns; the repayment of loans; proceeds from sales of the investment; and the compensation provided for in Article 4.[53] Transfers are to be made without delay at the market rate of exchange applicable on the date of the transfer.[54]

The Timor-Leste-Portugal BIT allows for free transfer of amounts related to investments. Examples given include capital for the maintenance and increase of the investments and investment returns as defined in Article 1(2) of the BIT.[55]

---

dessa Parte tratamento não menos favorável do que o concedido por essa Parte aos investimentos dos seus próprios investidores ou de investidores de terceiros Estados, consoante o que for mais favorável, no que diz respeito à restituição, indemnizações ou outros factores pertinentes."

Translated freely into English, this reads:

"Investors of one of the Parties who suffer losses on investments made in the territory of the other Party owing to war or other armed conflict, revolution, state of national emergency or other events considered equivalent thereto under international law will receive from that Party treatment no less favourable than that accorded by that Party to investments of its own investors or to investors of third States, whichever is more favourable, as regards restitution, compensation or other relevant factors."

52 Article 7(2) of the Timor-Leste-Portugal BIT provides that "As compensações previstas no número anterior devem ser transferíveis livremente e sem demora em moeda convertível."

Translated freely into English, this reads:

"Compensation foreseen pursuant to the previous paragraph shall be freely transferable without delay in convertible currency."

53 Article 5 of the Timor-Leste-Germany BIT provides that "Each Contracting State shall guarantee to investors of the other Contracting State the free transfer of payments in connection with an investment, in particular (a) the principal and additional amounts to maintain or increase the investment; (b) the returns; (c) the repayment of loans; (d) the proceeds from the liquidation or the sale of the whole or any part of the investment; (e) the compensation provided for in Article 4."

54 Article 7(1) of the Timor-Leste-Germany BIT provides that "Transfers under Article 4 (2) or (3), under Article 5 or Article 6 shall be made without delay at the market rate of exchange applicable on the day of the transfer."

55 Article 8(1) of the Timor-Leste-Portugal BIT provides that "Ambas as Partes, em conformidade com a respectiva legislação, garantem aos investidores da outra Parte a livre transferência das importâncias relacionadas com os investimentos, em particular, mas não exclusivamente: *a*) Do capital e das importâncias adicionais necessárias à manutenção ou ampliação dos investimentos; *b*) Dos rendimentos definidos no n.o 2 do artigo 1.o

7 *Investor-State Dispute Settlement*

Both the Timor-Leste-Germany BIT and the Timor-Leste-Portugal BIT foresee arbitration as a method of dispute resolution for investment disputes, but the content of the provisions contained in each treaty differs somewhat.

Pursuant to the Timor-Leste-Germany BIT, investment disputes are to be settled amicably in the first instance.[56] In the absence of an amicable settlement, the dispute may be submitted for arbitration at the request of the investor following a six-month cooling off period. Unless the disputing parties agree otherwise, the dispute shall be submitted to ICSID arbitration.[57] Interestingly, the BIT also provides that, "[d]uring arbitration proceedings or the enforcement of an award, the Contracting State involved in the dispute shall not raise the objection that the investor of the other Contracting State has received compensation under an insurance contract in respect of all or part of the damage".[58]

---

deste Acordo; *c*) Das importâncias necessárias para o serviço, reembolso e amortização de empréstimos, reconhecidas por ambas as Partes como investimentos; *d*) Do produto resultante da alienação ou da liquidação total ou parcial dos investimentos; *e*) Das indemnizações ou outros pagamentos previstos nos artigos 4.o e 7.o deste Acordo; *f*) De quaisquer pagamentos preliminares que possam ter sido efectuados em nome do investidor de acordo com o artigo 9.o do presente Acordo; *g*) Dos salários de trabalhadores estrangeiros, autorizados a trabalhar, em conexão com o investimento, no território da outra Parte."

Translated freely into English, this reads:

"Each Party, in accordance with its respective laws, guarantees to investors of the other Party the free transfer of amounts relating to the investments, in particular but not exclusively: a) Capital and additional amounts necessary to maintain or increase the investments; b) The returns defined in paragraph 2 of Article 1 of this Agreement; c) The amounts required for the service, repayment and amortisation of loans, recognised by both Parties as investments; d) The proceeds obtained from the sale or the total or partial liquidation of the investments; e) Any compensation or other payments foreseen by Articles 4 and 7 of this Agreement; f) Any preliminary payments that may be made in the investor's name in accordance with Article 9 of this Agreement; g) The wages of foreign workers authorised to work, in connection with the investment, in the territory of the other Party."

56 Article 11(1) of the Timor-Leste-Germany BIT provides that "Divergencies concerning investments between a Contracting State and an investor of the other Contracting State should as far as possible be settled amicably between the parties in dispute."

57 Article 11(2) of the Timor-Leste-Germany BIT provides that "If the divergency cannot be settled within six months of the date when it has been raised by one of the parties in dispute, it shall, at the request of the investor of the other Contracting State, be submitted for arbitration. Unless the parties in dispute agree otherwise, the divergency shall be submitted for arbitration under the Convention of 18 March 1965 on the Settlement of Investment Disputes between States and Nationals of Other States."

58 Article 11(4) of the Timor-Leste-Germany BIT.

Pursuant to the Timor-Leste-Portugal BIT, investment disputes are to be settled amicably in the first instance.[59] Where this is not possible, and following a six-month cooling off period, either party may submit the dispute to the competent courts in the territory in which the investment is located, to ICSID for conciliation or arbitration pursuant to the ICSID Convention, or to an *ad hoc* arbitral tribunal established pursuant to the UNCTAD Rules.[60] In other words, this treaty lists a variety of options for dispute settlement, such as recourse to the national courts, ICSID conciliation (in addition to arbitration), or arbitration under the UNCTAD Rules. This is a so-called "fork in the road" provision, since Article 11(3) of the treaty specifies that a decision to refer a dispute to one of the listed methods of resolution is irreversible.[61]

---

59 Article 11(1) of the Timor-Leste-Portugal BIT provides that "Os diferendos entre um investidor de uma das Partes e a outra Parte relacionados com um investimento do primeiro no território da segunda serão resolvidos, de forma amigável, através de negociações."

Translated freely into English, this reads:

"Disputes between an investor of one of the Parties and the other Party relating to an investment of the former in the territory of the latter shall be settled amicably through negotiation."

60 Article 11(2) of the Timor-Leste-Portugal BIT provides that "Se os diferendos não puderem ser resolvidos de acordo com o disposto no n.o 1 deste artigo no prazo de seis meses contados da data em que uma das partes litigantes o tiver suscitado, qualquer das partes poderá submeter o diferendo:

a) Aos tribunais competentes da Parte no território da qual se situa o investimento; ou.

b) Ao Centro Internacional para a Resolução de Diferendos Relativos a Investimentos, para conciliação ou arbitragem, nos termos da Convenção para a Resolução de Diferendos entre Estados e Nacionais de outros Estados, celebrada em Washington, D.C., em 18 de Março de 1965; ou.

c) A um tribunal arbitral *ad hoc*, estabelecido de acordo com as regras de arbitragem da Comissão das Nações Unidas para o Comércio e Desenvolvimento (CNUCED)."

Translated freely into English, this reads:

"If the dispute cannot be resolved in accordance with paragraph 1 of this Article within six months of the date on which one of the disputing parties raised it, either party may refer the dispute:

a) To the competent courts of the Party in whose territory the investment is situated; or.

b) To the International Centre for Settlement of Investment Disputes, for conciliation or arbitration, under the terms of the Convention on the Settlement of Investment Disputes between States and Nationals of Other States, concluded in Washington DC on 18 March 1965; or.

c) To an ad hoc arbitral tribunal, established in accordance with the arbitration rules of the United Nations Conference on Trade and Development (UNCTAD).

61 Article 11(3) of the Timor-Leste-Portugal BIT provides that "A decisão de submeter o diferendo a um dos procedimentos referidos no número anterior é irreversível."

8 *State-to-State Dispute Settlement*

The Timor-Leste-Germany BIT and the Timor-Leste-Portugal BIT contain similar provisions with regard to the settlement of disputes between the contracting States concerning the interpretation or application of the treaties.

Both treaties provide in their respective Article 10 that the contracting States should attempt to settle any such dispute. Where this is not possible, either party may submit the dispute to *ad hoc* arbitration. Unlike the Timor-Leste-Portugal BIT which provides for a six-month cooling off period,[62] the Timor-Leste-Germany BIT does not specify that a cooling off period needs to be respected.

Both treaties also provide for arbitral tribunals comprised of three members: two party-appointed arbitrators and a chairman nominated by the co-arbitrators.[63]

Translated freely into English, this reads:

"The decision to submit the dispute to one of the procedures referred to in the preceding paragraph is irreversible."

62 See footnote 60 above.

63 Articles 10(3) of the Germany- Timor-Leste BIT and of the Timor-Leste-Portugal BIT respectively provide that "Such arbitration tribunal shall be constituted ad hoc as follows: each Contracting State shall appoint one member, and these two members shall agree upon a national of a third State as their chairman to be appointed by the governments of the two Contracting States. Such members shall be appointed within two months, and such chairman within three months from the date on which either Contracting State has informed the other Contracting State that it intends to submit the dispute to an arbitration tribunal" and that "O tribunal arbitral é constituído *ad hoc*, do seguinte modo: *a*) Cada Parte designa um membro e ambos os membros propõem um nacional de um terceiro Estado como presidente, que será nomeado pelas duas Partes; *b*) Os membros serão nomeados no prazo de dois meses e o presidente no prazo de três meses a contar da data em que uma das Partes tiver comunicado à outra a intenção de submeter o diferendo a um tribunal arbitral; *c*) O presidente do tribunal arbitral tem de ser nacional de um Estado com o qual ambas as Partes mantenham relações diplomáticas." Translated freely into English, this reads:

"The arbitral tribunal is constituted *ad hoc*, in the following manner: a) Each Party shall designate one member and these members shall propose a national of a third State as president, to be appointed by the two Parties; b) The members shall be appointed within two months and the president within three months from the date on which one of the Parties notified the other of the intention to submit the dispute to an arbitral tribunal; c) The president of the arbitral tribunal shall be a national of a State with which both Parties maintain diplomatic relations."

9 Notable Trends

Given the limited number of BITs concluded by Timor-Leste thus far, it would be artificial to identify any particular treaty practice to date for this country. However, it bears noting that the two treaties that are publicly available offer relatively ample protection, containing wide definitions of investments and relatively wide definitions of investors, broad substantive protections, umbrella clauses, a generous scope of application and, importantly, recourse to international arbitration (which, in the case of the Timor-Leste-Portugal BIT offers different alternatives) in the event of a dispute between one of the contracting States and an investor of the other contracting State.

IV Multilateral Investment Related Treaties and Organizations to which Timor-Leste is a Party

Timor-Leste is not yet a party to many multilateral investment treaties. While it applied for membership of ASEAN in 2011, at the time of writing, the ASEAN Coordinating Council Working Group was still evaluating its application due to concerns of some of the ASEAN members over the youth of the country. Moreover, one precondition of membership is the establishment of embassies in all other ASEAN member States, a requirement which Timor-Leste is still to fulfil. If Timor-Leste accedes to the ASEAN Comprehensive Investment Agreement, one advantage would be that Timor-Leste investors and investors into Timor-Leste will have access to the dispute settlement mechanisms for investment disputes contained therein.

1 *MIGA*

Timor-Leste is a signatory of the Convention Establishing the Multilateral Investment Guarantee Agency (the "MIGA"). The MIGA is a development financial institution and a member of the World Bank Group. It was established "to encourage the flow of investments for productive purposes among member countries, and in particular developing member countries, thus supplementing the activities of the International Bank for Reconstruction and Development…, the International Finance Corporation and other international development finance institutions."[64]

MIGA offers political risk insurance and credit enhancement guarantees to investors of other member States. Investments eligible for guarantee are

64 Article 2 of the Convention Establishing the MIGA.

defined as including "equity interests, including medium- or long-term loans made or guaranteed by holders of equity in the enterprise concerned, and such forms of direct investment as may be determined by the Board [of MIGA]", provided they are made in the territory of a developing member country.

The Convention Establishing the MIGA foresees coverage of three generally accepted categories of non-commercial risk, namely: currency transfer risk; expropriation; and risk of war and civil disturbance, as well as, under certain conditions, risks of breach or repudiation of a contractual commitment by the host government to the investor.

The dispute resolution mechanism applicable to disputes arising under a contract of guarantee or reinsurance is to be arbitration, in accordance with the rules contained or referred to in the contract in question.[65]

Disputes between MIGA as subrogee of an investor[66] and a member of the Convention are to be settled in accordance with Annex II of the Convention or an agreement to be entered into between MIGA and that member on alternative dispute settlement mechanisms, but based in any event on Annex II.[67] Pursuant to Annex II, where negotiation has failed, and unless the parties, by mutual consent, opt to resort first to conciliation, disputes are to be submitted to arbitration.

The Annex provides that "[u]nless otherwise provided in this Annex or agreed upon by the parties, the Tribunal shall determine its procedure and shall be guided in this regard by the arbitration rules adopted pursuant to the Convention on the Settlement of Investment Disputes between States and Nationals of Other States."

Finally, disputes between MIGA and a member or agency thereof, or a former member, are to be settled in accordance with Annex II.

V Multilateral Dispute Settlement Related Treaties

Timor-Leste became a contracting State of the ICSID Convention in August 2002, shortly after gaining independence. However, as noted above, Timor-Leste is not a party to the New York Convention.

65 Article 58 of the Convention Establishing the MIGA.

66 Subrogation occurs automatically upon MIGA paying, or agreeing to pay, compensation to the holder of a guarantee – Article 18 of the Convention Establishing the MIGA.

67 Article 57(b) of the Convention Establishing the MIGA.

VI International Investment Arbitration Jurisprudence

With regard to the practical application of the investment protection provisions for international investors mentioned above, at the time of writing, at least one arbitration was initiated by two foreign investors (*Lighthouse Corporation Pty Ltd (Australian) and Lighthouse Corporation Ltd IBC (Seychelles)*) against Timor-Leste, as detailed below.

Lighthouse Corporation Pty Ltd and Lighthouse Corporation Ltd IBC v Democratic Republic of Timor-Leste (ICSID Case No. ARB/15/2)

Tribunal:	Gabrielle Kaufmann-Kohler (President, Switzerland) Stephen Jagusch (New Zealand) Campbell McLachlan (New Zealand)
Case Initiated:	14 January 2015
Award:	Pending (a memorial on the merits was filed by the Claimants on 14 March 2016).

VII Outlook: Anticipated Developments

Timor-Leste's economic growth, coupled with plans to expand the legislative framework and efforts made to encourage FDI since shortly after achieving independence, mean that investment protection and related dispute settlement mechanisms are areas that are expected to develop considerably over the next few years. The establishment of alternative methods of dispute resolution, including arbitration, form an express part of Timor-Leste's Strategic Development Plan 2011–2030 and are a key stated priority for the Government for the improvement of access to justice.[68]

68 See, for example, the report "Mediation and Arbitration in the Markets of the Community of Portuguese-Speaking Countries" (free translation) by the International Institute for Mediation and Arbitration, available only in Portuguese at http://www.aip.pt/irj/go/km/docs/site-manager/www_aip_pt/documentos/homepage/informacao/ILMAI_FernandoTonim.pdf.

CHAPTER 12

Vietnam[1]

I Introduction

The Socialist Republic of Vietnam is a single-party socialist republic on the Indochina Peninsula with a presidential head of state and appointed prime minister as head of government. Vietnam has a civil law system, similar to that of France, but has developed common law traits such as an increased reliance on judicial precedents by the Vietnamese courts.[2] Legislative power is vested in the National Assembly, which also appoints justices of the Vietnamese courts and supervises the activities of the People's Court and the People's Procuracy. Under the law of Vietnam, their courts render judgments independently, although they are not publicly published and it is difficult to obtain access to past judgments.[3]

In 1986, Vietnam implemented the *Doi Moi* policy in order to shift from a centralised economy to a socialist-oriented market economy, encouraging the establishment of private business and the promotion of foreign investment. From being one of the poorest countries in the world, with per capita income below $100, within a quarter of a century Vietnam has become a lower middle income country with per capita income of US $1,890 (2014) and GDP at US$186.2 billion.[4] Since the *Doi Moi* policy was introduced, the economy has undergone

1 This chapter has been drafted by Mr Vishal Melwani, with the assistance of Mr Tom Jackson, Mr Tegan Smyth and Ms Teresa Yuen of Eversheds LLP, Hong Kong, and reviewed by Mr Luu Tien Ngoc and Mr Le Tuan Anh of Vision & Associates, Hanoi, Vietnam.

2 "Doing business in Vietnam", Practical Law Company (1 November 2011): <http://uk.practicallaw.com/3-515-9149>, see also World Bank Group Doing Business 2016 – Vietnam available at: http://www.doingbusiness.org/data/exploreeconomies/vietnam/.

3 Article by Anh Luu published in July 2006 updated by Le Thi Hanh, Director of the Library of Information Centre, Hanoi Law University, Vietnam, in May 2013 (http://www.nyulawglobal.org/globalex/Vietnam1.htm).

4 The Voice of Vietnam, GDP gap between Vietnam and other countries in the region is threaten to broaden – 2015: http://vov.vn/kinh-te/gdp-cua-viet-nam-so-voi-cac-nuoc-trong-khu-vuc-nguy-co-bi-noi-rong-426539.vov, see also World Bank Group Doing Business 2016 – Vietnam available at: http://www.doingbusiness.org/data/exploreeconomies/vietnam/.

 DOI 10.1163/9789004335257_014

rapid growth and continues to be one of the fastest growing economies in the world, with a growth rate averaging 6.4% per annum over the past decade.[5]

The current objective of Vietnam's socio-economic development plan is for the country to become a modernisation-oriented industrial nation by 2020.[6] A key part of its strategy to maintain fast economic growth and improve the country's business climate, is the active encouragement of foreign investment. In this regard, Vietnam's new Law on Enterprise and Law on Investment came into effect on 1 July 2015. Full implementation of Vietnam's new system of investment laws and regulations is still underway. It is expected that the new legislation will provide a simplified and more efficient legal framework for investors doing business in Vietnam.[7] For example, the process of applying for an Enterprise Registration Certificate will become more user-friendly in that, among other things, less detailed information will be required.[8] Theoretically, enterprises are now free to conduct business in sectors not prohibited by law. Further, an enterprise is now permitted to have multiple legal representatives. This will bring about greater flexibility in business operations as compared to the previous position where no business could have more than one legal representative.[9]

Since the economic transition, the inflow of Foreign Direct Investment ("FDI") has increased dramatically with more than 18,991 active projects licensed in the period of 1988 to 2015, totalling in excess of US$265.65 billion

5 The World Bank, Vietnam Overview: http://www.worldbank.org/en/country/vietnam/overview.

6 Resolution No.13-NQ/TW, 'The 4th Conference of the 11th Central Executive Committee of Communist Party on Constructing System of Synchronous Infrastructure Aiming to Our Country Become a Modern-Oriented Industrial Country in 2020' <http://thuvien-phapluat.vn/archive/Recolution-No-13-NQ-TW-on-constructing-system-of-synchronous-infrastructure-vb144170.aspx>. For more information on Vietnam's development plan, *see* Vietnam Ministry of Planning and Investment, Foreign Investment Agency: http://fia.mpi.gov.vn.

7 See the article by Thao Nguyen, EU-Vietnam Business Network Consultant, dated 26 June 2015 (http://evbn.org/game-changer-for-foreign-investment-in-vietnam/); see also the article by Michael Lee, Partner of Tilleke & Gibbins dated 29 May 2015 (http://www.conventuslaw.com/vietnam-new-investment-and-corporate-law-a-step-forward-or-more-of-the-same/).

8 Article written by Dr. Le Net of LNT & Partners dated 30 June 2015 (see: http://lntpartners.com/documents/New%20LOE%20LOI%20Come%20Into%20Affect%20from%20Midnight%20_%20LNTpartners.pdf).

9 Article written by Michael Lee, Partner of Tilleke & Gibbins dated 29 May 2015 (see http://www.conventuslaw.com/vietnam-new-investment-and-corporate-law-a-step-forward-or-more-of-the-same/).

in implementation capital.[10] In 2014, the total FDI newly-registered and increased in the country topped US$21.92 billion, according to the Ministry of Planning and Investment's Foreign Investment Agency.[11] Although this represented a 1.9% decline compared with the same period last year, it still exceeded government targets. This figure demonstrates substantial year-on-year growth of USD$11.2 billion from 2013 which equates to a 6.2% increase.[12] Keeping this auspicious trend, US$13.3 billion have been newly-registered and increased and US$8.5 billion have been disbursed in the first 8 months of 2015.[13]

Among the 105 countries and territories investing in all 63 provinces or cities directly under central government in Vietnam, the Republic of Korea took the lead with US$42.89 billion with 4,615 projects, constituting 16.18% of the total FDI registered in Vietnam. It was followed by Japan (US$37.94 billion with 2,725 projects, representing 14.31%), Singapore (US$33.35 billion with 1,446 projects, representing 12.58%), Taiwan (China) (US$29.18 billion with 2,460 projects, representing 11%) and British Virgin Islands (US$18.92 billion, representing 7.13%). These countries account for 52% of the total registered capital and cover the manufacturing, construction, accommodation and real estate sectors.[14]

Vietnam is widely regarded as an attractive destination for foreign investors due to its relative economic stability, abundant and highly-educated labour resources, government incentives, and natural resources. Vietnam was ranked as the 11th top prospective host economy for the years 2013–2015 in terms of FDI inflow, by a survey of transnational companies conducted by UNCTAD.[15]

10 The Voice of Vietnam; Foreign direct investment enhance development of Vietnamese products – 2015: http://vtv.vn/kinh-te/doanh-nghiep-fdi-tao-dong-luc-phat-trien-hang-viet-20150731153729444.htm.

11 Foreign Investment Agency under Ministry of Planning and Investment: Situation of foreign investment in 2014: https://dautunuocngoai.gov.vn/detail/2704/Tinh-hinh-dau-tu-nuoc-ngoai-nam-2014.

12 General Statistics Office of Vietnam, Social and economic situation in eleven months of 2014: http://www.gso.gov.vn/default.aspx?tabid=622&ItemID=16113.

13 Foreign Investment Agency under Ministry of Planning and Investment: Situation of foreign investment in the first 8 months of 2015: http://fia.mpi.gov.vn/tinbai/3650/Tinh-hinh-dau-tu-nuoc-ngoai-8-thang-nam-2015.

14 Foreign Investment Agency under Ministry of Planning and Investment: Situation of foreign investment in the first 8 months of 2015: http://fia.mpi.gov.vn/tinbai/3650/Tinh-hinh-dau-tu-nuoc-ngoai-8-thang-nam-2015, https://drive.google.com/file/d/0BwilzYaS5B6cRW5QR1h6dkpqQ2M/view?pli=1.

15 UNCTAD World Investment Report 2013: Global Value Chains: Investment and Trade for Development, available at: http://unctad.org/en/PublicationsLibrary/wir2013_en.pdf,

Investors have however raised concerns as to the legal and financial infrastructure, and the potentially slow and bureaucratic decision-making process.[16]

II Vietnam's National Arbitration and Investment Legislation

1 *Vietnam's Arbitration Legislation and Institutions*

Vietnam's Arbitration Law

Vietnam's legal system is rapidly developing, and it is only in recent times that arbitration has received legislative recognition. The law governing arbitration proceedings in Vietnam is the 2010 Law on Commercial Arbitration No. 54/2010/QH12 ("LCA").[17]

Prior to the LCA coming into effect on 1 January 2011, the Ordinance on Commercial Arbitration was the first instrument on arbitration in Vietnam in 2003, establishing Vietnamese arbitration infrastructure. The LCA brings Vietnamese laws closer to international standards, by incorporating the provisions of the UNCITRAL Model Law of 1985, together with the 2006 amendments. Observers have welcomed the new arbitration regime as offering an attractive alternative to litigation before the local courts which are perceived as being inefficient and lacking transparency.[18]

The LCA broadens the scope of arbitrable disputes, giving arbitral tribunals competence to resolve three types of conflicts, including those: (1) arising from commercial activities; (2) arising between parties when at least one of them is engaged in commercial activities; and (3) where the law stipulates that disputes shall or may be resolved by arbitration.[19] Regarding the second type of disputes, "commercial activities" are defined beyond the sale and purchase of goods to also include investment activities.[20] Due to the 2005 Law on Investment No. 59-2005-QH11 as well as the current 2014 Law on Investment No. 67/2014/

---

although Vietnam has seen a drop in its rankings for 2015–2017, see UNCTAD World Investment Report 2015: http://unctad.org/en/PublicationsLibrary/wir2015_en.pdf.

16 2015 Investment Climate Statement: http://www.state.gov/e/eb/rls/othr/ics/2015/241793.htm.

17 Law 54 on Commercial Arbitration No. 54/2010/QH12, available at http://www.viac.org.vn/en-US/Document/Document/3.aspx.

18 The New Law on Commercial Arbitration in Vietnam: Some Positive Changes in Theory and How it Can Work Out in Practice (9 March 2012): http://terralex.org/publication/b4d64adddc.

19 Article 2 LCA.

20 Article 3.1 Commercial Act No. 36/2005-QH11.

QH13 ("LOI"), FDI falls under the third type of dispute, as the LOI provides that disputes with foreign investors relating to investment activities in Vietnam may be settled by arbitration or by the Vietnamese courts.

The LCA does not specifically define domestic and international arbitration but provides that "Foreign arbitration means an arbitration formed under a foreign law on arbitration and selected as agreed by the parties to settle a dispute outside or within the Vietnamese territory".[21] Arbitrations between Vietnamese citizens are in certain circumstances also considered "international". Specifically, the LCA provides "For disputes with a foreign element, the arbitration tribunal shall apply the law chosen by the parties. If the parties do not have an agreement on the applicable law, the arbitration tribunal shall make a decision to apply the law which it considers the most appropriate."[22]

The LCA has also overcome many of the perceived drawbacks of arbitration in Vietnam. For instance, the old Ordinance placed limitations on who could be appointed as an arbitrator and contained qualification requirements as to nationality, requiring the arbitrator to be a Vietnamese citizen unless the dispute involved "foreign elements". Instead, the LCA allows the parties the liberty to choose the arbitral tribunal and removes the requirement as to Vietnamese citizenship.[23]

The old Ordinance also provided that where there were "foreign elements", the parties could choose an applicable law to govern the dispute. However, such law would apply only insofar as it was consistent with the "fundamental principles" of Vietnamese law, thus creating uncertainty for the parties.[24] Parties to an arbitration involving foreign elements now have the autonomy to decide upon the governing law for the dispute.[25]

The LCA provides the tribunal with the power to decide on certain types of interim relief upon the application by a party.[26] Previously relief could only be granted by the Vietnamese courts, a procedure which caused delays and led to inefficiency.

---

21 Article 3(11), LCA.

22 *Ibid.*, Article 14(2).

23 The New Law on Commercial Arbitration in Vietnam: Some Positive Changes in Theory and How it Can Work Out in Practice (9 March 2012): http://terralex.org/publication/b4d64adddc.

24 *Ibid.*

25 Article 14, LCA.

26 *Ibid.*, Article 49.

Vietnam's Arbitral Institutions and Rules

There are currently eleven arbitration centres in Vietnam.[27] The main arbitral institution is the Vietnam International Arbitration Centre ("VIAC") at the Vietnam Chamber of Commerce and Industry[28] which was established in 1993 and, unlike its predecessors, is an independent organisation. Its establishment came after the merging of the Foreign Trade Arbitration Committee (1963) and the Marine Arbitration Committee (1964).[29] The objective of VIAC is to promote the dispute resolution method of arbitration and alternative dispute resolutions ("ADR") generally in Vietnam.[30] The VIAC administers its cases under its own Rules of Arbitration, the latest version of which came into force in 2012.[31]

The LCA also provides for the establishment of foreign arbitration centres and representative offices in Vietnam, although awards issued by such bodies are treated as foreign arbitral awards, which may affect enforcement as discussed below.[32] In addition, *ad hoc* proceedings are recognised under the LCA.[33]

The VIAC maintains a list of approximately 126 Vietnamese arbitrators,[34] and 17 foreign arbitrators[35] which has substantially increased in light of the legal reform. The VIAC has seen a considerable increase in the number of

27 Ministry of Justice, List of institutional arbitrations in Vietnam: http://moj.gov.vn/bttp/Pages/trong-tai-thuong-mai.aspx?Page=2. They include: Global Commercial Arbitration Centre (GCAC), Finance Commercial Arbitration Centre (FCCA), Saigon Commercial Arbitration Centre (SCAC), Nam Viet Commercial Arbitration Centre (NVCAC), Indochina Trade Arbitration Centre (ITAC), Can Tho Commercial Arbitration Centre (CCAC); ASEAN International Arbitration Centre (ACIAC); Pacific International Arbitration Centre (PIAC); Financial Commercial Arbitration Centre (FCCA); Vietnam Financial Banking Arbitration Centre (VIFIBAR); Vietnam International Arbitration Centre (VIAC); and Ho Chi Minh City Commercial Arbitration Centre (TRACENT).

28 *See:* http://eng.viac.vn/.

29 C. Nguyen, Arbitration in Vietnam: An Overview, *Journal of International Arbitration*, Kluwer Law International 2014, Volume 31 Issue 5, p. 676.

30 *See:* http://eng.viac.vn/about-us/gioi-thieu-chung-a164.html.

31 Vietnam International Arbitration Centre, Rules of Arbitration: http://viac.vn/Uploads/Quy%20tac%202012%20Eng%20-%20Final.PDF.

32 Chapter 12 Law on Commercial Arbitration No. 54/2010/QH12: http://vietlaw4u.com/download/Vietnam%20Commercial%20Arbitration%20Law.rar.

33 *LCA Art 2* provides "Ad hoc" arbitration means a form of dispute settlement under this Law and the order and procedures agreed by the parties."

34 VIAC List of Vietnamese arbitrators: http://eng.viac.vn/vietnamese-arbitrators-p2.html.

35 VIAC List of foreign arbitrators: http://eng.viac.vn/foreign-arbitrators-p3.html.

cases heard over its nineteen years of establishment, most notably in the last five years, with 99 disputes settled in 2013, 124 in 2014 and 146 in 2015.[36]

This is however a low statistic compared with other arbitration centres in Asia, such as, for instance, the Hong Kong International Arbitration Centre ("HKIAC") which heard 477 disputes in 2014,[37] 252 of which were arbitrations[38] or the Singapore International Arbitration Centre ("SIAC") whose caseload in 2014 was 222.[39] A 2007 survey by the Vietnam Chamber of Commerce and Industry and the Ministry of Justice of Vietnam[40] found that negotiation was favoured for resolving disputes over the infrequently used arbitration system in Vietnam. There was a clear lack of confidence and trust in arbitration, and a concern as to the enforceability of arbitral awards, which the LCA has sought to address.

Arbitration in Vietnam is still young and efforts are being undertaken to bring the arbitration regime in line with international standards. In particular, the Rules of Arbitration of VIAC were amended and came into force in January 2012. It was published together with the VIAC's Guidelines on Arbitral Proceedings, and both of them are inspired by the UNCITRAL Model Law and UNCITRAL Notes on Organising Arbitral Proceedings, in that existing standards in international arbitration, such as the principle of party autonomy, separability of the arbitration agreement, independence and impartiality of the arbitral tribunal, freedom of the arbitral tribunal in the conduct of arbitration proceedings, interim measures, and the final and binding character of awards, have been taken into account.[41]

Vietnam's Courts and Arbitration

There are a number of circumstances in which Vietnamese courts may become involved with arbitration proceedings. The LCA provides that at the request of an arbitral tribunal or by the parties to an arbitration, the courts may for

36 Numbers of Disputes in VIAC Over 17-Year-Period from 1993 to 2015: http://eng.viac.vn/statistical/numbers-of-disputes-in-viac-over-17-year-period-from-1993-to-2015-a274.html.

37 HKIAC Case Statistics 2014: http://www.hkiac.org/about-us/statistics.

38 *Ibid.*

39 SIAC Case Statistics 2014: http://www.siac.org.sg/2013-09-18-01-57-20/2013-09-22-00-27-02/annual-report.

40 Hew R. Dundas, "National Report for Vietnam (2012)", *International Handbook on Commercial Arbitration,*; and 'Report on Results of the Research into the Use of Arbitration in Resolution of Commercial Disputes in Vietnam', 2007 MJV/VCCI.

41 C. Nguyen, "Arbitration in Vietnam: An Overview", *Journal of International Arbitration*, Kluwer Law International 2014, Volume 31 Issue 5, p. 680.

instance assist in the appointment of arbitrators,[42] summons for witnesses[43] and the collection of evidence.[44]

One such circumstance is the grant of interim relief.[45] Article 102 of the 2004 Civil Proceedings Code ("CPC"), as amended and supplemented in 2011, sets out a number of reliefs, which, together with those set out in the LCA, constitute the types of interim reliefs that a party may request from the court once arbitration proceedings have been initiated. The types of relief available include freezing orders, interim payments of money and prohibitions on dealing with any of the assets in dispute.

There are also circumstances in which the courts may intervene in arbitral proceedings, such as for the purpose of assessing the jurisdiction of the arbitral tribunal,[46] challenging arbitrators[47] and reviewing decisions in respect of the validity of arbitration agreements.

Challenges to international arbitral awards can be made by a party with sufficient evidence lodging a petition to the court within thirty days of the award.[48] A challenge can only be made on the grounds set out in Article 68 of the LCA. The grounds for refusing recognition or enforcement of an award under the LCA follow closely those of Article 36 of the UNCITRAL Model Law.[49] Many of the grounds on which an award can be set aside are also grounds for denying recognition or enforcement of an award.

Pursuant to the LCA, Vietnamese courts can set aside an award, or refuse to recognise and enforce an award, on the grounds that the award is contrary to the fundamental principles of the law of Vietnam. This is instead of the equivalent ground for refusal under the UNCITRAL Model Law of it being contrary to public policy.

In theory the courts are not allowed to review the merits of a dispute already resolved by an arbitral tribunal. However, the fundamental principles of Vietnamese law have, in some cases, been relied upon to justify the retrial and reassessment of the merits of a dispute. Vietnam's Arbitration Law permits a party to apply to set aside an arbitration award, provided that the

---

42 Article 41(5), LCA.

43 *Ibid.*, Article 47(2).

44 *Ibid.*, Article 46(5)(and see Article regarding summons of witnesses).

45 *Ibid.*, Article 48.

46 *Ibid.*, Article 43.

47 *Ibid.*, Article 42(4).

48 *Ibid.*, Chapter 11.

49 http://www.uncitral.org/pdf/english/texts/arbitration/ml-arb/07-86998_Ebook.pdf.

application relies on sufficient evidence to support the grounds on which the arbitral award should be set aside.[50] A party may request a domestic arbitral award to be annulled within thirty days of the date the award was granted. When a request is tendered, the party must pay an application fee to the local Provincial People's Court and, when a review is conducted, the judicial standard of review is *de novo*.

2 *Vietnam's Investment Laws*

Vietnam proactively encourages foreign investment. Accordingly, specific laws have been introduced to facilitate and promote investments, albeit various restrictions and limitations exist.

For foreign investors investing in Vietnam, whether by: (i) incorporating a new company (either wholly or partially foreign owned); or (ii) contributing capital to or acquiring equity (whether 100% or less) in an existing Vietnam-incorporated company, the applicable laws are, firstly, the investment law, and then the specific laws to which the sectors where foreign investment is made are subject. In the course of the nearly 30 years from 1987 to the present, three investment laws have been introduced in Vietnam[51]. The investment law currently in force is the LOI, which simplifies many procedures relating to investment registration by foreign investors and focuses more on providing protections to all investors.[52]

Among other things, the LOI has for the first time codified[53] the laws prohibiting: (a) the 6 sectors in which no investment whatsoever may be made (e.g. certain drugs; specimens of endangered and rare wild fauna or flora; prostitution; purchase or sale of humans, tissues or parts of the human body, etc.); and (b) the 267 sectors in which foreign investment is subject to certain conditions or restrictions (e.g. accounting businesses, auditing businesses, legal practicing, commercial arbitration institution services, etc.). Other than these sectors, foreign investment can now freely be made.

---

50 Articles 68 and 69, LCA.

51 The first one is the 1987 Law on Foreign Investment in Vietnam, which applied only to foreign investments. The second one is the 2005 Law on Investment, which applied to both foreign and local investments. The currently valid one is the 2014 Law on Investment.

52 Law on Investment 2014 Law No. 67/2014/QH13: http://www.xaydung.gov.vn/web/guest/legal-documents/-/legal/TB4r/en_US/18/250755/55213.

53 Before that the sectors are provided by different laws and even under-law regulations, which created a lot of difficulties for all investors (particularly foreign investors) to know which are prohibited, conditional and free to do business.

While in principle, the requirements of approvals and investment registration certificates ("IRC")[54] are still in place for foreign investments which take the form of incorporating new companies in Vietnam, comparatively fewer regulatory approvals are required for foreign investments if they are made through contributing capital to or acquiring shares in existing target companies in Vietnam. In the latter case, a simple investment approval notification from the provincial Department of Planning and Investment ("DPI") of the locality where the target company is head quartered is required if: (i) the target company operates in sector(s) in which investment is conditional; or (ii) over 51% of the charter capital of the existing target company is being acquired, while no such investment approval notification is required in respect of acquisition of 51% or less of an existing company incorporated in Vietnam. To better respond to the actual needs of foreign investors, on-line registration facilities are now available, whereby theoretically all major information about investment projects registered by investors (including foreign investors) are now electronically recorded in and obtainable from a nation-wide database managed by the Ministry of Planning and Investment ("MPI").

If foreign investment is made in a service sector, the international commitments (both multinational and bilateral commitments) made by Vietnam (e.g. Vietnam's WTO Commitments, Vietnam's Schedule of Specific Commitments under ASEAN Framework Agreement on Services ("Vietnam's ASEAN

54 Under the 1987 Law on Foreign Investment in Vietnam, this was called "Investment License" which may be a combination of 2 parts: investment project registration and project company registration. Under the 2005 Law on Investment, this was called "Investment Certificate" which clearly combined 2 parts: investment project registration and project company registration. However, under the currently valid 2014 Law on Investment, the "Investment Registration Certificate" recognises only the investment project registration by investors. The project company registration is now recognised in the so called "Enterprise Registration Certificate". Article 38 of the 1987 Law on Foreign Investment in Vietnam stipulated: *"The application shall be considered by the State body in charge of foreign investment and its decision shall be communicated to the parties concerned within three months from the date of its receipt of the application. Approval shall be communicated by the issue of an investment license."*; Article 50.1 of the 2005 Law on Investment states: *"Foreign investors investing in Vietnam for the first time must have an investment project and perform the procedures for investment registration or evaluation of investment at the State administrative body for investment in order to be issued with an investment certificate. The investment certificate shall also be the business registration certificate."*; and Article 3.6 of the 2014 Law on Investment provides for: *"Investment registration certificate ["IRC"] means a written or electronic document recording information registered by an investor about an investment project."*

Commitments"), Agreement between Japan and Vietnam for an Economic Partnership) also apply.[55] Among others, there are also limits on the percentage of ownership of a foreign investor in certain service sectors. For example, according to Vietnam's WTO Commitments, there is a blanket 30% cap on foreign ownership in regards to foreign acquisition of equity/ shares in an existing target bank,[56] 51% for motion picture distribution, 49% for an electronic game business and 49–51% for relevant freight transport services amongst others.

In setting up a business in Vietnam, an investor should note that the above-mentioned limits on the percentage of ownership of a foreign investor, whilst consistent within the same service sector, vary from one international commitment to another; and normally specially favourable incentives are reserved for investors coming from other ASEAN member countries. For example: the limit on foreign ownership applicable to internal waterways transport services is 49% under Vietnam's WTO Commitments, but it is increased to 51% under Vietnam's ASEAN Commitments. This is significant because the LOI accepts 51% majority voting for almost all issues in a joint stock company (65% approval is required for a limited number of key issues), and with 51% ownership, foreign investors from ASEAN countries may better control the company and business in Vietnam. As minority shareholders, foreign investors can generally buy, without limit, shares from Vietnamese investors.

The LOI confirmed investment incentives (particularly tax and land-related incentives) in favour of foreign investors where the investment projects are conducted in preferential investment sectors and geographical areas.

Further, the LOI provides for a broad range of protections for foreign investors. Specifically, the State recognizes and protects the ownership of assets, investment capital, income, and other lawful rights and interests of all investors in Vietnam. In particular, assets of any investors shall not be nationalized nor confiscated by any administrative measures in all cases. In case of a compulsory acquisition or requisition for special purpose (e.g. national defence and security), full compensation will be made by the State, in accordance with the applicable laws.

---

55 International commitments do not apply to foreign investment in production sectors. To date Vietnam has only made international commitments in relation to trade in goods and services.

56 However, 100% foreign ownership is permissible to a bank newly established by foreign investors in Vietnam.

III Vietnam's Bilateral Investment Treaties

1 *Overview*

Vietnam is not a party to the 1965 Convention on the Settlement of Investment Disputes between States and Nationals of Other States (the "ICSID" Convention).[57] However, Vietnam is party to at least 62 Bilateral Investment Treaties ("BITs") of which 48 are currently in force.[58] These include, among others, BITs concluded with France, China and Singapore in 1992, with the United Kingdom in 2002, and Japan and South Korea in 2003. Vietnam's first BIT was concluded in 1990 with Italy, and came into force in 1994.

Over the last 23 years, at least 48 out of the 62 BITs concluded by Vietnam have entered into force.[59]

Most recently, Vietnam has entered into investment agreements in 2013 with the State of Palestine, and in 2015 with Turkey.[60] The number of BITs entered into by Vietnam is likely to continue to grow in order to provide an appropriate legal framework for investment. It is estimated that, at the time of

---

57 H.R. Dundas, "National Report for Vietnam (2012)" in Jan Paulsson (ed), *International Handbook on Commercial Arbitration*, Kluwer Law International 1984, Supplement No. 70, August 2012, p. 43.

58 UNCTAD 'Full list of Bilateral Investment Agreements concluded, 1 June 2013' – Vietnam has signed BITs with Algeria, Argentina, Armenia, Australia, Austria, Bangladesh, Belarus, Belgium and Luxembourg, Bulgaria, Cambodia, Chile, China, Cuba, Czech Republic, Denmark, Egypt, Finland, France, Germany, Greece, Hungary, Iceland, India, Indonesia, Iran, Italy, Japan Kazakhstan, DPR Korea, Republic of Korea, Lao, Latvia, Lithuania, Malaysia, Mongolia, Morocco, Mozambique, Myanmar, Namibia, Netherlands, Oman, Philippines, Poland, Romania, Russian Federation, Singapore, Slovakia, Spain, Sri Lanka, Sweden, Switzerland, Taiwan, Tajikistan, Thailand, Ukraine, United Arab Emirates, United Kingdom, Uruguay, Uzbekistan, Venezuela. See http://unctad.org/Sections/dite_pcbb/docs/bits_vietnam.pdf and http://investmentpolicyhub.unctad.org/IIA/CountryBits/229.

59 UNCTAD 'Full list of Bilateral Investment Agreements concluded, 1 June 2013' – BITs with the following states/territories have entered into force: Argentina, Armenia, Australia, Austria, Belarus, Belgium and Luxembourg, Bulgaria, China, Cuba, Czech Republic, Denmark, Egypt, France, Germany, Hungary, Iceland, India, Indonesia, Italy, Japan, Korea (Republic of), Lao PDR, Latvia, Lithuania, Malaysia, Mongolia, Mozambique, Netherlands, Philippines, Poland, Russian Federation, Singapore, Slovakia, Spain, Sweden, Taiwan, Thailand, Ukraine, Uzbekistan, Venezuela. See http://unctad.org/Sections/dite_pcbb/docs/bits_vietnam.pdf and http://investmentpolicyhub.unctad.org/IIA/CountryBits/229.

60 http://www.palestineembassy.vn/index.php?option=com_content&view=article&id=100%3Ainvestment-agreement-signing-ceremony&catid=14%3Aactivities&Itemid=10&lang=vi; http://www.moit.gov.vn/vn/tin-tuc/4594/quan-he-kinh-te---thuong-mai-viet-nam---tho-nhi-ky--mot-nam-nhin-lai.aspx.

writing, the Vietnamese government is negotiating agreements with a further 37 countries.[61]

2 *Definition of Investment*

The publicly available BITs signed by Vietnam generally provide for a relatively broad definition of investment. The majority of these BITs define investment to include any kind of assets and, in particular, though not exclusively, movable and immovable property rights and any other rights *in rem*, shares, stocks and debentures of or interests in the property of companies, claims to money or any performance having a financial value, intellectual and industrial property rights and business concessions.

The majority of Vietnam's publicly available BITs stipulate that the investments shall be made in accordance with the laws and regulations of the State in which they are made.

The Vietnam-Malaysia BIT requires the investment to be made in an approved project. In regards to an investment in the territory of Vietnam this requires it to be an approved investment project based upon Vietnamese legislation. In respect to Malaysia, this requires an investment in an "approved project" to be in accordance with its legislation and administrative practice by the appropriate ministry of Malaysia.[62]

The BIT between Vietnam and Denmark also requires that in order to qualify as an "investment", an asset should be acquired for the purpose of establishing lasting economic relations between an investor and an enterprise.[63]

3 *Definition of Investor*

The definition of "investor" in Vietnam's BITs most commonly includes "nationals" and "companies" of a Contracting State.[64] The former are generally defined as nationals of a State pursuant to the laws or Constitution of that State, and the latter as companies duly incorporated or constituted in accordance with the laws of that State. For example, in the BIT signed between Vietnam and China, "investors" (in respect of the PRC) are defined as "natural persons who have nationality of the PRC" and "economic entities established in accordance with the laws of the PRC and domiciled in the territory of the PRC."

---

61 Gerhard Wegen and Stephan Wilske, Vietnam chapter in "Getting the Deal Through – Arbitration 2013", available at: http://dzungsrt.com/wp-content/uploads/2013/10/A2013-Vietnam.pdf.

62 BIT between Vietnam and Malaysia, Article 1.

63 BIT between Vietnam and Denmark, Article 1.

64 Such as the Vietnam-China, Vietnam-India, Vietnam-Poland BITs.

In a number of cases, the definitions are broader to include individuals permanently residing in one of the Contracting States, and also to include associations, partnerships and other types of entities that may be with or without legal personality and with or without limited liability.[65] In the BIT entered into by Vietnam and Denmark, the definition of "investor" includes "Any entity established in accordance with, and recognized as a legal person by the law of that Contracting Party, such as corporations, firms, associations, development finance institutions, foundations or similar entities irrespective of whether their liabilities are limited and whether or not their activities are directed at profit."[66]

Some BITs entered into by Vietnam go further to include legal entities which are constituted under the laws of a third party state, but controlled by a national or company of a Contracting State or a company that is seated and has its economic activities in the territory of a Contracting State.[67]

4 *Scope*

Vietnam's BITs characteristically apply to investments made prior to and after the entry into force of the treaty.[68] All of Vietnam's publicly available BITs contain subrogation rights, and a number of Vietnam's BITs provide that, where more favourable rules exist either under international law, the law of the Contracting States and/or another agreement, then the more favourable rules shall prevail.[69]

5 *Substantive Protections*

Fair and Equitable Treatment

All of Vietnam's publicly available BITs at the time of writing contain a "fair and equitable treatment" ("FET") provision as an obligation on the Contracting State vis-à-vis qualifying investors and/or investments.[70]

---

65 Such as the Vietnam-Denmark, Vietnam-Japan, Vietnam-United Kingdom BITs.

66 BIT between Vietnam-Denmark, Article 1 (3)(b).

67 Such as the Vietnam-Australia, Vietnam-Netherlands, Vietnam-Romania and Vietnam-Sweden BITs.

68 However, in the case of some BITs concluded with Vietnam, such as those with Poland, Egypt, Romania and Bulgaria, the BITs only apply to investments made after the entry into force of the treaty.

69 Such as those concluded by Vietnam with Australia, China, Czech Republic, Indonesia, Singapore, United Kingdom, Korea, Poland, Romania, Egypt, Bulgaria, Cuba, Hungary, India and Sweden.

70 *See:* http://www.aseanbriefing.com/regions/vietnam.

Generally, Vietnamese BITs stipulate that investments of each Contracting Party shall be accorded fair and equitable treatment, and full protection and security in the territory of the other Contracting Party.[71] The Vietnam-France BIT stipulates that fair and equitable treatment is in conformity with principles of international law and it must be ensured that the exercise of this right is not impeded either in law or in fact. The provision provides that "Each Contracting Party undertakes to provide, within its territory and in its maritime areas, fair and equitable treatment in accordance with principles of international law, for the investments of the other Party's nationals and companies, and to ensure that exercise of the right so granted is not impeded either in law or in fact."[72] Vietnam's BIT with Sweden widens the ambit of FET to cover procurement of materials and an investor's right to freely sell products and select suppliers without interference.[73]

Non-Discrimination

Many of Vietnam's BITs prohibit arbitrary and discriminatory treatment of qualifying investors and/or investments by Contracting States. However, not all agreements have a specific "Promotion and Protection of Investment" section to prohibit unreasonable or discriminatory measures in the management,

---

71 Vietnam-Australia, Vietnam-Belarus, Vietnam-Bulgaria, Vietnam-China, Vietnam-Cuba, Vietnam-Czech Republic, Vietnam-Egypt, Vietnam-France, Vietnam-Germany, Vietnam-Hungary, Vietnam-India, Vietnam-Indonesia, Vietnam-Italy, Vietnam-Latvia, Vietnam-Malaysia, Vietnam-Philippines, Vietnam-Poland, Vietnam-Romania, Vietnam-South Korea, Vietnam-Sweden, Vietnam-Switzerland, Vietnam-Thailand, Vietnam-United Kingdom.

72 BIT between Vietnam-France, Article 3, translated from original FR. The actual provision reads "Chacune des Parties contractantes s'engage à assurer, sur son territoire et dans ses zones maritimes, un traitement juste et équitable, conformément aux principes du droit international, aux investissements des nationaux et sociétés de l'autre Partie et à faire en sorte que l'exercice du droit ainsi reconnu ne soit entravé ni en droit, ni en fait."

73 BIT between Vietnam-Sweden, Article 2(1), provides that *"Each Contracting Party shall at all times ensure fair and equitable treatment of the investments by investors of the other Contracting Party and shall not impair the management, maintenance, use, enjoyment or disposal thereof by unreasonable measures, such as restrictions on purchase of raw materials, components and units, auxiliary materials, energy and fuel as well as means of production and operation of all kinds. In connection with the procurement of such materials and services as mentioned above, the investor shall have the right to freely select the supplier on the most favourable terms available. The investor shall also have the right to freely sell products abroad and can sell products within the country in accordance with the laws and regulations in force and no hindrance on such sales or other measures with similar effect should be instituted".*

maintenance, use, enjoyment or disposal of investments in its territory of nationals or companies of the other Contracting Party.[74]

For example, the Vietnam-Thailand BIT does not discuss discrimination in the context of investment or expropriation/nationalization. By contrast, the Vietnam-United Kingdom BIT[75] states that the scope of anti-discrimination is to ensure that neither Contracting Party impairs the management, maintenance, use, enjoyment or disposal of investments in its territory by unreasonable or discriminatory measures. This applies equally to nationals and companies of the other Contracting Party.

Full Protection and Security

At the time of writing, many of Vietnam's publicly available BITs include a provision providing for the "full protection and security" of the investments of the other Contracting State. Some BITs such as those entered into by Vietnam with Australia, Romania and Switzerland, specifically provide that the protection accorded to the investor is subject to the Contracting Party's own laws and regulations.[76]

Expropriation

Nearly all BITs publicly available at the time of writing contain a provision generally prohibiting the expropriation, nationalization and any other measure except if such a measure taken by the host State serves a public purpose, is taken under due process of law, in a non-discriminatory manner.

Measures are in place to ensure the payment of prompt, adequate and effective compensation, whether this is calculated on the London Interbank Offered Rate ("LIBOR") basis from the date of expropriation[77] or shall amount

74 Discrimination only discussed in expropriation clause: Vietnam-Austria, Vietnam-Belarus, Vietnam-Bulgaria, Vietnam-China, Vietnam-Czech Republic, Vietnam-France, Vietnam-Germany, Vietnam-Hungary, Vietnam-India, Vietnam-Indonesia, Vietnam-Italy, Vietnam-South Korea, Vietnam-Latvia, Vietnam-Malaysia, Vietnam-Poland and Vietnam-Sweden BITs.

75 Similar provisions are found in the following BITs: Vietnam-Argentina, Vietnam-Belgium, Vietnam-Cuba, Vietnam-Denmark, Vietnam-Egypt, Vietnam-Luxembourg, Vietnam-Morocco, Vietnam-Romania, Vietnam-Switzerland, Vietnam-Venezuela. Vietnam-India and Vietnam-Indonesia both include promotion and protection of investment provisions, however they do not discuss anti-discrimination procedure.

76 Vietnam-Australia BIT, Article 3; Vietnam-Romania BIT, Article 3; Vietnam-Switzerland BIT, Article 3; http://investmentpolicyhub.unctad.org/Download/TreatyFile/2331.

77 Vietnam-Bulgaria, Article 5(2); Vietnam-Denmark, Article 5; Vietnam-Italy, Article 5(4); Vietnam-Latvia, Article 5(1)(c).

to the "fair" market value of the investment expropriated immediately before the expropriatory action was taken or became public knowledge.[78]

Umbrella Clauses

Some of the BITs signed with Vietnam utilise the so-called "umbrella clauses", through which a State's contractual obligations arising from the investment agreements falling under the protection of the relevant BIT can potentially be elevated to treaty obligations.[79] For example, the BIT between Vietnam and the Netherlands provides that "Each Contracting Party shall observe any obligation it may have entered into with regard to investments of nationals of the other Contracting Party,"[80] the BIT entered into between Vietnam and Japan provides that "In fulfilling the obligations under this Agreement, each Contracting Party shall take such reasonable measures as may be available to it to ensure the observance of this Agreement by local governments in its Area,"[81] and the BIT between Vietnam and Singapore provides that "If the legislation of either Contracting Party or international obligations existing at present or established hereafter between the Contracting Parties in addition to this Agreement, result in a position entitling investment by nationals of the other Contracting Party to treatment more favorable than is provided for by this Agreement, such position shall not be affected by this Agreement. Each Contracting Party shall observe any commitment in accordance with its laws additional to those specified in this Agreement entered into by the Contracting Party, its nationals or companies with nationals or companies of the other Contracting Party as regards to their investments."[82]

Most Favoured Nation and National Treatment

Most of Vietnam's publicly available BITs require that the treatment of investments of investors from other Contracting States be no less favourable than that granted to nationals or companies of third states.[83] This is commonly known as a "Most Favoured Nation" ("MFN") provision.

---

78 Vietnam-Korea, Article 5(1), Vietnam-Japan, Article 9(3).

79 Vietnam-Belgium, Vietnam-Germany, Vietnam-Morocco, Vietnam-Netherlands, Vietnam-Romania, Vietnam-Singapore, Vietnam-Korea, Vietnam-Thailand, Vietnam-UK BITs.

80 Vietnam-Netherlands BIT, Article 3(4);

81 Vietnam-Japan BIT, Article 22(1).

82 Vietnam-Singapore BIT, Article 15.

83 Vietnam-Australia, Vietnam-Belgium, Vietnam-Cuba, Vietnam-Czech Republic, Vietnam-France, Vietnam-Germany, Vietnam-Hungary, Vietnam-India, Vietnam-Indonesia, Vietnam-Italy, Vietnam-Japan, Vietnam-Latvia, Vietnam-Luxembourg, Vietnam-Malaysia,

Singapore's BIT with Vietnam has MFN treatment of general application, in that neither Contracting Party shall subject investments or returns of nationals and companies of the other Contracting Party in its territory to treatment less favourable than investments or returns of nationals and companies of any third State.[84] A number of Vietnam's BITs explicitly state that there is no obligation to extend to investments any treatment, preference or privilege resulting from a customs union, economic union, free trade area or regional economic integration agreement to which the Contracting Party belongs or provisions of a double taxation agreement with a third country.[85]

Some of Vietnam's BITs explicitly state that investors of the Contracting State are to treat qualifying investors and/or investments at least as favourably as their national investors or their investments.[86] The Vietnam-France BIT specifies that each Contracting Party is to provide to nationals of the other Party on its territory and maritime zones treatment that is comparable to that afforded to their own nationals and companies, and no less favourable than that of the MFN. Moreover, the vast majority of Vietnam's BITs stipulate that investments made by investors of each Contracting Party in the territory of the other Contracting Party shall receive treatment which is no less favourable than that accorded to investments made by investors of any third State.[87]

Likewise, a few of Vietnam's MFN provisions relate to how Contracting States are to treat each other in the event of force majeure. Investors of one Contracting Party suffering losses on the other Contracting Party's territory due to war, armed conflict, national emergency, revolt, insurrection or riot shall be given restitution in a way no less favourable than that of any third State.[88]

6 *Repatriation of Capital and Compensation for Losses*

Some of the BITs signed by Vietnam publicly available at the time of writing contain repatriation provisions to allow for the repatriation by the investor of

Vietnam-Morocco, Vietnam-Philippines, Vietnam-Poland, Vietnam-Romania, Vietnam-Singapore, Vietnam-Sweden, Vietnam-Switzerland, Vietnam-United Kingdom.

84 Vietnam-Singapore BIT, Article 4.

85 Vietnam-Australia, Article 4(b), Vietnam-Italy, Article 3(3).

86 Vietnam-Czech Republic, Article 3(1); Vietnam-France, Article 4; Vietnam-India, Article 4(1)–(2); Vietnam-United Kingdom, Article 3(1)–(2).

87 Vietnam-Australia, Vietnam-Cuba, Vietnam-Hungary, Vietnam-India, Vietnam-Indonesia, Vietnam-Italy, Vietnam-Japan, Vietnam-Latvia, Vietnam-Malaysia, Vietnam-Philippines, Vietnam-Poland, Vietnam-Romania, Vietnam-Singapore, Vietnam-Sweden, Vietnam-Switzerland, Vietnam-UK.

88 Vietnam-Malaysia, Article 3(2).

capital invested and investment returns.[89] Most of these Contracting Parties also include clauses providing for compensation of losses resulting from war (and other armed conflicts), revolution, a state of national emergency, revolt, insurrection or riot in the territory of the host State.

7 *Investor-State Dispute Settlement*

Many of the BITs entered into by Vietnam provide that where a dispute arises between a Contracting State and an investor, the parties should in the first instance try and resolve their dispute amicably in so far as possible.[90] In such circumstances, some BITs, such as that between Vietnam and Egypt, further provide that local remedies shall be available to the investor "on the basis of treatment not less favourable than that accorded to investments of its own investors or investors of any third country."[91]In comparison, the BIT between Vietnam and Japan stipulates that each contracting party shall, in its area, accord to investors of the other contracting party "treatment no less favorable than the treatment which it accords in like circumstances to its own investors or investors of any third country with respect to access to the courts of justice and administrative tribunals and agencies in all degrees of jurisdiction, both in pursuit and in defense of such investors' rights."[92] Where disputes cannot be settled amicably, they shall be submitted to arbitration or to the courts or tribunals of the Contracting State where the options to negotiate or engage in consultations have been exhausted. The period in which a dispute should be referred for arbitration is generally three[93] or six[94] months.

89 Vietnam-Cuba, Vietnam-Denmark, Vietnam-India, Vietnam-Indonesia, Vietnam-Italy, Vietnam-Malaysia, Vietnam-Singapore, Vietnam-Korea, Vietnam-UK.

90 BITs entered between Vietnam-Bangladesh, Article 7(1); Vietnam-Australia, Article 12(1), Vietnam-Bulgaria, Article 9(1); Vietnam-Cambodia, Article VIII(1); Vietnam-Chile, Article IX(1); Vietnam-China, Article 8(1); Vietnam-Cuba, Article 8(1); Vietnam-Czech, Article 8(1); Vietnam-Denmark, Article 9(1); Vietnam-Egypt, Article 8(1); Vietnam-Finland, Article 8(1); Vietnam-Hungary, Article 8(1); Vietnam-India, Article 9(1); Vietnam-Indonesia, Article IX(1); Vietnam-Japan, Article 14(1); Vietnam-Latvia, Article 7(1); Vietnam-Malaysia, Article 7(1); Vietnam-Netherlands, Article 9(1); Vietnam-Poland, Article 8(1); Vietnam-Romania, Article 9(1); Vietnam-Singapore, Article 13(1); Vietnam-South Korea, Article 8(1); Vietnam-Sweden, Article 8(1); Vietnam-Tajikistan, Article VIII(1); Vietnam-Thailand, Article 10(1); Vietnam-United Arab Emirates, Article 10(1); Vietnam-United Kingdom, Article 8(1).

91 Vietnam-Egypt, Article 8(2).

92 See also BIT entered between Vietnam-Japan, Article 3.

93 Vietnam-Austria, Vietnam-Japan, Vietnam-Netherlands, Vietnam-United Kingdom.

94 BITs signed with Argentina, Belarus, Belgium, China, Cuba, Egypt, France, Hungary, India, Indonesia, Italy, Latvia, Luxembourg, Malaysia, Netherlands, Poland, Philippines, Romania, Singapore, Sweden, Switzerland, Venezuela.

Some BITs additionally provide that where a tribunal is not appointed within 4 months from a party's initiation of arbitration, the initiating party may invite the President of the International Court of Justice to make any necessary appointments.[95] By contrast, where a party wishes to refer a case to the domestic courts, there is no prescribed period within which the party should do so.

Several of Vietnam's BITs provide that both Contracting Parties agree in advance and consent before commencing conciliation or arbitration.[96] The vast majority of BITs in Vietnam permit a submission of the dispute to the International Centre for the Settlement of Investment Disputes ("ICSID") for conciliation or arbitration proceedings, by either the investor or the host State, although as noted above, at the time of writing, Vietnam is not yet a party to the ICSID Convention.

Thus, the vast majority of Vietnam's BITs provide the investor with the choice of arbitration under the UNCITRAL Rules, though in some cases arbitration under the ICSID Additional Facility is specifically chosen.[97] In other cases, an investor generally has the choice of *ad hoc* arbitration. For example, under the Vietnam-Switzerland BIT, an investor may request arbitration in the host country or arbitration in a constituted *ad hoc* tribunal following the UNCITRAL Rules of Procedure. Further, Vietnam's BIT with Indonesia provides investors with three options for dispute resolution in the event that a dispute cannot be settled amicably. The parties may choose to settle disputes before the national courts of the Contracting Party, or by an *ad hoc* arbitral tribunal specially constituted by the two Contracting Parties or by any existing arbitral tribunals agreed upon by both Contracting Parties.

Where the two Contracting Parties are party to the ICSID Convention, they may at the request of the investor submit their dispute to the ICSID.

8 *State-to-State Dispute Settlement*

The majority of Vietnam's publicly available BITs stipulate that disputes between the Contracting States shall be resolved as far as possible through

95 BITs entered between Vietnam-China, Article 7(3); Vietnam-Netherlands, Article 12(2), (3).

96 Vietnam-Belgium, Vietnam-India, Vietnam-Luxembourg. In the case of Malaysia, the party intending to resolve such dispute through consultation and negotiation shall give notice to the other of its intention.

97 BITs signed with Belgium, China, Luxembourg, Poland.

recourse to diplomatic channels[98] or by the governments of the contracting parties.[99] Some BITs propose general consultations or negotiations in order to settle disputes about the interpretation and application of the agreements.[100] The BIT between Vietnam-Australia, for example, simply proposes that the Contracting Parties endeavour to resolve any dispute between them by prompt and friendly consultations and negotiations. In the event that diplomatic settlement fails, a dispute shall be submitted to an arbitral tribunal, generally where it can be foreseen that the dispute cannot be solved diplomatically within six months – or within a "reasonable lapse of time" (Vietnam-Netherlands).[101]

A number of the BITs require the establishment of an *ad hoc* arbitral tribunal constituted by two arbitrators appointed by each of the Contracting States (within two months) and a chairman appointed by the two co-arbitrators (generally within two[102] or three[103] months from the date of appointment of the two co-arbitrators). The Vietnam-Australia and Vietnam-Japan BITs contain shorter time periods for the appointment of arbitrators. Under these agreements, which have very similar provisions,[104] the arbitral panel is composed of three arbitrators, with each Contracting Party appointing one arbitrator within a period of thirty days and the third arbitrator to be agreed upon as President by the two co-arbitrators within a further period of thirty days, provided that the President is not a national of either Contracting Party.

98 BITs with Argentina, Belarus, Belgium, China, Cuba, France, Indonesia, Italy, Japan, Luxembourg, Malaysia, Netherlands, Philippines, Romania, Singapore, Switzerland, United Kingdom, Venezuela.

99 Vietnam-Bulgaria, Vietnam-Denmark, Vietnam-Egypt, Vietnam-Germany, Vietnam-Sweden.

100 Vietnam-Austria, Vietnam-Czech Republic, Vietnam-Hungary, Vietnam-India, Vietnam-Indonesia, Vietnam-Poland, Vietnam-Thailand.

101 This length of time is variable and can be as long as 12 months, as under the Vietnam-Romania and Vietnam-Switzerland BITs.

102 Vietnam-Argentina, Vietnam-Austria, Vietnam-Belarus, Vietnam-Belgium, Vietnam-Bulgaria, Vietnam-India, Vietnam-Luxembourg, Vietnam-Malaysia, Vietnam-Netherlands, Vietnam-Romania, Vietnam-Singapore, Vietnam-United Kingdom.

103 Vietnam-Czech Republic, Vietnam-Denmark, Vietnam-Egypt, Vietnam-France, Vietnam-Germany, Vietnam-Hungary, Vietnam-Italy, Vietnam-Poland. NB: The period in which a Chairman may be appointed in the Vietnam-Sweden and Vietnam-Thailand BITs is 4 months. Vietnam-Venezuela provides that a Chairman must be appointed within five months.

104 Article 13(2) of the Vietnam-Japan BIT available at: http://investmentpolicyhub.unctad.org/Download/TreatyFile/1738, and Annex A to the Vietnam-Australia BIT available at: http://investmentpolicyhub.unctad.org/Download/TreatyFile/168.

If, within the period specified above, the tribunal has not been constituted, most BITs provide that the Contracting Parties may invite the President of the International Court of Justice to make any necessary appointments. In the case of the Vietnam-France BIT, where there is a delay or failure in appointing arbitrators, one of the Contracting Parties may invite the Secretary-General of the UN to assist with the constitution of the tribunal. Where the UN Secretary-General is a national of one of the Contracting Parties, the last incumbent Secretary-General will be delegated this function.

In general, Vietnam's BITs permit the *ad hoc* tribunals to determine their own rules of procedure or apply the procedural standards called for by international law. For example, the BIT entered between Vietnam and China provides that in the case of State-to-State arbitration, "the arbitral tribunal shall determine its own procedure . . .", and the BIT entered between Vietnam and Denmark provides that "The arbitral tribunal shall apply the provisions of this Agreement, other Agreements concluded between the Contracting Parties, and the procedural standards called for by international law . . . ".[105] The tribunal will decide by majority, after which point the arbitral award is final and binding. The BIT between Vietnam and the Netherlands allows the tribunal to decide the dispute *ex aequo et bono* if the Parties so agree.

9 *Additional Provisions*

Several Vietnam BITs contain a provision that relates to application of "other rules and special commitments."[106] These provisions address the situation where matters are governed simultaneously both by the BIT and another international agreement to which both Contracting Parties are parties. Generally speaking, those BITs which contain such clauses provide that investors and Contracting Parties will not be precluded from taking advantage of whichever rules are more favourable to their case. For example, the BIT entered into between Vietnam and Egypt provides that "Where a matter is governed simultaneously by this Agreement and by another international agreement to which both Contracting Parties are parties, or by general principles of International Law, nothing in this Agreement shall prevent either Contracting Party or any of its investors who own investments in the territory of the other Contracting Party from taking advantage of whichever rules are the more favorable to his

105 Vietnam-Austria, Article 9(6); Vietnam-China, Article 7(5); Vietnam-Denmark, Article 10(5); Vietnam-Venezuela, Article 9(5).

106 Vietnam-Egypt, Vietnam-Czech Republic; Vietnam-India, Article 13.

case,"[107] and the relevant provision in the BIT entered between Vietnam and the Czech Republic is in substantially the same language.[108]

The Vietnam-Denmark BIT has a territorial extension clause so that the agreement shall not apply to the Faroe Islands and Greenland. However, the ambit of the BIT agreement may be extended to the Faroe Islands and Greenland as may be agreed between the Contracting Parties in an exchange of notes.[109] The Vietnam-India BIT has an entry and sojourn of personnel provision wherein a Contracting Party shall (subject to laws relating to the entry and sojourn of non-citizens) permit natural persons of the other Contracting Party and personnel employed by companies of the other party to enter and remain in its territory for the purpose of engaging in activities connected with investments.[110] The Vietnam-Japan BIT has an environmental provision in place so that investment is not encouraged where each Contracting Party has to waive or derogate from such environmental measures.[111]

10 *Notable Trends*

Vietnam's earliest BIT was with Italy, signed on 18 May 1990 (entering into force in 1994) but the first BIT to come into force was that with Australia on 11 September 1991. The majority of BITs entered into during the 1990s were with European countries, and some with countries in South East Asia, North and Central Asia. Interestingly, many of the BITs which were signed by Vietnam between 2000 and 2010 have not yet come into force.[112] Further, only

107 Article 10(1).

108 Article 10(1).

109 Vietnam-Denmark, Article 14: "The provisions of this Agreement may be extended to the Faroe Islands and Greenland as may be agreed between the Contracting Parties in an exchange of notes".

110 Vietnam-India, Article 11: "A Contracting Party shall, subject to its laws applicable from time to time relating to the entry and sojourn of non-citizens, permit natural persons of the other Contracting Party and personnel employed by companies of the other Contracting party to enter and remain in its territory for the purpose of engaging in activities connected with investments".

111 Vietnam-Japan, Article 21: "The Contracting Parties recognize that it is inappropriate to encourage investment by investors of the other Contracting Party by relaxing environmental measures. To this effect each Contracting Party should not waive or otherwise derogate from such environmental measures as an encouragement for the establishment, acquisition or expansion in its Area of investments by investors of the other Contracting Party".

112 BITs were signed with the following countries but never entered in force: Algeria, Bangladesh, Cambodia, Chile, Greece, Iran (Islamic Republic of), Kazakhstan, Korea, DPR, Morocco, Myanmar, Namibia, Oman, Sri Lanka, Tajikistan, United Arab Emirates.

2 BITs were concluded after 2010 but neither of them is in force at the time of writing.[113]

IV Multilateral Investment Related Treaties and Organizations to which Vietnam is a Party

1 *ASEAN – AEC – ACIA*

Vietnam joined the Association of South East Asian Nations ("ASEAN") on 28 July 1995 as its seventh member.[114]

It is one of the three fundamental principles of the ASEAN community to realize the end-goal of economic integration outlined in the ASEAN Vision 2020, which has been confirmed in the ASEAN Harmonization Declaration (Declaration Bali II), of creating a stable, prosperous and highly competitive ASEAN economic region in which there is a free flow of goods, services, investment and a freer flow of capital, equitable economic development, and reduced poverty and socio-economic disparities. Inspired by the EU model, ASEAN member states were aiming to establish an ASEAN Economic Community ("AEC") – an intergovernmental cooperative organization – by the end of 2015. Whilst a fully integrated single market and production base is unlikely to be achieved by this ambitious target date, there have been significant developments through the implementation of commitments in other Agreements on Trade signed with ASEAN member states.

The AEC's mission is to establish ASEAN as a single market and production base which is strongly competitive and which enhances development, and to enhance, deepen and broaden economic integration between ASEAN members so that ASEAN, as a single market and production base, will become more dynamic and a stronger segment of the global supply chain. In moving towards developing the AEC, ASEAN intends, inter alia, to institute new mechanisms and measures to strengthen the implementation of its existing economic initiatives including the ASEAN Free Trade Area ("AFTA"), ASEAN Framework Agreement on Services ("AFAS") and ASEAN Investment Area ("AIA"); accelerate regional integration in some priority sectors; facilitate movement of business persons, skilled labour and talents; and strengthen the institutional mechanisms of ASEAN, including the improvement of the existing ASEAN Dispute Settlement Mechanism to ensure expeditious and legally binding resolution of any economic disputes.

---

113 BITs entered by Vietnam with Morocco and Oman.

114 http://www.asean.org/asean/about-asean/overview.

Like the other ASEAN member States, Vietnam is a party to the ASEAN Comprehensive Investment Agreement (the "ACIA") which was signed on 26 February 2009 and entered into force on 29 March 2012. It aims to create a free and open investment environment through the consolidation and expansion of existing agreements between ASEAN Member States.[115]

The ACIA contains substantive investment protections commonly found in BITs, such as provisions on non-discrimination, MFN treatment, fair and equitable treatment, full protection and security, and expropriation. Where a dispute arises between an investor and a Member State, the ACIA provides for various dispute resolution options, including the submission of a claim under the ICSID Convention, under the UNCITRAL Arbitration Rules, or to the KLRCA or any other regional centre for arbitration in ASEAN.[116]

Beyond the usual provisions found in BITs, the ACIA also contains provisions aimed at enhancing cooperation between ASEAN States in the promotion[117] and facilitation of investment,[118] and to enhance ASEAN integration.[119]

2 *APEC*

Vietnam has been a Member State of the Asia-Pacific Economic Cooperation ("APEC") since 14 November 1998.[120] APEC's aim is to promote sustainable growth and prosperity in the Asia-Pacific region.[121] Among other APEC initiatives for free and open trade and investment, three key APEC investment-related instruments are the Non-Binding Investment Principles ("NBIP"), the Menu of Options, and the Transparency Standards on Investment.

The NBIP sets out twelve investment principles that are broadly similar to the core elements of international investment agreements concluded between APEC Member States, including provisions on transparency, national treatment, fair and equitable treatment, full protection and security, protection from strife, the transfer of funds, and the entry of key personnel. The Menu of Options (or the Options for Investment Liberalization and Business Facilitation to Strengthen the APEC Economies) lists policies for liberalization

115 http://www.aseanbriefing.com/news/2013/04/12/introduction-to-the-asean-comprehensive-investment-agreement.html.
116 Article 33 of the ACIA.
117 *Ibid.*, Article 24.
118 *Ibid.*, Article 25.
119 *Ibid.*, Article 26.
120 http://www.apec.org/about-us/about-apec/member-economies.aspx.
121 http://www.apec.org/About-Us/About-APEC/Mission-Statement.aspx.

and business facilitation. The transparency Standards on investment cover the publication, awareness and availability of investment laws and measures.[122]

3 *MIGA*

Vietnam is a party to the Convention Establishing the Multilateral Investment Guarantee Agency (the "MIGA") of 1985. MIGA is a part of the World Bank Group and a multilateral investment insurance system against political risks, which offers investment protection for cross-border investments against losses resulting from, *inter alia*, currency transfer restrictions, expropriation and a government's (or, in certain circumstances, a State-owned enterprise's)[123] breach or repudiation of a contract with an investor. Vietnam has been a member of MIGA since 5 October 1994.[124]

V Multilateral Dispute Settlement Related Treaties

1 *ICSID Convention*

Along with Mexico, Russia, India, Thailand, South Africa and Brazil, Vietnam is a non-signatory to the ICSID Convention although it has apparently been considering accession for a number of years.

2 *New York Convention*

Vietnam has been a party to the New York Convention on the Recognition and Enforcement of Foreign Arbitral Awards (the "New York Convention") since 12 September 1995.[125]

Although the New York Convention does not specifically addresses the issue of investment protection, it has central importance with respect to the enforcement of arbitral awards including in certain cases, those arising out of investments.

---

122 "Identifying core elements in investment agreements in the APEC region", UNCTAD Series on International Investment Policies for Development, United Nations (New York and Geneva: 2008), available at: http://unctad.org/en/Docs/diaeia20083_en.pdf.

123 Multilateral Investment Guarantee Agency (MIGA), *Investment Guarantee Guide*, World Bank Group: March 2012, p. 7 available at: http://www.miga.org/documents/IGGenglish.pdf.

124 http://web.worldbank.org/WBSITE/EXTERNAL/EXTABOUTUS/ORGANIZATION/BODEXT/0,,contentMDK:20122866~menuPK:64020025~pagePK:64020054~piPK:64020408~theSitePK:278036~isCURL:Y,00.html.

125 http://www.newyorkconvention.org/contracting-states/list-of-contracting-states.

Vietnam will apply the Convention only to recognition and enforcement of awards made in the territory of another contracting State. With regard to awards made in the territory of non-contracting States, this State will apply the Convention only to the extent to which those States grant reciprocal treatment. Furthermore, Vietnam restricts application of the Convention to differences arising out of legal relationships, whether contractual or not, that are considered commercial under the national law.[126]

Interpretation of the Convention in Vietnam by the courts or other competent authorities is subject to the Constitution and laws of Vietnam.[127] This reservation was recently reaffirmed in 2013 by a Vietnamese court in Decision no. 01/2013/QDST-KDTM. This insistence on interpreting the Convention under Vietnamese law appears to run contrary to the purpose of the Convention, which aims at unifying rules governing foreign arbitral awards on the international plane.[128]

VI International Investment Arbitration Jurisprudence

At the time of writing, Vietnam has been the respondent State in five investor-State disputes, all under the UNCITRAL Rules.

None of the cases are public and the information available is extremely limited. The descriptions of the cases provided below are based on the limited information currently in the public domain.

Trinh Vinh Binh v Socialist Republic of Vietnam (*UNCITRAL Rules*)

Tribunal: C. Mark Baker (President, United States)
Brigitte Stern (France)
Kaj I. Hobér (Sweden)
Award: Case discontinued following confidential settlement, March 2007

126 http://www.uncitral.org/uncitral/en/uncitral_texts/arbitration/NYConvention_status.html.

127 Decision no. 453/QD-CTN (1995), art. 1.

128 G.A. Bermann, *Recognition and Enforcement of Foreign Arbitral Awards: The Application of the New York Convention by National Courts*, July 2, 2014 draft, p. 12. available at: http://www.iacl2014congress.com/fileadmin/user_upload/k_iacl2014congress/General_reports/Bermann_-_General_Report_Recognition__Enforcement_of_Foreign_Awards_July_2_2014__2_.pdf.

Background Facts

The first case against Vietnam was introduced in 2004 by a Dutch investor of Vietnamese origin, Trinh Vinh Binh, under the BIT between Vietnam and the Netherlands. The dispute concerned unlawful confiscation of real estate and other assets without compensation. The case was eventually settled on confidential terms and no award was made.[129]

Michael McKenzie v Socialist Republic of Vietnam (UNCITRAL Rules)

Tribunal:	Neil Kaplan (President, United Kingdom)
	John Gotanda (United States)
	Campbell McLachlan (New Zealand)
Award:	11 December 2013 (Not public)

Background Facts

In 2010, an American investor, Michael McKenzie, owner of South Fork Co., brought arbitration proceedings against Vietnam under the BIT entered between Vietnam and the United States in 2010. The investor claimed that the government had wrongfully allowed mining activities to be carried out in a plot of land initially reserved for his resort development in Bac Binh District, Binh Thuan Province. The arbitral tribunal ruled against the investor who was ordered to pay the legal expenses of the Vietnamese government.[130]

Dialasie SAS v Socialist Republic of Vietnam (UNCITRAL Rules)

Tribunal:	Kaj I. Hober (President, Sweden)
	Jean-Michel Jacquet (France)
	Michael J. Moser (Austria)
Case Initiated:	July 2011
Award:	17 November 2014 (Not public)

Background Facts

A French investor, DialAsie SAS, initiated arbitration proceedings against Vietnam in 2011 under the Vietnam-France BIT. The dispute concerned the closure in 2006 of a dialysis clinic operated by DialAsie SAS in Ho Chi Minh City,

129 Case information available on italaw.com (http://www.italaw.com/cases/155).

130 "US Investor loses $3.7 bln case against Vietnam govt" dated 6 March 2014 (http://www.vietnambreakingnews.com/2014/03/us-investor-loses-3-7-bln-case-against-vietnam-govt/).

amidst a series of disputes with local health-care authorities. A decision has reportedly been made in November 2014 in favour of Vietnam but the award has not been published.[131]

RECOFI v Socialist Republic of Vietnam (UNCITRAL Rules)

Tribunal:	Bernard Hanotiau (President, Belgium) Stanimir Alexandrov (Bulgaria) John Christopher Thomas (Canada)
Case Initiated:	July 2013
Award:	Pending

Background Facts

A French food company, RECOFI, brought a case against Vietnam in July 2013 under the France-Vietnam BIT of 1994. The claim was brought in relation to losses apparently incurred by RECOFI in an assistance program that provided food and basic commodities to Vietnam when it was facing food shortages in 1987.[132] The case is not public but in May 2016 it was reported that Vietnam had prevailed in the arbitration.[133]

VII Outlook: Anticipated Developments

Vietnam is a party to the Trans-Pacific Partnership ("TPP") which was concluded in Atlanta, Georgia, USA on 5 October 2015, after five and a half years of negotiations. The TPP is a comprehensive, regional trade agreement that is widely expected to create new trade and investment opportunities for Vietnam in the Asia-Pacific region. The TPP brings together 12 economies from both sides of the Pacific, namely, Australia, Brunei Darussalam, Canada, Chile, Japan, Malaysia, Mexico, New Zealand, Peru, Singapore, the United States and Vietnam. Collectively, these countries represent 40% of global GDP,

---

131 See *IA Reporter*, "Dialasie SAS v. Vietnam Award: Vietnam's Justice Ministry Reveals that it Prevailed in Arbitration under French Investment Treaty", available at: http://www.iareporter.com/downloads/20150304.

132 Article by Lacey Yong and Sabastian Perry published in Global Arbitration Review titled, 'Vietnam wins treaty claim over medical facility' dated 16 January 2015 (http://globalarbitrationreview.com/news/article/33307/%vietnam-wins-treaty-claim-medical-facility/).

133 See, "Investigation: Vietnam prevails in UNCITRAL BIT arbitration with (another) French investor", *IA Reporter*, available at: http://www.iareporter.com/articles/investigation-vietnam-prevails-in-uncitral-bit-arbitration-with-another-french-investor/.

one-third of world trade, and comprise a population of 800 million, making the TPP the largest regional trade agreement at the time of writing.[134] Apart from offering new market access for Vietnamese goods and services and producers exporting to and investing in TPP markets, the TPP also reinforces the region's commitment to a rules-based trading system by updating international rules that apply to cross-border trade and investment.[135]

Vietnam already has existing bilateral Free Trade Agreements ("FTAs") with 2 of the 11 TPP partners and 3 regional FTAs.[136] The TPP represents Vietnam's first preferential trade agreement with Canada, Mexico, Peru and the US.[137] While the TPP has been concluded, it will only enter into force when at least six original signatories, accounting for at least 85% of the GDP across the TPP economies, have ratified the agreement. When the TPP comes into force, it will be interesting to see how this agreement will fit into treaty arrangements in Vietnam's existing FTAs, BITs, regional investment agreements such as the ASEAN Comprehensive Investment Agreement, as well as the widely anticipated Regional Comprehensive Economic Partnership Agreement ("RCEP") where negotiations are expected to be concluded soon.[138] While the TPP and RCEP might open doors to vast investment opportunities and a jump in FDI inflows to Vietnam,[139] these agreements at the same time afford investors in Vietnam with greater protection when investing in economies which did not previously have investment agreements with Vietnam.

VIII Conclusion

Thus far, Vietnam has entered into a larger number of BITs than FTAs. However, a notable recent development is the conclusion of the Vietnam-EU FTA. That FTA adopts the EU's international investment court mechanism,

134 Singapore Ministry of Trade and Industry, *Trans Pacific Partnership Free Trade Agreement* (TPP) *7 Things You Should Know*, available at https://www.mti.gov.sg/MTIInsights/SiteAssets/Pages/TPP/Seven%20things%20you%20should%20know%20about%20the%20TPP%20(Final).pdf.

135 *Ibid.*

136 http://webtr.vecita.gov.vn/.

137 http://fta.miti.gov.my/.

138 http://fta.miti.gov.my/index.php/pages/view/60?mid=39.

139 http://www.bloomberg.com/news/articles/2015-10-08/more-shoes-and-shrimp-less-china-reliance-for-vietnam-in-tpp.

which will be staffed by permanent judges (as opposed to *ad hoc* arbitrators) and provides for appeals on errors of law.[140]

In view of Vietnam's relative activity in terms of the conclusion of BITs, it remains somewhat unusual that Vietnam has yet to accede to the ICSID Convention, though it has reportedly been considering doing so in recent years.

140 Nottage, L., "The TPP Investment Chapter and Investor-State Arbitration in Asia and Oceania: Assessing Prospects for Ratification", *Sydney Law School, Legal Studies Research Paper No. 16/28*, April 2016, p.11.

Index